The Life of a Galilean Shaman

MATRIX
The Bible in Mediterranean Context

•

Richard L. Rohrbaugh
The New Testament in Cross-Cultural Perspective

Markus Cromhout
Jesus and Identity:
Reconstructing Judean Ethnicity in Q

Pieter F. Craffert
The Life of a Galilean Shaman:
Jesus of Nazareth in Anthropological-Historical Perspective

Douglas E. Oakman
Jesus and the Peasants

•

FORTHCOMING VOLUMES

Stuart L. Love
Jesus and the Marginal Women:
Healing in Matthew's Gospel

⊠ The Life of a Galilean Shaman

Jesus of Nazareth in
Anthropological-Historical
Perspective

PIETER F. CRAFFERT

◤ CASCADE *Books* · Eugene, Oregon

THE LIFE OF A GALILEAN SHAMAN
Jesus of Nazareth in Anthropological-Historical Perspective

Matrix: The Bible in Mediterranean Perspective, Volume 3

Cascade Books
A Division of Wipf and Stock Publishers
199 W. 8th Ave., Suite 3
Eugene, OR 97401

ISBN 13: 978-1-55635-085-6

Cataloging-in-Publication data:

Craffert, Pieter F.
    The life of a Galilean shaman : Jesus of Nazareth in anthropological-historical
    perspective / Pieter F. Craffert.

    xviii + 452 p.; 23 cm. — Matrix: The Bible in Mediterranean Context 3
    Includes bibliographical references (p. 425–451).

    ISBN 13: 978-1-55635-085-6

    1. Jesus Christ. 2. Jesus Christ—Biography. 3. Jesus Christ—Biography—History
and criticism. 4. Bible. N.T.—Social scientific criticism. 5. Bible. N. T. Gospels—
Criticism, interpretation, etc. I. Title. II. Series.

BT301.2 C70 2008

For my friend and colleague Pieter J. J. Botha, who has believed in this project from the very beginning, and the members of the Context Group, who constantly remind us that things can look differently when our ethnocentric lenses are replaced

Contents

Diagrams

Acknowledgments

THE RESEARCH REFLECTED HERE does not only claim to represent a paradigm shift in historical Jesus research but was itself an exercise in paradigm shifts. While it started in the first phase as the application of an alternative social-type model to the existing material and within the prevalent research paradigm, it turned out to offer different answers to new questions. The second phase, based on a different historiographical paradigm called an anthropological-historical paradigm, consisted of a re-writing or, at least, a reframing of most of the arguments. One of the most difficult tasks was the unlearning of taken-for-granted research truths and insights regarding historical Jesus research, and the self-realization of what it means to consistently treat the study of the historical figure as an analysis about an actual social personage. If Jesus was a Galilean shamanic figure as suggested, he was such a figure right from the start of his public life, and the sources emerged from the beginning of his career as about this kind of figure. Since a shift in paradigms opens up new terrain, this research is much more exploratory than definitive; it is suggestive as to where historical Jesus research can still go in future when exploring the cultural processes and social dynamics surrounding a social personage's life. All of this also explains why it has occupied more than a decade of my life.

This research has obviously touched on many lives and has accrued a social dynamic of its own. The shamanic model, when first introduced in seminars and in a journal article, was, understandably, met with resistance. Over the years there were more well-intended warnings than overt support. But it was the difficult process of acknowledging and processing the paradigm shift in my own thinking that contributed more to the delay in finalizing it than did any scholarly opposition to the project. What the counterarguments have achieved was to force me to bring the differences between the paradigms into sharper focus and to pay better attention to the implications of this paradigm shift for understanding the life of an ancient and foreign figure.

It was, however, the support and encouragement of several individuals that have contributed to the finalization of the manuscript. In the first phase of the research, the support of several friends and colleagues should be acknowledged. Gerd Theissen accepted the challenge to host me and my family in 1999–2000 as an Alexander von Humboldt fellow at the Ruprecht-Karls-Universität, Heidelberg. His hospitality and collegiality is highly appreciated, and I hereby wish to express my gratitude for the bold step of promoting a research project on Jesus as a shamanic figure when most would have turned away from the challenge. During seminars in Heidelberg, I have benefited not only from his comments and responses but also from those of Peter Balla and Harry Meier, fellow Humboldtians who made our stay in Heidelberg memorable, and from Annette Merz (at the time) a teaching assistant in Heidelberg. The financial support of the Alexander von Humboldt Foundation for the eleven-month sabbatical in Heidelberg is acknowledged, while sabbatical leave from the University of South Africa made it possible for me to focus on the research.

During this period, Bruce Malina read drafts of early chapters. Despite the fact that he did not agree with everything (in particular, with the term *shaman*), he encouraged me to continue the research. In many more ways than can be acknowledged here, his innovative research insights have motivated me to push through with these ideas. A visit to Nijmegen, on invitation by the late Sjef van Tilborg, for lectures on the topic resulted in his reading the first chapters. A stay with Sjef was always like visiting a sacred place, and in one of his very last letters he inspired me to complete this project.

The book is dedicated first to my friend and colleague at Unisa, Pieter Botha. From the beginning he saw the potential in the idea of the shamanic complex and as editor of a journal in 1999 was willing, against common opinion, to publish my first attempt. Most of the ideas expressed here have, over a cup of coffee, been echoed against his critical and supportive mind, while his own research has always been an inspiration for me to explore new avenues. His often unacclaimed and unrecognized promotion of the study of orality and oral cultures for understanding aspects of the transmission of the Jesus traditions has served as example of transformative thinking, while his meticulous attention to detail and context serves as a constant reminder for careful research.

Over the years members of the Context Group have mostly offered support for the idea, while their relentless and playful application of anthropological models in social-scientific interpretation have created the environment in which I have felt safe to explore my ideas. It is often in the remarkable novel ideas that emerge from this group that I found encouragement to pursue my own ideas of Jesus as Galilean shamanic figure. The friendship and collegiality that I have experienced over the years from members of the Context Group have kept me going against all odds, and I therefore also dedicate the book to this remarkable group of scholars.

The final manuscript was read and recommended by a number of scholars, some members of the Context Group. My deepest appreciation goes to Dick Rohrbaugh, Halvor Moxnes, Christopher Rowland, Stevan Davies, and John Lambert, who have either made valuable suggestions or provided the necessary inspiration to pursue its publication. They are not to be blamed for any shortcomings that remain in the text. From the editors at Wipf and Stock I have received the most friendly and professional support. From the first negotiations to the final editorial suggestions, editor-in-chief K. C. Hanson's engagement with the material has been exemplary in respecting an author's position, while copyeditor Jeremy Funk was considerate of my own style and preferences. Petra Dijkhuizen's proofreading skills have been invaluable.

Without the personal backup and encouragement from friends and colleagues, it would be so much more difficult to persevere with such a decade-long research project. It is with appreciation that I recall the friendship and collegial support of Johannes Vorster and Danie Goosen throughout this project.

The lives of the three people closest to me—my wife, Leona, and two daughters, Valmy and Leonette—have most severely been affected by this project. For ten years they have lived with the "shaman book," at times not even fully aware of what I was doing. The often-asked questions from my children in their early teens about what historical Jesus research is, not to mention what a shaman is, are indicative of their involvement and support for a father working in his study often in "family time." The pride with which they have explained to friends about their father's *book* provided more support and encouragement than what they will ever know. My deepest gratitude and thanks go to Leona who with her love and affection supported me. While it is easy to write a book confirming and supporting conventional viewpoints, love and loyalty are expressed during support for unconventional wisdom and research. Such support I have experienced more than deserved.

Introduction

IMAGINE THAT MOST OF what is written in the canonical Gospels is taken as reports about the life of a historical figure. Imagine that everything from the infancy narratives to the stories about an afterlife existence, from the healings and exorcisms to the claims about being a special emissary of the kingdom of God in his everyday activities, are seen as the residues of Jesus's life in first-century Galilee. Within the framework of current historical Jesus research, this is unimaginable because the canons of critical Jesus research state that a historical figure could not have been like any or all of the literary presentations available today. The historical figure is underneath the overlay of early Christian and church traditions that have transformed the stories about a historical figure into the mythical and literary compositions that they are. If the "miraculous," the "mythical," and the unbelievable reports in the Gospels are taken as belonging to the life of a social personage in first-century Galilee, a historical figure emerges who is incomprehensible in terms of the cognitive possibilities of most modern historical Jesus scholarship. This picture, however, is very much the product of a long interpretive tradition in critical Jesus research.

The aim of this book is to offer an alternative to both the existing historical pictures of Jesus and the historiographical paradigm by means of which such constructions are made. The aim is to offer a picture of the historical Jesus that from the start takes seriously that he was a social personage fully embedded in the cultural system and worldview of his time. What he said and did were said and done by a social personage embedded in the cultural processes and dynamics of the kind of figure that he was. Within the framework of what is called an *anthropological-historical perspective,* I will present a social-scientific picture of the historical Jesus as a Galilean shamanic figure. It is not a case of new answers to the old questions but of new answers to different questions since both what we are looking for (the historical figure) and what we are looking at (the literary evidence) as well as the research problem and the interpretive process are altered in this perspective.

The process of redescribing the historical Jesus problem and redefining the constituting components is the result of a variety of developments and insights. These did not take place all at once but emerged piecemeal under the influence of various factors.

Developments in social-scientific interpretation have been a constant influence in my thinking. Social-scientific interpretation as a major force on the interpretive scene focuses primarily on constructing appropriate first-century Mediterranean cultural and social scenarios for understanding biblical texts in their own setting.[1] But so far, Malina (2002b, 4) remarks, "there has been no 'life' of the historical Jesus based on social-scientific interpretations." As far as I know, this is still the case. One of the aims of this study is to redress that. If texts and documents are to be situated in appropriate cultural scenarios and social systems in order to know what they were saying, the same applies to a historical figure and the processes associated with the life of such a figure.

Some years ago I came across a book on shamanism and was struck by the similarities between the events and phenomena ascribed to the lives of shamanic figures and what is encountered in the canonical Gospels about Jesus of Nazareth. My first attempt at exploring the shamanic complex for understanding Jesus as historical figure was done within the framework of traditional historical Jesus research (see Craffert 1999a). The dominant theories about the sources as well as the distinction between the Jesus of history (the historical figure) and the Christ presentations of the Gospels were maintained, as it were. The shamanic model merely offered a different label (next to magician, Cynic, healer, prophet, and the like) for describing Jesus's social type with the suggestion that it could account for more of the elements and features ascribed to Jesus than the other models. Over time, that has changed.

---

1. Social-scientific interpretation has been under development for the last decade or two by members of the Context Group. It has been discussed in several studies dealing with the issue of the historical and cultural alienness of the New Testament documents and legitimate attempts to bridge those gaps (see Elliott 1993; Craffert 1994; 1995a; 1996; and for example, the essays in Neyrey 1991; Esler 1995; Pilch 2001; and Stegemann, Malina, & Theissen 2002).

Familiarity with social personages, such as shamanic figures, in many cultural settings raised important questions about the use of the social-type models in Jesus research (be this prophet, healer, wisdom teacher, Cynic, magician, rabbi, and the like). I was struck by the fact that very few, if any, of the models adequately cover all the data ascribed to Jesus of Nazareth, and if he was indeed such a figure (as assumed by the social-type model), that very little of the dynamics and cultural processes that would have colored his life are currently considered. Once the insights from anthropological and cross-cultural research about religious figures and social personages in real-life situations are taken seriously as a potential framework for grasping the nature and reality of Jesus as a historical figure, it becomes clear that historical constructions should include analyses of the way in which these constructions are constituted. The nature and character of such social figures are closely entangled with the cultural processes and dynamics associated with their lives. What is real and historical about such figures is closely connected to such processes and dynamics. If the conclusion of this study can be anticipated—if Jesus of Nazareth was a shamanic figure—he was so during his lifetime in Galilee, when he healed and taught, in what he said and did, and in how he was constituted and experienced as a social personage.

Engagement with reflections and developments in historiographical discourse led to a description of *anthropological historiography* as one approach beyond positivistic historiography. Like many other humanities scholars and social scientists, historians are grappling with the plurality of viewpoints and the multiplicity of reality systems that characterize the landscape of postmodern thinking. A major shift that took place in late-twentieth-century secular historiographical discourse is based on the acknowledgment of different forms of intellectual life as real and on the recognition that the strange and exotic in other historical eras can no longer be treated as the known and the common. Historiography became subject to the discourse of ontological pluralism and is looking toward models and insights from anthropology and cross-cultural studies to deal with its subject matter in a responsible way. These insights proved to be indispensable in a responsible historical interpretation of the strange features and alien phenomena ascribed to Jesus of Nazareth as a historical figure and social personage.

From this perspective it thus became apparent that much of the gospel material contains data that cannot be dealt with by means of the cultural system and reality construction of modern scientific societies. What Laughlin, McManus, and d'Aquili (1990, 155) say about Western science in general is equally true for historical Jesus research:

> The failure of modern Western culture to prepare individuals for an easy, fearless exploration of alternate phases of consciousness has the unfortunate consequence for science of not equipping most ethnographers with the experiential and conceptual material required for sophisticated research into the religious practices of other cultures.

Traditional historiography in general and New Testament studies in particular do not equip historical Jesus researchers to deal with the events or phenomena ascribed to the historical figure in a culturally sensitive way. More to the point, if Jesus of Nazareth was a cultural figure from a distant and alien cultural world (such as shamanic figures are to most modern Western societies), traditional Jesus research is inadequate to deal with either the historical figure or the historical remains that have originated as a result of such a social figure's life. In fact, if he was a shamanic figure (or the like), current historical Jesus research does not even have the sensors for picking up the clues in the texts referring to the historical and cultural reality of such a figure's life. From this point of view it became clear that despite variation and constant renewal in historical Jesus research, it remains trapped in the framework of the positivistic historiography from which the question first emerged more than one hundred and fifty years ago. Historical Jesus scholars are still trying to answer the questions and problems that gave rise to the quest at its onset. There is much renewal and puzzle-solving in the paradigm of historical Jesus research but very little renewal of the paradigm. It became clear that renewal will not follow from new answers to the old questions but will only be brought about by a new perspective, a new historiographical framework, as it were, and consequently, new answers to different questions.

One of the implications of this redescription of historical Jesus research is that the traditional views on the Gospels as being constituted in a linear and layered way are abandoned in favor of viewing the documents as residues of both his life as a social personage and the cultural processes and dynamics associated with such a life. If Jesus of Nazareth was a shamanic figure, the stories, reports, and accounts about his life from the very beginning probably included the features and characteristics of such a figure.

Therefore, they are to be treated as the residue, as cultural artifacts, about the life of a historical and social personage as well as the cultural processes accompanied by such a public life.

What makes a study such as this particularly difficult is that it is simultaneously an explanation of "how to" and a "do-it-yourself" manual. It is necessary to explain the how, why, and what of the paradigm while at the same time offering an exercise in doing it. It is like mapping and describing a road while still constructing it—the method has to be explained along the way while trying to cover the terrain. Therefore, as opposed to the well-known metaphors of the Schweitzerstrasse and the Wredebahn used to depict current historical Jesus research, the metaphor of *cultural bundubashing* will be used. This metaphor, taken from off-road driving, describes the adventure of going places where no roads have been built. Through an exploration of the cultural landscape of the first-century Mediterranean world in general and the reality system of shamanic figures in particular, cultural bundubashing will work toward the hypothesis that Jesus of Nazareth could plausibly be seen as a Galilean shamanic figure.

⊠ PART 1

A Paradigm Shift *in*

Historical Jesus Historiography

logical monism, the historian's worldview functions as the reality catalog. Ontological monism assumes a direct link or at least a continuum between the ancient and modern worlds. A common reality links the two worlds, so to speak, and for that reason, what they were talking about there (events of miraculous healings, special births, encounters with a heavenly Son of Man figure, encounters in a kingdom of God, to name only a few aspects), is assumed to belong to the world of common reality.

Other worldviews or cultural realities are disallowed the ontological status of "reality," and everything that does not fit that catalog is regarded as primitive, mythical, fictional, or not real. Whichever explanation is adopted, "reality" is viewed as monistic, and otherness is subjugated to or incorporated into this catalog. Whatever does not conform to the historian's *reality* catalog cannot be historical.

Within this ontological framework, positivistic and postmodern historiographies have developed unique configurations and practices of doing history. The components of these patterns form nested assumptions because, as Schinkel points out, the "way one thinks about reality has implications for the way one thinks about knowledge and truth. Ontology and epistemology are not philosophical islands, completely isolated, exerting no influence upon each other. On the contrary: epistemology and ontology support one another" (2004, 55).

Historiography on this continuum shares with Western thinking a second feature, which Fay describes as the "seesawing between the Scientific Attitude and the Rhetorical Attitude":

> In the former, language is something to be looked *through* to the Real, the given, the found; in the latter, language is something to be looked *at* as something which creates or structures what is called Real. The first attitude sees language as a means for getting to or connecting with what is extralinguistic; the second attitude sees language as the means by which meaningful reality is constituted. The former is referent-oriented; the latter is text-oriented. (1998, 3)[2]

Views on both language and reality are closely linked to the assumptions of ontological monism. Ontological monism finds expression in histo-

2. Fish remarks about these two attitudes: "But it would seem, from the evidence marshalled in this essay, that something is always happening to the way we think, and that it is always the same thing, a tug-of-war between two views of human life and possibilities, no one of which can ever gain complete and lasting ascendancy because in the very moment of its triumphant articulation each turns back in the direction of the other" (1990, 221).

riographical practices in what Tonkin describes as the "myth of realism" (1990, 25) and Malina refers to as the belief in *immaculate perception*: "the evidence is there for the picking, just read the sources!" (2002b, 5). Because a normative reality catalog is available, the natural veracity of any narrative is assumed while historians who use the recollections of others, Tonkin argues, "just scan them for useful facts to pick out, like currants from a cake" (1990, 25). Thus, documents are used as "transparent narrative or a quarry for facts."[3] This is a feature that postmodern historiography shares on an equal footing with traditional historiography. Historiography is conducted by simply "going there," to the world of the other via the testimonies about what has happened and what was said.

Positivist or Traditional Historiography

The scientific basis of positivistic or traditional historiography emerged during the nineteenth century and shared the optimism of the sciences that methodologically controlled research makes objective knowledge possible. In the first half of the twentieth century it shared with other sciences a broad positivistic attitude that reality is directly knowable by means of a correct method (see Fay 1998, 2) while a good deal of naive realism, which assumed that the historian simply discovers *how things were,* accompanied it (see Tosh 1984, 111–17). The hallmark of this approach is that historians "know things 'straight,'" as Wright describes it, because a picture theory of knowledge, which holds that truth is self-evident and beyond debate, underlies this position (1992a, 33). The influence of ontological monism is clearly visible here.

The basic task of the historian in versions on one side of the continuum can be described as a search for "realist factuality" or a "factual recreation or recovery of the past." It consists of arguing whether the data are reliable and sufficient to support a specific claim or not. Here, ontological monism finds expression in what Carr describes as the "fetishism of documents . . . If you find it in the documents, it is so" (1961, 16). This naive realism is supported by the idea that the documents contain testimonies. In picking out the testimonies, it is assumed that the sources reflect

3. The *myth of realism* as described here is not to be confused with the realism/antirealism debate mentioned above. The latter refers to two distinct philosophical positions regarding reality. The myth of realism, however, refers to the belief that facts can directly be extracted from evidence. The notion behind this belief is that the historian's narratives are empirically founded (see Lorenz 1998a, 314).

historical reality; just read and evaluate the sources, and historical factuality becomes apparent. This is the belief, as Collingwood argues, behind historical criticism, which offers a solution to a problem interesting to nobody but the practitioner of this kind of scissors-and-paste history; that is, the *history* "constructed by excerpting and combining the testimonies of different authorities" ([1946] 1970, 257). Scissors-and-paste history, he says, is based on the notion that the documents are testimonies to be questioned about their reliability:

> The presupposition of the problem is that in a certain source we have found a certain statement which bears on our subject. The problem is: Shall we incorporate this statement in our narrative or not? The methods of historical criticism are intended to solve this problem in one or other of two ways: affirmatively or negatively. In the first case, the excerpt is passed as fit for the scrap-book; in the second, it is consigned to the waste-paper basket. ([1946] 1970, 259)

In the history of historiography, the scientific attitude of positivistic or traditional historiography lasted for most of the twentieth century until it was challenged by the rhetorical attitude. During the latter part of the twentieth century the pendulum swung to what became known as *postmodern historiography*.

Postmodern Historiography

The basic idea of postmodern theory of history, Iggers says, "is the denial that historical writing refers to an actual historical past" (1997, 118). Without trying to give a full overview of this movement, the most significant feature certainly was an adoption of the assumptions of the Rhetorical position.

> That is, they highlighted the ways historians select events to figure in a narrative account (indeed, how incidents become historical events only by being brought within a narrative framework); how historians assign significance to events by placing them into a narrative context; and how historians themselves (rather than Reality) decide the basic form which a narrative will take. (Fay 1998, 5)

This is explicit in Ankersmit's claim that "we no longer have any texts, any past, but just interpretations of them" (1989, 137). For that reason, he says, history is like art and unlike science: "In the postmodernist view, the focus is no longer on the past itself, but on the incongruity between present and past, between the language we presently use for speaking about the past and the past itself" (1989, 153).

In postmodern historiography, ontological monism functions differently in what Fay calls "temporocentrism." That is the idea that "the modern historian is the master of ceremonies, so to speak, in wielding the power of reality and interpretation" (1998, 5). With the interpretive turn "a new form of intellectual hubris" has emerged in some circles, "the hubris of wordmakers who claim to be makers of reality" (Toews 1987, 906). Otherness and "the others" and consequently, *the past* are mastered by the worldview and cultural system of the *postmodern* interpreter.

Despite major shifts away from traditional historiography, Lorenz shows that this kind of postmodern historiography is an "inverted positivism" that remains attached to the fundamental conceptual structure of positivism (see 1998a, 312–20). Both the "either/or logic"[4] and the positivist opposition between literal and metaphorical language is maintained.[5] In setting up positivist historiography for its objectivist empirical viewpoint, he argues that postmodern historiographies retain, instead of reject empiricism:

> This inverted empiricism fulfills a crucial function in metaphorical narrativism because the plausibility of the fundamental theses on the fictionality of narrativity is completely dependent on its implicit contrast with empiricism . . . the identification of *all* interpretation with imposition, imaginary construction, and literary invention presupposes the possibility of *knowledge without interpretation*—and that is empiricism pure and simple. (1998a, 314–15)

The argument that historical narratives do not mirror the past in the way photographs and replicas do, presupposes this empiricist picture theory of knowledge and an empiricist theory of truth as direct correspon-

---

4. In history this logic, which Bernstein (see 1983) ascribes to the *Cartesian Anxiety*, finds expression in the following description: "either knowledge claims can be firmly founded in empirical data, or claims to knowledge are arbitrary and a sheer figment of imagination. *Fantasy* is thus presupposed to be the only alternative for and only opposition to *foundation*" (Lorenz 1998a, 313).

5. "This opposition between literal and metaphorical language—presupposed in positivism—is retained in 'metaphorical' narrativism in an inverted form: now descriptive statements are treated as mere information, hardly worth a serious philosopher's attention, and metaphorical language is upgraded to the real thing" (Lorenz 1998, 313).

dence.[6] But as Carroll says: "Obviously, historical narratives are not mirror images of the past; in general . . . they are not even pictorial, let alone perfect pictorial replicas of anything. But why should the fact that they are not pictures imply they are fictions?" (1998, 43).

Postmodern historiography introduced a strong criticism against the "soulless fact-oriented positivism" (Iggers & Von Moltke 1973b, xii) of traditional historiography. However, as Burke points out:

> It remains a pity that the majority of professional historians (I cannot speak for anthropologists and sociologists) have so far been so reluctant to recognize the poetics of their work, the literary conventions that they follow. There is a sense in which it is difficult to deny that historians construct the objects they study . . . It is equally difficult to deny the role of fiction 'in the archives' . . . On the other side, it is an equal pity that White and his followers, not to mention the theorists of narrative, have not yet seriously engaged with the question whether history is a literary genre or cluster of genres of its own, whether it has its own form of narratives and its own rhetoric, and whether the conventions include (as they sure do) rules about the relation of statements to evidence as well as rules of representation. Ranke, for example, was not writing pure fiction. Documents not only supported his narrative, but constrained the narrator not to make statements for which evidence was lacking. (1992, 128–29)

Historiography Beyond the Positivist–Postmodern Continuum

Within the framework of ontological monism the historian either creates or re-creates the historical subject straight, so to speak, because of the taken-for-granted reality catalog and the accompanied belief in immaculate perception. Precisely because of criticisms such as the above, the very continuum is questioned and is being replaced by approaches that take seriously an intellectual movement that has developed during the latter part of the previous century. Instead of "a dialectical middle ground" (Fay 1998, 11), which genuinely captures the truths of both sides, there is a movement in historiographical thinking beyond this dichotomy. It is in

---

6. A correspondence theory in historiography "sees historical statements as justified because they correspond to past events, and such correspondence is verified by the historian's establishing a foundation of hard facts upon which to base an interpretation, or around which to build a historical reconstruction" (Denton 2004, 163).

particular the replacement of ontological monism by some form of pluralism and the acceptance of multiple cultural realities, which are pushing historiography beyond the positivist–postmodern continuum.

Ontological Pluralism and Multiple Cultural Realities

The first development that has contributed to the movement beyond the positivist–postmodern continuum, and consequently to the possibility of reconceptualizing contemporary historiography, is a worldview development that consists of the recognition of multiple realities (worldviews) and some form of pluralism. A feature common to many thinkers today is the acceptance of some form of relativism, or a "celebration of contingency, fragmentation, fissures, singularity, plurality, and raptures" (Bernstein 1991, 307). This movement is characterized, on the one hand, by a reaction against ontological monism and, on the other hand, by a defense of multiple worldviews. A rejection of ontological monism is common to all thinkers in this movement for there is

> a willingness to emphasise the importance of the local and the contingent, a desire to underline the extent to which our own concepts and attitudes have been shaped by particular historical circumstances, and a corresponding dislike—amounting almost to hatred in the case of Wittgenstein—of all overarching theories and singular schemes of explanation. (Skinner 1985, 12)

The myth of realism that maintains the natural veracity of historical documents has been shattered with the recognition of multiple cultural realities. It is no longer obvious what the exotic or the alien documents are all about; texts and artifacts are contextually and culturally shaped and embedded where they belong to particular singularities. The philosophical foundation of this movement, Burke remarks, is "the idea that reality is socially and culturally constituted" (1991, 3). And this is true not only for the *postmodern* interpreter but particularly also for the alien and others encountered in the historical records and artifacts.

Since pluralism is open to many interpretations, it became necessary to qualify how it is to be understood because "not everything goes." Bernstein designs what is called *engaged fallibilistic pluralism*:

> For it means taking our own fallibility seriously—resolving that however much we are committed to our own style of thinking, we are willing to listen to others without denying or suppressing

the otherness of the other. It means being vigilant against the dual temptations of simply dismissing what others are saying by falling back on one of those standard defensive ploys where we condemn it as obscure, woolly, or trivial, or thinking we can always easily translate what is alien into our own entrenched vocabularies. (1991, 336)[7]

Among historians, Rüsen rejects "lazy pluralism" and suggests a pluralism as "a discursive relationship between different historical perspectives" (1993, 56), while Iggers argues for an "expanded pluralism" (1997, 140).[8]

In historical studies it was, in fact, scientific investigation that has destroyed the naive viewing of the past and foreign societies as if similar principles apply there as with us, Nipperdey points out (see 1978, 12). It resulted in a shift that takes seriously that cultural realities are expressions of the human spirit in its wide variety of forms.[9] It implies that the "dark, contrasting, strange, even exotic events, manners and forms of life are drawn into the attention of history" (Rüsen 1993, 210). But, the alien, the strange and the other can no longer be treated as the known, the common or the self as in the viewpoint of ontological monism. This is saying far more than that texts do not reflect reality in a one-to-one relationship—it is saying that distant texts should be treated as cultural artifacts or presentations of cultural realities that can no longer be evaluated by means of the god's-eye view or immaculate perception of a modern positivist worldview.

---

7. Lorenz refers to the insights of fallibilism and contextualism in the following way: "Contextualists recognize that all knowledge is relative to specific epistemic claims. And fallibilists recognize that *all* claims to knowledge are corrigible, and assume a hypothetical character, because there are no firm foundations of knowledge" (1998a, 350).

8. Bernstein suggests that some important distinctions are made: "For there is the danger of fragmenting pluralism where the centrifugal forces become so strong that we are only able to communicate with the small group that already shares our own biases, and no longer even experience the need to talk with others outside of this circle. There is *flabby* pluralism where our borrowings from different orientations are little more than glib superficial poaching. There is *polemical* pluralism where the appeal to pluralism doesn't signify genuine willingness to listen and learn from others, but becomes rather an ideological weapon to advance one's own orientation. There is *defensive* pluralism, a form of tokenism, where we pay lip service to other 'doing their own thing' but are already convinced that there is nothing important to be learned from them" (1991, 335–36).

9. Another shift was from the actions of great men to other forms of historical thinking, such as history of everyday life, microhistory, and cultural history (see Burke 1992, 38–43; Rüsen 1993, 170–80).

Beyond Objectivism and Relativism

The second development in pushing beyond the positivist-postmodern continuum was in philosophical thinking that, instead of the oppositional thinking, operates with the notion of dialog. Bernstein shows that the movement beyond objectivism and relativism involves the "practical task of furthering the type of solidarity, participation, and mutual recognition that is found in dialogical communities" (1983, 231). Instead of a middle position between the old scientific and rhetorical dichotomy (or subjectivism vs. objectivism, idealism vs. realism, or relativism vs. objectivism, to mention only some of the traditional dichotomies), this is a movement beyond these dichotomies that in a dialectical way deals with the insights from both sides—epistemologically and philosophically. In being beyond this dichotomy, this position is neither an oscillation nor a middle ground between them.

Within this viewpoint, the task of the historian can be formulated as a dialog with the past: "To be sure every historical account is a construct, but a construct arising from a dialog between the historian and the past, one that does not occur in a vacuum but within a community of inquiring minds who share criteria of plausibility" (Iggers 1997, 145).[10] But dialog assumes at least two voices or conversation partners, and in this perspective the historical past is recognized as an (alien) other.

Therefore, a distinction between the "two meanings of the word 'history'—between history as what actually happened and history as a collective *representation* of what happened" (Tosh 1984, 18)—is taken for granted. History as what actually happened remains an *other*, and in many instances a culturally alien other, while history as a representation is about that *past* as an other[11]:

> For although metaphorical narrativism surely deserves credit for the (re)discovery that historians produce texts and that history therefore possesses textual *aspects*, it is equally mistaken in its essential *identification* of history with its textual qualities . . . This is so because of a trivial but fundamental fact, namely, that his-

10. For three equally complex explanations of how the historical process of dealing with both interests and objectivity, with evidence and interests, at the same time, see Stanford (1986, 138–42), Rüsen (1993, 52–59), and Lorenz (1998b, 358–67).

11. If history is only what is written, what is created by historians, "then all elements of the historical field are equally real, since the real minds of historians create them" (Stanford, 1986, 34).

tory, contrary to all fictional literature, is always about something *outside* the text—the real past. This *referential quality of historical narratives* explains why the construction of narratives about the past is an activity with *disciplinary, intersubjective controls,* because the ways in which we refer with words to things are intersubjective. The fact that reference is not self-evident cannot be regarded as an argument contra the referential quality of language because reference is *never* a simple given. (Lorenz 1998a, 324)

These developments have not destroyed the historian's commitment to recapturing reality or his or her belief in a logic of inquiry. In fact, the historicity of strange, exotic, and alien forms of life, Rüsen says, "lies in their marring the common sense criteria of historical interpretation" (1993, 210). Therefore, it is necessary to capture some of the fundamentals of historical inquiry and historical knowledge presupposed by such a historiographical paradigm.

(Anthropological) Historiography in a New Paradigm

These movements result in a shift to a hermeneutic (interpretive) approach in the human sciences in general and in historiography in particular to do justice to the meaning, significance, and context of the people involved (see also Stanford 1986, 78).[12] Iggers refers to these movements as a "transformation of consciousness" (1997, 6).

The postmodern critique of traditional science and traditional historiography has offered important correctives to historical thought and practice. It has not destroyed the historian's commitment to recapturing reality or his or her belief in a logic of inquiry, *but it has demonstrated the complexity of both.* (Iggers 1997, 16; italics mine)[13]

---

12. This development is often associated with the so-called *interpretive turn,* which can be identified in a variety of disciplinary circles (see Craffert 1995b, 21–26). At least two assumptions characterize these studies: first, an incommensurability between cultures is assumed (which means that commensurability has to be argued or demonstrated instead of being assumed); second, since humans are all enmeshed in a particular culture, interpretation is a fundamental condition of being human. The first implies that humans are cultural beings, the second that they are interpretive beings.

13. It should be noted that Iggers uses the term *postmodern historiography* in a much broader sense than those classified above. Above, the term refers to historians who strongly ascribe to the Rhetorical Attitude and consequently see history only as what the historian produces.

In such a framework, the question of historical authenticity is not one of authentic snippets but of adherence to the context—historical and cultural: "If we want to make contact with another mind, we need not only some similarity of symbolic usage and of conceptual systems, but the understanding by both parties of the situation—or, more generally, the context" (Stanford 1986, 118).

Within these movements, historical studies developed new modes of defining itself—both internally and in relation to its subject matter. One such an approach, to be referred to as *anthropological historiography*, will be offered here. It is my attempt, based on the above developments in the world of historiographic discourse, to design an interpretive paradigm for historical Jesus research, which will avoid the pitfalls and shortcomings of current historical Jesus research.

The aim, therefore, is to describe and explain the complexity of such a historiographical paradigm. This paradigm is based not only on an avoidance of the inherent pitfalls and shortcomings of the positivist/postmodern continuum but particularly on what is missing from it. This transformation of consciousness indeed refers to a different worldview and philosophical viewpoint from which the historiographical task is undertaken. The result, therefore, is not merely a reformulation of either positivist or postmodern historiography but a development that can be seen as a movement beyond this continuum.

Historiography as a Dialog with the Past

The constitutive principle in doing history, Thompson reminds us, is "pastness" (1993, 262). The activity of doing history is an activity designed to answer questions about a past, which is construed in terms of its pastness and hence in terms of its difference from the present. It is to place texts, artifacts, events, and persons in a world different from the world of the present. The aim in historicizing material from the past, therefore, is to offer explanations of past activities in terms of their pastness and otherness. In historical Jesus research, it would mean showing how things were in the world (texts, events, phenomena, and social types), how things were connected, and how things hung together in the past and alien culture. Therefore, even though the historical other is also a construction, the dialog takes place between two partners, and the distant and alien other (or past) has to be recognized for its otherness.

Within this paradigm, the acceptance of ontological pluralism and the interpretive process as dialogical has a domino effect on both meanings of the word *history*. Against the notion that historians can recreate the past, anthropological historiography admits against a naive realism that there is no one-to-one referentiality (or representation of reality). But that does not mean realism is to be abandoned or referentiality is to be sacrificed. This is not to fall victim to naive realism (see Stanford 1986, 26; Lorenz 1998b, 351).[14] Pluralism affirms the existence and reality of alien and distant pasts, just as the alien and distant present is acknowledged as outside and different to the interpreter. Historians have learned that science and history are both representational but "not a simulacrum of reality," because "no matter how veridical a representation is, it is still a representation: a facsimile of reality and not reality itself" (Fay 1998, 8).[15] Discovery of the past, therefore, is not objective in the sense of re-creating the past. That is impossible, but in the sense of a reconstruction as approximation (see Iggers 1997, 145). Once it is accepted that history as representation of the past can never be a re-creation or recovery of that past event or phenomenon, then it is unnecessary to avoid the term *reconstruction*. "Construction" too often carries the notion of the historian *creating* the past. "Reconstruction" realizes it is only an approximation of the past reality with an open invitation to correct such reconstructions. Reconstruction of the past (history as representation) takes place within the setting of dialog with the past (of history as what actually happened).

From this perspective, the task of historians include, on the one hand, the ideal of recovering the past (in the sense of meeting the distant and alien other) and, on the other hand, the ideal of showing up falsifications (in the sense of misrepresentations) of the distant and alien other.

14. "*Realism is the view that there is a way that things are that is logically independent of all human representation. Realism does not say how things are but only that there is a way that they are*" (Searle 1995, 155). It is like distant galaxies, which remain beyond our reach but not beyond the possibility of our knowing them better (see also Hesse 1990).

15. Haskell makes this point well in a parable about maps. A map is not a territory, and when we want to go to, say, Paris, we know perfectly well that maps can help, and we also know that some maps are better than others. We also know that none of the maps actually is *Paris* (see 1998, 315). Or, in the words of Lorenz, "Historians themselves claim to represent the past and thus subscribe to the 'reality-rule'; the mere fact that the past is only known by us through a frame of description therefore does not entail the conclusion that the past *is* a description" (1998b, 366–67).

> This distinction between truth and falsehood remains fundamental
> to the work of the historian. The concept of truth has become im-
> measurably more complex in the course of recent critical thought
> . . . Nevertheless the concept of truth and with it the duty of the
> historian to avoid and to uncover falsification has by no means
> been abandoned. As a trained professional he continues to work
> critically with the sources that make access to the past reality pos-
> sible. (Iggers 1997, 12)[16]

It remains the task of historians to "recover some of our losses from
the past" as Stanford expresses it (1986, 50). At the same time, the historian is constantly on the lookout for forgery or falsification (either of the
sources or of representations). Again, this aim does not claim absolute
truth or knowledge. In practice, this philosophical position shifts the task
and focus of historians away from the problem of foundations for knowledge but to the issue of argumentation of claims to fallible knowledge (see
Lorenz 1998b, 350). This means that "when historians believe a particular
fact about the past, they assume it provides accurate information about
the world, even though they know (i) it is possible that the purported
fact is not true, and (ii) we have no independent access to the world to
know whether a particular description of the world is true" (McCullagh
2004, 26).[17]

The recognition of the fundamental plurality of worlds and realities
already includes a rejection of the *myth of the framework*.[18] As human beings we are not imprisoned in our frameworks, and the failure to find ways
of escaping them is an ethical and not a cognitive or linguistic one (see
Bernstein 1991, 336). The more vehemently we insist on the insight that

16. The task of the (anthropologically minded) historian remains "to establish as firmly
as possible events and states of affairs in the past; and to find the most appropriate words
in which to relate and describe—that is, to communicate—those findings to other people"
(Stanford 1986, 74).

17. In this view, it is accepted that "however arbitrary historical explanation might
be, it is nowhere near as arbitrary as such [postmodern] *ex cathedra* pronouncements of
canonizations or anathemas. In the end, those who advocate, or practice, history merely as
a form of moral rhetoric have no defense at all against those who disagree with them and
practice a moral rhetoric of another kind, one which for example praises Hitler as a friend
of the Jews, or damns Churchill as a warmonger and mass murderer" (Evans, 2002, 87).

18. Popper uses the term "the myth of framework" to describe the human condition
of being imprisoned in our language and categories: "I do admit at any moment we are
prisoners caught in the framework of our theories; our expectations; our past experiences;
our language. But we are prisoners in a Pickwickian sense: if we try, we can break out of
our framework at any time" (1970, 56).

we can only see from our perspectives, the more we will have to acknowledge that others also construct their realities and that the only access to such constructions is via socially interpreted reality. The stronger our insistence on socially constructed reality, the stronger our commitment should be to understand others' beliefs and practices within the framework of their socially constructed cultural systems and views of reality. Therefore, this paradigm emphasizes the need for practical ways of encountering the other and the alien but without pressing our standards onto them.

In all of this, the documents and artifacts of the past are not treated as re-creations of the past reality or with the view that they in any way provide direct or immediate access to the past. Instead, from this point of view they are seen as in themselves cultural artifacts produced by and in the sphere of a particular cultural system that is not that of the historian. Instead of treating the documents as testimonies, they are treated as evidence of culturally constructed realities.[19] To be precise, it is to treat the gospel documents not as either authentic or inauthentic collections of testimonies about Jesus of Nazareth but as cultural artifacts connected to a social personage and to a particular sociohistorical setting.

Historiography as a Cross-Cultural Activity

With the acceptance of this paradigm, a choice has been made for an interdisciplinary and cross-cultural historiographical process. In anthropological historiography it is realized that the unique can only be understood in a social context, and that requires an understanding of that context by means of theoretical constructs and comparative methods. As Stanford says, "for historians, perhaps more than any others, the truth must be seen in the context of time and place" (1986, 170). Or, as Rüsen describes it:

> Historical studies looks at cultures which do not belong to the tradition of western self-understanding and deliberately adopts its methods to accommodate these cultures, thereby even alienating itself from the western historical tradition in order to release the sparks of the alternative from its own history. (1993, 178–79)

Therefore, it acknowledges the interconnectedness between historical and anthropological interests:

---

19. Collingwood explains well the difference between treating documents as testimonies and as evidence (1970, 256–57).

> Historians and anthropologists have a common subject matter, 'otherness;' one field constructs and studies 'otherness' in space, the other in time. Both fields have a concern with text and context. Both aim, whatever else they do, at explicating the meaning of actions of people rooted in one time and place, to persons in another. Both forms of knowledge entail the act of translation. (Cohn 1980, 198)

Historians consult anthropological literature "not for prescriptions, but for suggestions; not for universal rules of human behavior, but for relevant comparisons" (Davis 1982, 273). It is one way of establishing the criteria of plausibility.

But anthropologists and historians have long recognized that the interpretive process escapes perfect description due to the inevitable tension inherent in it: identification and distancing. A process of bracketing, complemented with a process of comparing the other's world and one's own world, is more to the point in describing cross-cultural interpretation. Therefore, the cross-cultural interpretive process consists of at least three distinct but interconnected tasks: first, grasping the subjects' cultural system in the strongest possible light (thick description); second, paying attention to the interpreter's cultural system; and, third (by way of contrast), conducting cross-cultural comparisons and dialog.[20]

The Historian's Cross-Cultural Toolkit

It should be realized that this process, which can be taken apart analytically, is actually a closely intertwined process. In reality it does not follow a linear or logical track because the grasping of alienness (and of our own "strangeness") and the comparison and dialog between cultural systems often take place in the same moment.

CROSS-CULTURAL INTERPRETATION: RECOGNIZING DIFFERENT FORMS OF INTELLECTUAL LIFE

The objective of situating different tasks in the interpretive process places considerable strain on the hermeneutic circle metaphor, which is not suited to deal with it. Therefore, the cognitive metaphor of the hermeneutic circle can be supplemented with that of bracketing.

---

20. A full discussion of this process has been done elsewhere (see Craffert 1996, 457–61).

As has already been suggested, anthropological historiography recognizes the cultural reality of the "other." In fact, one of the pillars of all anthropological research (which is employed here) is the recognition that words, texts, gestures, and the like have meaning within a specific cultural system. In the words of two well-known anthropologists: "In order to construe the gestures of others, their words and winks and more besides, we have to situate them within the systems of signs and relations, of power and meaning, that animate them" (Comaroff & Comaroff 1992, 10–11). Therefore, as Nipperdey suggests: "It is part of the procedure of historians that they skillfully and critically distance themselves from their own presuppositions and perspectives" because "ancient, medieval or pre-modern man [*sic*] behaved in a way that was completely different to what we are inclined to think on the basis of our own experience" (1978, 12).[21] Grasping their ultimate presuppositions implies a temporary moratorium on those of the interpreter.

What this means is that in the evaluation of documentary sources, "before anything else can be achieved, the historian must try to enter the mental world of those who created the sources" (Tosh 1984, 116). To begin with, it is necessary to appreciate what the sources are about. The recognition of the reality of the native's point of view is the direct counterpart of the positivist historian's conviction that the study of documents is the means by which a true or real account of what *actually happened* can be constructed (see Cohn 1982, 241). A repetition of what the sources say is not yet historiography. As Tonkin says: it is misleading to use documents as

> transparent narrative or a quarry for facts . . . for we . . . who use life stories need to understand, and more precisely identify how, whether mythic or realistic, poetic or phlegmatic, they always have to be structured, according to known conventions, in order to convey the desire—fearful, hortatory, or ironic—of this teller to present a self to this listener, at this particular moment. (1990, 34)

It does not help to know only what the sources say but also to understand what they mean and assume. A responsible engagement with cultural artifacts replaces the practice of immaculate perception (or, what

21. Therefore, another cornerstone of historiography in this paradigm is that historians must grasp the absolute presuppositions, the unspoken assumptions, of the society under review, in order to understand what has occurred (see Stanford 1986, 93).

has been called the "myth of realism") where sources are merely used as testimonies.

CROSS-CULTURAL INTERPRETATION AS THICK DESCRIPTION: A WINK IS NOT A TWITCH

While the ancients are no longer available to be consulted on our grasp of the rules by means of which they lived, insulted, acted (im)politely, worshiped, or reproduced, the only controls in an anthropological historiographical interpretation over flights of imagination are "sensitive readings of ancient texts, attention to archaeological evidence, and a familiarity with religious cultures in other times and other places" (Eilberg-Schwartz 1990, 238). Cultural events (such as exorcisms and visions) and social personages (such as shamans) are firmly embedded in specific cultural systems. But for that reason cross-cultural and comparative tools, together with a truly interdisciplinary and interpretive approach that takes seriously the otherness of the ancients, are inevitable.

If cross-cultural interpretation implies a grasp of the otherness in its strongest possible light, the first task of the historian remains to grasp the cultural particularity involved. Geertz explains this with the example of two boys rapidly contracting the eyelids of their right eyes (1973, 6). In one instance it is an involuntary twitch, in another a conspiratorial signal to a friend; from an eyewitness perspective they are similar movements, but the one is a twitch and the other a wink—the differences are unphotographable. Descriptions can vary from "thin" (rapid contracting of eyelids—twitch) to "thick" (deliberate act of communication—wink). That is, "discovering and reconstructing deep layers of meaning in human interaction" (Walters 1980, 542), or in Burke's words, thick description "may be defined as a form of translation, a making explicit, for the benefit of non-members, of the rules implicit in a given culture" (1987, 6). It is part of the burden of the outsider (the historian) to grasp what is implicit, unsaid, taken for granted, or generally assumed in the reality system of the insiders. Thick description is the "stranger's exegetical recovery of intelligible clues and contexts that are acted out and interpreted—often unconsciously—within the culture studied" (Medick 1987, 87).

CROSS-CULTURAL INTERPRETATION AS DIALOG:
"MAKING SENSE OF" IS NOT THE SAME AS "SAYING IT MAKES SENSE"

The defense of pluralism contains an acknowledgment of the contingency of "the other," which is based on the realization of one's own contingency. And if the other can no longer be mastered, absorbed, or reduced to one's own, a new interpretive strategy is called for. With Bernstein it finds expression in a strategy of dialog, conversation, and debate within the framework of fallibilism (see 1983, 223–24).

An adequate cross-cultural interpretation can never stop at the point of examining (bracketing) the subjects' world since interpretation, by definition, is comparative, in that understanding has to take place in two worlds at once—that of the interpreter and that of the subjects. As Taylor reminds us, "it will frequently be the case that we cannot understand another society until we have understood ourselves better as well" (1985, 129). And if that is the case, then an adequate interpretation also includes a better grasp of ourselves as agents in the world—which means, at least in our case, in an industrialized, scientific world.

For cross-cultural interpretation also demands, as Bernstein points out, "the need to make critical discriminations and judgments" because not "all forms of otherness and difference are to be celebrated" (1991, 313). Elsewhere I have argued: "We can be passionately committed to the beliefs that regulate our actions when they are based on the strongest possible historically-contingent justifications. This is different from declaring our vocabulary final, immune to criticism, or the norm for evaluating others" (Craffert 1996, 464). The engagement with otherness in this paradigm, therefore, inevitably includes cultural dialog and criticism—of the other and one's own.

Pressing as far as possible toward making sense of the subjects' point of view is not the same as saying that the interpreter should adopt their point of view. Turning native is like swallowing the propaganda that created the interpretive problem in the first place: it not only amplifies an existing problem (in that it adds one more subject to be understood by outsiders); it also rules out the possibility of showing cultural beliefs or practices as wrong, confused, or deluded (see Taylor 1985, 123).

Making sense of the subjects' viewpoint is not the same as saying that their viewpoint makes sense. The challenge remains to grasp their view of cultural reality in its full force without having to ascribe to the truth of it. An example, to be discussed in detail, of a now-foreign viewpoint sensible in some past cultures are the ancient theories of embryology and sexology that, from a modern biological point of view, need no longer be accepted as a true reflection of procreation. What is "culturally" real and historical is not necessarily "comparatively" real and historical because of this comparative perspective.

Beyond a History-of-Ideas to Material and Cultural Dynamics and Processes

Another feature of the above continuum of historiography is often de- scribed as a *history-of-ideas approach*. It is concerned with the history of texts and ideas in the text but without engagement in the cultural dynamics and cultural processes behind the texts and ideas. What is extracted from the documents is a narration of events or ideas (see Barraclough 1978, 51; Burke 1991, 4) but without an involvement with the human and social processes behind them. This is the logical result of treating documents as testimonies—they contain valuable ideas or data divorced from bodies and life. In fact, they are read for the testimonies they contain about events or ideas.

When data are treated as true or false testimony, it is easy to also fall into the trap of a history-of-ideas approach. An example is treatment of the gospel documents for their testimonies about Jesus of Nazareth, about what he said and about what he allegedly did. Marsh's understanding of Wright's Jesus picture clearly illustrates the history-of-ideas hang-up, so to speak:

> If a sociological base for Jesus is hard to pinpoint in his account, then it suggests that the picture of Jesus being offered is less con- crete than may be supposed. Even if it can be argued that in the first century beliefs were much more praxis-oriented than they are in the present, *Jesus remains located (and locked, despite such statements . . .) in a world of texts and ideas* . . . . (1998, 83; italics mine)

When treated as evidence, documents immediately become entrance points to cultural worlds and processes. That is, to an understanding of the cultural dynamics, the social processes, and the social assumptions that the ancients took for granted. In this mode of historical thinking, which Rüsen refers to as "societal history," history "does not take place anymore on the level of intentional actions, but on the deeper level of structural conditions and presuppositions for actions" (1993, 174).

Despite the fact that Jesus of Nazareth is treated in current scholarship as a prophet or sage or wisdom teacher or the like, most analyses lack any appropriate treatment of the cultural dynamics and cultural processes that would have accompanied his life. Even if Jesus is seen as a prophet, teacher, or healer, the focus remains on what can be deduced from the testimonies regarding his words and deeds. However, if Jesus was a historical figure of such a nature (prophet, teacher, healer, or the like), his life was inscribed in social and cultural processes and not merely the result of atomistic sayings and deeds. It is an inclusion of these elements (i.e., social and cultural processes) in the historical construction that distinguishes a culturally sensitive construction from one based on a history-of-ideas; and these social and cultural processes are particularly lacking in historical Jesus research. What is missing from such constructions are the material and cultural settings that enable texts and ideas to be embodied in the real life of those concerned.

The Conscious and Self-critical Use of Anthropological Models

Unlike the linear and direct access to events and sayings (the testimonies) assumed in approaches influenced by ontological monism, a different interpretive process is imagined in a world of ontological pluralism and multiple cultural realities. Neither the temporal nor the cultural gap is directly bridgeable by simply "going there" because by going there, a foreign country is encountered. What they are doing and saying "there" can only be approached with reservation and caution. Some of the most powerful tools in conducting cross-cultural research, therefore, are cross-cultural models (which are often the product of previous processes of interpretations and comparisons).

From the perspective of anthropological historiography, the historical Jesus scholar is faced with a similar challenge as the historical anthropologist trying to understand a religious figure in a foreign, historical community. Therefore, it comes at a price. It requires an interdisciplinary vehicle carrying anthropological models, an appropriate cross-cultural toolkit, as well as a willingness to depart from the well-trodden roads of established research. Part of, or prior to, asking about historicity comes the question of what it is that is supposed to be taken as historical and, as this discussion shows, in a cross-cultural situation, that question hardly ever has a single answer.

Like the historical anthropologist and the anthropological historian, the New Testament scholar has far less information than the field anthropologist and therefore has to rely on the methods of historical anthropology, which is an attempt, on the basis of ideas about certain cultures and how they work, to imagine what the culture of specific historical people might have been like. Eilberg-Schwartz calls it a sort of reconstructive art (see 1990, 238). Anthropological studies provide the scenarios by means of which appropriate frameworks can be built for comparison and description. Anthropology "can widen the possibilities, can help us take off our blinders, and give us a new place from which to view the past and discover the strange and surprising in the familiar landscape of historical texts" (Davis 1982, 275). This task is like that of the detective: the more exposure one gets to different historical cultures, the better one is equipped for identifying the traces in a particular case; the more one knows, the more one sees!

The models to be used in this study (the shamanic complex and a model of alternate states of consciousness [ASCs]) belong to the category "homomorphic models" (Carney 1975, 9–11).[22] In contrast to isomorphic models, which are models built to scale as exact replicas (such as model trains or globes), homomorphic models reproduce only selected salient features of an object. These may themselves be abstractions, such as social

22. The acronym *ASC* is commonly used in the literature for "altered states of consciousness." This phrase is, however, not without its problems. Both the history of the term "altered" (it was first used to describe the states brought about by psychedelic drugs—see Austin 1998, 309–10) and its implicit pejorative (ethnocentric) connotation (these states represent a deviation from the way consciousness should be—see Zinberg 1977, 1 n. 1) discredit its continuous use. What is "ordinary" consciousness is not the same for all human beings, and on a cultural level, a distinction can be made between *baseline* (or normal) and *alternate states of consciousness*, and they will differ from culture to culture. In other words, there is no single distinction between *consciousness* and *altered state of consciousness* (with the implication that a fixed set of altered states exist for all human beings). In this study, the preference is for the term "alternate," because that word "makes it clear that different states of consciousness prevail at different times for different reasons and that no one state is considered standard" (Zinberg 1977, 1 n. 1). Or as Austin says, the term "alternate" states the obvious that "many optional states occur." It is hoped that it will be clear that even thought the term "alternate" and the acronym *ASC* will be used in this study, they do not contain any suggestion of states that are homoversally "altered" (1998, 306). In this study, as argued elsewhere (see Craffert 2002), *ASC* will be used for "alternate state of consciousness" and ASCs for "alternate states of consciousness."

systems or bureaucratic forms of government or the shamanic complex.[23] It can therefore be said that cross-cultural models operate in the territory between cultural systems and allow us to see both ways.

Besides the use of specific models, insights from other anthropological studies will also be employed—in particular, insights from medical anthropology—for grasping the strange and alien nature both of the documents and of what they contain.

The origins and dynamics of a specific model are linked to the original research from which it was conceptualized and abstracted, and future applications will have to deal with these qualities of the model.[24] This means that the question whether Jesus as historical personage can be understood by means of a specific model (e.g., as shamanic figure) is different from deciding whether that specific model is appropriate for understanding phenomena in the first-century Mediterranean world. Both aspects will therefore be considered.

The use of anthropological models in the interpretive perspective proposed here operates on the basis that models and insights from the social sciences (especially anthropology) are consciously employed in creating first-century scenarios for promoting understandings that do not present themselves otherwise. Modern authors do not provide their readers (and ancient authors did not provide theirs) with a quick guide for understanding the cultural script, the life processes, and the cultural dynamics presupposed in written documents. In short, texts do not *contain* but *presuppose* a certain common culture (a cultural script) and a notion of how the world works (worldview). Understood against this background, anthropological (or cross-cultural) models work against "home-blindedness" in sensitizing readers to understand what goes unsaid in a specific setting; they help out-

23. The metatheoretical principle of such models is that there are degrees of culture-boundedness that we are in principle capable of measuring (see Rosemont 1988). Admitting that we are imprisoned in our own cultural categories does not necessarily mean that we are always trapped beyond the point of escaping (see Craffert 1996, 454). Such being the case, we can also agree that some cross-cultural models can help us to discover similarities between various cultural phenomena.

24. In an evaluation of the "goodness of fit" of Wilson's sect model for use on New Testament material, it has been argued that too many features assumed in the internal dynamics of the model cannot be harmonized with the cultural system of the first-century world. These include the invention of a Jewish parent body from which the sects deviated, the assimilation of features from much later periods, and the postulation of an internal dynamic in sect movements that does not correspond to the general cultural system of the first-century world (see Craffert 2001a). See also the discussion of Botha (1994).

siders grasp the dynamics of foreign cultural phenomena. They are helpful in showing what is there, and what is assumed, not simply to label what is already known or can easily be identified. They are tools for conducting thick descriptions.

Cultural anthropology in general, and the shamanic complex in particular in this study, offer the New Testament scholar a range of scenarios about human activities, experiences, phenomena, and social types that are different from those taken for granted by modern Western exegetes. They can expose "home-blindness" by helping to bridge the cultural and historical distance and by capturing otherness, placing it in a comparative context (see Burke 1990, 270).[25]

The Nature and Construction of Cultural Realities

In anthropological historiography it is accepted that because of the social and cultural construction of reality, human beings live in a world partly of their own making. Everyday reality is interpreted and experienced in a cultural way. As Malina indicates: "*All human beings are entirely the same, entirely different, and somewhat the same and somewhat different at the same time*" (2001a, 7; italics his). The first emphasizes that human beings are all the same on a physical, anatomical, and sensate level. Our hearts pump blood and our brains function as the cognitive hub of our bodies. Each individual is a unique replica of being such a human body and being while given the cultural patterns of human actions, experiences, meaning, and feeling, there are identifiable patterns that are based on the same hardware (see Malina 2001a, 8–9).

But that does not tell us what the nature of such cultural experienced realities is like. Since the topic of this study is an understanding of a historical figure as a social personage, a threefold distinction will be applied in order to make sense of the variety of events and phenomena that contribute to the constitution of a social personage: those that are unique to a given cultural system, those that are only unique cultural interpreta-

25. The same principle is expressed in a warning when MacIntyre (1971, 226) says that the "crude notion that one can first learn a language and then secondly and separately go on to understand the social life of those who speak it can only flourish where the languages studied are those of the peoples whose social life is so largely the same as our own, so that we do not notice the understanding of social life embodied in our grasp of the language; but attempts to learn the alien language of an alien culture soon dispose of it."

tions or representations of normal human phenomena, and those that are cultural presentations of otherwise common human phenomena.

THE REALITIES OF ALIEN EVENTS AND PHENOMENA

The acknowledgment of multiple worldviews and reality systems is based on the insight that large portions of the real world, objective facts in the world, "are only facts by human agreement" (Searle 1995, 1). These are called *social facts* or *socially created reality* or *institutional facts* (they will be called *cultural reality* in this study), which are ontologically real, but they exist only within human institutions.[26]

These things are "objective" facts in the world in the sense that they are not a matter of your or my preferences, evaluations, or attitudes but are dependent on human institutions for their existence. In short, culture is real without being an objective "thing" (see Peacock 1986, 1–20). Cultural realities, such as the piece of paper in your pocket, which is a ten-dollar bill, Searle explains, are different from "brute" facts, such as the fact that Mount Everest has snow and ice near the summit, which is totally independent of any human opinion (see 1995, 1–3, 7–13). In order to show that cultural realities can be objective (based on the intersubjective agreement of a group of people), and still depend on human institutions and the role of language to be objective, he makes three useful distinctions.

The first is that between objective and subjective distinctions in an epistemic sense. An epistemic subjective judgment such as, "Rembrandt is a better artist than Rubens" can be contrasted with an epistemic objective judgment, such as "Rembrandt lived in Amsterdam during the year 1632," which is true or false independent of anybody's attitudes or feelings. The latter (if true) constitutes an objective fact.

The second distinction is between ontological subjective facts (such as pain, which is dependent on a sense perception) and an ontological objective entity (such as a mountain, which existence is independent of any perceiver or mental state). Judgments about such ontological objective entities can be epistemically subjective ("this mountain is more beautiful than that one") while epistemically objective statements can be made about ontological subjective entities ("I have a pain in my back!" can be

26. It is what Berger and Luckmann call the "reality of everyday life," which "is taken for granted as reality" by all people (1966, 37), and what Burke calls "the latent rules of daily life" (1991, 11) of how to be a father or a daughter, a ruler or a saint in a given culture.

a report about an epistemically subjective fact that does not depend on outside observers).

The third distinction is between intrinsic and observer-relative features of the world. An intrinsic feature of objects is that they have a certain mass and chemical composition independent of any observer, while observer-relative features do not add any new material objects to reality but add epistemically objective features. An object with a certain mass and chemical composition (independent of any observer) can be a screwdriver; that the object is a screwdriver is an observer-relative judgment (but this ontological subjective judgment can be more than a personal opinion and depend on intersubjective approval and thus be culturally real). These three distinctions cut across one another, but together they provide the conceptual tools for understanding the ontological status of cultural realities.

Cultural realities cannot be captured and described in the language of physics and chemistry. Searle explains this with the example of buying a beer in a restaurant in Paris: "There is no physical-chemical description adequate to define 'restaurant,' 'waiter,' 'sentence of French,' 'money,' or even 'chair' and 'table,' even though all restaurants, sentences of French, money, and chairs and tables are physical phenomena" (1995, 3). But all these are cultural realities that make up that part of human life that is real but not material or physical. Just as paying a restaurant bill with a piece of paper is a "real event" that consists of much more than the observable actions of the participants, an exorcism, demon possession, or heavenly journey can be a real cultural event within a particular cultural system, consisting of much more than the observable or material actions.

These cultural real things (events and phenomena) exist for us and for all other people on the planet. They are just radically different for different people. Examples include things like money, property, government, and marriages; but also experiences of consciousness such as out-of-body flights or possession experiences. The distinction between observer-dependent and observer-independent features also applies to social personages—some features are just not ontologically objective.

Anthropological literature shows that specific social types are often credited with particular cultural events and phenomena.[27] As Vitebsky (1995, 142), for example, says: "Shamanic cultures have particular as-

27. "Social type" refers to a person's social identity in terms of values, behavior, style, and habits. Social types represent patterns in cultural conduct. For details, see below, Chapter 5.

sumptions about what exists (ontology) and how things happen (causality). If one shares these assumptions, then the possibility of effective shamanic action follows." As in many traditional societies today, locals understand that certain social types (like shamans) "provide" the game or fish, provide protection or control the elements (like bringing rain), travel to other worlds in out-of-body flights and the like. Notions of controlling the elements, experiencing spirit-possession, controlling and commanding spirits, experiencing miraculous healings, recounting special births, and the like are stories that make sense in many traditional cultural systems and particularly in a shamanic worldview. For Jesus's compatriots, Jesus could control the elements, walk on the sea, provide food and drink, converse with the ancestors, return after his death, and so forth. Not once do we find an explanation in the texts about what is "actually" being conveyed. Other cultural events or phenomena ascribed to Jesus of Nazareth include his baptism, exorcisms, visionary experiences, and the ability to read and write. The "reality" of such events is appreciated as embedded in the complexity of the whole system and particular institution (see Craffert 2001b, 111–13). The challenge is on outsiders to grasp their otherness and to deal with the strangeness, and where necessary, to engage in cultural dialog.

A visitation by an ancestor or a heavenly being is a particular kind of cultural event in some cultural systems. However, the same event can also be viewed comparatively or cross-culturally (for example, as an ASC visionary experience, which is a possibility within the common realm of human experience). This becomes exponentially more complex in situations where large numbers of people are involved in the cultural event or experience (such as an exorcism, healing, or baptism scene), which can be described simultaneously by an alternative set of concepts. A soul flight by a shaman must be considered a historical event of some sort within specific cultural systems (as a cultural reality experienced by an individual that has an impact on a community), but from a comparative perspective the same event can be seen as an ASC experience with general human features and based on a common human potential and bodily features.

Determining the reality or plausibility of such cultural events and phenomena, therefore, places a heavy burden on any researcher because what can be viewed as culturally unique is simultaneously humanly common. Thus, depending upon whether the same event is explained either as a "heavenly soul journey" or as an ASC experience, the reality status of the event or phenomenon will be appreciated differently. Affirming each of these means affirming different things in each case. If it is taken within its cultural setting (for example, as a visitation by an ancestor), the answer can be, *yes! Such a cultural experience did take place!* Taken across cultures in a present-day or comparative sense, the same event can, for example, be seen as an ASC experience, and the answer can also be, *yes! It actually happened!* However, affirming *what* has happened will be radically different in these two cases. These can be taken as complementary or just different explanations or descriptions of the same events or phenomena. Affirming the reality means affirming two separate explanations of the same human event or phenomenon.

THE REALITY OF CULTURAL REPRESENTATIONS OF THE WORLD

Not everything that is, is the result of cultural constructs. From a critical realist perspective, it is accepted that there also exists a reality totally independent from any human representations. Therefore, there is also a world of things and phenomena of which different cultures make their own representations or descriptions, some of which are true and others false (or some of which are better and others worse).[28] Most aspects of the world are described by means of very many conceptual systems, and knowledge entails those descriptions where the world "fits" such descriptions. The terms used to denote these are "true," "fact," or "how-things-are-in-the-world" (see Searle 1995, 151, 165–67, 199–226 for a discussion of these issues). While it is true that all representations are always done from within some representational system, it does not follow that such representations are not about something.[29] However, not all representations of the same things or phenomena have to be accepted because it is necessary to offer arguments and justifications that take into account the notions of truth and knowledge that we also subscribe to.

An example of the "reality" that exists independently of human representation is the fact of procreation, or, if you will, the fact that babies are

28. It is true that humans divide the world up and can continue to imagine new ways of doing so, and "it is only from a point of view that we represent reality, but ontologically objective reality does not have a point of view" (Searle, 1995, 176).

29. The argument that different presentations are different demarcations or constructions presupposes an external reality. "Unless there is already a territory on which we can draw boundaries . . . From the fact that a *description* can only be made relative to a set of linguistic categories, it does not follow that the *facts/objects/states of affairs, etc., described can only exist* relative to a set of categories" (Searle 1995, 166).

made. This is one of the areas of reality that will be discussed in this study because of the conflicting variety of human theories about it together with the peculiar claims about Jesus's origins. There are, in fact, numerous other cultural constructions of common human phenomena in the Jesus traditions (for example, the healing accounts) that need special interpretive care.

Determining the reality of reports about common human events and phenomena clothed in cultural garb is very similar to the former, but with a very definite difference. While explanations in the former category are complementary, here they are contradictory. While it is possible to endorse the variety of cultural events and phenomena as historically real for each culture, the same cannot be said here. Contradictory explanations of common human features and phenomena are not easily reconcilable. For example, two features of the conception of the world of educated people in the twenty-first century, Searle (see 1995, 6) points out, are not up for grabs: the atomic theory of matter and the evolutionary theory of biology. From this point of view, the cell theory of procreation is not merely an alternative to all other cultural theories of where babies come from. The claim that babies actually are the gift from ancestors does not offer the same level of explanation as the two-cell theory, which is true of all conceptions, whether known and acknowledged or not.

This makes judgment about the plausibility of cultural accounts of common human events and phenomena tricky. What has actually happened (what can be taken as real) will often only be decided in the process of cultural dialog and criticism. In such a process it would unfortunately be necessary to say that certain claims about states of affairs in the world cannot be taken as true. Certain claims are, in short, historically impossible or simply false.

With regard to cultural representations of events and phenomena, the efforts can be appreciated as serious explanations for states of affairs in the world but not as true accounts of what the state of affairs is. Neither shamans nor saints arrive in the world without the prior connection of two cells. Some cultural theories (some of ours included) are wrong about the world and even some theories taken as truth today will in future turn out to have been wrong. Therefore, it is not a matter of sufficient evidence that can determine whether a specific account about a special birth is possible or plausible but something to be decided on in a process of cross-cultural dialog.

THE REALITY OF COMMON HUMAN EVENTS AND PHENOMENA

It goes without saying that the life of any historical figure and in particular a significant figure in a specific setting would also be constituted by means of normal human events and phenomena that are observer independent. That is to say, features that are common to all human beings, such as a date and place of birth, family relationships, and various childhood or adult experiences.

The debate whether Jesus of Nazareth actually was a historical figure is not one to be entered into here; enough evidence suggests that further questions about what kind of a figure he was could be asked. Therefore, if he was a historical figure, it can be accepted that he was born, had a family of sorts, grew up, and had an adult life (if he died at an age around thirty) filled with a series of historical events. Understanding those events and phenomena is what is at issue here. His life story would thus also contain normal historical events and common human biographical data such as the *when*, *where*, and *what* aspects of his life. In so far as these can be determined, the places and times of birth and death; the names of his parents, family members, and friends; his place of residence and occupation would be included.

This category of events and phenomena in a person's life normally are observer independent. In a literate and bureaucratic society, such information can be obtained by any interested party from documents such as birth, christening, and death certificates; from educational reports; and other documentary databases. Provided that a full record of data is available and collected, the same picture of biographical information can normally be drawn by any independent researcher by comparing sources, determining the most authentic, and weeding out the corrupted documents.

There is, however, no hard evidence (certificates, documents, or records of any nature) available about Jesus of Nazareth. In fact, all the documents about his life originated after his lifetime and with definite motifs. Furthermore, much of the evidence about biographical events that could be located here, are offered in the framework of the above category. The data are all wrapped in cultural garb and presented as cultural information. This makes it more important to be able to deal with the cultural nature of the information about him as social personage.

Still there are some aspects ascribed to his life story that are not totally dependent on the cultural system. These include such historical events as his trial and travels, his temple activities and teachings. Again, while the distinction with the former categories is not watertight, in principle it would be possible to identify historical events and phenomena that could be investigated without specific insight into the cultural system. The main concern would be whether or not there is sufficient reliable evidence available about such events.

While the separation from the former category is rather flimsy, the former refers to events and phenomena that are unique to specific cultures (although they probably all have bodily or material origins and connections) while the latter refers to events and phenomena that belong to all human beings, qua their humanity.

A culturally sensitive reading of ancient texts has to be alert to all kinds of cultural realities: those that are unique to a given cultural system, those that are only unique cultural interpretations or representations of normal human phenomena, and those that are cultural presentations of otherwise common human phenomena. Some events or phenomena ascribed to Jesus indeed belonged to his culture's construction and interpretation of reality (such as exorcisms) while others are merely their cultural representations of things that exist in the world (such as the way in which Mary was impregnated). Still others, which are normally taken as observer independent, turn out to also be culturally contaminated. In all cases, the establishment of the historical plausibility of these takes a different route in the interpretive process.

Concluding Remarks

There is evidence that the world of historiographical discourse is predominantly characterized by the features resulting from the worldview of ontological monism that operates with a single reality system. Despite serious criticisms over the years of positivistic or traditional historiography, criticism that resulted in revisions of the paradigm, little was done in changing the paradigm. Therefore, many versions of postmodern historiography share the assumptions and methods of traditional historiography. One of these is the notion that data from foreign cultures can still be read straight or be picked for their testimonies because of the assumption of the natural veracity of their contents.

It is the emergence of a whole new worldview that acknowledges the plurality of cultural systems, and consequently the multiplicity of cultural realities, that serves as a challenge to the paradigm. One version of such a paradigm shift is referred to here as anthropological historiography.

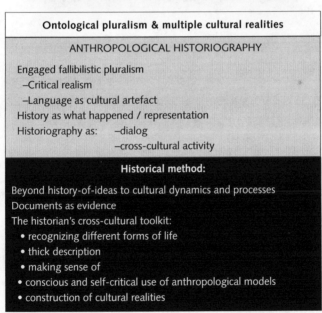

Diagram 1.1: Mapping the World of Historiographical Discourses

Anthropological historiography occupies on the historiographical landscape a different terrain from positivist and postmodern approaches because anthropo-

logical historiography operates under the banner of ontological pluralism and multiple cultural realities instead of under ontological monism. Therefore, anthropological historiography does not share in the dualisms that have developed in the theoretical discussions under the latter worldview. The recognition of cultural realities in the historical record and the acknowledgement of real cultural differences resulted in the emergence of an interpretive and cross-cultural historical method.

CHAPTER 2

An Analysis of Current Historical Jesus Research

Diversity in Current Historical Jesus Research

A CURSORY OVERVIEW OF critical Jesus studies indicates that scholars do not agree on exactly what they ought to investigate, where to start, how to proceed, which methods and models to use, or even which context to presuppose for his activities. In addition, given the nature and condition of the evidence, there is great uncertainty about how to talk about a historical figure ascribed with so many "unbelievable" features. The one element of continuity that spans the history of the quest from past to present, Kelber says, is "the diversity of Jesus images" (1994, 142).

One should be sympathetic when Hurtado points out:

> There are differences in the evidence chosen for framing Jesus' historical background, differences in what one sees as more influential in Jesus' historical matrix, differences in whether to use religious concepts and categories or social-scientific ones to understand Jesus (and, if the latter are chosen, which ones to emphasize), differences over the dating and evaluation and identification of Christian sources (intra- and extra-canonical, extant and hypothetical), and certainly differences in the personal hermeneutical agendas and concerns that lie behind and help motivate the task. (1997, 291)

There is no clear consensus on what exactly the aim of historical Jesus research should be and consequently no agreement on what the individual tasks consist. While most studies include a list or description of biographical and historical "facts" about Jesus's life, such as the list of his family members, his hometown, and his place of birth (see Sanders

1985, 11; Funk 1996, 32–35; Theissen & Merz 1997, 147–74), there is
no agreement on either historical details (e.g., the day and time of death
or the nature of his trial) or biographical details (e.g., about his public
performance). For some the quest is the search for "the personality, the
self-consciousness, the inner life of Jesus" (Fowl 1990, 329), while for others it "requires the reconstruction of his message and, to the degree that we
can get at it, his motives and goals" (Fredriksen 1995, 77). Others see it as
an attempt to construct a biography of Jesus, an accurate sketch of what
he taught and how he behaved (see Sanders 1985, 2; Johnson 1996, 105).[1]
Since there is no longer (if there ever was) a common *quest for the historical
Jesus*, the term "historical Jesus research" is preferred in this study.

Furthermore, there is no agreement on which sources should be used
or by means of which methods. If anything, the current debate about the
sources for constructing a historical picture of Jesus, is chaotic. Besides
disagreements about the validity of (mostly) extracanonical sources (e.g.,
the *Gospel of Thomas*),[2] scholars disagree on almost every detailed aspect.[3]
Furthermore, Crossan complains that with different inventories of sources
"we are not just ships that pass in the night, we are ships that pass on
different nighttime oceans" (1998, 143). There simply is no agreement on
the number, value, or priority of the sources to be used. This is illustrated
when Fredriksen points out that Mack cannot reasonably be criticized for
not taking large parts of the gospel tradition seriously in his reconstruction,
because, in his theory, it is part of the Christian overlay or was created by
the evangelists (see 1995, 80). Therefore, according to his description of
the research problem (and that of the Jesus Seminar), large parts cannot be
included in the database.

Disputes over what should have priority—the narrative tradition or
the sayings tradition—is symptomatic of different approaches sharing the
view that historical Jesus research should be based on *realia*. If the Synoptic
Gospels are taken as authentic, Arnal complains, it guarantees that the
narrative tradition will determine the portrayal of the historical Jesus.

---

1. Borg sees it as just "constructing an image of Jesus" (1999, 11). Most historical
Jesus scholars will, however, probably agree with Funk's rather neutral formulation of the
research problem facing them: "we expect to identify and describe a particular person who
lived in a particular time and place and who said and did particular things" (1996, 57).

2. For the divergent views on the date and value of extracanonical sources in historical
Jesus research, see, for example, Crossan (1998, 114–16) and Meier (1991, 123–39).

3. See Meier (1991, 41–44), Sanders (1993, 57–77), and the Jesus Seminar publications
(Funk et al., 1993, 3–34) for a discussion of the same issues.

However, in his view, "it makes more sense to begin with a mass of secure data and use it to generate conclusions than it does to use preconceptions about Jesus to determine what data are relevant" (1997, 202). Thus, the bedrock should be the authentic sayings.[4] Taking this body of material as the only authentic material surviving from Jesus himself, it places Jesus squarely within the wisdom tradition, and therefore the conclusion is obvious, Jesus was a wisdom teacher or sage (see, e.g., Funk 1996, 69–70).

This list is not only far from complete but also does not contain all the permutations of variables available in Jesus research. In a sense, each study consists of a unique configuration of these components. These could be conceptualized like the spokes of a wheel, which depart from the same axis but run in different directions; the only thing keeping the field of research together is that it is about Jesus of Nazareth as a historical figure. Therefore, at first sight, historical Jesus research seems to be remarkably diverse, as, on a certain level, it indeed is. But, as will be indicated, particular patterns can indeed be identified (using Wright's map of the *Schweitzerstrasse* and the *Wredebahn*). In fact, it will be argued that on a fundamental level (that of the historiographical framework), current historical Jesus research actually shows a remarkable uniformity.

A Remarkable Uniformity in Current Historical Jesus Research

It is often stated (with pride) that the results of two hundred years of critical Jesus research cannot simply be bypassed. And despite the variety mentioned above, there is a remarkable singularity in historical Jesus research over the two centuries, which finds expression in at least two identifiable patterns (the *Schweitzerstrasse* and the *Wredebahn*). In reality, historical Jesus researchers are still trying to answer the question posed more than two hundred years ago, by means of basically the same interpretive method, and based on the same philosophical assumptions. This shines through in the description of Du Toit:

> The Third Quest [in his view all current historical Jesus research] shares with the Second Quest most of its basic critical presuppositions: the quest for Jesus is conducted within the framework

4. This is the explicit viewpoint of the Jesus Seminar: "The parables and aphorisms form the bedrock of the tradition. They represent the point of view of Jesus himself" (Funk and The Jesus Seminar 1998, 9).

of modern historical criticism, assuming that the Jesus tradition should be subjected to historical analysis in order to reveal the Jesus of history covered by many layers of Christian tradition and dogma. As part of this process it holds a number of theoretical and methodological presuppositions in common with its predecessors. Jesus research since 1980 shares with the Second Quest the two-source hypothesis as a broad framework of the search for Jesus, furthermore the assumption of the arbitrary, that is, non-biographical arrangement of the Gospel material in Mark (and consequently also in the other Synoptics) and John, it similarly presupposes the kerygmatic nature of the Gospel tradition and the consequent stratified nature of the tradition. (2001, 99)

This summary contains the main features of critical Jesus research that have changed little over the decades. Implicitly it is accepted that historical Jesus research is a continuation of attempts to answer a question within the same framework in which it was first posed. This is confirmed by the following examples.

First, the initial objective of most current historical Jesus research is to secure authentic or original material from the post-Easter gospel portrayals of him.[5] Implicit in this strategy is the notion that each (at least canonical) Gospel contains a historical kernel and is constituted as a layered tradition: "the earlier the material, the more likely it is to bring us into contact with historical bedrock" (Wright 1999b, 20). It should already be noted that this strategy is based on the assumption that the documents (when "read straight") could not have been about a historical figure. The common wisdom in historical Jesus research is that the Gospels reflect a development over a long period in which authentic or original kernels or nuggets have been expanded into their existing formats. This is well expressed in the following commonly accepted viewpoint:

> How can we distinguish what comes from Jesus (Stage I, roughly A.D. 28–30) from what was created by the oral tradition of the early Church (Stage II, roughly A.D. 30–70) and what was produced by the editorial work (redaction) of the evangelists (Stage III, roughly A.D. 70–100)? (Meier 1991, 167; see also Theissen 1992, 1–5)

---

5. As Meier points out, a major part of the effort in Jesus studies is focused on determining "what material comes from the historical Jesus" (1991, 167), or, as Scott maintains, a "search for a firm foundation on which to construct a biography of Jesus has been an essential mark of all its stages" (1994, 255).

The so-called "distortions" of what comes from Jesus are caused by a variety of factors: some are the result of a post-Easter perspective and others were created by community needs, some result from creative mythologizing or redactional activities and others from unhistorical ascriptions to Jesus. It should also be noted that not all scholars subscribe to all of these reasons or give them the same weight. The following explanations are found:

(1) Some traditions reflect a post-Easter perspective.[6]

(2) The early Christians created stories and traditions out of Jewish scripture and tradition.[7]

(3) There is also material ascribed to Jesus that reflects the need and situation of the early church or the redactional activities of the evangelists and does not belong to the life of Jesus. Sometimes these two perspectives overlap and the early church is credited with stories that were created without any historical basis in the life of Jesus (Borg 1999, 6, mentions the story about the wedding in Cana as an example).

As will be indicated below, what scholars differ about is not whether but how much of the material can be considered authentic and how to decide on that. Therefore, the search for authentic material underneath the overlay of all sorts of additions is a structural feature of current historical Jesus research.

Second, common wisdom of two hundred years of Gospel and historical Jesus research holds that a historical figure could not have been like the portrayal of Jesus in the Gospels. There is a strong and a weak version of this assumption, but it is common knowledge that the quest for the historical Jesus started with Reimarus in the eighteenth century, with the distinction between the man Jesus and the Christ of faith (see Funk, et al. 1993, 2; Du Toit 2002, 96–97). What is said in the sources about

6. "Doubtless our Easter faith has influenced our traditions" (Theissen & Merz 1998, 99).

7. Sanders (see 1993, 62–71) points toward different ways in which the early Christians created new material about Jesus: they believed that Jesus still spoke to them in visions and during prayer, and they created new material from Jewish Scripture and tradition (they saw in Jesus the fulfillment of prophetic expectations). For an even bolder view of their creative imaginations, see Funk (1998, 6); and Funk, Hoover, and The Jesus Seminar (1993, 4–5).

the historical figure cannot and could not have belonged to the life of a historical figure. Therefore, the documents are treated in such a way as to discover the original nuggets, which are assumed to represent or contain the historical figure. The historical development of the texts is collapsed onto the historical life of Jesus, and in both instances the original has to be recovered from underneath the overlay.

Third, some fixed patterns, established procedures, and basic structures have developed around the identification of authentic material for describing Jesus as historical figure. These include procedures not only for identifying the authentic parts and for removing the overlay but for situating such authentic material in plausible settings. From "what we are looking *at* in the Jesus tradition," that is, the *stuff* or *material* available for historical study, scholarship moves to "what we are looking *for* through the Jesus tradition" or "the *object* of historical study, the thing we want to know and say something about, which is Jesus himself" (Holmberg 2004, 448). Therefore, another structural feature of this paradigm (to be referred to as the *authenticity paradigm*) is that the linear picture of the development of the tradition (Stage I through to Stage III) also constitutes, in reverse order, the linear process of returning via authentic material to pictures of the historical figure. As will be indicated below, different configurations of criteria of authenticity are employed in order to do this.

Two Configurations of the Authenticity Paradigm

Amidst the diversity, and given the fundamental uniformity, current historical Jesus research can be portrayed by means of some fixed configurations. The suggestion of Wright, who argues that critical historical Jesus research can conveniently be understood as developing along two highways (two distinct patterns in the paradigm), will be followed in this study (see 1996, 25, 79, 83–84). In his view these two do not represent watertight compartments but are heuristic aids to map currents of thought in the field: a *Wredebahn* and a *Schweitzerstrasse*.[8] These distinct roads are different configurations of the same paradigm. He shows that there are

8. When employing this kind of matrix for categorizing and ordering such a diverse field of study, which is made up of so many variables, it is wise to admit the limitations of the schema. No categorization model can do justice to all the current historical Jesus studies, and many studies will, due to a variety of reasons, not fit a particular track perfectly. There are due to be some casualties on these roads.

crossover points between the tracks, and some scholars move to and fro over the fine "Green line."

> The *Wredestrasse* insists that we know comparatively little about Jesus, and that the Gospels, in outline and detail, contain a great deal that reflect only the concerns of the early church. The *Schweitzerstrasse* places Jesus within the context of apocalyptic Judaism, and on that basis postulates far more continuity between Jesus himself, the early church, and the Gospels, while allowing of course for importantly different historical settings in each case. The two approaches are sufficiently distinct for us to be able to categorize current writings in two main groups. (Wright 1996, 21)

The Schweitzerstrasse can be identified with what is also known as the *third quest*. Despite admitting that what he has termed the "third quest" is still very open ended, Wright claims that that is "where the real leading edge of contemporary Jesus-scholarship is to be found" (1996, 84). He has a rather fixed idea of its travelers: they all locate Jesus within Judaism and specifically within "eschatological Judaism," and scholars from the Jesus Seminar (like Crossan and Funk) fall outside the orbit of this definition (see also 1992b; and Marsh 1997, 409). The term *third quest* will be used in this study in this original sense and not as a designation of all historical Jesus research since the eighties.[9]

Wright is not the only scholar who thinks that current historical Jesus research can be mapped by means of two distinct streams of research. Funk distinguishes between the "pretend questers" (that is the *Third Questers* of the *Schweitzerstrasse*) and the "reNewed questers" (that is, the members of the Jesus Seminar or the *Wredebahn*) (1996, 64).[10] The third questers belong to the *pretend* group because they pay only lip service to the distinction between the historical Jesus and the creedal Christ and accept the canonical Gospels as basically authentic. In his words:

> The point of their quest—to the extent that it can be called a quest at all—is to demonstrate that the canonical Gospels are completely or essentially reliable while denying that the non-canonical texts

9. For some scholars, the term "third quest" refers to all major Jesus research over the last two decades, including scholars like Crossan and Mack (see, for example, Theissen & Merz 1998, 10–11; Dunn 1999, 33; Meier 1999; Du Toit 2001, 98 n. 74).

10. Funk employs three criteria for distinguishing between them: whether the distinction between the historical Jesus and the Jesus of the Gospels (the Christ of faith) is taken seriously, whether sources other than the canonical Gospels are used, and whether any Christian claims are at risk in the quest.

tell us anything significant about Jesus . . . these questers in fact make the historical Jesus subservient to the creedal Christ. Third questers are really conducting a search primarily for historical evidence to support claims made on behalf of creedal Christianity and the canonical Gospels. In other words, the third quest is an apologetic ploy. (1996, 65)

Both the Wredebahn and the Schweitzerstrasse have more than one lane that allows some maneuvering and different driving experiences. They cover the same terrain, in many instances run together for a certain stretch of the way in order to part and get together again. This means that they share some features and sometimes offer the same scenic route but from different perspectives. They cross the same rivers and often run very closely together. Sometimes they give access to the same turnoff or highway facilities but otherwise offer totally different features and scenes and run in divergent directions.

It will also become apparent that despite some differences, distinct configurations of the authenticity paradigm are all examples of traditional historiography with its roots in the nineteenth-century positivistic sciences. The authenticity paradigm displays the typical modernist, ethnocentric and history-of-ideas features of traditional historiography that treats the documents as testimonies of what Jesus has *actually* said or done.[11] This is confirmed not only by the fact that current historical Jesus research is still trying to answer a two-hundred-year-old question but also in the similar structures of each configuration to that original question.

The Wredebahn on Jesus and on Gospel Presuppositions

First, the focus will fall on the assumptions about the gospel texts and the historical figure and then on the interpretive strategy on the *Wredebahn*. That is, first to be treated is the assumption about *what we are looking at* followed by *what we are looking for*, and then will come a glance at the nature and structure of the interpretive process.

---

11. Rohrbaugh shows that ethnocentric results in historical Jesus research often follow from unknowingly asking ethnocentric questions to and about the texts (see 2002).

Assumptions about Jesus and the Gospels

While these assumptions can be distinguished for analytical purposes, in actual interpretations they form a coherent network or a set of nested assumptions.

THE JESUS OF THE GOSPELS IS NOT THE JESUS OF HISTORY

The basic assumption, which functions as a programmatic structure for most of historical Jesus research, is that the historical figure was different from the Jesus (or *Christ*) portrayed in the Gospels. The Wredebahn represents the strong version of this theory.

The Wredebahn forcefully preserves the insight that arose during the early origin of the quest, namely, that a historical figure could not have been like the Gospel presentation of Jesus (that is, I would hasten to say, when read as if it belongs to a modern Western worldview); what is *incredible* could not have been historical. From this assumption a common discourse has developed about both the nature of the sources and the objective of historical Jesus research; one may describe this objective with the model of archaeological strata that assumes that an authentic kernel resides at the very bottom stratum. A real historical figure could only be found at the bottom layer once all the inauthentic additions have been removed.

Miller, for example, quite explicitly states that the heart of the search for the historical Jesus is the fact that "*the gospels are written from the perspective of belief that Jesus was raised from the dead*" (1999, 32; italics his). Therefore, when the early Christians talked or wrote about "the words and deeds of Jesus, they were not thinking about a historical figure from their past, but rather about the supernatural Lord living in their present." With this, the very nature of the Gospels, as seen in this approach, has been established: they "are assumed to be narratives in which the memory of Jesus is embellished by mythic elements that express the church's faith in him" (Funk et al. 1993, 4–5). And therefore, the gospel traditions are basically to be mistrusted: "The quest of the historical Jesus is an effort to emancipate the Galilean sage from the tangle of Christian overlay that obscures, to some extent, who Jesus was and what he said, to distinguish the religion *of* Jesus from the religion *about* Jesus" (Funk 1996, 31).[12]

12. Funk strongly argues that the real and critical engagement in historical study of Jesus distinguishes the historical Jesus from the Jesus of the Gospels and from the Christ of the creeds (see 1996, 65).

If Jesus was a "humble sage from Galilee" (1996, 162–63), Funk says, it is unthinkable that he could have said the things that John ascribes to him; he would not have called for repentance in view of some impending judgment, or have predicted his own death and resurrection as reported in Mark. These are newly acquired Christian convictions so powerful that they were read back into history and placed on the lips of Jesus. It is, however, significant that the Gospel authors found these convictions neither contradictory to the life of the historical figure nor unbelievable enough to leave them out of their portrayals.

LAYERED TEXTS

The model of stratification, drawn from archaeology, presents itself naturally when it is accepted that the tradition was preserved in layers. The general wisdom behind the notion of stratification is that "every story and word of Jesus has been shaped by the eyes and hands of the early church" (Borg 1987, 9). Consequently, the Wredebahn subscribes to two sets of assumptions regarding layers in the Gospels.

First, a distinction is made between material that belongs to Jesus as historical person and material created by the early Christian communities,[13] or, in the words of Miller: *the gospels are a blend of historical memories about Jesus and religious interpretations of him that arose after his death* (1999, 33; italics his).

To be even more precise, a threefold distinction is made in the development of the Jesus material and consequently between that material and Jesus' life. In the formulation of Crossan and Reed:

> the words and deeds attributed to Jesus in the New Testament gospels fall into major layers built successively one upon (that is, over, under, around, and through) another. Think of them as, first, the *original* layer, coming from Jesus' own words and deeds in the 20s; next the *traditional* layer, coming from the tradition's adoption, adaptation, and creation of the new material in the 30s, 40s, or even later; and, finally, as the *evangelical* layer in the gospels we now possess from the 70s through the 90s. (2001, 37)[14]

---

13. This assumption is based on the notion that "the gospels contain two kinds of material: some goes back to Jesus, and some is the product of the early Christian communities. To use an archaeological analogy, the gospels contain earlier and later layers" (Borg 1999, 5; see Sellow 1992, 141–43).

14. Elsewhere Crossan states: "All the gospel texts, whether inside or outside the canon, combine together three layers, strata, or voices. That is, in the earliest stratum, 'the voice

An important assumption behind the stratification metaphor is that the oral phase of the tradition contains the uncontaminated, genuine, and "close-to-Jesus" accounts of his words and deeds. The process as visualized by this model is that smaller units of tradition were orally preserved, or to put it differently, oral traditions preserved historical and *real* words and events. These units were employed in bigger narratives or used within larger frameworks, but the genuine and authentic original snippets remained intact. If they can be identified, these snippets lead us closer to the historical Jesus.

The second set of assumptions relates to the use of sources by some gospel authors. The presupposition (based on two hundred years of gospel research) is that the Gospels were composed out of different earlier sources, and that later Gospels totally absorb the earlier ones that they have used as sources (see Crossan 1998, 101). One such gospel, which together with the Gospel of Mark is taken as source for Matthew and Luke, is the Q Gospel (see 1998, 111). The result is that the gospel texts are also seen as constituted by consecutive strata or layers: Q and Mark, then Matthew and Luke, and finally John (see 2003a, 296).

What this also means is that the third stratum of the tradition (that of the evangelists) not only produced a set of texts that consist of consecutive layers (Q, Mark, Matthew, Luke, and John), but that the Gospels individually consist of three strata of tradition (the *original*, the *traditional*, and the *evangelical*). According to this construction, there are thus two different sets of layers in some of the Gospels: layers of source material (which might be from the original, traditional, or evangelical layers preserved in a source), plus layers of traditions (which might be from the original or traditional layers, or created by the gospel authors themselves). However, when treated *correctly* (that is, sifted through the sources by formal means and through the traditions by means of a process of elimination), the Gospels can give access to the first stratum, to the *original* words and deeds of Jesus (see Crossan & Reed 2001, 37–38).[15] As will be further

---

of Jesus.' There is as an intermediate stratum, 'the anonymous voices of the communities talking about Jesus.' There is, as the latest stratum, 'the voices of their [the Gospels'] authors'" (1998, 140).

15. Only a small section of the sources, which has multiple attestation in different source traditions, is taken as representing the historical figure. As Freyne points out, this picture is methodologically correct to the point of distorting the picture from the outset by limiting the field of vision (see 1997, 64). Theissen voices a similar objection: "if you raise a Jesus construction only on multiple testified traditions in canonical and non-canonical

discussed below, it is not surprising that Q is taken in these circles as "the most important source for reconstructing the teaching of Jesus" (Robinson 2001, 27).

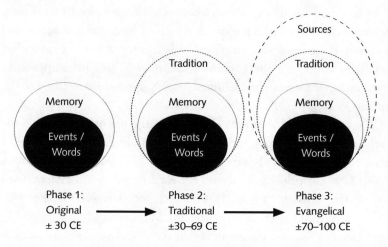

Diagram 2.1: The Stratified Model of the Wredebahn

The model of stratification supported by scholars on the Wredebahn resulted in a picture of the gospel texts as being constituted in various layers with the authentic or "earliest" stratum containing the "voice" and reports about the "deeds" of Jesus. These were embellished and elaborated first by the traditions of the early Church and then by the literary creativity of the evangelists.

The authenticity logic does not allow the inclusion of documents that can be dated late and that allegedly have no or little connection to the tradition stream. Besides some of the extracanonical texts, which on the Wredebahn are considered early, most of the documents are taken to have originated much later. The verdict about the infancy gospels is typical.

Borg, for example, calls the *Infancy Gospel of Thomas* "a fanciful tale which is the product of early Christian imagination," in which the divine status of the post-Easter Jesus is uncritically projected back earlier into his

---

sources, you are on the one side dependent on the random preservation of some words or deeds of Jesus on some fragments of papyrus and on the other side dependent on the rather biased selection of Jesus sayings in the Gospel of Thomas" (1996, 159). Also, Kelber asks whether any historian can base a picture of a historical personage on an extremely selective group of sayings attributed to that person (see 1994, 147).

life (1994b, 25). In the *Complete Gospels* of the Jesus Seminar, Attridge says, this Gospel "affords us a view of how Jesus was regarded in the unsophisticated religious imaginations of ordinary early Christians" (see Miller 1992, 370). The main concern in all these judgments is with what they contain; "there is virtually no historical information in any of these tales" (Funk and The Jesus Seminar 1998, 24).

More than anything else, these judgments are the result of a specific set of philosophical assumptions (to be discussed below).

The Wredebahn on *Historical* and Historicity

IF SOMETHING CAN BE SHOWN TO GO BACK TO JESUS,
IT "ACTUALLY HAPPENED"

Two strategies are very prominent in this configuration of the authenticity paradigm for determining historicity or what actually happened.

The first strategy is based on explanations of "the historical method." The favorite examples are the eyewitnesses to an accident and the reporter trying to figure out what has really happened at a crime scene. If you have four witnesses in a court of law describing a car accident that took place earlier, it makes a huge difference whether they are independent witnesses or whether they base their witness on hearsay. If a reporter got his information from bystanders and told the next two informants about it, and the fourth got his data from the previous three, in a court of law there would be only "one not-exactly-an-eyewitness and three sincere echoes" (Crossan & Reed 2001, 12–13). The historian, like the journalist, should not report as a fact based on unconfirmed evidence and should show what information they use. Similar to a lawyer, a historian should determine how good the memory, vision, and hearing of a witness are, and whether testimony is based on hearsay or first-hand experience (see Miller 1999, 35–37). The notion at work here is that more than one reliable witness can testify what has actually happened.[16]

As far as it goes, these are excellent principles for specific kinds of historical questions, such as, which words were spoken by someone at a specific point in time? or, who were present at a specific crime scene? But

16. In some instances it is explicitly stated, such as Van Aarde from the Wredebahn, who claims, "[t]o decide whether something is *historically plausible* demands, according to our insights today, independent multiple attestations. These witnesses should be attested to in documents that are chronologically stratified" (2001, 27; italics mine).

even if every single word ever spoken by Jesus can be determined very precisely, this determination only gives a picture of what he taught as a teacher of some kind. It cannot tell us what kind of social type he belonged to (unless, of course, all he did was teach). It has very limited value in answering other historical questions and, in fact, little value when dealing with cultural events and phenomena. The nature of a car accident or crime scene is such that a video recording would be very useful in determining what has actually happened and which witness is lying or telling the truth. As will be seen below, in the case of cultural events (such as an exorcism), even a video recording would be of little value to show "what has actually happened," if the cultural system in which the events took place is not grasped.

The second strategy of the Jesus Seminar is to collapse *what goes back to Jesus* onto *what actually happened*. In fact, it is given in the definition that the original layer contains Jesus's *own words and deeds*. One should be clear about how this functions in actual interpretations: if something does not belong to the first stratum, it did not actually happen, and something can only be historical if it can be shown to belong to the original stratum. For example, Crossan and Reed use the idea of layers for both the sayings and the deeds of Jesus. Coming to the infancy narratives, for example, they say the following:

> But in their infancy narratives both Matthew and Luke agree independently on the virginal conception of Jesus from Mary of Nazareth, a tradition that nobody else in the New Testament even mentions in passing. There was, then, an even earlier story claiming such a miraculous conception for Jesus. That story is at least somewhere in the second, or *traditional*, layer but was it created there *or was it from the very earliest layer, from the conception of the historical Jesus himself?* (2001, 46; italics mine)

They explain that since the Lukan infancy narrative contrasts Jesus's kingdom with that of the emperor, it actually comes from the traditional layer sometime after Jesus has publicly proclaimed the kingdom of God. Of significance is their last question. The implication is that had it been from the original layer, it had to have happened as described (then it must have been "from the conception of the historical Jesus"). It is clear that if the virginal conception were from the original layer, it would have made a claim about the actual *miraculous* conception of Jesus (but luckily, it is from the second, traditional layer and only makes a theological claim about whose kingdom is superior). The implicit assumption is that it is not a story about Jesus's actual virginal conception (it did not really happen because the material is not original), because the story only comes from the second stratum and therefore was only about authority in the early church. It seems reasonable to say that if a text with early multiple attestation on this topic were to be discovered, in this view, it has to be taken as from the original stratum and thus must be about Jesus's actual conception.

Admittedly, this is pushing the argument beyond its normal use because in actual fact it only functions to show what does *not* belong to the life of Jesus or what is not historical; material created in the second or third phases cannot refer to historical events or words of Jesus.

INCREDIBLE EVENTS CANNOT BE HISTORICAL

On the Wredebahn there is finally an explicit embracing of philosophical naturalism: incredible events cannot be historical. "The old deities and demons were swept from the skies by that remarkable glass [Galileo's telescope]. Copernicus, Kepler, and Galileo have dismantled the mythological abodes of the gods and Satan, and bequeathed us secular heavens" (Funk and The Jesus Seminar 1998, 2).[17] As Horsley points out: "The Enlightenment reduction of reality to what fit the canons of Reason and Nature, however, left theologians embarrassed about the Christian Gospels as sources for the historical Jesus" (2003, 55). Most elements simply do not fit the reality catalog of modern historians.

For example, because of the supernatural elements (the sky being ripped apart, the spirit descending like a dove, and a voice speaking from heaven), the baptism story as we have it is completely implausible, Arnal says (see 1997, 204). The historical kernel is underneath the mythological overlay. An eyewitness (or video camera), according to this viewpoint, would have seen two people in the water of the Jordan with the one baptizing the other in whichever way: this is the historical kernel, all the paraphernalia are supernatural embellishments.

According to the Jesus Seminar, the baptism story and the transfiguration story, where Jesus is seen walking and talking with some ancestors, are "biographical legends"; the birth stories have "no historical information"; they could not "identify a single report of an exorcism that they

17. Or as Lüdemann (1995, 135), for example, states: "With the revolution in the scientific view of the world, statements about the resurrection of Jesus have irrevocably lost their literal meaning."

believe to be an accurate report of such an event," and they "were unable
to endorse any of the nature wonders as historical events" (Funk and The
Jesus Seminar 1998, 16, 24, 33, 531). For Crossan, all the nature miracle stories are actually "credal statements about ecclesiastical authority"
(1991a, 404). In fact, he claims: "a large amount of the *deeds* of Jesus were
created within Exegetical Christianity. They believed in the historical Jesus
so much that they kept creating more and more of him out of biblical
type and prophetic text" (1994a, 20). This attitude also underlies Davies's
evaluation of the nature miracles: "I regard all reports that Jesus overcame
natural law as legends that arose after Jesus' lifetime" (1995, 67).

THE WREDEBAHN AND HISTORICITY

Despite multiple attestation and clear claims in the texts, scholars on the
Wredebahn also treat the texts as reports about events in their world, and
everything that is incredible is merely taken as a symbolic story.

Miller's reading of the sleeping saints who appeared from their graves
when Jesus died (Matt 27:51–53) is a good example of this pattern. It "did
not really happen," or this story is not historical: "On the one hand, we
have no objective basis for claiming that the event really happened. On the
other hand, we have strong clues from the way Matthew writes the story
that he never intended it to be taken literally" (1999, 141). His first argument is, generally speaking, quite fair: it is reasonable to expect, if such an
extraordinary thing ever happened (several dead ancestors have appeared
from their graves and have been reunited with their families), that more
sources would have mentioned it. This is a sound historical principle. But
it is based on the assumption that Matthew is telling about an event that
took place in time and space (similar to a car accident). It will be argued
that this is not necessarily the case, because people embedded in polyphasic cultures (see pp. 174–77 below for a description of polyphasic cultures)
accept as real and natural experiences and events that do not necessarily
happen in time and space (such as various kinds of ASC experiences)—
that is, even though they are offered as events and experiences in time and
space. It will later be suggested that this is exactly one of those experiences
and should therefore not be treated as if it belongs to a modern Western
conception of events and experiences in time and space.

Miller goes on to claim that Matthew never intended his story of
the risen saints, who appeared from their graves with Jesus's death, to be

taken literally, for it was intended "symbolically," to be understood for its "message." Is it not incredible that Matthew would tell a story that, as Miller says, "by any measure has to be the most amazing event of all time" simply to convey a symbolic message? By which measure would that have been an intended symbolic message? What if it never was a story about people appearing from their graves in time and space because it was an ASC experience (similar to many other such experiences) that were told as if they had happened in time and space because such experiences were taken as real experiences and events? Then it was not simply a story with a symbolic message but a cultural expression of something else, which might indeed contain a "message" but then a message connected to a cultural system and a certain experience of reality. In that case it was not simply a *symbolic message* conveyed by means of an *incredible story*. My suggestion is that both the claim of the symbolic message and the notion that it is the most amazing story of all time are the product of a reading of the story as if it was written in a modern Western cultural system and worldview and not in a first-century Mediterranean cultural system.

The basic pattern in these examples is that the documents are read as if they belong to a modern worldview and cultural system. From that point of view, many of the stories simply are incredible (such as the story of people emerging from their graves, walking on the sea, interacting with demonic figures and ancestors), and then a deeper meaning is to be found behind the story, either as a theological embellishment or a mythical overlay. It is sometimes maintained that behind many of the gospel stories or deeds ascribed to Jesus there might be a small historical kernel, which gave rise to the initial report, that was then embellished by means of a mythological overlay or by credal statements. Examples can be multiplied, but the point remains: a naturalistic view of the world is employed for evaluating the historicity of stories ascribed to the life of Jesus. What cannot be accounted for by means of naturalism is dismissed as mythic, legendary, or literary creations. *Historicity* and *historical events* in this perspective refer to those events and phenomena that could have been seen or photographed and are taken for real by "all human beings." These are typical features of a modernist (ontological monist) engagement with the world. This pattern, which is also applied to other texts (see Miller 2003, 175), clearly echoes the nineteenth-century formulation of D. F. Strauss that when "the narration is irreconcilable with the known and universal laws which govern the course of events," then "the matter related could not have taken place in the manner described" (1999, 97).[18]

The Structure of the Interpretive Process: From the Documents back to the Historical Figure

A small historical kernel of eyewitnesses' and ear witnesses' reports was embellished by the first followers and early church into a different kind of social type, which found full expression in the Jesus pictures of the evangelists as *the resurrected Christ* or *the Christ of faith*. The gospel portrayals contain very little material related to the historical figure and therefore the interpretive process follows the inverse order of the development process: from a small historical kernel identified by means of criteria of historicity and the historical method, the historical figure can be seen when these nuggets are put into a proper setting of Galilee in the early parts of the first century.

Crossan makes it clear that drivers on the Wredebahn believe it is impossible to go directly into the mound of Jesus tradition to separate the historical Jesus layer out from all later strata (see 1998, 149). Therefore, all that can be identified is the earliest discernible stratum of the tradition; that is to say, the oldest traditions and texts (which, according to Crossan, happen to be Q and the *Gospel of Thomas*, or what is called the "common sayings tradition"). Therefore, the first step in their quest for the historical Jesus for drivers on the Wredebahn (members of the Jesus Seminar) is to determine authentic material (see Funk 1996, 64, 139; Crossan 1998, 140–41; Borg 1999, 11).

In these studies, most gospel material is considered inauthentic, and authenticity has to be demonstrated. Authentic material is that which is early and historically plausible. In these studies, the criteria of authenticity

---

18. It is worthwhile to be reminded of the ethnocentric stance of Strauss already in the nineteenth century. In fact, his position was not different from many others who commented upon "the other" in that period. "When therefore we meet with an account of certain phenomena or events of which it is either expressly stated or implied that they were produced immediately by God himself (divine appearances, voices from heaven, or the like), or by human beings possessed of supernatural powers (miracles, prophecies), such an account is *in so far* to be considered as not historical. And inasmuch as, in general, the intermingling of the spiritual world with the human is found only in unauthentic records, and is irreconcilable with all just conceptions; so narratives of angels and devils, of their appearing in human shape and interfering with human concerns, cannot possibly be received as historical" (Strauss, 1999, 97).

function mechanically: the first and most important one is the criterion of multiple attestation. Something attested to in two or more independent sources, of which at least one is an early source, is taken as authentic Jesus material. Once a core has been established in this way, texts with single attestation—texts that are coherent with the core—are accepted (see Borg 1999, 12; Crossan 1994b, xiii).

Once such a core has been established, a good basis has been laid for constructing a picture of the historical Jesus. When such independent traditions with multiple attestation closely combine with the sharpest possible context constructed for the territories of Herod Antipas in the 20s CE, they provide the historical bedrock, and after Jesus's profile has been established from such a process, it can be used to determine other historical material in the layered texts. If those two "combine closely," it can be used to construct "a Jesus profile" that is used "to accept as historical all materials that coheres with it [the profile]" (Crossan 2003a, 298).

One should be clear about this assumption: if there is a fit between the oldest identifiable texts/traditions and context, the profile can be considered original or historical. As Crossan explains his methodology, "I am attempting a double-blind experiment with context and text in that order. That means a focus first on *context without text* and then on *text without context*. Only afterwards do I combine them in a very special manner" (2003a, 297–98). This means identifying the earliest textual evidence we have for the Jesus tradition, and if that evidence coheres well with the closest Galilean context, then it is taken as historical material (and a basis to evaluate all other material).

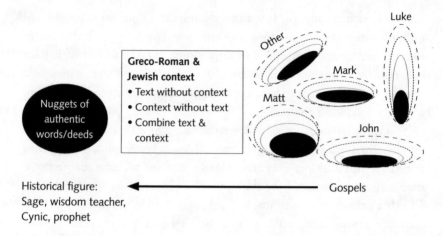

Diagram 2.2: Going Back to the Historical Figure via the Wredebahn

> *The first step in the interpretive process is the identification of the authentic nuggets in the various documents, which can then be used, via constructions of the historical setting, to identify the historical figure in the documents. The arrow shows the thrust of the movement back from authentic nuggets to histori- cal figure, while the little black areas represent the small amount of authentic material in the different Gospels.*

The Schweitzerstrasse on Jesus, the Sources, and Gospel Presuppositions

There is a second configuration of this paradigm that is particularly significant because it probably represents the majority of New Testament scholars. While neither a majority nor a minority is an indication of correctness, it is significant when mapping a specific area of research to know where the majority would belong.

Assumptions about Jesus and the Gospels

THE JESUS OF HISTORY AND THE CHRIST OF FAITH

Those on the Schweitzerstrasse take a weaker position on the distinction between the Jesus of history and the Jesus of the Gospels. As far as the argument goes, the Gospels (and Paul) present Jesus as a divine figure who is the risen Christ. The traditions were written from this perspective and therefore cover the reality of the earthly person. As Sanders, for example, says, no source gives us "the 'unvarnished truth'; the varnish of faith in Jesus covers everything" (1993, 73). However, the picture of the Synoptics is basically to be trusted. As Theissen and Merz express this assumption about the Synoptic Gospels: "we may also be confident that just as people are not perfect enough to hand on the pure truth, so they are not perfect enough to distort it totally" (1998, 120).

More recently, Dunn has offered a strong case for the reliability of the synoptic picture: "We should *not* work methodologically with any assumption that Jesus must have been different from the Jesus of the Synoptic tradition" (2002, 147; and see also 2003b, 130, 132, 134, 167, 241, 328). As will be argued later, in terms of the language of this study, this is just another ethnocentric version of ontological monism that, by means of a theological strategy, subsumes cultural realities under the categories of one's own cultural or reality catalog. On the Schweitzerstrasse ontological monism becomes visible in the claims that such stories as told about Jesus and ascribed to his life cannot be historical *unless taken as supernatural* or *sui generis*. As with the Wredebahn, what is missing is a consideration of the possibility that such features could not only have been historical (culturally speaking) but also have belonged to the life of a certain kind of social personage.

LAYERED AND LINEAR TRADITIONS

Dunn offers a good summary of the received view in this paradigm on the literary documents: "Few if any today assume that the written sources take the reader back directly to Jesus who worked and taught in Galilee three or more decades earlier. But equally, few if any doubt that behind the written sources there was earlier tradition" (2003a, 173). While it is accepted on the Schweitzerstrasse that the Synoptic Gospels were composed from different sources, it does not make much of an impact because it is also accepted that they are basically reliable, and the criteria of authenticity function only in identifying those parts that were created or added by the early church. What this means is that the Synoptic Gospels (minus the post-Easter additions) are taken as the basis for any further historical construction (see also Wright 1996, xvi).

It does not matter that some of the sources contain older parts. The criteria of authenticity are not used to deal with gospel sources but basically to weed out the post-Easter and early church additions to the tradition. Since the canonical Gospels are permeated with the Easter faith of the early church, they "must be carefully sifted with the criteria of historicity [authenticity]" (Meier 1999, 465).[19] Once that is done, an authentic basis has been created. Taken together with the assumption of the basic reliability of the synoptic tradition, the Synoptic Gospels serve as a reliable data basis for these constructions.

From the point of view of the Wredebahn, Crossan complains that scholars on the Schweitzerstrasse do not take the existence of Q as seriously as they should (1998, 111). While the validity of the *two-source* hypothesis is admitted, this hypothesis does not seriously impact on the historical value of the material because the scholars on the Schweitzerstrasse do not conclude from it that Q must be older and, therefore, more authentic than Matthew or Luke (or their versions of Q).

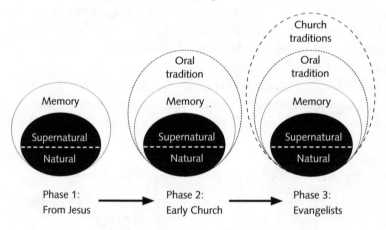

Diagram 2.3: The Stratified Model of the Schweitzerstrasse

Ontological monism on the Schweitzerstrasse includes the notion of supernatural elements that were present right at the first phase during Jesus's life. From the start, memory has remembered both the "natural" and the "supernatural" parts of Jesus's life. These were supplemented by early church tradition and by the evangelists' creative elaborations.

Based on the foundation of canonical priority, Dunn, for example, says that the value of other sources (starting with the Gospel of John)

19. In these studies, a different set of criteria is employed to determine the inauthentic parts. Notoriously demoted in these studies are the criteria of multiple attestation and independence of sources. Criteria with primary positions are the criteria of embarrassment, discontinuity, and coherence (see, e.g., Meier 1991, 168–77).

becomes "progressively slighter," but "we shall certainly want to call upon John's Gospel as a source, but mostly as a secondary source to supplement or corroborate the testimony of the Synoptic tradition" (2003b, 167). Although they often receive rather lengthy discussions, extracanonical sources do not contribute much to knowledge about Jesus mainly because they were written long after the events. In terms of this scheme of things, they were created independently from the tradition stream. Meier's verdict about the infancy gospels is typical; they are prime examples of fantasy: "if we can use the *Infancy Gospel of Thomas*, we can use *Alice in Wonderland* just as well" (1999, 464; and see 1991, 115).

The Schweitzerstrasse on *Historical* and Historicity

There should be no doubt that the Schweitzerstrasse bought into the idea of authenticity and historicity of the authenticity paradigm in more ways than one. One is by claiming that the Synoptic Gospels are authentic. An obvious example that has already been mentioned is that of the infancy narratives, which are read for their actual information about Jesus's birth (even though very little is taken as information about Jesus's birth, the documents are read for that purpose).

It is, however, the assumption that the historicity of events is based on multiple attestation in the sources, which will be highlighted here. Habermas, for example, formulates a general principle with regard to the miracles of Jesus: we first have to address the data in order to ascertain whether there is actual evidence for them (see 1995, 129). Craig bases his claim for the historicity of Jesus's resurrection upon relevant evidence; for him, the relevant body of evidence refers to those texts that can survive the tests of authenticity applied by the Jesus Seminar, such as multiple attestation (see 1995, 146, 158, 162–63). Determining historicity is fairly simple: what goes back to Jesus (phase 1) or has multiple independent attestations actually happened or was said by Jesus.[20]

Scholars on the Schweitzerstrasse share other assumptions from this paradigm: namely, a naturalistic view of reality and a reading of the documents, both of which claim that what is incredible can normally not be historical. But in this version of the paradigm, the reliability of the data

20. As can be illustrated with many examples, multiple independent attestation remains an important criterion with regard to specific events even on the Schweitzerstrasse (see Meier 1994, 290).

is immediately protected by an ideological (or theological) presupposition, namely, the addition of supernatural events and phenomena. What
is incredible, it is maintained, is normally not historical unless God has
performed or allowed something "supernatural" to happen, and in the
Gospels many "supernatural" events ascribed to Jesus of Nazareth are mul-
tiply recorded. Therefore, by means of the notion of *supernatural events or
phenomena*, of which God is the origin, events and phenomena in the life
of Jesus of Nazareth can be considered historical.

Jesus's birth and resurrection are cases in point. Virgins normally do
not give birth to children, but in the case of Jesus of Nazareth, Wright says,
something mysterious (*supernatural*) has happened (1999a, 176). Similarly,
something remarkable happened to Jesus's body three days after his death.
Wright again: "Any real scientist will tell you that science observes what
normally happens; the Christian case is precisely that what happened to
Jesus is not what normally happens" because what has happened is that his
body "had been transformed into a new mode of physicality" (1999c, 124).
Philosophical naturalism (which claims what happens normally) is supplemented in the case of Jesus of Nazareth by supernatural or mysterious
interventions (see also Craig 1995, 144–45; Swinburne 1997, 202).[21]

As will become clear, even scholars on the Schweitzerstrasse sometimes find it difficult to adhere to the notion of the supernatural. Jesus's
temptation in the desert is, according to many scholars, mythological (see
Sanders 1993, 113–14; Theissen & Merz 1997, 193). About the so-called
nature miracles Meier informs us, "they did not fare well in my testing. In
my opinion, only the feeding of the multitude has a fair claim to go back
to some remarkable event in Jesus' lifetime" (1999, 482). This is also the
case with some of the features ascribed to Jesus's birth, as Dunn remarks
with regard to Matthew's moving star, which is unlikely to be historical
(2003b, 343–44).

While these scholars are quick to claim that such *supernatural events
and phenomena* were objectively visible (that an eyewitness or someone

21. Sanders cogently summarizes this point: "Much about the historical Jesus will
remain a mystery. Nothing is more mysterious than the stories of the resurrection" (1993,
280). What cannot be accounted for by means of naturalism is comfortably ascribed to
a mysterious or supernatural intervention. Elsewhere I have argued that it is a fallacy to
claim that such a hybrid worldview (based on naturalistic philosophy supplemented by
"supernatural" elements) is actually very "biblical." As will be argued below, many so-called
supernatural events and phenomena were very "natural" within the worldview and cultural
system of first-century Mediterranean people (see 2001b, 109).

with a video camera would actually have been able to see Jesus after the resurrection or to see the supernatural phenomena that happened during his baptism), some of them are also the first to declare such phenomena out of bounds to the historian.[22] Questions such as whether God has indeed acted in a particular "miracle" go beyond the realm of history, Meier claims (see 1991, 220; see also Johnson 1996, 102–10; Dunn 2003b, 126–27).[23]

By way of summary, in the case of Jesus of Nazareth the observable, historical events and phenomena included natural as well as supernatural ones, and these make up the searched-after historical kernel, or *what we are looking for*. The Schweitzerstrasse's employment of the supernatural category to deal with incredible stories does not alter the basic assumption that many of the stories are by themselves too incredible to be taken as historical; the use of a supernatural category in fact affirms that position.

The Structure of the Interpretive Process: Hypothesis and Verification

The interpretive strategy on the Schweitzerstrasse is described by various (similar) concepts. The format of the interpretive strategy of the Schweitzerstrasse is designed to interpret the preestablished authentic material by means of what Wright calls "the scientific method of hypothesis and verification" (1999b, 22). The first move is not to discover which sayings or even what complexes are authentic but rather to look for an explanatory model or matrix by which to order the data (see Allison 1998, 36). The researcher, after a period of immersion in the data (the assumed "authentic material"—read, the "Synoptic Gospels"), emerges with a hypothesis, a big picture of how everything fits together.[24] Following

22. On the question of whether a video camera would have recorded the event of Jesus's resurrection, Wright responds: "Assuming that a camera would pick up what most human eyes would have seen (by no means a safe assumption), my guess is that cameras would sometimes have seen Jesus and sometimes not" (1999c, 125). Davis is even more blunt: "I feel no sense of embarrassment whatsoever in holding that a camera could have taken a snapshot of the raised Jesus, say, feeding the seven disciples beside the Sea of Tiberias (John 21:1–14)" (1997, 142).

23. How deeply scholars on the Schweitzerstrasse are trapped in a positivistic historiography is confirmed by these examples. Elements that cannot be considered historical in a modern scientific worldview cannot be taken as possible historical elements in the life of Jesus. They are taken as "Jesus as seen with the eyes of faith" (Dunn 2003b, 332).

24. Meier's viewpoint also explicitly expresses this process: "I think that the critically

the dictum of Meyer that "history is reconstruction through hypothesis and verification," Sanders is a prime example of this approach (quoted in Sanders 1985, 8–9, 47). He says, "We need to study the facts about Jesus and try to understand their significance in his context" (1985, 8). For him the temple controversy offers such a sound bedrock.[25]

When the documents are stripped from their editorial and traditional overlay, the authentic material fitted into the best hypothesis offers the best construction of the historical figure. It turns out that the Synoptic Gospels' portrayals are fairly close to the historical figure.

In perhaps the most extensive study of the criteria of authenticity on this road, Theissen comes up with a formulation of the criteria, which also postulates that a fit between the data and a historical context can be assumed to constitute historicity or authenticity. In a study with Merz the "historical criterion of plausibility" is formulated in the following way: "what is plausible in the Jewish context and makes the rise of Christianity understandable may be historical" (1998, 11).[26] To my mind, Dunn correctly points out that "Theissen's criterion of historical plausibility is more a restatement of historical method than a criterion" (2003b, 83). In fact, Allison argues that most historical Jesus scholars have probably all along been using an explanatory model or matrix (Crossan's *sharpest possible context* or Theissen's *plausibility of context*), by means of which the authenticity of traditions had been established (and claimed they were the

---

sifted data of the gospels demand that the depiction of Jesus as the eschatological prophet working miracles à la Elijah must be a key element in the reconstruction of the historical Jesus" (1999, 483). Similarly, Dunn starts with a "broad picture," his vision of the holistic method (see 2003b, 332).

25. Like the identification of authentic material that is in dispute, there is no consensus that the temple controversy offers such a firm historical bedrock (see Scott 1994, 266; Arnal 1997, 206–9).

26. In three studies, Theissen (1996; Theissen & Winter 1997; and Theissen & Merz 1998) evaluates the existing criteria of authenticity. It is argued that the criteria of multiple attestations and independence of sources (what, for some scholars, count as criteria of authenticity) are merely an index of the validity of sources, and that there are actually only two true criteria of authenticity: the criterion of difference and the criterion of coherence (see Theissen & Winter 1997, 17): "Unser Überblick über die wichtigsten Kriterien der Jesusforschung zeigt: Nur die zuletzt genannten Kriterien von Differenz und Kohärenz sind Echtheitskriterien im engeren Sinne, und unter ihnen hat das Differenzkriterium die grössere Bedeutung" (Theissen & Winter 1997, 18). In a reformulation of the criteria, the "plausibility of context" (*Kontext plausibilität*) and the "plausibility of influence" (*Wirkungsplausibilität*) are taken together as the historical criterion of plausibility as formulated above.

result of using criteria of authenticity) (see 1998, 36). But this procedure is, without a doubt, extremely arbitrary.[27]

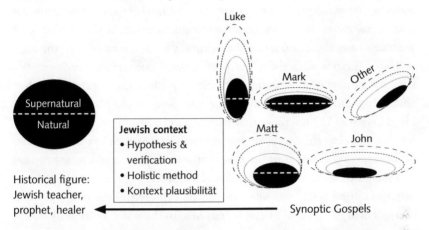

Diagram 2.4: Going Back to the Historical Figure via the Schweitzerstrasse

On the Schweitzerstrasse the Synoptic Gospels occupy the prime position as historical sources, and this is indicated by the large sections of authentic material. After their church overlay is removed, these sources are subjected to the hypothesis and verification process in order to identify the historical figure consisting of both natural and supernatural elements that made up his life in Galilee. The linear nature of the process is indicated by the direction of the arrow.

Current Jesus Research and the Historiographical Map

The question remaining is: How and where does current historical Jesus research fit into the above historiographical map? In my view, the answer is that it fits securely on the positivist/postmodern continuum. The strongest argument in support of this claim is the absence of reflection on what historical Jesus historiography, conceptualized as anthropological historiography, would be like. In this sense, the most remarkable feature of the reaction in Jesus research against positivism and the movements toward a postmodern historiographical discourse remain the absence of any discussion of the culturally alien nature of the data about Jesus of Nazareth as

27. Crossan has very cogently asked about the method of hypothesis and verification: why not hypothesize that John had it historically correct? Had they immersed themselves in that Gospel first, they would certainly have emerged with different hypotheses (see 1998, 97).

well as the fact that all the data originated from a worldview and cultural
system that operated with a different sense of reality. One of the striking
features, for example, in the work of Schröter, who pays considerable attention to issues of historiography in Jesus research, is the almost total
absence of any reflection about the culturally alien nature of both the texts
and what is reported in them (see 1996; 2001; 2002). He not only emphasizes the import of the postmodern view on historical constructions but
also points out such implications for our view on the historical sources.
He shows that the documents themselves are not pure reflections of the
historical reality they refer to but the product of memory and sources.
However, what is not considered is that what was or could have been remembered were the words and deeds of a cultural figure from an alien and
distant cultural system. While this will be explored in the next chapters,
two sets of arguments will be advanced here to show that current historical
Jesus research is firmly situated on the positivist-postmodern continuum.

First, either explicitly or implicitly, historiographical positions in
Jesus research are consciously situated on the positivism-postmodern
continuum.

It has to be appreciated that in the historiographical reflection of
current historical Jesus research, there are earnest attempts to avoid the
extremes of the positivist/postmodern historiographical continuum.
Special attempts are made to bypass the pitfalls of positivistic historiography, while the critique and insights of postmodern historiography are
often consciously embraced. At the same time, the extreme forms of postmodern historiography are avoided. This can be seen in Wright's adoption
of critical realism as an alternative to both positivism and subjectivity or
relativity (see 1992a, 32–36).[28] Crossan navigates between two modes of
historical reconstruction that he refers to as "one an impossible delusion"
(*positivism*), which imagines that you know the past without any personal
or social interference, and "the other illusion" (*narcissism*), where you think
you see the past but all you see is your own reflection (see 1998, 41–42).
The rejection of positivism is explicitly expressed in an adoption of postmodernism (or, as he calls it, *interactivism*).

28. For Wright, critical realism as an approach to historiography "is a way of describing
the process of 'knowing' that acknowledges the *reality of the thing known, as something
other than the knower* (hence 'realism'), while also fully acknowledging that the only access
we have to this reality lies along the spiraling path of *appropriate dialogue or conversation
between the knower and the thing known* (hence 'critical')" (1992a, 35, italics his).

These explicit maneuverings between the positivist and postmodern positions are supported by implicit struggles with issues on that very continuum. While a common feature of historiographical reflections in Jesus research remains the explicit avoidance of positivism, the entrapment in that continuum can be illustrated with a number of examples. The following themes are exemplary and not intended to be exhaustive.

One is a rejection of the correspondence theory of truth. The force of the argument is to show that historical constructions are not reproductions or reconstructions of the past (which is gone for ever) but mediated pictures (see Funk 1996, 58; Du Toit 2002, 120; Schröter 2002, 166).[29] Despite the fact that they are no longer naive fundamentalists who believe that everything written stands in a one-to-one relationship to reality (is a description of reality), scholars on both the Schweitzerstrasse and the Wredebahn still take for granted the natural veracity of the documents. The documents are still read straight, as if they are talking about events and phenomena in the world of modern exegetes. A historical figure could not have been like the portrayals, and, therefore, either somewhere underneath the overlay there must be some authentic kernel containing the real historical figure, or the Gospel portrayals are the deposit of truly supernatural interventions in history. However, as argued earlier, within the framework of anthropological historiography, the issue is no longer the foundation of knowledge but the arguments of claims regarding the fallibility of knowledge.

Another example is the claim that research results are tentative and open to further investigation.[30] The admission is, however, only a reserva-

29. Schröter argues for a *"Konstruktion von Geschichte"* and not a *"Rekonstruktion der Vergangenheit"* (2002, 167), while Du Toit suggests that a reconstruction is an illusion because the only option is "in reflektierender Verantwortung angesichts der fragmentarischen Quellen Geschichte in einem kreativen Akt zu konstruieren" (2002, 121). As will become clear below, it is unfortunate that they contrast construction with a caricature (or at least an outdated positivistic) view of reconstruction as recovery of the past ("wiedergewinnen"), resurrection of the past ("wirklichkeitsgetreu wiederauferstehen") or recovery of the past ("eine Wiederherstellung der Vergangenheit").

30. Over a broad spectrum of Jesus studies, it is today accepted that historical constructions are not fixed and final. Crossan's disclaimer emphasizes the delusion of positivism. Jesus reconstruction, he says, is always a creative interaction of the past and the present (and not possible without the interference from the historian's personal and social location) (1998, 41–45). Funk states that his picture of Jesus is "tentative, subject to further investigation and new information" (1996, 20). It often takes lengthy analyses to show to what extent Jesus books are in fact positivistic, despite such disclaimers (see, e.g., the discussion in Marsh, 1997, 411).

tion about the force of a construction and not a claim about its character or validity. The claim that a construction is preliminary and tentative is not the same as avoiding, say, a positivist approach.

Second, there is very direct evidence that current historical Jesus research is trapped in the positivistic framework (not even to claim the positivism/postmodern continuum). Three examples, painted with a broad brush, will have to suffice in showing from the foregoing overview of the Schweitzerstrasse and the Wredebahn that both are trapped in this framework. First, contrary to his own claims, Crossan is a case in point. He is taken as scapegoat because, as Horsley says (2003, 160 n. 1), Crossan has brought the standard approach to the historical Jesus to its logical and most sophisticated conclusion.[31]

Denton shows that Crossan's so-called *interactivism* has very few practical consequences for the way he does history (2004, 76). Based on the arguments that data cannot be controlled or applied until they are understood, and that they cannot be understood before they assume a role in a historical investigation, Denton unmasks the positivistic characteristics in Crossan's approach, showing that his "is a prime example of a method that presumes to understand, and evaluate, data apart from any public context" (see 2004, 124–25). Crossan handles the data on Jesus strictly as testimony, prior to a sensitive understanding of what the data are about (see 2004, 66). Precisely the results of centuries of gospel research conducted within a positivistic framework (as testimony) are claimed in the standard approach.

This is confirmed by Crossan's stated use of an interdisciplinary instead of a positivistic approach. His description of his version of an interdisciplinary methodology is multidisciplinary instead: "I started with historical criticism, next incorporated literary criticism, and finally added macrosociological criticism to form an integrated interdisciplinary model" (1998, 139). On all accounts, this is a multidisciplinary model, which is confirmed by the fact that each method is used independently from the others. It is nowhere better illustrated than in the fact that the social-scientific and anthropological models are applied to the data only after they have received their primary sense in his approach (see also Denton 2004, 183).

31. This is also the view of Denton, who says that "there is no historian of Jesus working today who has refined tradition criticism in a way more sophisticated than Crossan" (2004, 71, 176).

It is precisely positivistic historiography that assumes that data can be used (i.e., read straight) prior to or without an interpretive framework, and that is exactly what happens both in Crossan's tradition history and in his so-called interdisciplinary method described here.

Second, it has been shown that Jesus research is, broadly speaking, dominated by the search for authentic material, or, as Scott remarks, that the general trademark of Jesus research remains a search for a "sure foundation" or "bedrock" (1994, 275). Either a little core of purified evidence (by means of the radical application of specifically two criteria of authenticity: multiple attestation and early dating) or the bulk of the synoptic evidence (purified from early church overlay by means of a selection of criteria of authenticity) guarantees that the "real Jesus," or at least a reliable account of the historical figure, can be identified.

Scholars on the two roads differ about the number of complexes that go back to Jesus (for some the database is small and for others large) but not about the principle: the historical figure is to be found in the original or authentic material underneath the gospel portrayals.[32] However, as Horsley observes:

> 'Data' from the Gospels must be isolated, analyzed, and brought carefully under *control* in order then to be used in historical reconstruction. Only data that pass the test of modern reasonability/rationality can be used. Having already reduced the Gospels to religious bits and pieces directed to individuals, we then, by scientific screening, exclude the dross of anything miraculous, mythic, or fantastic, leaving the pure nuggets of reified sayings and parables we can test for 'authenticity.' (2003, 7, italics his)

Third, both the Wredebahn and the Schweitzerstrasse are trapped in a set of nested philosophical assumptions about how to deal with "the other." Neusner offers a well-formulated summary of these assumptions, which are tacitly assumed in most historical Jesus studies:

> These have been [1] historical fact, unmediated by tradition, themselves bear theological consequence, the gift of the Reformation

---

32. The tacit assumption is that if original words (or deeds) of Jesus have been ascertained, the researcher has a clear grasp of the historical person; the original words or deeds afford a direct and accurate link to the historical figure (see also Schüssler Fiorenza 1997, 345–52; Bloomquist 1997, 97–98, 1080, for critical discussions of these views.) In other words, both those who accept the sources as historically reliable and those who reject them share the same positivistic view of the sources—they only judge differently when it comes to their historicity.

(show me as fact in the source, e.g., Scripture); [2] historical facts must undergo a rigorous test of skepticism, the donation of the Enlightenment (how could a whale swallow Jonah, and what else did he have for lunch that day); and [3] historical fact cannot comprise supernatural events, the present of nineteenth century German historical learning (exactly how things were cannot include rising from the dead). (1994, 113)

As shown above, the assumptions of modern naturalism work differently on the two roads. In the case of the Schweitzerstrasse, they are supplemented with the notion of the supernatural, while on the Wredebahn they result in the verdict that what does not conform to the standards of scientific reasoning and its reality catalog is to be considered mythological. Whatever is encountered in the documents is filtered through the lenses of ontological monism, the worldview of modern science. These are typical features of traditional historiography that can be called by different names.

Social Types in Jesus Research

All Jesus studies include a notion about his social type. Therefore, a great variety of social types is used to capture his position as historical figure. As Gray remarks,

> there has been renewed interest in the question of how Jesus of Nazareth should be classified in terms of religious or social type. Should he be described primarily as a teacher, prophet, miracle worker, magician, Galilean charismatic, or militant revolutionary? The list of possibilities could be extended. These types are not mutually exclusive, and it is possible—indeed likely—that a given individual would have combined different roles. But it is still worth asking which single type best describes Jesus. (1993, 3)

While pointing out that it is worth asking which social type best describes Jesus as a historical figure (in this study this is fundamental to an understanding of Jesus as historical figure), Gray makes the common mistake of equating social role with social type. This is often the case when a *social type* merely functions as a label for categorizing preestablished features.

On finer analysis, it appears that at least two kinds of social types (each with its variations) can be identified in historical Jesus literature:

pictures based on a single social type and studies that operate with some kind of composite social type.

Single Social Types

The term *single social type* refers to the variety of social types utilized in the scholarly literature for describing Jesus as social figure (prophet, healer, magician, sage, teacher, and the like). These are usually the product either of some authentic material being identified or of bedrock material (usually some narrative material) being taken as starting point in identifying Jesus as historical figure. The normal pattern is that if the miracle tradition is given weight, Jesus emerges as magician; and when the sayings tradition is treated as central, Jesus emerges as teacher or sage; and when the prophetic and apocalyptic sayings are identified as authentic, he emerges as some kind of eschatological prophet (see, e.g., Telford 1994, 52–54).

There are two specific problems with these single social types. The first problem, which is obviously bound up with the identification of authentic material, is that none of the single-social-type models can deal with all the data. In some instances, everything that fits the initial social type (hypothesis) is taken as authentic. In others, the social type is the *conclusion* based on the identified authentic material (usually concluding, on the basis of the teaching material, that Jesus must have been a teacher or sage of some kind). Whichever way one works, the social type covers only selected portions of the data, and a large part is or has to be excluded from the picture.

The second problem is that (authentic) material is simply *added* onto the existing type. Sanders, for example, believes Jesus was an eschatological prophet but one who gained fame from miracles and was also a teacher. He then clearly illustrates the dilemma: while many scholars on the Schweitzerstrasse agree that *prophet* is the social type that best fits Jesus, they have to recognize that he was also a miracle worker and healer—elements that are not covered by any definition of a prophet. Not infrequently, he says, "one will read that he [Jesus] combined styles or types" (1985, 239).[33] What Sanders says about the prophet category is equally true about the other pictures: the price one has to pay for the single-social-type models

---

33. In his later work, Sanders continues to struggle with this dilemma. He maintains that "prophet" is the best "single" category for Jesus, but that he was also an "exorcist" and a "teacher" and a "miracle worker" (1993, 153–54).

is that in the end they contain people who differed substantially from one another, and who are ascribed many functions not associated with that type.[34] Wright solves this problem in an ingenious but invalid way by arguing that Jesus was not only an *eschatological prophet*, he was "more than a prophet" (see 1996, 196). Unfortunately, a *figure-more-than-a-prophet* is not known historically or cross-culturally, and it would be impossible to determine what the cultural dynamics of such a figure would have been like.

This problem is equally pertinent with drivers on the Wredebahn. For Crossan, the historical Jesus was a peasant Jewish Cynic, but he also acted as healer, exorcist, and miracle worker (see 1991a, 311, 347; 1994b, 93, 198).[35] Funk, who insists that based on the earliest evidence, Jesus was a teacher, at another point refers to him as "the itinerant teacher, healer, and exorcist" (see 1996, 124, 143). Did Cynic teachers actually heal and exorcise? No, Downing admits: "We do not have sufficient healer-figures to afford us any clear model, and there is no contemporary model of a Cynic healer" (1987, 447).

The dilemma with these single-social-type models is that when a pure social type is used, they cannot deal with all elements in the tradition.[36] When all elements are included, the social types no longer have a basis in history and culture. In other words, the category is stretched to the point that it becomes meaningless because it no longer covers historical examples.

---

34. In a sense, the problem is even bigger because neither in antiquity nor in modern scholarly discussions is there a clear-cut definition of what a prophet is (see Öhler 2001, 139). The discussion and literature on prophetism in Israel in the Second Temple period cited by Grabbe confirms this point (see 2000, 232–34).

35. In a rather amazing turnabout, Crossan says that *Jewish peasant Cynic* is not an "ancient social type" but "a modern scholarly construct" (1998, 334). Besides the question regarding in what way such a modern scholarly construct relates or gives access to an ancient historical figure, the point remains, how and where do healing, exorcism, and miracles fit into the type, whichever modern scholarly model or construct is used?

36. Another example is the utilization of the millenarian prophet as social type (see Allison 1998; Theissen 1999). It is important to note the differences between Theissen and Allison. Theissen sees Jesus as a prophet of a millenarian movement, and his basic argument is that the Jesus movement was a millenarian movement. Central to that argument is the notion that it was an inner Jewish revitalization movement. Allison sees Jesus himself as an eschatological prophet (see 1998, 44). In both instances, the type does not cover all the evidence.

Composite Social Types

In several studies, these *add-on* components reach the status of *composite social types.*[37] Various pictures of composite social types are found in the literature. Telford claims that "a combination of *teacher, prophet, healer* best captures historically his [Jesus's] social identity or role" (1994, 55), while for Theissen, Jesus was partly "a sensitive poet, partly an apocalyptic prophet, partly a miracle-worker and exorcist, a charismatic leader and an extreme ethicist" (1996, 172).

In Vermes's picture of Jesus as charismatic holy man, the traditions of healer, exorcist, and prophet-teacher are given almost equal weight (see 1973, 22, 58). One of the most interesting examples is Borg, who identifies five types of religious figures known cross-culturally as well as within the history of Israel: the religious ecstatic, the healer, the wisdom teacher, the social prophet, and the movement founder (see 1995, 8–10).[38] Jesus did not conform to a single social type since he "had characteristics of several different types of religious personalities" (1994b, 29).[39] The implication is clear: Jesus combined five social types known in history and cross-culturally.[40]

Four observations can be made about these composite social-types.

The first is that they are the best confirmation that the different categories of religious specialist are, indeed, distinguishable and in need of

---

37. Composite pictures are usually the result of taking the synoptic tradition as authentic, while single pictures follow from the tendency to identify a single strand of tradition as authentic (as bedrock).

38. Borg initially identified only four social types (see 1987, 16).

39. It should be noted that Borg admits that Jesus as a spirit person is foundational to everything else he was. Being a spirit-filled person (or a charismatic holy man) is to Borg (1987, 51, 71) "the key for understanding the central dimensions of his ministry: as healer, sage, revitalization movement founder, and prophet" (see also 1994b, 31).

40. It has to be admitted that not all scholars who describe Jesus by means of such a composite social type operate with the theological prejudices of Hengel, who maintains that Jesus did not conform to a particular type because his authority was so underivable: "Even within the characterization we have preferred, of an 'eschatological charismatic,' he [Jesus] remains in the last resort incommensurable, and so basically confounds every attempt to fit him into the categories suggested by the phenomenology or sociology of religion" (quoted in Telford 1994, 55 n. 84). Dunn expresses a similar opinion in that "Jesus' mission seems to have broken through all the most obvious categories by which his mission could be evaluated; he evidently did not fit with any degree of comfort into any of the pigeon-holes by which observers might have wished to label him" (2003b, 704).

distinction. It is implicitly accepted that healers can be distinguished from teachers (and so forth).

The second observation is that these composite social types confirm that social types in Jesus research are used merely as labels for naming certain identified functions. Did Jesus, in fact, combine the social types which, in the case of other (historical) figures, are distinct and separate? These combined social types do not provide any understanding of the social dynamics of Jesus as a figure or of his position as a social type because they have no confirmation through history-of-religion or cross-cultural parallels. In other words, they are not identifiable social types of historical figures but scholarly labels for selected functions.

The third observation is that, in using these composite social types, scholars admit that Jesus actually performed a variety of functions that cannot be captured by any of the existing social type categories used by New Testament scholars—it confirms that Jesus cannot be imprisoned in one of the existing social types: healer, Cynic, magician, prophet and the like. At the same time, they assert that he was a social personage engaged in a wide variety of cultural activities.

Finally, while a social type by definition differs from a social role, it is apparent that for these combined-social-type constructions, there are no clear historical or cross-cultural parallels. While scholars in other fields of research find distinct social types for the social personages that they investigate, in the case of Jesus of Nazareth it seems as if none of the categories quite fit.

The question, therefore, remains whether there is really no social type well established historically and cross-culturally that can account for the diverse functions and traditions ascribed to Jesus. Can this (artificial) combination of social types or the stretching of existing social type models to include all the functions ascribed to Jesus, be avoided? It is the hypothesis of this study that the shamanic complex offers such a model.

Social Type as a Label for the Historical Figure

With the exception of a few studies (e.g., Smith 1978; Davies 1995; Malina 1997), the pattern of identifying Jesus's social type is fairly common: from an identification of authentic material (or, connecting authentic material with a specific setting), it is concluded what kind of social type he belonged to: if he spoke about eschatology, he was an eschatological prophet; and if he uttered wisdom sayings, he was a sage or teacher of some kind, and so forth. In other words, it is the conclusion of an interpretive process that started with the identification of authentic material (either the Synoptic Gospels or a few authentic nuggets).

As has been pointed out, the dominant function of social types on both the Schweitzerstrasse and the Wredebahn is that they merely function as labels for naming preestablished features (clusters of original material) of the historical figure. In other words, they name features without adding any value to the analysis—with the result that the real value of the *social-type* category is lost.

Social types as labels and a history-of-ideas approach go hand in hand in these cases. Furthermore, the affinity between a history-of-ideas approach and the positivistic quest for authentic material should be apparent. In both cases, it is trust in the availability of a direct textual quotation or textual material that satisfies the demand of scholarship. This tendency can be explained by looking at the type of categories that are used in historical Jesus research. Jesus was a teacher (there are texts saying that he taught); Jesus was a healer (there are stories about his healing); he was a poet and prophet (because there is evidence to this effect). The logic is simple: a person who teaches is a teacher, and a person who prophesies is a prophet, and so forth. The kind of teacher or prophet simply depends on the identified content.[41]

Why is there no category of Jesus as "diviner" or as "mediator of divine power" or as "shamanic figure"?[42] There is no such category because there is no direct textual evidence confirming such pictures. But what analysis tells us is that Jesus probably acted as diviner and mediator to the divine world; he experienced visions and intervened in illness and demon

41. In some instances, this also applies to analyses that are not based solely on ideas but on specific social locations. Because Jesus operated mostly in the villages of Galilee within the household or family sphere, he must, according to Horsley, be understood as a prophetic leader of a movement of Israelite renewal based in these villages. The structure of the argument is, however, the same: Jesus's social type is a label that is added to a preestablished set of "facts" (1996, 189).

42. In an interesting suggestion that he does not explore, Sanders says that when looking at Jesus's view of his position in God's plan, it is that of the *viceroy*: "There was no title in the history of Judaism that fully communicated all this, and Jesus seems to have been quite reluctant to adopt a title for himself. I think that even 'king' is not precisely correct, since Jesus regarded God as king. My own favourite term for his conception of himself is 'viceroy.' God was king, but Jesus represented him and would represent him in the coming kingdom" (1993, 248). His reluctance to employ that concept confirms this point.

possession; and he mediated divine wisdom, power, and prophesies to mere mortals.

This point can perhaps best be illustrated from what is missing from Jesus research. First, there is very little (if any) discussion about what constitutes a specific social type in that world or about what the cultural dynamics of the various social types were. It is more often than not assumed that definitions of the term *prophet* or *sage* or *teacher* are self-explanatory and can be obtained from another text referring to such a figure. Consequently, it is accepted that the social dynamics of such figures are well known. The second missing point of discussion is that there are very few (if any) social analyses that inform the decisions about Jesus's social type. The impression is rather that since it is known what each of the social types are (because they are used to describe other historical figures), it is unnecessary to go into any serious social analysis.

The most common social type on the Schweitzerstrasse is Jesus as a prophet of some kind. Meier's viewpoint is typical: "I think that the critically sifted data of the gospels demand that the depiction of Jesus as the eschatological prophet working miracles à la Elijah must be a key element in the reconstruction of the historical Jesus" (1999, 483). What he means by "critically sifted data" has nothing to do with a social analysis of the evidence in terms of the social type and cultural setting but with authentic material receiving the appropriate label. Jesus proclaimed the kingdom of God and performed miracles (such as healings and exorcisms), and these functions need labeling—as is the case with social roles.[43] However, neither the eschatological prophet nor the miracle worker is a recognized social type in Israelite tradition. Like the social types used on the Wredebahn, these can only be found on the pages of New Testament publications.[44]

The fact that these social types are not cross-cultural models but are merely found in New Testament publications is further confirmed by the Elijah parallel. On what basis can Elijah be seen as a "typical biblical prophet" or as an exponent of a recognizable social type in the Israelite

43. The difference between *social type* and *social role* will be discussed below. Social type is more permanent, has a wider range, depends on an identifiable cultural pattern, and is established by means of a social-type analysis; a social role refers to a function or status of limited range (to teach, to heal, to minister). A social role is an official category that can be identified by anyone because of the position.

44. Crossan's Cynic who is also a magician/healer (see 1991a, 347, 421) and Funk's sage who is also a miracle worker (see 1996, 143, 252) are examples of social types from the Wredebahn.

tradition?[45] Furthermore, Elijah cannot be a social type for understanding Jesus's social type unless it has been established that Elijah himself belonged to such a recognizable type. Elijah himself is a figure in need of analysis and interpretation, and simply citing him as example does not contribute to the analysis or understanding of Jesus's social type. This cavalier citation of earlier biblical figures is indicative of labeling rather than analyzing. When trying to understand one figure in a culture, it does not help to simply cite more examples from the same culture unless they are based on a comparative analysis—either within the same cultural setting or across cultures.

The connection between social-type models and the history-of-ideas approach can also be illustrated with the following questions: if Jesus was a prophet, what would have been historical about his life? What would his life have been like, and how would knowledge about that life and public activity have been preserved and transmitted? Even though social-type models such as that of a prophet are used (in the wide variety indicated above), current historical Jesus research, generally speaking, does not take the social type as an analytical category to explore the social and cultural dynamics of Jesus's public life, had he been such a figure. The examples cited in this chapter confirm that historical-critical Jesus research operates with a fragmented linear and history-of-ideas approach, or better, with an atomistic, chain-like process of interpretation. The so-called social types are rather social roles added as afterthoughts onto the preestablished authentic material or identified functions in Jesus's life. The fact that social types enter the discussion usually as the last component of the portrayal of Jesus confirms the point that no social analysis takes place where the social type, its features within a particular cultural setting, the specific individual, and the sources are in constant interaction.

Conclusion

Toward the end of the previous century, Barraclough complained that "at least 90 per cent of historical work published today is resolutely traditional in method, subject-matter and conceptualization" (1978, 207). This

---

45. The question is whether Elijah should even be seen as a typical prophet from the Hebrew Bible. Israelite prophets were primarily social, moral, and religious reformers. For Josephus, much closer to Jesus, *prophets* were individuals with special insight into the future (see, e.g., Gray 1993, 164–65; Öhler 2001, 127).

is equally true for most historical Jesus research, which continues to play out the research program set into motion by the historical questions posed more than two hundred years ago. Despite renewal in the paradigm, it is dominated by a search for the authentic core (small or large) on which a historical picture of Jesus can be based.

It is no accident that current historical Jesus research can be seen as a continuation of the former quests, because it is still trying to answer the questions posed in the eighteenth and nineteenth centuries. The ways of treating the documents, of asking the questions, of structuring the interpretive process, and of dealing with a historical figure are all part of a positivistic historiographical paradigm that gave birth to historical Jesus research.

The notion that any picture of the historical Jesus should be based on hard evidence implies that the first (or at least the most important) step remains the identification of the authentic core and that is done within the philosophical framework provided by the previous ages. Despite a lack of agreement about the starting point and procedures of research, the focus on authentic material dominates most of the scholarly literature on the sources. In fact, much of what currently goes on in Jesus research is unimaginable without the search for or claim about original material. This discourse is so deeply ingrained that it is almost impossible to even imagine a critical historical Jesus study not participating in it. Central to this enterprise is the notion of a linear development from a single event or series of events that gave rise to traditions and that were then creatively employed in the tradition or by the gospel authors—that is, a linear model of event, tradition and gospel additions, or of original, traditional, and evangelical material. Another structuring principle in the authenticity debate is that there is a mixing of issues of authenticity (whether it belongs to Jesus) with issues of historicity (whether it actually happened). In fact, in a variety of ways these questions are treated on the same level, and conclusions about the first set of questions are used for the second. In short, if authenticity can be established, historicity (what has happened or was said) follows easily. But what if there never were such "single events" to begin with, but only cultural events with specific cultural features?

With regard to *historicity*, the Wredebahn and the Schweitzerstrasse are like nonidentical twins: they have the same naturalistic origin but unrelated appearances. Each version of the authenticity paradigm presupposes its own construction of the actual events that lie behind the gospel accounts. For those on the Schweitzerstrasse, there were natural and supernatural events that were remembered, recorded, and retold. For those on the Wredebahn, most of the episodes and scenes in the Gospels were acts of literary creativity or storytelling, with a (greatly reduced) historical event in some instances behind these processes. None of these interpretations treat the gospel scenes and episodes as possible accounts of *cultural events* inscribed in a cultural system or reality framework of first-century Mediterranean people.

While the use of new methods and models often challenge some of the fundamental assumptions of the traditional historiography, the basic paradigm remains intact, and it is nowhere more visible than in the assumptions about the origin of the Gospel texts. It is important to realize that the two hundred years of gospel research cannot be divorced from the questions and assumptions that started the process and still carry it (see also Du Toit 2002, 119; Tuckett 2002, 214). Jesus research went hand in hand with specific assumptions about how the Gospels came to be written, about how one Gospel used another, and about what could or could not have happened in reality.

What we are looking at, according to this paradigm, should be mined or penetrated in order to identify the historical figure (*what we are looking for*).[46] Treating the documents as testimonies, the historical figure is to be identified in the authentic nuggets (determined with multiple independent attestation) or in the Synoptic Gospels cleansed from post-Easter overlay. This constitutes what can be described as a linear, chain-like interpretive process.

---

46. As Crossan quite correctly remarks, the "validity of one's Jesus-conclusions stand or fall with that of one's gospel-presupposition" (1997, 351). And gospel presuppositions, he claims, are based on the general consensus of two hundred years of research (see 1988, 140–49). These two hundred years of scholarship basically allow us to see layered texts with small (or larger) authentic kernels at the bottom and the largest part of the documentary evidence as literary creations.

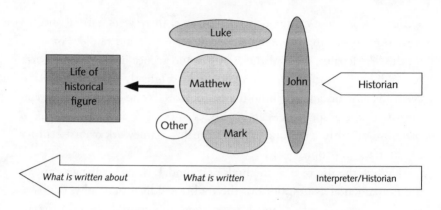

Diagram 2.5:
The (Linear) Chain-like Structure of the Authenticity Paradigm

Undoubtedly, as the variety in the authenticity paradigm shows, a constant revision of elements within the paradigm (or within different versions of the paradigm) is taking place but none which challenges the paradigm as such. There are many revisions, or as Kuhn says, puzzle-solving *within* the paradigm but very little revision *of* the paradigm.

It is, however, the movement beyond the positivist-postmodern continuum that has not yet been registered in historical Jesus research. It is precisely in the recognition of multiple cultural realities that a paradigm change in historiography is to be noted. Portrayals of Jesus within the authenticity paradigm are all based on *what the texts say* or *what a cluster of authentic material points to* and not what can be deduced from *what analysis reveals*. In other words, the documents are treated as testimonies instead of as evidence. Without a proper cross-cultural methodology and interpretive style it is impossible to deal with culturally alien texts and phenomena without distorting (mastering, absorbing, or reducing) them. In the remainder of this book it will be shown what anthropological historiographical Jesus research looks like. It consists of a new view on what we are looking at as well as what we are looking for, a different structure of the interpretive process and in fact, an alteration of the research question as such.

CHAPTER 3

A New Road for Historical Jesus Research: Cultural Bundubashing

Introduction

CURRENT CRITICAL JESUS SCHOLARSHIP is constitutionally incapable of dealing with culturally alien texts and phenomena in a sympathetic manner. The two roads in current historical Jesus research are inadequate for dealing with the cultural meaning and significance and are inattentive to the cultural processes assumed and described by the documents. *Cultural bundubashing,* as the track of anthropological historiography will be called, offers an alternative critical paradigm for historical Jesus research.[1] In an attempt to avoid ethnocentrism and anachronism while striving to do justice to the cultural and historical singularity of those involved, it takes historical Jesus research through the cultural landscape of both the documents and the historical figure reported in them. It is not a middle position between the Wredebahn and the Schweitzerstrasse, and it does not occupy a position somewhere between critical scholarship (which thinks most of the material was created by the early church) and the naive fundamentalist (who thinks that everything in the Gospels comes from the historical Jesus) but, like anthropological historiography of which it is an instance, operates altogether on a different terrain.

This track often runs parallel to—and can even cross—the other two roads but mostly covers a different terrain. It offers a view of the same

---

1. Bundubashing is the rough ride of off-road traveling for which an off-road vehicle and toolkit are needed. Travelers are bound to run into serious difficulties (like crossing rivers and mountains where there are no bridges and proper roads). But this is the real way to see the countryside and experience the cultural richness of the land, the initiates say.

scenery but from a different point of view. It starts with a uniquely conceptualized research problem, which is the result of a differently conceptualized terrain and results in an alternative interpretation of the data. It
does not offer alternative answers to existing questions but offers answers
to alternative questions and problems. It consists of a redefinition of the
questions instead of a rephrasing of the answers.

Cultural bundubashing is designed to take the historical Jesus researcher back to the strangeness of the cultural system and the pastness
of the historical world in order to grasp the meaning, significance, and
context of the events, phenomena, and people involved, while searching
within the framework of anthropological historiography for the historical
figure. Within this paradigm, the aim of historical Jesus research is to determine and describe across the historical and cultural gap what it was like
in the strangeness of their world, and how things were in the life of Jesus
in Galilee, and how that can be appreciated in a modern world. Cultural
bundubashing remains loyal to the ideal of capturing *what essentially happened*, or what the case (or state of affairs) in the past was, but realizes this
requires cross-cultural interventions.[2] In this view, history concerns itself
not just with *facts* but with the meaning of things and the interpretation of
details (see Malina & Neyrey 1988, 142). Instead of the search for criteria
of authenticity or historicity, cultural bundubashing focuses on two other
processes: the establishment of cultural plausibility and what will be called
contextual particularity, and both make use of thick descriptions.

It is the acceptance of multiple cultural realities and ontological pluralism that constitutes the historian's task; this is much more complex than
simply asking about what has happened as if a straightforward answer can
be offered. Within this framework, the rules of evidence of both positiv-

2. Iggers and Von Molkte point out, "Indeed Ranke's oft quoted dictum '*wie es
eigentlich gewesen*,' has generally been misunderstood in this country [the USA] as asking
the historian to be satisfied with a purely factual recreation of the past. Ranke's writing
makes it clear that he did not mean this. In fact the word '*eigentlich*' which is the key to
the phrase just quoted has been poorly translated into English. In the nineteenth century
this word was ambiguous in a way in which it no longer is. It certainly had the modern
meaning of 'actually' already, but it also meant 'characteristic, essential,' and the latter is
the form in which Ranke most frequently uses this term. This gives the phrase an entirely
different meaning" (1973a, xix). This is confirmed by Wilma Iggers's translation of one
of the relevant Ranke texts: "To history has been given the function of judging the past,
instructing men for the profit of future years. The present attempt does not aspire to such
lofty understanding. It merely wants to show how, essentially, things happened" (von
Ranke 1973, 137).

istic and postmodern historiography can no longer be applied. Within this view of historiography, the distinction between truth and falsehood remains fundamental, but the concept of truth has become "immeasurably more complex in the course of recent critical thought" (Iggers 1997, 12). The historian continues to work critically with the sources that make access to the past reality possible because the concept of truth and the duty to uncover falsification have not been abandoned.

The aim of this and the following chapter is to explain this complexity of dealing with alien and distant historical Jesus material in a culturally sensitive manner. Therefore, in this study the terms *historical* or *historical interpretation* have specific meanings. They refer, in the first place, to situating and understanding the texts, events, and the person *Jesus of Nazareth* as phenomena in their pastness and otherness. To begin with, this constitutes a totally different research question: not what has happened or which source is correct, but what are the sources and stories about?

A Redescription of the Research Problem

It was shown that in current historical Jesus research the interpretive process follows the inverse order of the linear development of the texts: interpretation moves backwards from the Gospels to the historical figure. Cultural bundubashing is based on a different interpretive process.

Abduction as Interpretive Process

Bernstein, following Peirce, describes interpretation as a cable-like process. In science, we ought to trust the multitude and variety of arguments rather than the conclusiveness of any one of them, he says (see 1983, 224; 1991, 327). Our reasoning should not form a chain that is no stronger than the weakest link, but a cable whose fibers, though ever so slender, by their sheer numbers and interwovenness make it much stronger. In this description the features of an interpretive versus a positivistic theory of science is visible.

This process of reasoning from hypothesis to data and back as many times as necessary to gain insight, is what the philosopher Peirce calls *abduction* (see Malina 2001b, 9).

> Abduction is reasoning that begins with data and moves toward hypothesis with the introduction of a new idea. *It is reasoning toward a hypothesis*; it deals with how a hypothesis is adopted on

probation, with reasons for suggesting a hypothesis in the first place. There are reasons for suggesting a hypothesis initially as a plausible type of hypothesis. The verification process makes known the approximation to reality of the suggested hypothesis. In turn, the hypothesis may render the observed facts necessary, or at least highly probable. (Malina 1991, 259–60; italics mine)

Working toward a hypothesis in a cable-like process (*abduction*) is complex because of the variety of fibers that are connected and that presuppose one another. Abduction differs from induction, which is an inference from a sample to a whole or from particulars to a general law. Induction classifies, while abduction explains.[3]

Scientific method, in this paradigm can "prove" nothing but tries to be "powerfully persuasive" (Lewis-Williams 1995, 3–4). It operates with the "best-fit" hypothesis, which accounts for all or most of the fibers that are interwoven, and is not based on a bedrock or foundation (such as an authentic kernel). In such a cable-like process, where interaction between many fibers make up the interpretive process, constant revision is a given, while certainty is not ascribed to a single link in a chain. Anthropological historiography is cable-like in that it does not depend on the prior identification of authentic material but consists of the testing and evaluation of several fibers in working toward the proposed hypothesis.

Within this understanding of interpretation, the question no longer is how to move from the literary documents (which are reporting about a specific social personage, and which are themselves the product of specific cultural processes) to the historical figure (which is ascribed with particular cultural events and phenomena presumably belonging to that social personage) but how to account for both the historical figure portrayed in the documents and the documents as cultural artifacts about a particular historical figure. That is, how to treat both the historical figure and the literary documents as cultural artifacts from a distant and alien cultural system. This question was already well formulated by Smith almost three decades ago:

What sort of man and what sort of career, in the society of first century Palestine, would have occasioned the beliefs, called into

---

3. Abduction "is an inference from a body of data to an explaining hypothesis, or from the effect to cause. . . . Abduction furnishes the reasoner with hypothesis while induction is the method of testing and verifying" (Malina 1991, 357 n. 27 quoting Fann). The *hypothesis and verification* method of the Schweitzerstrasse clearly belongs to the logic of induction.

being the communities, and given rise to the practices, stories, and sayings that then appeared, of which selected reports and collections have come down to us? (1978, 5–6)

Diagrammatically, it can be expressed in the following way:

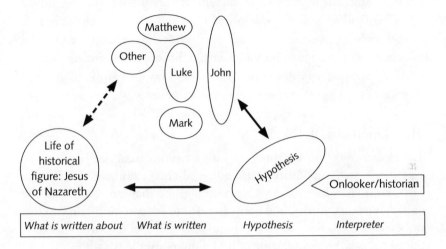

Diagram 3.1: The Cable-Like Structure of Cultural Bundubashing

This diagram captures a number of aspects regarding the interpretive structure of cultural bundubashing: (1) the texts and historical figure are configurations of each other (in being about a particular historical figure), while they were created in a historical continuum; (2) the hypothesis should account for both what is written (the documents) and what is written about (the historical figure)—expressed by the fact that hypothesis, historical figure, and documents are all represented as a similar type of geometrical figure (circle-like); and (3) the historian's lenses (hypothesis) highlights both the features of the text and the historical figure. It is via the particular hypothesis that the historical figure emerges from the evidence in the documents—evidence that itself is the product of the hypothesis.

Formulated in this way, the question presents a clear dilemma. It is necessary to know about Jesus's social type in order to understand the Gospel pictures about him, but that cannot be understood without a glimpse of his social type. Put the other way around, in order to know what the literary texts are talking about, it is necessary to have a grasp of the cultural plausibilities of the historical figure, while an understanding of the documents as reporting about a specific social personage is presupposed in reading them.

The interpretive process, therefore, is explicitly cable-like in that the same hypothesis should account both for what is written and for what is written about. The hypothesis provides the framework for working toward an understanding and explanation of what the historian encounters. It should, therefore, account for both the historical figure and the material evidence about the figure. It should explain the shape, content, and nature of the documentary evidence and also account for the nature, origin, and character of the historical figure reported in the texts.

The Hypothesis of This Study

The challenge is, can we come up with a hypothesis about Jesus's social type that is well established historically and cross-culturally; that fits the first-century Mediterranean Galilean setting; and that can account for the underlying traits, stories, and deeds ascribed to Jesus in his lifetime: traits, stories, and deeds that led to the origin of the Gospel texts and that continued to make sense in the life of his followers after his death?

The hypothesis of this study is that *Jesus of Nazareth can be seen as a Galilean shamanic figure*. This hypothesis should at least account for:

1. Jesus as a social personage described in the literary documents;

2. the events and phenomena in the documents ascribed to him as a historical and a cultural figure;

3. the cultural processes and dynamics associated with the life of such a historical figure; and

4. the origin and shape of the literary evidence as the product of such a life, as well as the cultural processes and dynamics set into motion by such a social personage.

As is, generally speaking, the case with ancient societies, there are serious difficulties in applying such a model to Jesus of Nazareth. It can hardly be overemphasized that the information about Jesus of Nazareth is extremely scarce, and none of his *biographers* were field anthropologists interested either in reporting the details of his experiences or in conveying the cultural information taken for granted by those sharing his cultural setting.[4]

Therefore, one should not expect complete ethnographic detail on the person or profile of Jesus.

It is nevertheless important to explore the potential of this approach for revealing the evidence that is available. The shamanic complex is the primary model to be employed in order to bring to the surface the categories and cultural logic in terms of which the process of abduction (to and fro movement between hypothesis, data, and construction of the historical figure) are to be conducted. It will provide the categories and concepts in terms of which sense is made of the data, and in terms of which a picture is painted of the historical figure in a particular cultural setting.

By way of summary, the interpretive process of abduction in cultural bundubashing can be illustrated in the following way:

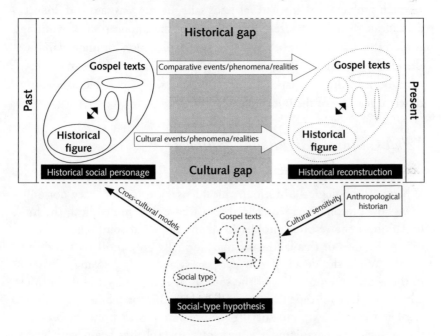

Diagram 3.2: Examining the Past via Cultural Bundubashing

There are both temporal and cultural gaps between the historian and the past.
What we are looking for and looking at are cultural artifacts from this foreign

4. Davies quite correctly remarks that we have perhaps 1 percent (more likely 0.001 percent) of the information available to us in the texts, [information] that an anthropologist has, who has done fieldwork in a particular culture (see 1995, 42).

*world, but the historical figure and the literary documents are seen as configura-
tions of each other (indicated by the similar geometrical [circle-like] figures in
the past). The gaps are to be covered by means of a hypothesis or cross-cultural
model that facilitates a cultural sensitivity and enables cross-cultural interpretation (indicated by the model in dotted lines at the bottom). What the historian
"brings back" is a picture of both cultural and comparative events, phenomena,
and realities associated with such a social personage. The historian's reconstruction here is again a dotted picture of both the social personage and the literary
documents, which are a configuration of the social personage mediated by the
hypothesis. Unlike the authenticity paradigm, this is no linear process of trying
to make sense today of what happened or what was said "there" but a roundabout way, by means of cross-cultural models and strategies of interpreting and
making sense "here" of cultural events and phenomena "there."*

The most important implication of this way of conceptualizing the
research problem is that whatever Jesus said and did was said and done as
a Galilean shamanic figure. This is precisely the implication of working
toward the shamanic hypothesis as the best explanation for understanding
the kind of social personage about whom such documents were created.
Already from these reshaped interpretive lenses, it is possible to identify
different features of the interpretive landscape.

What Cultural Bundubashing Allows
the Historical Jesus Researcher to See

When anthropological historiographical lenses are applied, they not only
show how preconceived lenses in the past have determined both the formulation of the research problem and the proposed solutions, but that
certain features of this landscape that normally go unnoticed stand out
clearly. While the detail of this perspective will only become apparent
in the actual interpretation of the sources, it is necessary to offer a brief
glimpse of the landscape that is revealed along this road. Since the culturally alien world, text, and social personage are absent from the view of
the authenticity paradigm, it is necessary to explicitly begin with what
cultural bundubashing allows the researcher to see regarding each of the
three components.

A Cultural Landscape with Cultural Artifacts

From the point of view of anthropological historiography, the Jesus scholar is, prior to reading any of the sources, confronted with the fact that these documents originated from and communicated in the preindustrial, agrarian, and preprint world of the first-century Mediterranean (see Rohrbaugh 1978; Botha 1992; Malina 2001a). This is not the place to discuss the content and internal dynamics of the first-century Mediterranean worldview (see below, Chapter 6). It is, however, necessary to become aware that cultural bundubashing takes us into a worldview landscape radically different from that of everyday life in a modern Western-oriented society. As Malina says:

> Jesus was socialized and enculturated in an eastern Mediterranean society uninfluenced by globalism, universalism, scientism, the modern city, the industrial revolution, the nation-state, the Enlightenment, international law, the Renaissance, Arab-European scholasticism, Justinian's Code, Constantine's Christendom, the talmudic Jewish religion, and the like. (2002b, 4)

Everything that is known about the context and worldview of Jesus of Nazareth shows that he lived in—and that the texts about him originated and communicated in—a world that is historically and culturally far removed from that of the modern Western reader.

There is the gap of the industrial revolution (with its differentiation of social institutions) and the divide of huge cultural differences that separate the modern from the ancient reader. They operated with specific notions about human beings and personalities (the "self" as consisting of a body-soul/spirit configuration). Their worldview (world) was populated with many beings other than humans, who influenced human life. Religion was embedded in politics and family life, and divine power was believed to be mediated by a variety of means: temples, human beings, and various objects. The separation between human and divine spheres was very flimsy. And they arguably lived in a worldview where experiences such as dreams and visions contributed significantly to knowledge about life and the world (to be described below as a "polyphasic" worldview).

None, if any, of these features is explicitly described or explained in the sources—they are taken for granted because they represent an accepted cultural script. They are part of the absolute presuppositions of the first-century world by means of which Jesus of Nazareth was constituted as a historical figure, and through which the documents originated as reports about such a figure.

Based on the earlier discussion about the reality and plausibility of cultural events and phenomena (see above, pp. 25–32), especially those events and phenomena connected to the lives of particular social personages, two important implications can already be noted.

CULTURAL EVENTS IN THE LIFE OF JESUS COULD HAVE BEEN REAL HISTORICAL (CULTURAL) EVENTS WITHOUT BEING "OUT THERE"

Of the events reported in the Gospels and ascribed to the life of Jesus, a very large part consists of *cultural events* that were experienced and that belonged to the first-century Mediterranean's specific cultural system. These events, therefore, could have been intersubjectively (*objectively*) there without being ontologically objective—they could not have been photographed or analyzed by physical or chemical analyses.[5] Treating reports about such events and phenomena as if they were commonly human is related to the so-called *fallacy of misplaced concreteness*—the tendency to mistake an abstraction for a concrete thing (see Peacock 1986, 20). An example pertinent to this study is ASC experiences, which are common to polyphasic cultures (to be discussed in detail below).

Both everyday and extraordinary events are experienced in ASCs, but this does not mean that they are necessarily everyday events (or extraordinary events) "out there." Even though such experiences include bodily events or human activities (such as hearing a voice or seeing an object or experiencing a sensation), this does not mean they are "out there." Therefore, even if a video recording of an exorcism or of the visitation by an ancestor or demon is made, most of the "reality" will not be seen. This can be illustrated with a remark by a Native American after a shamanic medicine ceremony: "The Whites don't catch anything when they take photographs, and therefore it is meaningless to photograph" (Hultkrantz 1967, 43). The fact that many such events cannot be photographed does not mean they are not real for the participants.

---

5. The dynamics of the *cycle of meaning* by means of which people construct such cultural realities will be discussed later (see Chapter 6 below).

WHAT "GOES BACK TO JESUS" IS NOT THE SAME
AS SAYING "IT ACTUALLY HAPPENED"

This paradigm also reveals that in historical Jesus research the direct link is mistaken between claims about "what goes back to Jesus" (apparent early dating) and claims about "what actually happened" (or what can be taken as historical). Not only is this connection based on a vicious circle, but determining what actually happened is much more complex than is assumed in the authenticity paradigm and registered in its reality catalog. In this view, *what actually happened* is a much more complex issue than either identifying authentic historical nuggets or declaring most of the material as literary creations.

There is a vicious circle in the layered model of Jesus traditions between dating the material and claiming such material as historical or authentic. The sound historical principle of early material turns, in historical Jesus research, into the fallacy of historical closeness: if it can be shown to go back to Jesus, it is taken as actual events or as historical.[6] It also works the other way around: what cannot be historical (what is not possible) cannot be early, and therefore the Gospels are dated fairly late.

From the point of view of cultural bundubashing, the reports about the deeds of Jesus are forced by the authenticity discourses into categories where they just do not fit. The basic pattern on both roads is that of normal events that can be seen, plus either supernatural elements or mythical literary creations. Historicity refers to the pure and actual core event behind the story (except in the case of the Schweitzerstrasse, it is claimed that supernatural events are indeed "natural" and historical—though extraordinary and unique—but visible and photographable). In both instances, the fallacy of misplaced concreteness can be seen at work. On both the Wredebahn and the Schweitzerstrasse, historicity or "what actually happened" is taken as what can be shown "to go back to Jesus" (to "Stage 1" or to "the original layer").

This is a vicious argument because the identification of early material does not depend on external evidence but is primarily based on the assumed development of ideas. Based on philosophical presuppositions or

---

6. Those on the Schweitzerstrasse take supernatural events together with natural events as observable events. Taken together with the assumed reliability of the synoptic tradition, these observable events are taken as belonging to the first stratum, or as going back to Jesus. In the case of the Wredebahn, all the elements that could not have been real do not belong to the small historical kernel and are ascribed to mythology or are regarded simply as stories created sometime in the tradition.

simply the reality catalogue of Western culture, it is already presupposed what could not have belonged to the life of a historical figure. Thus, common wisdom in critical Jesus research is that *how things were in Jesus's life* did not include a special virgin birth or a transfiguration experience or walking on the sea and the like (except for those who import the supernatural category). However, as shown above, determining the plausibility of an event or phenomenon is much more complex than simply determining its time of origin.

Plausibility does not depend on the number or age of the documents attesting to an event or phenomenon. How many independent accounts are needed, for example, to affirm the plausibility of an *extraordinary* cultural story, such as that the first shamans were not born but came to earth on a golden disk, or that Mary became pregnant without the intervention of a man?

Therefore, from the point of view of cultural bundubashing, events or phenomena can go back to the life of Jesus in Galilee as cultural events and phenomena without committing the fallacy of misplaced concreteness by claiming that they actually happened in time and space as described. How things were can include both the belief in and the experience of such things as a virgin birth or transfiguration. Things can go back to the life of Jesus without our having to accept that they actually happened exactly as described, Davies reminds us (see 1995, 16–17).

It is necessary to emphasize one conclusion from this. Even if Q and *Thomas* (or the Common Sayings tradition) or any other document were to be dated to the thirties of the Common Era, that does not make them, by definition, historically accurate or historically reliable regarding who Jesus was and what he actually did.[7] Within this framework, it is not chronological distance but, first and foremost, the cultural gap that separates Jesus as historical figure from modern understandings of him. Therefore, the crux of the historical problem is not the parallel texts but the historical and

---

7. Crossan admits as much: if there is a tight linkage between the context and the earliest layer of text, "that is the best reconstruction of the historical Jesus and his companions presently available" (1998, 149). The two pillars of the historical-critical approach are clearly visible here: the earliest gospel traditions transmitted in stratified layers have been uncovered over the last two hundred years of research. In undermining the assumption of the distinction between the historical figure and the mythical Christ, and rejecting the idea of authentic snippets of Jesus material, the argument presented in this study is that if a tight linkage can be found between a known social type and the gospel presentations, that is also the best historical construction available.

cultural gap. Even if a copy of one of the existing Gospels dated to the year 35 CE were today to be discovered, we would face the same interpretive problem: how to understand the events, phenomena, and features ascribed to Jesus of Nazareth. His virgin birth, Davidic ancestry, and visionary appearances would not suddenly become more real or historically true. They remain cultural phenomena embedded in cultural documents. Even if all the available documents can be dated as early as, say, five years after the life of Jesus, it still would not guarantee that anything happened as described because they are cultural material about a cultural personage from a distant cultural system.

Therefore, attempts to push back the dating of the written material also suffer from the *fallacy of chronological closeness* in suggesting that the written documents are actually to be dated much earlier than the generally accepted suggestions.[8] The fallacy is to assume that *early* material that can be connected to Jesus is historical or authentic, or that it conveys "what actually happened." Conversely, what can be shown to have originated in a later phase is taken as not historical.

From the perspective of cultural bundubashing, however, the position is that the historical figure is not to be found underneath the overlay of the literary texts but in them. Therefore, all *adequate* sources should be analyzed for what they are evidence for. If a historical figure could have been like the portrayals in the canonical texts, and the latter were not merely literary creations, all the documents that can, with some measure of certainty, be attributed to the beginning phase of the Jesus movement can be seen as residues of Jesus as a social personage.[9]

Jesus of Nazareth as a Cultural Figure

When anthropological historiographical lenses are applied, it becomes apparent that Jesus of Nazareth was a historical figure within a particular cultural system, and that parallels with similar figures are abundant. Cultural

8. Ellis, for example, argues for a considerable degree of probability for some written transmission of Gospel traditions from the time of Jesus's earthly ministry (see 1999, 32–33). See also Bauckham 2006.

9. The inventory of textual remains containing the canonical Gospels, other gospels (such as the *Gospel of Thomas*), gospel fragments, and infancy gospels, together with other sources, is impressive compared to any other ancient figure. Besides the discussions of the data in most of the standard historical Jesus publications (see, e.g., Meier 1994, 41–166; Theissen & Merz 1998, 17–89; Dunn 2003b, 139–70), these texts are available in translated collections (see, e.g., Schneemelcher & Wilson 1991; Miller 1992).

bundubashing, therefore, does not share the assumption in Jesus research that a historical figure could not have been like the portrayal of Jesus in the sources. The similarity between the Gospel portrayals of Jesus of Nazareth and social figures (such as shamans) in many traditional societies and well known from anthropological literature warrants the hypothesis that a historical figure in first-century Galilee could have been like this. In other words, cultural bundubashing does not necessarily accept that large parts of the tradition were retrospectively rewritten from a post-Easter perspective. This might have been the case, but it can no longer be assumed *a priori*. Such a distinction is much more a function of an interpretive paradigm than of the evidence. In fact, if many of the elements ascribed to Jesus can belong to the life of a historical figure, they need not be ascribed to post-Easter literary activities or the like.

Furthermore, all the canonical Gospels consist of composite pictures of Jesus as teacher, healer, prophet, sage, visionary, and the like. It seems clear that at least for them, it made sense to describe a historical figure who in a natural and normal way combined these features and functions. They never find it necessary to explain to their readers that there is a difference between the actual historical figure and the kind of character that they were describing as a human being roaming the pathways of Galilee.

Contra the Wredebahn, cultural bundubashing, therefore, does not *a priori* accept that the historical figure is somewhere *underneath* the layers of mythical or literary overlay; the historical figure is *in* the literary documents. Contra the Schweitzerstrasse, cultural bundubashing does not recognize the documents as reports about supernatural events and phenomena but as cultural artifacts about a social personage who could have been real and historical (culturally speaking).

Furthermore, from looking at the Gospels themselves, it is clear that a large amount of the material ascribed to Jesus of Nazareth belongs to the category of *cultural events and phenomena* or to the category of common human events and phenomena described by means of cultural jargon. The Gospel authors have no problem in ascribing a variety of stories, events, and deeds to Jesus as human being, which would strike modern Western readers as extraordinary. Apparently it was quite acceptable to the first readers to learn that a *real person* (historical figure) could do the things ascribed to Jesus (and, for that matter, ascribed in that world to several other persons), such as controlling the elements and the spirits, healing the sick, appearing in visions or dreams, and receiving visitations from ancestors. For both the authors and their readers, it was imaginable, and they could entertain the notion that a first-century figure in Galilee could act in the way Jesus did in the stories and have the attributes ascribed to him. The parallels with social types in other traditional societies (known from anthropological literature) are just too great to ignore.

In accordance with the exposition of the reality of cultural events and phenomena discussed in the first chapter, a rough but useful description of cultural figures can be presented by means of the components constituting such figures as social personages.

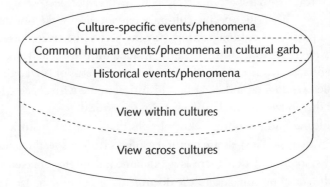

Diagram 3.3: Components Constituting a Social Personage

The life and reality of a social personage such as Jesus of Nazareth can be described as consisting of a particular configuration of at least three types of events and phenomena: (1) culture-specific events and phenomena, (2) common human events and phenomena clothed in cultural garb, and (3) historical events and phenomena from that world and worldview. In all instances, what is seen about such a social personage as culturally unique and particular (viewed within) can also be viewed comparatively and cross-culturally (viewed across cultures).

This spectrum represents a rough but useful framework for dealing with the reality of various kinds of events and phenomena ascribed to Jesus as a historical figure. There is a considerable overlap between the distinctions in this diagram because none is a watertight category. Furthermore, together they make up the biographical data of a human life, which does not fall into clean categories. Especially in the life of significant social personages there are many cultural realities that constitute such a life. The important point, however, is that the reality of these different kinds of events and phenomena cannot all be determined with exactly the same sort of methods and argumentation. Consequently, each category demands different criteria and procedures for establishing plausibility. As the diagram indicates, cultural events and phenomena can be viewed from different perspectives: as culturally internal and as cross-cultural events and phenomena.

The Gospels as Cultural Artifacts

Another feature that becomes visible from this perspective is that the Gospels, which ascribe specific cultural events to a specific kind of figure within a particular cultural setting, can themselves be treated as cultural artifacts referring to a cultural reality. In fact, all the ancient documents that originated because of the life and activities of Jesus of Nazareth belong to an alien worldview and describe a historical figure with specific features and are themselves cultural artifacts from that world.

Cultural bundubashing acknowledges that Jesus is a historical figure as well as that the Gospels are cultural artifacts from a specific (and alien) cultural system, and that there is a fundamental interconnectedness between the social personage and the documents as cultural artifacts reporting about him. This assumption does not tell us what kind of social figure Jesus was, only that there is a connection between the social personage and the literary documents that originated within a particular cultural system and because of his activities. This starting point suggests that Jesus's social personage and the Gospel texts are not independent entities but *configurations of each other* embedded in the same cultural system.[10] Therefore, Jesus is knowable as a cultural phenomenon (social type) embedded in certain cultural processes of a specific cultural system, while the gospel texts are reports about that cultural figure, but themselves are the products of certain cultural processes, some of which were closely related to the social personage they describe.

In a sense, it goes without saying that if the literary documents are not taken as organically connected to the historical figure, they cannot be used as evidence about that figure. In other words, if they were merely

---

10. The phrase "configurations of each other" I owe to Pieter Botha, who uses it to explain that, in a culturally sensitive reading, it is inevitable to see text and context as configurations of each other; they are constituted from the same elements and display the same nature (2000, 2).

literary creations about the ideologies, theologies, or aspirations of a later generation, they are useless as sources about the historical figure they refer to. This study explicitly wants to explore the possibility that they were configurations of each other and connected via the cultural processes that constituted the social personage, the oral traditions and the literary texts. This means that what we are looking at is fundamentally determined by what we are looking for. The shape, nature, and content of the texts are constitutionally linked to the kind of social personage that Jesus was as a historical figure. The historical figure is not at the beginning and the texts at the end of a developmental process. Even though the literary texts originated later in time, they are configurations of each other within the same cultural area. Therefore, before the question can be addressed regarding how to move from the former to the latter, it is necessary to explore the cultural processes and dynamics of both what we are looking at and what we are looking for.

From this perspective, the Gospels are seen as rather different either from reports about actual supernatural events or from literary or mythological fiction. From this perspective, they are the residue of cultural processes that are connected to the dynamics of the cultural figure they report about. What is seen by means of the lenses of cultural bundubashing is that the Gospels not only contain cultural stories about events, they contain cultural stories about cultural events about a specific social personage within a particular cultural system. The texts themselves are not merely neutral reports but cultural artifacts that need to be analyzed in terms of the dynamics and processes that link them to the social personage they report about. These arguments will be explored in the following chapter.

In this view, it is not necessarily chronological distance but cultural processes and realities (which probably started during the life of Jesus as social personage) that are to be blamed for the very nature of the stories the Gospels contain and for the differences between them. All the literary texts about Jesus of Nazareth are compromised by being cultural reports subjected to such cultural processes and dynamics, and not necessarily because they are chronologically removed from his life. Even if the Gospels were all written very soon after the events or soon after the death of Jesus, from this point of view the first and foremost problem is determining what they were about to begin with, or what their cultural reality value is.

Treating the literary documents as cultural artifacts and as evidence about the life of a particular social personage (asking what they are evidence for) has far-reaching implications for all aspects of scholarly beliefs about them. One is the question of which documents are to be used for working toward the hypothesis, and the other is about the date of the available documents. In short, which documents are to be taken as adequate for working toward the shamanic hypothesis.

As I have said several times, the database on the Schweitzerstrasse is primarily the Synoptic Gospels (cleansed from post-Easter overlay), and for the Wredebahn, the earliest kernels of Jesus sayings identified by means of multiple, independent, early attestation. In one way or another, the date of composition and the tradition history of the content are determinative in establishing the status of the database. With cultural bundubashing, it is not different—only that totally different considerations will play a role in establishing the database.

In cultural bundubashing, the historian is bound, like any other historian, to the first basic question about historical sources, namely, whether there is adequate evidence for the case (see Stanford 1986, 63–65); or as Iggers says, bound "to go to the archives" (1997, 16). That includes research about the age and manuscript history of documents: are they adequate sources for the case under consideration?[11] It is impossible to deal with these issues here in detail, but it is necessary to point out the implications of this discussion for the status of the database.

At present, the dating of the Gospels depends on a picture of what could have belonged to the historical figure, and on what was added as fictional or mythical material. It should be obvious that within the view of cultural bundubashing, the dating of all the Gospels could be reconsidered—that is, if it is accepted that what is normally taken as later elaborations and embellishments could have been part of Jesus's life (part of his constitution as historical figure) in Galilee or of the earliest oral traditions. Since the current dating of the canonical Gospels is so closely connected to the traditional pictures of Jesus that have been challenged, the best solution would be to accept as valid sources all those that can, with some certainty of manuscript history, topically be connected to the life of Jesus as a social personage. Until proven otherwise, all documents from antiquity claiming to be about Jesus of Nazareth should be reconsidered as

---

11. For the literary remains attributed to Jesus, this type of research is well known (see, e.g., Koester 1990). Since the development of ideas remains an important beacon in determining the origin and historical development of the documents, it should be kept in mind that existing studies reflect the picture of the authenticity paradigm.

some form of residue of his life as social personage. Creating fictional texts could have been part of this process, but then not because the content is judged to be mythological or historically *impossible*.[12]

Although the point will not be pursued here, this also applies to all other sources, such as the infancy gospels. As I have pointed out, in the authenticity paradigm the scholarly verdict about the infancy gospels is similar across the two roads: they are products of the literary creativity of early Christians. However, within cultural bundubashing, the *Infancy Gospel of Thomas*, for example, need no longer be seen as a collection of stories about a series of miraculous deeds by a young boy, Jesus, but as a cultural artifact that originated within the above interpretive processes. Thus, as an *adequate* historical source (based on the manuscript and other evidence) it could be seen as a cultural artifact that originated in the cultural dynamics of events, transmission, and enscripturation about a specific social figure.

The report in Luke (2:41–52), as well as other parallels to be discussed later (see below, pp. 377–80), suggests that the cultural event behind this account in the *Infancy Gospel of Thomas* could have been the creation and retelling of stories about the boyhood of a specific social personage during his lifetime. In fact, it can be understood within the dynamics of Jesus's life in Galilee that such boyhood accounts were ascribed to him because of his position as a social figure in that community. Seen in this way, these are not reports about Jesus's boyhood but boyhood accounts throwing light on a social personage in manhood.

Nevertheless, in this study mainly the canonical material will be used to work from and toward the hypothesis that, as historical and cultural figure, Jesus can be described as a Galilean shamanic figure. This is not a defense for the authenticity of the Synoptic Gospels but a practical choice—an interpretation must start somewhere.

---

12. It is worthwhile listening to the warning of J. A. T. Robinson: "I did not appreciate before beginning the investigation, how *little* evidence there is for the dating of *any* of the New Testament writings" (1976, 336). Because of the small amount of external evidence, it is well known that the current dating of the Gospels heavily depends on the constructed tradition history. For example, the destruction of the temple is not even sufficient to securely date the Gospel of Mark. After evaluating the arguments, pro and con, Kümmel concludes: "Since no overwhelming argument for the years before or after 70 can be adduced, we must content ourselves with saying that Mark was written *ca.* 70" (1975, 98).

Cultural Bundubashing and Historicity in Jesus Research

In cultural bundubashing, the notion of *historicity* itself has been rede-fined from a concern with factuality only (because of the testimony of more than one independent witness) to one concerned with the meaning of things and the interpretation of detail within a concrete setting. The historicity of strange and alien cultural phenomena confuses the criteria of positivistic historiography because, as Lorenz says: "When we talk about facts and reality, we therefore always refer to reality *within a specific frame of description*" (1998b, 355; italics his). Historicity is not something in itself, and even ten independent accounts of an event do not guarantee historicity or factuality (in the sense of whether something actually hap-pened when and as described) because multiple accounts of cultural events or phenomena are just that—multiple cultural accounts of cultural events or phenomena.

In a previous section, the notion of cultural plausibility has been nar-rowed down to the plausibility associated with a specific social type or hypothesis. That is, to affirm that historicity is not something abstract but concrete within a particular cultural system and related to concrete circumstances; in this case, historicity is related to a specific social per-sonage. The question is not simply whether specific reported events and phenomena (like those ascribed to Jesus of Nazareth in the documents) are historical in the abstract (because of multiple independent attestation), but whether they plausibly belong to the biography of a specific historical character—thus, whether they are historical as components of a particular type of life.

In this study, the shamanic hypothesis provides the main frame of description and the context for offering explanations of how things hung together in the life of Jesus of Nazareth. Historicity will be measured in terms of adherence to a particular social-type model: whether cultural events and phenomena ascribed to his life are considered historical will depend on this social-type model and framework. What is to be taken as historical or be labeled historicity depends on cultural plausibility in terms of this hypothesis.

In addition, it was earlier argued that the question of historicity in a cross-cultural setting normally results in at least two distinct answers; in a worldview of ontological pluralism, it requires cross-cultural interpreta-tion and comparison. In an interpretive process of abduction, historicity is caught in the interplay among the proposed hypothesis (frame of description), the cross-cultural gap, and the alien data; and different answers and descriptions can be ascribed to the same events or phenomena.

Therefore, the search for cultural plausibility and contextual particularity are neither criteria of authenticity nor a new set of criteria for historicity but tools for constructing historical and culturally sensitive interpretations of detail and explanations of how things were. That is, the meaning and interpretation of both the historical figure and the documentary data. The implication is that in such a cross-cultural setting there is a to-and-fro movement not only between individual episodes and the overall hypothesis but also between cultural plausibility and historicity.

Two reservations need nevertheless be registered.

Even a Perfect Fit with a Social-Type Model
Is No Guarantee of Historicity

There is no "final proof," even if the shamanic (or any other social-type) model can account for the content and nature of the stories ascribed to Jesus in the Gospels and for the social personage that is presented, that as historical figure he was indeed like that. Even with a perfect fit, it is possible that the historical figure could have been different from the Gospels' presentations. However, if there is a proper fit, it is also plausible that as a historical figure, Jesus of Nazareth was indeed such a social figure. In other words, if it can be shown that a specific model (in this case the shamanic model) can account for most of the content, features, presentation, and shape of the Gospels, then it is reasonable to assume that Jesus as a historical figure fits into that pattern. This is based on the following considerations.

Either the Gospel authors accidentally created it, or they were familiar with such a pattern. The alternatives are either to assume they had no knowledge of it and accidentally created it in describing Jesus as historical figure by means of such a coherent social-type model, or they operated with a model of a social type that was familiar to their world. The former means that they have described a configuration that would not have made sense in their world.[13]

13. In his perceptive way, Smith makes this point: "the fundamental antithesis, that between 'the Christ of faith' as a mythological figure and 'the Jesus of history' as a preacher free of mythological presuppositions, is anachronistic. Where in ancient Palestine would one find a man whose understanding of the world and of himself was *not* mythological?" (1978, 4). The pattern that he describes as mythological has been identified in this study as a culturally plausible pattern associated with shamanic figures. Would it make sense to

If they were familiar with it, either Jesus was such a cultural figure, or they thought it was plausible to depict their hero in terms of such a composite picture. Either Jesus was indeed such a figure (social type) while living in Galilee, or they merely utilized such a social type for describing his life. It is suggested both that they were familiar with a social type similar to this religious pattern and that Jesus as historical figure likely fitted into that pattern.

If such a social personage was a cultural plausibility, it obviously applies for both options as a historical figure or as a literary creation. It would be difficult, if not impossible, to distinguish between reports about a shamanic figure and made-up stories in the same cultural setting about such a figure. This challenge has to be admitted: it is difficult to distinguish such creations and additions to a reported tradition (say, about a shamanic figure) because, if Jesus was a Galilean shamanic figure, the additions and creations would presumably have been about him as precisely such a figure.

The Historical Figure Could Have Been Different from the Textual Presentations

Given the particular nature of the Gospel evidence—everything originated in the existing format in a subsequent historical period—the connection between the portrayal in the data and the historical figure is more precarious than in many other historical instances. It has to be admitted that all the available material can indeed be fictitious! In fact, given the nature of the data, it would be almost impossible to distinguish a report about an actual shamanic healing from a fictitious account of a healing by a Galilean shamanic figure. The Gospel authors, as embedded in their cultural system and communities, were probably perfectly capable of creating everything that they have written. In other words, it is possible that either in the oral transmission or during the enscripturation phase, most of the stories and descriptions could have been made up and are therefore unrelated to any historical figure (see below, pp. 118–20, for a description of the process of enscripturation.)

But, by the same token, it is equally possible that constructions on the Schweitzerstrasse, based on the *authenticity* of the Synoptic Gospels, could be mistaken—they could simply be fictitious and so also could be the ±20 percent *authentic* or *original* material identified by the Wredebahn.

describe someone by means of a social type that does not ft into their cultural system?

As indicated earlier, even in current historical Jesus research, the final judgment for authenticity rests with a fit between identified material and a constructed historical setting (see above, pp. 59–61). But, as has been pointed out, it is assumed that such a fit points toward authenticity; there is no guarantee that the corpus of material used (the Synoptics or the sayings gospel) is not fictitious. It is possible that the historical figure was totally different from any of these images (that of the Wredebahn, the Schweitzerstrasse, or cultural bundubashing).

But, if the documents can, via the proposed hypothesis, be connected to the life of a social personage, they need not be seen as fictitious or as literary creations. In fact, if the hypothesis facilitates understanding of meaning and the interpretation of detail, it can be taken as valuable and historically plausible.

This is the case not only for the canonical texts but also the extracanonical texts (which can be connected to the historical era) such as the infancy gospels. When seen as cultural artifacts produced within certain cultural processes, they can be taken as related to the life of a specific kind of social personage. This means that they not only contain material about a social personage, but that they are material evidence of the cultural processes associated with such a figure as well as of the processes by means of which they themselves were created. In general terms, it means that the documents are the product of cultural processes related to a specific social personage and not merely the product of (cultural) literary creations.

Concluding Remarks

Unlike the position that maintains that most of the material referring to Jesus of Nazareth is actually fictitious (for some, everything except a few sections from the Synoptics and *Thomas*, and for others everything except the Synoptic Gospels once stripped from theological overlay), cultural bundubashing assumes that the sources can be trusted that they are about a specific historical figure and offer cultural information of a historical nature about that figure. They are seen as the residue of a public life and cultural processes.

Two conclusions from this discussion need to be highlighted. One, if the Galilean shamanic model can account for both the historical figure and the content and nature of the sources, it is reasonable to assume that Jesus of Nazareth was indeed such a figure. Two, if the nature, shape, and contents of the documents can be accounted for by the proposed shamanic hypothesis, they need not be seen as fictitious or later mythical or literary creations. They can then be viewed as cultural reports or literary residues about the cultural processes related to a Galilean shamanic figure.

As indicated above, anthropological historiography belongs to the category of interpretive theories of science: it strives to be powerfully persuasive by accounting for both the individual elements and the overall design, for both the historical figure and the literary documents. Therefore, it is necessary to pay attention to some of the cultural processes and the dynamics associated with the life of such social personages as suggested by the shamanic hypothesis. Those are the processes regarding the life of such a figure as well as those associated with the transmission of stories and reports about such a figure in traditional societies.

CHAPTER 4

In the Beginning Was a Social Personage and Cultural Artifacts

Introduction

BEFORE ANALYZING THE DATA by means of the proposed hypothesis, it is necessary to elaborate on the scenery offered by cultural bundubashing. In the previous chapter an effort was made to show what the landscape of historical Jesus research looks like when viewed with a culture-sensitive lens. However, in a historiographical paradigm that emphasizes that things are culturally embedded, it is not only the strange and the alien that need to be accounted for but also the cultural processes and dynamics that created particular literary texts and specific cultural figures. Knowing what is culturally plausible contains valuable but limited currency in the search for the meaning of things and the interpretation of detail. It is also necessary to engage in the contextual particulars with regard to the historical figure as well as the documentary sources.

The first question, therefore, is what does it mean to say that as a historical figure, Jesus of Nazareth probably belonged to a particular type of social personage? Second, the claim that the literary documents are cultural artifacts containing reports or residues about a particular social personage does not display the whole truth. What is implied by the claim that the documentary sources are configurations of a particular social personage? How things were in this case include a notion of how they came about. Cultural bundubashing, therefore, is also concerned with the cultural processes and dynamics implicated in the origin and creation of both the social personage and the cultural artifacts. This will be done by analyzing three intertwined phases: (1) The processes of constituting a social personage; (2) activities of communicating about a social personage; and (3) what will be called the processes of *enscripturation*—that is the processes involved in the origin of the written documents as seen from the perspective of cultural bundubashing.

Cultural Processes Constituting a Social Personage

Compared to cross-cultural instances (to be considered later), and in view of the above discussion, it follows that if Jesus of Nazareth was a historical figure, the events and phenomena ascribed to him in the documents could have belonged to his life—thus could in a (cultural) sense have been real historical events and phenomena associated with this social personage.

When moving away from a history-of-ideas approach toward one of cultural realities, it is necessary to take account of the nature of such cultural events and phenomena as well as the kind of cultural processes and dynamics that are implied in the creation and expression of such a social personage. That is, to bring to the surface for outsiders what insiders take for granted (a thick description).

If the answers to Jesus's question, "Who do people say that I am?" is anything to go on, people very early on applied different models to represent him: Elijah, John the Baptist, Jeremiah, or someone else (see Mark 8:27–28 par.). The historical figure from the beginning was a culturally constructed and interpreted figure, and a number of processes are to be imagined here. This requires a thick description of the cultural events and phenomena ascribed to him as social personage, as well as the cultural processes that most probably played a role in that constitution. Besides the detail of his life as a historical figure, which will be considered later, at least the following features characterize the reality and constitution of a social personage.

Shared Experiences and the Sharing of Experiences as Cultural Events

From the point of view of cultural bundubashing, many of the events ascribed to Jesus in his lifetime (baptism, healings, exorcisms, transfiguration, ascension, resurrection) are clearly not objective events "out there" but cultural events and phenomena. Therefore, it is necessary to analyze them for their nature as plausible cultural events.

CONSTITUTING COMPLEX CULTURAL EVENTS AND PHENOMENA

In describing the dynamics of a shamanic ritual, Atkinson suggests:

> If one envisions a triangle composed of shaman, patient, and audience, it follows that the relationship of any two elements is dependent on the relationship of each element to the third. The ritual in question serves both as an occasion for healing and as an arena for shamans to establish themselves as influential 'men of prowess' or 'wielders of spiritual potency' for their local communities. (1987, 342)

Shamanic figures, for example, are social personages involved in cultural events and processes that go far beyond their individual activities or impact and that often have societal effects that are linked to the social type. Think about the shamanic function of guiding the hunt or fishing activities, which often involve the whole community. But whatever they do is inscribed in the cultural dynamics of their society. ASCs most often are part of a "public ceremonial occasion," and the experience at times is "more significant for the group that observes it than for the individual who experiences it" (Bourguignon 1972, 332–33).

This description gives a clue of how to view the cultural events ascribed to Jesus of Nazareth. They should be viewed as communal events and phenomena embedded in the dynamics of a particular cultural setting. Take the baptism stories as an example. An eyewitness (or video recording) probably would have noticed the people in the Jordan River, would have heard John the Baptist speak, and possibly would have seen some people in trance conditions. However, the event included at least some ASC experiences of Jesus himself, of John, and possibly of some bystanders: according to the sources, the cultural event included at least Jesus' experience of a vision, and probably John the Baptist's too, but also the reporting or retelling about the event. As a cultural event, it was a complex and multifaceted event with more than one participant right from the very beginning (an analysis of this episode will follow below).

What this implies is that as an event described in the Gospels, Jesus' baptism (and by implication other episodes such as exorcisms, initiation rites, journey experiences, or group trances) was co-created by the participants and the community. The nature of such events is dependent on culturally constituted conditions, parts of which are participant experiences of ASCs. As events they are, therefore, dependent on the shared experiences of participants but also on retelling of such experiences (which for the bystanders would constitute recognized and real cultural events). Thus, there are not only multiple retellings but multioriginality in the very constitution of the events. Two implications should thus be highlighted.

One, different eyewitnesses did not observe objective events (events in time and space) that could have been photographed or videotaped, but they were part of the creation of cultural events within a specific cultural system. Therefore, since cultural experiences and sharing of the experiences were part of the events from the very beginning, there could not have been *independent* witnesses reporting about objective or "photographable" events.

Two, the nature of many cultural events is such that there never is only one version of "what happened" because such events are complex cultural phenomena that depend on the shared experiences of the participants and the sharing of the experiences—that is, on community involvement from the beginning. Reports about such events are, therefore, subject to the cultural dynamics of experiencing and sharing about the events. The content has been established within the process of creation, and this includes the creation of the first witnesses.

If many of the events described in the Gospels were co-created by the participants, it should also be considered that such events were only fully constituted in the first sharing of the experiences. The total event became a public happening (whether visionary experiences during the baptism, or the exorcism of demons in an exorcistic episode, or the healing of a patient during a public gathering) in the actions, experiences, and sharing of the experiences. The event as a real event is only fully constituted and knowable in its collective experiencing, telling, and retelling, and historical reflection should account for all of these.

Consequently, as events they are constituted both by the multi-experiences and the communal telling about them. It would be fair to say that such events are created in the processes and dynamics of the event, which include the experiencing and reporting of the experiences. Whatever so-called *eyewitnesses* could remember never was a small historical kernel but a co-created or communal cultural event[1]—keeping in mind that it was always about Jesus as a particular kind of social personage.

1. This is contrary to the received view, which is in constant search for the core or authentic event. Even someone as progressive in his thinking about the tradition as Dunn continues to think about the core and stability of particular traditions.

Reporting About Complex Cultural Events And Phenomena

Oral or written reports about such events will therefore almost always be linear and one-dimensional reports about complex cultural phenomena or processes that often include several actors.[2]

From the *eyewitnesses* there will always be more than one version of such an event. What is seen, heard, and experienced by one participant might be totally different from the experience of other participants. In the case of cultural events and phenomena, the search for either *the* "authentic" or the "first" or "original" version in the life of Jesus is, therefore, in most cases by definition impossible. There never was a single story (at least not where more than one person was involved in the event), and reports even by bystanders were not necessarily about "objective events"—although they are about real culturally experienced events.

They represent, in other words, not only one image but the reports of several people's combined images in a story or report. To be clear about this point, a verbal or written report about an exorcism is a linear, one-dimensional version of visible events, auditory words, and the visions, images, and auditory reports of various participants. The reports should be respected for their cultural singularity and uniqueness, and this includes their experiential, their narrative, and their social nature as cultural events and phenomena.

But as already indicated, the Gospels contain reports and portrayals that are very similar to portrayals of social figures in many traditional societies. Thus, the eventual narrative—such as the "event" about Jesus's baptism—was created out of visible actions, multiple experiences, and the first telling of the experiences. It had an ontological independence in that the reported "event" was literally created out of the multiple experiences of various people and the retelling in narrative format of the verbal reports of the participants. Fluidity is guaranteed in the co-creation of observable actions and experienced realities that were combined in a narrative format that were transmitted by various ways—in oral and possibly even in written form.

From the point of view of cultural bundubashing, these are the kind of data about Jesus as historical and cultural figure that need to be factored into a historical interpretation. Knowing how things were requires grasp-

---

2. Compare anthropological reports about shamanic rituals or exorcisms in traditional societies today (e.g., Hultkrantz 1967, 37–43).

ing these cultural processes. Reflection about the sources will have to take into account the nature and reality of the cultural events described by them and ascribed to the historical figure. This will have to be part of the interpretation throughout and is not something that can be established at the beginning. Verbal reports are linear representation of complex multi-faceted cultural experiences. Establishing the historicity of such events and phenomena is a complex issue, but the intent here is merely to broaden the scope of vision of what should be considered biographical components of a social personage's life. But there is more to these dynamics. Both the cultural events associated with the social personage and the life of the particular social personage set into motion a whole set of further cultural processes.

Legitimation and Affirmation of Identity as Cultural Realities

It is virtually impossible to think about a social personage (such as a sha-manic figure) without taking into account the way in which such figures are partially constituted by means of communal involvement. Becoming a social personage in a traditional society is not based on the appointment by a committee or on the acquisition of a qualification (diploma or degree), but on the result of a set of cultural processes such as a personal call, com-munity recognition and sanction, and appropriate rituals of initiation. It is not based on official diplomas of performance or qualifications but needs "certificates" of approval and legitimation in order to function.[3] To quote Atkinson again: "Performers who seek reputations as shamans are faced with a vexing conundrum: successful shamans are individuals on whose spiritual powers others depend; yet performers are in fact dependent upon audiences to acknowledge their shamanic claims" (1987, 342). The removal or replacement of such figures, therefore, often follows the withdrawal of communal support, while disapproval takes the form of witchcraft accusa-tions or labeling of some sort, effective in that community.

What this means is that without community recognition and le-gitimation, such a social personage does not have a social existence and cannot operate effectively. Community recognition includes the active process of legitimation and recognition of the figure in the lore of the group. Some specific cultural processes, which would all be at home in

3. The phrase "legitimation in social thought" refers to the process of "explaining and justification" (Berger & Luckmann 1966, 111).

Jesus's first-century Mediterranean world and that could arguably be connected to his social personage, will briefly be described. While these processes can be distinguished, in real life they are interconnected fibers of a cultural system and the constituting network of social personages.

Honor was one of the core values in the first-century Mediterranean world; "Honor is the value of a person in his or her own eyes (that is, one's claim to worth) *plus* that person's value in the eyes of his or her social group. Honor is a claim to worth along with the social acknowledgement of worth" (Malina 2001a, 30). Such honor can be ascribed or acquired.

Honor and shame are forms of social evaluation in which persons are constantly assessed in relation to others. This cultural value is to be detected behind the questions about Jesus's family (cf., Mark 6:3; Matt 13:57; Luke 4:22; and John 7:40–42) and authority. The question in Luke: "Tell us, by what authority are you doing these things? Who is it who gave you this authority?" (20:2) is an example of a public challenge of honor. As Rohrbaugh explains: "Since the birth status of Jesus warranted nothing like the behavior he exhibited, the challengers naturally assumed the honor must have been *acquired,* i.e., bestowed by someone with the right to confer it" (1995, 186; italics his).

Honor can be acquired, and one of the ways in which it is won is by means of the pattern of social interaction known as "challenge and response." "Challenge and response is a sort of social pattern, a social game, if you will, in which persons hassle each other according to socially defined rules in order to gain the honor of another" (Malina 2001a, 33). While this pattern regulates social interaction between all in a village or community, it is obviously more pertinent in the lives of social personages. For that reason, it is not surprising to see that public assessment and honoring of Jesus is frequently reported in the Gospels, as in Mark 9:15: "When the whole crowd saw him, they were immediately overcome with awe, and they ran forward to greet him."[4] Another common way of ascribed honor was by means of an honorable family tree. Therefore, one of the main purposes of genealogies in the first-century Mediterranean world was "to set out a person's honor lines and thus socially situate the person on the ladder of statuses. A genealogy points to one's ascribed honor" (2001a, 32); or,

---

4. See also the following: Mark 1:22, 27–28, 45; 10:24; 10:32; 12:17; Matt 4:24; 9:31; 12:23; 14:1; 21:15–17; Luke 2:47; 4:22, 36; 7:17; 8:56; 18:43; 19:37; 23:47 for various versions of this social pattern.

as Rohrbaugh says, *"genealogies are honour claims"* (1995, 187; italics his). The basic belief behind this is "like father, like son."

The downside of such public assessment is also reflected in Jesus's public interactions where his authority is not acknowledged. According to some reports, this happened in his hometown, Nazareth (Mark 6:1–6 par.). Given the nature of a social personage (such as a shamanic figure) as embedded within a particular cultural system, it is not surprising that where Jesus's authority and position was not acknowledged, he was also ineffective. After the discovery of his family identity in Nazareth, his hometown, Matthew remarks: "And he did not do many deeds of power there, because of their unbelief" (13:58).

What the above examples, together with insight from the basic dyadic structure of personality, tell is that a social personage was not a given in that society but mutually constructed and recognized by the society.[5] What Jesus was as a social personage was partly created in the cultural processes of honoring and assessment.

Rumoring and Gossiping Jesus

Rumor and gossip research has been used to illuminate the history of the gospel traditions and to describe the flexible conditions of their origins. Botha shows that rumor and gossip represent realistic and historically plausible ways of conceptualizing the transmission of the Jesus stories. Implicit in his research, but not actively pursued, is the insight that rumors and gossip are not only mechanisms for the transmission of knowledge and information but ways in which knowledge and information are created and maintained, particularly in preprint societies. To be sure, they are not merely techniques of reporting or transmitting fixed data but rather cultural processes of creating knowledge and information.[6]

Far from being unreliable knowledge, rumors generally present themselves with pretensions to ideal verification; they *always* reach us through a friend, colleague, or relative (who is a friend of the firsthand witness). They

---

5. "The dyadic person is essentially a group-embedded and group-oriented person (some call such a person 'collectively-oriented'). Such a group-embedded, collectivistic personality is one who simply needs another continually in order to know who he or she really is" (Malina 2001a, 62).

6. Botha shows that "[i]n real life contexts the term 'relay' is inappropriate with regard to the rumour process, as no information is passed on unidirectionally" (1993, 214).

embody a social process in society—not only for dealing with a variety of situations but also for preserving its memories. Botha states:

> Rumours are improvised news resulting from a process of collective discussion entailing both an information-spreading procedure and a process of interpretation and commentary. In spreading and commenting upon presumed or ambiguous facts a group constructs one or two acceptable and valuable explanations. Changes in a rumour's content are not due to the failings of human memory, but rather to the development and contribution of commentaries made throughout the rumour's process. . . . Everyday communication, and thus exchange of rumours, is an interactional, reflective process and *not* like a linear relay line. Various concerned parties converse with each other, and the rumour is the final consensus of their collective deliberations seeking out a convincing, encompassing explanation. Rumours entail a subjective *construction* of reality. (1993, 212, 214; italics his)

The social dynamics illuminate how some of the Jesus traditions were transmitted, but they also confront us with an epistemological reality: truth is not something in itself; it is there, but always stands in relation to people.

> A rumour process is, in the end, only a speeded up version of the comprehensive, imperceptible process through which we acquire all of our ideas, opinions, images and beliefs. Rumour research leads us once more to the realization that reality is socially constructed. Certainty, in a final sense, is social: what the group to which we belong considers to be true *is* true. (1993, 227; italics his)

Gossip, which is part of the mystery of human conversation, is one of the methods of storing, transmitting, and retrieving information in all societies, but especially in nonliterate societies. Therefore, Botha says it cannot be called trivial but should be seen as part of the dynamic process of communication in society (see 1998b, 32). Rohrbaugh shows that there are at least twenty instances in Mark, and many more in the other Gospels, ·of reports about gossip and rumor distribution ascribed to Jesus's life (see 2001, 257–58). They are typically of the following nature: "At once his fame began to spread throughout the surrounding region of Galilee" (Mark 1:28) or, "And the report of this spread throughout that district" (Matt 9:26). According to these accounts, gossip and rumors were part of Jesus's everyday experiences and integral to his constitution as social personage. The dynamics of gossip in such societies are well expressed in the case when Jesus asks his disciples what the people are saying about him: "Now when Jesus came into the district of Caesarea Philippi, he asked his disciples, 'Who do people say that the Son of Man is?'" (Matt 16:13).

These cultural activities (gossip and rumors) fulfill definite functions in society. They were probably some of the most effective social processes in maintaining values, enhancing group boundaries, and performing public assessment in the early movements of Jesus-followers.[7] In leadership competition and public assessment, gossip is "manipulative talk" (Rohrbaugh 2001, 255) or "an unruly interplay of information and moral judgment" (Botha 1998b, 48).

Botha remarks that we may not gain more biographical details of Jesus when we think about the Jesus stories in terms of gossip dynamics, but our understanding of human nature is enhanced by knowledge of the characteristically personal subjects of gossip that are always part of a definite context (see 1998b, 48). However, in terms of the above distinction between the transmission of the gospel traditions and their role in creating knowledge and information in the life of a social personage in traditional societies, gossip dynamics indeed add biographical data in showing how things were (or could have been) in the life of such a public figure. According to the present argument, as historical figure, Jesus was partly constituted by means of rumors and gossip together with other processes, such as honoring. The many rumors and much gossip circulating about him were, in a literal sense, constructing Jesus as a cultural figure—they were part of what made him a social personage. If our concern is with how things were in his life in Galilee, these elements cannot be excluded from the picture.

Visioning and Prophesying Jesus

Who and what Jesus was as a social personage was also partly constituted by visionary experiences of his first followers. Since these will all be discussed in detail below, it will suffice to only mention them here. If the number of episodes of Jesus's visionary experiences, together with the many references to such experiences in Acts and Paul's own testimony, are taken into account, it is clear that such experiences were not limited to Jesus himself

7. A discussion of these components can be found in Botha (1998b, 36–42) and Rohrbaugh (2001, 251–56).

but were part of the cultural activities of both his first disciples and the first followers after his death.

A considerable portion of the reports about his life is based on alleged ASC experiences of his followers. Therefore, it is reasonable to include these experiences in our understanding of what Jesus was like as a social personage.

Historically speaking, it is a fact that for his followers, Jesus's life as a social personage did not end at his death. Some of the major sources about his life claim that it continued first in his resurrection and then in his continued presence with or visitations to his followers, and that he continued to influence their lives. In fact, it will be shown that these ASC experiences probably are merely a continuation of patterns and processes established during Jesus's own lifetime.

The continued envisioning of Jesus by his followers is part of the cultural process by means of which various of his followers worked through the process of his death. Such experiences are linked to the production and transmission of the tradition. Both Paul and the author of Acts provide plenty of evidence that soon after Jesus's death, his followers were engaged in cultural processes of vilification and labeling in order to control information. A case in point is Paul's own example (Gal 1:8–9) of the importance of his own visions and version of the tradition and the denigration of those of another conviction.

All this should come as no surprise because, according to some Gospel reports, some members of Jesus's close circle were involved in visionary experiences even during his lifetime (this will be discussed in detail below). Both the transfiguration story and the accounts of Jesus walking on the sea can be understood as ASC experiences by some of his followers and thus as referring to cultural events in the life of his followers. In both these accounts, certain properties of Jesus as social personage are established or generated in the experiences.

Except for naive fundamentalists who think that everything in the Gospels comes directly from Jesus, most scholars accept that prophecy played a part in the development of what is ascribed to Jesus. Boring shows that "Christian prophets contributed to the tradition of Jesus' words in a variety of ways: both primarily (creating new sayings) and secondarily (modifying traditional sayings), both directly (by contributing to it) and indirectly (by influencing the way others contributed to it), and at more than one moment in the trajectory of a saying" (1983, 109). While the debate continues between those who suggest that much of the gospel tradition was actually created in prophecy and those who argue that the gospel tradition contains only prophesies that agree with the "foundational Jesus tradition" as Dunn claims, it is agreed that prophecy played a significant role (2003b, 191).[8] What cannot be wished away is that visions and prophetic activities were naturally part of the ways of gaining and constructing knowledge in the early Jesus movement. Again, how things were in the life of Jesus of Nazareth could and probably did include prophetic and visionary activities.

Remembering Jesus

Prior to tape recorders, the inventions of film and video cameras, or the archival possibilities of modern literate societies, research about historical figures always implicated memory and remembering. Even if *authentic snippets* were to be identified, they would not be archival deposits of historical events or words of Jesus. At best, they could be the remembered versions of his followers. At least two aspects of memory and transmission should be taken into account.

The first is about remembering in traditional societies. The idea that people in traditional societies have better memories than people in literate societies is not supported by the evidence.[9] Claims in such traditional societies that information has been transmitted correctly also have nothing to do with the sentiments of an identity logic. "Verbatim" or "correctly" meant *traditional* (see Crossan 1998, 75). Research shows that even though subjects believe that a tradition has been preserved "unaltered," this is not necessarily the case. It has been preserved in line with the tradition and the guardians of knowledge by accepted cultural means.[10]

8. It is ironic that precisely the evidence of a lively discussion about false prophecy and the need for evaluation of prophetic utterances mentioned by Dunn can be taken as evidence for the vitality of prophecy as such. It is only where such practices are alive and well that such strong measures are also introduced to control them (2003b 189–91).

9. Rather there is a positive relation between schooling and memory (Crossan 1998, 49).

10. The belief that traditions are transmitted unaltered is not restricted to people in traditional societies. Among modern educated people, in cases where the correspondence between memories and events can be checked, there is no high correlation between accuracy and the vividness of memories—as is shown by so-called flashbulb memories (see, e.g., McCloskey, Wible, & Cohen 1994). One such study on how people heard about the Challenger shuttle explosion found: "When the subjects were tested over 2 and a half years

The second is about memory as such. The debate whether ancient people could remember better than modern people is, in a sense, trivial—obviously it is possible to improve memory by certain techniques and to record excellent recovery of information (like lists). The problem is much more fundamental, namely, the nature of memory as such. Unlike the storehouse metaphor that informs most popular (and New Testament scholarly) views about memory (namely, that events and data are stored or deposited on a clean slate that needs to be recovered), a more appropriate metaphor nowadays is the *correspondence metaphor of memory* (see Koriat et al. 2000, 483–85).

A proper way to think about memory and remembering is to accept that it is much less "accurate" than we tend to think and believe about ourselves. Bonanno points out that

> memory can no longer be thought of as an archival system of specific memories, an ever-expanding library consisting of full and complete records of discrete episodes, but rather as a *process* involving bits and pieces of information that are continually interpreted and reconstructed in the course of remembering. (1990, 175)[11]

Two of the many features of this research are particularly relevant to the present argument. One is the realization that memory has much in common with perception in that things can be remembered if they can be perceived; angels or ancestors can only be "remembered" where they can possibly be "perceived." Humans perceive in a cultural way (with their brains and not with their senses), and memory of images or sounds depends on these cultural processes of perception to be real. The second is the suggestion to think in terms of *overall faithfulness* instead of actual ac-

---

later, most described their memories as visually vivid; yet none was entirely correct, and fully half of them were substantially wrong in the memory reports" (Koriat, Goldsmith, & Pansky 2000, 512).

11. Research in psychotherapy, which works with the life narratives of subjects, increasingly points to the inadequacy of the archaeological metaphor for conceptualizing human memory. Remembering does not consist of the uncovering of a fixed deposit of memories, "not in the uncovering of objective facts and details of a life story, or historical truth, but rather in the production of an articulated narrative understanding or narrative truth" (Bonanno 1990, 176). This finding is confirmed by studies on hypnosis and memory that indicate that even different hypnotic versions of past events do not correlate. They are constructed versions of events and data based on a variety of current concerns (see Watkins & Watkins 1986; Piper 1994).

curacy. Both these findings force the debate back to the particular cultural system.

The question, therefore, should not only be, what was remembered about Jesus?" but, "how and as what was Jesus remembered?" We should abandon the search for the original or authentic sayings of Jesus or for stories about him that were somehow transmitted by his early followers.[12] Stories by the disciples, even the day after an event (so to speak), would already have been subject to the features ascribed here to memory and to the constraints placed by the cultural system on what can be remembered. Exorcism stories would even in their experiential phase be structured by cultural constraints and other well-known stories. Therefore, the fact that many of the miracle stories display similar features is not necessarily an argument that they were created late in the transmission process. As will be argued below, the Gospel writers experienced what they believed, and they believed what they experienced. Just as the shaman who knows in advance the land that is visited in a soul journey (vision), people experience exorcisms in terms of the cultural patterns and folklore available to them. In fact, possession takes place by means of culturally recognized entities—demons, or ancestors, or animal spirits, and the like. It is therefore not surprising that exorcism stories are experienced and retold within cultural expectations and patterns. Memory remembers culturally significant phenomena, and within cultural patterns. In fact, memory is one of the culturally structured tools for constructing and interpreting reality and, therefore, for constructing and interpreting how Jesus of Nazareth was constituted as a historical figure.

What We Are Looking For: A Culturally Constituted Figure

The gist of the discussion is that whoever and whatever Jesus was as a social personage, we should not be looking for a unique individual performing extraordinary or exceptional deeds and from time to time uttering some wise sayings, but for a cultural figure embedded in the cultural system and worldview of his time. What he did, what he said, and what he was

12. It is surprising that Crossan, who realizes the limitations memory places on the nature of remembered sources, does not apply that insight to his own view on the sources (see 1998, 68). His strongest application of these insights is to show that the oral tradition, which coexisted with the first written sources, cannot be championed ahead of them. But surely, all the information in the written sources (Q included, if it actually existed) is subject to the same constraints of memory?

were closely connected to the cultural processes and dynamics of his life and world. As historical figure, he was as much constituted by individual actions as by these cultural processes.

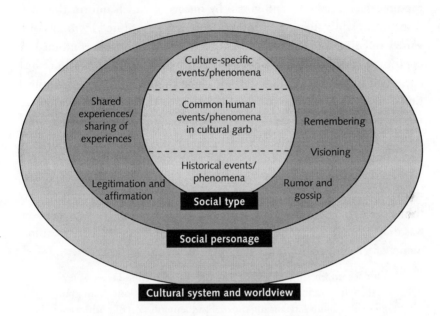

Diagram 4.1: Constituting a Social Personage

In cultural bundubashing, the scope of what could be considered plausible historical realities has been widened considerably, compared to the authenticity paradigm. It is not only events and phenomena with multiple independent attestation that could pass a common reality test, but all those events and phenomena that reasonably could have constituted Jesus as a particular social personage in a traditional society are to be considered.

From this perspective, it seems clear that there never was and could not have been an original, uncontaminated kernel of authentic Jesus material. Noll points out that "What is often understated in discussions of nonliterate societies by modern observers is that the cultural mythology is a *living* one. There are no written sources to validate religious beliefs, only the repeated, ritualized, re-experiencing of the sacred" (1985, 449). While the first-century Israelite world was not totally nonliterate, it was probably the case that most communication was of an oral nature (Bar-Ilan 1992; Craffert & Botha 2005, 21–31). And given the foregoing discussion of how Jesus was constituted as a social personage, it is also probably true that the oral tradition was a living one.

The documents themselves, as shown above, are full of references to the processes of rumors and gossip by means of which information was distributed, while the very historical figure was constituted by means of a variety of cultural processes. Visionary experiences probably continued to contribute to the knowledge about and images of Jesus as social personage. Such processes certainly did not come to an end once enscripturation started. In fact, texts such as the letters of Paul and *The Shepherd of Hermas* show that these cultural processes were well established long after Jesus' death. Therefore, there probably were living traditions from the beginning.

As shown above, in the view offered here it is difficult to even speak of *an originating event* or a single authentic saying.[13] It was argued that given the nature of many of the events and episodes ascribed to Jesus, there never was only a single version of what happened. Kelber suggests the tradition model of a biosphere for understanding the sayings of Jesus:

> Our search for singular originality concealed behind layers of textual encumbrances reveals much about the force of our desire, but falls short of understanding the oral implementation of multioriginality in the present act of speaking. Only on paper do texts appear to relate in a one-to-one relation to other texts. (1994, 164)

Probably there also was, right from the start, a multi- or plurioriginality in many of the events, phenomena and saying that constituted Jesus' life as a Galilean social personage. There probably were living traditions right from the beginning because the Gospels report about cultural events and words with multi- and plurioriginal origins.

Despite the processes of informal controlled tradition to be discussed next, it is unlikely that there was, during Jesus's lifetime in Galilee, a community that could exercise control over the tradition process. If the

13. Dunn emphasizes that there were events (an "originating event") and words spoken, but these were never captured in a single original tradition (see 2003a, 153). In a similar argument, Wright argues for an "informed but controlled oral tradition" by means of which the community would order its life and thought by telling and retelling important events (1996, 134). It should be emphasized that for Dunn the recognition of the phase of oral tradition is an attempt to do justice to the way in which the traditions were transmitted. The various oral traditions point toward words or events that were fairly stable but transmitted in an oral environment in a variety of streams. The oral transmission is used to explain the varieties in the traditions of the fixed words or events.

disputes among the disciples, between Paul and the other apostles, and the variety of public responses to the question who Jesus was are taken together, it rather seems that diversity ruled during the first few decades. Given the nature of the cultural processes discussed here, it is more appropriate to assume a spectrum of portrayals of Jesus as a social personage (or as a Galilean shamanic figure) during his lifetime.

Communicating a Social Personage: Informal Controlled Tradition

It is suggested above that ample evidence points toward cultural processes of the oral creation and transmission of stories and information about Jesus as a social personage. These included such processes as prophecy, gossip, and rumors. Given the generally agreed-upon fact that the written versions originated some time after these events, it has to be accepted that the traditions were orally preserved and transmitted up to that point.

Unlike others who make use of the insights of Kenneth Bailey to affirm the basic reliability of the synoptic tradition (the idea that oral tradition somehow preserved a reliable memory of the *originating event/ impact*), I am interested in the mechanisms and cultural dynamics with regard to the transmission of tradition to which he refers. In traditional societies, he points out, stories critical for a group's identity are repeated in public where a form of community control takes place over the "truth" (see Bailey 1995, 364). Second, while everyone in a community can be a reciter, there is also community control over the fact that the recitations in public gatherings and, thus, the preservation of an *official* tradition is accredited to significantly recognized figures in the community (see 1991, 40, 42). Third, the climax of an event or the core of a tradition is a negotiated truth (see 1991, 48–49).

It seems obvious from the foregoing remarks and those in the previous section that if anything was transmitted (orally or in writing) about the historical figure of Jesus, in the view of cultural bundubashing it must have been about the historical figure as a particular social personage (in this case, a Galilean shamanic figure). What was written down from the beginning, as with what was orally transmitted, was not authentic nuggets but the social personage or the cultural figure. The first followers did not transmit what they believed were authentic nuggets, but what they believed Jesus as a social figure was. As has been indicated already, what was created, transmitted, and remembered in the oral phase was the total package of reports and deposits of the cultural processes associated with Jesus as social personage. There never were merely authentic snippets. If Jesus had been a social figure of repute, as suggested by all the sources, from the very beginning, his followers talked and wrote about him as social figure.

In fact, one of the implications of the insight that a historical figure could have been like the portrayals in the documents is that, whether oral or written material, it was about a social personage. While current historical Jesus research takes most of the literary material as literary creations containing additions, falsifications, or elaborations, cultural bundubashing takes the documents as residues about the normal cultural processes associated with the constitution of such a figure. Whether written or oral, they can be seen as reports about the total package of social personage and cultural dynamics—oral reports were not more pristine or original.

An important implication of this is that even if earlier oral or written sources can be identified, they still are subject to this condition. To be blunt, even if Q existed, according to this view, it did not contain pure nuggets of authentic material but probably was as much the product of the above cultural processes and dynamics as any other document (or report). Even though it contains primarily sayings of Jesus, the idea has to be entertained that these sayings were subject to the above-mentioned cultural processes.

Enscripturating a Social Personage in Cultural Artifacts

Two features regarding the documents for Jesus research are common knowledge. First, no field reports or firsthand documents about Jesus's life are available since neither he nor his immediate followers left behind any material reports. Therefore, it is generally accepted that the literary texts were all created some time after his death. Second, scholarly beliefs about the processes of enscripturation vary considerably. As already indicated, those on the Wredebahn see the documents primarily as the products of literary creativity in which most of the material was *de facto* made up (created) by the authors (this even applies to the authors of the earliest identified sources). For them, the documents and their content are basically the products of this later stage. Scholars on the Schweitzerstrasse take the Synoptic Gospels as basically reliable reports (with the Easter overlay removed) but doubt the value of the Gospel of John or any other document as of much historical value. Therefore, scholars on the Schweitzerstrasse take the Synoptics as reliable sources, but they take the Gospel of John as well as the extracanonical gospels in the same way as do scholars on the Wredebahn—merely as literary creations.

However, as I explained earlier, the difference between cultural bundubashing and the authenticity paradigm is not only about what we are looking for but also what we are looking at. The position to be promoted here is that besides the cultural processes of enscripturation to be discussed, the written versions of the Jesus traditions are to be seen in continuation with the foregoing processes.

It should, however, be stated right at the beginning that treating the documents about the life of Jesus as cultural artifacts connected to that life needs much more research attention than would be possible here. As I said earlier, this interpretive process is being designed in the very process of trying to map it. For example, it would be necessary to reconsider the tradition history of the Jesus traditions if they are seen as part of cultural processes. In other words, tradition history becomes history of the tradition processes instead of history of individual texts, sayings, or accounts. Here the focus will only be on the cultural processes by means of which the literary documents could have been constituted and created if Jesus was a social personage of the kind suggested here. This means that in addition to the above-discussed cultural processes, many of which continued after Jesus's death, another set of processes are to be reckoned with.

Initially, two arguments can be offered in support of this view of cultural bundubashing.

First, the oral and the written material belong together (that is, if they were about Jesus as social personage). At least after the first written versions of Jesus's life appeared, oral and written versions thereof existed hand in hand. The imaginative scenario sketched by Dunn is probably as close to the historical situation as available evidence and insights allow us today:

> Was there no Jesus tradition known and used and circulated until Mark gave it life by writing it down? Of course not. Did Mark have to seek out ageing apostles or rummage for scraps in boxes hidden away in various elders' houses in order to gather unknown, unused tradition and set it out in writing? Of course not. Was the tradition gathered by Mark known only to Mark's church or circle of congregations? Surely not. And once Mark had gathered the tradition into his Gospel, did that mean that the tradition ceased to

be oral? Of course not. Or again, when Matthew received Mark's
Gospel, are we to assume that this was the first time Matthew
or his church(es) had come across this tradition? Of course not.
(2003a, 171)

At some point after Jesus's death, some of his followers started writing
down and collecting the stories, rumors, and reports that were circulating
about him. In fact, J. A. T. Robinson argues that "there is every reason to
think that both oral and literary processes went on concurrently for most
of the first hundred years of the Christian church. The writing was earlier
and the reign of the 'living voice' longer than we have tended to suppose"
(1976, 346).[14] One should therefore imagine a wide stream of traditions
right from the beginning and probably lasting for the whole first century.

Second, Mark probably was not the first to tell the story as a whole,
or to tell a whole story about Jesus's life. The logic of the cultural processes
described earlier is that the various fibers in the constitution and transmission of material about Jesus of Nazareth were all contributing to the life
story of a social personage or Galilean shamanic figure. Enscripturation—
the different processes of putting the reports into writing—were about the
same social personage. The following processes shall now be considered.

Selecting, Editing, and Arranging Transmitted Material

In view of the present considerations, the tradition history of most of
the gospel material will have to be reconsidered. Although that cannot be
done here, suffice it to say that in the perspective of cultural bundubashing, the enscripturation process was merely a continuation of the existing
cultural processes regarding Jesus as social personage. If the authors of the
literary texts were part of the Jesus movement, they were just as much
part of the above processes and could equally have participated in the
gossip, rumors, retelling, and prophetic or visionary activities, but also in
the transmission of fixed liturgical or teaching material in the process of
informally controlled transmission. But, given the body of material in the
communal memory, they also selected and arranged and probably edited
the material that they enscripturated.

---

14. Ellis argues that "the circumstances that gave rise to written teachings in early
Christianity was not chronological distance but geographical distance" (quoted in Robinson
1976, 346). Even so, there is no reason to think that the written versions were substantially
different from what went on in the oral tradition.

To be sure, each of these editorial processes was performed on the above-described material. In other words, the selection, editing, and arranging of material was done not on original or authentic material, but on the body of culturally created and transmitted material that was in circulation about a specific social personage, Jesus of Nazareth. As suggested above, the communal memory from the beginning probably consisted of a diverse body of culturally created material about a culturally constructed and interpreted social figure.

If Jesus was indeed a Galilean shamanic figure as suggested by the present hypothesis, then the material about his life from the very beginning was already about such a figure. Whether any of the Gospel authors added elements consistent with such a figure (visionary or mythical elements), is almost impossible to know. Given the cultural processes from the very beginning, it is impossible to detect which component was added later. For example, if legitimation by means of an honorable genealogy could possibly and plausibly have been part of a Galilean shamanic figure's biography, it could have been created very early when rumors about him circulated in Galilee. It also could have been added on later. Therefore, for what it is worth, after setting and testing a specific hypothesis against the available evidence, all the sources should again be scrutinized for possible elements that do not fit the life of the kind of social personage tested by means of the hypothesis. Editorial or creative additions from later settings can only be detected once a proper picture of the historical figure has been established by testing a specific hypothesis.

If this sounds like the well-known criterion of dissimilarity, it should be realized that there is a huge difference. Here it is not offered as a criterion to determine authentic material in advance. Any *additions* can only be identified as a secondary phase in the interpretive process of abduction. As an afterthought of what does not fit a particular hypothesis, the databases, so to speak, are to be cleansed.

Finally, one would also be mistaken to conclude that this is a new defense of the old position that historical Jesus research can only operate on the redactional level of the different Gospels. It is not an apology for the Gospels' portrayals against those who excavate for the authentic material within the Gospels. This is an attempt to understand the overall cultural processes associated with and linked to the social personage. The processes of enscripturation are not to be divorced from the foregoing cultural processes of constituting and communicating the historical figure.

Trying to find a social figure that fits is an attempt to give a reasonable and defensible answer for the whole complex process. If anything, this is an attempt to give a coherent account of a total process and not only the final product. And this is precisely the messy implication of an interpretive process of abduction: it is a constant to-and-fro movement working with, from, and toward a hypothesis in order to make sense of both the overall picture and the constituting components. And that process applies to both an understanding of the historical figure and the literary documents.

The Use of Sources

If the Gospel texts do contain some substantive reports about a historical figure and were not fictional creations, then the question remains why such different portrayals of the historical figure emerged. In fact, despite some scholarly optimism about the "remarkably consistent and coherent picture of Jesus" (Dunn 2002, 153) in the Synoptic Gospels, a comparison of the four canonical Gospels shows that each is a unique version of Jesus as historical figure from the "*communal memory*" (to use Dunn's term again). Such a comparison shows that each evangelist has selected, edited, and arranged the material in a unique and idiosyncratic way. Even reports about the same recognizable episode display significant differences. Furthermore, a surface scan of the canonical Gospels shows that either the authors made different selections from the large body of communal memory or some of them went about very liberally in creating or adding material to that body of knowledge.

If Luke and Matthew actually knew and used Mark (and Q) as claimed by the Two Source Hypothesis, the Gospels of Matthew and Luke are material evidence for the fact that those who claimed to transmit the Jesus story to later generations did not find it awkward to create their own special version of the life of the Galilean social personage. There is no reason to think that earlier versions (oral or written in the case of Mark) did it differently. Written material, in this perspective, is just a special case of all the material transmitted about a specific kind of social personage: culturally created reports and residues about a social personage.

However, enscripturation might even have included the use of written sources by the Gospel authors (Luke 1:1–4). Given the current state of Gospel research, it is almost impossible not to take a stance on the use of sources. It is possible that smaller collections first originated and served as written sources for later gospel authors (of which Q is a hypothetical example). From this point of view two remarks can be made.

First, if Q existed, the use of it can show how sources (written or oral) were treated in that world. At least, if current Q studies are anything to go on (see, e.g., the discussion by Dunn 2003a, 158–70), it is clear that ancient authors did not remotely share our modern view about either copyright or authorship. Matthew and Luke did not hesitate to raid Q for their own intentions and purposes. In addition, one might learn which pieces of written material were possibly older than the final written version, but unfortunately not what was historical. Even if older written sources existed, there is no reason to take them as more authentic or historical, for in terms of the construction offered here, the age of texts and even the relative age of sources (such as the supposedly earlier age of Q) is of little relevance prior to sorting out what the texts were about. The Gospels are the products of a larger set of processes that impacts on authenticity. It was well understood by Morton Smith:

> Of course in evaluating historical reports the question of priority is important and must always be considered, but it is not decisive. One must begin by establishing, from the reports, the main facts about a man's career, the when, where, and what. Only after this can particular stories be evaluated by their agreement with the main facts. (1981, 404)

Second, even if earlier (oral or written) texts existed, in terms of the above construction, they would not be more authentic but merely earlier versions of the same cultural processes. To be sure, even if Mark and Q were composed earlier than the other Gospels, they in all probability originated in the same cultural processes described above. They could also be written reports and deposits of the total stream of cultural processes creating and enscripturating a social figure. In this view, Q (if it existed) was not a collection of what Jesus said but subject to the same cultural constraints in terms of which all material about Jesus was from the beginning created and transmitted. If Q existed as a written document, there is no reason why it should not also be seen as an edited construction from even earlier material.

What We Are Looking At:
Cultural Products and Artifacts about a Social Personage

One of the basic principles of anthropological historiography suggests that the literary data should be treated for what they are about as cultural artifacts within their own setting. In accepting that the canonical Gospels were not merely literary creations (three with a similar narrative structure and style supplemented with short discourses, the Synoptic Gospels, and one substantially different from those, the Gospel of John, also with a narrative style yet with long discourses), it is assumed here that they were linked to the life of Jesus as a Galilean social personage. Seen in this way, the canonical Gospels no longer consist of an authentic kernel covered with traditional or church overlay but are seen as different configurations of the above cultural processes about the same historical figure. They are four versions of specific cultural processes about a specific social personage that already started during Jesus's lifetime. They are, so to speak, the literary residues of a Galilean shaman's life.

Not all processes influenced each text in the same way, but if it is accepted that the texts are about a real historical and cultural figure (and not merely literary creations), then some kind of a causal and cultural continuity between each text and historical figure can be assumed and these are to be conceptualized as embedded in the cultural processes. In this view, the historical figure is not *underneath* but *in* the literary documents.[15]

So what are we looking at? The canonical Gospels are the literary reports or residues about a social personage, and they are themselves the product of cultural processes. The transmission and enscripturation of events and stories were about the same social type constituted and constructed as a social personage. At the level of the events ascribed to Jesus, specific actions as well as cultural experiences and telling of such experiences were identified. The texts reflect deeds and phenomena ascribed to a specific social type. The transmission of those stories calls for different cultural processes that include rumors and gossip as the ways in which traditional societies create, preserve, and transmit knowledge about significant figures.

In this construction, the Gospel texts display a further phase in the cultural processes whereby a historical figure was constituted and even-

---

15. Chilton, who also maintains that there "is no 'primitive,' 'historical,' 'authentic,' or otherwise real Jesus apart from what texts promulgate," suggests that "Jesus is only knowable as a literary historical phenomenon: what the gospels point to as their source" (1999, 16).

tually enscripturated as a social personage. These cultural processes were configurations of each other in that each represented a different phase about the same figure and within a shared worldview and cultural system. From Jesus the historical figure as a particular social personage and from the gospel texts as cultural artifacts about that personage, there are at least three dynamic processes: constituting, communicating, and enscripturating the social personage. Over time these can be refined as identifiable processes linked to particular places on the continuum. Right from the start, there was more than one constructed Jesus, and in the end, more than one literary residue of the historical figure constituted in this way.

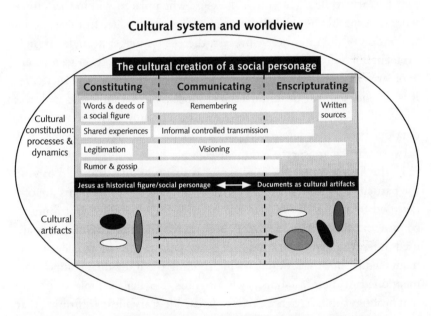

Cultural system and worldview

The cultural creation of a social personage		
Constituting	**Communicating**	**Enscripturating**
Words & deeds of a social figure	Remembering	Written sources
Shared experiences	Informal controlled transmission	
Legitimation	Visioning	
Rumor & gossip		

Cultural constitution: processes & dynamics

Cultural artifacts

Jesus as historical figure/social personage ⟷ Documents as cultural artifacts

Diagram 4.2: The Continuum of Cultural Processes and Products

The following insights are highlighted by this diagram: (1) There is a continuity from the cultural constitution of the social personage to the literary documents about that social personage. This is expressed in the similar shape but different shades of the circles representing the social personage. (2) There is a continuity from the cultural constitution of the social personage to the communication and enscripturation of that social personage via the different cultural processes that were all part of the same worldview and cultural system. The cultural construction(s) of a social personage by means of a variety of processes were enscripturated in the texts as residues about that social personage.

The Fibers of the Interpretive Cable
and the Scope of This Study

Working from and toward a particular hypothesis does not translate into a single interpretive activity but consists of various activities containing several sets of fibers. The plausibility of specific events or phenomena is dependent on the truth of the overall hypothesis, while such a hypothesis can only be evaluated by testing the plausibility and possibility of specific elements. That is, whether Jesus actually fits a specific social-type model depends on the overall construction of the individual elements ascribed to his life story, while these only make sense when placed within the framework of a specific hypothesis or social type about his life. In this conceptualization of the interpretive process, there is no longer a single research problem but a cluster of interrelated questions that mutually crisscross one another—all of which cannot be dealt with simultaneously.[16] Therefore, it is also not a linear or unidirectional process but, as indicated with the choice of abduction, a to-and-fro movement not only between model and data but between different components of the data and the model, and between particular aspects and the overall picture.

The first and obvious implication is that working from and toward the particular hypothesis implies that the individual components are understood by means of the particular hypothesis while they contribute to confirm (or disconfirm) the overall hypothesis. The sources collectively are used to test the hypothesis that they were about the life of a Galilean shamanic figure, but that is done by interpreting the individual components mentioned in them as about such a figure's life. For example, affirming that healings could have been part of Jesus's life story means affirming that

16. As an interpretive process, it is similar to what Chilton calls the process of pentagulation: "Our methods must reject the misleading analogy of archaeological strata, and attend to the historical unfolding of meaning by exegetical means . . . in a process akin to triangulation mapping, we may infer from our reading of texts what his [Jesus's] position must have been to produce what we read" (1999, 22–23). The process of triangulation in mapping means the measurement or mapping of an area by means of a network of triangles. The principal concern in this approach is not authentic material but what must be assumed about Jesus as a historical person in order to explain the nature and content of a given text. Compare also Hurtado's suggestion: "We should examine the variation in those sources for the Jesus tradition with strong 'external' claims as to age and general value, preferring that reconstruction of the historical Jesus which best accounts for the variations in the sources of early provenance" (1997, 294–95). This is implicit also in Davies's approach (see 1995, 43–44).

they were typical shamanic healings. Determining the plausibility of such healings means that they are evaluated as shamanic healings.

Establishing the historicity of specific elements in Jesus's life story in this case implies determining their historicity or plausibility as shamanic activities. Verifying the shamanic hypothesis can be done only via an evaluation of the individual components as typical shamanic activities and phenomena, while the evaluation of such individual elements is done in terms of the shamanic hypothesis.

Second, it follows from the above arguments that both the oral and the written material that were created in the earliest period of the Jesus movement were about him as social personage. This applies to all the written documents that can with some measure of verification be connected to the life of Jesus of Nazareth. All are to be treated in the interpretive process in the same way as potential sources of evidence for the life of a Galilean shamanic figure.

Although all the literary texts from the earliest phases of the Jesus movement should be taken as potential historical sources, the canonical Gospels are still the main sources of knowledge about Jesus of Nazareth. Together with some other sources, they are virtually the only entrance point to him as historical figure, but they have priority if only for the reason that they consist of accounts more or less covering his whole life (at least as a social personage). If for no other reason, the canonical Gospels will be taken in this study as the primary sources simply to test the proposed method and hypothesis. Given the interpretive process suggested here, interpretation should start somewhere, and the canonical Gospels, covering different aspects of the life of Jesus as social personage, will be used. Do they make sense as reports under the hypothesis that Jesus of Nazareth was a Galilean shamanic figure?

What Steve Mason suggests about historical reconstruction in general is applicable here. It is not a matter of choosing one source over another but an attempt to explain plausibly how each source came into being if hypothesis X is correct (see 1995, 466). Does the shamanic (or any other) model help to explain why, for example, the canonical Gospels originated and took the specific shape and content that they have? If Jesus belonged to a specific social type, do specific features in each source make sense, and how can each Gospel be seen as a representative of that social type and historical figure? For example, does the Gospel of John, when viewed as the residue of a shamanic life, make sense as a historical source for Jesus's life?

Part of this activity of working toward a hypothesis would be to put the question: Which elements do not fit the particular hypothesis or social type within the historical setting? In other words, which elements display features of later times or settings? Does the hypothesis help in understanding why each of the sources portrays Jesus in unique ways? This "test" should be applied to all the sources that, with some external verification, can be located in the early phase of Christian beginnings. For example, does this way of working toward a hypothesis help to explain the origin and content of the infancy gospels and the extracanonical gospels? If that was the only source available about Jesus of Nazareth, would it make sense in terms of the proposed hypothesis? Judgment on the validity of any source for the life of Jesus is dependent on an understanding of the social type and the events ascribed to him as well as on understanding the cultural processes that took place at different stages of source development. These questions are part of working toward a shamanic hypothesis but cannot all be considered in this study.

Cultural bundubashing is designed to deal with the data about cultural events (alien, culture-specific events and phenomena) and normal human events and phenomena clothed in cultural garb (cultural representations of events and phenomena). It has to be admitted that under the assumption that evidence about common human events and phenomena (such as detail about birth and death) is available, and that *realia* about Jesus's life can actually be established, many questions can be asked that, from the point of view of cultural bundubashing, cannot be answered (at least not with the available evidence). For the data on common human biographical aspects of Jesus's life (biographical information that is not necessarily created by the cultural system) different tools and methods are needed. But, as it turns out, no hard biographical information of the kind normally used to construct a social personage's biography is available. All the evidence about biographical information seems to be either influenced by or directly related to cultural information. For example, even information about Jesus's place of birth or family origin or level of literacy and the like are connected to his social type and social personage. It belongs either to the category of alien human events and phenomena or cultural representation of human events and phenomena.

There are also questions that require special tools and methods (such as questions about the procedures and events related to Jesus's trial and crucifixion). Appropriate tools and methods for asking and answering these questions are needed that will not be discussed here. Cultural bundubashing cannot answer all possible historical questions about Jesus as historical figure, but it has implications for asking most other questions because it sensitizes and equips us for dealing with evidence about events and phenomena from a distant and foreign cultural system and worldview. Once it is known what social type Jesus was, it might be easier to understand why many other biographical elements are ascribed to him. Certain biographical features belong, within specific settings, to particular social types (features such as special birth stories, which decorate some social-type figures). Therefore, knowing about a person's social type is knowing (something) about a personal profile and about a person's biography.

Since the interpretive process is a constant to-and-fro movement between the different components, these questions should be unbracketed at some point in time. With the risk of including data that actually belong to editorial or other additions, a preliminary portrayal has to be made just in order to return to it again for possible addition. Such information cannot be removed prior to a clear and crisp picture of what Jesus could have been like as a historical personage. Since this study focuses on the former process of working toward the hypothesis in the canonical Gospels, a working hypothesis will be followed that material used can always be removed if it can be indicated that it was created later. However, if material can be shown to fit the hypothesis, it is reasonable to assume that the historical figure was indeed like that.

Concluding Remarks

Cultural bundubashing offers a new framework for historical Jesus research that has far-reaching implications for the way questions are asked and answered. It confronts the researcher with a whole new set of realities. In fact, it should be clear that cultural bundubashing does not offer alternative answers to existing questions but offers answers to alternative questions and problems because its lenses show different objects (documents) to be interpreted and a cultural figure embedded in those documents. Cultural bundubashing situates historical Jesus research on a different terrain from that of either traditional or postmodern historiography. This can be illustrated by the following diagram.

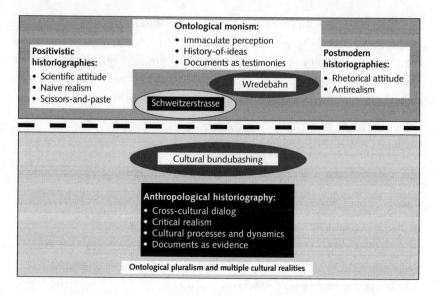

Diagram 4.3: Situating Historical Jesus Historiography

Seen against this diagram, the historiographical paradigms in Jesus research look like this:

Positivist—postmodern historiography

Schweitzerstrasse and the Wredebahn

- a historical figure could not have been like any or all of the gospel presentations of Jesus of Nazareth
- the Gospels emerged in a linear fashion as layered traditions with the authentic material in the earliest phase
- the interpretive process moves backwards from the identified authentic material by means of induction to the historical figure in the first layer

Anthropological historiography

Cultural bundubashing

- some historical figures, like shamanic figures, could be like the gospel presentations of Jesus of Nazareth
- each Gospel can be seen as the residue of a configuration of social processes instigated by the life of the social personage
- by means of abduction the interpretive process takes into account in a to and fro movement both the social personage and the cultural dynamics of the life of the hypothesized social type

The central activities imagined in current historical Jesus research are that Jesus's words were recorded and his deeds reported and a great deal of effort is invested in trying to (deter)mine those two. Instead of searching for authentic nuggets in a history-of-ideas approach, which is based on the correlation of ideas and texts, cultural bundubashing sees both the social personage and the literary texts as cultural artifacts that were produced in specific cultural processes within a particular cultural system. In creating Jesus as a shamanic figure, the cultural processes included, from the very beginning, processes of legitimation (recognition and rumoring), processes of memory (remembering), and processes of revisioning.

On the one hand, the literary texts can be seen as cultural artifacts containing descriptions, reports, and stories about a specific social personage. The Gospels are, thus, seen as the products of an alien and distant cultural system while they report about events and phenomena in the life of a social personage from that cultural system. They not only contain cultural stories about events, but they contain cultural stories about cultural events concerning a specific social personage.

On the other hand, the lenses of cultural bundubashing allow us to see that Jesus of Nazareth was a social personage embedded in a specific (foreign) cultural system. The cultural figure presented in the Gospels is ascribed with many activities, features, and phenomena that come across as strange but that have many similarities with social figures in traditional societies. The Jesus of all four Gospels performed *miracles* and healings; he is credited with a special birth and with appearances after his death (except in the Gospel of Mark); he is well known as a teacher and prophet of some kind, to mention only the most obvious features. Anthropological research confirms not only that a historical figure could have looked like this, but also that establishing the reality or plausibility of events in the life of such a figure comprises a complex cross-cultural task.

This way of looking at a social personage implies that a description or analysis of Jesus as historical figure should take into account not only his social type but also the specific kind of events and phenomena ascribed to him as a social personage. The rest of this study is an attempt to set and test, that is, to work toward, the hypothesis that Jesus was a Galilean shamanic figure.

PART 2

A Model *of*
Shamanic Figures

CHAPTER 5

The Shamanic Complex: A Social-Type Model

Introduction

The hypothesis of this study is that the *shamanic complex* offers a framework of a social type or religious entrepreneur that can best account for Jesus as historical person and social personage and for the content and nature of the literary sources. Therefore it is necessary to define the shaman and describe shamanism.

The *shamanic complex* is the shorthand phrase for the features and practices associated with an ASC-based religious pattern. It is a family of features that, as a regularly occurring pattern in many cultural systems, consists of a specific configuration of certain characteristics (ASC experiences such as visions, possession, or journeys) and certain social functions (such as healing, divination, exorcism, and control of spirits) that flow from these experiences.[1] These occur within a recognizable worldview pattern, and it is not so much the individual elements but the combination of a number of aspects that constitutes the shamanic complex as an identifiable phenomenon in many cultural settings. As a combination of regularly occurring features and functions, these do not appear in this pattern amongst other religious practitioners or entrepreneurs. Therefore, the shaman or shamanic figure is a recognizable social type distinct from other social types such as prophets, priests, healers, sages, or rabbis.

---

1. The biophysical dynamics of ASCs will be explained in the next chapter.

Social-Type Analysis

A social type can be defined as "a human prototype—a sociological summary of the typical characteristics of a particular group or of a category of human beings usually recognized and typed by the public and often granted a nickname" (Almog 1998, 5). It is an analytical concept or abstract depiction constructed from a number of real cases in order to reveal their essential and common features.[2] Social types can be identified in certain patterns of behavior and ways of thinking that make the members of the group resemble one another and distinguish them as a whole from others.

A social-type analysis is a useful way of understanding the characteristic features of a particular type of individual. Since human beings are unlike molecules, they can never be identical to one another. Such an analysis therefore does not look for perfect homogeneity but for similarities within the group or category characterized by the social type.[3]

Features Of Social-Type Models

The following features of the social-type model as discussed by Almog are relevant to this discussion (see 1998, 7–10).

A social type is different from a social role.[4] While they are similar in many ways, they are not identical. A role refers to the behavior expected from a certain status holder, while a type describes a fixed pattern of behavior or consists of a significant number of traits; a role is usually limited to a specific area of life, while a type covers a range of features; a single individual usually plays different roles but belongs to only one or two social types in a lifetime—the one is more temporary and the other more fixed; roles are usually evaluated in terms of efficiency or productiv-

2. The nature of ideal types (of which social type as described here is an instance) is such that "it is possible to identify and describe a social type without ever finding a single living soul who possesses the full range of features typical of the social type model" (Almog 1998, 6).

3. It may be asked how many features of a specific social-type model would be sufficient to connect an individual figure to such a model. There is no exact answer to this question, but it is important to realize that this question can be put to all social-type models (such as prophet or Cynic) and to most models about human beings and their conduct (see Almog 1998, 7 for a discussion of the problem).

4. Social types are also different from stereotypes, which often depend on the exaggerated similarities within groups.

ity, while a social type is perceived as a certain way of being and becomes a reflection of personality and a style of life. Sometimes, but not always, types and roles overlap (for example, in the healing role of the family physician), while performing a role does not always result in a fixed social type (for example, not everyone performing healing functions from time to time can be called a *healer* of some kind). Social types can be local (such as the *cowboy* or *astral prophet*) or can appear across cultures (like the *yuppy* or the *shaman*)—in that case, different demands are placed on an analysis. Although any social type is culturally determined, some find expression across cultural boundaries.

Features of Social-Type Analyses

The following indicators for social-type analyses are relevant to the present argument (see Almog 1998, 17–19).

First, what is needed is the building of a prototype model and the putting together of a database of the specific social types. In most cases, enough examples and cross-cultural models are available. (This is certainly the case for the shamanic model, which has ample cross-cultural verification and application.)

Second, it is necessary to develop a sociohistorical sense of the roots of the social type within a specific setting and an understanding of its cultural mechanisms and dynamics. This refers to the fibers connecting a social type to a specific cultural setting. In the case of Jesus of Nazareth, the social type has to be located within a first-century Galilean setting.

Third, an analysis of the various aspects of the social type within a specific setting is needed. In this case, these aspects under investigation are especially the nature and content of the sources. Certain types of stories and specific kinds of phenomena are ascribed to and associated with specific social types, and these need to be identified in each particular case. As for Jesus of Nazareth, an analysis of the sources (their nature and contents) cannot be divorced from the kind of social type that he was, and finding mutual links between, on the one hand, the sources and the dynamics of the transmission of the sources and, on the other hand, the social type provides an additional fiber supporting the overall construction.

With these remarks, a choice has been made against at least two other ways of using social-type models for understanding Jesus as historical figure.

One way that has been dismissed is to insist that only models or concepts from the original sources should be used (such as *prophet, teacher,* or *rabbi*). When a model helps interpreters to discover what is there and to identify the interaction and dynamics of cultural elements, it does not matter so much whether the concepts used are those of the natives or of the researcher. The problem with current historical Jesus research at this point is that whichever social type is used, it is done within a history-of-ideas approach.

For these reasons it is not better to use, say, the concept *prophet* (used in the Gospels) than that of *holy man* or *shaman* (not used in the sources). Because of the above features of assumed scripts, it is possible to use a local concept, such as *prophet*, without being able to identify or understand the cultural dynamics of the social type. Whether a local term (*emic*) or an outsider's term (*etic*) is used, interpreters have to learn how a specific world works, and how its internal dynamics are interconnected.

Comparison does not, in the first instance, take place at the level of concepts (which already assumes that within different settings the same concept has the same meaning) but at a more fundamental level of the underlying system and constitution. In a dialogical interpretive process, there will for any case be elements of cross-cultural translation that take place.

The second way to be avoided is to use anthropological models simply to add a new label to an already identified list of features in the Jesus tradition. In my view, very little has been gained if all the features associated with a particular model can be listed in the gospel traditions independently of the model and then can be compared to the features of the model (as drawn up from an overview of such a model). For example, the use of millenarian models for describing Jesus as millenarian prophet and the early Christian movement as a millenarian movement comes very close to being a new label for old lists of features.[5] A model should add value to existing insights and knowledge about the sources and the figure—it should allow us to make comparisons on the fundamental level

---

5. In my view, very little new light has been shed or insight gained when the Gospel list is compared to the millenarian list, and it is found that most features match (see Allison 1998, 61–74), or that at least some features are dissimilar (see Theissen 1999). The four features of Theissen's description of the Jesus movement as millenarian movement (*Revitalisationsbewegung, nativistischer Bewegung, prophetische Bewegung,* and *Heilsbewegung*) can in any case be established independently of any millenarian model.

and to understand the cultural dynamics as they manifest in this particular case. This is something different from the application of social-scientific or anthropological models after the data have been given their primary sense by the sources.[6] When used as evidence and not testimonies, the explicit and conscious (cross-cultural) models of the historian provide the setting for determining sense and meaning.

Summary

Being able to identify a historical figure with a specific social type in such an analysis is highly significant. It can help to distinguish that figure from other social types in that setting; it can provide insight into the underlying cultural dynamics of the figure's life and of the origin of the stories about the figure; and it can provide a handle to understand the features ascribed to the figure.

In this type of analysis, Jesus's social type not only needs cross-cultural verification and credibility in the first-century setting, but it should also be able to account both for all the strands of gospel evidence (e.g., prophecy, healings, and teachings) and the overall pictures of the Gospels (at least the majority of canonical Gospels). A social type is not simply added as a label, and neither does it *come up* after being immersed in the sources for some time. It has to be demonstrated that such a social type fits the first-century Galilean world of Jesus and makes sense as a background to the various strands of gospel traditions. A decision about Jesus's social type should therefore be the result of an analytical interpretive process in which various fibers interconnect: a picture of the first-century world and worldview, together with an interpretation of the gospel evidence within that context, play an integrated role.

The hypothesis of this study is that the model of the shamanic figure can indeed account for the variety of features and functions ascribed to Jesus and can even offer explanatory power to understand the cultural dynamics of such a figure behind the gospel reports. In fact, while all studies contain some picture of Jesus's social type, the critical issues are not only to include the totality of Jesus's activities in such a description but also to ground a description of Jesus's social type in a proper analysis

---

6. Denton clearly shows that in the documents-as-testimonies approach of the authenticity paradigm, models are applied after the sources have been given a sense by means of the tacit context of the historian (2004, 182–83).

of that social type, of the historical setting, and of the historical personage. In other words, the social type should not only label the features
and functions but also give explanatory power to understand the dynamic
processes associated with such a social type within the particular historical
and cultural setting. It will be argued that as a cross-cultural social type,
the shaman has a universal distribution in human cultures and consists
of a family of traditions about religious specialists who, in a natural and
regular way, combine the features and functions often attributed to Jesus
and can account for the whole spectrum of cultural processes constituting
Jesus as historical figure.

Making Sense of Shamanic Studies

The study of shamanism has proved "remarkably resilient" in a number of
academic disciplines (including among scholars of religion, anthropology,
archaeology, and psychology) and remains a favorite topic of many scholars
(see, e.g., Atkinson 1992). Defining *a shaman* and describing *shamanism*,
however, remain challenging tasks if only for the reason that these terms
belong to an "analyst's category" (Riches 1994, 382) that does not always
easily fit onto the real world.

A very basic feature of shamanism to be taken into account is that it
is not a religion but a complex of notions and practices within religions;
it is the complex of beliefs, rites, and traditions clustered around the shaman and his or her activities (see Hultkrantz 1973, 36; Siikala 1987, 208).
Therefore, one cannot belong to *shamanism*, but one can participate in or
benefit from this pattern of religious beliefs and activities, and in special
circumstances one can become a shaman. This feature constitutes the very
basic challenge in shamanic studies: how to identify and describe this complex, which exists only within a specific religious system or within various
specific religious systems. What constitutes this identifiable complex?

Within scholarly circles, there is no agreement on how the terms
shaman and *shamanism* should be used: whether they should be restricted
to the culture-specific and geographically limited area of Siberia where
the study of shamanism originated, or whether they should be applied to
various ecstatic types of religious practitioners all over the world.

Therefore, both the complex cultural phenomenon itself and the history of scholarly interpretation contribute to the difficulty of finding a
proper definition. Three specific challenges have to be overcome when

trying to make sense of the vast literature on the shaman and shaman-ism. First, *shaman* is a term with a history. Second, shamanism is studied by different academic disciplines and each offers its own set of concepts. Third, most studies of shamanism address "local shamanism rather than shamanism writ large" (Atkinson 1992, 321).

Shaman: A Term with a History

The term *shaman* has a quasi-emic (quasi-local) status that was first as-signed to a particular Siberian phenomenon but later transported to oc-currences in many other regions of the world (it achieved an etic status). The shaman was first recognized as a religious practitioner of specific Siberian hunting tribes. There is, however, no agreement about where the word *shaman* comes from and exactly what it means. It is commonly claimed that the term *šaman* (from which *shaman* comes) originated from the Tungus people of Siberia, meaning something like "one who is excited, moved, raised" (Walsh 1989c, 2; Lewis 1989, 45), while others argue that the meaning of the original Tungus-Mongol word *šaman* is "to know" (see Ripinsky-Naxon 1993, 69; Lee 1999, 22–25).[7]

As an analytical concept it was, however, soon applied to figures outside that region and even outside the realm of hunter-gatherers. Consequently, more than one type of definition is available today. A clear distinction, therefore, exists between those who believe the concept should be used for the Siberian region only and scholars who apply the term for phenomena outside that area.

The first group (culture-specific definitions) consists of scholars work-ing in the Siberian area (and some British anthropologists) who think that the term *shaman* should be restricted to that area and the culture-specific religious phenomena covered by the original definition.[8] Although it is to

7. There is, however, no certainty about the origin of this term in the Tungus language, which is spoken by about 6 percent of the inhabitants of Siberia (see Thorpe 1993, 19). It is also suggested that the word ultimately derives from the Vedic *sram*, "to heat oneself" (see Lewis 1984, 5). The situation, as Reinhard points out, is that "there is a Tungus word, its ultimate origin and meaning uncertain, associated with a Tungus phenomenon, its ultimate origin and original form uncertain" (1976, 14; see also Voigt 1984, 14–15; Thorpe 1993, 21–22). It is not even certain whether the modern term shaman is derived from the Tungus word. Some scholars propose that the modern European forms, for example in French or German, come directly from the modern Persian word *šaman* (see Voigt 1984, 14; Grim 1983, 15–16) or from Iranian origins (see Kingsley 1994, 195).

8. Kehoe (2000, 102), for example, states: "Good scholarship, good science, and

be expected that if the term is used in this sense, it would be easy to identify specific characteristics, this is not the case, since significant differences exist in scholarly circles with regard to every specific detail of shamanism in the Siberian area. It is furthermore clear that there are significant variations of shamanism even within the Siberian regions (see Kehoe 2000,16).[9]

A variation on this type of definition is sought by those claiming that the term *shaman* belongs exclusively to hunter-gatherer societies. In his analysis of magico-religious practitioners, Winkelman finds that the "shamanic healer complex," as he calls it, evolves with the socioeconomic evolution of societies.[10]

> The research here indicates that agriculture, sedentary lifestyles, and political integration are the social conditions that differentiate the shaman from the shaman/healer, the healer, and the medium, and are the conditions responsible for the change in shamanism. (Winkelman 1990, 313)

Different kinds of shamanisms are therefore identified within particular types of societies: respectively, shamans with hunter-gatherer

---

ethics oblige anthropologists to maintain the terms 'shaman' and 'shamanism' primarily to Siberian practitioners so called in their homelands."

9. A description of Siberian shamans reveals that they do not agree on the number of levels of the cosmos; not every group agrees on the number of souls a person possesses; the calling of the shaman has no fixed pattern; while some shamanic calling is inherited, other shamanic calling is received by means of special selection; amongst some groups, only men become shamans, and in others, men and women become shamans; the drum, which is an item of special importance in performing shamanic tasks, has disappeared from some groups; among some groups, the shaman functions as psychopomp, while it is absent from other groups (Eliade 1964; Thorpe 1993, 22–40). These variations depend on the indicators used, on the specific level, and on the cross-cultural section in which the indicators are identified (see Alekseenko 1984, 86; Voigt 1984, 14; Atkinson 1992, 308).

10. Within the shamanic complex, Winkelman distinguishes between shamans, shamans/healers, healers, and mediums (see 1990, 326–29; 1992, 25). The distinction, for example, between the shaman and the medium is that the shaman is the "form which ASC based magico-religious practitioners tend to take in hunting and gathering societies," while the medium is "the form these practitioners take in agricultural societies with political integration beyond the local community." In addition, Winkelman adds the sorcerer/witch category as practitioners involved in malevolent acts. The problem with this last category is that it disregards the fact that any magico-religious–practitioner role is also connected to social labeling: any shaman, magician, or other kind of practitioner has the potential of falling into disrepute. While the notion that one person's miracle worker is another person's sorcerer or magician is widely accepted nowadays, the other side of this coin is that the same person can fall out of grace with the community. Seen in a diachronic way, witches and sorcerers were often the shamans or medical practitioners of a community.

societies, shamans/healers with sedentary societies, healers with agricultural societies, and mediums with agricultural/pastoralist societies (see also Winkelman 1992, 28).[11] Of special significance is the fact that although Winkelman reserves the term *shaman* only for persons found in hunting and gathering societies, he quite aptly points out that all the practitioners labeled as shamans, shaman/healers, healers, and mediums share major characteristics in common, namely, involvement with the "shamanic healer complex" or biologically based ASC practices (see Winkelman 1990, 313, 332; 1992, 25–36, 46).

The second type of definition belongs to scholars who apply the *shaman* concept to worldwide phenomena outside the Siberian context. The result is that the term came to be used for a worldwide phenomenon (see Winthrop 1991b, 255; Gilberg 1984, 25).

Most influential were the publications of Mircea Eliade, who, according to Reinhard, captured the essence of shamanism for many to follow (see 1976, 14). Eliade limits his definition to specialists of the sacred "who know how to employ ecstasy for the benefit of the community," and this ecstasy is always linked to soul flights (1961, 153). To many scholars following Eliade, the shamanic journey remains the most important feature of shamanism (see Gilberg 1984, 23; Harner 1988, 9; Walsh 1989a, 26; Ripinsky-Naxon 1993, 92).

Whatever the origin of the term *shaman*, it has been widely adopted by anthropologists and scholars of comparative religion to refer to religious practitioners in diverse cultures (often using diverse English terms, including *medicine men, witch doctors, sorcerers, magicians, healers,* and *seers*; see Eliade 1961, 153; Gilberg 1984, 21; Walsh 1989c, 2; Winkelman 1990, 309).

Differences between Scholarly Traditions

The meanings of the terms *shaman* and *shamanism* vary considerably among different national and ethnographic traditions. In the Anglophone world, they have been widely adopted by American cultural anthropologists and generally have been avoided by British social anthropologists,

11. See also the counterexamples discussed by Townsend, which show that shamanism "is not a unique phenomenon limited to one cultural setting" (1997, 436).

who prefer terms such as *spirit mediumship* for probably the same range of persons (see Overholt 1985, 8; Lewis 1986, 78–79; Thorpe 1993, 7).

Furthermore, a variety of distinct discourses were created in scholarly circles to describe the same human phenomena encountered in shamanism. An instance of this is the almost unending (and insolvable) debate about trance, ecstasy, possession, and the like, which belong to shamanism. As Taves points out: "Psychiatrists most commonly refer to dissociation (or more distantly hysteria); anthropologists to trance, spirit-possession, and altered states of consciousness; and religionists to visions, inspiration, mysticism, and ecstasy" (1999, 7). In the above mentioned definition of Eliade the confusion is visible: shamans are religious specialists who know how to employ *ecstasy*, and ecstasy "always involves trance" and the trance is interpreted as "a temporary abandonment of the body by the soul of the shaman" (1961, 153).

For some scholars, it is important to indicate that ecstasy and trance are different phenomena,[12] while others maintain that they are "actually two words for the same thing; *trance* being a medical term and *ecstasy* the theological and humanistic term" (Hultkrantz 1988, 38).[13] Others wish to argue that possession differs from trance or ecstasy, and some believe that possession is not an ASC.[14]

There is no easy solution to these problems because what is an *emic* (local) term in one context is an *etic* (scientific) term in another.[15] It is therefore the case that definitions and field observations differ because observers differ about what constitutes different altered states, such as trance or possession (see Peters & Price-Williams 1980, 400).

Focus on Local Definitions of the Shaman

It should be apparent from the above definitions and descriptions that in many (most?) instances, definitions of the shaman and descriptions of

---

12. Pilch wants to make a distinction between trance and ecstasy. Not all trance is ecstasy, he argues; the "religious context of the experience" determines ecstasy (1995, 54). Reinhard points out that ecstasy often has the connotation of rapturous delight, and that trance is a more neutral term.

13. Bourguignon distinguishes between trance, possession, and possession trance as three distinct phenomena that characterize distinct kinds of communities (see 1968).

14. For Bourguignon, possession is not a type of ASC (see 1979, 249).

15. In the ancient Greek world, Burkert points out, ecstasy is a local term referring to an ASC ("das 'Heraustreten aus dem normalen Zustand'") (1962, 45).

shamanism are given from local perspectives and are not about them writ large. The legacy of Eliade (as seen above) is the insistence on the soul flight as the constituting feature of the shaman. It should, however, be noted that in Shirokogoroff's classic study of Tungus shamanism, the soul journey is absent from the definition, and spirit-possession and control of spirits form the essence of it (see Reinhard 1976, 14; Peters & Price-Williams 1980, 408 n. 1).[16]

The implications of this insight need to be emphasized. A local definition of a shaman cannot randomly be used in order to establish the existence of shamanism in a specific case. Case-specific definitions (local terms and definitions, or a singular emphasis on, for example, soul flights) are applicable in some instances but are not very useful as cross-cultural models. In addition, even if there were agreement on what constitutes the essence of shamanism, it would still remain a question how specific instances comply with that essence.[17]

What is needed is a cross-cultural model of the shaman and shamanism. The advice of Voigt on this issue is valuable:

> The shaman is neither a word nor a figure fulfilling some roles. It is a person living in a given society. The researcher of shamanism has to describe the person and the society in its entirety, including historical and psychological facts as well. A comparative picture of shamans can only give a solid basis for a valid systematization of shamanism as such. (1984, 17)

16. Lewis talks about engagement in mystical flights and other "out-of-body experiences" (1984, 9; 1986, 88). Hultkrantz insists against Eliade's definition that shamanism does not always include soul flights, since in some cases the ecstasy may be solely concerned with clairvoyance or the calling of spirits (see 1984, 34 n. 4). Winthrop extends the narrow definition to include "trance behavior and mystical flight" (1991b, 255), while for Peters and Price-Williams, the only attribute is "that the specialist enter into a controlled ASC on behalf of his community" (1980, 408 n. 3). For Walsh, shamanic altered states include traveling to other realms (e.g., soul journeys) and interacting with other entities (e.g., during spirit-possession) (1993, 742).

17. Despite narrow definitions, the historical identification of a specific individual as a shaman is not always easy. Gilberg, for instance, operates with a very specific definition of shamanism but admits that "it is not always possible to apply it absolutely, since some characteristics are shared with other types of religious specialists" (1984, 23). Definitions become blurred in empirical situations, Jones says (1976, 31). It is clear from most particular studies of shamanism that so-called classic definitions have been modified, altered, and adapted to local needs and cultural systems (see, e.g., Jones 1976, 53; Lewis 1986, 87; Thorpe 1993, 25–40). Another way of putting this is that the shamans of the narrow definition hardly ever exist, or that they existed in specific case studies.

It is therefore necessary to find a model with cross-cultural validity that can be used in a comparative project. It will be argued that a homomorphic model of the shamanic complex indeed offers these possibilities, but it is necessary to first look at the foundation of this complex.

ASC Experiences as the Foundation of the Shamanic Complex

There have been attempts to justify the universal distribution of shamanism on a theory of geographical migration (see Walsh 1989a, 29; Winthrop 1991b, 255). A weakness of such a theory, however, is the strange assumption that shamanism remained essentially consistent throughout its migration, while language and other social practices changed drastically (see Walsh 1989c, 7).[18] While such theories remain interesting, they cannot be used to justify the widespread distribution of shamanism as a homoversal pattern of religious practitioners.[19]

ASCs Are Complex but Normal Biopsychosocial Human Phenomena

The various definitions of the shaman and descriptions of shamanism show that for a long period of time scholars have realized that a common pattern underlies the variety of religious practitioners or shamans. Both the induction techniques and the observable outcome and manifestation point toward a biologically based potential for ASC as the common denominator.[20] Analysis of a large number of religious practitioners in the shamanic

18. It is often argued that shamanism was part of the culture of the Paleolithic hunting-and-gathering groups that migrated from Asia to populate the Americas some ten- to fifteen thousand years ago (see Winkelman 1990, 320; Thorpe 1993, 41). Therefore the term shamanism is often used by scholars involved in the study of prehistoric times (see Voigt 1984, 15).

19. The term homoversal was coined by Rosemont "to signify 'for all human beings, physiologically and mentally constituted as they are'" (1988, 52) and utilized to great effect, for example, by Krüger, as what is common to human beings on a physiological and mental level (see 1995, 160, 205).

20. Research shows that a variety of these ASC induction techniques lead to "a very similar alteration in consciousness, characterized by a state of parasympathetic dominance in which the frontal cortex is dominated by slow wave patterns originating in the limbic system and related projections into the frontal parts of the brain . . . Experimental and clinical studies . . . indicate that a wide range of 'transcendental states' are based in a common underlying neurobiochemical pathway involving a biogenic amine-temporal lobe

complex confirms that the universal foundation of these practices is the biologically based ASC and associated potentials (see Winkelman 1992, 9, 125).

It should be realized right from the start that what is experienced as the *normal* or *ordinary* state of consciousness in any given cultural setting is a construction and not a given—it is, in fact, the product of a variety of factors. Cultural forces are apt to select and prescribe from the broad spectrum of human potentialities those elements that are to be described as "normal" or "ordinary." As Tart says:

> Each of us is, however, born into a particular culture, and the culture may be viewed as a group of people who recognise the existence of only some of these potentials and have decided that some of those they recognize are 'good' and thus to be developed, while others are 'bad' and thus to be discouraged. (1980, 245)

The result is that what is experienced as normal or ordinary consciousness "is a *construction*, not a given, and a *specialized* construction that in many ways is quite arbitrary" (1980, 245). The important point is that in any society "a finite set of possible phases of consciousness is declared normal" (Laughlin et al. 1990, 142). This remark is substantiated by a large number of studies showing that within different cultures, various phases are taken as normal and ordinary, and people in that culture are socialized to consider those definitive of their own and others' mindsets. That the so-called *normal state of consciousness* is a cultural construct and not a given is agreed upon by a large variety of researchers in this field (see Zinberg 1977, 21).

Three features of ASCs will briefly be described: they are biologically based (*bio*psychosocial) states, they are psychosocial (bio*psychosocial*) phenomena, and they can be induced in a large number of ways resulting in a whole spectrum of different states of consciousness.

ASCs as *Bio*psychosocial Phenomena

Consciousness is not something inside the body; it is neither a property of the mind nor a separate phenomenon but a manner of existence in the world. It is not a "thing" but an ever-changing stream of being (see Cupitt 1995, 16–18; Kriel 2000, 93–94, 116, 122 ; Capra 2002, 33–37).[21]

---

interaction" (Winkelman 1992, 93).

21. Laughlin, McManus, and d'Aquili offer a similar definition: "we have said that

Human beings are neither machines nor merely biological or chemical entities but "biopsychosocial systems" (Goodman 1987, 282).

The existence of cultural homoversals has in recent years been analyzed as the product of the universality of the neurobiological systems (see d'Aquili & Laughlin 1975, 34). One such homoversal is certain ASC experiences. The capacity for awareness and consciousness, which are therefore essential products of human bodily evolution, include a broad spectrum of human potentialities of which so-called ASCs are "conditions in which sensations, perceptions, cognition, and emotions are altered" from the point of view of "ordinary consciousness" (Bourguignon 1979, 236).[22] Being born human, Tart says,

> we possess a certain kind of body and nervous system operating in accordance with physical laws governing us and our environment. Thus, there are a very large (although certainly less than infinite) number of potentials, thousands of potentials, which *could* be developed in us. (1980, 245)

It is within this framework that so-called ASCs are to be situated. Like sex, eating, or vocalization, Lambek says, ASCs are

> 'natural' in the sense that, under the right stimuli, it is a condition or activity (or range of conditions or activities) of which the human species at large is capable, the form or manifestation of trance [or ASCs] in any specific context is no more 'natural' (necessary, unmediated, given) than the model that guides it. (1989, 38)

Following Ludwig, ASCs will therefore be used as an umbrella term for

> those mental states, induced by various physiological, psychological, or pharmacological maneuvers or agents, which can be recognised subjectively by the individual himself [or herself] (or by an objective observer of the individual) as representing a sufficient deviation, in terms of subjective experience or psychological func-

---

consciousness is a term referring to the ongoing stream of experience that is mediated by a functional neural complex. This complex is a continuously transforming entrainment and disentrainment of neural networks which, among other things, models the world. The transcendental world that it models commonly includes the being as it operates in the world" (1990, 90).

22. "The physiological effects of ASC indicate a biological basis for practices which utilize such alterations of consciousness. A wide variety of procedures induce such changes, suggesting that shamanism and other ASC traditions are a natural manifestation of the human mind, and that multiple independent inventions of traditions have likely occurred" (Winkelman 1992, 109).

tioning, from certain general norms as determined by the subjective experience and psychological functioning of that individual
during alert, waking consciousness. (1968, 69–70)

ASCs as Bio*psychosocial* Phenomena

The *psychosocial* in the above heading claims that as a systems phenomenon, consciousness is not only a biological or neurological feature of human nature but also an embedded feature in psychosocial parameters that
co-determine it. In a study of the social and cultural patterning of ASCs,
it was found that such states exist in religious contexts in 90 percent of
the sample of 488 societies. In other words, in a very large percentage
of human societies for which data is available, ASCs manifest themselves
regularly within religious rituals (see Bourguignon 1979, 245). This means
that they have methodologically cultivated means of inducing ASCs.
While it is indeed shamans who enter such states on a regular basis, in
such societies many ordinary persons can do the same thing from time to
time (see Siiger 1967, 73).

Depending on which states of consciousness are taken as baseline, all
other states will turn out to be alternative. Thus, what is *altered* from one
point of view (cultural system) is *ordinary* from another. The psychology
of dreaming is a good example of this. In some cultures, people learn how
to manipulate the phases between the waking phase and the dream phase
(called the *hypnagogic* phase) and between the dream phase and the waking
phase (called the *hypnopompic* phase). While only a minority of people in
Western culture is aware of their dreams, people in the above non-Western
cultures have ritual acts by which they manipulate these phases, and, therefore, dream incubation is a common practice among them (see Laughlin et
al. 1990, 144). For example, for one traditional Native American, "'normal waking consciousness' is that unfortunate phase during which the soul
and the body are glued together," while in alternative phases, such as in
dreaming, "the soul is freed from the body so that it can fly and commune
with other souls and spirits" (Laughlin et al. 1990, 226).

There are at least two forces that determine the dynamics of this
process. First, culture provides the content of consciousness experiences
since they are grounded in a cultural environment (see Lewis 1989, 5).
Therefore, ordinary states of consciousness as well as the ASCs in a specific
setting are not stereotyped reactions to specific stimuli or neurological

conditions, but dynamic, goal-oriented processes that the individual has learned from the culture (see Van der Walde 1968, 64).

This is clearly demonstrated by the intake of hallucinogens by native people in eastern Peru. The first experience with the images and sensations of the drug *shori* is usually frightening.[23] The visions that these men see are learned from other men:

> Jaguars, snakes and beautiful women cannot be found in a veg-
> etable substance or located at nerve ends . . . The young men must
> learn to shape the visual illusion and the physiological sensations
> into the mold and the form of the spirits. (Siskind, quoted in
> Bourguignon 1979, 265)

Neither the drug nor the ASC contains its own "content" but only modify human consciousness for a time (see 1979, 241). The shaman, for example, is transported to a land beyond, "whose geography he already knows because he has heard it described innumerable times before; what he finds 'on the other side' substantiates the validity of tradition" (Furst 1972, xiii).[24] Referring to the way in which traditional scriptures are used in visionary material (clear references but no word-for-word quotations), Rowland (1982, 361) remarks that it "shows how a mind saturated in the scriptures can utilize the imagery to express the character of the vision. There is no conscious attempt to quote Scripture." This point confirms that images, stories (written or oral), traditions, and the like are both pres-ent and created in the dynamics of ASC experiences.

Second, the nature of these events as cultural events determines the dynamics of the stories and reports about such events. It is those people who have experienced the other side and have gone through the initia-tion who will around such experiences "amass stories and legends about *the way* a shaman acts and *what* he experiences" (Nordland 1967, 177). ASC experiences are by definition not public and objective but private and personal, and whatever a third party knows about them is revealed by the subject. Each and every ASC event or experience, therefore, is a cultural event and is relayed as such.

---

23. This is confirmed by reports about other ASC experiences.

24. This is similar to the Desana shaman who "needs to learn to see the Milky Way as a road, the hills and pools as communal houses of the spirits, and the animals as people" (Goodman 1987, 285).

ASC Induction and Spectrum of States

There are certain stabilizing mechanisms that keep any ordinary system of consciousness in place. It is clear that in order to maintain waking consciousness, an optimal level of exteroceptive stimulation is necessary (see Ludwig 1968, 70 and Tart 1980, 260). Despite these stabilizing controls, a great variety of techniques can be employed that will result in an alteration of the ordinary or baseline state of consciousness. Ludwig mentions at least seventy-five different forms of ASCs that are induced by means of five kinds of conditions:[25]

- reduction of exteroceptive stimulation (such as during solitary confinement);

- sensory overload or bombardment (such as drumming or chanting);

- increased alertness (such as with radar screen operators);

- relaxation of critical faculties (such as during meditation);

- alteration in body chemistry or neurophysiology (using pharmacological agents). (see 1968, 71–75)[26]

Besides the intake of hallucinogenic drugs, ASCs can thus be triggered by both sensory stimulation and sensory deprivation.

Specific techniques can be employed to bring about such alterations in any human being. In everyday language, they can follow from certain bodily conditions or experiences (e.g., highway hypnosis) or from certain illnesses (e.g., fever), from recreational activities (e.g., mood-altering drugs or long-distant running) or from religious practices (e.g., rituals). In other

25. Krippener identifies twenty states of consciousness. These are dreaming, sleeping, hypnagogy (drowsiness before sleep), hypnopomp (semiconsciousness preceding waking), hyperalertness, lethargy, rapture, hysteria, fragmentation, regression, meditation, trance, reverie, daydreaming, internal scanning, stupor, coma, stored memory, expanded consciousness, and normal consciousness (1972). Tart (1980, 243) remarks: "In more than 15 years researching the phenomena called altered states of consciousness, I have been repeatedly impressed with the incredible range of phenomena encompassed by that term and with the high degree of unrelatedness of most of these phenomena."

26. It should be noted that Ludwig lists all the alterations associated with each of these induction areas, immaterial of whether they are associated with an illness, with the intake of drugs, with ritual activities or with something else. While it is valuable to realize that similar alterations in specific subsystems of consciousness can be induced by a variety of techniques (or conditions), it is important to keep in mind that not all these conditions are either pathologies or illness conditions.

words, induction can be deliberate (e.g., meditation) or accidental (e.g., highway trance); it can be by artificial means (e.g., drugs) or within a natural setting (e.g., dancing or drumming); it can be spontaneous (e.g., during solitude, prayer, or illness) or planned in a group activity (e.g., ritual dance or chanting). The states can be common or exceptional, light or deep. Some states are religious, others pathological; some are cultural mechanisms and institutionalized, others dangerous and to be avoided.

Given this wide spectrum of ASC experiences, the debate whether trance and ecstasy are the same is really a linguistic dispute. Suffice it to say that different schemes can be employed for mapping the variety of ASCs (see Craffert 2002, 73–76).[27]

The discovery of opiate receptors and consequently of opiate-like neurotransmitters in the brain (known as *endorphins*) has played a significant role in understanding some of these induction procedures. It was found that under certain conditions the body/brain provides its own painkillers and euphoriants. Prince, for example, suggests that some rituals act as "endorphin pumps," which explains why pain can be alleviated under such conditions (see 1982b, 414; and see 1982a). The presence of these natural euphoriants in the human body, Lewis suggests, "makes Marx's famous epithet about 'religion as the opium of the people' literally and materially true in a most unexpected way" (1989, 34). The point, however, is that similar conditions can be brought about by a large variety of induction methods.

Religious traditions have long recognized the profound influence of bodily conditions on psychological or *spiritual* states. Within specific cultural settings, these are taken for granted and receive little direct attention in any description. Things like going up a mountain, remaining in solitude, keeping awake, and fasting are often only mentioned in passing; but on a bodily and experiential level, these are significant indicators of the type of experiences involved. In anthropological literature there is, however, a close connection between religious experiences and the human body. As Wulff points out, "spiritual discipline" is often directly related to the body: assuming certain postures, depriving oneself of food (fasting) or of sleep, submitting the body to certain discomforts or even control of breathing (1997, 49). The two main ways to achieve an ASC are by

27. The position is confirmed by the discussion by Hultkrantz, who concludes that there is no reason to assume in these studies an opposition between trance (or ecstasy) and possession (2004 [1908], 159).

means of physiological (sensory) deprivation or physiological (sensory) overstimulation.

In shamanic studies, a variety of techniques are described for inducing shamanic states of consciousness, including fasting, sleep deprivation, solitude, dancing, drumming, and drugs. ASC-induction agents include reduction as well as an overload of sensory input and can even include *normal* activities such as extensive running, hunger, thirst, sleep loss, and temperature extremes (see Winkelman 1990, 321; Ludwig 1968, 70–75; Walsh 1993, 744; Peters & Price-Williams 1980, 399; Lewis 1989, 34).

Restricted stimulation is the result of a variety of practices such as meditation or solitude. The examples of religious seekers retreating to mountains, forests, the desert, a hollow tree, a mountain cave, or the top of a pillar or pole are well documented. The inspirational effect of sensory deprivation implied in the stereotyped mystical flight into the wilderness counts amongst one of the other common techniques of inducing an ASC and has been well documented in laboratory experiments. It has been shown that a drastic reduction of environmental input can within a matter of hours result in depersonalization, disturbances of body image, auditory and visual hallucinations, and the like (see Nordland 1967, 169; Wulff 1997, 76).

The effects of sleep loss are well documented as resulting in symptoms such as delusions or visual or tactile hallucinations (see Wulff 1997, 75). Sleep deprivation takes on several forms in religious contexts, including vigils and solitary prayer while fasting—and, for that matter, *involuntary fasting*—appear in many religious traditions as a means of seeking prophetic revelations or visions.[28] In both instances, it results in nutritional deficits, which, whether actively sought or involuntarily encountered, can contribute to changes in the central nervous system, a system that

---

28. The term "involuntary fasting" refers to the often-experienced nutritional deficiencies or chronic malnutrition in traditional societies, which can also contribute to the induction of ASCs (see Winkelman 1992, 95). During the Middle Ages, Kalweit points out, "winter means involuntary fasting and vitamin deficiency . . . During these times, people's body chemistry turned ecstasies and visions into everyday occurrences" (1992, 83–84). Or as Huxley describes it: "After all, every winter in the Middle Ages there was a period of extreme vitamin deficiency; pellagra and other deficiency diseases were very common. On top of the involuntary fasting came the forty days of Lent, where voluntary fasting was imposed upon involuntary fasting, so that by the time Easter came around the mind was completely ready for almost any kind of vision" (1972, 42).

facilitates the induction of ASCs.[29] Several studies suggest that calcium deficiency might be responsible for culturally specific conditions such as *ukuthwasa* among Nguni people (see Wulff 1997, 74) or *pibloktoq* among the polar Eskimo (see Wallace 1972, 374–83). Fasting often goes hand in hand with other ritual activities.

Breath control finds expression in either rhythmic breathing or holding of the breath—both of which influence the intake of oxygen and the proportions of this with carbon dioxide in the bloodstream. An example of this includes the Trascodrugite practice, which Pilch argues can account for the finger-to-the-nose gesture in the book of Ezekiel (8:17) (2002a, 714).[30]

Physiological (sensory) overstimulation is encountered in ritual practices such as drumming, chanting, singing, and dancing. A number of researchers have suggested that the rhythmic music and drumming may affect neural functioning such as the electrical rhythms of the brain (see Wulff 1997, 85). In fact, in many settings the drum remains the shaman's main instrument.

Just as the hallucinations or images are learned from culture, the intake of certain drugs or the exposure to certain conditions conducive to ASCs will not necessarily result in the alteration of consciousness. Tart mentions that experienced marijuana users can, for example, frequently *turn off* the effects of the drug at will (see 1980, 263). It is also well known that the neophyte marijuana user usually has to be taught how to "get stoned," that is, how to get into the state of consciousness associated with marijuana. The transition from one state of consciousness to another can therefore also be learned (see Tart 1980, 264–65). In fact, Walsh remarks that the ability to access altered states "appears to be a learnable skill," and

29. Winkelman points out that food and water deprivation have a direct effect upon the pituitary and adrenal glands, which affect the hypothalamus and hypocampal-septal systems (1992, 95). In an abbreviated formulation, Wulff explains the physiology of fasting thus: "the brain is nourished exclusively by glucose (simple sugar), which the body cannot store for more than a few hours. During total fasts of even a few days, glycogen, the form in which carbohydrates are stored in the liver for future use, is exhausted, triglycerides (a combination of the trihydric alcohol glycerol and fatty acid) in body fat are broken down, a process that frees the components for use. Finally, when body fat is depleted, muscle protein is broken down into amino acids, most of which can be converted into glucose" (1997, 72).

30. Trascodrugites practice refers to the ritual practice of a particular sect group whereby worshippers are said to hold a branch to their noses in order to induce ASCs (see Pilch 2002a, 708–9).

practitioners may eventually learn to enter desired states rapidly and easily (1989b, 35). It also seems clear, both in the use of LSD and meditation, that the experiences differ for the same person under different historical, social, or psychological conditions (see Zinberg 1977, 32).[31]

A fascinating insight, as d'Aquili and Newberg indicate, is that neurophysiologically speaking, ASC experiences can be driven from the body up ("bottom-up") or from the brain down ("top-down") (1993, 5–6).

> Intriguingly, the same neurological mechanisms triggered by the physical behaviors of ritual from the bottom-up can also be triggered by the mind working in top-down fashion—that is, the mind can set this mechanism in motion, starting with nothing more substantial than a thought. (Newberg, d'Aquili & Rause 2001, 97)

In practice, solitude or meditative prayer ("brain-down"), just like drumming and dancing ("body-up"), can result in similar (or different) ASCs (see further Craffert 2002, 74–75).

From this overview, it should be apparent that at least three indicators can be used to identify specific practices or experiences as ASCs: the presence of deliberate induction techniques, external behavior, and claims by subjects; and when practitioners are members of a culture known to foster such practices, their claims can be fitted into such a framework (see Winkelman 1992, 22).

Above it was said that cultural events are experienced as real within specific cultural systems and, therefore, are objectively there without being ontologically objective. At this point it is, however, necessary to look at the dynamics by means of which people construct such cultural realities.

A Homomorphic Model of the Shamanic Complex

A homomorphic model is one that is not built to scale or as an exact replica, but that reproduces only selected salient features of an object or phenomenon. It is a model that has cross-cultural validity in dealing with phenomena in a variety of cultural systems (see above, pp. 23–24). It provides "an explanatory context for investigation rather than a definitive de-

---

31. Prince also points out that certain opiates do not necessarily create a euphoric state but operate as painkillers: "It is only a minority of subjects, including those who have a previous history of morpheme addiction and those with certain personality characteristics . . . that report an unusually pleasant state of euphoria after a single dose" (1982a, 312).

scription of the phenomenon" (Grim 1983, 11) and has several advantages to local models.

The Shamanic Complex

In an analysis of shamanism, Lewis shows that when the focus is shifted from the question, what is a shaman? to, what is the shamanic complex?,

> . . . all the features that have been distinguished as signifying separate phenomena associated with contrasting social formations (past or present) actually regularly occur together within a single cultural context . . . All these features, which others have seen as separate self-sustaining styles of religiosity, are in reality constituent elements in the composite shamanistic complex. (1986, 84–85)

In other words, the shamanic complex consists of a family of traditions, which, as a regularly occurring pattern in many cultural systems, consists of a configuration of certain features (controlled ASC experiences) and certain social functions (such as healing, mediating, prophecy, exorcism, and spirit control or possession) that flow from these experiences. Based on an overview of a number of studies of shamanism and shamans, two features appear to occur regularly: Shamans experience specific ASCs, which can include otherworldly journeys, visions, possession, mediumistic and transformation experiences; and, unlike any other religious social type, shamans appear to combine several functions or roles that are usually separate in other social types.[32]

This insight is confirmed by Winkelman's study of forty-seven societies, which points toward the universal presence of "magico-religious practitioners" (his term), grouped together in the *shamanic complex* (see 1992, 17, 47). He illustrates that shamans are the original representatives of a cultural adaptation to "biologically based ASC and associative adaptive potentials." He further shows that the pattern has remained stable despite the socioeconomic development of societies from hunter-gatherer

---

32. The following definitions of shaman and shamanism have been consulted: Eliade (1961, 153), Hulkrantz (1973, 34; 1984, 34 n. 4), Reinhard (1976, 16), Peters & Price-Williams (1980, 408 n. 3), Grim (1983, 11–12), Lewis (1984, 9; 1986, 88), Pentikäinen (1984, 127), Gilberg (1984, 22), Siikala (1987, 208), Walsh (1989c, 5), Winthrop (1991b, 255), Thorpe (1993, 6, 132–33), Winkelman (1992, 9), Townsend (1997, 431–33), and Lee (1999, 22–33).

or fishing societies through agricultural and sedentary societies to societies with permanent residency and political integration.[33]

Both the essential features and the essential functions of the shaman need, however, to be explored.

Essential Features of Shamanism: ASC Experiences

Shamans are nowadays commonly described as those religious entrepreneurs who enter some kind of ASC for the benefit of the community. As Townsend says, "the raison d'être of shamanism is to interact with the spirit world for the benefit of those in the material world" (1997, 431).

Employing the term ASC in the description of the model (instead of "local" terms such as trance, soul journey, ecstasy, or the like) has a definite cross-cultural currency because it covers the variously experienced states of consciousness. It provides a theoretical handle to understand the biopsychosocial dynamics of shamanism. It will also be argued that as a combination of regularly occurring features and functions, the constituting elements of the shamanic complex do not appear in this pattern amongst other religious specialists. The notion of the *biologically based ASCs* not only gives the shamanic complex the potential to go beyond any local labeling of phenomena but also adds explanatory power to it.

It seems clear from the different studies that journey experiences constitute an important characteristic of the shaman's type. To many scholars, following Eliade, the shamanic journey remains the most important feature of shamanism (see Hultkrantz 1973, 29; Gilberg 1984, 23; Harner 1988, 9; Walsh 1989a, 26; Ripinsky-Naxon 1993, 92). The shamanic journey can be described as the shaman's experience of separation from the body, largely losing awareness of the body and environment and traveling as a free soul or spirit to one of the worlds in the specific shamanic cosmology—the upper, middle, or lower world (see Walsh 1993, 748).[34]

---

33. Winkelman insists that the term shaman should be restricted only to those who belong to the pattern in the hunting-and-gathering phase. Other terms should describe the later development of the pattern. Also, in a randomly chosen group of forty-two cultures, Peters and Price-Williams find that the element common in all cases of shamanic magico-religious practitioners was controlled ASC on behalf of the community (see 1980, 408 n. 3).

34. The shamanic journey has many variations in cultures. Some ascend and others descend, while others take a trip into a river or lake (see Ripinsky-Naxon 1993, 94). The Eskimo shaman, for example, journeys to the depths of the sea in order to placate the angry goddess Takanakapsaluk, who withholds animals after breaches of taboo (see Walsh

In addition to journey states, another major shamanic alternate state is the possession state, which refers to "states in which the shaman's consciousness is experienced as being taken over to varying degrees by an ego-alien entity, usually believed to be a spirit" (Walsh 1993, 744; and see Lewis 1989, 49). Possession by demons, animals, the Holy Spirit, or tribal spirits, and mental states or trance states, Ludwig points out, "all take on the flavour of the predominant cultural values, beliefs, and expectations" (1968, 76). The shaman seems to be a master of spirits, with the implication that this inspired person incarnates spirits by becoming voluntarily possessed (see Lewis 1989, 45, 49).

It should furthermore be realized that not all shamanic ASCs consist of the same degree of intensity (some are merely experienced as visions, others as journeys or possessions) and not all shamanic experiences can be regarded as equivalent (see Ripinsky-Naxon 1993, 96–97). The shaman's state of consciousness may even vary perceptibly from journey to journey or from possession to possession (see Walsh 1993, 745). This explains why a single description (such as "journey state" or "possession" or "ecstasy") cannot capture all instances within this complex. This point confirms the value of the category of ASC experiences for this task.

An additional point of insight is that within the life of a specific shaman, changes and variation can often be detected. Lewis points out that the classical shamanic study of Shirokogoroff illustrates that ecstasy, possession, trance, and the like are phases in the life of a shaman and not adverse phenomena (see 1986, 90–91). This is confirmed by Loeb's observations regarding the evolution of the inspirational type of shaman (one who, in addition to ecstasy, is involved in prophesying and exorcism) from the noninspirational type of shaman, which Loeb called the seer (see 1929, 62). The seer is primarily involved in obtaining visions.

These examples show that within and between different historical and cultural settings, shamans actually experience a range of ASCs. Based on these ASC experiences, shamans perform specific functions that will here

---

1989a, 27). In some cultural traditions, journeys are to the middle world (that is, on earth) and sometimes to the upper world. Journeys usually have the function of intervening with spirits or gods on behalf of human beings. Journeys to the upper world often start from mountain- or treetops or from cliffs. The shaman may experience being transformed into a bird soaring to the upper world or climbing the world axis in the form of a tree, ladder, or rainbow (see Reinhard 1976, 17; Walsh 1989a, 27; Vitebsky 1995, 70–73).

be divided between, on the one hand, healing and the control of spirits and, on the other hand, teaching and education.

Essential Functions of the Shaman: Healing and Control of Spirits

All studies indicate that shamans combine in their activities a variety of functions that are also associated with various other distinct social types. These include healing, divination, prophecy, mediation, protection of spirits, retrieval of souls, exorcism, psychopomp, sacrifice, protection of the community, and the like. Given the variety of functions, it is not surprising that the shaman is described as a figure combining functions often separated among other religious practitioners. In the words of Ripinski-Naxon, for example, "in the person of the shaman is embodied, all at once, the community's healer, the mystic, and the intellectual" (1993, 64).[35] In modern jargon, Vitebsky says shamans "are at once doctors, priests, social workers and mystics" (1995, 10).

When looking at the functions ascribed to shamans, it is clear that when engaged in activities on behalf of a group or community, they center on healing, divination, and the control of all kinds of spirits, such as those of animals, of the weather, and of divine entities (see Voigt 1984, 16; Winthrop 1991b, 256; Gill 1986, 217; Winkelman 1990, 318; 1992, 9).

Similar to the other phenomena associated with shamanism, healing takes on the features of a particular cultural system. Healing mostly deals with the loss of the soul or attack by spirits (such as demons) and can also be the result of malevolence from other religious practitioners. Some shamans make use of natural remedies (see Winkelman 1992, 49), but most often the remedy is of a spiritual nature. The ASC-based activities (of the shaman) can also form the foundation of various therapeutic techniques. Usually being possessed by a spirit, the shaman is not the subject but the manipulator of spirits and, therefore, is also equipped as exorcist (in cultures where spirit-possession appears). Therefore, the shaman is often called a *healed healer*. It would be a mistake to assume that such figures only heal while in a trance, and that everything they say is received in an ASC (see Russel 1964, 161). It is necessary to grasp the dynamic processes in which

---

35. Many older definitions of shamanism indeed describe the shaman as a combined figure: priest, healer, and prophet at the same time (see Voigt 1984, 16; Pentikänen 1984, 127; Siikala 1987, 208; Dixon 2004 [1908], 11).

such figures are inscribed instead of focusing only on their reports (which usually highlight only the benefits for the community).

Since shamans are not private mystics, their ASCs are intended to serve their communities; or as Hultkrantz says, "a shaman's foremost task is to mediate between his [sic] human associates and the spirit world" (1988, 35). Therefore, shamanic divination comes in many forms (see further below). The content of their communication, like the realms of their flights and the images of their visions, is provided by the cultural tradition. The kind and content of the communication (teaching or prophecy) in each instance is determined by the cultural system and carries the features of the ASC-based experiences, and is not merely the product of learning.

Mediation also includes the obtaining of animals or fish and providing protection of all sorts (see Vitebsky 1995, 108–12). Because shamans provide direct access to divine or spirit forces, they act especially when need arises, or when ordinary people are powerless against hostile forces. In addition to these regularly occurring functions, the following special abilities are often associated with the shaman: weather control, immunity to fire, the ability to transform oneself into an animal, and death and rebirth experiences (see Gill 1986, 217; Winkelman 1992, 47–50). The logic is not that they can control natural elements, but that they can control the spirits in and of these elements. Animals, in this worldview, are not just animals; they have animal spirits, and so with the other elements of nature.

Since shamans often operate in small-scale societies, shamanic activities increase when the society comes under stress: for instance, with starvation, poor hunting, bad weather, and other crises (see Gilberg 1984, 25). The function of guiding people's souls to the hereafter in some instances has a counterpart in the function of assisting people on their brief journey of life (see Ripinsky-Naxon 1993, 96).

Essential Functions of the Shaman: Divination and Education (Teacher, Prophet, Sage)

Shamanic figures are widely experienced as both the creators and preservers of the myths, knowledge, and traditions of their societies. In traditional societies, not just anyone controls cultural knowledge, and not every individual can contribute to the creation of "new" knowledge. Remarks about the role that the shaman plays alerted me to the importance of this issue:

"As a historian, mythmaker, and storyteller, the shaman not only reflects the culture of his or her people but directs the development of that culture. The shaman is more knowledgeable, more adept, and more potent in dealing with unseen powers than everyone else in the community" (Krippner 1985, 454). As Hultkrantz says, among the Mohave, for instance, the shamans dream new myths (1985, 453). This is because someone with special qualities is needed to enter the realm where superior knowledge is kept. One of the reasons is that only certain figures know or have access to the cultural ways and means of doing that. Therefore, all shamans, Lewis claims, are mediums; that is to say, they function as a "telephone exchange" between humans and their gods (1989, 49).

Particularly in a world where knowledge is limited and often has to be "stolen" from the divine realm or from other human beings, access to knowledge (especially "new" knowledge for a community) is obtained by the appropriate means. "Since the knowledge held by animals, plants and other natural phenomena is inaccessible to man in his normal waking consciousness, the wise man develops states in which he can communicate directly with the nonhuman world" (Kiefer 1985, 454).

Research on a wide range of experimental laboratory studies indicates a functional role for ASC in eliciting creative thinking and psi abilities.[36] Such phenomena change ordinary experience, break up the habitual experience of the world, dissolve egocentric fixations, and alter the relationship between the conscious and the unconscious. Therefore, it may facilitate divination procedures by providing access to normally unconscious information that is revealed in dreams, or by providing connections between bits of information usually inaccessible in ordinary states of consciousness. In short, ASCs circumvent the normally cognitive processes in seeking novel solutions to problems (see Winkelman 1992, 117–19). Comparative studies indicate the same point:

> It is also interesting that the astrological information imparted to the seer is not a unique feature of Enoch, and merely evidence of its author's special scholastic, cataloguing, 'wisdom' interests. Information about the stars, planets, the cosmos is commonly imparted to shamans in their heavenly tours. They are gaining es-

36. The term psi is used for the profound unitary force underlying phenomena such as extrasensory perception and psychokinesis (see Winkelman 1992, 176–77 n. 1). For an excellent comparison between such phenomena and descriptions of "supernatural" phenomena in the ancient world, see the study of Dodds (1971).

sential knowledge of the universe, thereby establishing a 'larger' context from which to speak about socio-cultural matters. It is this sort of knowledge which lends them prestige and credibility as they report other aspects of their visions which are of more mundane, historical, and immediate concern to the community. (Niditch 1980, 162–63)

An instance of ASC experiences well researched today is that of near-death experiences (NDE). As one study indicates, "Patients' transformational processes after a NDE are very similar and encompass life-changing insight, heightened intuition, and disappearance of fear of death" (Van Lommel et al. 2001, 2040). The list of specific changes noted in patients who had such NDEs is significant: "greater concern for others (patience, tolerance, understanding), a reduction in death anxiety with a corresponding strengthened belief in an afterlife, greater transcendental feelings, a reduction in materialism, increased self-worth, greater appreciation for nature and increased awareness of paranormal phenomena" (Groth-Marnet & Summers 1998, 118).

Given these potentialities, it is understandable why the shaman can function as wisdom teacher, visionary, and prophet. While the shaman operates within a particular cultural system, his or her connection with the body of knowledge of that cultural system is usually different from everyday experiences. In the words of Nordland,

> The ability of primary-process thinking, of making unconventional combinations, like those of the child in his [sic] reflections on his surroundings, are important aspects of creativity. It is highly interesting that this ability is the most characteristic personality trait of the shaman. (1967, 184)

In fact, the very dynamics of polyphasic cultural systems is that fresh ASC experiences (such as visions) may result in new interpretations that transform existing conceptions (of cosmos, self, or others), and that such transformative processes are especially fluid in cases where textual material is not written (see Laughlin et al. 1990, 230–31). It will be shown below that significant changes in ancient Israelite cultural lore were often associated with such ASC experiences.

It is important to realize also that concepts such as *learning, teacher, knowledge*, and the like are all tightly embedded to specific cultural systems and cannot easily be divorced from their settings. When looking at Jesus as teacher or prophet, it is necessary to bring into account these cultural fibers. For example, not only *what* counts as knowledge, but *how* it is acquired, is culturally determined.

The Same Pattern Has Different Names

The discussion in the previous sections shows that the cross-cultural pattern of ASC-based religious practices is well established—despite the variety of terms used. It should therefore be realized that within the family of traditions, many religious specialists, who have unique labels in their own cultures, belong to this pattern.[37] In fact, it should be expected that local terms be used for describing similar phenomena belonging to the pattern. Therefore, it does not really matter whether the practitioner is called *shaman, nganga, isangoma, angaqoq, tietäjä* (or whatever the local term might be).[38]

From this perspective, one realizes that it is but by historical accident that we are considering *shamanism* and not, say, *ngangaism, isangomaism,* or *tietäjäism*. Had the pattern first been identified and studied in Southern Africa (or elsewhere), it might have been the case that one of the other concepts would have won the day (see Thorpe 1993, 7). Obviously, the choice of words can also be a way of making a distinction, and the terms *shaman* and *shamanism* are just concepts that are used for describing a pattern with multiple expressions.

Given the historical development from a culture-specific to a cross-cultural term, we "should not be afraid to call shamans shamans" (Lewis 1984, 10)—that is to name a religious specialist who experiences ASCs and who acts as inspired diviner and healer, and who can also control the spirits (see Lewis 1984, 9). For this reason, my suggestion is that the shamanic complex can also be used for understanding a first-century Galilean figure if the same pattern is present.

---

37. By referring to a family of traditions, Walsh brings to the fore the idea that there is variability among shamanic practitioners while the fixed pattern is maintained.

38. The *nganga*, as engaged in a wide range of activities and functions, is known in many Bantu languages (see Thorpe 1993, 80–101; Schoffeleers 1994, 74), while the *izingoma* is known in the Zulu languages (see Thorpe 1993, 102–25). The Finnish counterpart is called the *tietäjä*, and the Mehinaku Indians call their shaman a *yetamá*, while the word among the Iglulike Eskimo is *angakoq* (see Ripinsky-Naxon 1993, 72, 80). Not even all Siberian or inner Asian tribes use the term *shaman* for their magico-religious practitioner of this type (see Lee 1999, 23–24).

Some Benefits of the Shamanic Model

The shamanic complex shows how things hang together in the life of shamanic figures. Neither was the concept of the shamanic complex used, nor would it necessarily have been understood, by Jesus or his followers, because *shaman* was not one of the terms used to describe him. It is an analytical model for helping us—historians, removed in time, space, and culture—to grasp the dynamics and inherent features of the historical figure we are looking at.

In addition, in being of a social type, shamanic figures always operate within the confines of a community. Shamanism is not only the product of individual experiences and phenomena but also the product of community involvement and participation. The variety of functions ascribed to such figures is the result and product of the ASC experiences that constitute them. In working with and toward this model, at least three features of the model need to be highlighted: it is interpretive, it is cross-cultural, and it has explanatory power.

The Interpretive Power of the Shamanic Model

As a homomorphic model (not built according to scale), the shamanic complex is not constituted by means of a list of individual shamanic elements but is conceptualized as a pattern, and only within the pattern do the elements receive meaning. The constituting elements of the pattern are any number of a variety of ASC experiences, together with certain essential social functions.

According to this way of looking at shamanism, there is no list of "shamanic features" that can be identified (and checked off) in a specific case. The pattern is reshaped or remade in each and every specific cultural setting. Visions, trances, or any other ASC experiences are not necessarily *shamanic* but belong to the category of normal human experiences that can appear under many conditions and with many social types. However, when ASC experiences appear in a specific, identifiable pattern, this pattern can be called shamanism, and from within, this pattern offers interpretive power for understanding the dynamics of the social personage involved.[39]

39. This way of designing and employing the model is radically different from the other example applied to Jesus of Nazareth known to me. Lee identifies "shamanic elements," which are then identified in the ancient Greek world or in ancient Israelite society (see 1999, 116–87). The same principle applies to the analysis of the Synoptic Gospels. The

The Cross-Cultural Functions of the Shamanic Model

The shamanic complex allows a comparison of religious practitioners across cultures on the basis of adherence to the identified pattern. And as Smith, quoting Wittgenstein, reminds us, "comparison is, at base, never identity" (1982, 35). *Emic*, or local, terms can be used for one's own experiences but have little interpretive power when it comes to other cultural systems. For example, possession by an ancestral spirit is a useless category for cultural systems without strong ancestral involvement; a soul flight underneath the sea is not a very useful cross-cultural category when dealing with desert-located peoples. But when these phenomena are seen as biologically based ASC experiences, it is possible to see them as cultural versions of similar experiences.

Despite the many cultural variants among humans, the one thing we share with our forebears is the same body (i.e., brain and central nervous structure), which allows these kinds of ASC experiences. We can be fairly certain that they must have had similar experiences of out-of-body-ness, or visions and auditions that do not necessarily have any extrinsic source of origin. Thus, the identification of the biologically based potential of human beings of experiencing such phenomena goes much further in explaining the various phenomena found in different cultures than what any of the local cultural explanations do. It also, for example, means that a possession by a divine spirit, an ancestral spirit, or an animal spirit is all of the same kind; it is only the cultural lore that differs.

The Explanatory Power of the Shamanic Model

The category of ASC is not merely another way of describing trance, visionary, ecstatic, or journey experiences, but a way of understanding and explaining them since it offers an explanation of the cultural dynamics of ASCs. The shamanic model is not merely a new pigeonhole or matrix for fitting Jesus of Nazareth into it; it offers, first, an interpretive and explanatory framework for understanding him as a social personage, as well as the cultural dynamics that probably surrounded his life as a historical figure. In being a social personage, a shamanic figure always operates within the confines of a particular community. A shaman, however, is not only the product of individual experiences and activities but also the product of

---

"shamanic features in Jesus' exorcisms are minimal," it is said (1999, 264). But there is not necessarily a shamanic way of exorcism distinct from other ways of exorcism.

community involvement and participation. The model, therefore, goes a long way in avoiding the shortcomings of a history-of-ideas approach while illuminating the features needed for dealing with the cultural processes and dynamics associated with the life of a shamanic figure.

Shamanic figures are not social personages who heal and teach and engage in the control of spirits. Shamanic figures are those social personages who do these things because these shamanic functions or activities (healing, teaching, and control of spirits) are integrated with their ASC experiences, and all belong together to their being in the world (in a particular worldview and cultural setting). It is a certain way of being, which carries its own features and is not merely a way of categorizing existing phenomena. For example, shamanic healings are not merely healings that are labeled shamanic, but are part of the features belonging to the life and dynamics of someone being constituted and acting as such a figure. As people who often experience specific kinds of ASCs, they are effective within specific settings because part of the dynamics of their constitution and efficiency as figures is embedded in cultural communities. Shamans are shamans for specific people, and they are so within particular settings and by means of the symbols and traditions of those people. Shamanic activities are simultaneously community and communal activities.

The depiction of religious entrepreneurs as shamans (in other words as ASC-based specialists) thus goes beyond mere description—it adds specific explanations for understanding the dynamics and operation of such figures. The use of cross-cultural models in historical anthropology is helpful in comparing pictures but also in better understanding the dynamics associated with specific social types. Therefore, the shamanic model should also be able to show how the variety of features hung together in Jesus's life story, and how the cultural dynamics contributed to the creation of his social personage.

Conclusion

Based on these descriptions, a cross-cultural definition of a *shaman* refers to those religious entrepreneurs who enter controlled ASCs on behalf of their communities and perform certain social functions that center on healing, divination, and control of spirits. As Winkelman (1997, 394) claims, the shaman represents the "most widely recognized institutionalized use of ASC." It is not so much the individual elements but the combination of a number of aspects that constitutes the shamanic complex as an identifiable phenomenon in many cultural settings. According to this definition, shamanism is constituted by a combination of elements, elements that exist independently elsewhere but are integrated in this complex with a particular worldview, and that validate specific techniques. As a cross-cultural model, the shamanic complex contains fewer specifics of particular cases but has the advantage of covering more cases that belong to the same pattern.

This overview also shows that there is no such thing as *the shaman*, but there is indeed a universal pattern of religious practitioners associated with it. It means that the terms *shaman* and *shamanism* will be used in this study in very specific ways: as expressions of an interpretive model designed to deal in a cross-cultural way with a family of traditions related to a specific type of religious practitioner or entrepreneur. A shaman is that kind of religious specialist who experiences all sorts of ASCs and, because of that, performs certain tasks on behalf of a community. The definitional quandary should not lead to despair.

Finding concepts and definitions with cross-cultural currency is no easy task. It is also true that when the concept ASC is used, many of the locals will not (and will not be able to) identify with (or even understand) that concept. But that is the nature of comparative (analysts') categories, which need not comply with local terms. A cross-cultural model has been described that operates on a higher level of abstraction and that covers specific instances. It will always remain an issue (and perhaps for the good) that the search for the essence of shamanism should occupy academic studies. There is some consolation in the fact that the same applies to all other religious social types, be it the prophet, the priest, or the sage. A local definition in one context is not necessarily applicable to another.

There is not necessarily a contradiction between maintaining that, on the one hand, the shamanic complex as a pattern of religious practices can be described as a specific pattern within identifiable worldviews and cultural settings (based on ASC experiences), and that, on the other hand, shamanic modes vary between cultures and with specific individuals. The definition of shamanism adopted in this study favors the notion that it is remade in different historical and cultural settings but with the maintenance of the general pattern. Therefore, the shamanic complex refers to constellations of certain features and functions that recur in particular cultural systems.

In view of what has been said about the cultural processes and cultural dynamics that constitute social personages such as shamanic figures, it is worthwhile to consider a concrete example. About Khanty shamans in Siberian society, Balzer (1991, 61) points out that a "true shaman of wide reputation and power does not necessarily appear in every community or in every lifetime." One of the prerequisites to become a "big man" shaman is "the climate of adulation required for a shaman to build a following." The dynamics of the constitution of the shamanic figure are clearly visible:

- The appearance and success of the shaman are not determined by training or education but follow from reputation and the cultural dynamics of recognition and affirmation.

- Similarly, shamanic success in healing depends on communal involvement and on the dynamics of shamanic and community interaction.

- Shamanic events and phenomena cannot be isolated as atomistic entities, but they are integrated communal entities that exist only in their cultural complexity.

CHAPTER 6

Components of a First-Century (Shamanic) Worldview

Introduction

The historian John Tosh mentions that the worst kind of historical anachronism is psychological anachronism: "the unthinking assumption that the mental framework with which people interpreted their experience in earlier periods was the same as ours" (1984, 86). Therefore, as argued above, in the evaluation of documentary sources before anything else can be achieved, the historian must try to enter the mental framework or, as it will be called here, the worldview, of the people who created them. Jesus of Nazareth and his first followers, who created the documentary evidence, arguably lived in such a unitary cosmos or worldview. The aim of this chapter is to take the first few steps toward an exposition of that worldview and context.

In the view adopted in this study, context is much more a state of mind than a stage of interpretation. It is an awareness of and a sensitivity toward the fact that every aspect of life (ours and others') is embedded in some kind of context. It is not only the broader framework within which the interpretive act takes place but also the specific setting within which particular stories, phenomena, and events find their ultimate meaning and expression. Doing justice to the singularity of other people's lives means situating them within the systems of signs and within relations of power and meaning that animate them. It has to become the *second new language* of the interpreter—the taken-for-granted, ultimate presuppositions that change the historian, as it were, into an insider.

Context is not like a bag of tricks that can be emptied once and for all in order to form the "background" for interpretation. Context fibers are all-pervasive, which means that they should be present in each act or aspect of interpretation. It is, however, impossible to be comprehensive in fully creating the cultural system and taken-for-granted worldview of insiders together with the full picture of the social, economic, and political conditions of a case. On the other hand, all context fibers are linked—meaning that they belong together within a complex whole.

Interpretations have to negotiate between these two parameters. Context fibers cannot, however, be applied piecemeal. They should guide interpretations all the way: from trying to understand what the reports are about, to deciding what kind of figure Jesus was, to dealing with the differences between the sources—both what is written and what is written about should be covered by the context canopy.

As *cultural bundubashing* implies, this road takes its passengers through the terrain of cultural notions and practices. Therefore, the historical Jesus research toolkit should include tools and mechanisms that allow entrance to the cultural peculiarities of the first-century Mediterranean people. Context fibers are, therefore, the threads that ensure that each and every aspect of the ancient lives is considered as an element from their world. Placing Jesus of Nazareth and the documentary sources within a first-century Mediterranean worldview is a much more complex task than can be conducted here. Nevertheless, some contours of the landscape will be drawn.

Worldview as a Cultural Construct of Place

"Place" is not an empty, given context, but as Moxnes says, "something that is created and contested" (2000, 172), and part of a cultural whole.[1] Place is shaped by personal and communal experience and meaning; it is where we locate our sense of deepest meaning and from where we inter-

1. Following Moxnes, a distinction will be made between "situating" Jesus in Judaism and "placing" (2001, 35) him in a first-century Galilean religious landscape. Sanders, he shows, situates Jesus in Judaism as a system of religious beliefs without paying any attention to place as a geographical and cultural space. With some exceptions, common Judaism offers the scholarly framework for situating Jesus of Nazareth and for understanding his Galilean identity as a first-century figure. It also provides the framework for comparing Jesus and "Judaism." The interest here is not in Judaism as a religious system but in the Israelite religious landscape of which Judaism(s) as a religious system was a manifestation or manifestations.

pret reality. To place Jesus of Nazareth in a first-century Galilean religious landscape is to uncover the meaning-giving dynamics and realities of that location. The central question of context in this study is therefore not so much whether some specific historical setting can be identified for particular sayings or deeds or whether the political conditions under imperial rule can be captured, but first and foremost to get the cultural system and worldview right for understanding the cultural traits and overall picture of the specific social type and historical personage. It is an essential act of interpretation not only to exclude certain background knowledge but also to know what to include in each case of a successful interpretation. Therefore, it is always the case that certain aspects of context are framed in or out when interpreting.

People in a modern Western-oriented culture live in a world radically different from that of biblical people. Strenuous effort is required of a Western scientist, Laughlin, McManus and d'Aquili point out, "to realize that his [*sic*] concrete view of reality is merely a construct . . . and thus an impediment placed in the way of comprehending a unitary cosmos in which his cognized environment is only one of many alternative ways" (1990, 226). What ancient people believed about themselves and the world is not only different from what modern Western people think, but the way in which they acquired that knowledge is different from that of modern people.

Comparing Modern and Ancient Worldviews

In discussing the philosophical lenses of cultural bundubashing (see above, pp. 9–10) the notion of ontological monism which maintains that "the other" can be mastered, absorbed or reduced to the same, was rejected. The position of ontological pluralism and cultural plurality of worldviews and reality maintains that different cultural systems are different constructs or systems of reality that resists the assimilation of the one to the other. But that applies not only to the ethnocentric accommodation or absorption of ancient worldviews by modern scientific ones, but also the other way round. In other words, it also rejects the strategy of belittling modern scientific worldviews as reductionist in the face of ancient or traditional worldviews that allegedly operate with many levels of reality.

The idea that modern science has "reduced the West's view of reality" (Smith 1976, 96), with the result that other "levels of reality" become obscure is an equally ethnocentric form of ontological monism.[2] It is found, for example, in the notion that the biblical worldview contained "minimally two levels of reality" (Borg 1994c, 131), and the argument is that modern science actually has a limited view of *reality*—it is like a view finder that can only detect what comes in front of its beams (see Smith 1976, 8–9, 97).

The position of radical pluralism rejects ontological monism in whichever disguise. The position taken in this study is that it is necessary to understand the complexity and integrity of the ancient worldview in its own terms. That means, grasping their notion of ontology and reality, the features and facets that were constitutive of their unitary or interconnected worldview. The reason why the above position is a fallacious argument, at least from the philosophical point of view of engaged fallibilistic pluralism (or, cultural bundubashing), is because there is no *reality* or *base level of reality* from which modern science and traditional worldviews start (with the one constitutionally incapable of recognizing the other levels). The very notion of reality or a basic element of it, is constructed differently by modern science and by traditional worldviews. Put differently, they do not start with the same "material world" as reality, to begin with. The material world of modern science is described by means of at least chemistry and physics, cells and atoms. As said earlier, two modern scientific theories about the world are not up for grabs: the atomic theory of matter and the evolutionary theory of biology. While the natural sciences describe the nature of material entities in terms of physical, chemical, and biological components and processes, the modern worldview is not limited to those entities alone. In fact, a systems ontology goes beyond the atomistic view of the parts in describing the reality of systems that goes far beyond the material components thereof. In a systems ontology:

> Science is moving from viewing 'solid material bodies' as 'the paradigm of reality,' to viewing matter-in-systems as the paradigm of reality. . . . Something only becomes real, comes into existence, in a system. Nothing, neither a piece of matter, nor a word or an idea,

2. Borg shows that what is called the primordial tradition contains the "root image of reality which we find in the biblical tradition" (1994c, 131). "Root image" is another term for *worldview*. Unfortunately, Borg makes the common ethnocentric mistake of saying that the adoption of the primordial tradition implies for biblical people that there were two levels of reality—that of ordinary experience and that of another reality. However, as I have argued, there is no such thing as "ordinary" experience because for them ordinary experience included experiencing as real and concrete what for others is "another reality."

exists as an isolated entity. Subatomic particles are already energy/matter-in-complex-system. . . . reality is a hierarchy of complex systems in which each new level of complexity represents a new type of reality, a new manner of being which requires a unique explanatory discourse in which to express its unique structure and function. (Kriel 2000, 76–77, 130)

The material world described by these theories is, however, radically different from the material world or ontologies constructed in traditional worldviews (which will later be described as animistic ontologies).

The *Cycle of Meaning*: Experience, Expression, and Inherited Pattern

Laughlin, McManus, and d'Aquili show that there is a specific dynamic at work in the creation and maintenance of knowledge and worldviews in traditional societies called a "cycle of meaning" (1990, 227–29): experience, activity, and knowledge are part of a single process creating and maintaining the worldviews of people in preindustrial traditional societies (see also Laughlin 1997). Such worldviews are described by means of a specific structural composition in which worldview elements are symbolically expressed by means of different mythic means that lead to transpersonal experiences that are in turn interpreted in such a way as to verify or vivify the worldview elements. The mythic expressions can take the form of a personal quest, ritual enactment of shamanic interjection. In an adapted version of the diagram of Laughlin, McManus, and d'Aquili, it can be illustrated in the following way:[3]

---

3. While Laughlin, McManus, and d'Aquili use the term *cosmology*, that will be replaced here with the broader concept of *worldview*, which includes cosmology but also other worldview elements, such as the "self" and the "other."

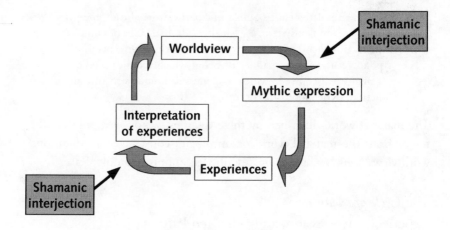

**Diagram 6.1: The Cycle of Meaning: Worldview,
Mythic Expression, Experience, and Interpretation**

*In the cycle of meaning, there is a constant circle where the worldview and
mythical elements are confirmed by the experiences allowed by the myths and
worldview, while the interjection of new knowledge follows the procedure of
culturally significant figures, such a the shaman, who introduce new cultural
knowledge.*

Worldviews do not exist "out there" but are cognized worlds or cultural constructs shared by members of a specific group. Before specific
features of such traditional worldviews are introduced, one more distinction between modern scientific and traditional worldviews need to be
mentioned.

Monophasic and Polyphasic Cultures

Much of ethnographic literature amply demonstrates that people in most
societies operate psychologically by accepting ASC experiences (such as
visions, dreams, and possession) as meaningful and normal human experiences (thus as everyday reality) for obtaining knowledge about the world
(see, for example, Bourguignon 1979, 245; Craffert 2002). Such people,
Laughlin, McManus, and d'Aquili say, "experience *polyphasic consciousness*,
and consequently their cognized view of self constitutes a polyphasic integration." Such realities in polyphasic consciousness "are frequently coded
as experiential" (1990, 155). This is opposed to most Western (North
American and Western European) people, whom Laughlin, McManus,

and d'Aquili characterize as subject to *monophasic consciousness*: the only *real world* experiences are those unfolding in the sensorium during the normal *waking* phase. The latter's connection to radical reflexivity should be obvious. A special development within the realm of monophasic cultures is the practices associated with modern scientific thinking. There are at least two reasons why modern scientific thinking should be followed.

The first is that modern sciences operate with a distinct epistemology, which Taylor calls "radical reflexivity" (1991, 304), and which, Spurrett explains, was bought at the cost of divorcing positional and experiential claims from real and apparent ones (2002, 192). He explains it with the common notion of "sunset speech," which we all ascribe to while knowing perfectly well that relative to the earth, the sun does not move; "sunrises are really earth-turnings" (the terms *real* and *really* are used synonymously in this paragraph). Things are not always as they seem to us or as we experience them, and this applies both to sunsets and to cosmology, to self-speak or to soul-talk. Radical reflexivity refers to that practice not only of having experiences but of scrutinizing them and subjecting them to reflexive thinking, or to "turns in on itself in self-awareness" (Laughlin et al. 1990, 236).

Second, unlike traditional worldviews, modern science as a controlled observation of nature does not offer an ontology that is experiential or functional in providing meaning to life. Modern science produces "a view of the world, a cognized environment, that is intentionally disconnected from the direct, everyday experience of people while profoundly affecting people's lives" (Laughlin et al. 1990, 233). For this reason, the resemblances between, for example, quantum physical cosmologies and traditional cosmological systems exist largely at a superficial textual level. Quantum mechanics is not involved in providing meaning for most people in their daily lives. In traditional worldviews and cosmologies, flying spirits, ancestors, and the like can be seen and are experienced (in visions or dreams) in a sense in which photons, electrons, and black holes are not and cannot be experienced, and are not part of everyday reality.

What is clear is that experiences in polyphasic cultures are very real for the participants: the deities encountered are "deities out there," and the worlds visited are "worlds out there," and the journeys undertaken are with a "real" soul or "real" body, as the case may be (see James 1902,

75; Laughlin et al. 1990, 132, 270).[4] In fact, as James points out, they are "as convincing to those who have them as any direct sense experience can be, and they are, as a rule, much more convincing than results established by mere logic ever are" (1902, 83). This is not only the case with people sharing such cultures, but as Nordland indicates (see 1967, 173), Western subjects under experimental conditions also experience such states as so real that they sometimes need psychiatric treatment afterwards. ASC experiences are as real as experiences in ordinary waking consciousness because, as Newberg, d'Aquili, and Rause explain:

> All perceptions exist in the mind. The earth beneath your feet, the chair you're sitting in, the book you hold in your hands may all seem unquestionably solid and real, but they are known to you only as secondhand neurological perceptions, as blips and flashes racing along the neural pathways inside your skull. If you were to dismiss spiritual experience as 'mere' neurological activities, you would also have to distrust all of your own brain's perceptions of the material world. On the other hand, if we do not distrust our perceptions of the physical world, we have no rational reason to declare that spiritual experience is a fiction that is 'only' in the mind. (2001, 146)

From the perspective of neuroscience, ASC experiences are just like any sensory perception in a normal waking state, blips and flashes within the neural pathways; whether vision or normal seeing, in the human brain they have the same character. A visitation by a god or an ancestor, a journey to another world, or the possession by a spirit or demon can be culturally real without being objectively "out there."[5] "Reality" is created in the brain and (dis)confirmed by society. But "normal" or "ordinary" consciousness is not an ontological given but a specialized cultural construction. Each culture teaches its members what is "normal" and "real," and therefore

4. The epistemological difficulties that these kinds of experiences create should not be underestimated. Even those involved in them must often think about the "reality" of what they experience. Jones tells us of the instance of a Limbu shaman when only the shaman's soul traveled up the ladder to another realm. Questioned, the shaman answered that "only his 'words' travelled since any fool could see that he never left the ground" (1976, 36). Even ancient people incorporated devices by which they wanted to confirm that what they had experienced had been objective. Is this because they also doubted whether their experiences were indeed objective (see Russel 1964, 163)?

5. The ontological status of such constructs cannot be determined by neuroscience alone. In other words, it cannot be concluded that such experiences are only blips and flashes in the brain (for a discussion of this problem, see Craffert 2002, 79–83).

such ASCs can have ontological or reality value for people in such cultures. In polyphasic cultures there will thus be no difference in quality between stories and reports about such experiences and about experiences "out there" (see Tart 1980, 245; Laughlin et al. 1990, 142). An encounter with ancestors or with neighbors will have the same "reality" value while voices in an ASC are as real as those in everyday conversation. In fact, subjects themselves often find it impossible to distinguish the one from the other. Therefore, it should be expected that stories or reports about such events will not be any different from those in everyday experiences.

Some Features of Preindustrial Traditional Worldviews

The first feature is that worldviews in preindustrial traditional societies tend to be *somatocentric* (see Laughlin et al. 1990, 216–17, 225–27), which can be explained by reference to the bodily experiences that accompany them. Taking seriously polyphasic consciousness or ASC experiences as part of everyday reality plays a central role in the cycle of meaning of such societies. The result is that there is an interplay between ontology and certain experiences. Such experiences are not meaningful simply as bodily experiences but are inscribed within the cycle of meaning. They are experiences embedded in mythic expressions and in a worldview framework, experiences that become meaningful cultural events.

The example of marijuana usage for recreational purposes—as opposed to ritual usage—confirms this point; the same bodily experience can lead to greater fragmentation in the first instance but to sacred meaning in the second (see 1990, 230).

Events and phenomena experienced within such a cycle of meaning (and worldview) are not *supernatural*. As Walsh points out about shamanic cosmologies, "if we examine shamanic technology and cosmology together [and not from our ethnocentric point of view], we will see that they form an integrated unit in which theory and practice, cosmology and technology, belief and technique are intimately linked in a meaningful and coherent whole" (1990, 88). Or, as Mutwa explains: "There is nothing supernatural, everything is natural. We in Africa know—and please don't ask me to explain further—that the human being possesses twelve senses—not five senses as Western people believe. One day this will be accepted scientifically—twelve" (1996, 30).

It is important to note the implication of this with regard to the nature of knowledge-categories. It is suggested that within the dynamics of the experience/expression spiral, none of their categories are purely analytical or reflective, they are experiential-reflective categories because they are caught up in this dynamic process. To oversimplify this dynamic: they believed what they experienced, and they experienced what they believed, and their expressed versions are a product of this process. In this regard, Hadot makes an important (and independent) remark regarding the nature of ancient philosophical texts:

> We think that ancient philosophers were above all theoreticians: they supposedly first put forward a theory of the world, and then, in addition, deduced some practical consequences from it, and thus proposed a morality, a way of living, that ensued from their theory. I believe that exactly the opposite was the case. In Antiquity, the choice of a certain way of living everyday life did not come at the end of a process of philosophical activity . . . but on the contrary at the very beginning . . . there is a certain experience of the human condition and an existential choice that corresponds to it . . . there is a reciprocal causality between theory and choice of life. (2001, 389)

One should be clear about the difference in nature between such a process and the method of radical reflexivity employed by modern science.

A second feature of the cycle of meaning is that, like the worldview it describes, it is never static because the very dynamics of such a system presuppose that it can all be transformed. Change may be accomplished at any given point; for example, fresh visionary experiences may result in new interpretations that transform the worldview. The transformative processes are particularly fluid in cases where textual material is not all written down (see Laughlin et al. 1990, 230). As I have indicated, shamans are some of the social figures entitled to interject new knowledge into the system.[6]

The third feature is that preindustrial, traditional societies are in a specific sense extremely undemocratic, in that not everyone is entitled to contribute to the body of knowledge of the society. It has been indicated above that shamans have experiences that are consistent with the myths of their cultural system (see also Walsh 1990, 90). Scientific communities also have rigorous rules for determining and evaluating knowledge, but in

---

6. The indication of ASCs and the avenues to new knowledge and problem solving in traditional societies is well known (see Ludwig 1968, 88).

traditional societies these are personalized. It is a cross-cultural feature that in these societies certain individuals are socially recognized and labeled as specialists in having legitimate experiences (such as traveling to divine realms) or specific powers to obtain knowledge. It is within such a framework that the cycle of meaning is also extremely fragile in that renewal is dependent on new legitimate experiences (Laughlin et al. 1990, 229).

A fourth feature is that visionary, travel, and possession experiences, as described above, are central features in the cycle of meaning of cultures ascribing to polyphasic consciousness. In other words, most shamanic worldviews not only legitimate such experiences, but these experiences contribute to the construction of such worldviews. In a very concrete sense it can be seen that they experience what they believe, and they believe what they experience, and all of these experiences have bodily connections. They are the product of specific neurological and brain structures.[7] Amidst the patterns of regularities and similarities among cultures, it is significant to notice that "all knowledge is mediated by structures inherent to the human brain" (Laughlin 1997, 474). Not only knowledge but also states of consciousness are mediated by these brain and neurological structures.

Finally, part of an understanding of the cultural dynamics by which such stories about ASCs come into being (i.e., the cycle of meaning), includes an appreciation of the difficulty of putting images into words. This is a topic often reflected on in other branches of research (such as memory research and psychotherapy), and highlights that images are not always directly translated or translatable into words (see Bonanno 1990, 182–84). Especially visionary and out-of-body travel experiences are, by definition, ways of knowing the world through images. Eliade, for example, explains "the features of funerary geography, as well as some themes of the mythology of death," which in all probability are the result of the ecstatic journeys of shamans who describe them in minute detail:

> The unknown and terrifying world of death assumes form and is
> organized in accordance with particular patterns; finally, it displays

7. It is a mistake to think that people in traditional societies cannot tell the difference between fantasy and sense perception. Kiefer points out, "their very expertise in fantasy cultivation proves that they can and that they consider the knowledge achieved this way [from the divine world] equal or superior in epistemological status to sense perception" (1985, 484). They only conceive of a different relationship between fact and fantasy or between visionary figures and ghosts. Put differently, the fact that people distinguish between visionary figures and ghosts (as in New Testament texts) does not mean that they make the same distinction that we do between fact and fantasy, or reality and delusion.

a structure and, in the course of time, becomes familiar and acceptable. In turn, the supernatural [*sic*] inhabitants of the world of
death become visible; they show a form, display a personality, even
a biography. (1987, 207)

Summary

The worldview of Jesus of Nazareth, of his first followers who created the
literary texts and of the people of the first century in general, probably
was a traditional, polyphasic worldview in which the cycle of meaning was
propelled by this kind of dynamic. The obvious and most common-sense
argument in support of this is to point toward the lack within the traditional polyphasic worldview of any of the features ascribed to the modern
scientific worldview. But it is in the exploration of specific elements of
the polyphasic worldview that this lack becomes unquestionably apparent.
Put differently, it is in reflecting about specific worldview elements that
the dynamics of a cycle of meaning can be seen in operation. Therefore,
the aim of this exercise is not only to give an impression of the terms and
concepts that they have used but also to grasp the nature of their concepts.
These were not merely analytical or reflective concepts (their mythology
about the world); they were experiential concepts belonging to the cycle
of meaning of their lives.

To invoke a metaphor of a *lens-shaped image*, specific ways of obtaining knowledge constitute ontology. It should not be expected that people
who are familiar with and who often employ ASC experiences live in a
world similar to ours. In fact, it is remarkable how much differently the
gospel traditions are understood once their cycle of meaning containing
bodily experiences, mythic expressions, and ontological realities is entertained. It is the contention of this study that the worldview and cycle of
meaning are the ways to enter the mental world of those who have created the literary texts about Jesus of Nazareth as well as to understand the
content of what they are referring to, as well as the content of what they
ascribe to Jesus of Nazareth.

Even though such worldview constructs can be presented as humanly
rational and reasonably coherent, as I have argued earlier, this still does not
mean we should adopt that viewpoint. We should respect it if we intend
to grasp their mental framework, but need not necessarily agree with the

people of the first century or, for that matter, with any other person coming from such a worldview.

Elements of a First-Century Interconnected (Shamanic) Worldview

The cycle of meaning is a useful tool for understanding specific worldview elements in preindustrial societies in general and shamanic worldviews in particular. As soon as specific elements are engaged, it becomes clear that *the way things are, the way things operate,* and *the way such worldviews are populated* form an integrated whole. It is, therefore, not surprising that such worldviews are referred to as *unified* or *interconnected* worldviews.

It is remarkable but not surprising to what degree the worldview often ascribed to Jesus of Nazareth, and to first-century Mediterranean people in general, conforms to that of typical shamanic communities. Therefore, instead of trying to prove that the New Testament worldview is a shamanic worldview, this model will be used to describe some elements of that shared worldview pattern. By doing that comparison, an additional fiber in the cable will be connected to Jesus as a typical shamanic figure.

A Three-Tiered Cosmos

The shaman's universe, Walsh points out, "is three tiered, comprises of an upper, middle, and lower world, and the upper and lower worlds may themselves be multilayered" (1990, 88; see Hultkrantz 1973, 30; Townsend 1997, 437).[8] This is remarkably similar to the picture of the cosmos that informed the people of the Israelite traditions (see Deist 1987; Cornelius 1994). The way the world (cosmos) is perceived to be is remarkably similar in such preindustrial, traditional worldviews.

In analyzing and comparing different shamanic worldviews, it becomes apparent how cultural events are both real and subject to the cycle of meaning of the specific cultural system. Shamans travel to worlds they already know and that they believe exist, and they encounter spirit entities known to their mythology or system. "Why would shamans learn to journey to the upper world if they did not already believe there was one?"

---

8. Although a three-tiered cosmos is often present, it is no prerequisite for the shamanic complex (see Lewis 1986, 82). There are, furthermore, many local cosmologies that are not intrinsically linked to shamanism.

Walsh (1990, 90) asks. At the same time, spirits as cultural entities and the accompanied cultural events constitute for them how things are in the world—that is, what is real.

Animism: Connected via a Spirit World

Within shamanic worldviews, all things that exist are alive because "all things are seen to be interrelated and interdependent—not just what people commonly call 'living' things" (Harner 1988, 10). The ethnological term for the religious pattern involving belief in spiritual beings and that all objects are invested with a mind or spirit is *animism*. Such spirits could take on varied forms, inhabiting trees, streams, or rocks; or these spirits could be guardians of individuals or of a household, or be the embodiment of hunted animals; also the wind and rain may be imbued with spirit (see Lenski & Lenski 1987, 120; Walsh 1990, 89; Winthrop 1991a, 10–11; Vitebsky 1995, 12).

It is a little misleading to call the spirit of something simply its "essence" because the spirit is more than its chemical or material properties as understood by the modern sciences. In fact, it does not result from an analysis of such material properties. Rather, the spirit resembles the thing: bears have big spirits, and mice small spirits; the spirit of a knife cuts and that of a pot contains (see Vitebsky 1995, 13).

At least two implications immediately follow from this pattern. One is the possibility of all sorts of spirit-possession and the movement, interaction with, and control of spirits. The control, replacement, or loss of a human spirit could result in illness or bad luck, while the spirits of animals, objects, and plants are equally vulnerable to control or replacement (see Vitebsky 1995, 12–13; and Townsend 1997, 437–38, despite the fact that she describes the material and spiritual as two distinct realities). How things are, in such a worldview, is that things (reality) consist of material and spiritual components. The second implication is that someone, an agent or spirit, is responsible for everything that happens: "Whatever happens—good or bad, fortunate or unfortunate, success or failure—is likely to be attributed to spirits" (Walsh 1990, 90). They are constantly intervening in human affairs, sometimes helping, sometimes harming (see Lenski & Lenski 1987, 120). There is a hierarchy of power or spirits and everything and everyone is enclosed in it. Not only nonhuman beings but also substances that are imbued with spirit can influence things higher or lower in the scale—the scale commonly known as the *great chain of being* (see Sanders 1993, 140; Borg 1994c, 130).

Bultmann shows that there are two different conceptions of animism in the New Testament world and texts (see 1980, 155–60).[9] In the one, a spirit is a personal power that, like a demon, can possess someone (the agent model); and, in the other, it is an impersonal power that, like a fluid, can fill a person or object (the container model). Both conceptions exist side by side, often in the writings of the same author, and it is not always easy to distinguish them.

A Densely Populated Cosmos

Not even a movie of the religious landscape would be able to do justice to a component that was so central to the ancient worldview. One reason is that this landscape was ever changing and should be seen in its complex variety in particular locations if justice is to be done to it. Therefore, when a single frozen picture from that movie is given, it is merely to offer a glimpse of what is to be expected and taken into account when dealing with that world. Doing this is like freezing the frame of a film while knowing quite well that on either side other configurations are possible.

THE GREAT CHAIN OF BEING

It stands to reason that the religious landscape of Palestine and the wider Greco-Roman world offers the conceptual environment available for the early Christians in order to construct their world, interpret their experiences, and express what kind of being Jesus of Nazareth was to them (see Riley 1997, 99). An important component of this environment, which was common culture to most (all?) people of the ancient world, can be described by the already-mentioned "great chain of being."

Riley argues that it was common culture at the beginning of the Christian era to accept that there are five classes of living beings: "gods, *daimones*, heroes, humans, and last of all animals" (1997, 31). When Plutarch expressed this idea at the beginning of the second century, he was merely echoing a cultural belief that goes right back in Greek thinking some eight hundred years. This idea offered a conceptual framework that

9. Although Bultmann uses the term *animistic* (as opposed to *dynamistic*) as one way to conceptualize the spirit, his distinction describes different ways of conceptualizing animism or the religious pattern involving belief in spirit beings.

was widely adopted all over the Mediterranean world and populated by culture-specific beings. In all instances, these beings (human and nonhuman) were linked in a hierarchy of power and influence stretching from the highest to the lowest order—aptly described as the *great chain of being*.

Initially, the *daimones* were believed to be the lesser divinities arranged below the Olympian gods. They were ambiguous characters in that the same *daimon* could bring on ill or good fortune. They could exchange places and after falling from grace (dying) could become underworld *daimones*. It was after the exile, and under influence of some Israelite traditions that were influenced by Zoroastrian ideas, that the category of *daimones* was dualistically distinguished between good (angels) and bad (demons) (see Riley 1997, 33–34, 129).

The Hellenistic category of the *hero* was ascribed to people with at least two characteristics: "distinguished courage as well as bravery and noble character" (see Riley 1997, 36). They belonged to the few who, because of their heroism, were after death elevated to the realm of divinity.

Another helpful way of looking at this great chain of being is to distinguish between mortals, immortals, and eternals. Animals and humans are the mortals, and the main gods of the different pantheons were the eternals. In between these there is the wide and diverse category of immortals—that is, humans who have managed to cross the divide from human existence to the divine world. These are the heroes, the divine men, the philosophers and great teachers, the healers and kings.

Originally, eternals were all mythical figures from the distant past (see Talbert 1975, 422–29), but then around the turn of the era, *eternal* also applied to rulers (Alexander the Great, Augustus), philosophers (Empedocles), and healers (Apollonius). They were the heroes who used to be mortals but at the end of their careers achieved the status of immortals. While the category is distinct and extensive, not many mortals ever reached the state of immortality (see Talbert 1975, 420, 429; Riley 1997, 57).

Heroes or immortals are typically endowed with two distinct characteristics (see Talbert 1975, 422). First is the claim that immortals were the offspring of a divine and a human connection: either fathered by a god with a human mother, or the child of a goddess and a human father. Most often, Riley points out, the liaison was between a male god and a virgin human female (see 1997, 39). The beauty, strength, or wisdom of successful people were culturally sufficient to justify the claim of divine lineage. Why else could Alexander the Great be so great?

The second claim is that the immortal was taken up in heaven. Either his ascent was witnessed, or his physical remains could not be found. Even if divine begetting is absent, Talbert shows that ascent into heaven is constant for immortals (see 1975, 422).

Just as the divine population never was stable, the internal relations never were fixed. In some cases in the ancient world the partition between the divine and the human world was strong, in other instance it was flimsy; crossover in some eras and areas was much easier than in others.

The First-Century Israelite Religious Landscape

One of the most dangerous (and damaging) interpretive constructs that is placed onto New Testament studies is the idea of *monotheism*, if only for the reason that in its application it is so open-ended that it can accommodate almost any definition. From some, claims and confessions of loyalty and worship of a single divinity (Yahweh), it is often concluded that the Israelite (Jewish) religious landscape was thoroughly monotheistic. That term and debate will be avoided here except to say that whatever term is eventually used to describe what probably was a development process, nevertheless, from a phenomenological point of view, an analysis of several aspects of Jewish texts and practices shows the existence of nonhuman or divine beings that influenced so many aspects of human affairs was simply taken for granted. Such beings were part of their everyday reality. What one such study concludes about the earlier Israelite period is equally true for Jesus's time: "The pattern of Jewish beliefs about God remains monarchistic throughout. God is king of a heavenly court consisting of many other powerful beings, not always under his control. For most Jews, God is the sole object of worship, but he is not the only divine being" (Hayman 1991, 15).

First-century Israelites shared the same conceptual framework with their Greco-Roman neighbors but populated it differently. In the Israelite tradition of the first-century period, Yahweh was accompanied by a host of divine or nonhuman beings: especially angels, demons, and spirits (see Smith 1978, 68–69). The angelic or demonic opponents of God were under the guidance of the leading evil angel or demon, which goes under different names in this period (names such as Satan, Mastema, Belial, Lucifer, and the devil) (see Grabbe 2000, 225, 231).

These good and evil spirits, demons and deities, it was believed, could enter and control the world of sense perception of humans (see Vermes 1973, 61–63; Sanders 1993, 141–42) and did so in many spheres of life. For example, illnesses could be the result of the interference by such beings (like demonic possession), and healing was often ensured by exorcism or control of the spirits. This is the nature of an animistic view of the world where *spirit* is considered a substantial substance of everything.

Several examples show that the category of immortals, especially associated with the figure of Moses, made inroads into certain Israelite circles at the time of the New Testament. Despite some reservations about calling them gods, both Moses and probably Enoch can be seen as instances of humans that were elevated to the status of immortals (see Talbert 1975, 423–25, 429).[10]

Unlike most attempts to find direct testimonies that Jesus was indeed understood or described as an immortal, the present aim is to argue that this pattern is helpful in offering a conceptual framework for grasping part of the cultural dynamics associated with his life as a social personage.

> It would seem, therefore, that the early Christians were aware of the Mediterranean concept of the immortals and utilized it in one way or another in their proclamation of Jesus. During the first one hundred and twenty five years of Christian history this mythology functioned initially as a significant christological category and then as an apologetic tool. (1975, 436)

Whether it was directly applied to his life is less important than the fact that in all probability this framework was available in the cultural mythology and thus inscribed in their cycle of meaning. The point of this discussion is not intended to find an identity but to create a framework within which the cultural dynamics of his life as a social personage can be understood.

---

10. It is to be expected that where such an intricate cultural concept exists as the potential of human beings to be transformed into another kind of being, discussions would ensue about the actual nature of such figures. Are they mere human beings transformed, or were they immortals all along, masquerading as humans? Did they die as humans, were they buried and transformed into immortals, or were they taken up as immortals after being transformed through resurrection? The placing of emphasis one way or another remains part of the cultural reality within the overall pattern where humans could end up as immortals. The texts about Moses's translation are interesting examples (see Talbert 1975, 424).

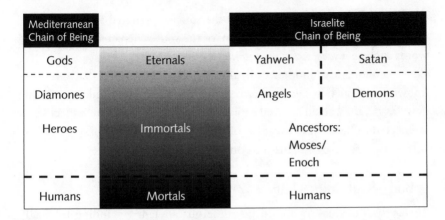

Mediterranean Chain of Being		Israelite Chain of Being	
Gods	Eternals	Yahweh	Satan
Diamones		Angels	Demons
Heroes	Immortals	Ancestors: Moses/ Enoch	
Humans	Mortals	Humans	

Diagram 6.2: The Denizens of the Great Chain of Being

The denizens who populated the Israelite ladder of mortals, immortals, and eternals were distinct from their Greco-Roman neighbors. In the Second Temple period, the Israelites conceptualized at least two reigns on the level of the eternals.

But worldview beliefs go much further than cosmology and the *others* or nonhuman inhabitants of the world. Worldview elements also include views on the self and others on earth.

The Human Being: Body and Soul/Spirit Components

An ontology created by modern science can be described as follows: "We live in a world made up entirely of physical particles in fields of force. Some of these are organized into systems. Some of these systems are living systems and some of these living systems have evolved consciousness" (Searle 1995, 7). This is radically different from the unitary (shamanic) universe of ancient people that did not describe the ontology of things in terms of chemistry or biological cells, but everything was composed of the four basic elements: fire, air (*pneuma* or "spirit"), earth, and water (see Wright 1995, 98–101). This included the human body and, as indicated above, ontology was not the product of radical reflexivity, but of experiential reflection. As Segal points out, "As in all ancient cultures, dreams, visions, and other religiously interpreted states of consciousness both gave the power to foretell the future and confirmed the culture's depiction of the afterlife" (2004, 207). And it is precisely in such depictions of the afterlife, as well as in descriptions of the soul as separated from the body in dreams and trances, that the nature of the soul is depicted by means of words such as *psyche*, *nefeš*, or *animus* (see 2004, 208).

Consequently, another difficulty of this discussion is that one unknown term (such as *soul*) has to be explained by another unknown term (such as *spirit*). And all cultural explanations of these terms are respectively connected to the cycle of meaning of the individual cultures of origin. This is true of all scholarly discussions on these topics.

A Body-Soul/Spirit Unity

The body-soul dualism found in numerous ancient (including biblical) texts should not be confused with the Cartesian dualism of matter versus nonmatter or of physical versus spiritual, because the soul (like the body) was composed of some substance that could be considered *stuff* (see Martin 1995, 115).[11] The logic is not one of ontologically separate components but of a symbiotic unity of entities. For first-century people (like most other ancients), the human being was a "commingling of substances" (1995, 25), and the primary substances were body-stuff and soul-stuff. But the human self (body and soul) was composed of the same elements as the universe, namely air (*pneuma*), earth, water, and fire (1995, 16). All things, including the variety of forms of life, were seen as various compounds of these basic elements, and therefore, materiality was a spectrum of more or less (or different configurations of these elements) and not in a dichotomy with nonmatter (see Wright 1995, 100; Martin 1995, 14). Therefore to say something was incorporeal (like a soul or spirit) did not translate to being immaterial. This conception of spirit is well expressed in the third-century text, *Pistis Sophia,* in which Mary talks about the Spirit visiting her in her house: "I was perplexed and thought that it was a ghost come to tempt me. And I seized him [the Spirit] and bound him to the foot of the bed which is in my house . . . and we went up together, entered the house, and found the Spirit bound to the bed" (v 61, Cullmann trans.).

---

11. Modern Western people are heirs of the Cartesian dualistic ontology regarding the human person. The central feature of this ontology is the notion that body and mind (soul) represent two distinct substances that were part of two radically different realms of reality. The one includes the body, matter, nature, and the physical; and the other, soul or mind, nonmatter, the supernatural, and the spiritual or psychological (see Martin 1995, 4–6; Vorster 2000, 105–6).

The "normal" human being therefore consisted of body, soul, and spirit. There was no fixed description of these or a single accepted view on this combination. It is rather the case that neither Christian writers (such as Paul) nor pagan authors (such as Plato) had a systematic or consistent picture of the human being. It is today impossible to speak of *the* Pauline, *the* Platonic, or *the* Aristotelian conception of the human being (see Aune 1994, 292; Martin 1995, 6–15). They all operated with various body and soul (and/or spirit) configurations.

Body/Soul/Spirit Configurations

In ancient conceptions, both soul and spirit were, like the body, composed of stuff, and part of nature, and neither would have been immaterial substances. None of the constituting components (body, soul, or spirit), not any configuration of them in combination was fixed in antiquity—neither in any specific tradition nor in the writings of any particular author.

This is not the place for a comprehensive treatment of any of these components but merely a site to note some of the general features that should be kept in mind when talking about the human being. Instead of trying to identify fixed conceptions on any of these, it is much better to go with the flow and to indicate the diversity of features ascribed by means of these terms.

As I have said, the human being in their view was an animated body, and a consistent debate shows that there was not a single or general conception of the nature of this entity. The body-soul, body-spirit, and even sometimes the body-soul-spirit relationship were expressed in many different ways. If it is remembered that the body-soul (or body-spirit) dualisms in the ancient world were not of the Cartesian ontological kind, it becomes interesting to note how these substances were thought to be united and related.

"Soul" (Greek *psychē* and Hebrew *nefeš*) is used primarily as a component of the animated human being. Human beings are, so to speak, *souled bodies*. Soul is the life principle and sometimes the consciousness of a human being. As it was in the rest of the Greco-Roman world, the soul could in Israelite tradition also be described as existing in a disembodied state after death (see Russel 1964, 146–47). But *soul* could also refer to the whole person, alive or dead (see Segal 2004, 279). Both the idea of premortal life and explicit references to the preexistence of the soul are the counterparts to the existence of a soul in a postmortem state (see Brown 1992, 161).

"Spirit" (Greek *pneuma* and Hebrew *ruaḥ*) was itself a kind of "stuff" that was the agent of perception, motion, and life itself: "it pervades other forms of stuff and, together with those other forms, constitutes the self" (Martin 1995, 21); it was the substance that gave form and quality (such as hardness, softness, density, or whiteness) to external objects. This wide-spread belief in the ancient world was equally shared by the Israelites, and therefore, not only human beings but also God, other heavenly beings, and natural phenomena had spirits (see Russel 1964, 148). Russel (see 1964, 154) shows that by the end of the Second Temple period, in much of the Israelite literature *soul* and *spirit* (when referring to human beings) were regarded as synonymous—which is also the case with Paul (see also e.g., *1 Enoch* 103:2–5). In other words, *spirit* could refer to the life force or consciousness and could also be described as a disembodied entity that ex-ists after death. This is the case in *Pseudo-Phocylides*: "For the souls remain unharmed among the deceased. For the spirit is a loan of God to mortals, and (his) image. For we have a body out of earth, and when afterwards we are resolved again into earth we are but dust; and then the air has received our spirit" (vv. 105–8, Van der Horst trans.). But when one describes this reality, it should be kept in mind that what Dunn says about *spirit* for Paul is true for other ancient authors: it is essentially an experiential concept; meaning, a concept "whose content and significance is determined to a decisive degree by his experience" (1975, 201).

The most significant difference between *soul* and *spirit* is that *soul* is used primarily as a component of the human being. *Spirit* has the same meaning when applied to human beings but is also used in a much wider context as the stuff that constitutes everything else. The most prominent feature of both the terms *soul* and *spirit* is that they were both used with a wide variety of meanings and often even interchangeably. That *spirit* was widely used is to be expected because *pneuma* was considered to be all around and was often spoken of as identical with air or wind. Given that *pneuma* was one of the components making up everything (including soul-stuff), the association between *soul* and *spirit* is natural.

A central feature about their construction of the body was that it was porous—its boundaries were penetrable from both inside and outside (see Vorster 2002b, 13–15). The body contained or consisted of many *poroi* ("channels" or "passages") through which blood, spirit, and other perceptions could flow. *Pneuma* was the life-giving stuff that filled the body. Similarly, perceptions of smell, taste, and the like were possible when something fitted into the correct *poroi*. In the words of Martin:

> *Poroi* are channels that enable external material to enter and pervade the body and constitute passageways within the body for psychic and nutritive (or destructive) matter . . . The concept of *poroi* in medical theory is one expression of the ancient assumption that the human body is of a piece with the elements surrounding and pervading it and that the surface of the body is not a sealed boundary. (1995, 17–18)

This principle is well expressed in the ancient art of physiognomics: the study of human character on the basis of how people looked and acted (see Malina & Neyrey 1996, 108). The surface of the body is an expression of the forces and movement inside the body, or a reflection of the soul and/or spirit as these "fill" the *poroi* of the body (see also Martin 1995, 18). It is probably this cultural notion about the body that can also be detected underneath metaphors of the body as a container as is found, for example, in the *Testament of Naphtali*: "For just as a potter knows the pot, how much it holds, and brings clay for it accordingly, so also the Lord forms the body in correspondence to the spirit, and instills the spirit corresponding to the power of the body" (2:2, Kee trans.).

Hierarchies were fundamental to the ancient worldview (see Martin 1995, 29–34), and so was the relationship between body and soul/spirit, all of which were different configurations of the same four elements hierarchically ordered. It is understandable that within the spectrum of ways in which the relationship between them was expressed, somewhere there would be a denigration of one of them. This is the case in some of Plato's writings where he refers to the body merely as the prison of the soul, and in later gnostic texts where the body is seen as intrinsically evil and the spirit as intrinsically good (see Aune 1994, 293, 296).

Some of the Functions of Pneuma

The fiber of spirit entities runs through many aspects of early Christian literature. It is impossible to understand many of the texts and phenomena referred to without a grasp of the ontology and functioning of the spirit world. It is even more complex because spiritual beings, according to the ancient Mediterranean worldview reside in some way in inanimate objects but are also a property of living human beings. For this reason it is necessary to reflect about their conceptions of spirit beings and the human self.

According to most medical theorists (and about everyone else who thought about the topic in the first century seems to have agreed), *pneuma* was the stuff of perception: "The body was able to see, hear, and feel due to the presence of the stuff of pneuma carried throughout the body by means of veins, arteries, or perhaps (in the opinion of some) nerves" (Martin 1995, 13). The debate about optics best illustrates this point. There were several theories about the role of *pneuma* in the optical system. For example, for some, the *pneuma* outside the body acted upon the *pneuma* in the eyes, which acted on the *pneuma* in the brain; others speculated about the *pneuma* that exited the eyes in the act of seeing—it literally pushes aside air to penetrate an object, which is seen (see Martin 1995, 22–24). Evil eye belief (the belief that the glance from a possessor of the evil eye can effect a person) is probably related to these notions (see Elliott 1988; Neyrey 1988; Derrett 1995).

The Role of "Spirit" in the Beginning of the Self

It is not only the bodily self and the social self but also the beginning or origin of the self (birth) that needs to be considered for the role of spirit. Sjef van Tilborg points out that in antiquity two forms of fertilization were well known: fertilization through copulation, and spontaneous fertilization (2000, 241 n. 112). Spontaneous fertilization will be discussed below (see p. 272).

Copulation implies semen, but only one of the various theories about the coming-into-being of semen is relevant here. According to the *hematogenic* theory (an influential theory that played a prominent role far into the Middle Ages), there was a very close link between spirit and semen.[12] As indicated earlier, blood and air (pneuma/spirit) flow into and through the body by means of *poroi*. "It was commonly believed that the arteries carried pneuma, either alone or mixed with blood" (Martin 1995, 22). Sperm or semen was thus seen as a foamy concoction of blood, other

---

12. The other theories are the *encephalo-myelogenic* theory, which held that there was a continuum of brains, spinal marrow, and sperm (hence "sperm is a drop of brain" [Van der Horst 1994, 207]); and the *pangenesis* theory, which maintained that sperm (like bones and flesh) was produced from all parts of the body (see Van der Horst 1994, 207–15).

bodily fluids, and spirit (see Martin 1995, 200–201; Vorster 2002b, 21). In the description of Peter Brown,

> To make love was to bring one's blood to the boil, as the fiery vital spirit swept through the veins, turning the blood into the whitened foam of semen. It was a process in which the body as a whole—the brain cavity, the marrow of the backbone, the kidneys, and the lower bowel region—was brought into play 'as in a mighty choir'. The genital regions were mere points of passage. They were the outlets of a human Espresso machine. (1988, 17)

The definition of sperm by the ancient medical theorist Galen captures this belief: "Sperm is bundled force (*dynamis*) in moist matter; or, according to another definition: sperm is moist matter from warm *pneuma* . . . ; or sperm is hot *pneuma* in moist matter, which moves from itself and has the potential to generate" (quoted in van Tilborg & Chatelion Counet 2000, 240).

The Astronomical Complex

Reflection about these issues will not be complete without some thoughts on the so-called *astronomical complex*. That is, the whole set of ideas regarding divine beings, celestial bodies, and deceased ancestors. The belief, which Israelites shared with most ancient Mediterranean people, is that the sun, moon, and stars were living beings (see Smith 1982, 204; Allison 1993, 22; Malina 1995, 6–8). Whatever substance composes the stars also composes the soul (see Martin 1995, 118–20). Therefore, it was possible, for example, to talk about the spirit (pneuma) of the stars as in *3 Enoch*: "[Come and I will show you] the spirits of the stars, which stand in the Raqia every night" (46:1; Alexander trans.).

The general features that followed from this belief were that celestial bodies have some kind of influence on affairs on earth, and that they can and should be approached for obtaining divine knowledge. No single or unified picture of these celestial beings existed in the Israelite world. There are two lines of evidence that are both based on this train of beliefs about the celestial bodies: one identifying the celestial bodies with divine beings (with immortals such as angels) and the other identifying heavenly bodies with deceased ancestors.

The first is the association of celestial bodies with deities or divine beings and, more specifically, the suggestion that the stars are angels and that Judean people worshipped (reverenced) angels (see Allison 1993, 22; Segal 2004, 265)—a viewpoint also expressed in Colossians 2:18 (see also Collins 2000, 88; Grabbe 2000, 222) and later Christian writings (see Roussin 1997, 90). This notion is further supported by depicting Yahweh, the sovereign god in Israel, with solar and celestial connotations (see Keel & Uehlinger 1998, 177–281).[13]

This process, called the solarization and astralization of Yahweh, consists of the identification of him with these celestial bodies and of his being depicted as the host of the heavenly bodies, where the traits of the sun god become attached to him (see Smith 1982, 204; Niehr 1995, 67–71). Herbert Niehr maintains that in the postexilic period, the notion of Yahweh as sun god was continued in Israelite thought (see 1995, 71; see also Smith 1982, 204–6). Perhaps more common was the worshipping or reverencing, if you like, of the sun, without the sun taking the place of Yahweh (or, of the Most High God). Bruce Malina points out that reverencing the living celestial personages and God's sky servants was proper behavior that was even portrayed in the heart of Judean temple religion: "The Jerusalem temple and its appurtenances served as a massive, nationally known billboard for astronomical lore" (1995, 15). This is the case if Josephus's description of the temple is taken seriously. He tells us that on the fine linen tapestry covering the gate of the temple was portrayed a panorama of the heavens, the signs of the living beings in heaven. Josephus tells us, furthermore, that the seven lamps in the holy of holies represented the planets while the loaves on the table, twelve in total, represented the circle of the zodiac and the year (*War* 5.210–18).

It is also clear that despite adherence to the prohibition of worshipping other gods, the Judeans whose views are preserved in the Qumran documents prayed to the sun and were at least involved in reverencing it.[14] They were not the only Judeans with an appetite for Helios since it figures prominently on *Jewish* magical amulets, often with inscriptions

13. Zevit argues that the figurines of goddesses indicate the existence of a sun cult or some form of celestial worship as part of Israelite religion (see 2001, 346).

14. Smith points out that the gold-plated staircase that is mentioned in the *Temple Scroll* was probably used for rooftop prayers to the sun (see 1982, 207). This viewpoint is supported by Josephus's remarks that the Essenes prayed to the sun, and that as "self-styled 'children of light' the Qumran sectarians had a special interest in luminaries and especially in the sun; this is shown not only in their prayers for sunrise, but also by their abandonment of the lunar calendar prescribed by the Bible in favor of one represented as solar" (*War* 2.128).

naming the deity and his angels (see Roussin 1997, 89). The zodiac in later synagogue decoration is probably a continuation of the same mental framework (see Hachlili 1977; Lesses 1998, 294–95, 363).

The second line of evidence has to do with the connection between celestial bodies and deceased ancestors. The dominant view in ancient Israel about the fate of the dead is that they descend to a netherworld, usually called *Sheol* (see Craffert 1999b, 45–48; Segal 2004, 134–36). While they were thought to enjoy a shadowy existence in *Sheol*, it was also pointed out that, at least in some circles, the deceased ancestors played a continuous role in community affairs.

In some Israelite circles of the late Second Temple period, the deceased ancestors were elevated to the heavenly realm of the immortals and consequently performed certain functions from there. They could either be consulted or visited by the living (see Friedman & Overton 2000, 39). But they (or their spirits/souls) could also take possession of the living.

It is today widely attested that ancestor veneration was widely practiced in ancient Israel, and that the tombs of especially the patriarchs and prophets were places mediating divine power and providing access to the divine world. Both the archaeological evidence and literary tradition give sufficient support to the notion that ancestral veneration was widely practiced in ancient Israel. The ancestors were, so to speak, a gateway to the divine realm and were considered a continuous influence in human affairs (see Jeremias 1958, 129; Smith 1990; Bloch-Smith 1992). The continuous practice to offer prayers at the tombs of the patriarchs (and matriarchs) confirms the insight that the ancestors (and their tombs) achieved the status of intermediaries with the divine world.[15] In fact, prayers could even be addressed to the deceased ancestors rather than to a divine being. Sometimes the term *Elohim* is used to refer to spirits of dead ancestors (see Van der Toorn 1996, 221; Friedman & Overton 2000, 43).

The common cultural physics of the day in the Mediterranean world insisted that stars and souls were of the same substance. According to Pliny, this discovery belongs to Hipparchus: "Hipparchus will never receive all the praise he deserves since no one has better established the relation between man and the stars, and shown more clearly that our souls are particles of

---

15. The case of Rachel the matriarch supports the assertion that the tombs of matriarchs were venerated. Her tomb at Bethlehem (recently excavated) became a place of pilgrimage, where barren women prayed for progeny (see Lightstone 1984, 74).

divine fire" (quoted in Segal 1980, 1349).[16] A host of texts indicate that humans could become angels or astral beings—that is, deceased ancestors continued life in astral format. The best-known figures probably are Moses and Enoch. In some Israelite circles, Moses was indeed seen as a divine being (see Van der Horst 1983; Lang 2002, 21), while *1 Enoch* (104) assures the righteous that they will one day shine like the lights of heaven—an idea also expressed in Daniel 12 (see also Collins 2000, 335). As Martin says: "The physiological common sense of this entire system thus underwrites the notion that the human soul after death will ascend to its natural level of cosmic substance and will become either a star or something like a star" (1995, 119). Not that everyone will achieve this status, but these instances validate that ecstatic and mystical experiences were part of the culture and represent for them the potential of human transcendence into an immortal astral/soul state.

In summary, the evidence shows that celestial bodies were living beings, that divine beings were closely connected to heavenly bodies, and that in some way these entities influenced human and earthly affairs. Therefore, the search for truth in the stars was a continuing theme in many Israelite writings (see Davies 1997, 40). That (divine) world was not accessible without special revelations such as heavenly journeys, visions, dreams, or the like (see Collins 1997, 50).[17]

16. The stars have fiery bodies according to *3 Enoch* (Alexander 1986, 299).

17. Astrology is concerned with the influence of heavenly bodies on terrestrial life. It operates on the assumption that human actions and natural phenomena alike depend on the movements of the heavenly bodies (see Ogilvie 1969, 54; Kuemmerlin-McLean 1992, 469; Rochberg-Halton 1992, 504). As Malina maintains, "It was common in the period to read the sky for information about nations as a whole or prominent individuals such as kings; or some sought general information about when to begin certain activities such as war, house building, buying or selling and traveling" (1995, 9).

CHAPTER 7

The Shamanic Complex and Ancient Societies

Introduction

IN THIS CHAPTER TWO related issues will be addressed. The first is wheth-er the shaman figure can be distinguished from other (religious) social types. How are they to be distinguished in cases where they all appear in the same cultural system and social location? Although this question has already been partially answered with the definition of the shamanic complex adopted above, it still needs some explicit reflection.

The second question is whether shamanism can be identified in the ancient world. It is today acknowledged that shamanism encounters a worldwide distribution on all continents (see, e.g., Thorpe 1993). Despite an often-repeated claim (which is probably a repetition of a claim made by Eliade; see 1961, 153) that it is a rare phenomenon in Africa, it is nowa-days accepted that ASC-based religious entrepreneurs are (or the shamanic complex is) widely distributed even there. But is it to be found in the ancient world?

Such a project is faced with a number of serious difficulties. Even for anthropologists to design a fieldwork program on shamanism today is no easy task (see Voigt 1984, 13). Not only are many of the aspects surrounding such figures enclosed in secrecy, but a rather small group of potential informants is involved in the ASC experiences of the shaman. Much of the information obtained from informants outside the circle of the shaman is the product of stereotypical presentations from within the cultural expectations.[1] It is furthermore difficult in principle to find the

---

1. See, for example, the study of Jones, who got much of his information on the Limbu shaman from an old man who never was a shaman himself (1976, 48). In fact, his

necessary information on such persons. A soul journey or heavenly trip is by definition personal and private, and unless the shaman tells people about it, nobody else has access to the content of such experiences. These experiences are strictly speaking not *public events* but secondhand accounts of personal and individual experiences. Add to that the insight that no shaman of worth, Harner says (see 1988, 12), would describe himself or herself as a shaman because of the humble realization that the powers involved are not their own.

From an analytical point of view (that of the anthropological historian), descriptions of the actual ASCs are important, while the potential beneficiaries (and those people for whom the influence of shamanic interventions is common cultural practice) are concerned about the divine insights, knowledge, and mediation of power that flow from such experiences. It is to be expected, therefore, that in most accounts the outcomes of a shamanic journey would be more prominent than the detail about the journey itself. This again illustrates the differences between the insiders' taken-for-granted knowledge and the outsiders' need for learning a second, new language or thick description. As with the application of the shamanic model to regions and cultures outside that of the original Siberian one, scholars also have to face up to the fact that local terms are commonly used in any reports. This is no different when looking at the ancient world.

Despite these difficulties, it is worth asking whether this pattern is visible also in the ancient world. It is not the aim here to give any comprehensive picture of shamanism in the ancient world, not even an overview of all the debates. The aim is rather to indicate that what is described as the shamanic complex and the shamanic figure (an ASC-based religious practitioner) is not at all unknown to either the Greco-Roman or the Israelite world.

Specifically, regarding the ancient Greek world, which would deserve a complete study on its own, the aim is merely to indicate what is going on in some research circles. The question of a comparison of social types will be addressed first, however.

---

knowledge was challenged by the shaman, since the deity had never come to the old man (see also Ripinsky-Naxon 1993, 21).

Shamans and Other Religious Specialists

In order to be a distinct social type, the shaman should be distinguishable from other religious specialists or social types. The argument here is that there is indeed an identifiable pattern among religious practitioners, which can be called shamanism or the shamanic complex. The dynamics of shamanism, it has been argued, are constituted by biologically based ASC experiences that find expression particularly in healing, divination (such as, teaching, prophecy and poetry), and control of spirits. Although shamans are not the only figures who experience ritually or religiously sanctioned ASCs, they are the only ones where this configuration of ASCs appears.

If this pattern can be identified in particular cases, it means that it should be possible to distinguish the shamanic practitioners from other religious specialists or social types in those cases. Although this can be demonstrated on a general level, the real challenge is to demonstrate this in a specific setting.

Based on two reasons it is often objected that such distinctions cannot be made: first, it is possible that the same person might fulfill different roles, and, second, that the shaman role, by definition, overlaps with that of other religious specialists[2] and is therefore not always so clearly identifiable.[3] It has, however, been argued that the shamanic complex represents an identifiable configuration of components, a configuration that, despite some overlap, does not occur in the same way with other religious specialists. The real challenge, as has been said, would be to describe these religious specialists as they appear in specific cultural systems. Here the task is to show that there are indeed examples of clear differentiation in scholarly studies between the shaman and other religious specialists, particularly the priest, the medicine man, the sage, and the prophet.

---

2. It has been argued that the functions of the shaman are healing (which overlaps with other types of healers or medicine men) and divination (which overlaps with prophets, visionaries, or holy men).

3. It has to be realized that in addition to the hundreds of concepts that members of traditional societies use, anthropologists and scholars of comparative religion have employed yet another large number of concepts to describe this pattern: these include *prophet, medicine man, sage, healer, holy man, seer, sorcerer, magician, wizard, wise man, wisdom teacher, exorcist, clairvoyant, divinator, fortune teller, medium, necromancer, witch doctor*, and the like.

Shaman versus Priest

Both priest and shaman are intermediaries to the divine world, but in different ways. In studies where the distinction is made, the following features of the priest clearly distinguish the two types (see Burkert 1962, 53–55; Grim 1983, 185–91; Gilberg 1984, 23–25; Overholt 1985, 9–10; Winkelman 1992, 28–46, 69–76).

The priest is a ceremonial performer who does not primarily have ecstatic experiences; the priest, Harner says, works basically in "ordinary reality" (1988, 9). Priesthood is often inherited and therefore part of the official political structure (priests usually serve as political leaders in their societies). The priest must learn certain fixed rituals, mostly associated with a sanctuary and the ceremonial cycle. Priests involved in religious rites are usually concerned about the protection of agricultural products via agricultural rites performed at commemorative feasts and at specific sanctuaries.

The priest type is usually associated with the formation of settled cultural centers, and the principal function of the priest is the performance of ritual sacrifice. The teaching function of priest is usually restricted to the preservation and transmission of the ritual and sanctuary information (traditional theology).

The shaman's sacred place is not restricted to one holy place but is connected to the shaman's bodily presence and immediate communication with the divine. Their functions are ASC-based and focus on healing, control of spirits, and teaching. The shaman's teaching is predominantly the intuitive explication of numinous experiences. Within the same cultural system, priests and shamans have different relationships to the godhead and the patron spirit(s). The summary of Grim is helpful:

> The most significant distinction between the priest and the shaman is that the priest is one who performs a traditional sacrifice based upon an acknowledged scripture or ritual formula, while the shaman is more spontaneous and less bound by traditions. Relying not on a verbal scripture or established theology, the shaman creates a personal, symbolic mode of sacrifice. (1983, 190)

Shaman versus Prophet

The prophet as social type can be distinguished both from the priest and the shaman. The primary function of the prophet can be described as "the one who speaks the divine revelation directly to the community" (Grim 1983, 180). Therefore, there are profound similarities between the shamanic and prophetic types.

The definition of Israelite prophets, as mediator figures claiming to have direct messages from a divinity, confirms this point. While sharing with shamans the ability to obtain ASCs (such as ecstasy), prophets had an authority founded on direct divine revelation and extraordinary personal qualities; they "use religion as a dynamic power for social and religious change" (Gilberg 1984, 24). The common view of the classical prophets of ancient Israel conforms to this picture: "these figures were . . . social, moral, and religious reformers" (Gray 1993, 164).[4] However, as indicated earlier (see above, pp. 72–73), very few, if any, of the prophets in the Israelite tradition ever acted as healers or diviners in the sense ascribed above to shamans or as ascribed to Jesus of Nazareth.

Shaman versus Medicine Man or Woman

The medicine man or woman, such as the other categories, is often vague and difficult to define or identify in reality. Nevertheless, it seems best to restrict the term to those practitioners who have knowledge of traditional medicine, and in a context where they operate together with shamans, they will take care of physical ailments such as broken legs or physical injuries (see Gilberg 1984, 24). In contexts where both medicine man and shaman types do not occur, it is difficult to distinguish which type is present. This is so because every shaman is also a healer, but every medicine man or woman is not necessarily a shaman. Not all medicine men or women have the features and functions ascribed to the shamanic complex above.

Shaman versus Sage or Teacher of Wisdom

The sage as social type, Grim says, can be found particularly in the humanist philosophical traditions of Greece and China (see 1983, 196). The most significant characteristic of the sage as social type is that of teacher.

---

4. The interesting contribution of Gray's study is that in Josephus's writings, the term *prophet* receives a new meaning: for Josephus, a prophet is someone with special insight into the future, and a "true prophet" is one whose predictions come true (1993, 165). This is interesting because if the evidence from a close contemporary of Jesus (i.e., Josephus) is taken into account, *prophet* had a very specific definition at that time.

It is in education that they impress people with their articulated ideas and comprehensive lifestyle.

Their orientation is not primarily with otherworldly concerns but with problems in the social and political spheres of their own time, which they try to rectify. For the sage, moral rectification is the way to reestablish basic harmony in the experienced universe.

The differences with the shaman are apparent. Teaching is at best only one aspect of the shamanic functions.

Summary

In order for *shaman* to be a meaningful category for identifying social types, it should in general be possible to distinguish the shaman from other religious practitioners. The differences and similarities within the Israelite tradition between visionaries, on the one hand, and priests and sages, on the other hand, are, therefore, equally illuminating (see, for example, Russel 1964, 173–77). It has to be acknowledged, however, that neither the historical identification of a specific individual as a shaman (or for that matter as any other social type) nor the distinction between shamans and other religious entrepreneurs is easy to make. Given the variety of definitions of the shaman (and, obviously, of other religious entrepreneurs) it is to be expected that the boundaries between them will often be very fluid. From the perspective of the shamanic complex, it is maintained that shamans are primarily defined by means of their involvement in ASCs on behalf of the community and by certain combinations of elements that do not appear in these configurations amongst other religious specialists. The challenge of the kind of historical identification suggested here would be to distinguish the shaman from other religious specialists in a particular cultural system.

If it is taken into account that not only the shamanic model but also that all other social-type models are of the homomorphic nature (i.e., they are not built according to scale), then it becomes easier to accept that a model cannot function as a die, or as a perfect matrix for identifying historical cases. The use of homomorphic models perfectly fits the nature of abduction; it is the interpretive force of the overall design that needs to be convincing.

The Shamanic Complex and the Ancient Greeks

In some scholarly circles, a number of the well-known Greek characters are described as shamans, including Empedocles, Pythagoras, and Orpheus (see Burkert 1962; Brown 1981, 376–81; Kingsley 1994; 1995, 217–32).

Empedocles, a student of Pythagoras in the fifth century BCE, for example, is a central figure for discussing shamanism in the ancient Greek-speaking world. He was based in Sicily but was very much a wandering charismatic who was known for his strange powers to perform miracles, control the elements, and raise the dead. The sources present him as poet, wisdom teacher, miracle worker, and healer.

Diogenes Laertius, in *Lives of the Eminent Philosophers* (8.69) tells about Panthea, a woman of Agrigentum, who had been given up by physicians but was cured by Empedocles. In the same writing, Diogenes (8.59) also tells us that Empedocles could provide drought and rain. Iamblichus, in his *Life of Pythagoras* (135–36), says that Empedocles was surnamed "the Wind-stiller" because he could still the wind—in addition to several other abilities: predicting earthquakes, terminating hurricanes, stopping hail from falling and rivers from flowing. He was also credited with bringing back from Hades a dead man's strength (Diogenes Laertius, "Empedocles," *Lives of Eminent Philosophers* 8.59). Dodds concludes his analysis of this figure with the following remark: "If I am right, Empedocles represents not a new but a very old type of personality, the shaman who combines the still undifferentiated functions of magician and naturalist, poet and philosopher, preacher, healer, and public counselor" (1951, 146). This is also the verdict of Kingsley: "Those who try to understand Empedocles as a phenomenon in his own right invariably end up describing him as an individual who managed to combine in himself the contradictory roles of magician and philosopher, wonder-worker and thinker" (1995, 231).

These descriptions are as close as one can get to the religious practitioners described above by means of the shamanic model. They give an indication that, when approached by means of the shamanic model, some ancient Greek figures closely resemble the shamanic type—even though they are, like shamanic figures the world over, often named by some local terms (such as *goēs* in the Greek literature).

In studies of the ancient Greek world there is, however, often a strong resistance to the application of the shaman terminology. Kingsley shows that often these objections are the result of terminological confusion or plain unwillingness to adopt the category. Referring to a remark by Kahn that was widely accepted (also by Eliade), Kingsley points out: "He [Kahn] argued that the peculiar claims of prophecy, healing and restoring the dead to life which we find in Empedocles' own writings would be genuinely shamanistic if, 'and only if', these feats had been performed in a state of ecstasy" (1994, 188). The same applies to the evaluation of whether Orpheus can be seen as a shaman. While admitting shamanic influences in this case, Kahn is bound to conclude that it is not a case of shamanism because of the typological divergence: during the soul flight, his soul does not leave his body—he descends "in flesh and blood."

Kingsley correctly remarks that with such nitpicking, there will be no shamans anywhere. As indicated above, within the life of any shaman there are variations in ASC experiences, and the defining feature is the ability of controlled ASCs of various sorts. The line of argument, further-more, shows a lack of understanding of ASCs. Not all shamanic journeys are soul flights, and even claims that they "were in the body" do not mean they were actually bodily journeys (as I have indicated earlier). In cultures adapted to ASCs, bodies just like souls (where there is a belief in souls) can not only travel but can actually perform several other activities.

It seems clear that at least in some instances in the Greek world, this pattern can be useful in identifying and describing some religious practitioners.

The Shamanic Complex and the Israelite Religious Traditions

Even though it cannot be investigated in any detail in this study, an interesting question worth speculating on is whether there were indeed shamanic figures in the ancient Israelite world.[5] Or, put more precisely,

---

5. Especially the Hebrew Bible is searched for shamanic elements (see, e.g., Kapelrud 1967; Goldammer 1972; Bystrina 1991). While many such elements are identified, they are often not sufficient to identify any shamans in the Israelite world. Grabbe's attempt to find an example of shamanism in the Israelite tradition suffers the use of a local definition (see 1995, 149). He adopts Hultkrantz's definition and claims that if we accept Hultkrantz's strictures (ecstatic experiences), shamans as such are not found in the tradition. But according to Hultkrantz's definition, many others who are identified as shamans will then also disappear from the scene. Methodologically, Overholt's approach is, comparatively, much more friendly for dealing with "prophet-like figures" in cross-cultural settings (see 1985, 4–7).

whether the pattern of the shamanic complex can also be identified among ancient Israelite social figures.

A number of studies have ventured into identifying the "shamanic elements" in the ancient Israelite world. Given the nature of the model described above (a homomorphic model) as well as the overlap with some other social types, it should be emphasized that the present aim is not to identify a list of "shamanic features." As has been indicated, there are no shamanic elements as such that can be listed (because shamans, for example, share many ASCs with prophetic figures), but within a specific combination, ASC elements contribute to define shamanic figures and to distinguish them from other social types. It will be indicated that there were many elements widespread in the Israelite world that are common in shamanism.

ASCs and Related Phenomena in Ancient Israelite Texts

Despite the fact that the Hebrew Bible refers to a religiosity dominated by a temple and its priests (who obviously saw any other form of mediation with the divine world as competition), several references show that ASC experiences were widespread in the Israelite tradition. In fact, the Christian Bible is filled with visionary stories, dream experiences, and other similar ASC experiences; it is too seldom emphasized what an important role visions, apparitions, journeys, and the like played in the Israelite traditions. Pilch points out that

> altered states of consciousness experiences fill the Bible beginning with Genesis when God puts the first creature into a deep sleep in order to create Eve, his helpmate (Gen 2:21) and ending with Revelation where John the Revealer repeats four times that what he reports is the result of experiences in trance (*en pneumati*: Rev 1:10; 4:2; 17:3; 21:10). (2002b, 691)

God often speaks to the patriarchs in dreams and visions. In Genesis 12:7 and 18:1, Abraham experiences visits from Yahweh (an epiphany), while in Genesis 15:1 he has only a dreamlike vision promising him multiple offspring. Isaac's wife, Rebecca, is protected from King Abimelech after he receives a visitation by Yahweh (Gen 26:3). Jacob encounters God in a dream and later calls the location of the encounter "the gate of heaven" (Gen 28:11–17), and in his future father-in-law's service, he receives instructions from an angel about rearing the goats (Gen 31:10–11), and in old age he receives a vision to move to Egypt (Gen 46:2). Joseph, the expert dreamer in the Hebrew Bible, has several dreams regarding his future greatness (Gen 37:5–9), and he turns out to be a dream interpreter *par excellence.*

The story about the beginning of the Israelite nation in the land of Israel is filled with visionary and epiphanic experiences of Moses—the shamanic type of figure who leaves Egypt after rivalry with Egyptian magicians (see Taylor 1985, 62). On Mount Sinai, Moses experienced several epiphanies and auditory revelations (see Exod 19; Num 12:7–8). In this same period we read: "And he said, 'Hear my words: When there are prophets among you, I Yahweh make myself known to them in visions; I speak to them in dreams'" (Num 12:6).

In the time of the boy Samuel, we learn that the "word of Yahweh was rare in those days; visions were not widespread" (1 Sam 3:1). But then a couple of chapters further, it is said: "Then the spirit of Yahweh will possess you, and you will be in a prophetic frenzy along with them and be turned into a different person" (1 Sam 10:6). Samuel clearly experiences ASCs that result in some form of transformation of his life.

It was normal for Israelite prophets to go into trances to receive a vision or to hear the words of God. In one of his visions, Isaiah sees Yahweh on his throne surrounded by heavenly beings (Isa 6:1–2). The distinction between a heavenly vision and heavenly journey in such a context is rather minimal. Jeremiah received his messages both as auditions (e.g., 1:1) and visions (e.g., 1:13). The Hebrew Bible ecstatic *par excellence* is Ezekiel (see Michaelsen 1989, 37; Grabbe 1995, 110). He often experiences divine possession (the "hand" or "spirit" of Yahweh comes upon him; see, e.g., Ezek 3:14, 22; 8:1); several times he has journey experiences (8:1–3; 11:1, 24) and is commanded to prophesy when the spirit falls upon him (4:7; 6:2; 13:2; 21:2). The other prophets with books named after them in the Hebrew Bible all claim to have had either visions or auditions (see Grabbe 1995, 78; Lee 1999, 135). Other examples include the seventy elders in Num 11:25 who start to prophesy when they become spirit-possessed, the prophet guild who can find lost objects, are rainmakers, and are consulted about sickness and war (see Kapelrud 1967, 91; Goldammer 1972, 278–80; Lee 1999, 137–38).

Israel's first two kings are both involved in several ASC activities. After consulting Samuel (a man of God who can dispense the spirit of God to kings) about lost animals, Saul is appointed king. On his return to the city, he meets with a group of prophets, enters an ASC ("became another person") and prophesies with them (1 Sam 9–10).[6] Later in his career when looking to kill David, he goes to the prophetic quarters, where he again becomes spirit-possessed and for a day and night lies naked while prophesying (1 Sam 19:9–24).[7] David is often associated with two prophet-seers, Nathan and Gad (see Grabbe 1995, 68).

In the Israelite tradition, Enoch, the sky traveler *par excellence*, has visions and dreams; he travels to heaven and on numerous occasions converses with God and the angles. A typical description of such a vision is the following: "I saw in my sleep what I now speak with my tongue of flesh and the breath of the mouth" (*1 Enoch* 14:2, Isaac trans.), or, "Again I saw a vision with my own eyes as I was sleeping" (*1 Enoch* 86:1, Isaac trans.; and see also 90:40). "Enoch's role is particularly reminiscent of the shaman," Niditch says (1980, 159). *First Enoch* is one of a large collection of books about other- or outer-worldly journeys in the Israelite tradition.[8] Together with the Hekhalot literature (a large collection of books within the Israelite tradition about heavenly journeys, which dates from the first to the sixth century CE), these form a formidable collection of mystical literature (see Niditch 1980; Lesses 1998). In an excellent study, Davila shows that the "descenders to the chariot" in the Hekhalot literature "closely resemble the model of shamanism" (2001, 306).

According to some Qumran exegetes, "God had revealed the mysteries of his servants the prophets to the Teacher of Righteousness, who was either the founder of the Qumran group or an early leader of it" (VanderKam 1994, 44–45). One such text clearly states that the Teacher of Righteousness received his knowledge from a vision:

> I will stand firm in my sentry-post, I will position myself in my fortress to see what he says to me, what he answers to my allegation. YHWH answered me and said: Write the vision; inscribe it on tablets so that [he who reads it] takes it on the run. (1QpHab 6.12–16, García Martínez trans.)

6. Like drummers or chanters in other traditions, the band of prophets used musical instruments (harps, tambourines, flutes, and lyres) while in an ASC (1 Sam 10:5). Pilch also describes other means of inducing trance found in the Bible (see 2002a).

7. Saul also consults a necromancer, the witch of Endor, on occasion before a battle (see 1 Sam 28). Only she "sees" Samuel, an indication that she is in an ASC.

8. For more examples of such ascensions or heavenly journeys in the apocalyptic literature, see Segal (2004, 407–8).

Lang suggests that a poem found in another Qumran document can be understood as referring to a heavenly journey by the founder of this brotherhood (see 2002, 195). The author (the Teacher of Righteousness?) claims: "besides me no-one is exalted," and he is "counted among the gods," and his "dwelling is in the holy congregation," where he is "counted among the gods" (4QMa 11.1, García Martínez trans.).

A related phenomenon is divination. The importance of divination in Israelite society, Grabbe says, "has generally been overlooked or ignored because of the assumption that divination is contrary to true biblical religion" (1995, 119). As his brief overview shows, this is far from the truth because all sorts of divination (including the Urim and Thummim and the Ephod, necromancy, and lecanomancy (observing the patterns of oil on water) are well attested.

Shamanic Figures in the Israelite Tradition?

It is impossible in this study to do a proper analysis of any other figure in the Israelite tradition. Allowing room for speculation, it may be suggested that at least two figures, Moses and Elisha do not easily fit into the *prophet* category and could possibly be seen as shamanic figures.

Moses's public career started with a vision of a burning bush (during a trip deep into the desert), where an angel commissioned him to his task (Exod 3:2). He received a magical rod, which was used in control of the elements (to divide the Red sea [Exod 14:16] and to provide water from a rock [Exod 17:5; Num 20:11]) and to determine the outcome of a battle (Exod 17:10–16). He is credited with several other "nature miracles," such as causing natural catastrophes (Exod 7–11), cleaning up bitter water (Exod 15:22–25), and providing food (Exod 16). Moses often ascends to a mountaintop (Exod 19:3, 24:18), where he remains in solitude and afterwards acts as intermediary between the people and the divine world (Exod 19–20). His life ends on a mountain (in solitude) and he is buried by Yahweh (Deut 34:6). Therefore, it is not surprising that Moses's heavenly ascent is a common theme in later Israelite literature (see Van der Horst 1983; Morray-Jones 1992, 13; Lang 2002, 20–21). Moses is presented as a "super prophet" (Lee 1999, 149) who often saw visions of God, and to whom God spoke directly (Num 12:8). He was a charismatic leader, lawgiver, prophet, miracle worker, and intercessor for his people (see also Goldammer 1972, 271–74).

The second figure is Elisha. Despite the application of a strict definition to the word, Grabbe could still find an example of a *shaman* in the
Hebrew Bible.

> Probably the figure most like the archetypical shaman is Elisha.
> He is able to harness the supernatural powers to perform miracles,
> to feed a large number from a small amount of food, to heal, to
> restore what is lost. He is able to see the supernatural world and to
> predict the future. (1995, 185)

He received his training from Elijah (2 Kgs 3:11), who is also portrayed as a shamanic figure (see Lee 1999, 138–40), and who is taken up
to heaven in a fiery chariot (Elisha's vision?). Elisha is also credited with
nature miracles (parting the River Jordan, making bitter water safe), with
healings, with reviving the dead, with feeding multitudes, and with finding lost objects. Elisha is a diviner and seer (his servant could not lie to
him) (see 2 Kgs 2–6).

Summary

While suggesting a close resemblance to the shamanic pattern, these examples also confirm that the typical features associated with the shamanic
complex can easily be identified in the biblical world. Various ASCs (such
as spirit or divine possession, flights or journeys to heaven or to other
designated areas, and healing and mediating functions associated with
such experiences) were well known (not to say common) among Israelite
religious figures (prophets, seers and mediums, kings, and the like).

It is also clear that certain culturally approved means of entering such
states could possibly be seen in the recurring theme of solitude in desert
areas or on mountaintops. Such figures in the Israelite tradition also operated parallel to the official temple cult practitioners. It would come as no
surprise if evidence for other shamanic figures were to be found in a thor-
ough analysis of the Israelite traditions by means of eyes sensitized by the
shamanic model—a position well demonstrated by Overholt (see 1985).

PART 3

Jesus *and the*

Shamanic Complex

CHAPTER 8

Baptism and Spirit-Possession Experiences

Introduction

THE INITIATION OF A shaman takes on various forms and follows along many different paths. In many examples, it starts with a disorientating illness accompanied by dreams or visions (see Thorpe 1993, 25–29). The most dramatic is initiation by lightning bolt; thus, many societies have the category of folks who become shamans after being struck by lightning; these are referred to as "lightning shamans." They are often venerated and feared as the mightiest shamans (see Kalweit 1992, 46–49). Also known are initiations that follow other accidents (such as falling from a tree) or a lengthy period of illness. In Limbu tradition, one becomes a shaman simply as a result of the possession by a deity (see Jones 1976, 47; Eliade 1964, 110).

Against the common assumption that shamanism follows an acute disorientating illness in the shaman-to-be, from the point of view of a homomorphic model it is perhaps more correct to say that the person experiences a "major life crisis" (Walsh 1993, 752), which kick-starts the process of becoming a shaman. The shaman's vocation, however, is normally announced with ecstatic behavior (see Lewis 1989, 48). While these incidents lead to a spontaneous vocation, a hereditary transmission of the shamanic profession is also known (see Eliade 1987, 202). It is clear that the call to become a shaman is part and parcel of the community orientation of the person and conforms to the worldview and mythical tradition of that group.

As far as I know, it is only with regard to Jesus's baptism that ideas of shamanism have been applied to the Jesus tradition. In his discussion of

Jesus as a person of spirit, Borg remarks that Jesus's baptism, followed by a testing in the wilderness is strikingly similar to what is reported of charismatic figures cross-culturally—specifically shamans (1987, 43). Somewhat earlier, Smith suggested that the stories about Jesus's wandering into the wilderness after his baptism (Mark 1:12–13 par.) resembled the session at the beginning of a shaman's career (see 1978, 104–6). But nowhere has this model been explored for the implications contained in such a remark. If what happened at his baptism was similar to the initiation experiences of shamanic figures, this could be the starting point for understanding the life of Jesus as a Galilean shamanic figure.

Jesus's Baptism: Initiation as a Shamanic Figure?

It is generally accepted that one of the most certain (and reasonable) facts we know about Jesus is that in his late twenties or around the age of thirty, he left Nazareth and became a follower of a wilderness prophet named John. In the words of Crossan, "Jesus' baptism by John is one of the surest things we know about them both" (1991a, 234). As has been pointed out, according to the Wredebahn, only the actual baptism by John can be taken as an authentic event. The rest was mythological additions (such as the voice and the vision). For those on the Schweitzerstrasse these "events" all count as supernatural events. But the baptism scene can be viewed differently.

Jesus's Teacher, John the Baptist

Known through a variety of early sources, John the Baptist stood in the "charismatic stream of Judaism" (Borg 1987, 41). Of the little information that has been preserved about him, his style of dress is known. According to Mark 1:6, he wore a camel skin with a leather girdle; this resembles to the garment worn by the prophet Elijah (see 2 Kgs 1:8). John is presented as a prophet and according to some traditions, regarded himself as the Elijah *redivivus*. Not only did Jesus in all probability join John the Baptist (see Webb 1994, 217–19), but it seems plausible that John was also Jesus's mentor. According to the Gospel of John (1:35), the first two followers of Jesus were initially followers of John the Baptist.

Jesus's First Spirit-Possession Experience

According to the Gospels, Jesus experiences an ASC during his baptism by John that contains several plausible shamanic elements. In a vision, he saw the sky opening and a spirit descending upon him like a dove, and he heard a voice declaring him to be a beloved son of God (Mark 1:10). The Lukan (3:22) and Matthean (3:16) versions are typical third-person accounts of a cultural event that was reported by someone having experienced it. They contain all the elements in the Markan version and report that after he had been baptized, Jesus saw the sky opened, and the Holy Spirit descended in the form of a dove (vision), and a voice came from heaven (audition). John's (1:32) version differs in that he adds the culturally logical thing that since those things happened, John the Baptist (and others) could also see and hear them. In cultures where visions and auditions are as real (and more real) than ordinary seeing and hearing, it is obvious that in their accounts, others could bear witness to them. It has to be borne in mind that in the human brain an objective observation and a vision register in exactly the same way; culture teaches us the differences between them.

It would be difficult to conclude from the little evidence that either John the Baptist or people in the crowd experienced ASCs. The evidence at least allows the conclusion that what happened at Jesus's baptism was his ASC experience and that besides visionary and auditory elements, it contained an experience of being spirit-possessed. John hints at it (the spirit "remained"), and the other sources implicitly assume that the spirit remained with him. In other words, he was in a state of spirit-possession because immediately he went on a spirit trip to the desert (Mark 1:12 and Matt 4:1). Luke is most explicit about the fact that Jesus remained spirit-possessed: "Jesus, full of the Holy Spirit, returned from the Jordan and was led by the Spirit in the wilderness" (4:1).

Solitary Stay in the Wilderness and ASC Experiences

Three of the Gospel texts claim that after the spirit-possession vision, Jesus was led into the wilderness by the spirit (Mark 1:12–13; Luke 4:1–13; Matt 4:1–11). A prolonged solitary stay in the wilderness (forty days) without food provides a fertile ground for more ASC experiences. As is to be expected, several such phenomena are reported for this period.[1]

In a single sentence, Mark (1:13) mentions three remarkable ASC features. For one, Jesus was tempted by Satan, and then the angels ministered to him. In between, Mark mentions that Jesus was with the wild beasts. Within this context and nested in between the devil's tempting him and the angels' ministering to him, Jesus's being with the beasts was most likely also the product of a visionary experience (see further below on Jesus's relationship to animals) rather than an encounter with real desert animals.

Matthew (4:11) also mentions that after the departure of the tempter (an adverse or evil heavenly being in the Israelite tradition of the late Second Temple period), Jesus experienced the presence of sky messengers (angels) who ministered to him. In other words, he had an ASC in which he either saw (in a vision) in his presence or otherwise experienced the company of heavenly messenger beings.

But it is the first mentioned feature that is most remarkable. Satan (in Mark 1:13), the tempter (in Matt 4:3) or the devil (in Matt 4:10 and Luke 4:3) visited Jesus in an ASC.[2] While the main point of these reports is the temptations by this evil heavenly being, they also contain information about the nature of the events: they were middle-world journeys. Since this is not the only clue to Jesus's ASC journeys, and because they are so central to shamanism, this topic will be discussed in more detail below.

Suffice it to note that the ASC encounter with Satan can be seen as a challenge to Jesus's obedience and thus to his status as son of God. What is remarkable is that while the challenge-riposte interaction was typical of the first-century Mediterranean world and usually required an audience, in these stories it is reported as an event that Jesus experiences in an ASC (see Malina & Rohrbaugh 1992, 41–42).

---

1. The idea of a forty-day fast in solitude in preparation for an ASC of different sorts was well established in all Israelite circles. Moses spent forty days on Mount Sinai to receive a revelation (Exod 24:18), while Elijah traveled for forty days to reach the same place in search of a revelation (1 Kgs 19:8). This is also the period mentioned in the *Apocalypse of Abraham*: "But for forty days abstain from every kind of food cooked by fire, and from drinking of wine and from anointing (yourself) with oil" (9:7, Rubinkiewicz trans.).

2. The names *tempter*, *Satan*, and *the devil* are all interchangeable for *the adversary* in the Israelite pantheon.

In summary, the baptism stories contain several elements analogous not only to shamanic initiation but to the shamanic complex in general: spirit-possession, visions, a soul flight, and an ordeal in the wilderness without food and in the company of wild animals. Perhaps it is not surprising that the baptism stories were the first (and only) part of the Jesus story that has previously been linked to shamanism.[3]

On all accounts, the baptism scene can be seen as an event of shared experiences, and the sharing of experiences constituted the event. It is also reasonably certain that it kick-started Jesus's public career.

Jesus's (Shamanic) Journey Experiences?

As has been said, to many scholars, the shamanic journeys (also known as *cosmic travels, soul flights,* or *sky journeys*) lie at the heart of shamanism.[4] All journeys are not to heaven; some may be to the underworld or the middle world (somewhere on earth). Other religious specialists may enter ASCs, minister, or heal, but it is the shaman alone who primarily engages in soul flights for the benefit of the community or group. Such journeys have a variety of functions: shamans journey in order to learn, to heal, to retrieve souls, or to help the community. Walsh points toward three phases in such a journey: a period of preparation and purification, the induction of the ASC, and the actual journey (see 1989a, 26). The initial phase may involve a period of isolation, fasting, and celibacy, or perhaps spending time alone in the wilderness or in a solitary hut. A variety of techniques may be used for inducing the trance and can include singing, dancing, drumming, drugs, or fasting and solitude.

Not all cosmic traveling can necessarily be described as a shamanic journey (see Hultkrantz 1984, 30). Walsh refers, for example, to a kind of cosmic traveling that all people experience from time to time: travel-

---

3. Since I first explored the shamanic complex as a model for understanding Jesus as historical figure (see Craffert 1999a), two studies of which I know have explored this model. The one is an application of the model to the Synoptic Gospels (see Lee 1999), and the second is a very brief excursus in a book on Paul as shamanic figure, which suggests that this might also be the case with Jesus of Nazareth (see Ashton 2000, 62–72).

4. In the description of the shamanic complex, preference is given to ASCs (instead of soul journeys) as essential for defining shamanism. Soul journeys as a form of ASC nevertheless remain one of the main indicators of this complex and one of the main features distinguishing the shaman from other social-type practitioners (or religious entrepreneurs).

ing that occurs in dreams (see 1989a, 29). Then there are other kinds of out-of-body experiences that are similar to such journeys but are not undertaken for the benefit of the community. As a general category, the idea of a soul journey in trance seems to be the covering concept, while astral journeys are one subsection of soul journeys and have in the Hellenistic age some specific functions and specific characteristics. Astral journeys can be seen as a subsection of the general category of the shamanic journey. While Eskimo shamans typically journey to the depths of the sea, Israelite "shamans" (astral prophets) typically traveled to heaven. Such journeys may be undertaken for a variety of reasons but are primarily to the benefit of the community.

In and around the first-century Palestine of Jesus, experiences of soul journeys or sky trips of a variety of kinds were well known in Israelite and Hellenistic circles (see Smith 1981, 410–15; Segal 1980, 1353–54). Paul's remark about such a journey (2 Cor 12:2–4) of which he does not know whether it was "in the body" or "out of the body," illustrates that such journey experiences could take on different formats. As an experience of dissociation from the body, a soul journey can be experienced either as a bodily journey or as an out-of-body journey. Whether a journey is experienced as the journey of a soul or spirit outside the body, or as a journey of the body itself traveling would depend on whether the specific culture describes a spirit or a soul (or both) as entities inside the body or whether a specific culture describes the spirit or soul (or both) as mere configurations of the body. Whether the experience happens in the body or out of the body, the author can refer to the "self" as traveling (see Russel 1964, 166 for examples). Other such travelers in the Israelite tradition, such as Enoch and Ezekiel, have been discussed earlier (see above, pp. 206–7).

The best-known astral traveler in early Christianity is the author of Revelation (see e.g., Rev 1:10, 4:1), who claims that he saw an open sky, heard a voice inviting him into heaven, and ascended by means of a spirit (see Malina 1995, 25–46). "In the Spirit," John often experienced such journeys—once into the wilderness and once to the top of a great, high mountain (see Rev 17:3 and 21:10).

Had Jesus experienced such flights, he must have told his companions about them (this also applies to all other ASC experiences mentioned), or they must have thought it fit to ascribe such journeys to him. There are a number of indications that Jesus indeed often experienced such journeys.

Middle-World Journeys during the Stay in the Wilderness

As has been said, during the temptations in the wilderness after his baptism, it is said that Jesus experienced an encounter with Satan in which the devil "took him" to different places. Guided by Satan, Jesus journeyed to the temple in Jerusalem and to the top of a high mountain (Matt 4:5, 8; Luke 4:5, 9).

In *The Testament of Abraham* there is an interesting parallel story of Abraham who, while on a heavenly journey in a chariot with the archangel Michael, also saw the whole world: "And the archangel Michael went down and took Abraham on a chariot of cherubim and lifted him up into the air of heaven and led him onto the cloud, as well as sixty angels. And on the carriage Abraham soared over the entire inhabited world" (10:1, Sanders trans.).

Unlike the journeys of John in the Apocalypse, Jesus's journeys were, not "in the Spirit" but in the company of an adverse spirit, the devil. The setting of this account contains all the hallmarks of an ASC experience (spirit-possession or visionary experience). Although neither Jesus nor his followers claimed that these journeys happened because he was possessed by a spirit, there is nothing unusual about an ASC journey experience in the company of a hostile (tempter) spirit. While some scholars admit that these could simply have been visions, the description of such experiences in this study is that they are ASC journey experiences.

Other Heavenly Journeys?

Are these "middle-world" journeys the only evidence available that Jesus experienced ASC journeys? Smith argues that a large but diverse body of evidence points toward the fact that Jesus in his lifetime believed himself to have ascended to heaven and must have told his companions about it: "Thus Paul, an early source used by John, and the early hymns quoted in Philippians and 1 Timothy, agree in accrediting Jesus with an ascent to the heavens" (1981, 429).

The plausibility that the text in John (3:13) where Jesus says to Nicodemus, "No one has ascended into heaven except the one who descended from heaven, the Son of Man" is referring to such an experience is confirmed by other interpreters (see Ashton 2000, 71).[5] Bernhard Lang

5. It can be said that Jesus's ability to ascend to heaven is here based on his assumed

shows that another Johannine text (John 1:18) can also be read as a major heavenly journey (2002, 196). (John 1:18 reads, "No one has ever seen God. It is God the only Son, who is close to the Father's heart, who has made him known.") Lang says that this idea is also supported by the *Gospel of Philip*: "Those who say that the Lord first died and then rose up are in error. For he rose up first and then died" (21, Schenke trans.).

There can be no doubt that Jesus's followers often anticipated or practiced ascent to heaven as their goal (see Smith 1981, 416–18 for discussion of some examples). "Christians not only believed that Jesus had ascended after his death, they also expected to do the same themselves" (1981, 418). He suggests that with such strong evidence of belief and expectation of heavenly ascent amongst the first followers of Jesus, this practice is likely to have been a continuation of Jesus's own teaching and practice.

There is no simple solution to the dispute about the identity of the "man in Christ" to whom Paul refers in 2 Corinthians 12:2. The majority of scholars take it as a self-reference of Paul's experience of a journey to the third heaven (see, e.g., Baird 1985, 654; Morray-Jones 1993, 272), while a minority take it as a reference to Jesus's heavenly journey (see Smith 1981, 425).

While each interpretation harbors some inexplicable elements, I find the minority view more convincing. The main objections to it include that it cannot account for v. 7a, which implies that the revelations referred to in v. 1 are in fact Paul's own (see Morray-Jones 1993, 272) and for how Paul could have spoken of knowing Jesus *in Christ* (see Ashton 2000, 71). The objection to the majority interpretation is that Paul clearly distinguishes the man about whom he will boast from himself (v. 5). An argument from silence (which can be highly suggestive in some cases) is that if Paul could claim such a heavenly trip for himself (especially in this context), he certainly would have done it. "The plain sense of the text has to be accepted: the man was not Paul" (Smith 1981, 427; and see Goulder 1991, 18–19).

If the majority viewpoint were to be accepted, it contains an interesting feature of such ASC experiences (whether a journey or a visionary encounter with the divine), namely, that of a personal transformation. If "the man in Christ" is a self-reference to Paul, it is a very strange way of speaking about himself. But as Morray-Jones argues, it should then be understood as a reference to the transformation of the visionary into

prehistory in heaven (see Segal 1980, 1374; see also Meeks 1972).

an angelic or divine being: "The 'man in Christ' is thus Paul's 'heavenly self' or 'apostolic identity,' which is conformed to the image of the enthroned and glorified Christ and therefore possesses 'power' and divinely conferred authority. 'This man' is contrasted with Paul's earthly, human self" (1993, 273).

Such personal transformations are part of the cultural dynamics of ASC experiences. They are not merely personal experiences, but have personal and social ramifications (see further below). Whichever interpretation is accepted, they both confirm that such heavenly journey experiences were well known to and quite natural for at least Jesus's first followers. As experiences with an impact on the life of a community, they constitutionally belong to the telling of such experiences.

Jesus's Visions

There are two direct reports in the Gospels of Jesus experiencing visions, and several others where his disciples had such experiences involving Jesus.

A Vision of Satan and an Encounter with an Angel

Besides the visions already mentioned (at Jesus's baptism), Luke reports in an isolated saying a vision that Jesus had: "I watched Satan fall from heaven like a flash of lightning" (10:18). Very little can be said about it, but as Rowland remarks, "Whatever its original setting in the life of Jesus, the indications are that Jesus here recalls a visionary experience which had important consequences for his understanding of his ministry" (1982, 365). It will be indicated below that within that world such ASC experiences indeed resulted in personal transformations, altered perceptions of the self and altered notions of power and authority. All of these are not only part and parcel of the self-identity of such figures but also the source and power of their public activities.

The second instance is more difficult to deal with. Luke (22:43) tells that while in agony before his arrest, Jesus was comforted by an angel who appeared to him. Despite serious text-critical questions about the Lukan text, it has remained in the tradition.[6] The conditions as described

6. "Nevertheless, while acknowledging that the passage is a later addition to the text, in view of its evident antiquity and its importance in the textual tradition, a majority of the Committee decided to retain the words in the text but to enclose them within double

were conducive for a vision: in agony over his situation, Jesus prayed in solitude (on the Mount of Olives according to Luke, but in the Garden of Gethsemane in the parallel texts in Mark 14:32–42 and Matt 26:36–46). Matthew states that Jesus fell on his face while praying.

The vision of an angel is quite understandable when the scattered evidence from different texts is read together. Pilch offers such a culturally sensitive reading of this episode:

> In such a scenario [Jesus falling on his face], whether this was a fac-tual event or whether the evangelists created it, Mark and Matthew present Jesus in a posture that could stimulate the nasal cycle. If Jesus were prostrate, lying with the right side of his face on the ground, he would be initiating uninostril breathing in the left nos-tril. This breathing would stimulate the right brain hemisphere, the locus of origin for ASC experiences. Then Luke's tradition about the angel appearing to comfort him is a plausible description of an ecstatic trance experience. (2002a, 716–17)

The Transfiguration Scene

One of the stories in the Gospels that modern Westerners find difficult to believe is that of the transfiguration. One of the strangest phenomena to a Western mind is the ease with which a story is told in which interac-tion with long-dead ancestors is conducted. Neither the disciples nor the Gospel authors, however, blinked an eye about ancestors (ancestral souls or spirits?) appearing in bodily form and engaging in conversation with contemporaries.

A common supposition in modern scholarship is that these are "misplaced resurrection stories" (Smith 1980, 41). While this remark was made with reference to the Bultmann school, it is still the view of mem-bers of both the Wredebahn and the Schweitzerstrasse. Jesus's "resurrec-tion-ascension accompanied by two heavenly beings was rewritten as his transfiguration accompanied by Elijah and Moses" (Crossan 1991a, 389 of the Wredebahn), while Theissen and Merz (of the Schweitzerstrasse) claim that "divine sonship grounded in Easter . . . is backdated in different ways: transfiguration and baptism" (1998, 114). Elsewhere they say about epiphanies (including the transfiguration scene) that "capacities exceeding

---

square brackets" (Metzger, 1971, 177).

anything human are attributed to Jesus . . . 'relics' have been fused into stories of the revelation of a superhuman being" (1998, 296).

But as Smith continues:

> It is historically unjustified to suppose that things unbelievable in modern Marburg could not have been experienced in ancient Palestine, or that the failure of Bultmann's disciples to see him robed in glory proves that Jesus' disciples must have been equally incredulous. What is really *kaum glaublich* is that such a statement should have been made by a modern teacher of religion, even if only of New Testament, who might have been expected to know something of the phenomena of ecstatic cults. (1980, 41)

It is exactly in ASC experiences that the transfiguration scene (Luke 9:28–36 par.) is to be placed. As indicated previously, none of the stories in the Gospels are field reports (in an anthropologist's sense of the term) and therefore lack any clear detail about the events. They are theological (or ideological) accounts of the implications (from their respective points of view) of the cultural events that took place on the mountain with Jesus and three of his disciples. Our challenge is to describe and understand the nature of the cultural events that are referred to prior to any judgment about whether they "actually happened as described" or not.

A number of remarks contain clear clues as to the nature of the reported event. To begin with, three elements in the story as reported are very typical of inducing an ASC. The party went up a mountain in solitude (according to all three accounts) with the aim of praying (according to Luke's account, only Jesus went into a serious prayer session because the disciples were heavy with sleep). The third point: the episode preceding this event was about the disciples' nagging one another, quarreling about Jesus's true identity ("Who do the people say I am?"). An ASC experience could be induced by all or any of these conditions (see also Pilch 1995, 61).

A second clue is given in the remarks that there "appeared to them" (Matt 17:3 and Mark 9:4) two ancestors, and Jesus's appearance was altered (his face shone and his garments became white). These can be seen as visionary appearances (it is, after all, only in ASCs that ancestors make appearances as cultural events), which is confirmed by the similarities with visionary appearances elsewhere (see Rowland 1982, 367). In fact, Matthew (17:9) says that when coming down the mountain, Jesus commanded them, "Tell no one about the *vision*" (emphasis mine).

It is, however, necessary to dig elsewhere in order to guess the exact nature of the described event. Pilch quite convincingly argues that it can be seen as a "double vision experience" (1995, 63).[7] According to him, Jesus experienced a vision that included seeing two ancestors, and the three disciples experienced a waking vision in which Jesus was conversing with two ancestor figures—all with either shining faces or shining clothing.[8]

As explained earlier, the content of ASC experiences is to be found in the folklore of a people, and the dynamics of such an experience should be filtered in into accounts trying to understand them. According to the reports, Jesus and only three of his disciples went up a mountain with the intention of solitary prayer. Moses and Elijah would only appear to (be identified by) those reared in the Israelite tradition, and such people would also be familiar with parallels to Moses, who experienced ASCs on his mountain trips. Shamans only travel to worlds they know and have encounters only with ancestors in their lineage.

This story contains one of the cultural options regarding deceased ancestors in the ancient world, namely, that the dead (or at least some significant ancestors) keep their human form while being transported to the heavenly realm and reside there as celestial or spiritual bodies (or as souls). A second cultural option about deceased ancestors—that they or their spirits could possess someone—will be discussed below. As discussed earlier, the idea of a spirit or soul was not that of an entity residing somewhere in the body, but in terms of the ancient Mediterranean view on corporate identity, a spirit or soul could represent the person or self in a different configuration. An individual can be present, in life and after death, in a variety of bodily formats. This is what vision and possession logic presupposes: an individual person can be present in various configurations of the basic constituting elements while each configuration constitutes a *bodily* presence. Consequently, deceased ancestors not only can travel and possess others but can also be identified and consulted. This is the consequence of the acceptance of a visionary logic in a culture—visions, as much as other sources, are equally valid sources of human knowledge.

7. See Hanson for examples of other (in his terms) "double dream-visions" (1980, 1415–19). Pilch calls Hanson's examples "waking visions" (1995, 58).

8. From a different angle, Smith argues that the transfiguration story indeed refers to the kind of event that could happen in that world; Jesus took three disciples up a mountain for an initiation ceremony that led through hypnosis to a vision of him and two other figures (1980, 43).

One other feature in the transfiguration story points toward the characteristics that often accompany ASC experiences, namely, the reference to the cloud that overshadowed Moses and Jesus with his disciples (Matt 17:5; Luke 9:34). The power of shadows was well known in antiquity (like in many other cultures) since they could heal or hurt human beings or could even impregnate women (see Van der Horst 1976/77). While the shadow was often seen as replicating the soul of a person, it might be a case that the cloud that overshadows is a euphemism for God's soul/spirit encountered in the vision. It is, in fact, from the cloud that God spoke to them.

If it is accepted that the transfiguration was indeed an instance of a "double vision" experience, then Jesus's vision experience can be taken as indicative of shamanic experiences. The texts confirm that the point of the experience was to establish Jesus's identity as God's beloved son. Smith offers a plausible suggestion of what Mark could have intended: "The point is driven home by the story that Moses and Elijah, the Law and the Prophets, appeared as Jesus's subordinates" (1980, 42). Perhaps more importantly they were the two great holy men in the Israelite tradition (see Borg 1987, 56 n. 50). Then God declared in a voice (from the cloud) that Jesus alone was his son, and he alone was to be obeyed. Similarly, Pilch describes the function of the visions as a vehicle for the disciples to lessen confusion about Jesus's identity as the chosen or beloved son (not only Moses or Elijah or any other prophet) (1995, 63).

ASC Experiences in the Early Jesus Group

In polyphasic cultures where ASCs are regarded as normal practices, rituals and ASC experiences are not only accepted by most members but are often experienced by them. While the shaman experiences them regularly on behalf of the community, other members might also do so. As Goodman remarks regarding some Pygmy groups in the Ituri rain forest in the Democratic Republic of the Congo, all adult men can easily switch into their culturally approved ASCs (see 1987, 285).

During his lifetime, members of Jesus's disciple group often experienced ASCs. That such experiences are often ascribed to them, sometimes even when he was with them, further supports the claim that Jesus could have had such experiences. They were part of his group's cultural expectations and experiences. When calling two disciples, the Gospel of John reports, Jesus promised Nathanael that he "will see heaven opened and the angels of God ascending and descending upon the Son of Man" (1:51). The casual way in which this is reported suggests that everybody accepted such visionary practices as culturally possible and likely.

The transfiguration scene is another instance where at least three of Jesus's followers had group ASC experiences in which they saw Jesus conversing with some ancestors. The ASC experiences of Jesus's followers after his death will be discussed in a later chapter (see below, pp. 400–403).

Another instance is the reports about Jesus walking on the sea (John 6:16–21; Mark 6:45–52; Matt 14:22–27). Malina shows that these reports can very appropriately be read as culturally plausible descriptions of ASC experiences of the disciples (1999). In other words, it makes perfect cultural sense to read these reports as reports of ASC experiences of Jesus's disciples (see also Craffert & Botha 2005).

In the episode of Jesus's walking on the sea, conditions were conducive for ASC experiences: it was nighttime and a sudden storm arose on the sea of Galilee; the disciples were exhausted because of the wind and the waves, they were sleep-deprived and were terrified. Their visions contained somatic, visual, and auditory elements: Jesus lost his "gravity determined, land bound limitations," which enabled him to walk on the sea in their vision; in addition, Matthew (14:28–30) reports that Peter had "an in-vision experience of altered physical bearing" (Malina 1999, 367).

Three aspects should be added to this discussion. The first is that Jesus did not walk on "water" (H_2O) but on the "sea" (Matt 14:25–26; Mark 6:48; John 6:19). The sea was essentially different from water.

First, natural elements for us, such as the wind and the sea, were person-like entities for ancient people; or put differently, they contained nonvisible person-like forces, powers, or spirits. "The Greco-Romans identified the 'living' sea with the important deity Poseidon/Neptune (Semites called this deity: Tiamat or Tehom)" (Malina & Rohrbaugh 1998, 128). To walk on the sea, therefore, is to trample on the being that can engulf people with its waves and swallow them in its deep. As Malina says, for Jesus to walk on the sea "is evidence of his place in the hierarchy of cosmic powers" (1999, 359).

Second, stories about gods and heroes who walked on the sea are not unknown in the ancient world. Poseidon/Neptune traveled the sea on a horse-drawn chariot, while the Israelite God also walked across the sea as well as trampled it (see Cotter 1998, 148–50). The prophet Habakkuk (3:15) says the following about Yahweh: "You trampled the sea with your horses, churning the mighty waters."

The stories about Israelite heroes who could part water are well known (Moses, Joshua, Elijah, and Elisha come to mind). Walking on the sea was not associated with any other hero but remained the prerogative of Yahweh. There are, however, a number of heroes in the Greco-Roman literature who were associated with sea-walking, while the idea is also found in literature on dream interpretation (see Cotter 1998, 160–63).

Third, the idea of group ASC experiences is not exclusive to the New Testament literature. Josephus (*War* 1.347) talks about the group frenzies when, during the siege of Jerusalem (70 CE), the populace became demon possessed in numbers (Lee 1999, 191–93).

Like cosmic travel experiences, visions are entirely dependent on the experiences and the retelling of them. In a very fundamental sense, the precondition for the reality of such experiences to be accepted as cultural events is the notion of visions as actual sources of knowledge. The disputed issues are the authority and legitimacy of the visionary.

Jesus as Spirit-possessed Person

There can be no doubt that shamanism and (spirit) possession are inextricably related. Spirit-possession refers to the invasion of an individual by a spirit (or entity) and is a cultural evaluation of a person's condition. Spirit-possession covers a wide range of cultural phenomena and, being an ASC state, refers to all sorts of conditions. In some instances, it refers to a dissociation of identity ("becoming another person"); it can refer to the dissociation of memory; "spirit-possession" can refer to loss of other faculties, a loss interpreted as the result of the invasion by an alien entity or spirit. In addition to these, spirit-possession can either be voluntary or involuntary—the result of being overpowered by the spirit. Equally, spirits can be of all sorts: ancestor, animal, or divine. The simplest solution is to accept spirit-possession if someone within his or her own culture claims to be possessed or is treated like that by members of that culture (see Bourguignon 1968; Salman 1968, 197; Lewis 1989, 40).

If the following three lines of evidence are considered, it seems clear that Jesus was spirit-possessed and often experienced or claimed such a state: explicit statements mentioning him being spirit-possessed, claims that he was a prophet, and disputes about his identity. Besides the baptism scene describing Jesus's first spirit-possession experience (which has already been discussed), these three lines of evidence will briefly be considered. Jesus is often called a prophet, which in the Israelite culture implies being possessed; he is accused of being either demon-possessed or possessed by the spirit of an ancestor; and the Gospel authors claim that he was possessed by the spirit of God.

Jesus Was Well Known as a Figure with Prophetic Properties

The cultural assumption in the Israelite tradition was that prophets were specially possessed by the spirit of God. Jesus's close followers as well as the crowds believed this about him (Luke 7:16, 24:19; Matt 11:9; John 4:19). In the words of a crowd in Matthew (21:11), "'This is the prophet Jesus from Nazareth of Galilee.'" Jesus's enemies mocked him as a prophet (Mark 14:65) while Jesus even seems to have used the term *prophet* self-referentially (see Davies 1995, 44). In his hometown, he is reported to have said, "Prophets are not without honor except in their own country and in their own house" (Matt 13:57; and see also Luke 13:33). From these claims, it is logical to conclude that his followers would have taken it for granted that Jesus was spirit-possessed.

The one feature that distinguished ancient prophets from their contemporaries was that of speaking their minds ("telling it like it is or ought to be"). This is the one feature that makes ancient prophets resemble individualistic-oriented persons in modern Western cultures, which in their context made them exceptional. Often this exceptional nature was the result of their experiences of God in ASCs, by being possessed or touched by a divine spirit (see Malina & Neyrey 1996, 216–17).

Jesus Was Not Himself but Someone Else—He Was Possessed

A number of references show that Jesus was thought and seen by outsiders as not always being himself but someone else.

The first strand of evidence comes from debates about Jesus's identity. Davies remarks that "it is somewhat rarely observed to what a remarkable extent the question of Jesus's identity is raised in Mark, and in other ancient Christian texts, " referring to the other canonical Gospels and also in the *Gospel of Thomas* (1995, 93–97). In most cases, these disputes about his identity were not about *whether* he was possessed, but by *whom*.

There are several references to alleged debates in his lifetime about his identity or more specifically about the source of his power. Consequently, the question of Jesus's identity is asked and answered in many different ways and contexts.

One line of argument connects his identity and consequent power to possession by an ancestral spirit. In Mark (8:27–28 par.) Jesus asks his disciples: "Who do people say that I am?," and receives the following answer: "John the Baptist; and others, Elijah; and still others, one of the prophets." The tacit assumption of the question is that Jesus was not thought to be Jesus but someone else, possessed by an ancestral spirit (see Davies 1995, 94). The cultural logic of the answer is that someone in Jesus's day could be possessed by an ancestral spirit and in that way assume the identity of that ancestor. This logic is confirmed by the report about Jesus's discussion with his disciples after the transfiguration scene. This is a summary of the discourse: "'Why, then, do the scribes say that Elijah must come first?' . . . 'But I tell you that Elijah has already come. . . .' Then the disciples understood that he was speaking to them about John the Baptist" (Matt 17:9–13). The same logic is also apparent in the question to John the Baptist himself when the Levites from Jerusalem reportedly asked him: "Who are you? . . . Are you Elijah?" (John 1:19–21), and in a remark attributed to Jesus in Matthew (11:14): "he [John the Baptist] is Elijah who is to come." According to their cultural logic, John the Baptist was not actually himself either but he was possessed by the ancestral spirit of Elijah.

Exactly how ancient people thought deceased ancestors could reappear in their time is not explained (but, as has been explained earlier, it was indeed one afterlife option available in their cultural repertoire). Herod's alleged response to the question of Jesus's identity might suggest that they thought ancestors could be raised: "But when Herod heard of it he said, 'John, whom I beheaded, has been raised'" (Mark 6:16). Despite this direct claim, the logic probably is that someone possessed by the spirit of an ancestor is no longer him- or herself but becomes that ancestor. They had the example of Elisha, who received the spirit of Elijah and when seen by the prophets in Jericho received the response: "The spirit of Elijah rests upon Elisha" (2 Kgs 2:18).

That the answer probably lies in the logic of spirit-possession as an ASC experience is confirmed by a second line of response to the question of Jesus's identity. In Mark, Jesus's family went out to seize him because people thought he "has gone out of his mind" (3:20–21). Sanders remarks that this must be the remnant of a larger body of knowledge about Jesus's erratic behavior (see 1993, 153). The explanation of the scribes from Jerusalem was that he was actually possessed by Beelzebul (15:22), and Mark's answer to that was, as Davies summarizes it:

> it is not the case that Jesus was possessed by Beelzebul, Satan, or any other unclean spirit. Rather, it is the case the Jesus was possessed by the Holy Spirit; to deny this and offer instead the demon-possession hypothesis is an unforgivable sin. (1995, 96)

Twice in the Gospel of John it is reported that contemporaries accused Jesus of being demon possessed: "Many of them were saying, 'He has a demon and is out of his mind. Why listen to him?'" (John 8:48; 10:20).

Possession by an ancestral spirit or by a demon or by the Holy Spirit is a cultural interpretation of a possession experience. Ancient people disagreed about the identity of the possessed entity; what they did not disagree about was *that* Jesus was or could have been possessed. What these reports about Jesus's identity suggest is that he had possession experiences that were, depending on their relationship with him, duly interpreted by his Israelite contemporaries in different culturally accepted ways: as possession by an ancestral spirit, by a hostile spirit or by the Holy Spirit. As reports, they are well in line with the cultural assumption during the late Second Temple period that deceased ancestors through their spirits could act in and through a living being.

Explicit Mentioning of Jesus as Being (Holy-) Spirit-possessed

Explicit mention of Jesus being spirit-possessed or in the power of the Lord or the Spirit is made in some texts. After the ordeal in the wilderness, Luke says: "Then Jesus, filled with the power of the Spirit, returned to Galilee" (4:14). He also states that Jesus could heal because "the power of the Lord was with him to heal" (Luke 5:17). In this context, expressions from the Hebrew Bible such as "the hand of the Lord" or the "power of the Lord" can be seen as synonymous with the "spirit of the Lord" (see Bultmann 1980, 158).

The impression from the already-quoted claim in Luke (4:1) that Jesus was "full of the Holy Spirit" is that of an impersonal force filling up a person. The above-mentioned references, together with many others, operate with the alternative view that the Holy Spirit was a personal power or entity that could take possession of a person. Matthew (12:18) once used a quotation from Isaiah to make this point: "I will put my Spirit upon him," while Luke, in a different context, uses another quote from Isaiah to confirm it: "The Spirit of the Lord is upon me" (4:18). Both being "filled with" or "possessed by" a spirit assumes the notion of a porous body.

Possession Logic in the Israelite Tradition

The logic behind such remarks is that of ancient Israelite possession identity. How are we to understand this cultural logic? How do we make sense of the claims and reports that someone was possessed by a spirit, being full of the spirit or no longer him- or herself?

Davies argues that it should not be understood as "possession of" (which he ascribes to Smith) but as "possession by" (1995, 91).[9] He operates with a body-persona duality in which the same body can harbor different personalities: "this body may have in it persona *X* most of the time and yet the same body may have in it the supposedly supernatural persona *Y* some of the time" (1995, 208). Within the same body there could have been either of two identities or spirits in control. Or as he explains the logic of spirit-possession, "'I' the individual gives way and another 'I: the spirit' comes to be" (1995, 23). This model clearly reflects a modern dualistic view of body and spirit/soul, which also finds expression in the phenomenon of multiple personality disorders. There is, however, a third way of seeing it.

At this point, the interconnectedness of ancient Mediterranean views about body and soul/spirit and their cultural ASC experiences can be seen. In terms of the dominant view of a body-soul unity of biblical Israelites asserted earlier, the issue of how to understand first-century Israelite possession beliefs can be seen neither as a matter of *possession of* nor as *possession by* but rather as a matter of *being spirit-possessed*. Being spirit-possessed was

9. It should be noted, however, that Smith ascribes to both Jesus "possessed" and Jesus "being possessed" (see 1978, 104).

a way of being; or, put differently, being spirit-possessed determined the way the identity of the "I" was expressed. Being spirit-possessed was a way of being in the world or a way of being an "I," in contrast to being an "I" as the result of being born by means of a life-giving spirit. This could be experienced according to the container model (being filled with) or according to the agent model (being possessed by). This is what is implied in the claims that Jesus was not himself but someone else. Also, in Paul's remarks about spirit-possessed persons, this conclusion can be drawn: "If the Spirit of him who raised Jesus from the dead dwells in you, he who raised Christ from the dead will give life to your mortal bodies also through his Spirit that dwells in you" (Rom 8:11). In Galatians where he does not explicitly mentions spirit-possession, Paul says that "it is no longer I who live, but Christ who lives in me" (Gal 2:20).

Both possession and visionary experiences enter the tradition as reports about bodily experiences, and they become cultural events by means of the processes of affirming identity, which include the assessing and rumoring of a social personage. As cultural experiences, they are, therefore, integrated in a network of cultural assumptions.

Indicators of ASC Induction Techniques

The most popular induction technique in many forms of shamanism is undoubtedly drumming or rattling or taking psychoactive drugs. In some religious traditions, however, solitude, meditation, and prayer are equally well established induction techniques. The Israelite visionary, mystical, and magical traditions know several means of inducing the proper conditions for either receiving revelations and dreams or for experiencing other forms of ASCs. These include fasting or special diets, praying, solitude, abstention from sexual intercourse, and ritual baths (see Russel 1964, 169–73; Gruenwald 1980, 99–102; Smith 1984, 104–5; Lesses 1998, 117–60). In this tradition there is no evidence of the widespread use of hallucinogenic drugs.

Very early in the Gospel of Mark (1:35), it is said: "In the morning, while it was still very dark, he got up and went out to a deserted place, and there he prayed." The episode about Jesus walking on the sea is preceded by the remark that after taking leave of the disciples, "he went up on the mountain to pray" (Mark 6:46), while Luke often tells about Jesus going "into a lonely place" (4:42) or that he "would withdraw to deserted places and pray" (5:16). Luke also says Jesus went "out to the mountain to pray; and all night he continued in prayer to God" (6:12; see also, 9:18, 28–29; and 11:1).

Borg points out that

> verbal prayer is only one form of prayer in the Jewish-Christian tradition. Indeed, it is only the first stage of prayer; beyond it are deeper levels of prayer characterized by internal silence and lengthy periods of time. In this state, one enters into deeper levels of consciousness; ordinary consciousness is stilled, and one sits quietly in the presence of God . . . One enters the realm of Spirit and experiences God. (1987, 45–46)

It is said of other Galilean holy men of the time that they also often "still their minds" in order to direct their hearts toward heaven (see 1987, 44). It seems clear that solitary prayer for long hours, sometimes on a mountain and even all night, is often ascribed to Jesus in the Gospels. It is reasonable to assume that such practices resulted in "the experience of communion with God" (1987, 45).

Regarding one such event ascribed to Jesus, the struggle in the Garden of Gethsemane (Mark 14:32–42 par.), it has been pointed out that it could have resulted from a bodily posture that could stimulate the nasal cycle.

Abstaining from food (for forty days) in anticipation of an encounter with God (or Satan) was well known in the Israelite tradition: Moses, (Exod 34:28), Elijah (1 Kgs 19:8), and John the Baptist come to mind. This was also ascribed to Jesus after the baptism episode, while the motif of a forty-day (plus one) fasting period is well documented in the magical papyri—see the examples cited in Neufeld (1996, 160) and the Hekhalot corpus (Davila 2001, 96–97).

In one tradition, fasting is directly connected to the ability to exorcise certain spirits. After the disciples' inability to exorcise a demon, Jesus responded to their question: "This kind can come out only through prayer [and fasting]" (Mark 9:29).[10] The parallel with the magical papyri, where fasting is used for preparation for all sorts of ASC experiences, is remark-

---

10. The textual witnesses are split on whether the phrase "and fasting" should be included. A similar split characterizes the parallel text in Matt 17:21, which is excluded by the twenty-sixth edition of Nestle-Aland. What cannot be removed is that at least in some of the early manuscripts the connection between fasting and exorcism was accepted.

able. In one other tradition regarding Jesus's teaching about fasting, it is claimed that the goal of fasting is that "your Father who sees in secret will reward you" (Matt 6:18). It is reasonable to think that the goal of fasting is to encounter a divine experience.

Taken together with the other ASC experiences ascribed to Jesus, reports about his prayer life and remarks about fasting confirm that his relationship to God was one of extreme familiarity—a confirmation that he probably often had ASC experiences of intimate communion with God.

Implicit Shamanic (ASC) Indicators Ascribed to the Galilean Jesus

While the search for explicit references and indicators of ASC traits is fairly easy, there are also a number of tacit features that confirm that the figure described and reported about could have experienced such phenomena that can be linked to the shamanic complex. Such features are to be found in the presentation of the figure; put differently, they are to be found in the kind of things ascribed to his social personage.

Four such features of Jesus's life will briefly be discussed: his sense of divine identity, traits of sexual asceticism, the characteristics of an Israelite ḥasid (specifically, divine Sonship of a heavenly Father), and, finally, astral prophecy. Instead of post-Easter creations, these elements can reasonably be assumed to be part of a Galilean shaman's personage and could therefore have been part of Jesus's life in Galilee.

A Sense of Divine Identity: Mystical Transformations

As seen above, transformational experiences are very typical of people who have experienced various ASCs. Such experiences (possession experiences, visionary encounters, or journey experiences) can turn an ordinary, culturally well-adapted figure into an extraordinary (culturally well-adapted) figure who speaks and acts in different ways. As the above discussion of Jesus's (or Paul's?) heavenly journey (reported in 2 Corinthians) indicates, one of the features of persons having had such religious ASCs is a personal transformation—an awareness of a divine or spiritual identity of authority. In other contexts, it is often called a *prophetic identity* but can in this setting be described as a *shamanic sense of identity* or a shamanic awareness. It is a personal and social sense of power and authority; of being elevated among humans because of a calling, a special relationship with the divine world, because of encounters with the divine world. There is indeed a whole range of indicators in the traditions suggesting that Jesus had such an identity.

In other Israelite visionary texts, it is a constant theme that the person having had ASC experiences is transformed into a *supernatural being* (see Smith 1981, 410–11). One such example is Enoch, who during his encounter with the "Antecedent of Days" says: "I fell on my face, my whole body mollified and my spirit transformed" (*1 Enoch* 71:11, Isaac). Smith, furthermore, shows that statements in which a magician claims to be or become a divinity are of the most characteristic elements of magical material (1978, 125–26). The things ascribed to Jesus are also the things magicians said, such as, "I am the one who is from heaven" (*PGM* IV: 1018), or "I know you, Hermes, and you know me. I am you, and you are I" (*PGM* VIII: 49–50, Betz). This same idea is expressed by Paul in 2 Cor 3:17–18: "Now the Lord is Spirit, and where the Spirit of the Lord is, there is freedom. And we all, with unveiled face, beholding the glory of the Lord, are being changed into his likeness from one degree of glory to another; and this comes form the Lord who is the Spirit."

Once it is accepted that a person has traveled to heaven and has been given a message to act as a heavenly messenger, the power of that person becomes virtually unlimited. This is confirmed by an analysis of various Israelite visionary and mystical texts:

> The traditions examined above suggest that a variety of mythical and historical figures were credited with having achieved such a transformation . . . such a transformation was also considered possible, if only temporarily, for exceptionally holy individuals in this life. Such men were gifted with supernatural power and knowledge, and became intercessors between the divine and human worlds, because they had become conformed to the divine Image. (Morray-Jones 1992, 26)

ASC encounters with God and ASC experiences of possession by an ancestral or other spirit create a human being who acts and speaks with authority and power. Since there are enough other indicators that Jesus often experienced various kinds of ASCs, these indicators can be taken as clues to the effect they must have had on him (and his compatriots). It is, therefore, the indirect evidence of the power and divine authority in the reports ascribed to him that concern us here. It is reasonable to argue that if Jesus had such experiences, and if one finds such clues, that he also experienced such a transformation in his lifetime.

The *ego-eimi* sayings ascribed to Jesus constitute one such example. According to the received wisdom, all utterances in which Jesus is equated with God in one way or another were post-Easter creations. These include the *ego-eimi* sayings in the Gospel of John and the "I-say-unto-you" type of sayings in the Synoptics. However, Morray-Jones indicates that in these sayings, Jesus (or his followers) claimed to be "an embodiment of the divine Name" (1992, 14).[11] Davies quite convincingly puts forward the thesis that these types of sayings can be understood as sayings of the spirit of God, or of Jesus as possessed by the spirit of God (see 1995, 151–69). As Jesus of Nazareth, he mostly spoke in the way reported in the Synoptic Gospels, and as a spirit-possessed person he spoke in another way (as reported, for example, by the "I-am" sayings). Whether Davies is correct in this distinction is another matter. The important point that Davies has grasped is that a historical figure could speak in the way reported in the *ego-eimi* proclamations. Nobody speaks in one way only, and especially spirit-possessed persons could utter such words. The present suggestion is that these sayings make sense as elements in Jesus's life story precisely because they naturally belong to the typical transformational ASC experiences.

A Disdain for Sexual Activities: An Unmarried Life of Celibacy

One of the few certainties about Jesus's life is that he was not married—at least, there is no piece of evidence pointing in that direction. In Israelite life, this was unusual for a man of his age (see Vermes 2000, 254). There is no indication why this was the case, but read in conjunction with a disdain for sexual activities, it might have something to do with religious experiences, as Vermes suggests.

Abstinence from sexual intercourse is not only one of the features often ascribed to the induction of ASCs, but it was believed that abstinence made the body "a more appropriate vehicle to receive divine inspiration" (Brown 1988, 67). This is perfectly understandable in terms of one of

11. Kelber points out that, similar to proclamations of other prophetic figures in the Greco-Roman world, these proclamations are a manifestation of the divine figure being revealed: "In a comparable, though extravagant sense, Jesus the speaker of words of revelation acquires the status of revelation himself" (1987, 112–13).

the embryological theories, the *hematogenic* theory, discussed earlier (see above, pp. 192–93). According to this theory, there was a very close link between spirit and semen where semen was seen as a foamy concoction of blood, other bodily fluids, and spirit. In terms of this cultural logic, abstinence had nothing to do with the avoidance of "worldly pleasures" or possible "sins" in the sexual act but with the prevailing view regarding the nature of seminal emission. In the words of Brown:

> Possession was an intimate and dramatically physical experience. It involved a flooding of the body with an alien, divine Spirit. Hardly surprising, such an experience was thought to exclude the warm rush of vital spirits through the body, traditionally associated with intercourse. (1988, 67)

Abstinence from sexual intercourse is well attested in historical cases related to visionary experiences. Prior to receiving the vision on Sinai, Moses was told not to have sexual intercourse for three days (Exod 19:15). According to Philo of Alexandria, after his encounter with God on Sinai, Moses had come to disdain sex "for many a day, and almost from the time when, possessed by the Spirit, he entered on his work as a prophet, since he held it fitting to hold himself always in readiness to receive oracular messages" (quoted in Brown 1988, 67). Other Israelite traditions confirm this view. In one of the rabbinic commentaries on Numbers, it is told from a woman's point of view:

> Moses' sister, Miriam, noticing her sister-in-law's neglected appearance, asked her why she had ceased to look after herself. Zipporah answered:
>
> > 'Your brother does not care about the thing [sexual intercourse].'
>
> The same passage of the document also notes that when it was announced that the two Israelite elders, Eldad and Medad, had started to prophesy, Miriam overheard Zipporah's muttered remark: 'Woe to the wives of these men!' (Vermes 1973, 101)

In 1 Corinthians 7, Paul makes a strong case for either abstaining from marriage or from sex within the marriage for purposes of worship. Martin shows that Paul's statements "repeatedly reveal that he advocates celibacy, while allowing marriage only as a necessary option for the weak" (1995, 209). The ideal condition, in his view, is to be like himself: celibate.[12]

These examples confirm the cultural perception and reality that ASC experiences were generally regarded as a sex suppressor. Vermes remarks that against such a background, "namely that the prophetic destiny entailed among other things a life of continence, Jesus' apparent voluntary embrace of celibacy, at any rate from the time of his reception of the holy spirit, becomes historically meaningful" (1973, 101). A number of references come to mind.

There is the saying ascribed to Jesus only in Matthew (19:12) that some people make themselves eunuchs "for the sake of the kingdom of heaven." It will later be argued that "kingdom of heaven" can be understood as the result of various kinds of religious experiences, including ASC-related experiences. In this verse, it can be understood that Jesus was saying that some people deliberately avoid sexual activities in order to have religious or ASC experiences or because they have had such experiences. This Matthean saying "certainly does teach that sex is not necessary for all, and that in certain circumstances abstinence will accord with the divine will" (Allison 1998, 176). Allison discusses three other passages that demand restraint with regard to sexual desire and that envisage perfected human nature as doing without the sexual component (see 1998, 176–88).[13]

A Sense of Divine Sonship: Son of God the Father

Two related features that are ascribed to Jesus in the tradition suggest that it was indeed the case that he experienced mystical transformations because of ASC experiences. The first is his habit of calling God "Father" and even "*Abba*," and the other is the fact that in many reports, Jesus is called a "son of God." In this, Jesus resembles the picture that exists of other Galilean *Hasidim* or pious miracle workers in the late Second Temple period. Both features characterize the Gospels' depiction of Jesus's relationship with God as one of extreme familiarity; both features are characteristic of only

12. It is said that Maximilla and Priscilla, who were leaders of the charismatic Montanist group (some of the few female leaders in the early church), were prophets who "from the time when they were filled with the Spirit . . . left their husbands" and propagated divorce (Eusebius, quoted in Goulder 1991, 36).

13. Within his framework of things, Crossan suggests that a preference for celibacy could have been retrojected onto Mary and Joseph's marriage and the conception of Jesus (see 2003b, 688).

one group of people in the Second Temple period, namely, the Ḥasidim. In other words, there was a cultural convention of which these features were a part, and when applied to Jesus, they conveyed information about his position and role in the Israelite society of Galilee.

In the Hebrew Bible mention is made of three types of *sons of God*: heavenly or angelic beings, Israelites or the people of Israel as such, and, third, the kings of Israel (see Vermes 1973, 194; Sanders 1993, 161). In the late Second Temple period this changed when the Ḥasidim (Israelite charismatics or pious individuals) are referred to with the intimate description of "my son." The Babylonian sage Rav said about Ḥanina ben Dosa: "The whole universe is sustained on account of *my son* Hanina; but *my son* Hanina is satisfied with one kab of carob from one Sabbath eve to another" (quoted in Vermes 1973, 206). In Ḥasidic circles, Safrai concludes, "the relationship of a Hasid to God was not just one of 'child of God,' but of a son who can brazenly make requests of his father that someone else cannot make" (1994, 7).[14]

"The Hasid addressed God as '*abba*,' 'my father,' or 'my father in heaven,'" Safrai points out (1994, 7). Whereas the typical form of address in prayer in the Second Temple period was something like "Lord of the universe," it is the Ḥasidim, when involved in their rainmaking and other miracles, who address God as *abba* or "my father" (see Vermes 1973, 210–11 for examples).

In numerous texts, Jesus is called a "son of God." It is used both as self-identification and by others in the context of exorcisms and miracles (see Vermes 1973, 200–206). At two of the ASC experiences of Jesus mentioned above, a voice from heaven declared him to be a son of God. At his baptism, the content of the audition was: "You are my Son, the Beloved; with you I am well pleased" (Mark 1:11 par.). Again, the content of the audition during the transfiguration scene states the same point: "'This is my Son, the Beloved; with him I am well pleased; listen to him!'" (Matt

---

14. The *Ḥasidim* in this context refers to a movement close to the Pharisees (if not to the Pharisees themselves) who had a peculiar religious outlook and were credited with all sorts of miracles, such as causing rain to fall, healing the sick, and exorcising demons. The best-known among them were Ḥoni the Circle Drawer and Ḥanina ben Dosa (see Vermes 1973, 69–78; Safrai 1994, 4, 7). Looking at these figures as *Ḥasidim* does not imply a specific sect or organized group. The so-called Ḥasidic hypothesis (Davies 1977, 127), presupposing a well-defined group or sect, does not, therefore, apply here.

17:5; Luke 9:35). In both cases ASC experiences are explicitly linked to claims about being a son of God.

If the cultural custom of the time was indeed as indicated by the discussion above on the Ḥasidim, it is perfectly possible that the content of Jesus's vision during his baptism could contain the content of a *bath kol* ("heavenly voice"). It is also not surprising that the reported reactions of several demon-possessed persons (people experiencing possession ASCs) were to identify Jesus as a son of God. In one of his early summary remarks about Jesus's activities, Mark (3:11) states: "Whenever the unclean spirits saw him, they fell down before him and shouted, 'You are the Son of God!'" This is also the case with the demon-possessed person(s) in the country of the Garasenes: "What have you to do with me, Jesus, Son of the Most High God?" (Mark 5:7; and see Matt 8:29; Luke 8:28). It also arises in other miracles, like the ASC experience of Jesus's walking on the sea: "And those in the boat worshipped him, saying, 'Truly you are the Son of God'" (Matt 14:33). In the Matthean account of Peter's confession (16:13–20), three interesting features are connected: Jesus's question about who he actually is (possessed by which spirit?), Peter's answer that Jesus is the Christ and the "Son of the living God," and the remark that this confession is the result of a revelation by God. While this is another instance of a visionary or auditory ASC by one of Jesus's followers, it also supports the view that his followers referred to him as a son of God.

Since ASC experiences always display the features and myths of the host culture, it is not surprising that Jesus both experienced being a son of God and was described as such by other people involved in ASC experiences in which Jesus was also involved.

There are dozens of references in the reported teachings of Jesus in which God is addressed in an intimate way as "father," "my father," "father in heaven" or the like (see Dunn 1975, 21–26; Safrai 1994, 6). Besides the many instances in which the usage differs from the usual way of addressing God in the late Second Temple period, there is one reported instance in which Jesus actually said, "Abba Father" (Mark 14:36).

Jesus's Sonship with the Father is just one more consequence of someone who has had several intimate interactions with the divinity in prayer, heavenly journeys, and visions. Contrary to the view of both the Schweitzerstrasse and the Wredebahn that the "title Son of God was given to Jesus only on the basis of the Easter experiences" (Theissen & Merz

1998, 554; and see Funk 1996, 281), it makes perfect sense to accept that if Jesus was a shamanic figure, this could have been part of Jesus's life in Galilee. It was part of Jesus's identity because of the transformational ASC experiences that he had. As Davies remarks: "An individual who, it is universally assumed, believed himself to have some sort of special relationship with 'the Father' might well have referred to himself as 'the Son'" (1995, 157).[15]

Paul also makes the connection between those possessed by the spirit of God and those calling God "*Abba.*" According to Romans (8:14–19) those who are spirit-possessed (filled by or led by the spirit) are sons of God and they call God, *Abba*. In Galatians (4:6) Paul also connects sonship and spirit-possession but in an inverted order. Now he claims that spirit-possession follows their adoption as sons. Both ways, calling God Father and being called sons of God, are related to being spirit-possessed. Thus, very early in the movement it was accepted that all of them could become sons of God by means of ASC encounters with the divine realm.

A Sense of Divine Knowledge: Astral Prophecy

A final set of clues indirectly link Jesus to involvement in visions and/or heavenly journeys, and thus with the shamanic complex, namely, the discourses on astral prophecy. Astral prophecy, according to Malina,

> refers to those ancient narratives reporting the interaction of prophets and seers with star-related, celestial personages and the outcomes of that interaction. These narratives might describe both the initial circumstances of such interactions (i.e., visions, dreams, ecstasies and other altered states of consciousness), the interaction proper (what the prophet or seer hears and sees, i.e., alternative realities, the very secrets to be revealed), as well as the outcomes of the interactions (impact or meanings of celestial phenomena). (1995, 19)

---

15. It is within the context of the same cultural logic that the discourse about Davidic sonship (Mark 12:35–37) makes sense. The cultural assumption behind the scene is the notion that as a shamanic figure, Jesus has already been (in heaven) with God. Having been there, he could have had conversations with David, who had addressed him appropriately as lord—namely, as the one being up there with God. The report about the calling of Nathanael (John 1:51) assumes the same cultural logic: that for Jesus, the entrance to heaven (God) is transparent. Nathanael is promised a vision in which angels will visit the son of man and return to heaven. Here it is not Jesus himself but God's messengers who will ensure that divine communication channels remain open and active.

The story of Jesus as found in the Gospels from beginning to end, Malina points out, tells of the impact of sky events and sky personages on the people inhabiting the land (see 1997, 83). Together with Revelation, Ezekiel, Daniel, Enoch, and other Israelite texts, Jesus's so-called eschatological discourses (Matt 24; Mark 13; and Luke 21) belong to the category of astral prophecies. The triple tradition seeking signs from the sky (Mark 8:11 par.) and the frequent reference to a being who will one day come down from the sky, the "Son of Man," all carry the typical features of astral prophecy; Jesus was remembered as having spoken in this way (see Malina 1997, 85–86).

The resemblances between these discourses and other Israelite astral documents are just too obvious to disregard. Together with astral terminology, they all share with Revelation the unfolding sequence of wars, international strife, famines, earthquakes, persecution, and eclipses. "What is common to these events is that the ancients saw them all triggered by celestial entities and celestial events" (Malina 2002a, 55) because, in their view of things, sky events (such as lightning, thunder, cloud bursts, and comets) and sky entities (such as angels, immortals, and deities) impacted the earth and its inhabitants. Malina sums up his findings as follows:

> Jesus' final discourse in the Synoptics has the vocabulary and phraseology of first-century astronomy/astrology; its sequence of events follows Israelite tradition, his repeated reference to the cosmic personage known as the Son of Man and his highly focused concern on the fate of Jerusalem all point to astral prophecy. (1997, 92)

Although this is no proof that Jesus undertook a soul journey in order to obtain such prophetic knowledge, it is highly plausible that someone so deeply entrenched in astral prophecy with its visions, sky trips, and interaction with sky entities/personages indeed undertook such journeys. When looking at some of the features in the Jesus tradition and the book of Revelation, it is clear that both Jesus and John fit this pattern: John certainly did, and Jesus probably also undertook astral or soul flights (in ASCs) for the benefit of their communities.

There is an instance in the Synoptics where the claim of divine sonship is explicitly connected to the possession of divine knowledge that was revealed to Jesus: "All things have been delivered to me by my Father; and no one knows the Son except the Father, and no one knows the Father except the Son and any one to whom the Son chooses to reveal him" (Matt 11:27; Luke 10:22). Jeremias's suggestion that the aorist (*paredothē*) could be taken as a reference to Jesus's baptism cannot be proven, but as a technical term for the transmission of divine lore, together with the use of *apokalupsai* to refer to other instances of divine lore, points toward Jesus as a medium of divine knowledge (see 1971, 61). John is also quite explicit about Jesus's role in conveying divine knowledge: "He whom God has sent speaks the words of God, for he gives the Spirit without measure" (3:34). He is also the one receiving angelic information about the exaltation of the divine name (John 12:28–29). Typically, the shamanic function is like a telephone exchange with the divine world.

Conclusion

Taken together with the other indicators, the four features discussed above confirm that Jesus can plausibly be seen as a shamanic figure who from the first spirit-possession experience was transformed in his self-perception and social presentation. What can be taken for granted from the above discussions, in the words of Sanders, is that Jesus "thought that he had been especially commissioned to speak for God, and this conviction was based on a feeling of personal intimacy with the deity" (1993, 239). If Jesus was not a shamanic figure, the tradition was particularly meticulous in ascribing a great variety of clues about the experiences of such a figure into his life.

From the point of view of anthropological historiography, such clues about transformational and related ASC experiences are not merely descriptions of beliefs or reports of what actually happened, they are much more. They are an entrance point to explore the cultural dynamics of what is affirmed about Jesus's life, namely, that Jesus was someone who had such intimate experiences and encounters with the deity. It is not merely as singular events (such as a baptism) but as dynamic cultural processes (such as initiation and spirit-possession experiences) that such reports are of significance for understanding how things were in the life of Jesus as social personage. If anything, Jesus was partly constituted as historical figure by such events and phenomena. The above examples all point toward a life touched and influenced by ASC experiences and an involvement in the shamanic complex.

As indicated, the aim of the shamanic model is not to find a new way of identifying authentic material or to discover new historical information about Jesus. Its aim is to uncover a whole cultural dynamics and the working of a cultural system within which such figures operate in a specific way. It is based on a cable-like interpretive process where biographical elements are not divorced from the kind of figure or from the social dynamics that accompany such a figure.

In addition to the labels (*son of God, son of man,* and *Messiah*) used to constitute Jesus as social personage, there are a number of other labels that were used to describe his functions and activities as shamanic figure. These include *prophet, teacher, rabbi, healer, and exorcist.* These will all be discussed later.

CHAPTER 9

Healing, Exorcism, and the Control of Spirits

Introduction

THE CENTRAL FUNCTIONS OF shamanic figures are, on the one hand, healings, exorcisms, and control of spirits; and, on the other hand, the mediation of divine knowledge—that is, teaching, prophesy, and all sorts of divination. If Jesus was a shamanic figure, it would not be surprising that together with the accounts about his teachings and prophecy, the reports about healings, exorcisms, and control of spirits constitute the bulk of the material ascribed to Jesus's activities as a historical figure. In this chapter, the focus will be on an understanding of the healings, exorcisms, and control of spirits as potential shamanic activities.

Since the control of spirits will be considered in the second part of this chapter, attention will first be paid to the healing and exorcism accounts. If Jesus was a shamanic figure, as proposed by the hypothesis of this study, then healing, exorcism, and the control of spirits must have been part of his life story in a normal and natural way. But these reports constitute one of the most difficult challenges in historical Jesus research. In fact, there is a double challenge here. On the one hand, understanding the Gospel accounts as shamanic healings and, on the other hand, allowing for the dominance of the modern biomedical paradigm in all matters of illness and healing, it is no simple task to get a grip on what is implicated in such shamanic healings.

Thus, testing the hypothesis that Jesus was a Galilean shamanic figure depends on an understanding of the healing and exorcism stories as typical shamanic activities. It depends on a confirmation that the available reports are typical of shamanic figures. But that implies a clear notion of what shamanic healings and exorcisms are like. Put the other way round, knowing whether Jesus's healings and exorcisms can be taken as evidence for the shamanic hypothesis implies that they were shamanic healings and exorcisms. But knowing whether they indeed were shamanic healings and exorcisms implies more than simply applying the shamanic model to the available data. In a cable-like interpretive process, this contains a dual task, or as explained earlier, it brings to the surface the dilemma of abduction as an interpretive strategy: it is necessary to understand the healings and exorcisms as shamanic activities in order to work toward the hypothesis, but it should be known what shamanic healings and exorcisms are like in order to do that.

This is where the other challenge starts, because the reigning model for dealing with matters of health care—the biomedical paradigm—assumes that illness and healing are homoversals, that is, universal and similar for all human beings. It does not have a category for shamanic healings as distinct from biomedical healings, and, therefore, in one way or another, the reports are read by means of biomedical assumptions. As has been argued earlier, the aim of cultural bundubashing is not merely to establish whether there are multiple, independent attestations of a particular account and whether Jesus performed the healings and exorcisms as, when and where the documents state. Nor does cultural bundubashing imply that the shamanic model can simply be applied in order to grasp the nature of these activities. The historicity of this part of the data (as of other parts) is not something in itself, but can only be determined in terms of a specific context or hypothesis. To claim historicity includes that plausible cultural events and phenomena also fit a particular social personage; in this case, that they in a natural way belonged to the life of a Galilean shamanic figure. The challenge is to grasp the nature and reality of shamanic healings and exorcisms in a way that is not dominated by the biomedical paradigm.

The first step, however, will be to give an overview of the data, and that implies an engagement with existing research.

Healings and Exorcisms Attributed to Jesus of Nazareth

Despite the scarcity of evidence, there is little dispute about the kind of illnesses connected to Jesus's healing activities. First are the so-called *leprosy* stories. For the other two, it is not necessary to go beyond the categories employed by Davies: "healings of somatic disorders" and "exorcisms of supposedly possessing demons" (1995, 69). In addition to the summary remarks about Jesus's activities that state that he went about all the cities and villages healing every disease and infirmity, or that all the sick and possessed came to Jesus, this constitutes the bulk of the evidence.

Leprosy: A Repulsive Scaly Skin Disease

The New Testament contains only two lengthy stories about the cleansing of people with *leprosy* (Matt 8:1–4 par.; and Luke 17:11–19). In the reports about such patients, sometimes a single person (such as in Mark 1:40–42) and, at least once, ten lepers at a time (see Luke 17:11–19) were cleansed.

According to the World Health Organization, about twelve million people in the world today suffer from leprosy or Hansen's disease. They live with a stigma and are shunned by many people (see Zias 1991, 149).

Leprosy, or Hansen's disease, is a chronic, slowly progressive, bacterial infection due to *Mycobacterium leprae*. It affects not only the skin but also other bodily tissues, but this might not be observable by the uninformed observer (see Sussman 1992, 10). Because leprosy produces characteristic lesions in the bones, notably in the skull, it can be detected in palaeo-pathological records (the skeletal remains from ancient times) (see Hulse 1975, 89).

The following description of leprosy gives a clear indication of its nature:

> The disease is only mildly contagious. It is rare that spouses or children contract it, and the disease is not sexually transmitted. No one has ever died from leprosy; those who suffer from it have the same life-expectancy as anyone else. Neither do fingers and toes rot and drop off. The disease deadens nerve endings, and with a lack of feeling, cuts and other sources of infection often go undetected until the infection spreads to the bones which in turn are gradually destroyed. Physical deformation does not occur unless the disease is untreated for fifteen or twenty years. (Pilch 1988, 62)

In the Greco-Roman period, the Greek word *lepra* referred to a variety of skin diseases such as fungus psoriasis, infections, dermatitis, or eczema.

Hansen's disease was referred to in the ancient world in Greek as *elephas* or *elephantiasis*. It was already known in India in 600 BCE and was probably brought to the Mediterranean world by the armies of Alexander the Great. It was in the eighth century that an Arabic author first made the mistake of describing Hansen's disease with the word *lepra*. The rest is history, because wherever the word was used in ancient times, it was then interpreted as referring to Hansen's disease. This is how the word *lepra* as used in the Greek translation of the Old Testament and in the New Testament was then interpreted (see Hulse 1975, 88–89; Sussman 1992, 10).

Archaeology has contributed to overthrowing the belief that biblical *lepra* ("leprosy") was the same as Hansen's disease and was very common in ancient Palestine. Palaeopathological studies conducted on large numbers of bodily remains that have been excavated indicate that it was not very common in Palestine (see Zias 1991, 149).

The medical evidence indicates that the Greek *lepra* and the Hebrew *sara'at* must be very similar, if not identical. The New Testament gives very little information about *lepra,* while the Hebrew Bible contains considerable information about *sara'at*, which are the two words used for biblical "leprosy." Biblical *sara'at* could occur in humans, buildings, and clothing and could progress quite quickly. Where it is discussed in the Hebrew Bible in detail, it is furthermore clear that the main concern was not the illness as such but uncleanness (Lev 13–14). The priest declared a condition *sara'at* by looking at the bodily signs. Several skin diseases could produce signs that could be interpreted thus (see Hulse 1975, 91, 93, 99).

What is presupposed by references to scaly skin conditions is that lepers were ritually unclean and therefore excluded from normal social intercourse. This is a belief that was already established in ancient Israelite times where one of the reasons mentioned for excluding someone from the camp of the Israelites was a repulsive skin disease or a bodily discharge (see, e.g., 2 Sam 3:29). In other words, people with certain skin infections were considered unclean and therefore excluded from normal social interaction and especially from cultic activities. A person with *sara'at* posed no serious medical threat to society but, because of the experienced conditions, such a person posed a social threat by being unclean (see Lev 13:45–46).

A Variety of Somatic Disorders

Jesus is said to have healed a variety of somatic disorders. These include three cases of blindness (e.g., Mark 10:46–52 par.; Matt 9:29–31) and at least one each of the following: paralysis (e.g., Mark 2:1–12 par.; Matt 8:5–13), excessive menstrual bleeding (e.g., Mark 5:25–34), a withered hand (Mark 3:1–6), lameness (Luke 13:10–17), fever—Peter's mother-in-law (Mark 1:30–31 par.), deafness-muteness (Mark 7:31–37), a man with dropsy (Luke 14:1–6), and a boy who was moonstruck (Matt 17:15). Very little can be said about these conditions allegedly treated by Jesus. The best guess would probably be to accept that most of these accounts describe conditions as they appeared to his contemporaries.

With a few exceptions, no symptoms or conditions are described. For example, the Gerasene demoniac was uncontrollable, screaming, and hurting himself (Mark 5:1–7), while another spirit-possessed boy fell to the ground with foam coming from his mouth while grinding his teeth (Mark 9:14–29). For the rest, the reports do not even resemble ancient diagnostic reports. If attempts are made today to identify any of these as generic diseases (such as possible cases of epilepsy), it is worth listening to Fabrega's (1971, 390–91) warning that there are few diseases that can clearly and unequivocally be diagnosed in field studies without the aid of laboratory tests—the more so as little information is provided in the accounts.

Despite attempts to get closer to diagnoses, the information is so scant that the basic detail about the accounts themselves cannot even be ascertained (for example, whether Jesus healed one (Mark10:46) or two (Matt 9:27; 20:30) blind men, and whether it happened on his way into or out of the city; whether there were one (Mark 5:2) or two (Matt 8:28) demoniacs at Gerasa/Gedara). It is, however, remarkable, as Davies points out, that the majority of these cases resemble somatization disorders as described in modern psychiatric manuals (see 1995, 69–71). While in his viewpoint they are described as *psychosomatic illnesses,* a slightly different spin can be put onto that interpretation.

Demon- or Spirit-possessed Persons

The third category consists of the healing of demon- or spirit-possessed persons. Six accounts of explicit exorcisms are reported.[1] However, a distinction can be made between demon or spirit-possession as the explanation

1. These are (1) "an unclean spirit" (Mark 1:21–28; Luke 4:31–37), (2) Gadarene demoniac (Mark 5:1–20; Matt 8:28–34; Luke 8:26–39), (3) mute and blind demoniac (Mark 3:19–30; Matt 12:22–32; Luke 11:14–23), (4) Mute demoniac (Matt 9:32–34), (5) Syro-Phoenician's daughter (Mark 7:24–31; Matt 15:21–30, (6) moonstruck boy (Mark 9:14–29; Matt 17:14–21; Luke 9:37–43).

for certain common experienced illnesses (e.g., dumbness and lameness) and demon or spirit-possession as an explanation of an identifiable illness in itself, namely, demon possession. Demons are, for example, credited with being behind the condition of the dumb man in Matthew (9:32–33) and also with the cause for the curvature of the spine of the woman who suffered from it for eighteen years (Luke 13:10–11).

There are other instances where demon possession is ascribed to conditions that cannot be regarded as "common" illnesses but belong to the cultural category of demon possession (for example, the case of the Gerasene demoniac with wild and abnormal behavior). Demon possession is also ascribed to the mute boy who, when in a state of possession, falls to the ground in a state of convulsion (Mark 9:20) with foam coming from his mouth, while the daughter of the Syrophoenician woman is described as "possessed by an unclean spirit" (Mark 7:25). The cause of the boy who was moonstruck (Matt 17:15) is assumed to be demon possession only because Jesus rebuked a demon in healing him, as was the case with the man with "an unclean spirit" (Mark 1:23–25). The best guess is that these people were all probably commonly diagnosed by their contemporaries with the condition *demon possession*.

From this evidence and the many summary remarks in the Gospels saying that sick and possessed people came to (or were brought to) Jesus (e.g., Mark 1:45) or that Jesus went about all the cities and villages healing every disease and infirmity (e.g., Matt 4:23–25; 9:35; 15:30–31), it can be suggested that sick people apparently streamed to Jesus of Nazareth in order to be healed. Therefore, the question arises: how are these reports (or the authentic ones for some) actually understood in current historical Jesus research?

Jesus's Healings and Exorcisms in Current Research

Even skeptical researchers admit that if anything can be known about Jesus's activities, it is that he was a healer and exorcist (see discussion by Blackburn 1994). In fact, even the fellows of the Jesus Seminar agree that Jesus healed people and drove away what were thought to be demons (see Funk & The Jesus Seminar 1998, 60). Also, as can be seen above, the body of data on Jesus's healings is fairly well defined. With the exception of scholars on the Wredebahn, who from the outset exclude stories without multiple attestations, the majority agree on the data to be considered here.

The literature on Jesus's healings and exorcisms is so extensive and well covered elsewhere that it is unnecessary to repeat it here (see, e.g., Twelftree 1993; Davies 1995; Theissen & Merz 1998, 281–315). This analysis will focus on two features of the scholarly literature virtually unmentioned elsewhere.

The first is that most current discussions on Jesus's healings and exorcisms explicitly or implicitly assume a biomedical paradigm for understanding these accounts. This is the case both for the assumed sickness conditions and for the healing activities. It will be argued that current research is trapped in the framework of the biomedical paradigm, which sees disease as physical, the solution as technical, and the spectrum of human illnesses as universal.

Second, despite a general agreement that Jesus was indeed a healer and exorcist, there is very little agreement on what he actually did when he healed people and exorcised demons and spirits from afflicted persons. Excluding for the moment the lane on the Wredebahn where most of the healing and exorcism accounts are taken as literary creations in *marketing the messiah*, within the same framework scholars find a range of explanations on what it is that Jesus supposedly did in his healings and exorcisms. Viewpoints vary from miraculous healings to merely the provision of therapeutic comfort to psychosomatic healings. Despite an apparent variety, it will be argued that all of these explanations nevertheless fit comfortably in the framework of the biomedical paradigm. While sharing the biomedical paradigm, which provides the framework for defining sickness primarily as disease and healing as some kind of a technical intervention, there is still a variety of explanations within that biomedical framework, as applied by New Testament scholarship, to explain what Jesus supposedly did, and what the outcomes of Jesus's healings and exorcisms were.

The Framework of the Biomedical Paradigm

The dominant framework for understanding human illness and healing in the Western world is described as the *biomedical paradigm*. In this paradigm, the body is seen as a machine that sometimes breaks down (Weiner & Fawzy 1989, 9). This paradigm is firmly embedded in the Cartesian mind–body dualism, in which the body is seen as part of the physical world and separated from the mental or social worlds (see Rhodes 1990, 161; Heron 2001, 190–92). This not only leads to two healthcare systems—one treating purely bodily diseases and the other providing treatment for disembodied minds (see Weiner & Fawzy 1989, 15–16)—but also to a discourse in which the human being is constantly separated into these two entities: body and mind. A supporting assumption of this view is that the individual is seen as prior to and autonomous from society and culture (see Kleinman, Brodwin, Good et al. 1992, 9). Three features of this paradigm need to be highlighted here: disease as physical, healing as technical, and the spectrum of human illnesses as universal.

The first is that disease (or sickness) is primarily seen as a physical problem. Symptoms of distress are the result of disordered somatic processes such as biochemical or neurophysiological dysfunctions (see Good & Good 1981, 170); disease is to be accounted for by a deviation from the norm of measurable biological or somatic variables.[2] In addition to real bodily diseases, there is a category of mental or psychosomatic diseases, but biomedical dogma, Engel says, "requires that all disease, including 'mental' disease, be conceptualized in terms of derangement of underlying physical mechanisms" (1977, 130).[3]

Second, proper healthcare should contain some form of technical intervention. When carried to its extreme, "this orientation, so successful in generating technological interventions, leads to a veterinary practice of medicine" (Kleinman, Eisenberg & Good 1978, 252). The sick body or body parts are to be treated. Treatment "consists in the repair or replacement of parts (surgery), or in destroying the noxious causal agents . . . with the aid of 'magical bullets,' notably chemical drugs" (Worsley 1982, 321; and see Engel 1977, 131). Some of the successes of biomedicine, such as the "wonder drug" *penicillin*, have arguably contributed to this belief.[4]

2. As Good (1994, 70) complains: "I have been struck by the enormous power of the idea within medicine that disease is fundamentally, even exclusively, biological."

3. As others complain, disease is seen as an "entity invading organs in the body, altering their structure and function" (Weiner & Fawzy 1989, 9; and see Fabrega 1971, 969), or it is "a material entity and can be completely described in physicalist language" (Kriel 1997, 184).

4. During World War I, many soldiers who were wounded in combat died of septicemia (or blood poisoning), while as much as 18 percent of American soldiers died of pneumonia. Many others died during the war, of infections such as strep throat, syphilis, gonorrhea, or tonsillitis without sustaining any war injury. All of this changed in the early 1940s after the discovery and application of penicillin called the "wonder drug" because the percentage of

Third, if all humans have similar bodies, and sickness is primarily biological, physical, or organic, then it logically follows that sickness conditions are universal to all people. Consequently, the spectrum of physical illness and mental (or psychosomatic) illness applies to all people.[5] That is why cross-cultural psychiatrists "have often sought to establish that culture-bound disorders are known psychiatric diseases in cultural garb" (Good & Good 1982, 143).

By way of summary, the biomedical paradigm maintains that the spectrum of human illnesses (consisting of bodily diseases and psychosomatic conditions) is universal; society, culture, and the *mind* have very little to do with illnesses that are bodily and biological, and proper intervention is technical in order to repair the ill body.

Each and every assumption of this paradigm has been challenged. Starting with the mind-body dichotomy, biomedical practitioners within Western healthcare and medical anthropologists for cross-cultural situations have overturned the notion of sickness as primarily biological and physical, as well as the notion of healing as basically some form of technical intervention. As Eisenberg says, the "restricted and incomplete disease models" (1977, 15) of the biomedical paradigm have been criticized and replaced—both from inside the biomedical paradigm and by medical anthropologists.

Before that development is reviewed, it is necessary to look at the impact of the biomedical paradigm on Jesus research. Surprisingly, it is the mental framework that still dominates reflections in Jesus research on the healing and exorcism stories.

The Biomedical Paradigm and Current Jesus Research

It will be the aim of this section to show that current Jesus research on the healing accounts is firmly trapped in a biomedical framework. At least four explanations are available on how to understand the healing accounts ascribed to Jesus of Nazareth—all of them sharing in the framework of the biomedical paradigm.

---

deaths by these infections was lowered to less than 1 percent.

5. Like the mind–body dichotomy, this concomitant pair of physical and mental carries the ethnocentric construction of personhood and of biomedicine (see White and Marsella 1982, 5).

JESUS'S HEALINGS AND EXORCISMS AS MIRACULOUS ACTIONS

Scholars on the Schweitzerstrasse typically consider the healings as supernatural or miraculous deeds. A case in point is Meier (1994, 512), who
thinks that all the healing accounts are reports about extraordinary deeds
or miracles, which he defines as follows: "unusual, startling, or extraordinary events" that are readily visible to everyone but without any "reasonable explanation in human abilities or in other known forces that operate
in our world of time and space" (and see 1994, 646–61, 678–727). In line
with the scissors-and-paste approach to historiography, his actual historical question (the issue of historicity) is: "did the historical Jesus actually
perform certain startling, extraordinary deeds (e.g., supposed healings
and exorcisms) that were considered by himself and his audience to be
miracles? Or did such reports come entirely from the creative imagination of the early church . . . ?" (1994, 617).[6] In the majority of cases, the
data points toward extraordinary healings performed by Jesus without and
prior to any advanced medical techniques—indeed, a man of miraculous
healings![7]

The above conclusions are not only the result of ethnocentric assumptions about supernatural events and the result of the employment

6. In a similar but slightly different argument, Dunn advances a congruous position
with regard to Jesus's so-called miracles of healing and exorcism (see 2003b, 461, 672).
Treating the documents as testimonies of what was remembered about Jesus, he maintains
that Jesus was indeed a great exorcist and healer, and that these remembrances clearly
point toward him performing miracles. In Dunn's words, "We must say, the first 'historical
fact' was a miracle, because that was how the event was experienced, as a miracle, by the
followers of Jesus who witnessed it" (2003b, 672). The thrust of his argument is to show
that when read as remembered stories, the accounts of the healings and exorcisms show
that Jesus performed miraculous deeds. But, as will be seen, that is to treat the documents
as testimonies for miracles, while from a cross-cultural perspective, it is precisely this
interpretation that is in question. It is like looking for sufficient witnesses in order to
conclude that a shamanic figure has indeed undertaken a (real bodily) heavenly flight.

7. In the case of the individual exorcism and healing stories, the overwhelming majority
of reports, in Meier's view, indeed go back to historical events in Jesus's life (see 1994,
646–61, 678–727). Throughout, the pattern is the same: read at face value, the aim is
to determine whether a specific report can be taken as an extraordinary event in the life
of Jesus, or whether it was a literary creation. In a few cases, where there are only single
attestations of a particular healing, he admits a non licet because the data are too meager.
Elsewhere it is confirmed that in Meier's view, the healing miracles could have only been
actual miraculous healings. It is nonbelievers who would think in terms of psychosomatic
illnesses and the consequent interventions of a charismatic personality or by means of
autosuggestion (1994, 727).

of criteria of authenticity to determine the reliable witnesses, but also the result of the tacit assumptions of the biomedical paradigm.[8] These must have been physical diseases, and if the necessary modern medical aid is not available, healing such conditions as claimed by the texts constitutes *miraculous healings*. Since Jesus was no medical practitioner, what he did, according to Meier, constituted miraculous deeds without *explanation in human abilities or in other known forces that operate in our world of time and space*. This answer is totally dependent on what he believes the conditions that Jesus had encountered (physical diseases) actually were and how healing of such conditions normally takes place. They were obviously real bodily diseases or illnesses, which, if they were healed by Jesus in the ways described, surely constitute startling or miraculous events. This is clearly expressed in the words of Theissen and Merz, who say that in healing-miracles "the healing is brought about by the transference of a miraculous energy from the miracle-worker to the sick person" (1998, 293). After all, *real* diseases can only be cured by *real* medicine, or by miraculous deeds!

JESUS'S HEALINGS AND EXORCISMS AS PSYCHOSOMATIC HEALINGS

A variety of scholars (some closer to the Wredebahn) maintain the historicity of the healings albeit as psychosomatic healings. The best-argued case is that of Davies, who says that as a spirit-possessed healer Jesus probably healed the kind of disorders (psychosomatic illnesses) in the way described by the texts. In his view, Jesus acted as *faith healer* who healed people who believed in his power to heal while Jesus's self-presentation was such that he had power to do it (see 1995, 66–73). Stories about Jesus healing blindness, deafness, paralysis, dermatitis, and excessive menstrual bleeding are thus seen as the healing of psychosomatic illnesses. Or as Davies says, to use "more precise terminology than 'psychosomatic,' faith healers can be expected to cure problems produced by 'conversion disorders'" (1995, 69–70).[9]

---

8. According to Meier, historical research cannot resolve what Jesus did in performing the miracles, only that he did them: "the historical fact that Jesus performed extraordinary deeds deemed by himself and others to be miracles is supported most impressively by the criterion of multiple attestation of sources and forms and the criterion of coherence" (1994, 630; and see 1994, 661, 727, and 831). He has little doubt that Jesus performed miraculous healings that would not otherwise have been possible, and his conclusion finds support from all the other criteria of historicity.

9. A conversion disorder can occur when an individual, because of actions for which he

As seen above, Funk (1996, 253), who does not allow many of these events into the life of Jesus, also claims that the ailments mentioned in the texts can be understood as "psychosomatic in nature." Theissen and Merz employ psychosomatic categories of modern mental disorders, such as psychosis, dissociative disorders, and multiple personality disorder, where possession or demons are at stake (see 1998, 311). Even though they admit that sicknesses are defined by each society, and that leprosy and blindness, for example, are not to be equated with modern understandings, psychosomatic categories are used to explain most of the accounts. While admitting that *psychosomatic* is a modern category, and that there is no precise overlap with the ancient world, the point to note is that psychosomatic conditions remain trapped in the mind–body dichotomy and are consequently of a less serious nature. Psychosomatic diseases are only mental, and not really physical diseases that need real medical attention. In these cases, an explicit use of the dichotomy of the biomedical paradigm is employed to maintain the historicity of Jesus's healings and exorcisms. They could be historical because such (merely) psychosomatic conditions can be treated effectively by faith healers.

JESUS'S HEALINGS AND EXORCISMS AS THERAPEUTIC COMFORT (HEALINGS, NOT CURINGS)

The third proposal is represented in historical Jesus research by Crossan, who is primarily dependent on the work of Pilch (see 1998, 331). Since the early eighties, Pilch has published a series of articles on Jesus's healings, which were brought together in a book (see 2000). His understanding of the healing accounts in the New Testament is fundamentally determined by the distinction between "illness" and "disease," on the one hand, and the distinction between "healing" and "curing" on the other hand. Disease, in his view, reflects a biomedical perspective that sees abnormalities in the structure or function of organ systems. New Testament documents were not concerned with disease but with illness, which reflects a sociocultural perspective. Conditions referred to thus reflect not diseases but illnesses—

---

feels guilty, accepts the guilt and interiorizes it (see Davies 1995, 70). Conversion disorders were of two kinds: those of a "short duration with abrupt onset and resolution" (1995, 71) and those that take place over a longer period of time (known as somatization disorders). On a scale, these dissociative phenomena will range from somatic (fever, excessive menstrual bleeding, etc.) to sensory (deafness, blindness) to radical changes in persons' self-identity (multiple personality disorder) (see 1995, 72).

even though, underlying the illness experiences were incurable or uncured diseases. The rule of thumb, therefore, is that curing is to disease as healing is to illness. Healing involves the provision of personal and social meaning and therefore "all illnesses are always and infallibly healed" (2000, 93). Pilch claims that Jesus could not cure but only heal. Therefore, what Jesus did was to reintegrate people into society: "He restored meaning to the lives of these collectivistic persons" (2000, 142).

By explicitly employing insights from medical anthropology, Pilch subscribes to the notion that the people encountered by Jesus were healed but not cured; since the real medical aid to ensure curing was not available, Jesus could only offer meaning or healing as opposed to curing. Crossan is explicit that the blind, the lame, or the deaf were suffering from some kind of common *disease*.[10]

> I presume that Jesus, who did not and could not cure that disease or any other one, healed the poor man's illness by refusing to accept the disease's ritual uncleanness and social ostracization. . . . By healing the illness without curing the disease, Jesus acted as an alternative boundary keeper in a way subversive to the established procedures of his society. (1994b, 82)

By this Crossan is also saying what Jesus was doing in his healing *miracles*: his healings were merely

> ideological, symbolic, and material resistance to oppression and exploitation. Such resistance cannot directly cure disease, as vaccines can destroy viruses or drugs can destroy bacteria, but resistance can heal both sickness and illness and thus sometimes indirectly cure disease. (1998, 331)

It is clear that Crossan thinks the stories are about people with specific diseases (sickness conditions that can be ascribed to a specific biological or organic defect), and that Jesus could not cure diseases and, therefore, what he actually did was to offer therapeutic comfort. As Crossan says, "for disease you are better off with the doctor and the dispensary, but for illness you are better off with the shaman and the shrine" (1991a, 336).[11]

---

10. There are only three healing stories, together with the Beelzebul controversy, that Crossan takes "as not typically but actually historical" (1991a, 332). That is because they are supported by multiple independent attestations from his earliest textual strata.

11. In admitting that faith heals, he states that real people with real ailments were indeed healed at ancient shrines or by ancient healers (see Crossan 1998, 297). But his overall thesis does not explore this possibility.

As will be seen below, when the restricted definition of disease is replaced by a definition of disease that includes the biological, psychological, social, immunological, and other factors causing sickness, illness can no longer be seen as merely the subjective experience of *a generic disease* but (if the illness/disease distinction is applied) as the subjective experience of a biopsychosocial condition. Similarly, healing or curing can then be seen as the cultural or particular interventions in culturally experienced biopsychosocial ailments.

It is perhaps more the absence of this perspective in these New Testament studies than the claims made about Jesus as merely provider of therapeutic comfort that highlights the biomedical ideology. The biomedical assumptions nevertheless remain clear in these interpretations: sick people suffer from physical diseases that are subjectively experienced as illnesses, and for disease you need medical treatment, while someone like Jesus could only offer therapeutic comfort for the subjective experience, thus leaving the actual disease unaffected. So, in this viewpoint, what he did—if he did what the documents claimed he did—was only to offer therapeutic comfort to first-century Galileans' experiences of disease.

JESUS'S HEALING AND EXORCISM AS LITERARY CREATIONS: MARKETING THE MESSIAH

The fourth kind of explanation sees the data on the healings and exorcisms as merely the literary creations of Jesus's later followers. As indicated with regard to other aspects of Jesus's life, many scholars within the confines of the Wredebahn cannot be faulted for what they do not claim about Jesus as historical figure. In those constructions, the historical reality that can be known and described is the literary creativity of Jesus's distant followers (members of the Jesus movements). It is not necessary to discuss the extreme cases on the Wredebahn, who by definition exclude most of the healing stories from Jesus's biography. Funk, for example, considers Jesus only a "minor miracle worker" (1996, 253) because the believing community ascribed to his life most of the healing and miracle stories. Therefore, very few of them are based on actual events. In a process of missionary propaganda described as "marketing the messiah," Funk claims that they ascribed to his life all the things other charismatic miracle workers did (see 1996, 241). If most of the texts are to be seen as the product of mythmaking, storytelling, or marketing by early Christian communities, most of what they wrote cannot be used as historiographical evidence about the events they purport to write about (see also Martin 2004, 269–70).

But it should be noted that in conjunction with the tradition, critical analyses (which, as was shown, depend on the documents as testimonies and on a prior understanding of the events recorded), the Jesus Seminar's verdict that most of the accounts are literary creations marketing the messiah is also based on a particular understanding of what the healing accounts are about. In line with their general philosophical position, these healings could not have been historical because that is not the way healings take place. Even if deduced from the total lack of a consideration of the possible historicality of such healings as traditional healings, it can be assumed that part of this verdict depends on the assumptions of the biomedical paradigm: healings do not take place as reported in traditional societies, and therefore, these must have been literary creations after the example of other such *stories* in the ancient world.

Conclusion

In the authenticity paradigm it is standard practice to accept that those Jesus encountered were suffering either from a *physical* disease (in the biomedical sense) that could not be treated without biomedical interventions (and Jesus was no medical doctor), or from psychosomatic conditions, which could be treated by a traditional healer such as Jesus of Nazareth. If he did what the texts claimed he did, therefore, three solutions are offered (what is considered historical): he actually performed miracles, he only offered therapeutic comfort, or he merely treated psychosomatic conditions. The fourth solution—that the Gospels are merely literary creations—explains nothing about Jesus the historical figure (except in claiming he obviously did not perform such deeds because they are in principle impossible) but only about what later followers did in creating healing and exorcism stories in a process of mythmaking.

Even though the diseases cannot, due to a lack of information, be identified, both miraculous curing and cultural healing (provision of meaning) assume that the people mentioned suffered some kind of medical condition that could normally only be treated and cured by biomedical intervention. Either explicitly or implicitly, therefore, scholars take it for granted that the sickness conditions mentioned in the gospel accounts were all well-known generic conditions that were only differently labeled then. Jesus's actions are thus seen as appropriate for dealing with the assumed conditions: since he was no medical doctor, these were either miraculous deeds or he did, medically speaking, nothing about their disease conditions.

It is hardly ever appreciated that these conclusions not only depend on the available data but more so on the interpretive paradigm employed to understand them. To be precise, these conclusions are the product of the biomedical paradigm. Whether Jesus did what the texts claimed he did, and how he did it depend on what it is assumed that he could have done about the diseases while not being medically trained.

Beyond the Biomedical to the Biopsychosocial Paradigm

If has by now become apparent that what is believed about Jesus's healings and exorcisms is codetermined by the medical paradigm used (in the above cases, the biomedical paradigm). This point will be pressed home once more when the same data is screened by means of the biopsychosocial paradigm. In order to do so, it is necessary to explain this paradigm in some detail.

A New Healthcare Paradigm

The *biopsychosocial paradigm* offers an alternative framework for dealing with illness and healing in Western as well as in cross-cultural situations (see Engel 1977; 1997). In fact, it acknowledges that all sickness conditions are configurations of various factors, and that healing (curing) is an equally complex cultural practice containing a variety of elements. This paradigm does not totally abandon the insights of the biomedical paradigm but expands them and goes beyond them.

The biopsychosocial paradigm is based on a rejection of the mind-body dualism. Human beings are not machines; they are far more complex than machines (Engel 1977; Moerman 2002, 138). As Heron says: "a human body is not just an objective reality, part of the autonomous furniture of the universe; it is a subjective-objective reality" (2001, 191–92). In addition to the biological components, "it is also comprised of meaning, experience, knowledge and practice" since biology and culture interact, and "are equal partners in who and what we are" (Moerman 2002, 109, 154). It should be realized that this way of thinking represents an altered ontological basis from that assumed by the biomedical paradigm. As Kriel shows, reality itself is at once material, biological, conscious, and social (2000, 42–43). In this systems view of reality, reality itself (and the human being) is seen as a hierarchy of levels of complexity, and it is self-conscious human beings who become sick and receive treatment in order to become healthy again. From this perspective, both illness or disease and health or healing are differently described.

First, disease is no longer seen as primarily biological in nature because the biomedical definition of disease breaks down on several points—it cannot cope with the complexity of sickness conditions (see Cheetham & Rzadkowolski 1980, 322; Weiner & Fawzy 1989, 11). The biopsychosocial paradigm sees health and illness as "interlocking processes that are determined by biological and environmental, as well as psychological factors" (Fabrega 1971, 389). This paradigm

> views illness and disease as a breakdown in biological adaptation, which may or may not lead to anatomical lesions. The breakdown may occur at a variety of levels of biological organization from the psychological to the immunological; it may take many forms and lead to the same disease through different pathways. (Weiner & Fawzy 1989, 18)

It is perhaps with infectious diseases, the exemplary case of the *disease* model, that the shortcomings of the biomedical paradigm are best illustrated. The biomedical paradigm has, indeed, illuminated a host of entities unidentified in many other healthcare systems, which sometimes contribute to sickness. But instead of the disease model, which limits sickness to physical conditions, in the biopsychosocial paradigm it is acknowledged that some people have a *disease* but are not sick; others are sick but have no *disease*.[12] Normal, healthy people typically harbor many different colonies of viruses and bacteria that are not pathogenic (disease producing) primarily because they are kept in check by the human immune system (see Dubos 1977, 34; Brown & Inhorn 1990, 190).[13] Therefore, laboratory documentation may indicate the potential, not the reality, of a

12. A case in point is tuberculosis. The specific agent Mycobacterium tuberculosis is a necessary but not sufficient condition to contract the sickness. A whole host of factors play a role in its development and onset (see Solomon 1979, 74; Wallace 1972, 382–83; 396–97; Dubos 1977, 35; Brody 1988, 155).

13. In traditional societies, a given population and a given set of diseases have coexisted for many generations and, due to natural resistance and immunity, have achieved some kind of balance. In the face of a killer disease for outsiders (such as malaria), these people might have a good chance of survival because of their natural immunity (see Horton 1967, 56).

specific sickness (see Engel 1977, 131, 133). Furthermore, the relationship between a particular virus and sickness is complex in many instances.[14] So is the relationship between clinical profile and diagnosis.[15] Illness is no longer a matter of "having" or "getting" a disease but a matter of degree occurring at one particular place on the health/illness spectrum.

Second, in the biopsychosocial paradigm, health and healing receive new descriptions:

> If the human organism is viewed as composed of a number of hier-archically organized subsystems (particles, molecules, cells, organs) and itself belonging to larger systems (family, group, organization, society, nation, ecological environment), with each system relating reciprocally to the others, health will be understood as a dynamic balance of the systems and illness as a disequilibrium. (Cheetham & Rzadkowolski 1980, 322)

Health, according to this view, "is not defined in absolute terms—as the absence of disease—but rather, as a successful psychobiological adaptation to the environment" (Weiner & Fawzy 1989, 16). Similarly, the misconception that "a technical fix is the potential solution to all" (Eisenberg 1977, 14) is avoided. Without denying the great achievements of biomedical healthcare, the biopsychosocial paradigm recognizes healing as much more the result of a complex set of factors than merely medical, chemical, or surgical intervention (see Engel 1977, 131). Moerman identifies three factors working together in every healing process (see 2002, 16): autonomous responses, specific responses, and meaning responses (see further below).

Illness and Disease, Healing and Curing?

The illness/disease and healing/curing distinctions have indeed been employed in medical anthropology for designating the differences between the personal and cultural experiences of ailments and the identification

14. For example, the hepatitis B virus can be linked to a variety of outcomes: elimination of the virus by the body (i.e., no disease), or clinical or subclinical acute hepatitis. Acute hepatitis can have several outcomes, such as complete recovery or chronic hepatitis, which may or may not lead to cirrhosis and even carcinoma of the liver (see Weiner & Fawzy 1989, 11).

15. Depending on the belief system of the healer, a patient with a particular clinical profile can be diagnosed with "chronic hypertensive disease" and remain a chronic patient for the rest of his or her life, or can be diagnosed with reactive hypertension due to several environmental and social conditions and after treatment loses the status of patient and becomes well again (see Pfifferling 1981, 211–12).

of such ailments from, say, a biomedical perspective. They are, however, fraught with the ideology of the biomedical paradigm and turned out to be of little value in cross-cultural interpretation.

On the one hand, these distinctions are simply a continuation of the biomedical dichotomy between physical and mental (or body and mind). The following descriptions confirm this point. Disease is the "malfunctioning or maladaptation of biologic and psychophysiological processes," while illness refers to the "personal, interpersonal, and cultural reactions to disease and discomfort" (Kleinman et al. 1978, 252).[16] Disease is physical and illness is mental.[17] But that is to universalize disease as common to all people. This distinction is a perfect replication of the Cartesian dualism in disguise with *disease* the actual (material) cause of sickness and illness only the subjective (mind) experience thereof (see the criticisms of Lock & Scheper-Hughes 1990, 52–53; Rhodes 1990, 161).

Attempts to overcome this problem insist that neither illness nor disease is an entity, but both are concepts (see Fabrega 1971, 390; Kleinman et al. 1978, 252; Pfifferling 1981, 210). Unfortunately, as Hahn observes, the distinction "has been made inconsistently from work to work, and even within works" (1984, 1). Consequently, these attempts "are paradoxical in first relativizing the notion of disease to the Western medical paradigm and then universalizing disease and giving it primacy—something to which illness is a secondary and culturally variable reaction" (Pfifferling 1981, 10). This inevitably results in multiple meanings of the same concepts, while remaining trapped in the Cartesian dichotomy. In fact, once it is admitted that disease is not a *thing* (see Eisenberg 1977, 20), there is no *thing* that illness can merely be the subjective cultural experience of.

On the other hand, these distinctions have turned out to be inadequate for dealing with ailments and healing across cultures. By universalizing disease, it is assumed that non-Western people only experience illnesses (while not even knowing they have a disease) and traditional healers only treat illnesses and are ineffective against *diseases*. Although some medical

16. See the same ideology in the definition of Eisenberg: "patients suffer 'illnesses'; physicians diagnose and treat 'diseases' . . . illnesses are experiences of disvalued changes in states of being and in social function; disease, in the scientific paradigm of modern medicine, are abnormalities in the structure and function of body organs and systems" (1977, 11).

17. Fabrega also distinguishes between "purely physical factors (i.e., neurophysiologic, neurochemical) factors [disease] as opposed to symbolic factors, namely psychological and social factors consisting of behaviors, feelings, etc. [illness] of the person" (1982, 39).

researchers make a distinction between illness and disease to describe the distinction between sickness conditions and their subjective experiences by patients, it is clear from the lively discussion among medical anthropologists (see, e.g., Young 1982; Hahn 1984) that they are not close to agreement on what is meant by the terms or how the distinction can be applied in cross-cultural settings without being ethnocentric.

	Biomedical paradigm		Biopsychosocial paradigm
Human being is:	Body	Mind	Biopsychosocial unity
Sickness is:	Disease: physical	Illness: Psychosomatic/ mental	Biopsychosocial disequilibrium
Health care is:	Curing	Healing Therapeutic comfort	Autonomous responses/ specific responses/ meaning responses
Health care system:	Biomedicine/ medical doctor	Traditional health care/ shaman	Biopsychosocial interventions: medical doctor/shaman/healer

Diagram 9.1: The Biopsychosocial Paradigm

In order to grasp the implications of the biopsychosocial paradigm for dealing with the sicknesses and healings accounted in the Jesus traditions, it is necessary to explore this framework a little more.

Human Sickness in Biopsychosocial Perspective

No medical paradigm has contributed more to an understanding of the wide spectrum of human illnesses than the biomedical paradigm. However, instead of the restricted disease model, the biopsychosocial paradigm offers a different framework for understanding human sickness in general and in particular culture-specific conditions across cultures. Five insights are significant to begin with.

First, only about 10 to 20 percent of reported human sickness conditions are life-threatening (see Gumede 1989, 327; Kleinman & Sung 1979, 16). With these conditions, which are mostly caused by viruses, bacteria or fungi, or defects in a bodily organ, patients without appropriate treatment would normally die. In most traditional societies (like that of the first-century Mediterranean world), we hear very little about these patients for the simple reason that they would be found on the mortality list rather than the patients' list.

Second, what is true today about the USA is probably the case in the rest of the world as well as in past times: pain is the most frequent complaint brought to the rooms of physicians (see Kleinman et al. 1992, 1). It should be remembered that pain cannot be measured or seen; there is no "pain thermometer," which means that it is impossible to determine whether or how much pain is experienced, and when and under which conditions it has been removed: "there is no objective knowledge, knowable apart from subjective experience" (Kleinman et al. 1992, 6; and see Moerman 2002, 16). While most diseases are accompanied by experiences of pain, all bodily pain is not sickness related. Conversely, all sickness does not result in bodily pain—in fact, sometimes the patient is unaware of a certain disease (like hypertension in some cases) because there is no pain experience, while at other times the pain register arrives too late as a meaningful warning signal (as with some fatal diseases like cancer). The example of pain can, however, be helpful in understanding sickness (see below).

Third, research shows that 50 to 70 percent of patients who visit their family physician are ill or have pain but have no disease or are complaining without an ascertainable biological base (see Kleinman et al. 1978, 251–52; Weiner & Fawzy 1989, 23; Brown & Inhorn 1990, 190). The implication is that in a large number of cases a firm diagnosis is impossible, but the patients are sick or in pain. It has been like this since time immemorial: "But even from earliest times there were people who behaved as though grief-stricken, yet seemed not to have suffered any loss; and others who developed what for all the world looked like wounds or fractures, yet had not been subjected to any known trauma" (Engel 1977, 133). Many people who seek the help of a healer or physician are sick but have no *disease*; they complain but have no structural or infectious *disease*; they have pain but it is not caused by an injury or a virus, bacterium or fungus. It seems reasonable to conclude that a large percentage of people who visit a healer are ill with complaints that either have no identifiable biological or organic base or cannot be described as a specific disease. Thus, bodily and physical ill health conditions cover a much larger spectrum than only those conditions that result from identifiable biological or physical diseases.

Fourth, it has been demonstrated that changes in lifestyle (such as better sanitation, nutrition, and birth control) and not necessarily the advancement of medicine best account for improvements in health over the last two centuries (see Capra 1982, 135–37; Brown & Inhorn 1990, 196). People who practice good health habits (such as eating a balanced diet, getting enough sleep, and maintaining appropriate weight) are likely to be in good health. Today virtually every disease, as well as a shorter life span, is associated with poverty and low socioeconomic status. Furthermore, single, divorced, and widowed persons are more susceptible to a variety of sickness conditions than married persons. Bereavement that is not properly coped with is associated with a great variety of diseases (see Weiner & Fawzy 1989, 21–22, 25–26). Ironically, as Weiner and Fawsy point out, the inverse is also true: that stable societies impose a minimum of adaptive tasks on their members and consequently, tradition and stability protect persons, for example, from myocardial infarction. Good health is not always merely a matter of the strongest antibiotics; neither is protection from viruses and bacteria the only safeguard for good health.

Finally, while sickness is universal, how, when, and why people experience ill health remains particular—it depends on context and culture. This is the aspect to be explored further. Context and culture play a significant role in what sickness and pain are; they are definitive in delineating but also in experiencing sickness. Sickness follows cultural patterns, and even pain is subject to cultural beliefs. Consequently, both nosology (the classification) and symptomatology (the collective elements) of sickness are determined by cultural systems.

Pain and Sickness as Complex Biopsychosocial Phenomena

Pain and sickness, like human suffering, are homoversals. It is easy to see that most human-inflicted suffering includes the whole person.[18] It is not always apparent that pain and sickness have a similar structure—they are conditions of the human person attached to a particular setting. Put differently, sickness and the experience of sickness are cultural phenomena. It is here that a reflection on pain can illuminate the nature of sickness.

Although pain and sickness can be described in terms of various language games: body language (*bio*), mind language (*psycho*), and person language (*social*), these descriptions of sickness should not be separated.

---

18. The scope of human suffering is alarmingly wide. It includes human-made suffering because of war or revolution to natural disasters, and suffering that result from dehumanizing poverty, discrimination, abuses (such as slavery, child or female abuses), and different forms of violence (see Kleinman et al. 1992).

If it is done, it is done for the practical reason that everything cannot be dealt with at once.

PAIN AND SICKNESS IN BIO- OR BODY LANGUAGE

The biomedical paradigm offers by far the most advanced set of concepts to deal with body-language.

The most common theory of pain today is known as the *gate-control theory*, in terms of which somatic input is subjected to the modulating influence of a gate, before pain perception and responses are registered. According to this theory, the small nerve fibers in the spinal cord conduct most pain signals (say from a thumb hit by a hammer), while other nerve fibers conduct other sensory information (see Moerman 2002, 101). This view is closely associated with the biomedical paradigm, in which pain is seen primarily as the experience of an individual, an experience that results from "change in 'material' structures: sensory receptors, afferent neuronal relays, way stations in spinal cord, mid-brain, or higher cortical modulating systems" (Kleinman et al. 1992, 9). Despite some advantages,[19] this theory is unsatisfactory to explain the complexity of the pain experience.[20]

Since no segment of human behavior is free from biological bias, it is generally speaking the case that human bodies place the constraint on pain and sickness conditions and, for example, provide the basis for certain

19. An advantage of this viewpoint is that pain itself can be seen as a beneficent warning signal that something is wrong on the biological level (see Dow 1986, 64). The experience of pain protects the body from fatal injuries and is a learning device by means of which life-threatening situations can be avoided (not to touch a red-hot piece of steel). It is also useful in that it explains how the pain gate can be closed: for example, by applying ice to a thumb hit by a hammer, or by taking chemical drugs.

20. One problem with the gate-control theory is that pain is not experienced at one end of the nervous system and registered at another; pain is experienced throughout the entire system (see Degenaar 1979, 287). Pain infiltrates the whole consciousness and disrupts human existence. The "rich texture of the reality of pain," to use a phrase of Degenaar (1979, 284), is far more complex than is assumed by this theory, and so is the alleviation of pain. A number of cases reveals that often pain is more than mere bodily experiences and always are person experiences. A prominent example is that of pain in the so-called phantom-limb cases. Often people who have limbs amputated still experience pain in those phantom limbs, because such pain can be induced by the brain. Then there is the case of the soldiers with gaping wounds who would not experience any pain—in fact, in a particular instance, only a quarter of them had pain enough to ask for treatment (see Degenaar 1979, 290–91; Moerman 2002, 101). A plausible explanation maintains that healed soldiers can continue combat, while seriously wounded soldiers are relieved from participating in combat.

somatization processes. But the biopsychosocial paradigm emphasizes that no human behavior is free from psychocultural overlay (see Cheetham & Rzadkowolski 1980, 325).

In all of these, it is not a body that is suffering but a person; it is not a matter of having a body in pain or distress but of being a body in pain or distress. In a very fundamental sense, pain is an aspect of the human self (see Aldrich & Eccleston 2000, 1640). Therefore, pain is not merely having certain sensations but taking a certain attitude toward them, and thus making a human response to pain (see Degenaar 1979, 289). In terms of body language, pain refers to the unpleasant experiences in terms of tissue damage but is always more complex; pain should therefore also include mind- and person-language in order to describe the phenomenon.

PAIN AND SICKNESS IN PSYCHO- OR MIND-LANGUAGE

In terms of mind-language, pain hurts a person (and not merely a body). A neurological sensation is at the same time something experienced by a person; pain is not one or the other but simultaneously a mental and physical thing, an emotion and a sensation. While the pain of a toothache is localized in a particular tooth, the unpleasantness is a holistic conscious experience (see Degenaar 1979, 288). Similarly, it is realized that complex processes "transform painful relationships and pained feelings into chest pain and, vice versa, transform chest pain into a painful world" (Kleinman et al. 1992, 9).

In this discussion, the mind-body unity is maintained, and it is accepted that the mind fundamentally influences the body. In fact, the picture of pain that emerges from this is not one of a body in pain (although that is sometimes the case) but of the bodily person in a particular setting who is in pain. It is the person in pain who consults a healer. A good example is the case of chronic pain, one of the most common causes of visits to physicians today. Chronic pain often has no biological basis. The term *somatization* refers to the process where people employ physical symptoms in order to communicate personal distress (see Kleinman et al. 1992, 12). There is a large body of research pointing toward people with chronic pain conditions that can be connected to life situations (see Degenaar 1979, 293). In these cases the chronic pain or illness becomes the language of inner feelings, emotional distress, or social suffering.

Sickness, like pain, is a human phenomenon. This is confirmed by the cultural dimension (or when person-language is employed).

SICKNESS AND PAIN IN SOCIAL OR PERSON-LANGUAGE

The impact of society, culture, and the human mind on sickness conditions is extremely wide ranging. It includes what can be called *cultural iatrogenesis* (i.e., the importance of culture in the onset of sickness) to patterns of sickness shaped by culture and somatization as the bodily manifestation of psychological, social, or cultural problems. A few examples can be used for illustration.

Sickness patterns and pain experiences follow cultural beliefs. In different countries, people are diagnosed with conditions that either do not occur a lot elsewhere or would be seen as malpractice. For example, in France people are routinely diagnosed with liver-related conditions; in Germany they are diagnosed with heart-related conditions. "Germans, but not French, British, or Americans, regularly diagnose and treat low blood pressure . . . the Germans have nearly the same rate of heart disease as do the French and English, but they use *six times* the amount of heart medication as their neighbors do" (Moerman 2002, 82). In the United States there are a number of virus and low-grade virus diagnoses that do not appear in other comparable countries (see 2002, 77).

In some cultures non-life-threatening diseases such as malaria, measles, and whooping cough are deemed to be part of everyday living and are not constructed as illnesses that need specific treatment (see Worsley 1982, 336). The point is that people live in their bodies in distinct cultural ways (because of cultural beliefs or healthcare practices), which make a difference in their sickness profiles and treatment patterns. The example of the longevity among Chinese Americans, depending on their birth year confirms this point. Based on a complex cultural system, Chinese astrology ascribes certain features to specific years, and if one contracts a disease of an organ that is related to the year in which one is born, longevity is reduced up to 7 percent. No such correlation exists with other Americans born in the same year. The conclusion in clear: longevity is not due to Chinese genes but to having Chinese beliefs and sharing Chinese knowledge about the world (see Moerman 2002, 78). There is, furthermore, ample evidence that the experience of pain follows cultural patterns (see Kleinman, et al. 1992, 2).

There is a whole spectrum of conditions that can either directly or indirectly be ascribed to cultural beliefs, convictions, or patterns. In what Kleinman calls *"cultural iatrogenesis"* (1986, 36), the importance of culture in the onset of sickness can be seen. The best-known example from anthropological literature of the influence of social and psychological conditions on the human body is the extreme of bodily death in the so-called *voodoo death*. *Voodoo death* refers to the phenomenon, well known to anthropologists, that in many cultures a person put under a curse actually dies a short time later. This phenomenon is widely described as an extreme form of the body's response to fear and panic.[21] In its milder form, the same dynamic is at work in cases where guilt or damaged social relationships cause sickness.

Even infectious diseases are strongly influenced by behavioral, cultural, and a whole range of environmental factors for their effectiveness. These include population density, the presence or absence of domestic animals, and natural factors such as moisture, altitude, or temperature, which promote the onset and transmission of these diseases or, conversely, prevent their occurrence.[22] To be sure, the biopsychosocial approach does

---

21. Victims of the curse neither fight nor flee since they are convinced, along with their social group, that imminent death cannot be averted. Not only do their bodily functions fail to react in a positive way, but they refuse food and drink (thus further reducing the body's potential to fight), and the belief is reinforced by their group, who usually withdraws. Since the victim has given up the will to live, a form of "social death" is experienced (see Cannon 1942; Dubos 1977, 37; Csordas & Kleinman 1990, 23; Helman 2001, 14).

22. Whether people are infected depends not only on human biology but often much more on ecology. For example, measles with its short, virulent infection resulting in lifelong immunity must have a host population of at least half a million (see Van Blerkom 1991, 196), while others put the figure between three hundred- and four hundred thousand people (see Avalos 1999, 4). Social factors such as population size and density play a role in the onset and transmission of viral disease. Or as Van Blerkom shows, on cultural patterns: "Most of our infectious diseases came to us recently in our evolution, and from other animals. Some infections (e.g., herpes, colds, malaria, poxvirus infections) evolved along with us, with related strains in other primates. But entirely new human diseases are most likely to be either new strains of existing human pathogens (by mutation or infection of bacteria such as staph or strep by toxin-producing bacteriophages) or microorganisms acquired from an animal population. Therefore cultural practices that favor the transmission of zoonoses should also favor the evolution of human infections. The Old World's greater reliance on domesticated animals and higher tolerance of large commensal rodent and primate populations in human settlements contributed to the large number of epidemic diseases native to the hemisphere" (1991, 197). She, in fact, argues that epidemic diseases (such as smallpox, measles, typhus, and influenza), that killed many Native Americans, probably had zoonotic origins and were transferred to the New World via the explorers (see 1991, 198). Similarly, the movement of troops to and from the East probably was responsible for the serious plagues and epidemics in the Roman world, with the soldiers bringing these into the cities and hometowns (see Avalos 1999, 5).

not deny the great influence of those factors identified by the biomedical paradigm (such as genes, enzymes, organs, microorganisms, and the like) but situates them differently. In fact, it accepts that damage can occur at various levels—be it molecular, cellular, organic, or environmental—upsetting and creating disharmony in numerous systems (see Cheetham & Rzadkowolski 1980, 322).

A Biomedical Map of Human Sicknesses

If the category of human sicknesses consists of both common human conditions (always culturally experienced) and culturally constructed and experienced conditions, it is to be expected that no single map will be able to cover all sicknesses. This point is important for the biomedical paradigm assumes a common human map for disease and psychosomatic conditions. From the biopsychosocial perspective, it is no longer possible to assume either that disease is universal or that mental or psychosomatic illnesses are easily comparable. Before turning to the first-century Galilean situation, these implications will briefly be illustrated.

Besides its successes as a healthcare system, no other system has analyzed and investigated the human body in the same minutest detail as the biomedical paradigm, and consequently the biomedical paradigm has identified sickness conditions not even recognized by most other healthcare systems. The following is an incomplete list of the spectrum.

The first is trauma, such as accidents and injuries. Compared to other animals, the human body is fragile. Our skins are not thick enough or properly covered with hair to withstand normal temperature variations, while we are prone to injuries both from the natural environment and humanly constructed tools, weapons, and objects. Accidents and injuries, which often cause pain, contribute to the spectrum of the human experience of bodily suffering.[23]

Second, congenital and hereditary conditions are present in all societies. In all societies, there are some people who are unfortunate to be

---

23. Most societies have developed procedures to deal with broken teeth or limbs, with injuries or wounds. In fact, as Moerman indicates, it does not require much insight to set a broken arm or to remove a decayed or broken tooth—there is some evidence that even chimpanzees used sticks to remove loose teeth (see 2002, 54).

suffering from an organic defect or malfunctioning. In former eras, such people never even survived early childhood.

Genetic diseases also fall into this category: those conditions that only came to light with the insights of advanced biomedical, biological, and genetic research, and for which no cure has yet been discovered. Huntington's disease is such an example.[24] Not a single case of this disease has yet been cured (see Ridley 1999, 62). Other incurable conditions such as schizophrenia and Alzheimer's disease probably left the patients in traditional societies at the mercy of natural processes of dying.

Autoimmune conditions such as, for example, rheumatoid arthritis, have probably always been associated with old age. With far lower life expectancy in most traditional societies, fewer people are for any case subjected to these conditions.

Third, a number of diseases are directly related to the body's need of particular nutrients that it cannot produce and that are contained in food (see Bogin 1991, 158). These are referred to as nutritional-deficiency diseases and include vitamin and mineral deficiency syndromes (see Brown & Inhorn 1990, 200). Avalos points out that malnutrition was probably a constant cause of diseases during the first century (see 1999, 5). Ironically, a number of food-related diseases in industrialized societies (like bulimia and anorexia nervosa) occur despite the abundance of food.

Fourth, infectious diseases in humans are the result of a host of biological agents, such as viruses, bacteria, fungi, and parasites.

> Biological agents, ranging in complexity from microscopic, obligate intercellular viruses to large and structurally complex helminthic parasites, are the cause of infectious diseases in humans. Disease occurs when the interaction between the host and the infectious

---

24. Huntington's disease is identified with the repetition of more than thirty times of a specific gene on chromosome 4. If the gene is missing, the condition is known as Wolf-Herschhorn syndrome, and sufferers die very young. Most people have about ten to fifteen repeats of the specific "word" in that gene. Huntington's chorea is different: "If the 'word' is repeated thirty-nine times or more, you will in mid-life slowly start to lose your balance, grow steadily more incapable of looking after yourself and die prematurely. The decline begins with a slight deterioration of the intellectual faculties, is followed by jerking limbs and descends into deep depression, occasional hallucination and delusion. There is no appeal: the disease is incurable" (Ridley 1999, 55).

agent, or the host-parasite relationship, is no longer symbiotic, shifting in favor of the agent. (Brown & Inhorn 1990, 203)

Typically, infectious diseases are categorized into two major types, acute and chronic.[25] Acute infections, like measles and influenza, generally have a sudden onset and rapid resolution, either through death or through the self-limiting nature of the illness.[26] However, acute infections tend to burn themselves out before wiping out whole populations. Chronic infectious diseases (such as schistosomiasis and tuberculosis) are endemic in that they are constantly present in a community, associated with high morbidity, and incapacitating members of the community, but they are not epidemic (see Brown & Inhorn 1990, 205–6).

It would not be unreasonable to assume that even minor infections often result in early deaths in most traditional societies. It is claimed that malaria has killed more people on this planet than any other single disease (see Brown & Inhorn 1990, 196). In fact, Brown and Inhorn (1990, 188) point out: "infectious diseases still represent the major cause of morbidity and mortality in nonindustrial societies." The estimate that about 5 percent of the deaths in the ancient Israelite world were caused by dental infections (see Botha 1998a, 13) confirms that infectious diseases caused even by minor injuries were not properly controlled.

Fifth, a growing cause of disease in Western biomedical treatments is the negative effects of medication or medical intervention, referred to as the iatrogenic causes of disease. This could include the side effects of medication or the unforeseen outcome of surgical intervention. It is, however, not only biomedicine that produces such effects. Ethnographic literature shows that many traditional practices and interventions result in equally serious damages or diseases (see Brown & Inhorn 1990, 202).

And finally, mention has been made of cases where bodily pain, discomfort, or incapacity appears without any identifiable organic or biological cause. These can be described as *culture-specific syndromes* and

25. For an overview of the classification and modes of transmission of infectious diseases, see the summaries in Brown and Inhorn (1990, 203–6).

26. The self-limiting nature of infectious diseases takes on many formats. Whole communities can become immune in what is known as "herd immunity" (Brown & Inhorn 1999, 205), when natural immunity is acquired subsequent to infection.

can be seen as conditions that are reactive to psychosocial and cultural circumstances and therefore atypical versions of common human potentials (see discussion of Fabrega 1982). This wide spectrum of conditions is included today in, for example, the *Diagnostic and Statistical Manual of Mental Disorders* (DSM-IV).

In modern times laboratory tests or clinical examination would find no support for such complaints. According to the DSM-IV (see DSM-IV 1994, 446–50) *somatization disorder* covers a whole spectrum of bodily sites of pain or discomfort (head, abdomen, back, joints, extremities, chest, and rectum), while the clinical symptoms listed include nausea, vomiting, diarrhea, intolerance of food, excessive menstrual bleeding, urinary retention, sexual dysfunctions, paralysis, blindness, deafness, seizures, amnesia, fainting, difficulty swallowing, a lump in the throat, and hallucinations. While at least four of these have to be present in order to diagnose somatization disorder, it remains a fact that all of these (and more) bodily conditions are well-documented possibilities of human sicknesses without biological or organic causes.

Under this category could also be placed the so-called diseases of civilization or affluence, such as the diseases of obesity, hypertension, cardiovascular disease, and some forms of cancer; serious bodily illnesses are the result of conditions that are closely associated with lifestyle and excessive or harmful nutritional practices (see Brown & Inhorn 1990, 199–200). Although pathogenic organisms or genetic predispositions might be present in some of these conditions, their onset cannot be divorced from the culturally constituted environmental and psychological conditions. Thus, they are culture-specific or context-specific syndromes.

Trauma/ injuries:	Congenital/ hereditary:	Nutritional-deficiency diseases	Infectious diseases	Iatrogenic conditions	Culture-specific syndromes
• broken limbs • broken teeth	• genetic • auto-immune	• Vitamin deficiency • malnutrition	• acute • chronic	• medication • health practices	• DSM-IV • Psychosomatic • Diseases of civilization

Diagram 9.2: A Biomedical Map of Sickness Conditions

A Cross-Cultural Map?

The above map is not without value for dealing with the healing accounts in the Gospels because it gives a profile against which those sicknesses can be measured. The question is whether and in what way the biomedical map can be applied across cultural boundaries. That will be answered by first looking at another instance of a cultural sickness map.

In the traditional Zulu (an indigenous South African culture) map of sicknesses, there are two broad categories: natural and *ukufa kwabantu* conditions. The latter refers to "those particular culture-bound syndromes which the Zulu people themselves believe are unique or peculiar to their people in the sense that their etiology, diagnosis and treatment are all inextricably bound up with the traditional Zulu and African world views of sickness" (Edwards, Cheetham, Majozi et al. 1982, 82). On analysis it is clear that most of these syndromes even have similarities with psychiatric disorders as identified in the Western manuals of mental disorders, but they are not to be identified as such. In fact, even in clinical conditions it is impossible to identify them with the categories of such manuals (see Edwards et al. 1982, 83–85; Wessels 1989, 96–108). The *ukufa kwabantu* syndromes are deeply ingrained in the specific culture and cannot easily be identified with other culture-bound syndromes—therefore, they are not merely mental illnesses in cultural garb. Thus, when superimposed onto the biomedical map, *ukufa kwabantu* as culture-bound syndromes, do not precisely cover the culture-bound syndrome of that continuum.

However, such an analysis further shows that there are certain problems of living common to all people in all cultures and, therefore, from a broader cross-cultural perspective, many culture-specific syndromes are very similar (though not identical) between cultures (see, e.g., Edwards et al. 1982, 86; Wessels 1985, 51). Sickness profiles faithfully follow cultural patterns. Culture-specific syndromes are specific configurations within particular biopsychosocial systems, where both nosology and symptomatology are determined by that system. Therefore, culture-specific syndromes are not merely disguised versions of the standard DSM categories (see Hughes 1985). The variety of phenomena called sickness is itself the result of a variety of factors, which, in different configurations, are part of the human condition. Instead of claiming that disease is universal and illness the cultural and personal experience thereof, it is suggested here that sickness (as disease and illness) itself is objectified into a variety of identifiable and experienced phenomena, each with its own status and structure. Given the cultural and social settings, people experience sickness as the result of such biopsychosocial configurations.[27]

Patients and Sickness in the Gospel Stories

From the above discussion, three negative and two positive concluding remarks can be advanced regarding the sicknesses and patients encountered in the Gospel accounts.

The first is that it can no longer be assumed that any of the patients encountered by Jesus was in fact suffering from some kind of disease (a universal human sickness that can only be treated by medical means or by miracles). Different cultures not only have unique maps of human sickness conditions but different principles of mapping, which result in different cultural experiences of ailments. Not only are there different explanations for the causes of sicknesses, but the experiences of sicknesses vary. Thus, although all humans are subject to a similar range of illnesses, illness maps are not identical, and even the same sickness is still experienced in unique cultural ways; an identical sickness (e.g., measles) follows cultural patterns, and even pain is subject to cultural beliefs. It is particularly the culture-specific syndromes that show how culture and context play a significant role in what sickness and pain are. Culture is determinative in defining but also in experiencing sickness. Consequently, both the nosology of sickness (i.e., the classification of diseases) and symptomatology of sickness (i.e., the systematic discussion of symptoms of illness) are determined by cultural systems.

Second, it can no longer be assumed that the biomedical map of culture-bound syndromes (DSM-IV) can be applied to other cultural systems. First-century Galilean people (like twenty-first century traditional Zulu people) were subject to their own map, and they probably were not suffering from common physical *diseases* or from psychosomatic conditions listed in modern diagnostic manuals. In view of the biopsychosocial

27. This argument is based on what I hope is the implication of the insight that Degenaar advances with regard to pain. He says: "I hold therefore that the word 'pain' is not only an abstract concept applicable to a variety of phenomena, but that the variety of phenomena is itself the result of a variety of approaches to a reality called pain as it is pre-scientifically experienced. By means of these approaches, the reality of pain is objectified into a variety of phenomena each with its own status and structure. Thanks to the variety of approaches, to which a variety of phenomena correspond the rich texture of the reality of pain can be expressed" (1979, 284).

paradigm, it should be said that they were suffering from first-century Galilean (biopsychosocial) conditions or sicknesses. They were human beings who became sick by means of first-century Galilean sickness conditions, and some of these physical conditions were described as demon possessions or as illnesses caused by demons or evil spirits.

Third, although culture-specific syndromes seem to overlap on different healthcare maps, they cannot easily be taken as identical to those identified by the modern biomedical map. There are no signs of a "highly developed typology of illnesses" (Avalos 1995, 268) in the Israelite tradition in general or in the Gospel accounts in particular. This is no different from either other ancient societies or modern traditional societies (as was seen from the example of the Zulu culture). Nevertheless, as indicated above, even under clinical conditions, it is virtually impossible to identify culture-specific syndromes with categories employed in the biomedical paradigm. This is supported by the fact that high levels of misdiagnosis or faulty procedures occur even where doctors have access to advanced diagnostic techniques (see Cousins 1989, 158–61). This leaves us with nothing more than educated guesses and inferences about the illnesses in the New Testament, and some generalized conclusions. It is fairly obvious that we just do not know and cannot know, based on the existing data, what those people were suffering from. Since the Gospel reports do not even contain the minimum evidence often found in ancient diagnostic reports (such as about the smell, color, or taste of certain bodily fluids), specific diagnoses are impossible.

Fourth, if sickness conditions in other traditional societies are anything to go by, it is clear that almost 90 percent of patients who visit traditional healers have non-life-threatening diseases or conditions with no biological or organic cause (see Kleinman & Sung 1979, 16; Cheetham & Griffiths 1982, 955). Thus, they probably are culture-specific syndromes in the particular setting.

A remarkable feature of the healing episodes is that none of the healings ascribed to Jesus contains a reference to an injury or serious bodily wound (with the exception of the episode where Jesus replaced a soldier's removed ear). Not a single instance of mending a broken limb or of taking care of a serious injury is reported among Jesus's healings. As far as the reports go, there is also no indication of serious infections or of the mentioned organic and genetic diseases. A number of the healings ascribed to Jesus are not only very similar to the list ascribed to folk healers today, but they are very similar to those ascribed to other ancient healers like Apollonius of Tyana and Ḥanina ben Dosa.

Finally, people suffering from culture-specific syndromes are really ill—that is, if one accepts that somatization, bulimia, anorexia nervosa, hypertension, cardiovascular disease, or demon possession are serious (bio-psychosocial) illnesses in different settings. Contrary to the biomedical paradigm, where sickness is principally restricted to identifiable biological diseases (sometimes with an addition from psychosomatic or mental conditions), the biopsychosocial perspective reckons with sickness or ill health as a spectrum of unsuccessful biopsychosocial adaptations in which genetic, immunological, nutritional, psychological, and social or cultural factors could play a role in the onset and experience of a sickness. The general starting point of this paradigm can be expressed in the following way: "It is likely that numerous emotional and physical factors, many of them yet to be delineated, influence health and disease, probably in different ways for different individuals. There is no single, simple factor that causes or cures cancer and other major illnesses" (Cousins 1989, 215), and one could add, any minor culture-specific illness. Maladaptive bodily conditions (for whatever reason) are, in other words, serious illnesses.

It would not be possible to go further than claiming that Jesus's *patients* were indeed sick people who, in most instances, could approach Jesus themselves or were in such a state that they could be brought to him whenever he happened to be around. Some probably were chronically ill—that is, they had been suffering from these conditions for a long time without their lives being threatened (in one case, a patient had already been suffering for eighteen years).

The simple truth is that in terms of their understanding and expectations, those people were suffering from sickness, distress and/or pain: they were first-century people in pain or distress and sickness. Jesus's patients were sick (suffering from unsuccessful biopsychosocial adaptation); this sickness affected their whole system or biopsychosocial makeup, and they approached a recognized and highly rumored healer.

Some Insights Regarding Human Health and Healing

After the above discussion, it goes without saying that just like illness, health and healing also are subject to cultural patterns and beliefs. This will be confirmed in the discussion below.

But from the above description of sickness and from what has been said above about health and healing in a biopsychosocial perspective, a second insight can be highlighted, namely, that in certain classes of ailments, technical procedures are ineffective or misleading because they "misdirect" healing efforts (see Eisenberg 1977, 19). This is the case for illnesses in all cultural maps but particularly for many culture-specific syndromes.

A third insight is that in every healing process there are at least three factors working together: autonomous responses, specific responses, and meaning responses. An implication to be highlighted from this is that no technical or therapeutic intervention goes without human meaning responses. But this will become apparent in the discussion of each of these three responses.

Autonomous Responses: The Body Is the First Healer

For ordinary healthy people, most sicknesses are self-limiting in that they will disappear, even if nothing is done about them, because many years of evolutionary development have resulted in sophisticated bodily processes of restoring or maintaining bodily health (see Moerman 2002, 12).[28] In the words of Cousins: "the human body is its own best drugstore for most symptoms" (1989, 168). Some medical experts say that 85 percent of illnesses fall within the body's power to heal (see Remus 1997, 112). Prior to the application of any healthcare, the body activates a number of systems working toward healing. One of the results is that most diseases or symptoms will, in any case, change over time (see Ernst 2001, 19). It is well known that some chronic diseases, including multiple sclerosis and some cancers, "exhibit a relapsing, remitting course" (Kleinman, Guess & Wilentz 2005, 15). All of these refer to the body's autonomous response to loss of health.

Today much more is also understood about the body's production of endogenous morphine, commonly known as endorphins, which are a class of neurotransmitters acting as painkillers in the brain (see Moerman 2002, 102). There is a growing body of research showing that brain activity can change under various placebo manipulations (see Kleinman et

28. One field of research exploring these interactions is known as psychoneuroimmunology (PNI), which illuminates the close interconnectedness between body and mind (see, e.g., Friedman, 1990; Clow 2001). The new science of PNI, Fenwick says, investigates the principles of how "thoughts, feelings, meanings, desires, etc. are organizing principles that lead to the emergence of control functions within the body as a whole" (2001, 218).

al. 2005, 13). Certain bodily functions are also subject to change from ritual stimulation, be it, drumming, dancing, preaching, and the like (see Wedenoja 1990, 285–86; Newberg et al. 2001, 83). Endorphins influence not only bodily pain but a large number of other systems: "they play important roles throughout the entire organism, affecting everything from respiration to urination, from eating to exercising, from the immune system to the heart" (Moerman 2002, 138). The production of endorphins does not account for all the effectiveness of healing rituals but because "endorphins are potent pain reducers, ritual behavior that releases them would be effective against pain" (Dow 1986, 59). Moerman (2002, 154) concludes his study on placebo and meaning responses with the following remark: "Certain biological systems of great evolutionary age are probably the mechanisms responsible for much of the meaning response." As will be illustrated below, the meaning response is a significant bodily response affecting pain and sickness.

But it should not escape our attention that under normal circumstances the body as such (the interconnected network of bodily systems) strives toward equilibrium or healing.

Specific Responses

Specific responses refer to the highly (and sometimes not so highly) developed procedures, techniques, and medications that form the body of medical interventions. Most societies have developed some kind of technical procedure to deal with things like broken teeth or limbs, wounds or injuries, and birth pains.[29] Specific responses can vary from herbal and hallucinogenic plants to chemical pills and drugs, from laying-on of hands to inserting a scalpel, from ritual dances and magical words to laser therapies.

There can be no doubt that the level of technical intervention (the specific means) of the biomedical paradigm is superior to any other healthcare system. Statistics and experience prove that biomedicine is by far the best option available today for treating life-threatening conditions (see Horton 1967, 58; Kleinman & Sung 1979, 24). However, it does not excel in the case of culture-specific syndromes (see Cheetham & Griffiths 1982, 956;

---

29. As Moerman indicates, it does not require much insight to set a broken tooth— there is some evidence that even chimpanzees use sticks to remove loose teeth (see 2002, 54).

Wessels 1985). This is probably also the case with many diseases of affluence. If sickness is the result of failure to pray to ancestors or the result of
distorted social relations, then medication would be of little help: "prayer
and repentance, not penicillin, cure sin" (Snow in Helman 2001, 9).

This is not the place to deal with the spectrum of possible medical interventions available in the world or to evaluate the efficacy of any. This is
also not an attempt to deny the power of Western technical medicine—its
successes speak for themselves. But suffice it to say that all cultures have
developed specific techniques in order to intervene medically. What is not
always realized is that the very first level of specific intervention can be
described as the *symbols of competence* of the healer. Even before or sometimes without the application of any therapy, these function to facilitate
healing.

Meaning Responses in the Healing Process

Of special interest here is the third factor in the healing process, namely,
the *meaning responses*. The *meaning response* in the healing process can be
defined as the "psychological and physiological effects of *meaning* in the
treatment of illness" (Moerman 2002, 14). If belief can make ill and kill
(such as in voodoo death), then surely it can heal as well.

Providing meaning in healing is not the aim of the process—meaning is part of the method and therapy, or the means, of healing. In other
words, there is no such thing as symbolic healing (which provides only
meaning or healing to the patient instead of curing, as some would have
it) as opposed to other forms of healing.[30] All forms of healing have a
symbolic component or meaning response, and it contributes to healing
(see Csordas & Kleinman 1990, 11).

From a biopsychosocial perspective, there is very little surprising
about the idea of mind affecting body, mental phenomena affecting physical ones, because it is only in the discourse and conception of biomedicine
that, following the Cartesian dualism, mind and body have been separated. In the biopsychosocial perspective, mind and body are part of many
interacting and integrated systems—all of which have a biological basis,

---

30. Symbolic healing as used by Dow (1986) and others in medical anthropology
does not refer to a kind of healing as opposed to, say, biomedical healing or curing. If I
understand them correctly, their point rather is that there are aspects of symbolic healing
or symbolic transfer in each and every encounter.

but some are merely the products of such physical entities (see Withers 2001, 115). Even the taking of active medicine or surgery always contains an element of a meaning response, which contributes to the effect: "Meaning affects life; Life affects meaning" (Moerman 2002, 150).

Of special interest in this study are the meaning responses that can be called *the total drug effect* and the *doctor as drug*. Both refer to factors that are present in most healing accounts and that play a silent but significant role in the healing process.

MEANING RESPONSE AND THE TOTAL DRUG EFFECT

The *total drug effect* describes all the factors influencing the effect of a drug on the human body (see Helman 2001, 4–5). Taking a pill is a complex meaningful action in which many factors contribute to the relief of pain or symptoms. In a study, patients' reaction to various painkillers was tested. Taking medication, even inert medication, works better for pain than doing nothing. Taking a branded placebo, however, is even more effective. Yea so was taking a branded aspirin more effective than taking the same aspirin without knowledge of the branded name (see Moerman 2002, 18–20). Knowledge about the medication (via advertisements or gossip) impacted on its efficacy.

Beliefs are significant in the application of medication. Besides the active ingredient, which accounts for much of what medication achieves, the form, shape and color of medication contribute significantly to its effectiveness. While different forms and colors of medication do make a difference in their effectiveness (e.g., pills or capsules), it is clear that effectiveness for different people is also related to the form of medication: "Americans 'know' that shots work better than pills and so, they give shots" (Moerman 2002, 79)—in fact, percentage-wise, European doctors and patients (more than American doctors and patients) are satisfied with pills (and see Ernst 2001, 25; De Craen et al. 2001, 181–83). Furthermore, two inert pills are more effective than one; capsules are more effective than tablets and inert injections more effective than inert pills (see Moerman 2002, 47–53).

The history of medication itself offers an interesting insight into the impact of belief in medication on its effectiveness. The replacement of old medications with new ones is a common feature of biomedical medicine. In a study on the effectiveness of medication for the same condition after a new medication came onto the market, it was found that the old medication became progressively less effective as the new medication became popular. Therefore, Ernst says: "Until recently, the history of medicine was a history of placebo" (2001, 27; see also Brody 1988, 157).[31] What patients know and what things mean, Moerman concludes, account for the effectiveness of much of medical treatment (see 2002, 46).

The meaning response is also present in surgical procedures, such as the surgical procedures applied for coronary artery disease. In the Western world, one of the most common causes of death is myocardial infarction or heart attack.[32] A milder form of coronary atherosclerosis is known as angina pectoris, a pressing pain beneath the sternum. Based on the *rusty pipe* theory, several surgical procedures have been developed in order to alleviate these problems.

One such procedure is bilateral internal mammary artery ligation (BIMAL), in which some of the affected mammary arteries that are fairly easily accessible are ligated (tied off) in order to improve blood supply to other arteries. Since not everybody believed this theory, double blind studies were conducted in which the trial group only received the small incisions on the chest, but no arteries were ligated. In two of these studies, "the patients with sham procedures did as well (maybe even a bit better) than those with the complete procedure" (Moerman 2002, 59; and see Johnson 1994, 1140).[33]

31. Moerman mentions two common procedures that were applied in Western medicine during the nineteenth century: the application of calomel (mercurous chloride) and venesection, or the laying on of steel, which was a symbolic operation. While they were part of the medical treatment of the day, they did have an effect (see 1991, 136).

32. "The traditional biomedical understanding of disease is that it is caused by ischemia, a lack of adequate blood flow to some region of the heart, which is in turn caused by atherosclerosis, which is a build-up of lipids or fatty tissue in the coronary arteries, the arteries that supply blood to the heart itself . . . These fatty tissues, of course, are said to be due to excess cholesterol in the body, due presumably to people eating too much red meat. These lipid build-ups, or atherosclerotic plaques, cause lesions on the blood vessels. The heart attack is typically understood to be caused by thrombosis, that is, the blockage or the narrowed artery by a blood clot (thrombus) . . . these clots block the artery; the heart muscle, deprived of oxygenated blood, dies, creating an area in the muscle known as an infarct of the myocardial muscle (hence the technical name of a heart attack, a myocardial infarction or 'MI')" (Moerman 2002, 55–56).

33. Another procedure is based on the theory that blood flow to the heart should be improved in what is known as transmyocardial laser revascularization (TMR). An incision is made between two ribs, and the heart muscle is exposed, and between thirty and fifty channels are made into the heart with a controlled laser beam. The idea is that this will

This is not to say that the specific treatment or procedure is unsuccessful but to show that even with highly technical surgical procedures, bodily healing is a combination of specific and general therapies. There are many studies showing that surgical procedures are effective but not always necessarily for the reasons they are performed. These examples confirm that medical treatment, whether medical or surgical, can be effective treatment for a variety of reasons, one of which is because of the meaning response of the patient (see Moerman 1991, 136). In fact, the majority of patients react positively to sham surgery as well as to sham acupuncture (Ernst 2001, 25). Johnson boldly concludes that "one third of the effect of surgery is placebo" (1994, 1141), but that might be misinterpreting statistics.

That meaning contributes to the effect of medicine is perhaps best illustrated not with studies of inert medication, but when the same medicine is administered to informed and uninformed patients. In a study on the effect of a potent painkiller (naproxen) for cancer patients, it was found that "naproxen worked better than placebo in treating cancer patients. But both naproxen and placebo worked substantially better for the patients who had been told about the experiment than they did for the patients in the dark about the procedure. Indeed, in the informed patients, the placebos worked much better than did the naproxen in the uninformed patients" (Moerman 2002, 71).

The meaning response is also confirmed by the regular intake of medication. In a study of patients treated for cancer contracting secondary infections, there was no big difference between those receiving antibiotics and those receiving placebos: 22 percent of antibiotic patients and 27 percent of placebo patients got infections or fever. The great variation came with patients taking their medication regularly or not: only 18 percent of good adherents taking antibiotics had infections, and among the placebo patients 32 percent of the good adherents. Three times as many bad adherents of antibiotics and twice as many bad adherents of placebos got infections (see Brown 1998, 72). "So it is clear that 'antibiotics work,' and

---

make a sort of substitute artery, providing oxygen-rich blood to the heart muscle. There is much debate about why this procedure actually works, because the artificial channels close up within hours. In a placebo-controlled trial, the procedure was performed on the control group only without the actual laser beams being fired. "The percentage of patients who improved in two or more classes on the Canadian scale ranged from 25% (high dose) to 33% placebo to 39% (low dose). Frequency of angina declined, and physical functioning and disease perception scores increased, in all three groups" (Moerman 2002, 64).

protect against infections. But so does taking all your drugs, or placebo, as the case may be" (Moerman 2002, 117).

What all of this shows is that healthcare interventions work for more reasons than for their chemical or surgical purposes. They contribute to the overall experience of meaning by the patient and consequently have definitive bodily effects. Since sickness is not merely the defect of an organ or bodily system, healing is not achieved by mechanical, technical, or medical means only. Therefore, traditional healers the world over do have a bodily effect on the patients in their environment (see Kleinman & Sung 1979; Ward 1989, 134).

THE DOCTOR AS DRUG

Many interesting studies confirm the effect of the healer or doctor on the experience of pain and discomfort of patients. With confidence in the doctor, patients who received sham surgery to treat arthritis of the knee reported relief; patients treated by a sympathetic doctor need fewer narcotics to do the same job;[34] patients recover more quickly if they believe the doctor is in control;[35] drugs are more effective when healers believe in their efficiency.[36] In studies where both groups are given the same inert medication (placebos), but the difference is in the attitude and actions of the doctors, it was reported that "skeptics can heal 30% to 40% of their patients with inert medication, while enthusiasts can heal 70% to 90%" (Moerman 2002, 39). If medical doctors can heal with placebos, then why not traditional healers?

Given this insight, it is not surprising that even within the biomedical system, reference is made to the "doctor as drug" or to the magic of "faith in one's doctor" (Krippner 1988, 107). Within biomedicine of Western

34. For example, when preoperative patients received a visit from an anesthesiologist who emphasized nonmedical means to control postoperative pain, who expressed concern, and who offered a frank explanation of what pain to expect, the patients required half as much narcotics and were discharged two days earlier (Brody 1988, 150–51).

35. "In a recent study of 200 patients with physical complaints but no identifiable disease, doctors at the University of Southampton in England told some that no serious disease had been found and that they would soon be well; others heard the cause of their ailment was unclear. Two weeks later 64 percent of the first group had recovered, but only 39 percent of the second group had recuperated" (Brown 1998, 72).

36. In a study in which all patients received a placebo for dental procedures, the only difference between groups was that the clinicians knew that the one group would only receive placebos and the other group might receive an active drug. There was a remarkable difference in the experienced pain between the two groups (Moerman 2005, 82).

culture, faith in a physician is established and maintained by means of word of mouth (rumor and gossip in the positive sense); faith in the physician is symbolized by the degree certificates displayed on the walls of the consulting room; faith is confirmed by the doctor's dress (such as a white coat and stethoscope); and confidence in the physician is affirmed by the doctor's manner (enthusiastic or not), personality, style, and language (see Moerman 2005, 41, 81; Helman 2001, 9; 2004, 213–14). All of these, *symbols of competence*, contribute to the meaning response of patients and thus to the healing (curing) effect of treatment.

Shamanic Healings and Exorcisms

Within traditional cultural settings, a person can become a great healer because he or she has "acquired a reputation as a great healer" (Remus 1997, 113), which is expressed in the healing stories about such a healer. Healings and stories about healings ascribed to a particular healer are therefore interconnected in the same dynamics: healings can be performed because of the "reputations as a 'big man'" (Balzer 1991, 64). Avalos (see 1999, 79) points out that in the Greco-Roman world in general, reputation, more than anything else, was the key in identifying a healer. Reputation can furthermore be symbolized by dress and style of life. In a predominantly oral world, the symbols of competence are less material and written than oral and verbal.

It was indicated above that healing and exorcisms are central to most descriptions of shamanic figures. While some make use of remedies or herbs, the majority of shamanic figures heal by spiritual means or while in a trance or spirit-possessed. That is to say, they wield the symbolic means and meaning responses in particular cultural systems.[37]

With regard to the employment of séances, which play a role in this setting for healing, Balzer says:

> Complex beliefs enable performances of séances and help shape not only the personality and power of the shamans, but also the culture of curing in a given community . . . During a traditional séance, an enormous amount of communal energy was directed at solving a spiritual emergency, with an extended family often actively participating in chants and dancing . . . The Khanty sha-

---

37. Although he formulates it in terms of a strong distinction between disease as the actual sickness and illness as only the cultural experience thereof, Kleinman offers a helpful description of the role of meaning in the process of healing (see 1986, 34–35).

> man, whether male or female, was and to some extent still is able
> to fulfill mediating roles and to manipulate important Khanty
> symbols of communication. (1991, 61–62)

Two features important for understanding shamanic healing appear from these remarks. The first is the importance of communal involvement and the mustering of communal energy in shamanic activities. The second is the fact that shamanic figures employ, and manipulate if you wish, cultural symbols in a community. In an effective way, they employ and mediate the systems and symbols of meaning already available in their communities. It is because of the limitations in their technology, Eisenberg indicates, that shamanic and other traditional healers are more responsive to the "extra-biological aspects of illness" (1977, 14), which they can manipulate.

Furthermore, what Balzer says about Khanty shamans in Siberia is probably true for other shamanic figures: "An absolute prerequisite for an effective shamanic cure is faith" (1991, 67). Healings and stories about healings ascribed to a particular healer are therefore interconnected in the same dynamics: healings can be performed because of the reputations of and belief in the "big man."

An Ethnography of Jesus's (Shamanic) Healings from a Biopsychosocial Perspective

It was suggested above that the *patients* in Jesus's healings and exorcisms were probably suffering from first-century Galilean conditions of bio-psychosocial maladaption—they were sick but not necessarily from any life-threatening conditions. An ethnography or thick description of Jesus's healings will show that it is likely that he could have healed these people. This will simultaneously give answers to the questions, how did Jesus heal? and what were the outcomes of his healing activities? In other words, which therapies were used, or what treatment was applied, and what was the result of his healing activities?

In answering these questions, it will be suggested that the individual reports can indeed be seen as containing typical shamanic healings and exorcisms. By working with and toward the shamanic hypothesis, it will be indicated that the healing and exorcism accounts can be added as strong support for the hypothesis that Jesus could have been a Galilean shamanic figure. As argued earlier, this approach can prove nothing; it attempts to be powerfully persuasive in showing how things were and how they hung together.

In a cable-like interpretive process with a constant to-and-fro movement between, on the one hand, the individual reports read in terms of the hypothesis and, on the other hand, the overall picture constituted by means of the individual episodes thus interpreted, there is no obvious starting point. The procedure will be to establish the plausibility of the individual reports (that is, whether they can indeed be seen as typical shamanic healings and exorcisms) while such accounts will be used to sustain the overall hypothesis.

Finally, from all the accounts it is clear that no medical means were used in the healing accounts ascribed to Jesus of Nazareth. There is no evidence that he distributed any traditional medicine. But that does not mean that he did not employ methods and means of healing significance. Viewed in terms of the above distinction between autonomous, specific, and meaning responses, it can be said that Jesus employed both specific and meaning methods in order to effect bodily healing. Together with the body's autonomous responses, these means contributed to healing effects on the first-century Galilean conditions the patients were suffering from.

People are sick when they suffer from an unsuccessful biopsychosocial adaptation and healing is effective when it addresses the appropriate contributing factors for that maladaption. Faith, symbolic actions, and the meaning response are the therapies to be investigated here.

Meaning Responses:
The Mediation of Cultural Symbolic Means

According to the preserved reports, Jesus employed at least four types of means that in his society could be considered effective means of creating and establishing a meaning response under illness conditions. The first three will be considered here while the fourth, the controlling of evil spirits or demons, will be considered in a next section.

MEDIATING DIVINE FORGIVENESS OF SINS

In some Israelite circles, a close connection between sickness and sin was presuposed from the earliest times. It is God who restores the health of the faithful and who sends sickness to the unfaithful and disobedient (see Kee 1992, 660). For the people of the covenant, there is an even more direct link between sickness and ritual impurity (see, e.g., 2 Kgs 5 and Deut 28:15, 20).

The connection between sin and suffering appears to have been a cultural option in some Israelite thinking. This seems to be the tradition behind the reasoning regarding those suffering from Pilate's actions or those who were killed under the fallen Siloam tower (see Luke 13:1–5). It is clear that at least in some cases, illness was also understood to arise from God's punishment for individual sins, and the solution given was God's forgiveness of sins (see for example, John 9:2). That forgiveness could heal is implied in this cultural logic and in these examples. In a cultural system where sickness is expected to also result from sin, absolution or forgiveness will be effective in bringing relief.

Where people believed that afflictions could have resulted from sin, forgiveness was a prerequisite for healing. The normal prescription for forgiveness included a sacrifice for rectifying the disturbed relationship. This sums up the system monopolized by the temple priesthood and must have placed a heavy burden on the poor (who wanted to conform to the system but could not afford the sacrifice) or on those physically removed from the temple. That Jesus could be ascribed such power is a different matter but in terms of the shamanic hypothesis it is perfectly plausible. As a folk healer, Jesus must have mustered enough public support among the powerless to replace that system by offering forgiveness without the additional burden of a sacrifice (see Davies 1995, 104; Crossan 1991a, 324). This is exactly the kind of dynamics to be expected from a shamanic figure.

EMPLOYING FAITH COMMITMENTS: HEALING AND FAITH

In some of the healing stories attributed to Jesus, the faith of the patient or of someone else (person[s] bringing the patient to Jesus) is emphasized (see, e.g., Mark 2:5; 5:34; 20:51–52). In these instances, *faith* refers to trust or confidence that Jesus can heal (see Remus 1997, 36; Davies 1995, 69). As shown above, acknowledgement of the power to heal ("the doctor as drug") is a strong healing agent.

The role of faith is strongly emphasized in the report about the woman with the hemorrhage, who touched Jesus's garment in an attempt to be healed (Mark 5:28–29). In the Greco-Roman world, the implicit assumption of touching or of laying-on of hands was the widespread idea that power resides in and emanates from certain individuals and objects.

This was the case with so-called divine men or miracle workers and also with certain objects, such as amulets (which were often inscribed) and statues. Although the author of Mark tries to underplay the possibility that Jesus's garment had magical power by having Jesus say that it was her faith that made the hemorrhaging woman well, this remark of Jesus is clearly an antimagic statement, a statement opposed to the notion that magic resides in objects. The same logic is operative in the early Christian story about the shadows of the disciples (see Acts 5:15), which had healing powers (see Van der Horst 1976/77). In one of the typical summary remarks about what Jesus did when encountering a group of people, Luke explicitly refers to such a feature in Jesus's life: "And all in the crowd were trying to touch him, for power came out from him and healed all of them" (6:19). Belief in the healer or in the healing instruments is a powerful means of symbolic and meaning transfer. Such beliefs could be seen as equal to the symbolic power of the medical prescription mentioned above.

To sum up, it is fairly easy to conclude that faith can heal, and that in an extreme case, faith can kill. Belief in the ability of the healer to heal has been one of the hallmarks of healing practitioners over the centuries. Therefore, it is perfectly possible that if Jesus was a Galilean shamanic figure, he could indeed heal some of the people who trusted his ability and power to heal.

HEALING BY MANIPULATING RITUAL CLEANLINESS:
THE CASE OF LEPROSY

As indicated above, it cannot with any certainty be said what the *lepra* of the New Testament was. It has become commonplace to accept that the cases of leprosy in the New Testament do not refer to Hanson's disease but rather to an unidentified kind of flaky skin condition. It is also generally acknowledged that Jesus cleansed rather than cured those who were leprous (see Pilch 1981; Crossan 1994b, 78–80; Davies 1995, 69). Jesus did nothing medically; he merely intervened ritually in declaring them clean. Thus, contrary to those who claim that Jesus intervened miraculously, others now claim that he only intervened ritually.

Each culture has a system—called the purity system—that organizes matter as in place (pure) and as out of place (impure). This purity system applies to objects, people, times, and places. Milgrom (1989, 106) shows that the rationale for declaring someone or something impure in the Israelite tradition relates to the avoidance of death. For example, the loss of blood and semen, which both represent the forces of life, symbolize death; impure skin diseases symbolize death. Impurity is the description of a visible condition that could have been caused by a variety of factors (see Malina 2001a, 161–97).

The puzzling aspect about the role Jesus played in the leprosy stories is his interference on the terrain of the priests. It was the prerogative of the Jerusalem temple priests to declare someone clean. One explanation is that Jesus had a considerable reputation as a healer, and that people who suffered from these skin diseases came to ask his opinion on whether they were still unclean. This gave Jesus the opportunity of touching them and declaring them clean (see Davies 1995, 69). However, in these stories we find an interesting paradox: Jesus, who acted as a wandering person, mediated divine power by intervening on the traditional terrain of the temple authorities. He declared people clean and, therefore, reinstated them into the community, as he understood it. This action in itself is not uncommon for a figure who could act as a divine mediator in different spheres. In fact, if Jesus was a Galilean shamanic figure, it would not be unusual for him to also replace the official priests in their function of declaring people clean. This view finds support in the other stories about Jesus's crossing of boundaries and his bypassing of the purity system. He does not observe the rules of the Sabbath (time) or the rule of persons: Jesus touches unclean persons, menstruating women, and corpses (see Pilch 1981, 111; Malina & Rohrbaugh 1998, 72–74).

While accepting the line of argument that Jesus intervened ritually, I want to suggest here that he also effected healing in that way. In other words, this is to reject the assumed dichotomy of the biomedical paradigm between healing and curing that Jesus offered only ritual purity without any curing effect. The suggestion is that precisely the manipulation of the purity system can be seen as a symbolic shamanic activity that could affect bodily conditions. If sugar pills can remove pain, control infection, or cause hair to fall out, why can the powerful manipulation of the system of purity not remove *leprosy*, that is, the visible symptoms of what could have been some form of somatization?

It is the visible skin condition (whatever it was) that caused uncleanness to begin with. Therefore, within that system, it would also be the removal of the condition that would serve as a visible sign of purity. It is illogical to assume that the system would on the one hand tolerate the visible signs that cause the impure state to remain but on the other hand would appreciate the declaration of purity (by someone like Jesus of Nazareth or a priest). Therefore, it is suggested that the healing stories of Jesus can be seen as instances of the symbolic manipulation of ritual cleanliness in order to affect bodily skin conditions.

Specific Responses: Magical Means and the Laying-on of Hands

A number of the gospel healing stories are unusual in that Jesus not only acts as faith healer or forgiver of sins, but actually employs ancient techniques or practices that were well-known in magical circles and among other folk healers. In short, his use of gestures and material means resembles that of other healers, and this includes touching, spitting, mud application, the recommendation of taking a bath in a supposedly medicinally effective pool, and magical words (see Davies 1995, 77; Aune 1980, 1537). That does not make Jesus a magician of his time but does point to the use of magical means in some of the healings.

THE USE OF SALIVA

In several of Jesus's healing stories, saliva is applied. In the case of the deaf and dumb man (Mark 7:31–33), it is impossible to know whether the saliva was applied to either his ears or tongue, while Mark says that in the case of the blind man (8:23), Jesus actually spat on his eyes. In the Johannine version of the healing of the blind man, saliva is also applied to his eyes but only after having been mixed with mud (9:6).

Regarding the healing of the blind in Mark 8, Sussman suggests the following:

> Jesus spat in his eyes and laid his hands on him. When he could see again, the man reported that, 'I see men; they look like trees but they walk about.' Jesus then laid hands on him again and he began to see things clearly. After removal or displacement of the lens, the retinal image is markedly increased so that people will look much taller . . . In very advanced cataracts the lens may become displaced out of the line of sight, either spontaneously or by a very minor blow or disturbance. This suggests that Jesus may have cured the man's cataract by rubbing the eyes and so displacing the lenses. (1992, 12)

In the case of the blind man, where Jesus applied mud made of spittle and commanded him to wash in the pool of Siloam (John 9:1–7), Rousseau and Arav suggest that

> A common disease in the Near East, then and now, is trachoma, an infection of the conjunctiva, which causes suppuration and inflammation of the eyelids. The eyelids become so swollen that the ill person cannot open them. The plaster used by Jesus would have absorbed the pus; after the washing with clear water the inflammation would have diminished and the eyelids would have opened. This treatment, however, would not destroy the germs causing the infection; the relief would have been only temporary. (1995, 323)

However, saliva and the act of spitting were commonly believed to have magical powers to protect and to heal. Spitting was a common action to ward off evil, specifically as protection against the evil eye (see Malina & Rohrbaugh 1998, 225). Paul himself refers to the practice of spitting as protection against the evil eye (Gal 4:14). The Roman author Pliny the Elder (23–79 CE) reports that the best safeguard against serpents is the saliva of a fasting human being, while the saliva of a fasting woman is judged to be a powerful remedy for bloodshot eyes. Other uses include spitting on epileptics during a seizure, spitting in one's hand to increase the force of the blow and applying it to various sores (see Rousseau & Arav 1995, 323). Saliva, carried with the finger to behind the ear, was believed to be a remedy to calm mental anxiety. These prescriptions are all given in the context of several other substances, such as human urine, with supposedly magical powers (see Pliny the Elder, *Nat.* 28.7, Jones).

While it is known today that saliva has no specific medicinal properties, this does not mean that these techniques could not have been effective. Given the cultural context in which saliva was ostensibly believed to be powerful, when applied by a healer with reputation, it could indeed affect healing. Whether technical or symbolic, it seems clear that in the case of these episodes it is reasonable to accept the human instead of the magical explanation. Even if used as a technical procedure, it is clear that saliva also had symbolic and, therefore, meaning functions in Jesus's day.

THE USE OF MAGICAL WORDS

In healing episodes a number of times words are spoken in a foreign language (e.g., *Ephphatha* [Mark 7:34], the Aramaic for "be opened" and *Talitha koum* [Mark 5:41], the Aramaic for "girl, arise"). The use of Aramaic words in a Greek text has the flavor of magical texts where such words are sprinkled throughout these texts and, if translated, would lose their power (see Malina & Rohrbaugh 1998, 225; Remus 1997, 19). There is no clear answer whether these were indeed meant as foreign words with power, but they do focus attention on the speaker and thus on his power (see Sanders 1993, 145).

One of the features of many traditional healers is that they employ whatever means they can master and what their culture allows them to use. Therefore, suggesting that Jesus employed magic next to the other means is not an attempt to paint him as an ancient magician. It is rather an acknowledgement that if he was a Galilean shamanic figure, he employed a variety of means available in his culture.

TOUCHING OR LAYING-ON OF HANDS

In ancient healing and magic, touching or laying-on of hands is a common practice. In fact, it is one of the oldest therapies in human history. While there is no evidence for laying-on of hands in the Hebrew Bible or rabbinic literature, there is the example in the Dead Sea Scrolls (*Genesis Apocryphon* 20:16–17) of Abraham healing the Pharaoh in this way. The Pharaoh, who was plagued by an evil spirit, was healed in an exorcism by Abraham through the laying-on of hands. According to Flusser, it provides evidence that this therapy was known among Israelite people (see 1957; see also the discussion in Vermes 1973, 66).

Physical contact with sick persons, especially through the hands, is very common in Jesus's healing stories. As in the case of the blind man (Mark 8:23) and in a report about the sick daughter of a ruler (Matt 9:18), which Luke (8:41, 54) relates as a ruler of a synagogue, Jesus only took her by the hand. The request by this ruler, "Come and lay your hands on her, so that she may be made well, and live" (Mark 5:23), also shows that people generally believed that laying-on of hands could be a curative therapy. Laying-on of hands is also confirmed by a summary report about Jesus's activities in his home town, Nazareth: "And he could do no deed of power there, except that he laid his hands on a few sick people and cured them" (Mark 6:5).

If laying-on of hands or the therapeutic touch, as it is also called, is not seen as a therapy of "doing something" to another person but a way of "being with" (Wright & Sayre-Adams 2001, 173), then it is clear that as a meaning method, it can have significant effects, particularly on the immune system (see Clow 2001). Especially if the sickness is the result of a breakdown in biopsychosocial harmony, the therapeutic touch should obviously be a prime candidate for healing.

The exorcism (healing) of the woman who suffered from the curvature of the spine for eighteen years became effective as the result of laying-on of hands: "When Jesus saw her, he called her over and said, 'Woman, you are set free from your ailment.' When he laid his hands on her, immediately she stood up straight and began praising God" (Luke 13:12–13). It is difficult not to see the resemblance with this story told by a modern medical practitioner.

> Warren is bent over, grunting with his back pain. He even finds it difficult to climb onto my examination couch. His back is in spasm, he says, and it's so painful that he can hardly move. . . . He's rigid, racked with pain. And that is why his cure, when it comes shortly afterwards, is so miraculous and unexpected. For after a brief examination, some sympathetic words, a prescription for painkillers and a medical certificate entitling him to miss work for another two weeks, he is cured. Completely . . . Just after he's limped so painfully out of my room and staggered down the stairs, I can see him striding across the park next door . . . His movements are free now and fluent as a bird's. He looks happy. It's a miracle cure, no doubt of that . . . Once again, I compliment myself on my healing powers and the extraordinary, almost mythical power of my signature. Combined with it, the effects of those little scraps of paper are truly magical! (Helman 2004, 143–44)

The symbolic power of the healer's activities of writing and signing a prescription are equaled by the symbolic meaning attached to the laying-on of hands in the Jesus story.

Stories of Healing and the Cultural Dynamics of Healing Stories about Jesus

As indicated elsewhere in this study, from the point of view of cultural bundubashing, the issue of historicity or of what actually happened is fairly complex. It is not simply a matter of determining the factuality of events or phenomena but of grasping both the cultural plausibility and the comparative insight when looking at such events and phenomena. In the foregoing discussion, indications of the cultural plausibility of Jesus's

healings and exorcisms have been given. If he did what the texts said that
he did, what did he do? According to the stories, it can be claimed that
he intervened by means of either specific or meaning methods in order to
facilitate the return of health.

But that is not the final word on what actually happened or what the
state of affairs was during his stay in Galilee. While the analytical scalpel
separates different techniques and procedures of the healing process, in the
actual life of a great healer, therapeutic touch, belief, story, rumor, and the
like are all interconnected. In the end, it is the "great healer" who heals or
affects recovery or impacts on bodily conditions. In a bold and brave con-
jecture (which he did not explore), Crossan suggests that although there
is no evidence for it, it is possible that Jesus acted as an entranced healer,
using trance as a therapeutic technique (see 1994b, 93). Even if this was
not the case, in terms of the present understanding, a whole set of cultural
dynamic and activities should be included in the framework for understanding the healing stories. If Jesus healed—and the evidence is clear that
he probably healed several first-century Galilean people who suffered from
some kind of (mostly culture-specific) sicknesses—he did so as a shamanic
figure. In other words, his healings and exorcisms are to be seen as closely
connected to who and what he was; as a shamanic figure he could heal
because he also had close interactions with the divine world, had often
experienced various ASCs, was spirit-possessed and was acknowledged by
his followers and the crowds as a Galilean shamanic figure. Jesus's social
personage includes not only his self-understanding as a shamanic figure
who has direct interaction with the divine world, but also the dynamics
and force of healing stories that brought about a public sense of faith and
the actual belief of people in the healer.

Since Jesus had no particular training or apprenticeship as a healer
that we know of, it is obvious that the symbols of competence constituting
him as healer were not certificates of qualification or the white coat and
stethoscope of the modern medical practitioner. Instead, the stories and
rumors about him as a powerful and effective healer were the symbols
of competence. A remark attributed to the woman with the hemorrhage
for twelve years expresses one aspect of this dynamics: "She *had heard*
about Jesus, and came up behind him in the crowd and touched his cloak"
(Mark 5:27, emphasis mine). The rumors about Jesus as healer put this
healing into motion because she acted on what was believed (rumored)

to be a healing opportunity in her context: a great shamanic healer was passing by.

Understanding what happened or what the state of affairs was in Galilee includes taking into account the healing stories and reports and rumors about healing as part of the healing activities (or dynamics). These were part of the meaning-creating means and symbols that impacted sick bodily conditions. In this regard, the summary remarks in Matthew's Gospel give a remarkable impression of how things could have been and what the dynamics could have been around Jesus's life in Galilee.

> Jesus went throughout Galilee, teaching in their synagogues and proclaiming the good news of the kingdom and curing *every disease and every sickness among the people. So his fame spread throughout all Syria*, and they brought to him all the sick, those who were afflicted with various diseases and pains, demoniacs, epileptics, and paralytics, and he cured them. And *great crowds followed* him from Galilee, the Decapolis, Jerusalem, Judea, and from beyond the Jordan. (Matt 4:23–25, emphasis mine)

> *Great crowds* came to him, *bringing with them* the lame, the maimed, the blind, the mute, and many others. They *put them at his feet*, and he cured them, and he healed them. (Matt 15:30, emphasis mine)

If these remarks are not read for their testimony about specific events, places, and persons, they can be seen as carrying information about the dynamic processes of communal and community-driven healing processes that accompanied the life of a shamanic figure. The hype around the healings and the crowd involvement with the rumors are part and parcel of shamanic healings. Reputation, rumor, and recovery of the sick were and are part of the cultural dynamics of healing.

A construction of how things were in the life of Jesus of Nazareth should also include an imaginative picture of how and where all these patients succeeded in finding him. As a wandering shamanic figure, he had no consulting rooms or visiting hours. The simple dynamics of who could reach him where and when is to be taken into account in our portrayal of the healings.

While there is not a single verse offering direct information about the way people found him, the summary remarks in the Gospels may also give clues in this regard. The picture offered above is of spontaneous mass movements of people (the crowds) who gathered whenever he was in the area. Rumors not only followed but also preceded the Galilean shamanic healer on his wanderings around Galilee. Therefore, from this point of view, the account in Mark (2:1–12 par.) carries all the hallmarks of an authentic shamanic healing: the crowd involvement, faith (extraordinary belief that Jesus could offer healing), and the mediation of cultural means for symbolic purposes (the forgiveness of sins) that were all woven into healing reports. Healing was as much the result of the healing reports and stories as of the symbolic interventions of Jesus himself.

> When he returned to Capernaum after some days, it was *reported* that he was at home. So *many gathered around* that there was no longer room for them, not even in front of the door; and he was speaking the word to them. Then some *people came, bringing to him* a paralyzed man, carried by four of them. And when they could not bring him to Jesus because of the crowd, they removed the roof above him; and after having dug through it, they let down the mat on which the paralytic lay. When *Jesus saw their faith*, he said to the paralytic, "Son, *your sins are forgiven.*" Now some of the scribes were sitting there, questioning in their hearts, "Why does this fellow speak in this way? It is blasphemy! Who can forgive sins but God alone?" At once Jesus perceived in his spirit that they were discussing these questions among themselves; and he said to them, "Why do you raise such questions in your hearts? Which is easier, to say to the paralytic, 'Your sins are forgiven,' or to say, 'Stand up and take your mat and walk'? But so that you may know that *the Son of Man has authority* on earth to forgive sins"—he said to the paralytic—"I say to you, stand up, take your mat and go to your home." And he stood up, and immediately took the mat and went out before all of them; so that *they were all amazed* and glorified God, saying, "We have never seen anything like this!" (Mark 2:1–12, emphasis mine).

Shamanic healings are not technical but symbolic and meaning interventions in the lives of people sharing symbols and a cultural system with the shaman. That Jesus could probably do the things ascribed to him has nothing to do with supernatural or miraculous powers (although the participant could and probably did experience them as miracles). These healing accounts also need not be rejected as mere mythmaking or as stories (although healing stories were probably part of the rumors and gossip from very early on in his public activities). From the perspective of cultural bundubashing, the healing accounts can be seen as normal and typical activities of someone controlling and manipulating the symbols of meaning in his cultural world, and in that way affecting sick people—this is precisely what shamanic figures do all the time.

Shamanic Functions: Controlling of Spirits

In a worldview where spirit entities are ever present and powerful in controlling good and bad fortune, "ordinary people are largely helpless victims of these spirits" (Walsh 1990, 90). One of the main functions ascribed to shamans include relief from everyday calamities or distress (see Eliade 1964, 181–84) by means of placating or controlling these spirits. From this perspective, it is not surprising that in addition to the control of evil spirits in exorcisms for healing purposes, a large number of stories are ascribed to Jesus of Nazareth in which he encounters, controls, or placates spirits (evil spirits or demons) of all kinds.

The Controlling of Evil Spirits: Exorcisms as Healing

Exorcisms represent in the world of shamanic figures the most vivid and explicit form of spirit control. Although only six proper exorcism stories are told about Jesus of Nazareth in the Gospels, exorcisms represent the most prominent type of cure attributed to him (see Vermes 1973, 22; Sanders 1993, 149). By word of mouth, Jesus drove out the spirits from many who were demon possessed, and healed those with many diseases (see Matt 8:16; Mark 1:34; 9:24). In other instances (see, e.g., Luke 6:18), it is said that those troubled by evil spirits were cured (no demons were cast out). It is apparent that in healing, no clear distinction is made between those who were demon possessed, were afflicted with evil spirits, or had some other illnesses only attributed to evil spirits. Consequently, the distinction between healing and exorcism is blurred in many of the gospel accounts (see Twelftree 1993, 55). From the summary reports found throughout the Gospels, also no clear distinction was made between the different kinds of healings and exorcisms.

In both the six proper exorcism stories ascribed to Jesus and the other healings described as the casting out of demons or evil spirits, Jesus is presented as an authority in control of such entities.[38] Of interest at this point is the way in which he controlled the spirits. Jesus typically subdued

---

38. It is unnecessary to discuss the whole body of exorcism material ascribed to Jesus. Over a wide spectrum, scholars agree that Jesus can be seen as an exorcist (see Sanders 1993, 149; Twelftree 1993, 225).

the demons by using strong language; he rebuked and commanded them with language such as, "Be silent, and come out of him" (Mark 1:25). A more proper translation would be "Shut up, and get out!" which does more justice to the term that is used. It is the same word used to constrain an animal.

Although folk healers often used a variety of techniques (recall the use of an amulet by Eleazar to pull a demon from someone's nose (Josephus, *Ant.* 8.47), Jesus relied on the Spirit of God and word of mouth. The same word used in Jesus's command of the unclean spirit is often used in the magical papyri for silencing spirits in exorcism (see Remus 1997, 27).

The accounts where Jesus sent out his disciples contain explicit references that he also equipped them with "authority" ("and power") to control evil spirits or demons. "He called the twelve and began to send them out two by two, and *gave them authority over the unclean spirits*" (Mark 6:7, emphasis mine; and see Luke 9:1). Control of spirits is neither a technique nor a skill; it is a cultural action based on claimed and acclaimed authority.

The cultural reality of the control of spirits does not consist of a simple observable activity that can, for example, be photographed. Instead, it consists of particular cultural beliefs, certain cultural activities by a figure of authority (such as a shaman), the creation of specific stories of the control of spirits together with certain actions and reactions of the affected community.

Encounters with Ancestral Spirits

In order to give a more complete picture of Jesus's spirit encounters, some of the previously mentioned episodes need to be mentioned again. Ancestral spirits could be controlled, or at least encountered, as the transfiguration scene implies, while the disputes over Jesus's identity and the accusations that he possessed the spirit of either John the Baptist or one of the ancient prophets show the belief in ancestral spirit-possession. Given the practice of ancestral veneration in the Israelite tradition and the belief in the continued existence of some ancestors (*souls* of ancestors) as astral beings or immortals, it is not surprising to find so many references to ancestral spirits (or ancestors in spirit form) in the Jesus traditions. The presence of ancestors or ancestral spirits claimed to be active in both John the Baptist's and Jesus's activities is sufficient evidence for the assumed belief in the availability or the ability of ancestral spirits to interfere in human affairs (e.g., Mark 6:15).

Controlling the Spirits of Nature

Stories that are often relegated to the fringes of the Jesus tradition on the assumption that they were post-Easter creations include the so-called nature miracles. As indicated earlier, both the Schweitzerstrasse and the Wredebahn consider most of them fictional literary creations. However, from the perspective of cultural bundubashing, they provide for interesting reading.

It should be kept in mind that when modern Western people consider events in the sky, such as lightning, tornadoes, thunder, or cloudbursts, they see atmospheric phenomena. For ancient people, these phenomena were signs of activities by celestial entities (gods, spirits, and the like), that impacted human affairs (see Malina 1997, 94). In fact, all things beyond human control (including fertility, disease, and weather patterns) were believed to be controlled by nonhuman persons or entities. For this reason they interacted with these phenomena in a totally different way: the latter could be controlled and manipulated by the right people or ritual acts.

Within shamanic settings it is common practice to ascribe the control of natural entities to the shaman. As indicated, game-finding (fish or game) is one of the prime functions of the shaman in societies dependent on fishing or hunting. In short, the shaman controls the spirits in natural elements such as weather patterns, game, fish, and plants.

It was common knowledge in ancient Israelite mythical thinking that "the sea was regarded as the haunt of demons . . . and the mastery exercised over these malign sea-devils" (Ashton 2000, 65–66) could be performed by subduing or silencing and muzzling them. The Greek and Hebrew terms correspond and appear in similar contexts. It is also used in the episode of stilling the wind on the rough sea (Mark 4:35–41): Jesus commanded the wind to be silent and to muzzle itself. In the Matthean (8:26) and Lukan (8:26) versions of this story, Jesus commanded both the wind and the sea (waves). The same terms are used in the exorcistic scene of casting out a demon in Mark (1:25).

The episode of Jesus's walking on the sea (Mark 6:45–52 par.) has earlier been mentioned. Jesus's walking on the sea can be seen as an indication of his place in the hierarchy of cosmic powers since it is a story about a powerful person trampling on the nonvisible person-like forces or spirits of the sea. Therefore, several of the reports about controlling the elements of nature can be read as reports about the controlling of the spirits of the sea and the wind respectively.

Whatever the symbolic meaning or the message of the story, the cursing of the fig tree (Mark 11:12–14, 20–25) displays the feature that by word of mouth, that is, by speaking a curse, it was claimed that Jesus could harm the tree. That is, he could kill the spirit of the tree by means of a curse or command.

When read not for their alleged factuality as events in time and space but as reports about the activities of a Galilean shamanic figure, all these so-called nature miracles contain a wealth of information about the content of the life and stories about Jesus as a social personage. It would be surprising if all of these merely reflect the literary creativity of a later generation. As part of the dynamics of the life of a shamanic figure, these stories make perfect sense as belonging to his life story in Galilee.

Controlling the Spirits of Animals

Besides having a close relationship with animals in agrarian societies, the shaman is often sought out to intervene when game (or fish) becomes scarce. Finding food in traditional societies is very much related to those with the ability to ensure success at finding game or fish or providing food. From this perspective, it is significant how often stories about control of food resources are ascribed to Jesus.

Three different stories are very typical of the game-finding abilities of shamanic figures. In two different contexts the Gospels contain stories about Jesus's ascribed ability of game- or fish-finding. In the Lukan version of Jesus's calling of his first followers, Jesus acts in a typical shamanic fashion when directing them to lower their nets:

> When he had finished speaking, he said to Simon, "Put out into the deep water and let down your nets for a catch." Simon answered, "Master, we have worked all night long but have caught nothing. Yet if you say so, I will let down the nets." When they had done this, they caught so many fish that their nets were beginning to break. (5:4–6)

The Gospel of John also ascribes the attribute of locating fish to Jesus but in a totally different setting: "He said to them, 'Cast the net to the right side of the boat, and you will find some'" (21:6). So they cast it, and now they were not able to haul it in because there were so many fish. The result in both cases is a miraculous catch of fish. The control over animal "spirits" is also ascribed to Jesus in the account of the fish with the shekel in its mouth, which was needed to pay the temple tax: "However, so that we do not give offense to them, go to the sea and cast a hook; take the first fish that comes up; and when you open its mouth, you will find a coin; take that and give it to them for you and me" (Matt 17:27). The cultural logic is not that of an experienced game warden but that of a controller of animal spirits.

Jesus is also credited with the multiplication of food for feeding large crowds (Mark 6:37–44; 8:1–10 par), which in the kind of advanced agrarian society of first-century Palestine, is certainly related to the ability of game-finding. In addition he is credited with the ability to change water into wine (John 2:1–11). Riley shows that the turning of water into wine was the signature miracle of Dionysius, who was well known in Galilee: "The sheer quantity of wine produced, after the host's own supply has already run out, is significant: it can only have been for the purpose of rendering guests quite drunk, quite possessed by the spirit of wine" (1997, 128).

The resemblance between Jesus's baptism experience and the shamanic initiation has already been mentioned. While Mark records Jesus's being tempted in the wilderness by Satan for forty days, his version of the story does not contain any detail about the temptations, but adds that Jesus "was with the wild beasts; and the angels ministered to him" (Mark 1:13). Scholars who at all bother to pay attention to this remark are quick to assign it to legendary material (see e.g., Bultmann 1980, 28). However, as Ashton asks: "Could the spirits tormenting Jesus have assumed the form of savage animals, as is the case in many accounts of shamans' trials, and once he had overcome them was he comforted by the angels?" (2000, 67). Reading such clues with an open mind as to the features ascribed to and expected from shamanic figures (those who control all sorts of spirits) indeed confirms this suggestion. In fact, it would also explain why much later traditions were linked to Jesus, as is the case with the *Gospel of Pseudo-Matthew*, which states that on the third day after his birth, "an ox and an ass worshipped him." Again, on their trip to Egypt, it is said that "lions and leopards worshipped him and accompanied them in the desert . . . the lions went along with them, and the oxen and asses and the beasts of burden which carried what they needed, and they harmed no one" (14, 18.2, Cullmann trans.).

Jesus could also give his disciples "authority" over serpents and scorpions and over all the powers of the enemy (Luke 10:19). This is explained as "that the spirits submit to you" (Luke 10:20). Again, it is the same cultural logic at work in all of these examples: a Galilean shamanic figure could control the spirits of animals.

Recovering the Spirits of the Dead

The Lukan version of the raising of the daughter of Jairus is explicit about the cultural assumption that is implicit in the other versions and other stories about Jesus's abilities to resuscitate the recently deceased: "Her spirit returned, and she got up at once" (Luke 8:55).

One of the typical features of shamanic figures is the recovery and bringing back of the soul of the dead. Despite beliefs in astral immortality and resurrection, in these Israelite stories there is no mention of the recovery of the soul—Jesus is simply accredited with the ability to resuscitate recently deceased people (John 11:38–44; Mark 5:21 par.; Luke 7:14). The Lukan text mentioned above assumes that he did it by manipulating her spirit (by bringing back her spirit). This is the counterpart of exorcising evil or hostile spirits from a possessed person, because in this case he simply caused her own spirit, which they believed could depart from the body under all sorts of conditions (such as by traveling to heaven or by undergoing death), to return to her own body. Without mentioning it, it is possible that the other stories of resuscitations assume the same cultural logic of the time.

Malina and Rohrbaugh suggest that the story about the restoration of life to Lazarus in the Gospel of John (11:1–44) is the outward event that reveals something of the honor status of the God of Israel and about Jesus as his broker (1998, 200). It is, however, in the Lukan story (7:11–17) of the raising of the dead son of a widow that we see where the ancient mentality lies in these stories. In modern sensibilities such an "event" would reach front-page news for weeks on end. In their world it is used to focus on the plight of a widow whose loss of her only son would mean that her own life expectancy afterwards would be extremely short. Therefore, using a story about bringing back a young man's life spirit, the critical point in the episode is Jesus giving him back to his mother and therefore, "causing her *resurrection,*" as Malina and Rohrbaugh explain it (1992, 330).[39]

Pinpointing clinical death is no easy task, and in a culture where death is seen as a transition between two forms of existence (one in a fleshly bodily form and the other in a spiritual or other *bodily* form), it is even more difficult. It is therefore not surprising that in none of the texts about bringing persons' spirits back to their bodies is there any discussion about whether the persons were really dead. In fact, differences between their evaluations of the person's condition are mentioned in passing. Such is the case with Jairus's daughter, who was declared "dead" by the crowd; but according to Jesus, "The child is not dead but sleeping" (Mark 5:39).

It is, therefore, not surprising that in one of the reports about the sending out of the disciples, raising the dead (bringing back the spirits of the dead) is mentioned in conjunction with the other acts of spirit control, namely, healing and exorcism: "Cure the sick, raise the dead, cleanse the lepers, cast out demons" (Matt 10:8).

Assistance of a Helper Spirit

Closely related to the control of spirits are the reports about Jesus's helper spirit, which he also transferred to his followers. It has already been indicated that Jesus was depicted as being spirit-possessed and is often portrayed under the influence of a Holy Spirit. His baptism, it was said, can be seen as his initial spirit initiation experience, and the exorcisms were performed "by the Spirit of God" as Matthew (12:28) explicitly states. The belief that Jesus performed exorcisms with a spirit helper is also ascribed to his opponents, as in the following remark: "But the Pharisees said, 'By the ruler of the demons he casts out the demons'" (Matt 9:34). They tend to agree that Jesus was spirit-possessed and thus performed some of his deeds aided by a helper spirit.

Jesus is furthermore presented as the one who can pass on the spirit that he is possessed with, as in John (20:22): "When he had said this, he breathed on them and said to them, 'Receive the Holy Spirit.'" Perhaps the episodes where Jesus commissioned his followers also fall into this category. When sending out the twelve followers, Jesus gave them "authority"

---

39. Stories about resurrections in the early years of Christianity were not unusual. Irenaeus, bishop of Lyons in France toward the end of the second century, reports that resurrections were performed when the whole church in a particular area assembled, fasted, and prayed (see Remus 1997, 115).

over the unclean spirits (Mark 6:7; Matt 10:1) or over all demons (Luke 9:1) as well as the power to exorcise, heal, and to bring back the spirits of (i.e., to raise) the dead (Matt 10:8). In the Lukan report about the return of the seventy followers, it is stated (as mentioned above) that the demons and spirits are subject to them when they act in Jesus's name (authority). According to Luke (10:21), the result is that Jesus was ecstatic with joy (extremely joyful) "in the Holy Spirit" after the return of the seventy disciples who acted with authority over the spirits (see Dunn 1975, 188). As shamanic figure, he was, overall, a spirit-possessed person!

The Gospel of John explicitly talks about the Spirit of God as a helper spirit (14:16, 26). The *paraclētos*, who acts as an advocate or helper, will teach the disciples and act as witness. This is the same idea found in the Synoptics of the spirit as guardian who will speak on their behalf: "When they bring you to trial and hand you over, do not worry beforehand about what you are to say; but say whatever is given you at that time, for it is not you who speak, but the Holy Spirit" (Mark 13:11; see Luke 12:11; and Matt 10:20).

A Figure Acting with Authority over Spirits and in the Spirit

Many of the actions ascribed to Jesus resemble the conduct of typical shamanic figures who are not afraid of the spiritual powers or spirits associated with sickness and death or of the taboos categorized as impure. In other words, they represent the conduct of a social personage who is not intimidated by the spiritual forces keeping the cultural boundaries in society intact. In addition to Jesus's interaction with the sick and those with contagious skin diseases, the following actions confirm his position as such a figure:

- Jesus touches corpses without fear of being defiled (e.g., Luke 7:14);

- Jesus has contact with all sorts of dubious characters in society without being threatened—these include people such as prostitutes (Luke 7:37, 39; Mark 14:3; Matt 26: 6–7), tax collectors and sinners (Matt 11:19; Luke 7:34; and Matt 9:10; 21:32);

- Externals do not defile or threaten (Mark 7:15).

Finally, in a typical shamanic fashion, Jesus is ascribed the ability to find invisible objects, places, and people. His disciples find the Passover room on Jesus's command by following a man carrying a jar of water (see Mark 14:12–16); the Gospel of John explicitly talks about the Spirit of God as a helper spirit (14:16, 26).

If these clues are read for their information about actual events or *supernatural* abilities, we are probably missing the cultural clues about how Jesus was perceived, experienced, and depicted by his contemporaries. These abilities and features do not necessarily describe outside characteristics but the construction of a typical shamanic figure. Within the type of cultural system in which he lived and which can be seen as a typical shamanic worldview controlled by spirit forces, all of these ascriptions give an indication of the dynamics in society and of the role he played and was ascribed in his world. Shamans typically control, and are not controlled by, spirit forces.

Summary

If Jesus did the things ascribed to him in the texts, what did he do? On the one hand, there is no reason to doubt that he acted as a healer, exorcist, and controller of spirits. And there is no reason to doubt that if he did the things recorded in the Gospels, he did them as and was constituted as a shamanic figure. As understood in the above way, these stories report about a shamanic figure and indeed constituted him as such. On the other hand, if these things belonged to his biography as a shamanic figure, what he did was both to perform certain cultural deeds and to be caught up in the dynamics and processes that constituted such a kind of figure. Being a shamanic figure and acting as one, it has by now become clear, was not constituted simply by means of specific identifiable actions but by means of being inscribed in a set of cultural beliefs and in the dynamics associated with such a figure.

From the foregoing overview, it is clear that if Jesus was not a shamanic figure, the first tradents or gospel authors had in mind (accidentally?) a very coherent picture of the functions and activities of such a figure when they created the reports about him. Given the many clues and pieces fitting the puzzle, all of these offer strong support for the hypothesis that Jesus was indeed such a social figure.

Finally, it should be obvious that there is a great difference between a social type that combines these features and functions in a normal and natural way because of the identifiable ASC-based experiences, and the combined social types identified in traditional New Testament scholarship. In suggesting that Jesus was a shamanic holy man who combined certain features and functions on a regular basis, and who was constituted as religious specialist because of ASC-based experiences is something different from saying that he was either a teacher/healer/exorcist/sage or a teacher who also healed and exorcised (or a prophet who also healed and taught). It is the social type that contains its own identity and dynamics that helps us to see the elements in the material within a comprehensive whole. It will not give us a combination of a healer, prophet, teacher and so forth but will allow us to see Jesus's healings, prophecies, and teachings in terms of the comprehensive picture as that of a typical shamanic figure.

CHAPTER 10

Teaching, Preaching, and Prophetic Activities

Introduction

IN CURRENT HISTORICAL JESUS research, there is little doubt that Jesus of Nazareth was a teacher, prophet, and preacher, and that besides the *kingdom of God*, the most common phrase ascribed to his teaching was the term "Son of Man." However, despite very strong scholarly support for the idea that Jesus was a teacher (or prophet) of some kind, there is little agreement on how these themes should be understood or what the content of his teachings was.

However, it does not seem as if there was a single coherent picture of any topic in Jesus's teachings. As Davies points out: "If he [Jesus] had a coherent message and neither we nor his known near contemporaries know for sure what it was, he ought not to be thought, first and foremost, to have been a great and challenging teacher" (1995, 13). Against this general trend, he remarks: "These teachers, professors by trade, should wonder if there is not a bit of a Jesus-Like-Us in their constructions . . . perhaps he was not primarily a teacher at all" (1995, 10, 11).

If Jesus of Nazareth was a Galilean shamanic figure, as proposed, he was not a teacher but a shamanic figure, who, as a shamanic figure, also spoke, taught, and prophesied. Shamanic figures are the creators and mediators of knowledge and wisdom based on their connectivity to the divine world. As indicated earlier, one of the functions of shamanic figures centers on divination and education, or mediating divine knowledge and teaching divine insights. As storytellers and mythmakers, they mediate new knowledge to society and function as the telephone exchange to the divine world; they are the teachers of wisdom and poets in societies where they operate. If Jesus was a shamanic figure, he did not teach for the sake of teaching nor did he act as a teacher, preacher, or prophet for the sake of being that, but whatever he said (or did) was said (and done) as a Galilean shamanic figure. In other words, if we want to understand Jesus's teaching, preaching, and prophetic activities within the framework of cultural bundubashing, these should be seen as that of a particular kind of social personage—a shamanic figure.

When working toward the shamanic hypothesis, the interpretive dilemma of abduction again appears on the horizon. As a cable-like approach, abduction consists of a complex to-and-fro movement in the interpretive process. In order to show that Jesus's teachings support the shamanic hypothesis, it should be indicated that they can be taken as belonging to a shamanic figure. In other words, it should be shown that Jesus's teachings could have been expressed and could have been taken as shamanic utterances. But in order to show that Jesus's teachings were shamanic utterances, it should be known what shamanic teachings are or were like; and if they are taken as shamanic sayings, how are they to be understood? Everything cannot be done here, and a detailed analysis of all Jesus's teachings as shamanic teachings will have to be done later. The question is not whether the "kingdom of God" and "Son of Man" sayings give testimony that Jesus can be seen as a shamanic figure, but whether, when understood within the framework of the shamanic hypothesis, they offer support for the hypothesis. In other words, it is not (only) what the texts say, but what an analysis of the sayings by means of the shamanic model tells us. As argued over and over, within the interpretive process of cultural bundubashing, the shamanic model is a way for us of understanding and interpreting Jesus's (teaching) activities then and there without assuming that they are directly translatable or transferable to our world. That is, to understand them within the dynamics of a Galilean shamanic figure then and there—this entails both how Jesus was *teaching, preaching,* and *prophesying,* and how what he said is to be understood.

Before turning toward these issues, the first step in this discussion will again be to engage existing research. Besides putting the data on the table, it will serve as backdrop to show that insights from the standard approach cannot be applied unproblematically to this study.

The State of the Debate in the Authenticity Paradigm

As with Jesus's healings and exorcisms, the authenticity paradigm is also in this arena the dominant framework for making sense of his life. However, the challenges in dealing with Jesus's teachings are different. In a sense, there is a much larger diversity in the scholarly constructions because of the greater variety in the data and no shared model (such as the biomedical paradigm) exists for interpreting the data. Nevertheless, Jesus's teaching, preaching, and prophetic activities are firmly trapped in the basic interpretive structure of the authenticity paradigm. A number of the standard features are easily identifiable. The data is scanned for a complete list of testimonies that he was a teacher and for what he taught, while the interpretive principles of the authenticity paradigm are ever present: the identification of the authentic sayings, a search for their tradition history, together with the application of ontological monism for making sense of the two dominant themes—the "kingdom of God" and "Son of Man" sayings. These features will briefly be introduced.

A Teacher, Preacher, or Prophet of Repute

There is strong scholarly support for the claim that Jesus was indeed a teacher (and, for some, a *preacher*) of repute. Most historical Jesus researchers will probably agree when Vermes says: "Whatever else he may have been, Jesus was unquestionably an influential teacher" (1993, 46). *Teacher* is, in fact, the most common descriptor used for Jesus in the Gospels, Dunn points out (2003b, 697), while he is also called *rabbi* and *prophet*—labels referring to his teaching activities. It is natural for scholars to think, therefore, that teaching and preaching were central activities of Jesus's career, and that he had a clear agenda (mission or curriculum, if you prefer) for teaching and preaching.[1] Thus, the conclusion: he was a renowned teacher, preacher, or prophet. As Ehrman puts it: "By calling Jesus a rabbi I do not mean to say that he had some kind of official standing within Judaism but simply that he was a Jewish teacher. He was, of course, not only a teacher; he can perhaps best be understood as a 'prophet'" (2005, 219 n. 3).

---

1. This is confirmed by the natural way in which scholars affirm Jesus's teaching and preaching activities: "Jesus put the kingly rule of God in the centre of his eschatological message" (Theissen & Merz 1998, 240); or, "Jesus was remembered as preaching about the kingdom of God and that this was central to his message and mission" (Dunn 2003b, 387).

Not all will, however, follow Mack, who gives priority to Jesus's teachings: "For the first followers of Jesus, the importance of Jesus as the founder of their movement was directly related to the significance they attached to his teachings" (1993, 1). This view is supported by Keck, who says that Jesus "was not a healer who found he had something to say but a teacher who found it necessary to heal" (quoted in Dunn 2003b, 696 n. 387). These studies tend toward the single social type label of Jesus as teacher, prophet, or sage.

Scholars operating with a composite social-type model obviously emphasize different configurations. For example, Crossan, while acknowledging Jesus as teacher, puts the emphasis on Jesus's deeds. He argues: "If all he had done was talk about the Kingdom of God, Lower Galilee would probably have greeted him with a big peasant yawn." Therefore, he says, Jesus did not only talk about the Kingdom, "he enacted it" (1994b, 93). In a similar vein, Sanders points out that it is wrong to think Jesus was primarily a teacher; his *fame* came as the result of healing, especially exorcisms (see 1993, 154). Horsley also sees Jesus primarily as a prophet but claims that it surely is in the role of Jesus as a prophet leading a popular movement to perform healings and exorcisms (see 2003, 104).[2] Vermes, who has a strong antenna for cultural processes, argues that it was Jesus's "personality, his presence, the power of his voice, his awe-inspiring reputation as a wonder-worker" (1993, 74), which ensured that his words were accepted.

Some scholars maintain that the words and deeds of Jesus cannot be separated into neat packets of information because they are inextricably bound together in the Gospel traditions (see Meier 1994, 451). There is, nevertheless, no attempt to integrate these so-called teachings with the rest of his life. The teacher remains a social type added onto healer, prophet, and the like (clear examples of the composite model of social types). The belief driving even this position is that Jesus cared passionately about what he wanted to communicate: "Whatever else Jesus was, he was an effective

---

2. This is also the position of Herzog, who relies on the definition of Grabbe in this regard (see Herzog 2005, 115–16). Grabbe certainly, in a very generalized way, indicates that many prophets have the reputation to perform signs and wonders (1995, 117). But he also, more carefully, argues that such a definition is not without its problems (see 2000, 233–36). And given the other categories of religious and cultural personalities that he discusses, it is probably wise not to ascribe everything to the *prophet*. See also the discussion earlier of the difficulties regarding the *prophet* category (see above, pp. 72–73, 201).

teacher who cared passionately about communicating what he believed and convincing people of its truth" (Meier 1994, 270).

Not surprisingly, the current state of the debate on the two main topics in Jesus's teaching confirms this point. In fact, it will be shown that the very nature of the authenticity paradigm creates its own insurmountable problems for dealing with the data.

The Content of Jesus's Teaching, Preaching, and Prophetic Activities

There is a remarkable agreement in current scholarship that Jesus was a teacher of repute who primarily spoke about the kingdom of God and the Son of Man. However, there is no agreement on what he said about them or on how what he allegedly said should be understood.

There is general agreement that the *kingdom of God* was central to Jesus's teaching (see Borg 1986, 89; Funk 1996, 149). That he talked about the kingdom of God, Sanders says, is evident simply from the ubiquity of the theme (see 1985, 139). Therefore, the "centrality of the kingdom of God (*basileia tou theou*) in Jesus' preaching is one of the least disputable, or disputed, facts about Jesus" (Dunn 2003b, 383). Sayings about it are found in all the gospel documents (see Duling 1992, 56–62) and are related to a wide variety of topics.

A number of features about the scholarly discussion should, however, be mentioned. Scholars agree that the theme should be seen against the background of Israelite consciousness of being God's people and being under his rule or kingship (see Perrin 1976, 16–32; Duling 1992, 49–56). Whatever specific content is added, on Israelite ears of the first century, the idea of God as king was well established in the Hebrew Bible and Israelite tradition. Two meanings are, therefore, generally taken for granted: it is *God's domain* if a place is intended, and *God's rule* when an activity is required by the context (see Funk 1996, 149). Put differently, it clearly contains spatial or territorial as well as power connotations (see Dunn 2003b, 388–92). But the matter is more complex than this because another feature of the reports is the cause of a great variety in the scholarly debates: the theme "kingdom of God" in the texts refers to a whole spectrum of entities, and nowhere is there a systematic or coherent exposition of it. Summarizing the spectrum of issues regarding the "kingdom of God" sayings, Sanders points out: "The kingdom is either here, in heaven or both.

It is either now, future or both" (1993, 170), and scholars do not agree on which string(s) of the tradition are to be taken as authentic. Whatever it was, the kingdom of God in Jesus's teaching was an extremely diverse entity. Sorting out the possible permutations given by this diversity has been the hallmark of the debate. How can a something be here and still to come, how can it simultaneously be present and future, how can it be on earth and also in heaven? What on earth or in heaven is the kingdom of God? For a long time the debate about the kingdom as already-present but yet to come has dominated the discussion (see Perrin 1976, 34–40; Theissen & Merz 1998, 252–64; Dunn 2003b, 405–17).

In summary, while there is a consensus that the kingdom of God forms the center of Jesus's teaching, "there is a controversy over how to interpret it" (Theissen & Merz 1998, 240).

The second most common phrase in the Jesus tradition (next to "kingdom of God") is "the Son of Man" (see Dunn 2003b, 724). It occurs almost exclusively in the Gospels and appears in effect only on the lips of Jesus (see Nickelsburg 1992b, 142; Dunn 2003b, 737). There is, however, no agreement either on how they should be categorized or which category or combination of categories is to be taken as coming from Jesus.

The sixty-six "Son of Man" passages in the Synoptics can, according to Vermes (see 1973, 178–79), be divided between those with no reference to Daniel (the majority, sixteen references, if parallels are counted together) and those with either direct or indirect reference to the heavenly figure in Daniel (two with direct reference to the Danielic Son of Man and five with indirect references to the Son of Man coming in glory or on clouds, etc.). For Sanders, the references to the Son of Man are used in three major ways: sayings related to (1) Jesus's earthly activities, (2) Jesus's death and resurrection, and (3) Jesus's *return* or future life (see 1993, 246–47). In the view of Theissen and Merz, these sayings can also be classified into three categories: (1) those about the Son of Man active in the present, (2) sayings about the future Son of Man, and (3) sayings about the suffering Son of Man (see 1998, 546–48).

Clearly, there is no agreement on how these sayings are to be classified or understood. In fact, about the ongoing "Son of Man" debate, Dunn says, it is "one of the greatest embarrassments for modern historical scholarship, since it has been unable to produce any major consensus" (2003b, 725). This embarrassment is clearly illustrated by the analysis of Theissen and Merz, who show that: "Despite a vast amount of work, scholars are not yet in a position to make a well-founded decision between the possibilities sketched out above" (1998, 550). And the possibilities are whether all three or only some of the categories of the "Son of Man" sayings identified (by them) are authentic.

There is ample reason for embarrassment. It is, however, a question whether more effort along these lines will result in a consensus on the topics as the results given are answers to questions asked in the linear interpretive strategy of the authenticity paradigm.

Some Features of the Interpretive Strategy

Three remarkable features about the data (or the way it is understood) can be connected to particular features of the interpretive strategy in which Jesus's teachings are dealt with in the authenticity paradigm.

THE TOPICAL ARRANGEMENT OF UNSYSTEMATIC SAYINGS

The first feature about the data is that there is little or no systematic or coherent teaching reported about Jesus of Nazareth. None of the major topics or themes ascribed to his teaching are systematically explored or thematically elaborated. One searches in vain for a critical or extensive engagement with existing Israelite literature or tradition; there is no lengthy discussion of the law or of Israelite customs and traditions. Jesus did not develop any of the major themes of the Hebrew Scriptures, and neither did he speak about them directly. Taken together, his teaching, preaching, and prophetic activities do not seem to form a coherent whole or *curriculum*.

However, scholars create coherence of themes and build systematic connections that are not directly available from the sources. In principle, there is nothing wrong with this because this is what analysis and interpretation is about (at least in part). But it is the nature of the scholarly presentations that is noteworthy. Scholars are seldom aware that some scheme shapes their constructions. Moxnes, for example, shows how the modern historicist preoccupation with time has skewed scholarly constructions of the kingdom of God (see 2000, 110).

But as mentioned above, the main feature of this strategy is to list and categorize all the sayings about a particular topic. These categorized lists then serve as basis to describe Jesus's teachings about each individual topic. However, as Horsley points out, the topical arrangement of Jesus sayings in the chapters of books "has only the most general relation to the historical circumstances in which Jesus lived." The Jesus who spoke becomes in current scholarship, he says, "a dehistoricized 'talking head'" (2003, 56) because the topics are all treated in isolation from one another and from local circumstances.[3] More precisely, they are treated separately for what Jesus supposedly taught about each of them. The lists of his teachings on each topic are organized into neat systematic chapters that have no or little relation with the historical circumstances or communication context in which they were spoken. In addition, not only are the individual topics separated into neat chapters, but Jesus's teachings are treated as teaching for the sake of teaching rather than as the teachings of a particular type of social personage.[4]

IDENTIFYING THE AUTHENTIC SAYINGS

As is to be expected in the authenticity paradigm, there is the ever-present search for the authentic sayings of Jesus. Did Jesus actually say this or that about the kingdom of God, and can these or those sayings about the Son of Man be put into Jesus's mouth? For Vermes, authentic "Son of Man" sayings that can be linked to the historical Jesus are those that are independent of Daniel 7:

> The only possible, indeed probable, genuine utterances are sayings independent of Daniel 7 in which, in accordance with Aramaic usage, the speaker refers to himself as the *son of man* out of awe, reserve, or humility. It is this neutral speech-form that the apocalyptically-minded Galilean disciples of Jesus appear to have 'eschatologized' by means of a midrash based on Daniel 7:13. (Vermes 1973, 186)[5]

3. Instead, what is needed is to take into account the historical conditions, the cultural traditions, and finally the texts as we have them, as coherent wholes. Horsley emphasizes that what Jesus communicated about the kingdom of God was done within the sphere of Roman imperialism. In his view, Jesus was a prophetic leader of a resistance movement, who, in the face of Roman imperialism, with its Israelite partners and in the light of Israelite traditions of protest and resistance, pronounced the judgment of God by means of the "kingdom of God" sayings. His aim was the restoration of the Israelite village communities as covenantal communities (see 2003).

4. This criticism obviously does not apply to scholars who, from the start, take only or mostly the teaching material as authentic and thus describe Jesus as a kind of teacher—Cynic, prophetic, or wisdom.

5. Part of the problem is that the things ascribed to Jesus where "the Son of Man" is used out of humility or reserve are the kind of things that someone who has had visionary encounters with the divine world and who carries a self-perception of being God's agent would in any case have claimed.

The reasoning is clearly based on applications of the tradition history of Daniel 7 and what disqualifies the implicit references to it in the Synoptics is the notion that the belief in the second coming or Parousia originated after Jesus's death (see Vermes 1973, 185).

There are others who remove most of the "Son of Man" sayings from the database beforehand because these are not considered authentic (see Crossan 1991a, 454–56; Borg 1994a, 84–86).[6] Regarding most of the texts referring to the coming of the Son of Man on the clouds, Nickelsburg says:

> It is far more problematic to maintain that any of the sayings which identify Jesus as the Son of Man are genuine sayings of Jesus. To accept them as genuine more or less in their present form, one must posit that Jesus cast himself in the role of the suffering prophet or sage and, more important, that he believed that his vindication from death would result in his exaltation to the unique role of eschatological judge. (1992b, 149)

However, in other circles (the Schweitzerstrasse), there is great confidence that Jesus used the phrase "Son of Man" for himself (see Theissen & Merz 1998, 548; Dunn 2003b, 759–61).

As long as the identification of the authentic sayings is done in isolation from the total picture of the historical figure, it is to be expected that this diversity and disagreement will persist and even increase.

A HISTORY OF ISRAELITE TRADITIONS IN A HISTORY-OF-IDEAS APPROACH

A third feature of the data is that none of the major terms ascribed to Jesus's teaching is defined or explained. As Funk points out about the "kingdom of God" theme, his language was highly figurative, nonliteral, or metaphorical; Jesus was constantly comparing the kingdom of God to mundane things without telling his hearers what the exact point of comparison was. In fact, it is generally agreed that the one topic central to his teachings—the kingdom of God—is neither defined nor explained

6. According to Borg (1986, 88), the "coming Son of Man" sayings are no longer considered authentic: They "were the product of Christian scribal interpretation of Dan 7:13–14 *in the decades following Easter*" (italics mine). One cannot but wonder how many decades are required for people to make the connection between Jesus's use of the term "the Son of Man" as self-referential to this type of elaborated interpretation: one decade, or perhaps only five minutes?

but taken for granted in all the documents. It is elaborated on by means of parables, illustrated by way of comparisons, and brought into conversation in passing but never clearly defined or explained.

It is taken for granted by the Gospel authors, and presumably by Jesus himself (if the "kingdom of God" material was part of his sayings), that their audiences would know exactly what was said, or at least be able to construct the meaningful communication. Speaker, or author, and audience thus shared a common understanding that modern scholarship does not have. One of the main efforts in this field of research, therefore, is a focus on the history of traditions in Israelite documents. Although all scholarship, broadly speaking, starts with what is taken as the *common* understanding of these terms in ancient Israelite tradition, constructions still run in diverse directions.

Two familiar interpretive moves in the authenticity paradigm are followed in order to deal with the problem that the Gospel authors use the two terms "kingdom of God" and "Son of Man" without defining or describing them in detail. We are faced with the fact that these two terms, which are fairly difficult to understand today, were apparently perfectly understood by first-century people. To cope with this problem, one interpretive move of the authenticity paradigm is to look for the history of a specific term in the traditions of Israel, and the second is to apply the principles of ontological monism in order to say what the documents were talking about. That is to say, to find a referent for the term "kingdom of God." Often these strategies go hand in hand with explaining the meaning of Jesus's teachings on the "kingdom of God," or the "Son of Man" sayings.

Since "kingdom of God" and "Son of Man" both originated from common Israelite traditions, it is natural to assume that as ideas they have traceable tracks and were employed by Jesus as concepts with a meaning or meanings compatible to those tracks. In other words, based on the notion that ideas existed in and for themselves as significant entities in these texts, it is important to establish the history of traditions as they originated in Israelite thinking and were employed and reemployed in the texts. The search for how to understand the term "kingdom of God" perfectly illustrates this issue.

Perrin shows that for more than a hundred years the debate has been "bedeviled by a concern for Jesus' *conception* of the Kingdom" (1976, 33). It assumes that the term had a well-defined or constant meaning, at least in Jesus's mind or usage. Instead, Perrin suggests that the kingdom of God should be seen as a symbol that evokes the myth of the activity of God as king, and this activity can take on many different formats. This distinction between *conception* and *symbol* is still valid and roughly coincides with the existing scholarly divide—with emphasis on different sides of this spectrum.

Scholars on the Schweitzerstrasse adopt the distinction but emphasize the *conception* part of it (see, e.g., Dunn 2003b, 401–4).[7] Metaphor is a way of speaking about a reality that cannot be described otherwise, and the kingdom of God is such a reality. The reality to be spoken of is given by Israel's grand narrative about God's rule as well as by their hope of God's future actions. It was not merely a symbol, but referred to an alternative reality. Jesus was teaching or preaching in metaphorical language!

Meier similarly argues that the symbol "kingdom of God" carries the full weight of God's kingship in the Hebrew Bible and Israelite tradition (see 1994, 240–42, 269–70). He sees no reason why the symbol as concept cannot be taken to contain the "richly textured, multilayered and never-fully-captured reality" of God's whole history of divine rule in the Israelite tradition. Even when spoken of as a symbol, it is an idea or concept full of meaning and history. Sanders is another example on this road. He argues: "We should all agree that 'kingdom' is a concept with a known core of meaning: the reign of God, the 'sphere' (whether geographical, temporal or spiritual) where God exercises his power." It is not a "conceptionless symbol" (1985, 126). The upshot of this point is to insist that Jesus did have some ideas: the concept referred to "*the ruling power of God*" (1985, 127). The implication of seeing Jesus's teaching about the kingdom of God in this way is that it is taken as a set of ideas that were linked to Israelite notions of God's rule, which Jesus explored to create his specific message about it. In Meier's words:

> Jesus did understand the central symbol of the kingdom of God in terms of the definitive coming of God in the near future to bring the present state of things to an end and to establish his full and unimpeded rule over the world in general and Israel in particular. Although the urgent tone of Jesus' message emphasized the immanence of the kingdom's arrival, Jesus, unlike much apocalyptic literature and like his master John the Baptist, did not set any timetable for the kingdom's appearance. (1994, 349)

7. Dunn subscribes to Perrin's distinction but prefers the term *metaphor* (2003b, 486).

Jesus's teaching about the kingdom of God was a central feature of what he wanted to communicate about this concept. He announced a program, so to speak, about God's kingly rule. On this road it is common practice to take both the present and future sayings as authentic and part of the program (see, e.g., Theissen & Merz 1998, 253).

This is probably the dominant view of the kingdom of God: Jesus was talking about something that could be seen and that either existed or will in the future exist in time and space. The opposite viewpoint claims that it is merely symbolic (*mythological*): Jesus used a symbol to express ideas.

A scholar such as Borg on the Wredebahn adopts the above distinction between *conception* and *symbol* but complains that Perrin did not take it far enough (see 1986, 92–94). Talk about the kingdom of God and *another* world was for first-century people not merely an article of belief but a known reality that they experienced in religious settings. The notion of a symbol should be taken further, Borg suggests. The kingdom of God was a myth (a story that speaks about the other world and its relationship to this world) for first-century people:

> Put most simply, within the framework of the primordial tradition, 'kingdom of God' was for Jesus a symbol pointing to the kingship of God—the divine power and sovereignty, compassion and justice. The reality of God as king could be known, and the power of the Spirit (God acting as king) could flow into this world. Kingdom could also refer to the way of being engendered by that reality—joy, compassion, purity of heart . . . Finally, kingdom was also a symbol for the final state, 'paradise restored' . . . Jesus did not emphasize a future act of God (the end of the world), but emphasized the present kingly power of God and invited his hearers to 'enter' it and have their lives shaped by it. (1986, 94–95; see also the summary of King 1987, 53)

This is typical of scholars on the Wredebahn, who take only preidentified authentic material as the basis for construction.

It has to be noticed that on both roads the kingdom of God (either as symbol or as conception/symbol) is treated in a history-of-ideas manner. It was a set of ideas linked in Israelite tradition that Jesus employed in his teachings in his own unique and idiosyncratic way. Despite Borg's claim that it was not merely an item of belief but an experienced reality, his final description of what it meant to Jesus remained that of a symbol that carried admirable values.

Let me use one (random) example from the "Son of Man" debate to illustrate that this linear thinking about the history of ideas (the question of whether certain ideas already existed in Israelite thought or not) is used to argue for (in)authenticity. In pointing out that the section in *1 Enoch* that says that the Son of Man will judge humanity cannot be shown to be pre-Christian, Sanders says that "we cannot say that Jewish eschatology had already established the idea that a heavenly figure called 'the Son of Man' would judge humanity at the end of the normal history" (1993, 246). The implication is clear in these arguments: if the idea had not yet developed, in this case, *in Jewish eschatology*, then it probably cannot be authentic. One should note how a history-of-ideas approach dominates this argument—the development of concepts or ideas independent from cultural practices is the focus.

All these examples show that the main themes of Jesus's teachings are treated as those of a talking head, and of one who connects his employment of his teachings to the Israelite stream of ideas and merely elaborates or continues with them. There is more to this way of understanding these concepts.

MAKING SENSE OF FOREIGN CONCEPTS FROM THE
POINT OF VIEW OF ONTOLOGICAL MONISM

Something that is already present in the previous section needs to be highlighted. The assumption that in the Israelite history of ideas the background of Jesus's teachings is to be found includes the notion that those were easily-understandable ideas about entities or phenomena that we can grasp today. In other words, the challenge is to link onto an existing (easily understood) set of ideas and concepts that refer to knowable entities (e.g., to "a Son of Man") while identifying the novel applications of these ideas or concepts. All of this is possible because of the assumption of ontological monism.

Ontological monism assumes a single worldview and reality system for all people (past and present); and from that point of view, the aim is to express what was said there in the past in a clear and meaningful way here in the present. In doing so, the *apparently* strange and alien is translated or transferred into the meaning system of modern people, often by means of artificial and forceful strategies. But since the assumption is that people were communicating in a single reality system, the challenge for us is to make sense of what reality (or part of reality) they were talking about there in ancient Galilee. The temporal and cultural gap is bridged by assuming direct access to what they were talking about. In addition to direct identification of authentic sayings by mechanical means (multiple, independent attestations), therefore, it is assumed that what Jesus was talking about in his world (a "Son of Man" and "the kingdom of God") can directly be translated into words and concepts having meaning in our world. This practice of directly transferring what they were talking about into words and practices that have meaning in our contemporary world is already apparent in the history of research mentioned above, where the main concern is whether "kingdom of God" is a concept or a symbol, what its content is ("domain or rule"), and what it communicates today. Three random examples from prominent scholarly discussions will show that most current understandings of "the kingdom of God" are probably all trapped in this framework. Before offering these examples, let me just pose the question, what if "kingdom of God" and "Son of Man" sayings were from the beginning cultural terms referring to particular kinds of cultural experiences that were expressed as the indigenous knowledge of first-century Israelite people?

Here is the first example: Of all the many sayings about the kingdom of God, Crossan's understanding of the kingdom of God is based on twelve complexes only (see 1991b, 265). Although he realizes that for "first-century Jewish ears" the term could have been understood as an apocalyptic term (implying armed revolt and with cosmic destruction) or as a sapiential term (as a present ethical state), he opts for the latter. For him, the kingdom of God is not a place but a state: it "is power and rule, a state much more than a place" (1991a, 266). As he says elsewhere, "But what is actually at stake is not kingdom as place, be it here or there, but rule as state, be it active or passive. The problem in plain language, is power: who rules, and how one should" (1991a, 287).[8]

---

8. Elsewhere Crossan puts it a little differently, though not entirely more understandably: "The Kingdom of God is people under divine rule—and that, as ideal, transcends and judges all human rule. The focus of discussion is not on kings but on rulers, not on kingdom but on power, not on place but on process. The Kingdom of God is what the world would be if God were directly and immediately in charge" (1994b, 55).

If I understand Crossan correctly, it is that we today can take Jesus's authentic "kingdom" sayings and show how life can be on earth if God is in power. The "kingdom" sayings claim to be an expression of a different ideology: God's empire instead of Caesar's. His explanation ascribes to Jesus a clear anti-imperial program in which it is proposed what life would be like if Yahweh were to take over the government. Jesus, in this schema, is talking about entities and realities to which we have direct access (we share the same reality system). But what if Jesus were talking about cultural entities and phenomena (visionary experiences of divine encounters) that only in an indirect and roundabout way could have been seen as anti-imperialist?

The second example is even more explicit (and far more problematic) in its application of ontological monism. Borg's notion of the *primordial tradition* has already been introduced (see above, pp. 171–73). Applied to the kingdom of God, Borg says:

> First, in addition to the visible material world disclosed to us by ordinary sense perception (and modern science), there is another dimension or level or layer of reality. It is the image of reality as having, minimally, two levels, 'this world' and a 'world of Spirit.' Second, and very importantly, the 'other world' is not simply an article of belief, but an element of experience . . . Israel spoke about the relationship between the two worlds with its story of the king-ship of God. (Borg 1986, 93)

Jesus's use of "the kingdom of God" is, therefore, a symbol of this "other" reality. As shown earlier, in Borg's view, the problem, however, is not with ancient people but with modern people, who employ reduction-istic models or pictures of reality, and for that reason cannot appreciate this "other world" and reality. Ontological monism parades here as the primordial tradition of which modern people only have a limited grasp, but the effect is the same. If we only supplement our limited understand-ing, it will be possible to grasp the entities, phenomena, and meanings Jesus was talking about and referring to.

The philosophical position adopted in this study is that there is no reality or natural world that contains both the material world (as seen by us) as well as such an "other world" (appreciated particularly by ancient people). On the contrary, all people and all cultures live in a (i.e., in their) reality that they take as normal and natural and that consists of the world as constructed as a material world, plus elements ("cultural entities") added by means of their social construction (see Chapter 2). Demons, ancestors, spirits, actions of divine beings, and the like all fall into this category of constructed cultural entities. The challenge is not to convince outsiders that there is a reality out there that they do not perceive (as suggested by Borg and by the example of Sanders below), but to explore the reality value of such cultural entities in a cross-cultural perspective.

On the Schweitzerstrasse, the continual presence of ontological monism can be illustrated by an example that is typical of this road. Scholars on the Schweitzerstrasse are prone to take almost everything in the Synoptics as authentic, and, therefore, the main feature of their constructions is a comprehensive picture that includes every possible aspect mentioned in the texts. But this creates another dilemma: how can the diverse sayings be kept together?

After discussing the so-called eschatological dimension of the kingdom of God, Sanders says: "If Jesus 'like his contemporaries' expected an eschatological drama, then it would have been 'an event in the course of time' which he expected" (1985, 130). This perfectly illustrates that in Sanders's view, the kingdom of God was a reified entity, a future reality to be seen by all—an event in time and space (talk about a kingdom, about rule, about power, about imperial domain must be about phenomena visible and knowable to us all). He furthermore clearly formulates the dilemma that scholarship has created: since the kingdom of God must be a *thing*, the surprising aspect is that the same term ("kingdom of God") is used to express different meanings (different *things*), some with a present meaning and others with future meanings (see 1985, 150–52). He solves the problem in the following way:

> The passages are just not clear enough to allow us to think that Jesus claimed that the kingdom which was present was the same as the kingdom which he expected to come, nor can they overcome the firm evidence that he expected a future kingdom. It is better to distinguish the referents of the word 'kingdom.' (1985, 155)

Consequently, he suggests that Jesus used the same word with totally different meanings (some*thing* present and some*thing* of a different nature still to come); unfortunately, Jesus just did not explain this to everyone else. In fact, in this construction, none of the Gospel authors picked up the potential problem that the same word was used for such diverse meanings or *things*.

These examples will suffice to show how deeply current historical Jesus research is entrenched in the positivist framework of the authenticity paradigm. All three examples illustrate the basic interpretive tendency of trying to make sense (to ourselves) of foreign sayings and phenomena there in ancient Galilee by directly bringing their words, phrases, and concepts over here as if we already know what they could be about (they must be about known entities or phenomena). But what if both these topics were experiential-reflective concepts that were closely linked to the cultural experiences of people embedded in a particular cycle of meaning that included ASC experiences?

One of the most important challenges from the perspective of cultural bundubashing in rethinking Jesus's teaching, preaching, and prophetic activities is to put the data into a cross-cultural setting that does not take their words and phrases as referring to a world that we all share. "Kingdom of God" and "Son of Man" sayings are to be interpreted as cultural realities and put into cross-cultural dialog for us to make sense of, but without assuming these sayings were talking about things in a shared worldview and cultural system. Cross-cultural models, as I have said, are vehicles allowing us to cross the temporal and cultural gaps in a way that enables us to grasp their unique cultural experiences in their own light but simultaneously as homoversals—as that which is common to human beings.

Summary

Most scholars are convinced that Jesus was a teacher, and, in fact, many think his significance can precisely be attributed to the importance of his teachings and what he had to say. His sayings, therefore, need to be carefully systematized and analyzed for the clear message about the central topics of his teaching. Based on the identified authentic data, sayings about the kingdom of God and the Son of Man can be systematized in order to know what Jesus said about these two knowable entities. From the fact that Jesus reportedly often talked about the kingdom of God and the activities of the Son of Man, it is taken for granted that he had a *message* that he *taught* and *preached*, the content of which was in one way or another about God's kingly rule and also (at least for some) about activities of the (or *a*) Son of Man. The scholarly discussions remain trapped in a view that the documents in some way contain Jesus's teaching and preaching about these topics, topics that should be analyzed for their authenticity and then systematized in order to find the coherent sense.

The current debate displays the common features associated with the authenticity paradigm, namely, treatment of the documents as testimonies about everything that Jesus taught, a history-of-ideas reading that focuses on the content that needs to be clarified from everything said by Jesus (the authentic words), and a tendency to take the teachings as referring to ideas that should immediately make sense in our world (concepts or metaphors knowable because of the notion of ontological monism). When one looks at the above constructions with the philosophical-critical lenses designed earlier (i.e. with cultural bundubashing), a very specific and highly significant feature of the debate emerges: in different ways, the "kingdom of God" and "Son of Man" sayings are treated as some kind of real entities with identifiable features and can somehow be directly transferred to our world.

All these arguments share the implicit separation of words and deeds and share furthermore a tendency to treat each topic of Jesus's teachings (the "kingdom of God" sayings, the "Son of Man" sayings, etc.) in isolation from one another and from the kind of social personage that he was. Therefore, scholarly attempts in the authenticity paradigm are focused on making sense of the coherent (or incoherent) set of ideas that Jesus expressed about topics that were central to his teaching.

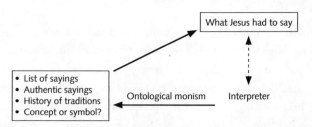

Diagram 10.1: Determining Jesus's Teachings in the Authenticity Paradigm

> *The same interpretive pattern can be identified across the authenticity paradigm. The list of authentic sayings is systematized by means of various categories; the Israelite history of ideas is mixed into the process, while ontological monism ensures that what was said there in Galilee comes out here in some kind of meaningful expression. The "kingdom of God" and "Son of Man" sayings refer to entities that we can fairly easily grasp today. There is just no agreement on how they should be understood.*

Recently, a number of scholarly voices have challenged some of the assumptions of this interpretive paradigm by situating Jesus's teachings in concrete social, political, and communicative settings in order to give a more appropriate picture of Jesus's teachings (see below). Cultural bundubashing links up to these studies but pushes their insights a bit further. What Jesus said (and did), he said (and did) as a social personage and, in the case of this study, as a Galilean shamanic figure. This means that he was not simply talking about the kingdom of God and the Son of Man within a particular context, but he did so as a Galilean shamanic figure (if this hypothesis is correct). In addition to situating the sayings in concrete social and political contexts, it is necessary to pay attention to the experiential-reflective nature of Jesus's teachings. Whatever else can be said about them, they were not teachings in a pure sense but the sayings of a particular social personage subjected to certain cultural processes, and even the content and topics of his sayings are linked to the kind of figure that he was.

The "Kingdom of God" and "Son of Man" Sayings in an Israelite Setting

In line with the general aim of this study, the focus will not be on a detailed understanding of all the sayings as shamanic sayings (that is a study for another day) but on seeing whether the teaching, preaching, and prophetic activities ascribed to Jesus of Nazareth support the hypothesis that he can be seen as a Galilean shamanic figure. As already stated, in a cable-like approach of abduction, there is a complex to-and-fro movement in the interpretive process. In order to show that Jesus's teachings support the shamanic hypothesis, it should be indicated both that they were used by Jesus of Nazareth and that they can be taken as belonging to a shamanic figure. In order to support this thesis, it should be known what shamanic teachings are like or were like; and if Jesus's sayings are taken as shamanic sayings, how they are to be understood.

Unlike the authenticity paradigm, where the authenticity of the "kingdom of God" and "Son of Man" sayings is dependent on early and multiple independent attestation supplemented by a connection to the tradition history of the phrases, cultural bundubashing takes a different route. Whether these phrases were used by Jesus of Nazareth depends on whether they fit the shamanic figure; and whether they can be associated with such a social personage depends on whether they can be interpreted as potentially shamanic kind of sayings. This discussion will start with the latter question, and will show that these phrases were not only common to Israelite visionary texts but also make perfect sense when placed within an Israelite cycle of meaning. It is to be suggested that precisely the two most common terms in Jesus's repertoire—the "kingdom of God" and "Son of Man" sayings—were widely used in other visionary texts, and were (it seems) the preferred terms for describing part of the experience of Israelite figures having ASC experiences such as heavenly journeys or visionary experiences. For this reason, it is imperative to grasp the dynamics of such terms within the cycle of meaning, particularly the dynamics of visionary experiences.

It should be kept in mind that the interpretive strategy of cultural bundubashing is to make sense of the distinct cultural world, in an approach known as abduction, by means of cross-cultural models (in this case, by means of the shamanic model) that give modern people access to the homoversals that have culturally specific manifestations then and there in the past culture. Put in different language, the shamanic model, capturing particular kinds of human experiences and phenomena, will be used to make sense of the experiential-reflective phenomena described by the documents. That is, making sense today of the distinct cultural world by crossing the cultural and temporal gaps to that world by means of a cross-cultural vehicle that allows us to deal with the data there in a cross-cultural way. If the data are framed by means of the shamanic hypothesis, then the "kingdom of God" and "Son of Man" sayings appear to be the residue of particular cultural processes associated with someone like a shamanic figure.

The Kingdom of God and Son of Man in an Israelite Cycle of Meaning

It was already mentioned that both the "kingdom of God" and "Son of Man" sayings were well-known phrases in Israelite tradition. Although the idea of God as king is well established in Old Testament texts, the explicit use of "kingdom of God" (or derivatives) is scarce. It is, however, remarkable that "kingdom of God" surfaces prominently in Israelite visionary (or so-called apocalyptic) texts (for details, see Duling 1992, 50–51; Caragounis 1992, 417–20). It is also remarkable that although the term *son of man* was used in the Old Testament as a circumlocution for "I," it is in the same corpus of texts (in fact, mostly in the very same documents and contexts) that a *son of man* figure appears in connection with the *kingdom of God* theme (see Nickelsburg 1992b, 137–41 for a discussion of these instances).

It is noteworthy that the only place in the New Testament outside the Synoptics where "Son of Man" is used to describe a heavenly figure is also in a visionary text: "Behold, I see the heavens opened, and the Son of man standing at the right hand of God" (Acts 7:56). The other instances in the New Testament that refer to Jesus as *the son of man* are, not surprisingly, in the visionary text of Revelation (Rev 1:13, 14:14).

Visionary experiences, as already explained, are inscribed in the cycle of meaning of a particular cultural system and worldview. Visionaries see, hear, and encounter what is already known to them but what often results in a novel or innovative exposition (because of the lateral connections and cycle of meaning). Three features of these visionary experiences within the Israelite cycle of meaning (which also happen to contain references to the kingdom of God and the Son of Man), are to be highlighted here as background for our understanding of Jesus's teaching, preaching, and prophetic activities as potentially those of a Galilean shamanic figure.

The Vision as Message versus the Message of the Vision

In some cultures, visionary or other ASC travel or audience encounters with divine beings or ancestors are experienced as direct encounters of the visionary with such beings. In the Israelite tradition, however, visions or otherworldly journeys normally contain third-person, apparently unattached reports about a heavenly scene (of which the visionary is the privileged observer). The visions of Enoch are examples of these extended descriptions of the visionary scenes (see, e.g., *1 Enoch* 21, 62).

Since time immemorial, Israelite people had reservations about direct encounters with Yahweh, and in the case of Moses, for example, the visionary encounter was mediated (by a burning bush in Exod 3). Congruent with Israelite beliefs in real life, the divinity is removed and not named, described, or directly addressed (God is called "the Lord of the Spirits" in e.g., *1 Enoch* 63, Isaac). But such a visionary experience or heavenly journey (otherworldly journeys in Israelite lore are to *heaven*), is precisely the kind of experience that is described in the reported vision, namely, an audience with the divinity. It is to be considered that the significance of such reports is not first and foremost the content of the reports but rather the experience itself, which is reported. Put the other way around, what the Israelite visionary texts make clear is that in Israelite tradition, the visionary encounter by means of a trip to heaven (in a vision) is narrated by means of a modest account as if reporting about a third-person figure (heavenly being) having the divine audience. If *son of man* was a modest or reserved way of referring to the self in Israelite culture, such an account in visionary texts is a modest way of relaying a heavenly journey or encounter.

Formulated in terms of cultural dynamics, the content of a vision is but the vehicle to report about having been to heaven and having seen, heard, and encountered the divinity. Sometimes in no uncertain terms it is made clear that the account is about the visionary himself—as Enoch emphasizes: "I, Enoch was in the heaven of heavens" (*1 Enoch* 71:5, Isaac trans.). An ASC heavenly journey was an experience that gave an Israelite person access to the divine world—a terrain under normal circumstances out of bounds, except for the (high) priests—and modesty and humility were to be expected.

In addition, it should be kept in mind that in a cultural landscape where the normal and regular access to the divine world is via the temple and its priesthood, any such direct or extraordinary encounter with the divinity (if accepted as legitimate) would count as a special or significant event. In Israelite culture, it would be appropriate to say, a significant cultural event, such as a heavenly ASC journey, is experienced and presented in a roundabout way. The content of the vision is the indirect way of relaying the significance of the visionary experience itself.

It is via the message in the vision that the very point (i.e., the message) of a vision as an audience with the divinity and what that implies was communicated. The basic truth about a vision or heavenly journey experience is that it is not a description of an objective scene (of a Son of Man or of any other heavenly being encountering the divinity). Instead, the subject, the one reporting on the vision is also the one having the experience or vision of the encounter with the divinity. While the content of the vision or ASC experience is given in terms of the cultural lore, it is the experience itself that is significant. The point to be stressed is that in many Israelite visionary texts, it is the message of having the visionary encounter—and not the content of the vision—that is to be appreciated. The vision as message is to be appreciated!

But, in addition to the point of such ASC experiences, it is also necessary to look at some of the contents of such experiences. Two features in
particular are significant for this discussion.

The Visionary as the Protagonist in (Some) Israelite Visionary Texts

Keeping in mind that the person having the divine encounter is reporting
about a protagonist who meets the divinity (or his servants, angels, or nonhuman beings), it is significant that in a number of instances the visionary
is directly identified with the protagonist in the vision. From the single
reference in Daniel (7:13) to one "like a Son of Man," it is impossible to
conclude definitively on this issue, one way or another. The argument that
the term *son of man* cannot be taken in its circumlocutional use (as defended by Vermes 1973, 170) is defeated by references to "the Son of Man"
in the rest of Daniel 7 (in the singular). Given the other instances, it could
very well have been an instance of a humble identification of the visionary
with the privileged protagonist. In the case in the book of Ezekiel, where
the prophet having the visionary experience is himself thirty-three times
addressed as "Son of Man," it seems clear that the visionary himself is also
the protagonist in the vision.

The protagonist in *1 Enoch*, Nickelsburg points out, "is a transcendental figure known as 'the righteous one,' 'the chosen one,' 'the anointed
one,' and 'this/that Son of Man,' who functions as champion of 'the
righteous and the chosen' and as judge of their antagonists, the 'kings
and the mighty'" (1992b, 138). It is, however, most significant that in
one particular instance Enoch himself is identified as the Son of Man,
the protagonist of his own vision: "You, Son of Man, who art born in
righteousness and upon whom righteousness has dwelt, the righteousness
of the Antecedent of Time will not forsake you" (*1 Enoch* 71:14, Isaac
trans.). For Nickelsburg, this turn of events "is totally unexpected," and
he claims that the "text is probably an addition to an earlier form of the
Book of Parables" (1992b, 140). If these texts are taken seriously as reports
about life-changing experiences (as has been indicated earlier, ASC experiences often result in life-altering experiences) and not merely as fictional
or literary creations, then the fact that Enoch is being identified as that
Son of Man is not unexpected. The ASC experience (vision) itself is the
life-altering event, and not what it contains. Visionary experiences change

people and, more than that, change the makeup of shamanic figures who often have such experiences.

What the foregoing examples show is that a heavenly son-of-man figure seen in a vision can indeed be the visionary himself. It would be difficult, furthermore, to imagine that the above-mentioned Israelite texts were not part of the cultural lore known to later generations having such experiences. In fact, instead of seeing the circumlocutional use of the *son of man* and these visionary (heavenly) figures as two distinct references, I suggest that (at least some of the visionary heavenly figures?) can be interpreted as instances of circumlocution in the vision. The employment (or better, experience) of a third figure or divine or heavenly agent (as *son of man*) in the vision—who acts as divine messenger, agent, or viceroy—can be seen as a modest way of relaying the same content: *the divinity, Yahweh, has a viceroy who will act on his behalf; I, the visionary, have been there!*

There are not only a number of direct and indirect references in the Gospels to the Danielic "son of man" figure, but there are also cases where Jesus is ascribed with the functions of someone who has had direct access to the divine world (see below).

Israelite Shamanic Figures (Visionaries) as the Creators of Traditional Knowledge

A history-of-traditions approach assumes some kind of linear process of development of ideas in which authors, as composers of new texts, make use of motifs, ideas, or traditions from earlier texts. If these Israelite visionary texts are indeed residues of visionary or ASC experiences, a different cultural process can be imagined, namely, the creative employment of ideas by way of lateral thinking. As I have explained with regard to the cycle of meaning, ancient people experienced what they believed, and believed what they experienced. If we develop a sensitivity for the experiential-reflective nature of many of ancient knowledge categories, it is easy to see that talk about the Son of Man and the kingdom of God is not merely a discussion of a set of ideas or beliefs, but the residue of creative and innovative cultural processes in which known ideas are redeployed. The dynamics are precisely that traditional material is adopted and adapted, transformed and linked in novel ways in visionary experiences as well as in the lives of such figures. Within the cycle of meaning of Israelite people, the "Son of Man" figure must have been part of the mythology associated with visionary texts, while such themes were creatively employed by those reshaping the cycle.

In view of this, a second feature of the content of some of these Israelite visionary texts containing *son of man* references needs to be considered. This concerns the fact that within such visionary texts, it often is difficult (if not impossible) to determine the history of tradition, simply because there was no history transmitted or developed from text to text.[9] Although Nickelsburg, for example, still treats the Enochic Parables (*1 En* 37–71) in terms of the development and utilization of ideas by later authors or narrators, he notes that there was no simple transmission of existing ideas but a "creative development and mutual modification of complimentary traditions" (1992b, 139). Thus, if these texts are taken seriously as the residue of visionary experiences, instead of thinking that authors have merely utilized earlier texts in a linear fashion, one should consider as the actual dynamics behind the texts the innovative employment of traditional material and the creation of new cultural knowledge by way of ASC experiences. For example, the emphasis Nickelsburg notes on the judicial function in some of these visionary texts constitutes the creation of new cultural knowledge based on lateral thinking (see 1992b, 141). In his actual description of these modifications, it is more a case of the creative employment and innovative connection of nonexisting ideas in the tradition than simply a development of ongoing tradition. This is the kind of cultural process to be associated with shamanic figures.

Authors of texts within that same cultural tradition can obviously create such ideas and arrive at the same point via literary creativity and innovation. However, these texts all claim to be the residue of visionary experiences and, as argued earlier, that is also the case with texts about Jesus of Nazareth. This suggestion is not without scholarly support. Segal suggests that Daniel's exegesis of Isaiah 66 was no exegesis at all; it was a visionary revelation: "The medium of this combination of passages is a prophetic, revelatory vision, which combines passages from all over the Bible, not in casual fashion but in a very complex and sophisticated man-

9. This model is clearly in the mind of Nickelsburg (1992b, 138) when he discusses the composition of the *Parables of Enoch*: "The Parables' portrait of this agent of deliverance [a "Son of Man"] draws much of its language and imagery from three biblical sources or traditional interpretations of these sources . . . Through the use and elaboration of this material, the author has created a composite figure."

ner . . . It is a vision that the seer has received after vivid study of the text" (2004, 264).

It should be kept in mind that based on the nature of ASC experience, there was quite literally no entity, figure, or being (no *Son of Man*) "out there" that could be seen or encountered, but the seeing or hearing (vision or audition) itself was the experience that included the Son of Man. There was, to begin with, no heavenly or human figure out there that later authors could have referred to or seen. The Son of Man in Daniel 7 (even if he was a heavenly being other than the visionary himself) was not "there" in any objective sense so that Jesus or anyone else could refer to him, but he was "there" as part of the Israelite cultural lore. Therefore, later visionaries could, based on this lore, see a *son of man* in their own ASC experiences.

The dynamics presupposed in this study are a little different from those presupposed in literary tradition history. The dynamics are the creative and innovative employment of traditional material in or after ASC experiences. The guiding principles here are ruptures and gaps, the innovation of tradition, and the creation of new cultural knowledge that takes place within the cycle of meaning.

Conclusion

From this very cursory overview of the two well-known phrases in Israelite literature, at least the following suggestions can be made: First, the "kingdom of God" and "Son of Man" sayings were closely connected to the life of Israelite visionaries—persons who could in other accounts easily be compared to shamanic figures. Second, these phrases were not only cultural terms in origin, but particular cultural vehicles for both experiencing and expressing ASC or visionary experiences. It seems clear that these phrases had their origin not only in Israelite tradition, but in the hands (or rather *heads*) of Israelite visionaries; they were phrases that actually expressed the ASC experiences. They were, in a very literal sense, experiential-reflective categories that often, if not exclusively, were associated with particular kinds of ASC experiences in Israelite settings.

If Jesus had ASC experiences as already suggested, it would come as no surprise that these phrases could have been closely connected to his life. It would be normal for these two concepts to form part of the cycle of meaning to which he was exposed as a Galilean shamanic figure. What he had to say cannot be divorced from the fact that if he had said anything, it was said as a Galilean shamanic figure (according to the present hypothesis). This finds support in the already-mentioned fact that major parts of the teachings ascribed to Jesus of Nazareth, the so-called eschatological teachings, are similar to the astrological texts associated with the life of astral prophets.

The Teaching, Preaching, and Prophetic Activities of a Shamanic Jesus

If Jesus was a shamanic figure, it is to be expected that what he did and said were closely associated with the kind of figure that he was. If he attracted a following as a shamanic figure and because he was such a figure, whatever he had to say (and did) was said (and done) in his capacity as such a figure. If Jesus of Nazareth was a Galilean shamanic figure, his sayings probably did not result from a "talking head" but were produced by the talking mouth of a shamanic figure. If he spoke about something, he spoke as a shamanic figure, and that means that his "teachings" were integrally connected to his life as such a figure. His teachings were part of what he was and did as a shamanic figure.

If, as already indicated, he did not follow a fixed *curriculum* or a systematic exposition of any single topic, how, when, and where did the shamanic Jesus teach? The short answer is that these activities were closely connected to his life and activities as a shamanic figure. His teaching, preaching, and prophetic activities were, in a sense, accidental or always situational, connected to the activities of a shamanic figure embedded in the cultural dynamics of being a shamanic figure. At least, that is one of the features of the data described previously.

Therefore, instead of a systematic presentation of the acclaimed topics in Jesus's teachings, the aim in this section is to explore some of the clues in the documents, clues that show that they fit into the picture of a shamanic life. Once the data are not raided for the possible authentic nuggets but placed within the life of a social personage, the "kingdom of God" and "Son of Man" sayings offer a picture of teachings, preaching, and prophecies; it is surprising how many features point toward the pragmatic activities of someone with no fixed curriculum or teaching agenda but who went about his activities as an integral part of who and what he was.

Once a Son of Man, Always in the Kingdom of God

The parallel texts in all the documentary data on the "kingdom of God" and "Son of Man" sayings constitute a special problem in the authenticity paradigm. Besides the already-mentioned problems (for example, that an *entity*, such as the kingdom of God, cannot simultaneously be present and future, here and not yet), the parallel texts create another problem: did Jesus actually use the specific phrases, or were they ascribed to him? In other words, can his authentic teachings be identified by looking at the use of the particular phrases?

Did he use the term *Son of Man* if parallel texts simply have an "I," or did he actually use the "I," and can the references in either case be taken as authentic? An example is the parallel texts on the question of who the people thought Jesus was. Mark (8:27) and Luke (9:18) have "I" ("Who do the crowds say that I am?"), while Matthew (16:13) reads, "Who do people say that the Son of Man is?" Five other parallel texts contain variations between "I" and the "Son of Man."[10] Did Jesus actually use the term when it appears in parallel texts that disagree, or was it later added in the text containing the words (see King 1987, 82–89 for examples)?[11]

With regard to the "kingdom of God" sayings, the amount of data is far to complex to deal with here, but a similar pattern can be detected.[12] One example will, however, suffice to show that a theme can be introduced as explicitly connected to a "kingdom of God" saying, while the exact phrase is absent from the parallel versions. In a warning against temptations, Mark's version is: "And if your eye causes you to stumble, tear it out; it is better for you to enter the kingdom of God with one eye than to have two eyes and to be thrown into hell" (9:47). The Matthean version (5:29), which places this saying in a different setting (but in the

10. One time Mark (8:31) has "Son of Man" and Matthew (16:21) and Luke (9:21) merely "I"; Mark (10:45) and Matthew (20:28) agree once on "Son of Man" against Luke's "I" (22:27); in parallel texts between only Matthew and Luke, Luke twice contains "Son of Man" (6:22 and 12:10) against "I" (Matt 5:11, 12:32), while Matthew (19:28) once contains "Son of Man" against Luke's "I" (22:30).

11. In the view expressed in this study, the exercise of determining how each Gospel has changed the terminology and gist of specific sayings can only be conducted once a clearer picture has been established of how these concepts could have functioned in the life of a shamanic figure.

12. In addition, this term is far more complex because, besides "kingdom of God," several synonymous phrases are used (including "kingdom of Heaven," "kingdom of the Father," or simply "the kingdom") in parallel texts (see Caragounis 1992, 425–26).

authenticity paradigm supposedly copied it from Mark), does not use the phrase "kingdom of God."[13]

Two implications seem to follow from these examples. The first is that in their representation of the tradition, none of the authors considered it important to replicate *Jesus's words*. If they thought "Son of Man" and "kingdom of God" were particularly authentic Jesus speech, or that his authentic teachings were connected to the use of these particular terms, they did not care to uphold it—even when allegedly copying from earlier texts. In the mind of these authors, Jesus's teachings (even if ascribed to him by the authors) were not directly linked to the use of particular words or phrases. The variations between the documents show that in the mind of these authors, the ideas of a Son of Man and the kingdom of God were present (or represented) in the figure, without using the phrases.

A possible explanation from the point of view of cultural bundubashing is that if Jesus was a social personage (a shamanic figure), he was that not only when he has used certain words or phrases. If he was a Galilean shamanic figure, if he was considered someone who had special connections to the divine world, the idea could be present without specific words or phrases. If either or both of the "kingdom of God" or "Son of Man" labels were part of his life, they were so for everything else he did or said. In simple terms, if Jesus of Nazareth was once identified or self-identified or proclaimed as a Son of Man, then he was always and everywhere a Son of Man. This is precisely how social labels function.

A second implication is that who and what Jesus was as a historical figure was right from the beginning characterized by his social constitution as a social personage, and this also applies to his teachings. If Jesus was a kind of social personage who was once ascribed with a label such as "the Son of Man," then in the minds of his contemporaries (and those enscripturating his life), he always was a Son of Man. And if the kingdom of God was part of his way of talking about experiences in the world, it was always potentially there. As already indicated, the specific words or phrases need not be present for the concept or idea to exist in a particular case, but once a son of the kingdom (or a Son of Man), always a man connected to God. This is precisely what is confirmed by connecting Jesus's teaching, preaching, and prophetic activities to his other activities as a shamanic figure.

13. Examples can be multiplied, but King's analysis shows many examples where the *Gospel of Thomas* contains the phrase "kingdom of God," while the Synoptics omit it in parallel texts, and vice versa (1987, 82–91).

It should be kept in mind that while this analysis to a certain degree distinguishes between the "kingdom" sayings and the "Son of Man" sayings, in the data they often are closely connected, and if they are taken as sayings of a shamanic figure, they probably were interconnected.

Jesus's Teaching Linked to His Everyday Shamanic Activities as Healer and Exorcist

Jesus's activities and those of his followers are repeatedly described by linking the kingdom of God with healing the sick or with exorcising demons. The summary remark of what Jesus was doing after his initial spirit-possession experience (baptism) contains the content of what he talked about: "The time is fulfilled, and the kingdom of God has come near; repent, and believe in the good news [the gospel]" (Mark 1:15 par.). The rest of the reports make it clear that what he was doing (as a Son of Man) was preaching and healing (see Mark 1:39). The good news (gospel) was closely linked to the kingdom of God; believing the gospel was sharing in the kingdom.

In Matthew the connection between what Jesus talked about and what he walked (did) is even more explicit: "proclaiming the good news of the kingdom and curing every disease and every sickness among the people" (4:23). Talking about the kingdom of God goes hand in hand with healing the sick and with exorcising demons, which are all shamanic activities and related to and resulting from ASC experiences (see also Matt 9:35). What Jesus did, according to Matthew, was to go about "all the cities and villages, teaching in their synagogues, and proclaiming the good news of the kingdom, and curing every disease and every sickness" (9:35). In the minds and memory of his first followers, being a teacher was merged with doing wonderful things: "Rabbi, we know that you are a teacher who has come from God; for no one can do these signs that you do apart from the presence of God" (John 3:2). This is also Luke's (9:11) description of Jesus's activities: "And he welcomed them and spoke to them about the kingdom of God, and healed those who needed to be cured."

A Lukan account where Jesus reportedly said that he has to "proclaim the good news of the kingdom of God to the other cities also" (4:43) is preceded by a report of what he did when preaching in synagogues: he preached, healed, and exorcised demons. It is difficult to avoid the impression that preaching and bringing the good news of the kingdom of God was never intended as a talkative activity. Bringing the good news of the kingdom of God again and again appears in the context of healings and exorcisms (see also Luke 8:1). Receiving the good news was, it seems, not simply hearing a message but sharing an experience of and with God's mediator of power.

Elsewhere the connection between message and experience is more explicit. It is reported that Jesus's activities as an exorcist are associated with the presence of the kingdom of God: "But if it is by the Spirit of God that I cast out demons, then the kingdom of God has come to you" (Matt 12:28; also Luke 11:20). The same connection is made in the story of the healing of the centurion's slave. Someone with trust (faith) in Jesus's ability to heal is promised a share in the kingdom of God with Israel's ancestors, Abraham, Isaac, and Jacob (Matt 8:11).

As indicated in the previous chapter, these shamanic activities were not restricted only to Jesus. He equipped his followers and gave them power and authority to also engage in kingdom activities and preaching—that is, to talk about the kingdom of God while healing and exorcising. The many reports about the sending of his followers to act in his name and on his behalf contain the same refrain: "Then Jesus called the twelve together and gave them power and authority over all demons and to cure diseases, and he sent them out to proclaim the kingdom of God and to heal" (Luke 9:1–2; and see 10:9; and Matt 10:1, 7–8; Mark 6:7–13). Walking and talking the kingdom of God was a unified act that was closely associated with mediating divine power—one of the things a shaman does.

But if he was a shamanic figure, speaking and doing never were isolated things: it was the shamanic figure who spoke, and the same figure who healed and exorcised. In view of this, a suggestion Borg makes that "life in the Spirit is life in the Kingdom of God" (1987, 199) can be pushed further. For Jesus, life in the Spirit started with his first spirit-possession experience and marks his whole public career. It is neither a place nor an activity but something to enter into as an experience linked to his shamanic activities. And his shamanic activities included talking and doing.

Jesus's Teachings Linked to Divine Mediation: The Shaman as Viceroy

If he was a shamanic figure whose life was changed because of his ASC experiences and who started a life of mediating divine power in everyday settings (healings and exorcisms) and called 'that' the kingdom of God, it would come as no surprise that he also offered services linked to that life and refer to these as the activities of the Son of Man.

There are a remarkable number of sayings that, in one way or another, ascribe to Jesus as shamanic figure the functions of someone who has had close encounters with the divine world and, thus, who can act as a mediator or divine viceroy.

If Jesus was a Galilean shamanic figure, it goes without saying that in his public persona, he represented and offered access to the divine realm and mediated power that in Israelite society resided with the temple and its officials. A full analysis of this dynamic will take us far beyond the scope of the present argument. However, it is remarkable that a whole range of teaching, preaching, and prophetic activities are presented in exactly such a mode. Three examples will briefly be mentioned.

The cultural dynamic of "forgiveness of sins" is not the cancellation of moral transgressions as it is often understood to be in introspective, guilt-oriented cultures. Instead, forgiveness "had the character of restoration, a return to both self-sufficiency and one's place in the community" (Malina & Rohrbaugh 1992, 63). Therefore, forgiveness by God means being divinely restored to one's position. In Israelite society, this was normally done at the temple and mediated by the priests. Israelite society of the Second Temple period did know of forgiveness that was mediated in ways other than by the temple rituals, namely, a noncultic forgiveness of sins based on confession (see Theissen & Merz 1998, 527–28). If Jesus started his public career with John the Baptist as suggested earlier, he was embedded in a setting where a ritual bath mediated God's forgiveness.

Therefore, it is not surprising that shortly after his baptism experience, in which he had a divine encounter, Jesus could offer God's restoration to people without any form of ritual. Not only does the scene of the healing of the paralytic link the forgiveness of sins to the healing of the man, but there is also an explicit reference to the mediating authority of the Son of Man: "But so that you may know that the Son of Man has authority on earth to forgive sins" (Mark 2:10).

Sin is to God as debt is to others: "Sin is a breach of interpersonal relations" (Malina & Rohrbaugh 1998, 174). This is what Luke makes explicit in his version of Jesus's prayer: "And forgive us our sins, for we ourselves forgive everyone indebted to us" (11:4). This condition of indebtedness was the result of a particular economic and political system that caused the peasants of the first-century world much suffering. Removing debt (as in the parable connected to the story of the sinful woman [Luke 7:36–50]) is paralleled by being forgiven by God, and this forgiveness is what Jesus mediated. In the Matthean version of this account (18:23), it is said that this is how it is supposed to go in the kingdom of heaven.

It is in the context of telling about Jesus becoming (in the public view) a son of God because of an ASC experience ("I saw the Spirit descending from heaven like a dove, and it remained on him" [John 1:32]) that Jesus is called the one ("the Lamb of God") who will take away the sins of the world (1:29). Because he is spirit-possessed, he is attributed with the mediating power to make things right with the divine world.

This brings us to the second example. The "Son of Man is lord even of the sabbath" (Mark 2:28) refers to a powerful dynamic in the life of a shamanic figure. This little phrase, after Jesus's disciples had breached the Sabbath conventions by plucking grain, refers to an issue that would not be unexpected in the life of someone with regular and direct interaction with the divine world.

While there were various sentiments in Israelite society about how the Sabbath regulations should be applied (see Sanders 1993, 207), it is not surprising to find Jesus on the side of those who did not strongly subscribe to the traditional authority figures. In fact, if he was a wandering shamanic figure, it should be realized that Jesus's natural access to public life and gatherings was very much restricted to community gatherings—that is, synagogue communities on the Sabbath, because in a peasant society there is little time for recreation, relaxation, or socialization in everyday life.

Several healing accounts take place in such Sabbath gatherings in *synagogues* (see Matt 3:1–6; Luke 13:10–17; 14:1–6; John 5:1–9; 9:1–12). The teaching, if any, followed the healing, and if the Son of Man (explicit in some accounts but implicated in all such stories of divine mediation) could act on God's behalf in healing, it is a clear sign that he could also be master of God's day.

The third example refers to the sense of authority and mission of the Jesus portrayed in the texts. As will be indicated below, part of being a shamanic figure has to do with the awe and the accompanied construction as social figure by outsiders, by the faithful crowd and by the close circle of disciples. But the position of shamanic figure does not go without a sense of self-identity and awareness of the position. The shamanic life starts with an initiation ceremony (in the case of Jesus of Nazareth, with his baptism) and is confirmed by other ASC experiences, and strengthened by being a divine instrument in healing and exorcisms, a shamanic figure obviously has a personal sense of being a shaman. In the words of Sanders (1993, 239): "he thought that he had been especially commissioned to speak for God, and this conviction was based on a feeling of personal intimacy with the deity."

It is this kind of self-identity that is expressed in a variety of stories that portray Jesus as a viceroy and, more often than not, as explicitly connected to the "Son of Man" phrase. The shamanic *son* (of God or man) reveals the Father and has total wisdom of and from him. Jesus invited people to follow him because the Son of Man can bring them in close contact with the glory of God (Mark 8:34–38). The often-repeated claims of Jesus's sense of a mission capture precisely the idea of a divine viceroy who acts with a divine commission. In different contexts, it is often expressed by the phrase "I have come . . . ," as in "I have come to call not the righteous but sinners" (Mark 2:17).[14] These notions are supported by the claim on Jesus's lips of a complete revelation from God of everything that he said: "All things have been handed over to me by my Father" (Matt 11:27). Sayings such as this express not only the idea of "the divine telephone exchange," but also a sense of being the revealer of divine knowledge.

Jesus's Teaching and Social Interaction: Impromptu Reactions to Rumors and Gossip

As a public figure, Jesus was constituted mutually by his actions, self-definition, and the reaction of the people. Social personages are not appointed or promoted but constituted by means of cultural processes of legitimation, social construction, and recognition. None of the labels applied or functions ascribed to him can be seen independently from such cultural processes. To be a social figure is to be involved in such cultural processes.

There are a number of reports that link Jesus's "kingdom of God" talk to social processes of gossip and rumors. In fact, much of Jesus's teaching about the kingdom of God is reported as responses to questions from others.

---

14. This phrase appears in John at regular intervals (5:43, 10:10, 12:47, 16:38, 18:37) and is also ascribed to John the Baptist (1:31). In the Synoptics, it is equally well attested (Matt 5:17; Mark 10:45; Luke 12:49–51), while at least twice in Luke, it is the Son of Man who comes (7:34 and 19:10).

There are a number of examples where Jesus's teaching can be seen as almost impromptu reactions to questions from a given audience. Sometimes it is the Pharisees and the scribes who are credited with asking questions (see, e.g., Mark 7:5; Matt 16:1), other times simply people in the crowd ask questions (see, e.g., Mark 2:18), and again, the disciples often question Jesus (see, e.g., Matt 15:12). At one point, Jesus reacts to a question by some Pharisees who have heard and participated in kingdom gossip. Jesus's reply is that the "kingdom of God is not coming with things that can be observed; nor will they say, 'Look, here it is!' or 'There it is!' For, in fact, the kingdom of God is among you" (Luke 17:20–21). As indicated, kingdom of God and its derivatives must have had a familiar sound to first-century Israelite ears: God's reign or a divine theocracy. Therefore, it is not surprising that people were curious about this coming reign of God and how it would be recognized. The vague answer to the question, based on rumors, points in the direction of its origin and connection to Jesus's social life: it is among you where the Son of Man is present.

In another instance, Jesus tells a parable of a nobleman who went into a far country to receive a kingdom, in order to counter the impression, created by gossip and rumor, of people who "supposed that the kingdom of God was to appear immediately" (Luke 19:11). It is likely that many of his contemporaries understood the kingdom of God in the conventional way of a new theocracy or of a claim by Jesus that he was to restore a political Israelite kingdom.

There must have been many questions about this "kingdom of God" talk. As already indicated, after Jesus had healed a crippled woman on a Sabbath, his adversaries were put to shame and the crowd "was rejoicing at all the wonderful things that he was doing" (Luke 13:17). Immediately, a connection is made about what the kingdom of God is like, and Jesus tells the parable of the mustard seed and the leaven (Luke 13:18–21).

The situational nature of Jesus's teachings (against the idea of a self-acclaimed proclamation) is perhaps nowhere as clear as in the question of paying tribute to Caesar (Mark 12:13–17 par.). Most scholars acknowledge that it was a question aiming to trap Jesus, in an attempt to get him arrested (see e.g., Horsley 2003, 99). As imperial criticism, this pericope is not only fairly innocuous but also does not seem to represent a very strong anti-imperial campaign or proclamation. It does, however, give evidence that what Jesus had to say was often less part of a clear program and more often impromptu responses, given his social position.

Jesus's (Shamanic) Teaching Was Done with Authority

Jesus was not an educated or trained teacher who belonged to any teaching group (see Vermes 1993, 46). Nevertheless, astonishment with his teaching is often expressed in the documents, as in Mark 1:22: "They were astounded at his teaching, for he taught them as one having authority, and not as the scribes."[15] Whatever else remarks such as this one convey, they point toward the general dynamics in nonliterate societies that only someone with (divine) authority can introduce new knowledge into the society. Not everybody can contribute new knowledge, and this is implied by the inquiry from the chief priests, the scribes, and the elders: "By what authority are you doing these things? Who gave you this authority to do them?" (Mark 11:28).

Jesus's authority is indeed not given from any institution or from learning. Sanders points out that, in contrast to a rabbi or a teacher of the law, who derived authority from studying and interpreting the law, Jesus's authority was not mediated by any human institution or even by Scripture. In effect, he said: "Give up everything you have and follow me, because I am God's agent" (Sanders 1993, 238). Being an agent of God is closely related to his ASC experiences and his transformed mentality as a divine mediator. This is confirmed by two related features of Jesus's reported style of talking that are noteworthy.

The first is his use of "Amen" to introduce particular sayings: "Truly [*Amen*] I say to you . . . ," which is extended in the Gospel of John to "Truly, truly [*Amen, amen*] I say to you . . ."[16] The second is the formula "I say to you . . . ," which is often found in antitheses.[17] This is the style of someone claiming to talk with a personal authority—a feature typical of shamanic figures, who base their authority on the transformational experiences in their lives and on the continued awareness of being such a social personage.

15. See Dunn for a list of all the instances (2003b, 698 n. 399).

16. See Dunn for lists of all these instances (2003b, 702 nn. 418–19).

17. Theissen and Merz demonstrate that Jesus's ethic on the law can be seen as a deliberate transcending of the Torah: "One can fulfil God's will only if one does not just fulfil his commandments by one's behaviour but also lets one's own will, down to the innermost emotions, be governed by them" (1998, 364).

Jesus's Teachings and the Socio-Political Conditions under Roman Rule

Social figures in general and shamanic figures in particular always operate within the boundaries of their specific cultural systems and local circumstances. This is clearly confirmed by the central phrases in Jesus's teaching, preaching, and prophetic activities: they are all culturally commonplace words. Thus, instead of looking for the complete list of everything that Jesus could have said about two otherworldly entities (the kingdom of God and the Son of Man), cultural bundubashing supports the understanding of Jesus's sayings as engaged communication within concrete circumstances. He was not teaching for the sake of conveying information but was talking for the sake of illuminating and expressing a reality with local and specific qualities present there and then.

Under the import of the social sciences in New Testament studies, several attempts have recently been made to avoid the linear interpretive strategy associated with the authenticity paradigm (presenting Jesus's teachings as those of a "talking head" for the sake of teaching). In particular, the horrible conditions for ordinary people in greater Palestine under the yoke of the Roman empire and its local elites have been extensively explored.

It is within the historical setting of oppression by foreign powers locally supported by the Israelite political elites that Jesus, according to Horsley, talked about the kingdom of God in two particular ways (see 2003). One is as a judgment of the rulers, and the other is as a restoration and renewal of Israelite village communities.[18] Evidence for Jesus's condemnation of the Roman imperial order is rather flimsy, while evidence for Jesus's direct criticism of the temple and priestly elites is much stronger.

Horsley's portrayal of Jesus as a prophetic political leader with a social-political program replaces the "talking head" with a "communicating prophet and activist" against Roman imperialism. In line with the previously mentioned fact that Horsley sees Jesus as a prophet who also healed and performed signs, it is not surprising that he treats the healings and exorcisms as bodily symbolic actions of resistance to Roman imperialism. For example, "when Jesus brings the seemingly dead twelve-year-old girl back to life just at the time she has come of age to reproduce children, he is mediating new life to Israel in general. In these and other episodes

---

18. See, however, the objections to this last thesis (Moxnes 2003, 151).

Jesus is healing the illnesses brought on by Roman imperialism" (Horsley 2003, 109).[19]

Already in the 1980s, Moxnes offered an interpretation of Luke's understanding of kingdom features by situating them in the context of social and economic relations of first-century Mediterranean Palestine (see 1988). Although that study was done on the narrative level of Luke's Gospel, it shows that Jesus's proclamation of the good news and the kingdom of God offered an alternative structure of social and economic relations for the people of God. Luke was not offering Jesus's sayings about the kingdom of God as a list of teachings about the topic, but by means of kingdom language was addressing the social and economic relations in society as such.

In a second study, which consistently avoids the dominance of the temporal perspective for understanding Jesus's kingdom sayings, Moxnes shows that a number of atypical figures are often associated with the sayings: these figures are eunuchs, barren women, and presexual children (see 2003, 91–107). Kingdom sayings are not to be read for their information about the future or the end of time, but are to be interpreted as an imagined place where different social relations and power structures operate. This is supported by images of the kingdom in which Jesus's followers as displaced persons (those who follow him as a wandering preacher) are encouraged by being "re-placed," so to speak, in a new kind of divine household, where God is not king but father (see 2003, 108–24). This becomes the new place in the world where they live from—a "new home place."

But ultimately, it is also the political implications of Jesus's kingdom sayings that interest Moxnes. Particularly in the analysis of Jesus's exorcisms as discourses of power relations in Galilee, he shows that the connection between exorcism and kingdom sayings contributes to establish positions of power in the Galilean society—together, kingdom sayings and exorcisms claim that the kingdom of God becomes "experienced place" in Galilee (see 2003, 125–41).

It is, however, Malina who has most forcefully shown that Jesus's "kingdom of God" sayings were a response to the perceived and experienced life within the Roman empire. For him, the kingdom of God

19. Davies (1995, 79) considers "preposterous" the theory that Jesus's healings and exorcisms were disguised forms of criticism. As I have argued earlier, the cultural mechanisms of spirit-possession and the reasons for sickness were much more varied, and, consequently, the exorcisms and healings certainly were much more than simply disguised imperial judgments.

belongs to the realm of political religion, that is, religion embedded in the elite political power system; and the problem to which Jesus's proclamation of the kingdom of God was an answer was "Roman political economy as appropriated by local Israelite aristocracy" (2001b, 34). Under the eastern Mediterranean Roman empire, the local Israelite elites failed in their traditional role of caring for the non-elites (the poor, hungry, and destitute), and the solution would be that the God of Israel would take control by means of the kingdom of God; in the coming of the kingdom of God, the Father in the sky, or the divine patron, would intervene on their behalf. In Malina's words: "Jesus proclaims his message, describes his task, and directs his symbolic actions at the pillars of politically embedded Israelite Yahwism" (2001b, 94).

But in a world where economics, too, was embedded in politics or kinship, Jesus's proclamation of the restoration of Israel also addresses the problems experienced by the "poor"—that is, by those members of society suffering from unfortunate personal circumstances and thus, the socially impotent (widows, the sick, the handicapped). The proclamation of the kingdom of God, Malina says, therefore, also addresses the issue of redistribution of honor and dignity, or the ability to participate in community activities (see 2001b, 111).

Finally, the good news of the kingdom of God finds expression in becoming part of the Jesus group. Malina shows that the numerous references to self-denial and family denial were part of the recruitment strategies of Jesus as faction founder (see 2001b, 113–37). Membership of the Jesus group became a substitute for former family and group allegiances and loyalties, and a strong motivation for this connection is Jesus's access to God's patronage. This group formed a new collective, the house of Israel, or the "true" Israel.

These studies are a long distance away from the "Jesus as talking head" portrayals. They are also very useful for grasping something of the communication intended in the original settings of local politics and cultural system. But it is still Jesus's message (or communication, or teachings) that forms the basis of the analyses of what he has said. Instead of the talking Jesus, the communicating Jesus is still seen as someone with a particular and powerful message (or prophecy) that characterized who and what he was as a historical figure (a communicating prophet). But Horsley, Moxnes, and Malina are all helpful in treating Jesus's teachings as part of the engagement of a shamanic figure in a particular world. In the picture portrayed above, his teaching, preaching, and prophetic activities were not so much communicating specific ideas as engaging with people as a Galilean shamanic figure; and that engagement took place in a particular political and social setting.

"Kingdom of God" and "Son of Man" Sayings Constituting a Galilean Shamanic Figure

This is not the first attempt to link the "kingdom of God" sayings to Jesus's experiences. Borg suggests that what Jesus said about the kingdom of God becomes clear once seen within the whole of what he was as a spirit person (see 1987, 198–99). Therefore, speaking of the kingdom was a way of speaking about the power of the spirit: "Entering the Kingdom is entering the life of Spirit." Life in the Spirit is life in the kingdom of God, and these two concepts (i.e., *life in the Spirit* and *kingdom of God*) speak of the same reality in Jesus's world. Similarly, Davies proposes that "*the kingdom of God is a form of experience*, an altered state of consciousness directly related to Jesus's career as a healer" (1995, 115, italics original). This does not mean that as a present experience it was clearly defined by the texts (see 1995, 134). In fact, the state was probably "experienced by unique individuals uniquely," Davies says (1995, 136).

Based on the foregoing discussion, the suggestion of this study is that neither the "kingdom of God" nor the "Son of Man" sayings are unconnected to Jesus's shamanic activities and experiences. To be more precise, the above analysis shows that these teachings can be linked to at least three distinct features: first, to the experiences of being a mediator figure by whom and through whom divine power and knowledge are mediated in people's lives; second, to the self-understanding and interpretation of such experiences, as a mediator figure (that is, in becoming a viceroy or representative in doing divine things on earth—such as interacting in sickness and distress, providing divine knowledge, acting as judge and divine evaluator of sociopolitical conditions, and the like). Third, the "kingdom of God" and "Son of Man" sayings are linked to the cultural dynamics of a (shamanic) figure being experienced as divine agent, broker, or entrepreneur. The first two links account for the features and functions ascribed to the Son of Man in the documents and for the nature of the kingdom of God, which is closely linked to the activities of a Son-of-Man figure. The last link accounts for the random nature and accidental structure of the teachings ascribed to Jesus of Nazareth.

It is suggested, therefore, that in most instances the term *kingdom of God* (or derivatives) can be seen as the *experience of the powerful presence of God in and through the life and activities of Jesus as a shamanic figure.* "Kingdom of God" is a code word, if you like, for the state or condition of God's powerful presence mediated by Jesus's (shamanic) activities, and is closely connected to all his other activities; his talk and his walk were a unity. In short, the kingdom of God can be seen as the experience of the powerful presence of God in the life and activities of a Son of Man who has had direct heavenly encounters. The "Son of Man" describes the self-designation of someone who believed and experienced himself being a broker of divine power and knowledge, and who could act as God's viceroy on earth. The "Son of Man" in the gospel documents does the kind of things that at least some people in the Israelite traditions with visionary experiences, and the consequent transformed self-understanding, do. Once perceived or self-understood as a Son of Man, always a Son of Man.

From this perspective, Jesus was not talking (teaching) about the kingdom of God as either a conception and symbol or as a place or a state in the meanings taken for granted by first-century Israelite people, but about his own encounters of the kingdom of God in personal shamanic experiences and the impact of these experiences on his position as a mediator figure. Within the cycle of meaning of the shamanic experiences, well-known concepts, words, and phases were transformed into the *teachings, preaching,* and *prophetic* sayings of the shamanic figure. This argument can account for the authority of his teaching as well as the unconventional and unsystematic nature of it.

If this understanding of the two major themes in Jesus's teaching, preaching, and prophetic activities is accepted as a reasonable reading of the data, it seems to support the hypothesis that Jesus could indeed have been a Galilean shamanic figure. From what has been presented here, it seems that despite the significance of the imperial setting and the economic/political importance of kingdom language, both "kingdom of God" and "Son of Man" sayings have their origin in the personal ASC experiences of Jesus of Nazareth, in who and what he was as a shamanic figure, and not in any systematic proclamation or anti-imperial sentiments. While they are applied to the concrete conditions of the local Galileans suffering from the power of the Roman empire and the Israelite local elites, both sets of sayings are the product of Jesus's experiences of divine encounters, of his being a viceroy, of his having direct interaction with the divine world, and of his mediating that world to people in the activities of his social personage. Since those activities took place in the imperial setting of first-century Galilee, they speak to the living conditions in their actuality. In this sense, his activities were closely linked to the imperial setting. But there is a sense in which Jesus's "kingdom of God" sayings had nothing to do with who was actually sitting in the seats of power in Rome and Jerusalem, because the kind of kingdom he was talking about was not intended to overthrow that kind of kingdom. What Jesus had to say as a shamanic figure certainly had social and political implications, and this way of living surely had serious consequences. But if it had been a systematic anti-imperial program, it was well disguised.

Conclusion

It should be emphasized that this is not another attempt to put what the Gospel authors have said into meaningful words here in our world (ontological monism), but by means of the shamanic model this is an attempt to say what we here can make of what they were saying there in ancient Palestine. Thus, "kingdom of God" and "Son of Man" sayings are not in the first instance about known entities or recognizable features or figures in our world, but an expression of cultural realities and experiences in their world. They are not and can not be known in themselves but can by means of cross-cultural models (such as the shamanic complex) be understood and explained as culturally unique manifestations of homoversals there.

The suggestion of this chapter is that if the "kingdom of God" and "Son of Man" sayings are placed within the framework of the shamanic hypothesis, they can be seen as two sides of the same coin expressing who and what Jesus of Nazareth was as a Galilean shamanic figure. The sayings were not used to describe two entities but, it is suggested, both were used to describe the activities and experiences of Jesus as shamanic figure. Both sets of sayings have their origins in the sphere of visionary experiences and were, therefore, inscribed in Jesus's cycle of meaning. Seen in this way, the content and meaning of the terms *kingdom of God* and *Son of Man* are not simply given or drawn from tradition or the past, but created (or re-created) in the use by a Galilean (Israelite) shamanic figure. That is to say, they were created in the life and activities of a shamanic figure in a particular (Israelite) setting and are not simply the product of a teacher, prophet, or preacher teaching, transmitting, or relaying existing material from earlier tradition.

If the question is, about what kind of figure were such teaching, preaching, and prophetic activities ascribed? then the answer here is: they could well have belonged to the life of a Galilean shamanic figure. In this view, the content of what Jesus said cannot be divorced from who and what he was as a social personage and historical figure. Thus, instead of seeing Jesus as a teacher who, in addition to some other topics, also taught about the kingdom of God and communicated about the Son of Man, this study sees Jesus as a shamanic figure who also spoke and taught, and what he had to say was closely related to who and what he was.

In terms of this analysis, the dichotomy between teaching and healing does not exist and cannot be defended, not even to claim that Jesus was primarily a healer who also taught. He was a shamanic figure for whom teaching and healing together constituted who and what he was as a social personage. It is likely that precisely such sayings would have been ascribed to, and belonged to, the life of a shamanic figure; and if understood by means of the lenses of the shamanic complex, both the "kingdom of God" and "Son of Man" sayings seem to support the hypothesis of this study.

AUTHENTICITY PARADIGM

Jesus was a teacher of sorts who had something to say, teach or preach

Approach:

Analysis follow the history of traditions

Topical arrangement of unsystematic sayings

"Talking head"

Search for authentic sayings imperative

A history-of-ideas approach: focus on ideas divorced from concrete setting

Ontological monism the vehicle for making sense over here of their words then and there

About the kingdom of God:

Kingdom of God is either place or thing

Categorized lists according to topics

Kingdom of God: present, future, not yet

In search of a referent: metaphor, symbol, or concept

About the son of man:

Son of man: danialic and non-danialic; present or future

Son of man is either circumlocution ("I") or reference to Daniel's heavenly being

CULTURAL BUNDUBASHING

Jesus was Galilean shamanic figure who taught in addition to and as part of other functions

---

Diagram 10.2: Summary of "Kingdom of God" and "Son of Man" Sayings

CHAPTER 11

Constituting a Galilean Shamanic Figure by Means of Infancy Narratives

Introduction

A BIOGRAPHY COVERS THE life of a person but might ordinarily start with her or his birth. Being conceived and born are normal human phenomena (homoversals), but the cultural accounts about such events are far from uniform. Therefore, the infancy narratives—which traditionally cover the conception, the birth, and the early childhood stories of Jesus of Nazareth—will be considered as normal human phenomena in cultural garb.

Some texts claim a divine conception of his mother without any interference by a male, while other texts ascribe a normal birth to him as a preexisting divine being. The actual birth accounts in Matthew and Luke contain several smaller events or claims about the state of affairs that make up these accounts. These include references to:

- the place of birth (Bethlehem);

- the date of birth (during a census by Quirinius, 6 or 7 CE or during Herod's reign, prior to 4 BCE);

- the Davidic ancestry and genealogy;

- a postbirth visitation by foreigners (by magi who were guided by a star in Matthew, and by shepherds directed by an angel in Luke);

- the killing of children by Herod.

These episodes are accompanied, on the one hand, by the virgin-birth claims and, on the other hand, by the single report in Luke's Gospel about Jesus at the age of twelve as a superchild in the temple. The discussion of these three sets of stories (first the actual birth-related stories, then the virgin-birth claims, and last the childhood account) will follow the same pattern. The first will be an indication how each set of stories is treated in the authenticity paradigm, then how such stories could form part of the life of a shamanic figure, and lastly, what light they shine on such a life.

The Birth Stories

The overarching impression of most of the discussions of a historical nature regarding Jesus's birth accounts is that the data are consistently treated as reports about events that actually took place (or did not take place because of inconsistent or insufficient evidence). There is very little evidence that the data are treated as data from a distant cultural system that might contain different kinds of information. The challenge from the side of cultural bundubashing is to see how the data can be interpreted as belonging to the life of a Galilean shamanic figure while doing justice to the cultural beliefs and convictions of the time.

The Birth Stories in the Authenticity Paradigm

The infancy narratives in Matthew and Luke are so dissimilar and even contradictory that the Jesus Seminar not only claims they "must have been composed independently of one another," but also that they are considered the last part of the gospel tradition to have been created and therefore consist mostly of fictional stories (Funk & The Jesus Seminar 1998, 502, 533). On the side of the Schweitzerstrasse, there is generally speaking a trust in the authenticity of the canonical Gospels, or at least an argument that the specific texts go back to traditions earlier than the Gospels or indeed to earlier events. In addition, the category of the supernatural is liberally applied in these accounts to ensure that the historicity of specific episodes can be protected. The surprising aspect about the current authenticity debate is that this is where members of the Schweitzerstrasse often agree that what is presented does not reflect historical reality but literary creations.[1]

---

1. Discussion from the sides of the Schweitzerstrasse includes Brown (1977) and, more

The pattern in the authenticity paradigm repeats itself over and over in dealing with the different elements belonging to the birth accounts. The texts are appropriated with the aim of establishing what actually happened at Jesus's birth. The one surprising feature, however, is that in some of these episodes even members of the Schweitzerstrasse find it difficult to salvage some of the stories by means of intellectual gymnastics or supernatural intervention. Four features characteristic of the approach in the authenticity paradigm will briefly be mentioned.

One, the birth accounts are read as reports about Jesus's birth. For example, on his alleged Davidic ancestry, although conclusions again run apart between the Schweitzerstrasse and the Wredebahn, the same objective is pursued, namely, to weigh the testimonies in order to determine whether in fact he was or was not from Davidic ancestry. Given the present status of the data about Jesus's Davidic descent, Miller argues that it is impossible to say one way or the other whether Jesus actually was a descendent of David (2003, 187). On the side of the Schweitzerstrasse, Brown is more confident that although certainty is not possible, such a claim can be maintained (see 1977, 511). The point is not to engage in the specific arguments here but to show that up to the minutest detailed element, the accounts are treated as potential reports about the actual conditions or states of affairs.

Two, the different textual accounts on matters of detail are compared in search of the authentic nuggets. For example, if the texts are read as potential reports about Jesus's place of birth, not even Brown can reconcile the discrepancies between Matthew's version that Jesus was born in Bethlehem because his parents were living there (2:2, 5, 8, 16) and Luke (2:1–6), who provides the excuse of a census that brought them to Bethlehem (see 1977, 513–16). In his view, the evidence for a birth in Bethlehem is rather weak. The shift of birthplace to Bethlehem (from Nazareth, which was his hometown), Theissen and Merz say, is "a result of religious fantasy and imagination" (1998, 165) because according to Scripture, the Messiah had to be born in Bethlehem. When read as a report about Jesus's place of birth, critical scholarship has clearly indicated that there are serious problems to accept the Bethlehem suggestion offered

---

recently, Theissen and Merz (see 1998, 153–66, 194–95); and Meier (see 1991, 208–52). A recent publication from the Wredebahn is the very comprehensive study by Miller (2003), while the Jesus Seminar publication on the acts of Jesus can also be consulted (see Funk & The Jesus Seminar 1998, 497–526).

by Matthew and Luke (see Miller 2003, 181–83.). But are they reports testifying about his place of birth?

Three, individual scenes are treated as reports about events or phenomena at the birth of Jesus and evaluated for their potential historicity. The best examples include Matthew's story about the magi and the star that led them to Bethlehem. Few reports in the infancy narratives have attracted more attention than this one from scholars searching for a natural basis for the report about the star.[2] Even Brown finds the story of a star moving to Jerusalem and then south to Bethlehem, and coming to rest above a specific house, an extraordinary and miraculous story that has no factual basis (see 1977, 36). The point, however, is that the report is read as if it reports about an actual astronomical phenomenon, and since this cannot be determined, the second-best option is followed in ascribing the story to literary creation.

Therefore, fourth, what cannot be pinned to the birth of Jesus as historical is considered much later literary creation. For example, read with a view to Jesus's actual ancestry, there is widespread agreement that the two available genealogies of Jesus (Matt 1:1–16; Luke 3:23–38) are not actually family lists but were probably created by the evangelists (see Brown 1977, 66; Miller 2003, 71–85). As Sanders says about the birth narratives in general, they represent the "clearest cases of invention" (1993, 85). What cannot be pinned to the life of Jesus, must have been fictional literary inventions ascribed to him at a much later stage.

In summary, by comparing the texts, searching for authentic kernels (or "nuggets of information that can qualify as historical," to use Miller's phrase [2003, 178]) and arguing about the authenticity of specific texts, the Schweitzerstrasse and the Wredebahn each display there own version of the authenticity paradigm, which attempts to identify *what was historical* about the birth accounts. In other words, the texts are analyzed as reports about extratextual events (such as Jesus's conception and birth in Bethlehem) or about states of affairs (such as his Davidic ancestry) during Jesus's conception, birth and childhood— the texts are constantly treated as testimonies.

---

2. All these studies search for a scientific explanation for the astronomical phenomena. The three most common theories identify the star with a supernova, a comet, or an unusual conjunction of the planets (see Brown 1977, 170–73; Stenschke 2002; Miller 2003, 102–3).

Cultural bundubashing offers a different way of dealing with the data. Once the tyranny of the authenticity paradigm is rejected and historicity is not longer equated with "it actually happened like that," or with, "if it belongs to Jesus's life it must have happened as described," it becomes easy to see that many of these episodes can be ascribed to the biography of Jesus without claims that they actually happened or that they describe features of Jesus's actual birth. In fact, the complex notion of historicity adopted here can tolerate events and phenomena being part of the cultural processes during Jesus's lifetime without claiming that they actually happened as described. Things can be historical in the life of the Galilean shamanic Jesus without accepting that they were events or phenomena in the world "out there," because cultural bundubashing is also interested in the meaning of the data.

Jesus's Genealogy

As I have said, while most of the clues for treating these textual sections as evidence for how things were in the life of the Galilean shaman are already available in the debate (Matt 1:1–17; Luke 3:23–38), they are not used to pursue such an argument. In cultural bundubashing, the texts can be read as literary deposits of at least three cultural processes, and the question is whether these texts can be used to establish something about how it was during Jesus's lifetime. Are they perhaps evidence that during his lifetime Jesus as shamanic figure was credited with a special genealogy? The following insights, when taken into account, suggest indeed something like that.

Shamans in many cultures often claim (or are ascribed) an ancestral pedigree going back to the founding fathers or shamans (see Kalweit 1992, 7–17). The same social dynamics could have been part of the legitimation of a shamanic figure (a *son of God* or a *son of man*) in the Israelite tradition in Galilee. It is, therefore, conceivable that already during his lifetime in Galilee there were cultural processes by means of which claims about his genealogy were credited to his biography. Cross-cultural parallels suggest that such a cultural process could have been part of his life in Galilee.

This is supported by a feature of ancient Israelite (and Greco-Roman) genealogies that is well known in the literature, namely, that they were not family lists but were employed to establish identity and undergird status (see Brown 1977, 65). The example of Zadok's genealogy referred to by Miller (see 2003, 186) perfectly illustrates this point that it was designed to offer legitimacy for his priesthood (as high priest, he required an Aaronite pedigree) and was no record of his ancestors. They were at best "certificates of status," as Van Aarde calls them (2001, 149). Such family registers had the purpose to set out Jesus's social status and ascribed honor as Malina suggests (see 2001a, 32). In that society they were testimonies of the male's status as bearer of rights in the community in telling who belonged socially with whom, and ascribing a social standing (see Malina & Rohrbaugh 1992, 25).[3] As Brown emphasizes, it was possible to have conflicting genealogies of the same person if those genealogies served different functions (1977, 85).[4]

It is therefore not surprising that significant public figures were attributed with special births or childhood experiences in the ancient and first-century Mediterranean world. If this insight is already well known about such texts, why try to use them for what they never intended to be, or cannot offer, namely, information about actual ancestors?

It should furthermore be taken into account that for purposes of historical reconstruction, "only the last three generations in genealogies from oral societies are likely to be accurate" (Malina & Rohrbaugh 1992, 25). In the case of Jesus's grandfather, the sources do not even agree two generations back. According to Matthew (1:16), Jesus's paternal grandfather was Jacob; but according to Luke (3:23), it was Eli. A detailed comparison of the two genealogies shows that neither is a historical record of actual ancestors (see Miller 2003, 71–85 for a discussion of the historical problems), and none of the arguments to reconcile them is successful (see Brown 1977, 503–4).

---

3 Malina and Rohrbaugh point out that in antiquity "the description of the birth and childhood of notable personages always was based on the adult status and roles held by the person. It was believed that personality never changed and that a child was something like a miniature adult. . . . Great personages were seen to have certain characteristics from the very moment of birth, which remained with them throughout life" (1992, 27–28). Or as Brown explains: "It is common instinct in many cultures and literatures to make the boy the father of the man by creating boyhood stories for great figures, stories that anticipate the greatness of the subject" (1977, 481–82).

4. This is very much in line with what Van Unnik says about the history writing in antiquity in general: "it is beyond doubt that in antiquity history-writing was not an art for its own sake. It was always aimed at something; it wanted to be useful for ethical or political instruction, to give amusement or to enhance the glory of families, towns or individuals" (1973, 12).

It is therefore in principle, and factually, impossible that they could contain the actual information about his family tree. Why then treat them as family lists with the question of finding possible nuggets of historical information if they were not different family lists but different certificates of status and honor? And as such, they could have belonged to his life story from very early on.

Davidic Descent

Sanders points out: "No one could trace his genealogy for forty-two generations, but if he could, he would find that he had *millions* of ancestors (one million is passed at the twentieth generation)" (1993, 86). The import of this remark is particularly significant when dealing with claims about Jesus's Davidic descent.

If David was indeed a historical figure, not only Jesus of Nazareth but most of his first followers could probably have made the same claim about Davidic descent.[5] It was not done not because they could not make such a claim, but because Jesus's followers were not significant social personages. The historically significant data about Jesus would not be to confirm or deny such a genetic or DNA connection to David, but to confirm the reality and impact of such claims on his life. The point is neither the available text nor that more of the same kind of texts can provide evidence to claim historical probability in this case, as Miller tries to do. The point is plain and simple: no one could claim Davidic ancestry definitively (it was and is impossible), but all could claim it potentially (who would do it for what purposes?).

In view of these insights, the attempts to use the evidence about Davidic ancestry to either establish or deny that Jesus was actually from the house of David is misplaced. It is not on the basis of these or any other textual evidence that it can be established. Neither this evidence nor ten more texts claiming the same feature can be used to establish Davidic ancestry. If it is deemed necessary (such as in the case of a significant social personage), it can be done on the basis of the general principle that people in a given population are all related to long-bygone ancestors, but

---

5. This makes the arguments about possible historical inferences rather obsolete. Not only tens of thousands of people, as Miller says, but most Israelites at the time of Jesus could have claimed some genetic connection to David (see 2003, 187).

this evidence cannot establish Jesus's family origin any more than that of Peter or Paul.

While Jesus's genealogies and Davidic ancestry cannot be taken as a reflection of actual descent, they can be read as historical components making up his public life in Galilee. In a typical shamanic fashion, they can be seen as a reflection of what it was like (what was historical) in the life of such a social personage. Within the cultural dynamics of such figures' lives, certain activities lead to such certificates of legitimation, while such certificates contribute to the social success and greatness of the social personage. In other words, it is easy to see as a cultural event behind these accounts the social legitimation of Jesus by those who were touched by his life and activities. Seen in this way, the Gospel genealogies are not reports about his life but possible constructions of identity and honor during his life.

The events or circumstances of the genealogies' creation are not Jesus's actual conception and birth but the cultural processes associated with his life. There is, however, no way to know for sure whether the present accounts of Jesus's certificates of status existed in their present format during his lifetime, or whether they were only created much later. What remains is that at whatever time they originated, they were from the first not genealogies but certificates of honor and status. In the envisaged process of cultural event, cultural communication, and cultural enscripturation there could have been many developments, and their present format might very well have been formulated in the enscripturation phase. There is, however, by the same token no reason why a genealogy and claims of Davidic descent could not have been part of Jesus's life already in Galilee. This is suggested by the reported disputes over his Davidic descent (see Mark 12:35-37 par.).

In view of the cultural purpose they serve, it is a misreading to even consider whether the genealogies contain any direct factual historical information about Jesus's ancestry. They do not contain direct factual information because they could not—that is not what they were intended for if they were certificates of honor. But that does not make them historically obsolete. They do not contain historical information, but they are themselves historical information for his life as a shamanic figure. The Wredebahn is correct to assert that they do not contain historical information; but the Wredebahn scholars are wrong in simply attributing them to the literary invention of the evangelists. In light of the foregoing arguments, the Gospel genealogies could have been and probably were residues of cultural processes activated by Jesus's life as a shamanic figure and thus could have been part of his career already in Galilee (see Craffert 2005a for a detailed discussion of these issues).

Birth in Bethlehem?

Both versions of the birth narrative contain the claim that Jesus was born in Bethlehem (e.g., Matt 2:1; Luke 2:4). Taken together with the above features and read within the framework of cultural bundubashing, these claims can be treated as part of the certificates of status and honor that could have belonged to Jesus's life as shamanic figure in Galilee. Seen in this way, these texts offer information of a different kind, namely, about his life ascribed with a messianic birth. In their current formats they undoubtedly contain elements that originated either during the communication or the enscripturation processes. But they can also be seen as reflecting a historical event during Jesus's life when he was credited with these special features.

The only other place in the canonical Gospels where Bethlehem is mentioned reports a public outcry among the people about Jesus's place of origin. Some ask whether the Christ is to come from Galilee when the Scriptures say he should come from the city of David, namely, Bethlehem (John 7:40–43). It is imaginable that if the label of a Bethlehem birth was attached to this Galilean shamanic figure, not everybody in society would have respected it. If anything, this report from the Gospel of John is an excellent instance of the kind of social processes to be expected in and about the life of a shamanic figure.

Reports about Visions, Dreams, and Angelic Visitations

Both birth accounts are packed with reports about visionary or dream experiences. Matthew structures his plot around dream experiences: Joseph is commanded by an angel in a dream to take Mary as his wife (1:20), an angel directs him in a dream to flee to Egypt (2:13) and again to return to the land of Israel (2:19). The magi are warned in a dream not to return to Herod (2:12). Also Luke's account is structured around angelic visionary experiences: Zechariah experiences a vision in the temple (1:11), Mary experiences a visitation by the angel Gabriel (1:26, 28), and the shepherds are directed to Bethlehem by an angel (2:9). Can there be much doubt about the taken-for-granted cultural codes for understanding these accounts?

Both dream and visionary experiences were natural cultural experiences to first-century people. But the differences between Matthew and Luke as well as the setting within the other elements of legitimation (such as the certificates of honor) suggest that these are not reports about such events prior to Jesus's birth but are part of the legitimation of him as social personage during his lifetime. Indeed, they are stories about him told in terms of the cultural script of the time in which his current position is explicated.

Scholars generally do not seek to explain the dreams and visions of the birth stories as if they actually happened. Instead, it is easily accepted that by means of such cultural events something can be conveyed about a social personage in that world. It is clear both from the differences between Matthew and Luke and from the nature of the events they report about that these scenes could have originated as legitimation accounts or stories about a social personage. The cultural events, therefore, were not the actual dreams or visions (which could have been possible) but the social construction of public character by means of such reports. That this could have been part of a social personage's life is confirmed by the many parallels, as well as by the other elements in these accounts, which all point toward their nature as certificates of honor and status.

What makes this suggestion different from others is that these accounts, while seen as part of the legitimation of Jesus as Galilean shamanic figure, are not taken as literary or mythological creations years down the line. It is suggested here that, similar to the other components making up the birth narratives, these stories of dreams and visions could have been elements in the cultural process right at the heart of his career.

The Bethlehem Star

When they read Matthew's infancy narrative within the authenticity framework, scholars go to great lengths to identify the astronomical phenomenon that could have given rise to the report in Matthew about the magi being directed by a star to a house in Bethlehem (2:2, 9).

It is well known that comets and special stellar constellations were interpreted in antiquity for their political and social implications.[6] The

---

6. It was written that with the death of Alexander the Great, not only an eagle but also a star was seen falling from heaven, and that both were seen going back to heaven carrying another brilliant star (see Talbert 1975, 426).

appearance of anything new or unusual in the heavens was interpreted as a portent about the rulers (see Miller 2003, 104–5 for examples), which led to the belief that the births and deaths of great men were marked by heavenly signs (see Brown 1977, 170–71). Therefore, rulers acted upon specific interpretations of heavenly phenomena.

But this is only part of the story because much *star-talk* in antiquity had nothing to do with the stars and planets up there as we know them today, but with visionary experiences by and about (human) stars down here on earth. Since the heavenly bodies were seen as living beings (angels for Israelite people) that influenced human affairs (see the discussion of the astronomical complex above, pp. 193–96), an episode about magi who were renowned for star gazing, is not out of place in a construction of Jesus's social personage. As indicated earlier, much of the prophetic material in the Gospels ascribed to Jesus connects him with astral prophesy and, therefore, a character report about his social personage could certainly include a connection with other astral prophets or magi. If his public activities started with the baptism scene where Jesus had experienced his first heavenly or astral travels, it is not out of place to connect these astral phenomena to his birth accounts.

Summary

Liberated from the dichotomy of claiming that either events actually took place at the birth of Jesus or were literary creations by the evangelists long after his life, it is possible to treat most of the scenes, episodes, and phenomena in the birth narratives as cultural events or processes in the life of a Galilean shamanic figure. Part of the cultural process included character building and legitimation of the social personage, and that was done, according to these scenes, well within the boundaries of their cultural system.

As cultural events and phenomena, all of the discussed Gospel scenes and phenomena could well have been part of Jesus's life in Galilee, and all, in fact, fit very clearly into the profile of a shamanic figure. That Jesus's life is not unlike the life of other shamanic figures, as shown in this study, is strongly supported by the evidence. As with the rest of the Gospel accounts, this is exactly how the reports portray these elements: as if they were normally and naturally part of his life.

Mary's Virginal Conception of Jesus

Despite many differences in detail and setting, Matthew and Luke agree on at least three aspects, which all point in the same direction. Mary became pregnant while she was still a virgin, Joseph was not responsible for the pregnancy, and Mary was impregnated by the Holy Spirit. Luke explicitly states that Mary was a virgin (1:17), while it is mentioned in Matthew (1:23) as a quotation from Isaiah 7, which was given to Joseph in a dream. Joseph's innocence in this pregnancy is expressed in Matthew (1:19) by the remark that Joseph wanted to resolve the unwanted pregnancy by quietly divorcing Mary; Joseph's innocence is noted as well by the extended explanation from an angel about why Joseph should not divorce Mary quietly (1:20–25). In accordance to the angel's message, Joseph then does not have sex with Mary until Jesus is born. Luke (1:34) exonerates Joseph indirectly when Mary states to the angel that she cannot be pregnant because she has no husband. Luke (1:35) claims that Mary was impregnated when the Holy Spirit came over her, and when the power of the Most High overshadowed her, while Matthew (1:18) simply states that Mary was found pregnant from a spirit (the Holy Spirit).

Together and individually, these testimonies are scrutinized and analyzed in great detail in attempts to answer whether Mary indeed had a virginal conception.[7]

The Virgin Birth Debate in the Authenticity Paradigm

The current debate about Jesus's virginal birth in the framework of the authenticity paradigm is conducted within a framework adhering to the same interpretive principles. Both sides, the Wredebahn and the Schweitzerstrasse, appropriate the sources as if they were reports about Mary's conception without any male intervention. The evidence is, therefore, scrutinized in order to determine whether there is sufficient testimony to conclude that Jesus of Nazareth was indeed conceived with or without a human father.

On the side of the Wredebahn, strong emphasis is placed on the argument that the only testimonies are relatively late. As Miller says: "Since the earliest parts of the New Testament (Paul, Q, and Mark) show no trace of

---

7. The terms *virginal birth* and *virginal conception* are used interchangeably in reference to the claim that Jesus was born to a virgin who had conceived him without intercourse with a biological father.

it, the belief is unlikely to have existed long before Luke wrote his gospel" (2003, 205). Within this scheme of things, evidence from either the traditional or evangelical phase (Phases II and III) cannot belong to the life of Jesus. Lengthy discussions about whether Matthew actually meant "virgin" or only "young woman," and whether conception *by* a spirit would exclude a human father are all directed to answer only one question: "is Matthew using these words in their normal sense or is he describing a miracle?" (2003, 202). Is the virgin birth supported by the testimonies or not?

The supporting argument for why the virgin birth is not a historical fact is based on the historiographical principle that demands public knowledge for any historical claim. Miller rules out the possibility of finding such evidence: "By its very nature a virgin birth is the kind of phenomenon for which there can be no public evidence";[8] and Miller therefore concludes: "In short, since a virginal conception cannot be an object of public knowledge, the virgin birth of Jesus cannot be historical knowledge" (2003, 210; see also Funk & The Jesus Seminar 1998, 504).[9]

On the side of the Schweitzerstrasse, there is, generally speaking, a trust in the authenticity of the canonical Gospels or at least an argument that the specific texts go back earlier, or to events earlier than the Gospels themselves. In addition, the category of the supernatural is applied liberally in order to ensure that the historicity of specific episodes is protected. Here one also finds the argument of public knowledge, but employed to confirm the reality of the virgin birth. For example, the truth of the claim that Jesus was virginally conceived by the power of the Holy Spirit, Meier says, "was hardly verifiable even when Jesus appeared on the public stage as an adult, is a fortiori not open to verification today" (1991, 230)—because, in his view, it refers to a supernatural or divine intervention. Although this is also the conclusion of Brown, he makes it clear that, in his view, it is very likely that the virginal conception stories originated because "that is what really took place" (1973, 65; see also Wright 1999a, 176).

---

8. See also Crossan and Reed, who argue: "But a virginal conception depends, positively, on the mother's word and, negatively, on the father's assurance" (2001, 48). Virginal conception, according to this position, is an event that cannot be verified historically.

9. The signs of ethnocentrism are inscribed in the very method of distinguishing between an exegetical and historical dimension. The first is what the stories mean to their original authors and audiences, and the second, "which parts of the stories are historically reliable" (Miller 2003, 1). "Historically reliable" means (as is clear from Miller's exposition) that which concurs with "our" view of reality.

Public evidence in these arguments is the equivalent of a reality check or 'how things are in our world,' which characterizes positivistic science and historiography. It is an example of what the anthropologist Delaney describes:

> The construction of the problem as an example of a type is a way of assimilating another culture to our own, a way of saying it is not so different from ours. The motive may be admirable, but the method is not; it glosses over significant differences and blinds us to the peculiarities of our own beliefs. (1986, 501)

The infancy narratives in general and the virgin birth reports in particular are appropriated as reports about Jesus's actual birth. This is explicitly the case on the side of the Schweitzerstrasse and implicitly on the side of the Wredebahn, which uses the reports to deny knowledge about Jesus's birth, and dates these reports very late. Both sides of the debate take it as far as this approach to the historical problem can go. However, as Stevens shows, perhaps "we misread the infancy narratives if we understand them as asserting Mary's physiological virginity" (1990, 49). Cultural bundu-bashing (which accepts neither the tyranny that what goes back to the life of Jesus must actually have happened as described, nor that texts from an alien cultural system are reporting about events or phenomena that necessarily makes sense in our world) poses different historical questions.

The following historical questions are to be addressed: Read as texts within their own cultural system and system of reality, what were the virgin birth reports about? What did Luke and Matthew probably believe about what they were claiming? How could we possibly react to their claims from the point of view of our views of reality? Can these reports plausibly be seen as reports about how things were in the life of Jesus as a shamanic figure in Galilee? In short, what are Luke's and Matthew's stories evidence for?

A Special Birth as a Confirmation of Shamanic Status

Typically, a shaman receives a calling, which means that there is a specific onset of the shamanic career. Moreover, in many cultures the career of a shaman contains references to the "mythical" origin of the first shamans in that culture or to a special birth of some kind. It is a historical and cultural fact that shamans are often subjected to a special birth or infancy narratives.

According to the Limbu tribe of eastern Nepal, the first shaman descended from the sky. He was sent by the creator god and appeared in the rays of the sun and descended to earth where he landed in a great body of water. He swam ashore and wandered the earth (see Jones 1976, 32). According to the traditions of the Cuna, who live on Panamanian islands in the Caribbean, their first shaman arrived on a golden disk that landed in a treetop. Later, ten more babies arrived in a similar way, and they were raised by virgins and became the first shamans of their tribe. The Buryats, around Lake Baikal in Siberia, claim that the first shaman among them was born after a sexual encounter between an eagle and a sleeping woman under a tree. The eagle had intercourse with her and soon a son was born (see Kalweit 1992, 11). He was the first shaman while, according to another variant of the story, that honor belongs to her. It is significant that one finds variant stories within the same cultural and societal setting. The idea of a virgin or a "clean, good woman" who has nothing "dark about her, and no shadow could fall on her body or bones" (1992, 11) visited and impregnated by a divine being is not uncommon in such stories about shamans. These are not reports about how things were at the actual conception or birth of the shaman but are elements in the life story of the shaman in real life. In fact, the notion that sexual intercourse can occur between mortals and supernatural beings is one of the most widespread of human beliefs (see Lewis 1989, 51).

Ancient literature abounds with infancy narratives about important men in which divine entities participated in the generation of that hero. These include stories about historical figures and mythical figures. In some instances, the god is disguised as a snake (the case of Atia, the mother of Augustus, where Apollo appeared as a snake); in another instance, Zeus appeared disguised as a golden shower (in the case of the conception of Perseus, who was also conceived virginally).[10] Two standard features of these Hellenistic life stories, Miller points out, are "1) the hero is the son of a god; 2) the greatness of the hero can be seen early in his life" (2003, 133). The pattern of these stories is similar to that of the first shamans: divine conception, special births and often a virgin mother. Like that of shamanic figures in other cultures, these should not be read as reports about actual

---

10. These stories are well known in New Testament research (see, e.g., Riley 1997, 39–41, 74–70; Crossan 1998, 28–29; van Tilborg & Chatelion Counet 2000, 236–39; Funk & The Jesus Seminar 1998, 501–7).

events or states of affairs but as historical moments of ascribing identity and honor to the social personage.

Miller points out that Iamblichus's *Life of Pythagoras* illustrates that "some ancient people knew full well that stories about a god who fathers a child were created to explain a man's extraordinary achievements" (2003, 151). The fact that their proof was the man's virtue or greatness of soul rather than something about the biological condition or sexual history of the mother does not take away the strong belief that some mortals were in fact believed to be fathered by a divine being. The significance of one of the examples from the ancient world should not escape our attention. The honor of a special birth was bestowed on Pythagoras during a celebration of his birthday; that is, during his lifetime he was honored and credited with a special birth (see Miller 2003, 151).

If Jesus was a first-century Galilean shamanic figure, the following aspects give context and profile to the virgin-birth accounts. That is, these aspects are helpful in understanding them as historical accounts within a specific historical setting and culture, and in expressing the significance of their cultural experiences about Jesus as a social personage while illuminating the cultural dynamics of the events and accounts in their setting. Such accounts, it is suggested, existed within the cycle of meaning of their worldview.

Ancient Sexology on Conception and Pregnancy

Van Tilborg remarks that modern exegetes have, generally speaking, a very poor idea of the enormous differences between our knowledge of sexology and that what was taken as state of the art in antiquity (in van Tilborg & Chatelion Counet 2000, 241 n. 112). In fact, in an ethnocentric way it is far too often taken for granted that all people, past and present, make the same causal connection between sexual intercourse and pregnancy that we as late twentieth and early twenty-first century people make. It is sobering to realize with Bryson that "at the beginning of the twentieth century, and for some years beyond, the best scientific minds in the world couldn't actually tell you, in any meaningful way, where babies come from" (2003, 351). This remark makes sense in light of Bryson's overview of the history of the discovery of the cell and the stuff of life. Our own not-so-distant ancestors did not have the mechanics right in their claims about conception. This becomes particularly clear in the above debate and will be illustrated here.

SEXUAL INTERCOURSE AND PROCREATION

The fact that first-century Mediterranean Israelites made a connection between sexual intercourse and procreation (as we twenty-first-century Western educated people do) does not mean that they made the same connection as all other people. In fact, very few people on the planet make the same connection as we do. The relevant facts of the last hundred and fifty years of biological research states: "Any complete human being begins life by the union of an ovum from a female human being and a spermatozoon from a male one" (Peacocke 2000, 62). This "duo-genetic model" (Delaney 1986, 509) of procreation proposed by modern scientific theories is very young and shared by a small percentage of the world's population.

According to this (modern) *sperm–ovum theory of conception*, procreation takes place when, as the result of sexual intercourse (and nowadays, also by means of *in vitro* fertilization), a male sperm cell fertilizes an ovum in the Fallopian tubes. In fact, prior to the discovery of the microscope in the seventeenth century, it was known that women have ovaries, but not ova (see Van der Horst 1994, 205).[11] Consequently, there were many theories about procreation, but none that granted women the role of co-creators and equal partners.[12]

This is also the case with many other people on the planet. Prior to contact with Western missionaries, the Polynesians of Bellona Island in the British Solomon Islands, for example, believed that children come from the abode of the gods, which lay somewhere below the eastern horizon. They were brought by ancestral spirits and implanted in the womb of a woman. A woman became pregnant not because of copulation, but because the deities and ancestors of her husband had sent her offspring; the Bellonese believed a marital alliance produced progeny "*not* by or because of the man's copulation with the woman, but because the patrilineal

11. In fact, the *discovery* of the ovum by Von Baer in 1827 follows the invention of the microscope by many decades (see Delaney 1986, 508).

12. Despite this scientific recognition that a woman provides half the genetic material in each pregnancy (obviously plus being the *container*), there is not yet a recognition of this fact in much of Western popular speech and attitudes. In a remark such as, "Speaking as a *man*, the act of procreation takes on a divine dimension," paternity as a cultural construct still does not acknowledge the equal role of women as co-creators of life (see Stevens 1990, 50–52).

ancestors and the deities of the patriline" were pleased with the alliance (Monberg 1975, 36). In their view, sexual intercourse was a social game, while the procreation of children was a serious matter involving the activities of deities and ancestors. This can be referred to as the *spirit-child theory of conception*.

Evidence is available for a similar notion about procreation among Tully River Blacks in Australia. They are ignorant about physiological paternity and ascribe pregnancy to a variety of causes, such as sitting over a fire while roasting a particular black bean given to the woman by the prospective father, or she may have dreamed of having a child put inside her (see Spiro 1968, 242).

It is widely acknowledged that in biblical literature there is no suggestion of a divine being masquerading as a human lover impregnating Mary (see, e.g., Funk 1996, 288, 294; van Tilborg & Chatelion Counet 2000, 241). If deities, however, could affect all other natural phenomena known to humans, they surely could impregnate earthly women.[13] It was unusual and extraordinary but not impossible or *supernatural*. In fact, Israelite history is full of women whose wombs have been opened or shut by God—these include the infertile mothers of Jacob (Gen 25:21), Samson (Judg 13:2–25), and Samuel (1 Sam 1:1–20), whose wombs had been opened (see Miller 2003, 224–25 for details). Especially if the close connection between spirit (*pneuma*) and semen (semen as "hot pneuma in moist matter" or as "bundled force" discussed earlier; Chapter 6) is taken into account, it is a small step, by means of a seed-child theory of conception, to the idea of a divine being impregnating a woman (the divine paternity of a child). Therefore, it is necessary to consider first-century Mediterranean beliefs about sex.

FIRST-CENTURY MEDITERRANEAN SEXOLOGY

It is not surprising that ancient Mediterranean people also had several views on both the causes of pregnancy and the processes leading to it. The ovum theory of conception was not one of the options available in their

---

13. But it should not be assumed that within the cultural logic of first-century Mediterranean people such a divine conception would have resulted from the god actually having intercourse with the woman. This displays our modern prejudice regarding conception because, as Plutarch points out, the act could be accomplished through the agency of the spirit of the god (see Talbert 1975, 433 n. 66 for details).

inventory of explanations. When they discussed reproduction, it was done by means of at least three other theories.

One was the so-called *double-seed theory*, which maintained that both men and women contributed sperm or semen. By all accounts there was, however, a qualitative difference between the semen of men and of women (see Van der Horst 1994, 207–15). While the idea of the female sperm was widespread, it occupied a lower position and in some cases a very inferior role as expressed, for example, in the distinction that men (with greater bodily heat) could boil blood to become semen, while women could only produce menstrual blood. As Van der Horst indicates, it is probably this theory which lies behind the notion of Sarah's seminal emission (Heb 11:11).

A second theory can be called the "monogenetic theory" of procreation (Delaney 1986, 496), which restricted the role of a woman to that of a container: "Her reproductive system is metaphorically transformed into the language of the land, waiting to be ploughed, waiting to receive potent blobs of power, capable of causing life, but needing the passive receptivity required for the germination, growth and nurturing" (Vorster 2002a, 295). Not only was this the dominant conception of procreation in early Christianity, but it was embedded in a whole set of assumptions about human physiology and ontology (see Vorster 2002a, 290–97).[14] What the man deposits, in this viewpoint, is a "seed-child" for which the mother only provides the container for it to grow, and so this theory can therefore be called the *seed-child theory of conception*.[15] Or, as the first-century Seneca says, "In the semen there is contained the entire record of the man to be" (quoted in Malina 2001a, 147).

This viewpoint was very common even among Western scientists up to medieval times. After the discovery of the microscope in the seventeenth century, one respected Dutch observer claimed that he was convinced he saw "'tiny preformed men' in sperm cells." He called the little beings "humunculi," which confirmed the old idea that "all humans—indeed, all creatures—were simply vastly inflated versions of tiny but incomplete precursor beings" (Bryson 2003, 333). This viewpoint is understandable

14. Delaney shows that this view was not confined to Christianity and indeed continued to dominate in some Mediterranean circles until the late twentieth century (see 1986, 496–500).

15. This point is further confirmed by the fact that in antiquity in general, and in the Israelite tradition in particular, infertility was always due to a defect in the female (see Miller 2003, 225).

in the light of ancient theories about the coming-into-being of semen as a concoction of blood and vital spirit boiled in the male body.

The third theory of sexology in the ancient Mediterranean world was that of spontaneous fertilization. Examples, as mentioned by Aristotle, include fertilization via "dew, grass, dung, figs, fir, mud, putrefaction, sand, rock hollows, sea-water, snow, vinegar, wax and wood," and van Tilborg adds: "the shadow of the power of the Most High would not really be out of place in this list" (2000, 241 n. 112). The kind of worldview belief behind these examples is that of a shadow as not merely the place where sunlight cannot penetrate but as a power in its own right or as the soul of a person or at least as a very vital part thereof. In a study on ancient beliefs about the power of shadows to heal (compare Peter's shadow in Acts 5:15), to injure, or influence, Van der Horst shows that there is enough evidence that the power of the shadow was also believed to include sexual efficacy: "if a shadow can damage or heal a person, why should the shadow of God not be able to impregnate a woman?" (1976/77, 211–12).

From the point of view of the duo-genetic model, however, all the above theories about pregnancy are misguided. Just as most people from the first-century Mediterranean world believed their theories about conception, many if not most of them firmly believed that some significant persons were indeed fathered by a god. However, the firm belief of people that an eagle or an ancestral spirit or a divine being fathered a child is not sufficient evidence that some people, past or present, were in fact conceived in any way other than by means of the fertilization of an ovum by a sperm cell. That is to say, they were wrong about the biology of conception and pregnancy that they subscribed to, which does not mean they were irrational. Such theories may have made perfect sense within specific cultural assumptions but cannot be taken as description about actual pregnancies or as evidence for events "out there" for all others. They are, at best, cultural representations about common human phenomena.

Given the notions prevalent about procreation in the first-century Mediterranean world, it would be fair to say that people of that time firmly believed that the Holy Spirit could indeed have impregnated Mary. Or, put more correctly, they firmly believed a (Holy) Spirit could implant a divine seed-baby in the female container called Mary. If the idea of *pneuma* as the life-giving source of semen (the creating fluid) and the notion of God as the ultimate creator of everything are included, it is easy to see that this theory plays a role in the description of Mary as a container for a divine seed-baby. But there is more of the cultural script assumed in Mary's conception. This conclusion finds support in the notion of paternity implied in these reports.

Sexual Intercourse and Divine Paternity

If there is not necessarily a link between sexual intercourse and pregnancy in all of the above theories (pregnancy can be the result of various other factors, according to these theories), there definitely is not a direct link between sexual intercourse and views about paternity.

The above-mentioned theories might be ignorant about certain biological realities; this does not mean they are either irrational or not culturally real accounts about paternity (see discussion in Spiro 1968, 244–45), because paternity does not necessarily describe a physiological link between a man and a child but is a cultural construct about a relationship.[16] Paternity in the face of the duo-genetic model can be established by means of a DNA test because it is directly linked to biological offspring. Irrespective of biological conception, divine paternity can be claimed without such a direct link. This realization that paternity is a conceptual and social relationship and not a physical one needs to be grasped in the debate about Jesus's so-called divine conception.

Delaney suggests that Mary's virginal conception should be seen as a spiritualized version of the folk theory (called the monogenetic theory of procreation) that has dominated the West for millennia. It should be read as a story not about physiological procreation but about paternity, and paternity is a cultural construct that is neither about the physiological link between a man and a child nor based on an awareness of the link between sexual intercourse and pregnancy: "Even though the father is divine, the meaning of paternity is the same as for a human father; even though Mary is unique among women, the meaning of maternity is epitomized by her" (1986, 496). Paternity is not the semantic equivalent of maternity (the physical link between a mother and the child that she bears). Regardless of whether conception occurs by seminal word or physical seed, it remains that the child comes only from one source—the father (see 1986, 500).

---

16. The notion of paternity as cultural construct is not precisely in line with scientific knowledge about procreation: "Paternity is a concept, the meaning of which is derived from its interrelations with other concepts and beliefs; it is not a kind of categorical entity, the presence or absence of which can be established empirically" (Delaney 1986, 495).

Four Accounts of Divine Parentage

At least three points of agreement between them confirm that the virgin-birth accounts were about Jesus's divine parentage: Mary was a virgin, Joseph was not involved, and the Holy Spirit impregnated her. Despite some scholarly attempts to show that Paul and John did not know about the virginal conception, Paul and John nevertheless agree about Jesus's divine origin or parentage.[17]

In so far as the first chapter of the Gospel of John (1:1) can be taken as a notion about Jesus's birth, it claims that Jesus was a son of God from all eternity (see Miller 2003, 233). His turning into human form can be seen, just like the appearances of other shamanic figures, at his point of birth. But this is claiming little more than that a divine seed-baby was placed into the container, Mary, the virgin.

According to Van Aarde (2001, 104–5), Paul's view of Jesus being the eternal child of God who had experienced a brief life and remarkable suffering because he was born of a woman cannot be reconciled with the idea of a divine birth (although I prefer to talk about his divine conception and paternity). But this is not the only plausible interpretation. While Paul agrees that Jesus was born of a woman (see Gal 4:4), he also holds that Jesus was already at birth the preexisting child of God. Paul can thus be read as verbalizing one way in which a resurrected hero (a continuous living shamanic figure) came into the world, namely, as an eternal son of God, born by means of a normal birth.

The monogenetic theory of procreation makes males the sole powers of creativity and the authors of life who ensure that the patriline is continued. A virgin (a female who has not been filled with a male's deposits) is just another way of confirming that the patriline—in this case a divine patriline—is continued (see Stevens 1990, 50). Therefore, the suggestion is that conception by means of a divine seed-baby as well as a *normal birth* of a preexisting divine being are two sides of the same monogenetic theory of procreation. Paul's understanding of the birth of Jesus as a preexisting divine being is just a cultural variant of Matthew's and Luke's divine-conception accounts.

---

17. It is "such an important topic" that Paul "would have referred to it" if he had known about it, because "a virgin birth is not the kind of information one forgets" (Miller 2003, 228; and see Van Aarde 2001, 104).

The four diverse versions of a special birth confirm that birth stories with different emphases developed because they were reporting not about observable events but about the life story of a social personage—they were not about biology but biography, told within the framework of ancient sexology and paternity. None is a historical description of an actual birth or conception; all are, however, cultural accounts about Jesus's life. The question remaining is whether such claims would have been made during Jesus's lifetime.

When read not as testimonies about either Mary's physical condition or Jesus's prebirth existence but as what they are evidence for, all these accounts seem to fit into the pattern or cultural package by means of which social personages (such as heroes) entered the world and exited as immortals. Invention in current historical Jesus research means literary creations long after the fact. The present argument is that the birth accounts were cultural inventions within the framework of specific cultural processes and dynamics. Divine parentage (similar to astral immortality) could be ascribed to a life that was understood and experienced as especially touched by divinity.

If all the biases created by the history of research are bypassed, an interesting question remains whether such stories could have been part of Jesus's life story even while he walked the dust roads of Galilee.

If Paul is taken as an example, it seems clear that such stories could be created when needed (such as Paul's account of Jesus's divine paternity). If Jesus was experienced as a son of God and a son of man because of his shamanic functions, there is no good reason why stories about his divine paternity (and origin) could not have been circulated very early on in his career (similar to what Josephus did in his autobiographical remarks—see below). In fact, the ease with which both Luke and Matthew could tailor these stories (or reports about previously tailored stories?) indicates that such stories hung together with the whole social dynamics and cultural processes associated with the personage and the cultural system.

Claiming something belonged to Jesus's lifetime is not claiming that it actually happened as described. But the different versions of a special birth of the shamanic figure point toward a creative act of ascribing to this figure a special birth, one way or another; and this ascription of special birth was something that had an impact on Jesus's interaction with people in Galilee, just as the stories about his healings and exorcisms did, and those about his being a son of God. In fact, part of being a holy man could have included a special birth claim because that is exactly how the cultural dynamics of such figures operate elsewhere and what the evidence shows could have been the case here.

Whatever else can be deduced from these arguments, one fact remains: namely, that the biblical authors actually believed what they claimed to believe. They simply were not aware of the duo-genetic theory of procreation and therefore were not talking about a divine deviation from that form of pregnancy (divine procreation, in their view, was no exceptional instance of the "normal" duo-genetic form of procreation). The Gospel authors were giving an account of a birth in terms of both their accepted theories of conception and their idea about paternity.

Conclusion

Comprehending the cultural processes of such events and phenomena in the life of a first-century Galilean shamanic figure not only requires an understanding of the cultural script in terms of which they are offered but also includes the notion of cross-cultural dialog and criticism. From the perspective of cultural bundubashing, the virgin-birth accounts are not reports about Jesus's actual conception. In so far as they make a claim about his conception, the claim is made by means of the cultural constructions of conception and procreation of the time. The Gospel birth accounts as cultural constructions can be seen as a combination of at least three specific cultural assumptions: the notion of a sperm-child theory of procreation, the notion of divine paternity, and the idea of spirit fertilization (by means of a shadow or overshadowing). Thus, when read by means of the cultural scripts of the time, the Gospel virgin-birth accounts are not evidence for Mary's physiology.

Cross-cultural studies and the philosophical embracing of radical pluralism liberate us from such ethnocentric remarks as, the Gospel authors "did not intend them [the virgin birth stories] to be historical accounts" (Miller 2003, 176–77). As an instance of a spirit-seed-baby explanation, the virgin-birth claim is as *historical* as any of the other ancient theories or claims about special shamanic births. It is one option of what ancient Mediterranean people would and could have claimed about conception of a significant social personage.

But not all otherness is to be celebrated. Just as other reports about seed-babies or spirit-babies are reports about what other people thought happened in real life, these are meant as historical reports. (In all cultural accounts, biblical ones included, the people involved are fully convinced that what they present are accounts of how things are in real life.) So, as modern people sharing a dual theory of conception informed by modern biological insights, we need not endorse culturally remote points of view, even if we try to understand or accept them as true cultural accounts of their times. The biblical accounts are indeed reports about what ancient Mediterranean people thought the facts of the matter were; but from the point of view of insights into procreation today, the people of that time had the biology wrong in believing that a spirit could do the job. They had the biology wrong (like most other ancient accounts about conception and pregnancy) but the paternity right, because paternity is a cultural construct that is not dependent on a specific biological connection. They were factually and biologically wrong about paternity (both in the case of Mary and in the case of every other pregnancy at the time) but right about their cultural construction of paternity.

If Jesus was a shamanic figure, as suggested here, the Gospel reports about Jesus's virginal birth can be seen as reports about his shamanic life in Galilee and are not to be taken as historical reports about Mary's condition. If the only evidence available for a claim about a virginal birth is the cultural accounts in terms of their cultural theories about conception and pregnancy, the debate should center on the question of the persistence in arguing about Mary's physiological virginity instead of about cultural paternity.

Childhood Stories about the Shamanic Jesus

That Jesus had a boyhood is a historical fact (at least if he was a human being). On the principle that what one becomes in adult life was already there in childhood, and if what one becomes is identified in adulthood, then in his culture it would have been normal to ascribe the greatness back to childhood—a cultural event of creating and ascribing such stories to Jesus's life story are to be expected as part of his life story in Galilee. In the canonical Gospels, there is only a single episode about this boyhood, namely, Jesus's teaching in the temple at the age of twelve (Luke 2:41–52). It is easy to dismiss this as a legendary or literary creation (meaning useless, unhistorical material), but it is much more challenging to view this story as part of an ancient life. That is to say, to see it as a story accompanying and decorating Jesus's public persona.

Such stories were fairly common in ancient biographies. Figures whose life stories incorporate such accounts include Alexander the Great and Apollonius of Tyana, but the two best known in the Israelite tradition are Moses and Josephus. About himself, Josephus writes: "While still a mere boy, about fourteen years old, I won universal applause for my love of letters; insomuch that the chief priests and the leading men of the city used constantly to come to me for precise information on some particular in our ordinances" (*Life* 9 Thackeray trans.). Legends contemporaneous with the New Testament attribute to Moses extraordinary knowledge as a boy (see Brown 1977, 482). At least in Josephus's case, his story was part of his autobiographical description—a clear indication that it could be part of a social personage's self-conception.

It should be obvious that the preceding discussion is no argument in favor of the Lukan story being told about Jesus at twelve or being considered a report about events at that stage. It is suggested here that this Lukan episode points toward special boyhood stories ascribed to Jesus during his adult life. Biographies are always written after the life (or the fact), but that does not mean that everything reported is also created at the time of writing. What is suggested by the ease with which such an incident as the boyhood story in Luke is included into his life story is that what was a normal cultural practice about significant or great figures even during their lifetimes could also have been part of Jesus's life: boyhood stories attached to (or because of) his life story. If the boyhood story of Jesus in the temple could easily have been included in Luke's version of his life story, why could it not have been in the folklore and gossip during his career?

Given the cultural script of the time, it seems fairly plausible to accept that some time after Jesus's baptism and first public activities, stories and rumors were being created and distributed about his precocious boyhood. If Jesus was experienced as a shamanic figure and as a mediator to the divine world, who was called a son of God and a son of man because of his numerous interactions with the divine world, then it is reasonable to assume that ancient Mediterranean people would also have credited him with a special birth and a significant childhood.

In the case of other miracles or healings ascribed to Jesus, attention has been drawn to specific cultural events that are implicated in the origin of such stories. The cultural event or process described above is not something that could have been videotaped had such an instrument been around. As the example of Josephus shows, a voice recording at the marketplace meeting or synagogue gathering would have been able to pick up the roots of the process; namely, after a visit to the village or the performance of a healing, the gossip and rumors could have included also accounts of his special boyhood.

In fact, it is easy to imagine that a variety of such stories were created and ascribed to him as part of the cultural processes linked to his being a shamanic figure. These were distributed by means of rumor and gossip and even by historical memory of other stories. The fact that the canonical Gospels were not interested in his boyhood (except for the single episode in Luke) is not evidence against such stories being part of his life story. The *Infancy Gospel of Thomas*, for example, is evidence for this inclusion of boyhood stories.

As indicated earlier, current scholarly verdicts focus on the fanciful and fantastic features of the *Infancy Gospel of Thomas* and therefore consider it historically totally useless. Meier supports his rejection of this Gospel with the following remarks:

> The portrait of this sinister superboy belongs more in a horror movie than a gospel. If nothing else, it is a healthy reminder that much apocryphal material stems from 'pop' rather than learned Christian circles and reflects neither early reliable traditions nor elevated theology, but instead curiosity, fascination with the bizarre and miraculous (not to say magical), and sheer desire for 'religious' entertainment. (1991, 115)

However, if the *Infancy Gospel of Thomas* is no longer treated as a report about alleged miraculous deeds by the boy Jesus but as part of the cultural processes surrounding a shamanic figure in Galilee, it can be useful as a historical source for that life. It is true that the tone of the stories in this infancy gospel is different from that in the other, canonical Gospels. But where were these "pop" Christians with money to compose, copy, and preserve the manuscripts of this Gospel? Evidence for the existence of this kind of stories are as old as that of any other kind of story attributed to Jesus (see Koester 1990, 311–12 for a discussion of these issues), while they are no more *bizarre* than some of the miracles or astral visions described in the canonical Gospels (if stories are to be evaluated by that criterion). Why should the creation of live birds from clay be more fanciful than the impregnation of a female by a divine spirit?

The transmission history of the *Infancy Gospel of Thomas* (such as that argued about the Synoptic Gospels if we accept the two-source hypothesis) shows that even after being fixed in writing, such stories were not reliably transmitted as received. Rather, as Koester indicates, "traditions about the childhood of Jesus constantly grew, were altered, and attracted new materials during a history of many centuries" (1990, 313–14). We should see in the reworking, paraphrasing, condensation, and even deletion of some stories, as Hock suggests, the cultural dynamics at work about such stories (see 1995, 86, 92). Even during the enscripturation phase, they were part of dynamic cultural processes about a specific kind of social personage. To me, it seems obvious that not only does the *Infancy Gospel of Thomas* contain stories that cannot be taken literally in our sense of the word, but the stories were themselves part of a specific cultural dynamic of telling and retelling stories about a particular kind of historical figure.

With a proper cultural sensibility for the cultural processes surrounding such figures within the type of worldview Jesus occupied, such judgments (viewing the stories as *bizarre*, fascination with the magical) are shown to be extremely ethnocentric. Obviously, they were not bizarre for those who created and preserved them, and compared to similar miraculous stories ascribed to shamanic figures, they were part and parcel of a specific worldview. Anthropologists would not even dream (no pun intended) of arguing about the "historicity" (in the sense of whether something actually happened as described) or the bizarre nature of such stories.

Historical questions include not only those about the historical information or the historicity in the reports (did the first shamans indeed arrive from heaven on a golden disk, or were they conceived because of intercourse between an earthly women and an eagle?) but also those about the historical reality and cultural dynamics of such reports ascribed to living and acting shamans. Is it imaginable and plausible that such stories were ascribed to Jesus during his lifetime (that is, if he was such a figure), just as they are ascribed to other shamanic figures? The impact of such stories is not dependent on their being reports about objective events but on their being inscribed within the cultural processes of creating and maintaining the stature and status of a significant figure.

Conclusion

Cultural bundubashing starts with an understanding of the mental world of those who created the sources in order to determine what things could have been like for them. Part of what things were like for them was the possibility of a social figure living with a special-birth and precocious-boyhood account. On all accounts, this must have been a significant feature of any social figure's life. From the hypothesis developed in this study, these stories need to be put into the setting of a son of god who was experienced as a mediator figure (a son of man), who on a regular basis intervened between human and divine affairs, and about whom many stories of contact with the divine world were circulated in Galilee. This is the kind of figure about which there are reports that his mother was a virgin during his conception and that he had special abilities, already as a young boy.

Second, cultural bundubashing reads the infancy narratives as cultural stories about cultural mentalities. When looking at the first-century infancy accounts referred to, a highly interesting pattern emerges. Matthew and Luke each operate with the virginal conception resulting in divine paternity (i.e., with the type of birth ascribed to immortals in that world), but are not at all interested in factual correctness (at least both cannot be factually correct). Paul and John operate with the normal birth of a preexisting divine being (i.e., with the birth of an eternal). Instead of reading these accounts as objective information about Mary's conception and Jesus's actual birth, they can be seen as cultural accounts about his life story. The Josephus reference shows that such biographical claims could indeed be made during a person's lifetime.

But cultural bundubashing also contains a comparative perspective. Just as ancient texts cannot be taken as evidence that babies in that period were in fact seed-babies or spirit-babies deposited in the fertile containers of females, the texts in this format and condition cannot be taken as evidence that a virgin became pregnant without male intervention or that at the age of twelve, Jesus performed all sorts of miraculous deeds. Therefore, the question is asked, what are the infancy narratives historical evidence for?

The narratives about Mary's virginal conception are not about pregnancy but paternity—divine paternity—and are historical evidence that a special birth could have been part of Jesus's life story. On the question, when did the birth and childhood stories about Jesus of Nazareth originate, and when were they told? one can only speculate. Since there is no concrete evidence to go on, the logical answer in terms of the shamanic model is, very soon after his baptism and public activities. Wherever the stories originated, they cannot be taken as evidence about Mary's physiological or gynecological condition or about the biology of Jesus's conception, but they can provide evidence about Jesus's life story. The infancy narratives are as far removed from a duo-theory of procreation as Bellonese pregnancy by an ancestral spirit is. If there is any miraculous element involved here, it is probably the fact that a theological construct about Jesus's *virgin birth* and divine paternity could have been built on top of a faulty (cultural) notion about procreation.

CHAPTER 12

Afterlife for Someone Like a Galilean Shamanic Figure

Introduction

THERE IS PROBABLY NO other topic in Jesus research that creates such controversy and inspires more seminars than that of Jesus's resurrection. This is also the place where the lines between the Wredebahn and the Schweitzerstrasse are drawn most sharply. But, as with the other aspects of Jesus's life, there is also a remarkable singularity in the basic assumptions underlying the apparent divergent answers.

As with previous chapters (e.g., accounts of Jesus's healings and exorcisms), the argument of this chapter is dependent on an understanding of what the texts are evidence for. Therefore, a first step would be to determine what the (cultural) reality of the resurrection accounts is. Only then can it be asked whether such a cultural reality could plausibly be connected to the life story of Jesus of Nazareth. Is it likely that as a Galilean shamanic figure, Jesus's life story was also decorated with a resurrection experience? Finally can the question of the historicity and actuality of *Jesus's resurrection* be considered?

Cultural bundubashing is based on the idea of ontological pluralism and acknowledges the possibility of multiple cultural realities and consequently that real differences exist between various cultural systems on the planet—all of which do not share the same ontological reality and afterlife notions. From this point of view, the basic problem within the authenticity paradigm is that culture-specific data, or data about a culture-specific reality and phenomena are treated as evidence (or lack of sufficient evidence) for an apparent homoversal reality. It will be shown that the

contrary is true, namely, that resurrection really is a culture-specific notion about the afterlife and dependent for its reality on a whole range of
cultural assumptions. Therefore, it is to be suggested that the documents
are in the first place not testimonies about *Jesus's resurrection* as if that can
be taken as a homoversal human phenomenon.

In this way, the three components of the interpretive process of cultural bundubashing (a sensitive engagement with the cultural script of the
other, an acknowledgement of one's own cultural system and engagement
in cross-cultural dialog and critique) are all activated. They are implement-
ed, as described earlier (see above, pp. 17–21) by means of a nonlinear
interpretive process consisting of a culturally sensitive engagement with
the other, cross-cultural comparison, and often at least two answers to the
question of historicity and historical factuality.

This strategy will be followed by first advancing an argument about
resurrection as one possible afterlife configuration for first-century Israelite
people. Then it will be suggested that accounts of Jesus's resurrection can
also be seen as such a cultural reality for some first-century Israelite people,
but that is not necessarily evidence that resurrection as an afterlife option
was a homoversal reality as such or was in the specific case a universal
historical fact. It means that what had been taken and experienced as a
cultural reality by some first-century Israelite people (it was one afterlife
option for some of them) actually could have been a reality in the specific
case of Jesus of Nazareth. In this regard it will be suggested that the idea of
resurrection as an afterlife option for Jesus as a social personage has indeed
a high probability. This will be substantiated by means of a general argument about social figures being ascribed an afterlife existence, as well as by
specific features in the data supporting such a claim. If Jesus was a Galilean
shamanic figure, it is likely that such a feature belonged to his life story,
and since such characteristics are ascribed to his life, it is perfectly understandable that it would have belonged to the descriptions of a shamanic
figure. Such a position, however, calls for cross-cultural dialog in order to
deal with the issues of historicity and actuality.

Jesus's Resurrection in the Authenticity Paradigm

Since *Jesus's resurrection* is such a central issue in historical Jesus research, it
is necessary to first offer a brief overview of it as presented in the authenticity paradigm. The claim that the authenticity paradigm is trapped in the
view of ontological monism and the framework of positivistic historiog-

raphy is nowhere more clearly illustrated than in the endless stream of seminars, debates, and publications to the effect of "Jesus's resurrection: historical event or theological explanation?" The question is answered in either of three (ethnocentric) ways: yes!, no!, or, it is a category mistake to ask the question. The Wredebahn and the Schweitzerstrasse roughly cover what Crossan refers to as the twin sides of the same (rationalist) coin. The secular rationalist reaction is to declare the resurrection stories fraudulent while for the fundamentalist rationalists they represent unique, divine events: "one side said they could never happen, the other side said they happened only once" (1999, 32). In this spectrum can be seen the components of an interpretive paradigm struggling to become established or prove that and what was really real (and thus historical) about Jesus's resurrection. In all instances it is accepted that the documents are testifying about a common human event in time and space, namely, *Jesus's resurrection*.

Like all other aspects in historical Jesus research, the debate in the authenticity paradigm on Jesus's resurrection is completely trapped in the framework of traditional historiography. Ontological monism and consequently the strategy of reading the testimonies straight, as if they were about events and phenomena in a commonly shared world, reign supreme. It is assumed that what the texts are about can be approached directly while the challenge is to weigh and evaluate the authenticity of claims and to find multiple testimonies affirming (or denying) the historicity of what is encountered in the documents (when read straight), namely, whether Jesus rose from the dead in a bodily fashion or not. The question scholars are addressing is whether there are reliable (authentic) and sufficient testimonies on the basis of which it can be decided whether certain things happened after Jesus's death that indicate that he was resurrected from death. If there were a video camera present, would it have been possible to collect evidence that he was no longer dead but alive? The answer of the Wredebahn is, no! and that of the Schweitzerstrasse (even if sometimes a little tentatively), yes, indeed it was a real event in time and space!

Three components that appear on both roads and that confirm captivity to this paradigm will briefly be discussed. These are (1) the spectrum of real and unreal in ontological monism, (2) notions about seeing the resurrected Jesus, and (3) ideas about the nature of Jesus's resurrected body.

What Is *Real* and *Not Real* in the Framework of Ontological Monism

One of the central issues in the authenticity paradigm is how to put into words something as extraordinary as the claim that someone has returned from death or became alive after having been declared dead. In looking at these attempts, it should not escape our attention that within this paradigm it is taken for granted that the testimonies are about such an extraordinary event in the world and the different attempts are all struggling with the same dilemma of how to bring into words what is real and actual but not normal. This finds expression in scholarly debates in a variety of oppositions: literal/metaphorical, mysterious/normal, myth/history, factual/fictional, actual/symbolic, and concrete/abstract, to mention some. A few examples will suffice.

When confessing that nothing about the historical Jesus is more mysterious than the stories of his resurrection, Sanders is clearly expressing this attitude: even after carefully weighing the testimonies, we are confronted with the fact that they present information about events that are not normal and human but mysterious (see 1993, 280).[1] But, the act of declaring events or phenomena mysterious, assumes a clear and definite picture of *common human reality*. Such stories, if judged authentic, belong to life's *mysteries*. Wright is even more explicit in this assumption. For him, the testimonies about an empty tomb and apparitions were not merely about well-known phenomena after someone has died (apparitions) but they refer to "some extraordinary physical things" (Wright & Crossan 2006, 37),

---

1. Theissen and Merz advance a similar argument about the meaning of the Easter event. In doing this, they assume the same rationalistic (modern) worldview. They claim, in principle there are two possibilities of translating Easter faith for our time: "either the Easter event is interpreted in such a way that it can be integrated into the world of modern convictions, or modern premises are modified in the light of the Easter faith" (1998, 504). Or, as they put it elsewhere, the basic question is, "should the Easter event be interpreted with analogies from our world of experience—or as an unparalleled breakthrough of something 'wholly other' should it widen that world?" (1998, 508). They do also find one reason for leaving our world of analogies when confronted with the Easter faith: "Easter is grappling with death," and in the resurrection of Jesus, "an enigmatic power manifests itself which overcomes death." In other words, translated into a discourse about death and the impossibility of finding human analogies to deal with it, the resurrection of Jesus can be dealt with as a historical reality. In this argument, the discussion is reduced to a philosophical level: resurrection is treated as a philosophical concept about overcoming death. It is in contrast to see it as a cultural category of experiential-reflective nature that this reduction can be appreciated.

or as he insists in a debate with Crossan, they are "accounts of something exceedingly strange and unprecedented in the real world" (2006, 18). In these accounts it is clear that there is a single continuum of what is real and what is not, and this continuum includes the supernatural category— some concrete, physical things are real but extraordinary or supernatural, and Jesus's resurrection belongs to them. Although unprecedented, it now belongs to the category of (supernatural) common human reality.

Even scholars on the Wredebahn, who dismiss Jesus's resurrection as mythical talk, share these assumptions about reality. The difference is, stories about such mysteries are mythical and did not actually take place. While a different answer is given, the data are used to answer the same question, namely, whether it was a real event in history. Crossan, for example, advances a distinction between literal and metaphorical modes of speaking: "one type of language is literal, factual, actual, or historical (Jesus is the peasant from Nazareth) and another type of language is metaphorical, fictional, symbolic, or parabolic (Jesus is the Lamb of God)" (2006, 171). This distinction, he claims, is universal and, therefore, allows entrance into our dealing with Jesus's resurrection: "Ancients knew just as well as moderns the distinction between, say, myth and history, fable and parable, or literal and metaphorical language" (2006, 180). The implication is clear that resurrection language was not literal but metaphorical and fictional. After affirming that these oppositions are commonly universal between ancient and modern people, he denies that this distinction has anything to do with real and unreal: "I insist, of course, that literal and metaphorical are not the same as real and unreal. I never, ever, confuse or equate the literal with the real" (Crossan 2006, 183). But on the very opposite page he asks whether ancient Romans would take the claim that Caesar Augustus was divine, a Son of God, Lord, Savior, and the like, as literal or metaphorical. That could either mean they took it to be real or unreal, or that they assumed it was real for them, and in being real, they could have more or less literal or metaphorical (whatever such affirmations about a reality could mean) beliefs about Caesar. Thus, literal and metaphorical, in his explanation, are transcultural while real and unreal are culture specific.

Ancient people indeed made a distinction between real and unreal, and literal and metaphorical and between fantasies and reality (and all the other dualities), but they did not make the same distinctions that some other people (for example, modern Western people) do. Not only what was real for them, but also what was literal or metaphorical, concrete or extraordinary, was culturally determined. People living in polyphasic cultures take as real much of what those in monophasic cultures would not consider as real, and while people in polyphasic cultures who, say, believe in the existence of ancestors or angels as real could take a specific instance as metaphorical, they would certainly take most such literal references also as real.

How deeply the authenticity paradigm is submerged in the assumptions of ontological monism is perhaps best seen in the next two categories.

Seeing Jesus after His Death

Since a significant portion of the evidence for *Jesus's resurrection* is based on the fact that he was *seen* after his death, it is necessary to reflect about how the data are treated. Those on the Schweitzerstrasse depart from the assumption that the *seeing* refers to normal, optical activities that in some instances can be supplemented by extraordinary or supernatural capabilities to see, while those on the Wredebahn most often depend on the idea of visions, but then as hallucinations or delusions.

On the Schweitzerstrasse, the argument is that if (or since) Jesus's body was resurrected, "normal vision" (*seeing*) was involved. It is also the kind of seeing assumed by many who maintain that Jesus's resurrected body was some kind of glorious or eschatological physical, material body (the fundamentalist rationalists). For example, on the question whether a video camera would have been able to record the event of Jesus's resurrection, Wright responds: "Assuming that a camera would pick up what most human eyes would have seen (by no means a safe assumption), my guess is that cameras would sometimes have seen Jesus and sometimes not" (1999c, 125). Davis is even more blunt: "I feel no sense of embarrassment whatsoever in holding that a camera could have taken a snapshot of the raised Jesus, say, feeding the seven disciples beside the Sea of Tiberias (John 21:1–14)" (1997, 142).

In some cases it is admitted that the *seeing* was some special event and therefore the category of *objective vision* is utilized. A *subjective vision* is when someone claims to have seen something that no one else can see because the item purportedly seen is not real or objectively there, while an *objective vision* is when someone sincerely claims to see something that no one else can see because God enables that person alone to see the real and objective presence of a thing. Subjective vision equals hallucination (in the sense of delusion) while objective vision equals normal vision because of God's grace. Therefore, the latter is also called *grace-assisted vision* or *grace seeing*, and it contains images that can be photographed (see Davis 1997, 127). According to these definitions, objective visions and normal seeing are of the same kind—the only difference is that in the case of objective vision, a person is individually (divinely) picked to see something that others cannot see.

While those on the Wredebahn take a different stance, the framework of ontological monism that assumes a common spectrum of human visionary experiences remains in tact. While at first sight it seems as if Crossan has moved beyond the ethnocentric views on *seeing*, he does not escape its claws. In his view it is "part of reality" to know which is which, which is vision and which is hallucination, which is dream and which is delusion (see 1999, 6). A dream becomes a delusion when you call 911 after a nightmare in order to have someone come and remove the big monster in your backyard, and a vision or apparition of the archangel becomes hallucination when you keep on insisting that everybody else should go and see the angel on the mountain top, he says. But to firmly believe and to act in a polyphasic culture because of a dream or the apparition of an archangel, ancestor, and the like, is neither delusion nor hallucination.

The Nature of Jesus's Resurrected Body

Treatment of the nature of Jesus's resurrected body or an afterlife existence on both roads of the authenticity paradigm is no less ethnocentric because on both, ontological monism rules supremely. On the Schweitzerstrasse, the supernatural category dominates procedures. The most popular viewpoint on this road is that something mysterious has happened to Jesus's body after his death. As Wright, for example, says: "The resurrection body is thus not identical with the original body; it has not, that is, merely been resuscitated; it is, rather, the *transformation* of the existing body into a new mode of physicality . . . It is . . . a *transformed* physicality, with new properties and attributes but still concrete and physical" (1999c, 120). Also, according to Davis, Jesus's resurrected body was a material object that took up space, occupied a certain location, and could be seen (see 1997, 133, 139–140, 142). O'Collins even claims a "consensus viewpoint," which states that "Jesus was translated at his resurrection into an entirely new mode of existence" (1978, 11).[2] At the other end of the same mystifying spectrum are those who explicitly rely on supernaturalism as an explanatory principle: "It seems that an omnipotent being would have it well within its power to make a human body materialize in a room" (Davis 1997, 134). An omnipotent God can either resurrect a material body or create a new kind of body. A revived version of this position Peters describes as FINLON: "the first instantiation of a new law of nature" (2006, 166).[3]

On the Schweitzerstrasse, the supernatural category or divine intervention overrules everything: If the seeing is normal, the body is special, if the body is normal the seeing is special or supernatural. Ironically, those on the Wredebahn share some of the same ethnocentric assumptions but reach a totally different conclusion.

While the secular rationalists for obvious reasons do not speculate about the nature of Jesus's resurrected body (they do not think it happened), they operate with the same notion of *seeing*. If a video camera could not have recorded anything on film during one of Jesus's appearances (which it could not have, according to these sentiments), it obviously was no historical event (see, e.g., Lüdemann 1995, 134 and Funk 1996, 258, 273). The implication should be clear: since there was no resurrected Jesus to be seen *normally* according to them, the resurrection was not a real historical event, and speculation about his resurrected existence is obsolete. One example from this road will have to suffice.

While trying to avoid such an outright rationalist response, Crossan's suggestion remains one of the most ethnocentric. He is well aware that the ancient world was filled with stories about gods, goddesses, spirits, immortals, and the like, which often assumed *bodily* forms. They had *bodies* but not flesh, and therefore, he claims, those were "seeming-bodies, play-bodies, in-appearance-only bodies" (1998, 37). The bodies with which these divine beings appeared were "like our special-effects movies today.

---

2. According to O'Collins, Jesus occupied a "glorious body "after the resurrection (see 1978, 49), while Craig describes it as "an immortal, powerful, glorious, Spirit-directed body, suitable for inhabiting a renewed creation" (1995, 157).

3. As will be argued below, I have in principle no objection to such a position because that would represent just another absolutization of a modernist position. However, in practice the obligation on any scholar or scientist claiming that a new "law of nature" was discovered would at least include that all other natural explanations for a particular phenomenon have been investigated. Resurrection as a cultural reality for ancient people normally does not even feature in these claims.

Sometimes we see body but not flesh" (1998, xxviii). His explanation of Jesus's bodily resurrection is that it "has nothing to do with a resuscitated body coming out of its tomb," instead bodily resurrection means "that the embodied life and death of the historical Jesus continues to be experienced, by believers, as powerfully efficacious and salvifically present in this world" (1999, 46). What precisely this last description means is not at all clear, but this kind of mystification ("the embodied life and death of the historical Jesus continues to be experienced") does not help one bit in unraveling the meaning of cultural realities that existed as lived and experienced realities for other people.

The experience of deceased ancestors in polyphasic cultures is embedded in a specific cycle of meaning where it constitutes a cultural reality on which people base their everyday lives and some of their ultimate beliefs.[4] In a solution similar to the above solutions, Crossan takes the discussion at this point away from the actual road (i.e., away from the question of whether resurrection accounts are about actual events) and shifts the debate to another topic, that is, to the meaning of the road signs (i.e., to the metaphorical value of the resurrection stories). The cultural gap is short circuited from the modern view of reality because the modern view of reality neither takes seriously as cultural reports the resurrection accounts in the literary sources nor grapples with the reality value of what the resurrection stories were about. An explanation about special-effect bodies is used in order to substantiate a claim about eschatological apocalyptic notions regarding a general resurrection. However, something can be real without being objective and can *be seen* without being *out there* (for a video camera to pick up) or without being the result of modern special-effects technology. What if none of these stories were merely providing information in our world about the resurrected Jesus?

4. It should be noted that in this example, the meaning of *resurrection* is reduced to a meaning dependent on a philosophical choice. In an attempt to answer the historical question of what Jews meant by resurrection, Crossan and Reed reduce the analysis to ideas about resurrection (see 2001, 255). The proper meaning of the term that "*God raised Jesus from the dead was to assert that the general resurrection had thereby begun*" (2001, 260). Therefore they claim that resurrection was not the same as resuscitation, apparition, or exaltation but was based on the stories of the seven martyrs in the Maccabean books. Crossan and Reed argue that for first-century Jews, resurrection was "an utterly eschatologico-apocalyptic concept" (2001, 258).

This has been picked up by Segal, who clearly identifies the rational-istic problem even though he does not succeed in escaping its claws. Segal quite perceptively remarks:

> I believe the whole enterprise of trying to prove that the resurrec-tion is a historical fact is a category mistake . . . I am not even sure that such a category [a literal resurrection of transformed flesh] is even valid . . . This small scholarly consensus—really a school of scholarship—is beside the point because the vast majority of modern historians looking at the very same story would say that *no evidence at all would ever demonstrate that a unique resurrection took place.* The resurrection is neither probable nor improbable, it is impossible to confirm historically. (2006, 135)

This is indeed the case if the reports were about *the resurrection*, or about a homoversal event in time and space—an *event* that modern historians can encounter straight.

Against all of these views, cultural bundubashing avoids the myth of realism in assuming the natural veracity of the reports—there was no *the resurrection* to begin with, but reports about an afterlife existence for Jesus of Nazareth and they were presented in the language and categories available and operative at the time. Modern historians from the anthropo-logical historiography paradigm (cultural bundubashing) will first make sense about what the data is evidence for. The first step would be a thick description of the ultimate presuppositions and cultural system of the people involved. Responsible historiography can no longer short-circuit the alien and distant gap and bypass the worldview of the documents. And explanations of special-effect bodies in the video sphere of modern virtual culture will not do.

Summary

Both roads in the authenticity paradigm short-circuit the cultural gap by assuming that the documents are talking to and about a common human reality. The myth of realism, which assumes the natural veracity of these texts, is nowhere more prominently present than in the resurrection dis-cussions. Those on the Schweitzerstrasse short-circuit the cultural gap of the resurrection stories by utilizing at least three mechanisms: application of the supernatural category, a rationalist definition of *seeing*, and mysti-fication about the nature of the resurrection body. Their position is that if Jesus was *seen* after his death, he must have occupied a *material physical body*, and all of that was the result of a divine (supernatural) intervention. Those on the Wredebahn disregard the cultural uniqueness of these reports in a similar way but reach opposite conclusions.

The authenticity paradigm contains no sense of a cultural gap between the stories and modern historians' understanding of the world and, consequently, does not attempt to understand such accounts as belonging to a different worldview, cultural, and reality system. The result is a presentation of extremely idiosyncratic arguments trying to justify what *Jesus's resurrection* was all about.

The aim of this study is not to offer an answer (not even an alternative answer) to all the above positions but to ask a different set of questions. The interpretive structure of cultural bundubashing creates the opportunity for asking different questions about the stories of Jesus's resurrection. To be precise, it does not participate in the question whether Jesus's resurrection was a historical event or fact, but whether as a cultural event and phenomenon, Jesus's resurrection supports the shamanic hypothesis. In order to answer this question, it is necessary to grasp the cultural reality of the reports and what the reports were reporting about. What is needed, first and foremost, is a thick description of what was taken for granted in that world when resurrection language was used to talk about an afterlife option.

Israelite Afterlife Options as First-Century Cultural Realities

A common feature in first-century Mediterranean communities is that many (if not most) people shared some notion of an afterlife. As Sanders says, for most Israelites of the Second Temple period, as for their pagan compatriots, "death was not the end to everything" (1992, 298). Like those of all their neighbors, Israelite afterlife options were cultural realities closely connected to two features, namely, a notion of the human being as consisting of some kind of body-soul dualism (or body-soul-spirit tripartite) and the acquisition of experiential knowledge in a cycle of meaning.

Another feature, almost the direct product of this, is that most societies contained a spectrum of afterlife beliefs. This is also the case with first-century Israelite afterlife beliefs, which, within the first-century Mediterranean world, overlapped but were not identical to that of any of their neighbors. Any particular afterlife option was created in a cycle of meaning where experiential knowledge and specific notions of the human self were interconnected to the idea that death was not the end of everything.

Afterlife, the Human Self, and Experiential Knowledge in a Polyphasic Culture

First-century Mediterranean cultures were earlier described as polyphasic in nature, which means that various states of consciousness in a cycle of meaning contributed to the acquisition of knowledge. Knowledge was experiential knowledge because of the feedback interaction between experiences, expressions, and mythological patterns.[5] Most cultural systems make distinctions between real and unreal, literal and metaphorical, and so forth; but it is only within polyphasic cultures and their cycle of meaning that ASC experiences contribute to knowledge about what is real and unreal, what exists and what not. While monophasic cultures are based primarily on knowledge acquired through waking phases of consciousness and reflexive thinking, it does not mean everything taken for real is only material or homoversal. In polyphasic cultures the cycle of meaning formed the basis for at least two sets of knowledge that are relevant for this discussion.

The first concerns the various notions about the human being. Beliefs about the body and the potentials of human existence were created and confirmed by bodily experiences. The cycle of meaning confirmed this relation between beliefs about the body and bodily experiences. The astronomical complex, which included beliefs and convictions about the human being and body (consisting of various body-soul-spirit configurations—see above, pp. 187–91) were culturally interconnected to beliefs about the stars and angels (in the astronomical complex—see above, pp. 193–96). Bodies, or humans in some *bodily* format, could fly to heaven, or could experience heavenly journeys; then there were the notions that someone in Jesus's day could be possessed (or filled) by an ancestral spirit or soul and in that way could assume the identity of that ancestor. A host of ancient texts indicate that humans could be turned into angels or astral beings after death. The idea of human beings transformed into astral beings belonged to the same *astronomical complex*—that is, the physics and physiology of the day, which

5. In his discussion of the development of afterlife options in Israelite history, Segal suggests a similar cultural dynamic as what is suggested here: "Experiences grow out of texts, and texts grow out of experiences (see 2004, 326).

insisted that the stars, souls, and angels were of the same substance. In all these cases, the particular belief is dependent on or at least supported by specific ASC experiences—be it out-of-body travels, possession experiences or visionary experiences. As Segal says, for example, the "separation of the soul from the body in sleep and in mystical ascent was the demonstration of the immortality of the soul" (2004, 345). These phenomena are an indication of the experience-expression cycle of meaning and belonged to the cultural world of first-century Mediterranean people.

The second set of knowledge contains the spectrum of afterlife options: "As in all ancient cultures, dreams, visions, and other religiously interpreted states of consciousness both gave the power to foretell the future and confirm the culture's depiction of the afterlife" (Segal 2004, 207). When taken together, the idea of a cycle of meaning can be expanded to suggest that within polyphasic cultures there is a circular and feedback interaction between the particular ways of obtaining knowledge and views on both the human being and afterlife options. It was *experienced* souls in *souled* or *spirited* bodies that also encountered afterlife experiences.

Within the cycle of meaning, these components hung together in providing the framework within which various accounts about afterlife activities are to be situated.

The Cultural Reality of a Postmortem or Afterlife Existence

Based on the notions about human beings and the acquisition of knowledge by means of ASCs, first-century Israelite people shared a similar reality spectrum, but it was not everywhere populated in the same way. Like all other peoples of the time, they had a spectrum of what exists and what not. Underlying, but not precisely overlapping such a spectrum, was another continuum of what is real and unreal. In other words, among the things that they took to exist in the world, there were things that were real and others not real (but which still existed). Applied to figures or beings, this spectrum could contain:

- people in everyday encounters (e.g., neighbors or family),

- deceased people and non-human beings encountered in other than everyday experiences or awaken conditions (e.g., ancestors, demons, angels),

- spirits (deceased or living persons' spirits could be encountered),

- ghosts (such as the one referred to in the stories of Jesus walking on the sea).

When these four categories are placed on a continuum, a fascinating picture of culturally approved beings becomes apparent:

living people—deceased people—nonhuman beings—spirits—ghosts

This spectrum is no obvious given, because socially approved or disapproved judgments always accompany it. Therefore, these entities could be either real or not real, either exist or not exist in a given instance. Paradoxically, while they might be taken to exist, they are not necessarily considered to be real. This seems to be the case with the reference to "spirit" in the Lukan resurrection account (24:37): while they see something that exists (Jesus), uncertainty about its reality is apparent.

"Spirits" and "ghosts" (as in Matt 14:26/Mark 6:49) invoke a subject common to popular culture in many societies, namely, the belief in ghosts, or "shades" or "spirits" of some kind (see Segal 2004, 451). Although the categories appear in many cultural versions, the description of either a "spirit" or a "ghost" is local and particular. The experience of a deceased person without knowing the precise nature or identity of the person, invokes the category of "ghost" while recognizable figures seem to be "spirits." Ghosts exist, but are not necessarily considered real or real in the same way as ancestors, who are recognized, or demons and neighbors, who are identifiable.

Two other features that apply to all the beings on the spectrum, except the neighbors and the ghosts, confirm that these beings were culturally real.

The first is that the language used in ancient sources and followed by modern authors is that the dead could easily be recognized by the living or other deceased. As Riley says,

> One common characteristic of the dead is that they are easily recognized by both the living and other deceased. The dead keep their recognizable form and appearance apart from their bodies because the surviving soul bears the 'image' . . . of the body, and is an essential attribute of the soul. (1995, 48)

But the language of recognition assumes direct knowledge of or a picture (photo) of a deceased person, which obviously did not exist in ancient times. A case in point is Paul's recognition of Jesus of Nazareth, a person whom Paul, on all accounts, had never met before. Instead of recognition, it is perhaps better to describe the dynamics as that of identifying in the sense of giving identity to a visioned entity. Visioned beings were identified (or is it *identitied?*) beings—a confirmation that visions provided access to, or created, what was taken as real.

Second, people in afterlife existence or postmortem states could still perform a variety of activities. On the one hand, there is ample evidence in the Greco-Roman world pointing toward the deceased as able to engage in sex both among themselves and with the living. In addition, some of the wise, brave, or significant deceased resumed a position of protection for the living (see Riley 1995, 54). On the other hand, even so, there was no agreement on the materiality of such afterlife figures, which is confirmed by the disputes about whether they could be touched or not. On occasion the dead could touch the living for good or ill, and even sometimes be touched (see 1995, 55). These dead bodies or beings, in whichever format conceptualized, could eat, drink, and talk to the living (see Riley 1995, 47 for examples). These examples do not point toward a modern idea of materiality but to the cultural reality of ASC-experienced bodies or to the reality of beings whose materiality was culturally conceptualized. In all of these, one of the basic principles of such ASC experiences is merely confirmed, namely, that the experiences are furnished with a sound and visual track from cultural belief system and tradition (see Pilch 2004, 4–5).

Although the Greek view of afterlife went through considerable changes and variation, and not all finally agreed on the same view, "the notion that the immortal soul separates from the body . . . is the innovation normally attributed to Greek authorship" (Segal 2004, 205).[6] In the Roman period, it was expressed by means of the journey to the heavens that contained a great deal of the astronomical complex. Some significant figures would travel to heaven and resume an immortal existence as and among the stars. It is within this framework that the cultural reality of various afterlife options is to be evaluated.

Afterlife in Israelite Tradition

The dominant view in Israelite tradition of the First Temple period was that life should be enjoyed and that the dead continued a shadowy existence

6. For another description of the variation in Greco-Roman thought, see Riley (1995, 23–58).

in Sheol (see Alexander 1986; Friedman & Overton 2000). A remarkable feature about Israelite afterlife options in the Second Temple period, and thus during the first century, is that they were of the same nature as those of their neighbors but displayed a different spectrum.

During this period the traditional view was gradually replaced first by the idea of resurrection as a beatific afterlife and then by notions of the immortality of the soul (for a discussion, see Segal 2004, 248–81). The idea of resurrection by means of astral transformation entered the Israelite repertoire of ideas via the visionary prophetic revelations of Daniel, and not via mere exegesis. As already indicated, the idea expressed in Daniel 12 opened the way for some significant people (the "wise" or the "leaders") to be transformed into stars and/or angels—an implementation of the astronomical complex in Israelite thinking (see above, pp. 193–96).

An interesting development in the ideas about the afterlife is added around the turn of the era. In some Jewish texts the idea of resurrection as recompense for the martyrs is replaced by the notion of immortality as reward for the martyrs. The future resurrection of the body is replaced by immortality and an eternal life, which begins the moment of death (Nickelsburg 1992a, 686–87; Riley 1995, 15–22; Segal 1996, 391–92).

For the Qumran community death was not a theological problem since they believed they had already transcended death by becoming a member of the community. Life as member of their community was already experienced as in conjunction with the angels and, therefore, resurrection was not really an issue since they had already reached immortality in this life with the angels (see Collins 1983, 72; VanderKam 1994, 80).

In summary, while some people did not speak about any afterlife or rejected it outright (because of the traditional Israelite beliefs), the majority in the first-century period fall into a spectrum of beliefs that included either immortality of the soul, astral immortality, or resurrection of a body or some kind of combination of these. All three beliefs are related soul or spirit entities and connected to bodily experiences and can be fitted into the cycle of meaning of Israelite people. The sources reflect a diversity of opinions among the different groups and a great variety of ideas within some groups (see Riley 1995, 22). That is to say, each notion was created in a particular Israelite cycle of meaning. Put the other way around: none of them described objective reality or how things were after life, but offered particular cultural constructs thereof. It should be remembered that all afterlife descriptions are made by and from the perspective of the living on this side of death.

Within the interconnectedness of an Israelite cycle of meaning (the interconnected framework of experiences, beliefs, and knowledge expressions), resurrection thus originated as one viable afterlife option for some Israelite people. Beliefs about the human body/being coexisted with a variety of experiences, which, within the polyphasic culture of first-century Mediterranean people, allowed for a whole spectrum of notions about human life and resurrection was one of them. But something more significant emerges from this brief overview: each of these options is a unique configuration or the product of particular cultural forces and beliefs.

Jesus's Resurrection as an Afterlife Option within a First-Century Israelite Cycle of Meaning

All four canonical Gospels, as well as Paul, provide evidence that Jesus did not simply die and was buried, but that something more happened after his death. He resumed an Israelite continued existence, described as a *resurrection*, which was based on stories that his tomb was found empty and that he was encountered (seen) by his followers after his death. There can be little doubt that the New Testament data claim that some time after his burial, Jesus was no longer dead but alive. That is, Jesus's followers were convinced (and reported accordingly) that he had entered an Israelite afterlife existence. None of the sources claim anything about the event itself; in other words, none describe an event of resurrection or offer any testimony as to witnesses to such an event. All affirm in different ways that the buried Jesus was no longer dead in his grave but alive and well in an afterlife existence.[7]

Two features of this cultural reality as presented in the documents are, however, significant here. The first is the remarkable role that ASC experiences (in particular, visions) play in their presentations. The second is the diversity of presentations of apparently the same postmortem resurrected figure, Jesus of Nazareth. Within a similar cycle of meaning, equipped

---

7. As far as I know, no New Testament scholar has done more than Pilch to describe Jesus's resurrection in cultural context as experiences and appearances in alternate reality (see 1998). While this description does not follow his reasoning, it has been influenced by his research in a way more than can be acknowledged here. It is a way of thinking about these cultural realities that I have learned from him.

with the same cultural entities of the human being and ASC experience, the different authors came up with different descriptions of the resurrected Jesus and of the experienced reality.

They Had Seen Visions . . . : The Role of ASC Experiences

The two disciples on the road to Emmaus reported that some women in their company went to Jesus's tomb early in the morning and could not find his body but "they had indeed seen a vision of angels" (Luke 24:23), from which they learned that Jesus was alive. This report is explicit about what is tacitly assumed in the other (cultural) reports, namely, that what is reported about, is actually a series of visionary experiences. Either the expression "he appeared to" or "they saw him" could be technical terms for visionary experiences.

Furthermore, there is little dispute over the fact that the technical language used by Paul refers to visionary experiences (see Segal 2004, 406). This is confirmed by his claim in the Letter to the Galatians (2:12, 16) that his knowledge is based on a revelation (a vision or ASC experience) and an explicit reference to a visionary appearance to him (1 Cor 15:8). The foundation of Paul's argument about Jesus's resurrection is not only that it is true because it is preached to them, but it is true because Jesus had appeared to them. Paul (in 1 Cor 15:5–8) is convinced that he, like the host of other visionaries, has really seen the resurrected Jesus (this *soma pneumatikon* of Jesus). And these are experiences that, for people in a polyphasic culture, give access to knowledge about their world.

Several other cultural clues in the reports support the argument that the basic format of knowledge about Jesus's assumed resurrected or afterlife existence was based on sightings or visions—thus ASC experiences.

First, there are the angels who act as the first informants about Jesus's resurrection: a young man, dressed in a white robe (Mark 16:5); explicitly an angel in Matthew (28:2), whose visit is announced by the experience of an earthquake while his "appearance was like lightning, and his raiment white as snow" (28:3); two men in dazzling apparel in Luke (24:4); and two angels in John (20:12).

Second, there are the typical strong emotional experiences that accompany such ASC experiences: trembling and astonishment in Mark (16:8); in Matthew the women are comforted by the angel not to be afraid, but the guards tremble (28:4–5); and in Luke the disciples were startled and frightened by the experience of Jesus's suddenly appearing to them (24:36). It should be realized that where such experiences are taken as real, part of the content is given in the experience; the experience is the knowledge or content creating event. The emotional reactions are not experienced after the event (because of the event), but can be relayed as part of the event. That is to say such experiences are holistic experiences in which no distinction is made between what is said in the vision or audition and what the vision or audition as such produces. As said earlier, often the ASC experience is the message; it is the person having the experience who is the one transmitting the knowledge or message.

Finally, there are also the features ascribed to Jesus and to the heavenly messengers that point toward ASC experiences. In many of the accounts, Jesus is presented as a figure subject to shape shifting. That is, in these experiences, he could take on a variety of appearances and even be present in disguise. In Matthew, some of the disciples doubted when they saw him (28:17), while in John, Mary Magdalene "saw Jesus standing there, but she did not know that it was Jesus" (20:14). The longer ending of Mark explicitly understands the tradition that he *appeared* "in another form" (16:12) to two of his followers. A different way of saying that they did not recognize him is to claim that (whatever it might mean?) their eyes were "kept from recognizing him" (Luke 24:16). As a report in waking consciousness—a perfectly recognizable Jesus unrecognized—this does not make sense, while as an account of a visionary experience of some sort, it makes perfect sense that Jesus could interact with two of his followers, walk with them and talk with them, while they did not recognize him.[8]

When taken as actual reports about visions or merely as claims that knowledge is based on a vision or sighting, it remains impressive to see how many such visionary encounters are offered in the sources in support that Jesus had resumed an afterlife existence. The following summary of the data is helpful.[9]

---

8. This should not necessarily be seen as a report of a visionary experience by any one or both of these two disciples. It rather makes sense as a typical report about a visionary experience by one of the disciples, which was offered as cultural evidence for Jesus's afterlife presence. While the idea of group trance experiences is often questioned by the uninformed, it is clear that such phenomena are not uncommon to anthropological literature (see Pilch 2004, 15).

9. Another way of looking at the data is to distinguish visions at the tomb from visions elsewhere—which would include those two followers at a later stage (see Pilch 1998, 57).

MARK	JOHN
1. Vision of angel(s) - 3 women* → young man (16:5)	1. Vision of angel(s) - 1 woman* → 2 angels (20:12)
2. Visions of Jesus Jesus appeared to: - Mary Magdalene (16:9) - two followers (16:12) - eleven disciples (16:14)	2. Visions of Jesus Jesus appeared to: - Mary Magdalene (20:14) - two followers (16:12) - ten disciples (20:19) - ten disciples and Thomas (20:26) - seven disciples (21:1)
MATTHEW 1. Vision of angel(s) - 2 women* → angel (28:2)	
2. Visions of Jesus Jesus appeared to: - the 2 women (28:9) - eleven disciples (16:14)	**PAUL** 2. Visions of Jesus Jesus appeared to: - Cephas (1 Cor 15:5) - twelve disciples (1 Cor 15:5) - five hundred men (1 Cor 15:6)
LUKE 1. Vision of angel(s) - 3 women* → 2 men (24:4)	- James (1 Cor 15:7) - all the other apostles (1 Cor 15:7) - Paul of Tarsus (1 Cor 15:8; Gal 1:12, 16)
2. Visions of Jesus Jesus appeared to: - two followers (24:15–16) - eleven disciples (24:37)	

* The list of women constantly changes:
>   Mark: Mary Magdalene, Mary the mother of James, Salome
>   Matthew: Mary Magdalene and the other Mary
>   Luke: Mary Magdalene, Joanna and Mary the mother of James
>   (and the other women)
>   John: only Mary Magdalene
>   Paul: no women.

When taken as reports about a series of visions or merely as claims about visionary experiences, the point remains the same: the resurrection accounts are filled with a cultural reality based on a culturally approved way of gaining knowledge. It is possible that some of the appearance accounts really are forms of legitimation of specific disciples by means of visionary reports and are not accounts of visionary experiences. On the basis of the current data, it is almost impossible to tell the difference between an account of an actual ASC experience (vision) and an account of a legitimation of a specific group of followers by means of an appearance story as an

ascribed vision—either way, *visions* as basis for knowledge play a remarkable role in the foundation of their claims. Either way, it is confirmed that
Jesus's presence with them is connected to or finds support from visionary
experiences. Put differently, for them, visionary experiences—actual or
reported about—were a sufficient basis for claiming an afterlife existence
for Jesus of Nazareth.

One of the most difficult things for people not socialized in a polyphasic culture is to accept the ease with which even normal human phenomena (such as eating or speaking) are reported in such visionary accounts
as what has happened. But this is precisely what is encountered in these
reports: accounts of normal human phenomena together with phenomena
common to their cultural system (such as encounters with angels).

The Features of a Resurrected (Afterlife) Body

Within their cycle of meaning and given the large number of appearances
of Jesus, none of these authors doubted Jesus's postmortem existence, and
they all describe it by means of *resurrection* language. Resurrection was not
an impossibility, but (in a Greco-Roman context, where the preferred notion was the immortality of the soul) was an exceptional afterlife option.
Since it was first *revealed* to Daniel (see Segal 2004, 262–65), resurrection
became an established afterlife option in some Israelite thinking. The potential for resurrection was already established in their spectrum of afterlife
options, and it had entered the cycle of meaning by means of a revelation.
This does not mean its characteristics were fixed. They were not, because
like all other afterlife options, these were also created in the dynamics of a
cycle of meaning where ASC experiences played a major role. The result of
this can clearly be detected in the New Testament data.

Although it might be explained by the fact that his experiences took
place long after Jesus's death, for Paul Jesus's resurrected body was some
kind of pneumatic entity. To be sure, Paul agreed that Jesus's afterlife existence was the result of resurrection (after all this was what had been
delivered to him via the tradition). Elsewhere I have argued that besides
some other features unique to ancient conceptions of the human body,
Paul's notion of Jesus's resurrected body as a *soma pneumatikon* should
indeed be seen as both bodily and material (see Craffert 2005b). As Martin
argues, Paul could not conceive of a "noncorporeal" or a "nonbody body,"

only of different kinds of bodies all made up of the same "stuffness" (see 1995, 128).

The canonical Gospels, on the other hand, deny what Paul affirms, namely, that the resurrected Jesus existed as a pneumatic body (a *soma pneumatikon*). It is Luke (see 24:39) in particular who emphasizes the flesh-and-bones body. In the Gospels, two other features of the resurrected Jesus are emphasized. He could easily move through closed doors, despite the fact that he had flesh and bones. While locked up in a house, the disciples experienced a vision where Jesus appeared to them (John 20:19) and showed them the wounds on his body.[10] There can be little doubt that they would have "seen" his body as it was, wounded and "real." All of this is confirmed by the report about Thomas's vision eight days later when again Jesus appeared through shut doors and Thomas could touch Jesus's body (John 20:26–27). As in dreams, in other ASC experiences, people have the same sensory perceptions as in waking states; that is, feeling, touching, smelling, hearing, or seeing what they take to exist.

Within a world where no ideas about afterlife existence were standardized, except for the cycle of meaning within which each configuration was created, it is not surprising to find such a diversity in the claims about the resurrected Jesus (or his resurrected body). In different ways the sources describe his afterlife existence by means of the tools and resources available in their particular configuration of the cycle of meaning. Flesh and bones did not constitute the resurrected body but was the format in which the reality of a resurrected body was expressed and experienced by some authors.

Resurrected bodies, in this scheme of things, belong to the categories of bodily format that are created and maintained in the cycle of meaning based on a certain set of beliefs about the human self, combined with a range of bodily (ASC) experiences. A resurrected body was (for them) a real and concrete afterlife form of existence; it was both real and it existed. This is something different from saying the documents were describing a body of transformed physicality or a divinely created supernatural body. Trapped by the *myth of realism*, scholars have as a result made all sorts of claims about Jesus as resurrected figure and about the nature of his resurrected body as some kind of supernatural entity. If they were describing

10. Within the parallel versions of Greco-Roman afterlife options expressed by means of immortal souls, even these disembodied souls retained the imprints and marks of their death wounds (see Riley 1995, 50–51).

a body of *transformed physicality* (a new format of bodily existence), the Gospel authors were doing a lousy job because they were couching it in the terms encountered in other afterlife accounts of the day. Instead, a resurrected body belonged, just like a possessed or a traveling body, to the features and bodily formats that could be created in their cycle of meaning while assuming their beliefs about the human body and the acquisition of knowledge.

The understanding offered here is radically different from the authenticity paradigm (in particular that of the Schweitzerstrasse). Based on the same evidence, those on the Schweitzerstrasse take the emphasis on the *materiality* of Jesus's resurrected body (flesh and bones, touching, eating fish) as indications that it was a *real* material body with supernatural qualities (it could appear and disappear and move through closed doors). All sensory stimuli can be part of ASC experiences. In ASCs, people can travel in or out of the body; or can experience touch, smell, or taste. ASCs can be taken as extremely real (a basic feature of polyphasic cultures), so there is nothing exceptional about the emphasis of the resurrection stories on Jesus's materiality as a feature encountered in visionary or other ASC experiences. Given the afterlife options available and the cycle of meaning of first-century Israelite people, they were convinced that he was no longer dead, but alive and well in the realm of the ancestors, immortals, or other divine beings. For some, he probably existed as a star somewhere among the other stars (angels, immortals, and divine beings).

It is beyond the level of this study to even discuss the question whether these visions were hallucinations or not.[11] They are taken as culturally legitimate (and approved) means of obtaining knowledge about their world, and in this case, about Jesus as a shamanic figure (a son of man and son of God for his followers) who is sitting at the right hand of God.[12] In Paul's mind, for example, there could have been no doubt that

11. In the realm of the study of shamanism in anthropology, the debate is, generally speaking, beyond the point of quarreling about whether shamanic ASC experiences are hallucinations or pathological (see, e.g., Boyer 1969). In the circle of New Testament studies, it is often still introduced (even in order to put down such a suggestion as an option (see, e.g., Segal 2005, 406–11).

12. Although Paul never uses the term *son of man*, Segal argues that he clearly identifies the Christ with the "son of man" figure. He argues: "Paul made an explicit analogy with the stars, which are both spiritual and bodies at the same time. And the analogy is not merely adventitious. It links the transformational process with the passage in Daniel 12 yet again, since Daniel 12 described the wise as transformed into stars. The transformed in Christ

Jesus was alive and well, living among the divine beings and immortals, and that Christians will one day be changed into spiritual bodies and exist among the stars.

Jesus's Tomb Was Empty

The canonical Gospels emphasize another feature that needs to be considered: Jesus's tomb was found empty. Luke confirms that it was the women (three mentioned by name in this account, together with the other women) who found the tomb empty of the body (24:3). In John it is Mary Magdalene alone who discovers the empty tomb and reports it to Peter and the disciple Jesus loved (20:1–2). Only after they have confirmed her observation at the tomb do they go back to their homes (in Galilee?). Thus, support for the visionary knowledge about Jesus's afterlife existence comes in all four canonical Gospels with the claim that Jesus's body was not found or was no longer in the tomb.

It should be emphasized that, as the earliest sources already indicate, an empty tomb, as such, is no convincing evidence that a resurrection has taken place. The polemic against opponents, who countered the claims of Jesus's resurrection with the explanation that his body was stolen by the disciples (Matt 28:11–15), confirms this point. As this polemic confirms, the Gospel authors probably knew perfectly well that an empty tomb, as such, is no evidence for a resurrection because the body could have been removed or stolen—that is, on the assumption that they knew in which cave or grave the body had been deposited in the first instance. Those of the house of Israel who did not accept the validity or legitimacy of these visionary accounts could easily have countered them with a story about a tomb raided by the disciples.

An empty tomb would have convinced nobody in the first-century world about the reality of an afterlife existence (most people were already convinced about that); it was only a means of selling a particular format of afterlife existence, namely, that of a bodily resurrection of a particular social personage. While the majority of Greco-Roman (and Israelite) afterlife options did not require a body, it becomes apparent why such a claim needed additional support. The idea of a resurrected body was not an impossibility, but it was a culturally abhorrent one, at least for many

---

will have, in short, the same substance as stars, which are luminous and spiritual in nature" (see 2004, 426–28).

Romans; after all, who would want a continued existence in this earthly body (see Riley 1995, 23)? An empty tomb was within that world no evidence for the reality of an afterlife existence it was the consequence of having a bodily resurrected afterlife existence. Where bodily resurrection is weaved into the cycle of meaning, seeing the deceased at the tomb was immediate confirmation that the tomb was empty.

Summary

Segal suggests that "for the evangelists, Jesus' resurrected body was a literal, physical body revivified" (2004, 442). I would agree, as long as *literal* and *physical* are taken as their culturally dependent notions about the body and reality. Within their cycle of meaning, bodies could travel or could become possessed and, by the same logic, resume an afterlife existence. For his cultural contemporaries, Jesus's body was resurrected as a real and truly first-century Israelite resurrected body that after Jesus's death, happened as a cultural event and via cultural phenomena. For people with strong beliefs in some form of postmortem existence, death is no end but a transit; it represents a step-over from one format of existence to another. It is to be suggested that within the cycle of meaning there is a larger unity of beliefs that hung together. The same kind of experiences and the exact beliefs about the human being (or self) underlie travel, possession, and afterlife experiences.

From this brief overview, it seems apparent that the New Testament authors firmly believed that Jesus did not remain entombed but continued an afterlife. The question remaining is whether such a position would in any way support the shamanic hypothesis.

Resurrection as an Afterlife Option for a Galilean Shamanic Figure?

It has been suggested above that the New Testament data provide very firm evidence that the belief that resurrection as a postmortem existence was ascribed to Jesus of Nazareth. All the documents mentioned claim in one way or another that he was no longer dead but assumed a resurrected afterlife existence. They were convinced that his tomb was empty and that he was enjoying a postmortem life. The question remaining is whether it is likely that such an afterlife option would have been ascribed to Jesus of

Nazareth or would have belonged to his life story. Many have argued that it could have been the product of literary or mythological creativity that it was ascribed to his life, but it is likely that in a very real sense his life as shamanic figure continued beyond the tomb. Two arguments will be advanced in this regard.

A Postmortem Existence for a Galilean Shamanic Figure?

The first is a general argument claiming that a postmortem existence would not be out of place in the life of a Galilean shamanic figure. Although resurrection is not a particular feature of shamanic figures, they often could, due to the shamanic worldview, fall into the category of figures who would be elevated to the level of the *living dead* (ancestors) while continuing to influence the community in all affairs.

Most people's biographies (life stories) end with their deaths. This is, however, not the case with everybody, because there is ample testimony that in some cultural settings religious leaders, healers, or other significant people are believed to continue their existence as living ancestors or as *the living dead*. In anthropological literature, it is not unknown that a healer becomes a supernatural figure or resumes a postmortem existence (see Dow 1986, 61), and in many contemporary church movements in the third world, it is not uncommon for the church founder, after death, to be elevated to such a position (see Obeng 1992, 94; Schoffeleers 1994, 83). The veneration of the burial sites of saints in both Christian and Jewish circles confirms this practice and so does the cultural lexicon that maintains that the holy ones continue their influence on the living (see Pilch 1998, 55–58).

The context in which resurrection entered Israelite thought (Dan 12), which has already been discussed, suggests that there will be those people who just live and die and experience no resurrection; while others, the wise and those giving instruction (providing revelations?), will be rewarded with resurrection (see Segal 2004, 291). An example from many years later shows another group from the ancient world where afterlife (in this case soul immortality) was not an option for everybody but only for some: "Jesus said, 'The souls of every human generation will die. When these people, however, have completed the time of the kingdom and the spirit leaves them, their bodies will die but their souls will be alive, and they will be taken up" (*Gospel of Judas* 43; Kasser, Meyer & Wurst trans.).

It is not necessary to offer more examples, and within a cable-like interpretive process the aim is not to find sufficient direct authentic testimonies claiming that Jesus of Nazareth was rewarded with an afterlife option. Instead, the point is a very general one: it is neither unknown for significant figures to be ascribed such a feature, nor unexpected that, if Jesus was a Galilean shamanic figure, it would have happened to him. Speaking generally, an afterlife option would not be out of place for a Galilean shamanic figure.

But there are particular features suggesting that resurrection as an afterlife option could very easily have been ascribed to Jesus of Nazareth. In fact, it is to be suggested that at least three streams of evidence suggest that it could have been the product or result of a shamanic life.

Resurrection as the Product or Result of a Shamanic Life

Afterlife in general, and resurrection in particular, must have been known to Jesus and his first followers. It would be difficult to argue otherwise because the very practice of secondary burials and the changes with burial practices during the first century of the common era suggest that first-century Israelite people were not dependent solely on Daniel and the Maccabean accounts for their belief in resurrection as afterlife option (see, e.g., Rahmani 1982).

In addition to the general argument that Jesus was, at least for his followers, a significant social personage, there are three lines of argument suggesting that it would not be inappropriate to connect Jesus's life to resurrection—lines of argument, in fact, that point to a variety of dynamic processes that could have contributed both to the ascription of an afterlife to him and to the accompanied postmortem experiences of him by his followers.

HEAVEN WAS FAMILIAR TERRITORY FOR JESUS OF NAZARETH

A sense of divine sonship, it was argued, is a feature ascribed to figures in the Israelite world with close and intimate relations with God, and, therefore, *son of God* is a designation that could have been linked to Jesus as a social personage (see above, pp. 238–41). The "kingdom of God" and "son of man" sayings closely associated Jesus with astral prophecy and with being involved in the heavenly realm on a regular basis. If he was a shamanic figure, as suggested by these features, it is likely that he has had intimate relations with the Israelite divine world. In short, he seems to have been highly familiar with the heavenly territory.

For that reason it is not surprising to find explicit references that Jesus expected to be lifted up (John 12:32). While "lifted up" could be seen as a reference to the crucifixion (as is suggested by v. 33), the context of this saying is that of the glorification of the Son of Man: "Jesus answered them, 'The hour has come for the Son of Man to be glorified' . . . The crowd answered him, 'We have heard from the law that the Messiah remains forever. How can you say that the Son of Man must be lifted up?'" (John 12:23, 34). Its primary meaning, Brown contends, is exaltation (see 1994, 1484).

The same idea is expressed a little later in John when Jesus promises his followers that he is on his way to his Father's house: "In my Father's house there are many dwelling places. If it were not so, would I have told you that I go to prepare a place for you? And if I go and prepare a place for you, I will come again and will take you to myself, so that where I am, there you may be also" (John 14:2–3). The idea of going and coming back from the divine realm is explicitly assumed. The very least that can be said about this is that within these sayings the gap between the divine and human world is narrow, and transit readily available. There was no huge and unbridgeable divide.

If the heavenly territory was not unfamiliar to Jesus as a social personage (as a son of man and a son of God), and if his own experiences included the transition (heavenly journeys), it would not be unreasonable to accept that death, in his view, was no serious threat. In fact, Jesus as a social personage would be precisely the kind of figure suitable for postmortem life in the heavenly realm.

JESUS'S AFTERLIFE EXPECTATIONS AS PREPARATION FOR ASC EXPERIENCES AFTER HIS DEATH

There is a whole body of data pointing toward the fact that as a son of man, Jesus expected, after his death, to resume a postmortem existence as a resurrected figure. That is the material normally treated as the *passion predictions*.[13] The most important are the threefold predictions in the synoptic parallel texts (Mark 8:31; 9:31; 10:33–34 and parallels) together with the threefold Johannine "Son of Man" saying about being lifted up

---

13. Brown (see 1994, 1469) offers a list of all these texts.

(John 3:14; 8:28; 12:34). Taken together with the other allusions to a violent death, "these statements point to death with suffering, sometimes in figurative OT or parabolic language" (Brown 1994, 1473).

Within the authenticity paradigm, these sayings are dealt with on a spectrum from "extraordinary or miraculous foreknowledge" (Brown 1994, 1468) to post-Easter creations or, as Theissen and Merz say, "prophecies after the event" (1998, 429). I have no desire to engage those discussions or to add another view on the possible tradition history of sayings that obviously have some family resemblances. Instead, if Jesus was a social personage of the type suggested here, it is very likely that he would have expected confrontations with the authorities, which could end in a violent death. My interest is not in whether these sayings were old and authentic, but whether they make sense as elements within the life of a Galilean shamanic figure. Do they have historical probability as belonging to the life of such a social personage?

Jesus probably started his public career after encounters with John the Baptist and from the very beginning must have realized that a similar violent death could become his destiny. On all accounts, the proclamation of the kingdom of God must have sounded like high treason to Roman ears, while the constant stream of opposition from other Israelite groups (temple authorities and Pharisees) could not have been encouraging for a wandering social personage such as Jesus.[14] It is even likely that someone in his position would have utilized the knowledge and references to Israelite sacred texts on the destiny of the prophets. It would only have been a socially illiterate person who, in Jesus's situation as a Galilean shamanic figure, would not have considered a violent death at the hands of the authorities as a likely outcome of his life.[15]

The explicit references to the "kingdom of God" and "Son of Man" themes in these *predictions* would not be out of place for someone identifying himself as a son of man, that is, for someone like a Galilean shamanic figure. The focus here is not to repeat all the arguments (especially not to

14. Jesus's proclamation of the kingdom of God was very much a threat and challenge to the Israelite theocracy (see Malina 1991b, 144–49).

15. What has not even been considered in this study are the clashes of religious institutions or forms of religiosity as well as the various levels of power incompatibility that Jesus's activities represent. On all accounts, Jesus of Nazareth represented a threat to several institutions: "it is not difficult to understand that Jesus was an irritant to the systems of power in Galilee, based on Antipas's administration, on the temple and Torah, as well as traditions of and structures of authority in village and household" (Moxnes 2003, 130).

show that these probably were authentic Jesus sayings) regarding Jesus's expectation of a violent death.[16] Instead, it is to create an awareness that the precarious nature of life must have been part of their (of Jesus's and his first followers') daily existence.

While I do not see these discourses (the passion predictions) as predictions, prophecies, or statements of foreknowledge, it is remarkable that they all contain a postmortem expectation. As Brown summarizes the evidence: "All three Synoptic predictions involve Jesus's ultimate victory; to rise or be raised. All Johannine predictions involve his exaltation to God" (1994, 1485). Especially in the context of the "kingdom of God" and "Son of Man" terminologies employed, it would not be out of place for a Galilean shamanic figure to anticipate such an afterlife existence. Given the references already mentioned that deceased ancestors from time to time interacted with Jesus and his followers, and that Jesus himself may have had some forms of heavenly engagements, and given the above arguments that Jesus probably identified himself as such a figure, it is reasonable that he also anticipated a postmortem existence for himself.

The suggestion here is that such expectations could very well have contributed to the ASC experiences after his death. While all these so-called predictions could have been created after his death, it is also possible that they in fact reflect the memory of an anticipation of Jesus as Galilean shamanic figure. But in addition to the above evidence, it is suggested that such expectations would have been particularly conducive to the visionary experiences after his violent death on the cross. The passion predictions, when seen from this perspective then, are not creations after the fact (by the evangelists or the early church) but could very well be seen as part of the dynamics of why his followers suddenly became subject to ASC experiences.

AFTER DEATH ASCs AS THE CONTINUATION
OF SUCH EXPERIENCES DURING JESUS'S LIFETIME

It is well known that visionary experiences often occur during states of mourning and sadness and especially after a violent and unexpected death. It is equally well known that such theories have been applied to explain the resurrection appearances (see, e.g., Lüdemann 1995, 93–95). However, it

16. Brown provides a good description of most of the issues (see 1994, 1484–89), while I agree with much of what Balla concludes about Jesus's foreseeing a violent death for himself (see 2001).

remains remarkable that according to the reports, soon after his death, the dominant form of cultural experience of Jesus's followers was various forms of ASCs and, in particular, visionary experiences. Not only did Paul start his career with such visions and John, in Revelation, report about such experiences, but the Acts of the Apostles is packed with ASC experiences (see Pilch 2004).

Given the already-discussed ASC experiences connected to Jesus and his public activities and the continued pattern of such experiences ascribed to Jesus's followers, it is suggested that the visionary resurrection experiences of Jesus after his death were not the product of his death but rather of his life as a shamanic figure. It seems as if a cultural pattern of such experiences was well established during his life and was merely continued after his death. Seen in this way, Jesus's postresurrection appearances are the continuation of the cultural practices that were part of the dynamics of their lives prior to his death with the one significant difference that now, Jesus himself, in some instances, becomes the content of their ASC experiences. Instead of the significant ancestors from the distant past, Jesus appeared in their visions; the *seer* became the *seen*.

Conclusion

Most people in the first-century Mediterranean world would have agreed on some kind of postmortem existence, but not on the shape, format, or entrance requirement thereof. The same elements in the cycle of meaning produced more than one afterlife option. Postmortem existence came in various formats, and neither resurrection of the body nor the immortality of the soul existed outside the cycle of meaning in which they were taken as real.

Second, the thrust of this argument is that resurrection was ascribed to Jesus of Nazareth because of who and what he was as a shamanic figure and not the other way around (marvelous features were not ascribed to his life because he was resurrected). He was resurrected and resumed an afterlife existence in the dynamics of his group precisely because of who and what he was as a shamanic figure. Both the resurrection and appearance reports as well as the *passion predictions* can be taken as remembered accounts (residues) about this life. Not as free-floating events or phenomena but as cultural events that were closely weaved into the fabric of his life as a Galilean shamanic figure and understandable as cultural realities connected to the dynamics of such a life. Jesus of Nazareth was indeed resurrected and probably precisely because of who and what he was prior to his death. In this sense, the *historicity* of Jesus's resurrection is strongly attested as belonging to his social character.

Resurrection in Cross-Cultural and Comparative Perspective

One of the implications of the above position is that in the ancient world everybody would not have accepted everybody else's notions about the afterlife. The different cultural options about the afterlife would have been exclusive categories of thought and experience for those not sharing the particular cultural assumptions and specific cycle of meaning. For example, the reality of resurrection as an afterlife option was disputed right from the beginning—as is confirmed by the often-reported disputes between the Pharisees and the Sadducees (see, e.g., Acts 23:6–11).[17] Rejection of resurrection was virtually given with its cultural construction, because the same cycle of meaning produced more than one afterlife option.

But it is precisely the structure of this belief that opens it for further cross-cultural and comparative analyses. Postmortem existence (then and today) was no free-floating idea. Postmortem existence was attached to a cycle of meaning, and the cycle of meaning included beliefs about the (dualist or tripartite) bodily existence of human beings; the cycle of meaning also included experiential-reflective knowledge acquisition common in polyphasic cultures. What happens when these cultural assumptions no longer apply? This is what constitutes the real difficulty in accepting the reality of Jesus's resurrection as a homoversal truth or general fact of history: it becomes nonsensical or a cultural impossibility. Three arguments can be advanced in this regard since cultural bundubashing acknowledges that part of the interpretive process includes the world of the interpreter or historian and asks for cultural dialog and criticism.

---

17. Segal offers an insightful analysis of the presence of afterlife notions in different Israelite groups of the first century based on the social location and the corresponding beliefs of different groups. The Sadducees, for example, did not have a belief about the afterlife because they did not need one. As the wealthy members of society, they had "a paradise on earth in the back gardens of their estates" (2004, 378) and, therefore, would not long for some kind of afterlife reward, but it was different with other groups.

The Embodied Self versus the Disembodied Soul

It has been indicated that the concept "soul" is a complex concept with a long and intricate history. Modern *soul*-talk often takes place in two contexts: as a description of the human being ("human capacity and experience") or as that "part of the self that continues beyond death" (Brown 1998, 100). The latter is the remnant of our ancestors' beliefs in the disembodied soul.

What our ancestors called "the *soul*" is today often called "the *self*," but that does not necessarily include talk about a part or entity that can continue beyond death. This is the case because although the history of soul- or self-talk is characterized by various forms of dualism, lately a "growing support for a monist, or physicalist, account of the human being" (Green 1998, 149) has been recorded.

Monism[18] or *physicalism*[19] is the cultural position that realizes that the self (although it can be separated from the body in the experience of the self or in language) is embodied and connected to practices. The "self" is constituted in interaction with a specific environment and in conversation with others; it is an engendered and bodily self within a social environment. Who we are, according to this cultural construct, is not the disembodied soul or self somewhere in the body but the self as bodily manifested in the world.[20]

The categories used to explore this monistic position are as diverse as the ancient dualist positions. They include the idea of a human self as constituted in conversation as a "dialogical self" (Taylor 1991, 314), as a

18 *Monism* in this sense as the opposite of *dualism* has nothing to do with ontological monism as the philosophical position that acknowledges only a single cultural reality and worldview as normative. Here, *monism* can be replaced by *unitary, holistic*, or *nondualist*.

19. Physicalists believe, among other things, that "our mental and spiritual lives are wholly dependent upon the workings of our brains" (Harris 2004, 208). While some reduce consciousness to the mere materiality of the brain, it is also possible to see all of this in a systems ontology, which sees consciousness as the emerging property of a complex bodily system.

20. From this point of view, the self or consciousness (or soul) is not "something inside the body. It is a manner of existence of certain highly complex animals, a manner of being-in-the-world of certain animal species. . . . Being conscious is related to material processes, but has a reality that cannot be ignored. Consciousness is a non-spatial aspect of biological reality" (Kriel 2000, 93–94). Far from reducing reality to materiality, this position is based on a systems ontology which acknowledges that reality is not located in building blocks (material entities) only, but is "variegated and essentially organized as levels of complex systems" (2000, 80).

"distributed coalition of agents" (Spurrett 2002, 216), or as *nonreductive physicalism* that asserts that the embodied soul is a "dimension of human experiences" that arises out of personal relatedness (Brown 1998, 101). The self is a way of being: bodily, socially, and culturally and is neither a component of nor equivalent to any of these. For a transplant of this self or consciousness (or soul, if you like) to any known or imaginable form would depend far more on the structure of the body and the world in which it lives than is often assumed: "If who we are depends a lot on the bodies we are, and the environments we are in, then being us in a new incarnation depends as much on information beyond the brain as it does on structures and content in the brain" (Spurrett 2002, 216).[21] An immortal soul manifestation or a bodily resurrection of this self elsewhere in the universe will have to replicate far more than is possible in order for this self to be who and what it currently is. This kind of self is at home not only in this body, but also in this social, cultural, and environmental setting. Despite the ability to experience (or describe in language) the self (or soul) as separate from the body, it is no separate entity (thing) but a nonmaterial reality inscribed into (or the result of) a complex bodily and environmental system.

So much for the notion that a disembodied soul was part of the ancient cycle of meaning. There is a second component of the Israelite cycle of meaning that no longer sits comfortably in a modern world.

Radical Reflexivity versus Experiential-Reflective Knowledge

The cultural position that promotes a monistic position Taylor ascribes to "radical reflexivity" (1991, 304), while Spurrett says it was bought at the cost of divorcing positional and experiential claims from real and apparent ones (2002, 192). Spurrett explains it with the common notion of sunset-speech, which we all ascribe to while knowing perfectly well that relative to the earth, the sun does not move; "sunrises are really earth-turnings" (the terms *real* and *really* are used in this paragraph in the same meaning). Things are not always as they seem to us or as we experience them and this applies both to sunsets and to self-speak or soul-talk.

---

21. In this regard, Harris argues that "unless the soul retains all the normal cognitive and perceptual capacities of the healthy brain, heaven would be populated by beings suffering from all manner of neurological deficit" (2004, 278 n. 3).

Radical reflexivity refers to that practice not only of having experiences but of scrutinizing them and subjecting them to reflexive thinking. Self-speak ("I said to myself . . .") and experiences of the self (like sunsets) will not go away, and neither will the ability we have as language-using animals to make our bodies and our selves objects of description and reflection.[22] However, even if one can in experiences (or language) still distinguish the "self" or "soul" as separate from the body, no longer should this distinction lead to a dualism of entities. Such experiences are no longer the sole source for constructing knowledge about the self.

The cultural position of monism is based on the practice of radical reflexivity plus a systems ontology in which experience is not the only source of knowledge, and reality is not equal to the existence of material entities or to the experienced entities only. This is something different from the experiential-reflective way of obtaining knowledge in the ancient cycle of meaning. The notion of experiential-reflective knowledge in a polyphasic culture no longer applies to the conditions in many modern societies. It should go without saying that the elements of this cycle of meaning cannot be purchased piecemeal in order to satisfy needs in other cultural settings. Notions about resurrection or immortality of the soul go hand in hand with the knowledge generating practices and experiences that have created them in the first instance as well as with the ideas about the human self. It is today difficult to affirm any of the cultural assumptions that made belief in resurrection (or, for that matter, in the immortality of the soul) as afterlife options viable for first-century Israelite people.

And to take sides with the Sadducees, who rejected the idea of resurrection, or with the Qumran community, who had no cultural need for it, is one way of saying that as a cultural option, it is no longer viable. The rejection of resurrection as a plausible afterlife option is neither a modern scientific phenomenon nor the result of a closed worldview, but more likely happened because the specific configuration of cultural beliefs, experiences, and practices is not shared between cultures.

The different positions can be summarized by means of a comparative table.

22. In the words of Kriel, "I can *be* my lived body or I can *observe* my body—step back (metaphorically speaking) and see (experience) my body as an object in the world. I can distinguish in language between myself as a lived body, and my objectified body. But when I am my lived body, I do not have a consciousness, *I am my conscious body*" (2002, 143; italics his).

EXPERIENTIAL-REFLECTIVE KNOWLEDGE	RADICAL REFLEXIVITY

Experiential cycle of meaning:
 	
• Dualism(s): body-soul/spirit
• Disembodied soul/spirit
• Afterlife options: —resurrection
                —immortality
            of the soul
	Physicalist/monisms
	
	• Afterlife:—mystery
	          —reserved silence

Beyond Afterlife Speculations to Afterlife Skepticism

It should be emphasized that part of the foregoing argument is to affirm the cultural reality of resurrection as one afterlife option for first-century Israelite people. But affirming the reality of cultural events and phenomena is something different from claiming that such accounts are universally or homoversally valid and applicable. Affirming the cultural reality of any of their afterlife options is a very limited affirmation of reality because it contains a yes supplemented by a strong no. It is little more than the acknowledgement of a reality for them that does not affirm a homoversal reality or phenomenon.

Today it is more appropriate to say that what happens after death is a mystery. When modern thinkers affirm "that we simply do not know what happens after death" (Harris 2004, 208), it should be taken seriously. Paradoxically, it means that nobody, literally nobody past or present, can claim with any degree of confidence to know what *afterlife* is like; at the same time, it means that specific human claims about an *afterlife* can also be evaluated as the cultural constructs within a particular cycle of meaning. In other words, a reservation about such knowledge does not keep us from rejecting cultural claims that no longer make (cultural) sense or that pretend to know the mystery.

Conclusion

There can be little doubt that the canonical Gospels offer sufficient evidence for the conviction that Jesus was not dead and enclosed in a grave but alive and well at the right hand of God and in the company of other Israelite ancestors. In short, the reports and stories about Jesus's resurrection are evidence for his continued life as a Galilean shamanic figure after his death in the realm of the living dead. But that is something different from saying that *Jesus's resurrection is a historical fact*, because these cultural reports and claims have to be placed in a cross-cultural and comparative perspective in order to make sense in the modern world.

Resurrection, for first-century people, was no unexpected or inexplicable event in history, an event that was treated as a mystery. It was one of the available (although, for the majority people, not the preferred) afterlife options constituted by means of an existing Israelite cycle of meaning. In contrast to those who take the testimonies as pointing toward a real instance of extraordinary events in which a dead body was transformed into a new mode of physicality (as something exceedingly strange and unprecedented in the real world), too may features merely point toward culturally stamped accounts of a culturally approved way of accounting for the events. The "real resurrection of Jesus from the dead, the real event itself," Lüdemann says, is not described in any New Testament text (1995, 24). I have suggested that from a culturally sensitive point of view, the "real" cultural event was indeed described in the documents because it was a cultural event clothed in their cycle of meaning, which made sense to them.

Conclusion:
Someone Like a Galilean Shamanic Figure?

WITHIN A REAL PARADIGM change, Kuhn (1970, 109, 111) says, "there are usually significant shifts in the criteria determining the legitimacy both of problems and of proposed solutions. . . . What were ducks in the scientist's world before the revolution are rabbits afterwards." Anthropological historiography represents such a change in historical Jesus research because, despite a great variety and apparent constant renewals, there is a remarkable singularity in historical Jesus research. It remains trapped in the historiographical framework from which it emerged more than a hundred and fifty years ago and is limited to the positivist/post-modern historiographical continuum. This is confirmed by the nested assumptions shared by the majority of historical Jesus researchers. These include the idea that a historical figure could not have been like the Gospel portrayals and consequently that the Gospels have developed in a linear and layered fashion from the authentic kernels to the elaborated literary constructions as they are known today. The aim of historical Jesus research, therefore, is to identify the authentic material from which the historical figure as a social type underneath the overlay is constructed. The social type identified in such constructions remains a talking head who spoke some authentic words and a disconnected actor who performed some pub-lic deeds, depending on the interpretive strategy, either within the setting of first-century Judaism or that of the Roman imperial rule.

In contrast, this book contains two distinct arguments. The one is that based on developments in historiographical discourse, an alternative interpretive framework can be conceptualized for historical Jesus research, and the other is that within this framework, the historical Jesus of Nazareth can be seen as a Galilean shamanic figure.

Anthropological historiography as an alternative theoretical paradigm offers a way out of the impasse in current historical Jesus research. It does not occupy a position somewhere in between positivist and postmodern historiography but represents an alternative paradigm that acknowledges multiple cultural realities and the existence of other forms of life as constitutive of the historical subject and the historical record. It offers an interpretive framework for a culturally sensitive understanding of Jesus of Nazareth as social personage embedded in his social system and worldview and by employing cross-cultural and anthropological models strives to cross both the temporal and cultural gaps faced by the historian.

The shamanic complex as an ASC-based religious pattern refers to a family of features that appears in many cultural contexts. It describes those religious entrepreneurs who, based on regular ASC-experiences, perform a set of social functions in their communities that are often separated from other social-type figures. As an identifiable pattern in the anthropological record, shamanic figures not only perform healings, exorcisms, and the control of spirits, but they also act as prophets, teachers, and poets in their communities. This is a social-type model that without much difficulty can account for the wide spectrum of gospel evidence ascribed to Jesus of Nazareth.

Jesus's baptism by John the Baptist resembles the initiation of a shamanic figure and probably introduced a life characterized by ASC experiences. It could be seen as the first of a series of spirit-possession and other ASC events that determined both his self-understanding and the dynamics of his public life. These set a pattern of experiences and events that were continued by his followers even after his death.

Like all shamanic figures, Jesus was credited with numerous healings, exorcisms, and various forms of spirit control. It is typical of shamanic figures to control spirit entities in the cultural settings in which they operate, and the bulk of the evidence regarding Jesus's public life could be interpreted in such a way as to show his control of spirits. The other side of a shamanic figure's public life includes being a telephone exchange to the divine world in order to convey knowledge, information, and divine wisdom. The two central concepts of his teaching, the "kingdom of God" and "Son of Man" sayings, both fit into the dynamics of a Galilean shamanic figure's life.

Like other shamanic figures, Jesus was plausibly attributed with a special birth that could have included unusual features of his mother's pregnancy. As features of a shamanic life, the infancy narratives are not seen as reports about how things were during his birth or early childhood, but these reports were part of the dynamics of a shamanic life: thus, they were the residues of some cultural processes associated with such a life.

In contrast to most historical Jesus research that ascribes many of the features in Jesus's life to the creativity of his followers after his death, this study argues that the resurrection can be seen as the product of a shamanic life instead of the ascribed mythical life being the result of a resurrection. This argument takes seriously the cultural and social dynamics associated with the kind of figure that is portrayed in the Gospels, and reasons that an afterlife would fit such a social personage.

The success of anthropological historiography as alternative framework for historical Jesus research is independent from the success of the shamanic complex for constructing the life of the historical figure. Even if the specific hypothesis is not endorsed, this framework offers a renewal of the paradigm. In constructions of Crossan and the Jesus Seminar, on the one hand, and in works of scholars such as Meier, Wright, and Sanders, on the other hand, positivistic Jesus research has been taken to its logical and sophisticated limits. Different constructions within that framework can only emerge from new configurations of authentic nuggets.

In my view, a fairly persuasive case has been made that the shamanic model allows an integrated interpretation of the variety of traditions as belonging to the life of a social figure and the dynamics associated with such a figure. If Jesus of Nazareth was not a shamanic figure, the portrayals in the available sources closely resemble the life of such a social personage. If Jesus was a Galilean shamanic figure, he was such right from the beginning of his public career and wherever and whenever he acted. That is to say, he acted as a shamanic figure and was socially constituted and maintained as such a figure once his public and social personage became known. The shamanic model is not a label that was applied to preidentified authentic words or deeds but is a heuristic tool that has allowed us a comprehensive and coherent understanding of the life of a social personage. More still needs to be done in exploring this hypothesis in order to obtain a full description of the life of a historical figure who is not easily captured by historical thinking.

Abbreviations

ABD	*Anchor Bible Dictionary.* Edited by David Noel Freedman. 6 vols. New York: Doubleday, 1992
AGAJU	Arbeit zur Geschichte des antiken Judentums und des Urchristentums
AmAnth	*American Anthropologist*
ANRW	*Aufstieg und Niedergang der römischen Welt*
ARA	*Annual Review of Anthropology*
BA	*Biblical Archaeologist*
BibIntSer	Biblical Interpretation Series
BTB	*Biblical Theology Bulletin*
BZNW	Beihefte zur Zeitschrift für die neutestamentliche Wissenschaft
CSSH	*Comparative Studies in Society and History*
CurrAnth	*Current Anthropology*
ER	*The Encyclopedia of Religion.* 16 vols. Edited by Mircea Eliade. New York: Macmillan, 1987
Forum	*Foundations & Facets Forum*
H&T	*History & Theory*
HTR	*Harvard Theological Review*
HTS	*Hervormde Teologiese Studies*
JBL	*Journal of Biblical Literature*
JJS	*Journal of Jewish Studies*
JSJSup	Journal for the Study of Judaism Supplements
JSNTSup	Journal for the Study of the New Testament Supplements
Neot	*Neotestamentica: Journal of the New Testament Society of South Africa*
NTS	*New Testament Studies*
NTTS	New Testament Tools and Studies

PGM	*Papyri graecae magicae: Die griechischen Zauberpapyri.* 2 vols. Edited by K. Preisendanz. Leipzig: Teubner, 1928.
R&T	*Religion & Theology*
SAMJ	*South African Medical Journal*
SCJ	Studies in Christianity and Judaism
Scrip	*Scriptura: International Journal of Bible, Religion and Theology in Southern Africa*
SJT	*Scottish Journal of Theology*
ThTo	*Theology Today*

Bibliography

Primary Literature

Quotations from *Apocalypse of Abraham*, *1 Enoch*, *3 Enoch*, the *Testament of Abraham*, *Testament of Naphtali*, *1 Enoch*, and *3 Enoch* are all from: James H. Charlesworth, editor. *The Old Testament Pseudepigrapha*, Vol. 1: *Apocalyptic Literature and Testaments*. Garden City, NY: Doubleday, 1983.

The quotation from *Pseudo-Phocylides* is from: James H. Charlesworth, editor. *The Old Testament Pseudepigrapha*, Vol. 2: *Expansions of the 'Old Testament' and legends, wisdom and philosophical literature, Prayers, Psalms and Odes, Fragments of lost Judeo-Hellenistic works*. Garden City, NY: Doubleday, 1985.

Quotations from the Bible are from the New Revised Standard Version (NRSV).

The quotations from *The Gospel of Philip*, *The Gospel of Pseudo-Matthew*, and *Pistis Sophia* are from: Wilhelm Schneemelcher and R. McL. Wilson, editors. *New Testament Apocrypha*, Vol. 1: *Gospels and Related Writings*. Rev. ed. Louisville: Westminster John Knox, 1991.

Quotations from the Qumran library are from: Florentino García Martínez. *The Dead Sea Scrolls Translated: The Qumran Texts in English*. Leiden: Brill, 1994.

The quotation from the *Gospel of Judas* is from: Rudolphe Kasser, Marvin Meyer, and Gregor Wurst. *The Gospel of Judas: From Codex Tchacos*. Washington DC: National Geographic, 2006.

The quotation from Josephus is from: H. St. J. Thackeray, editor and translator. *Josephus*, Vol. 1: *The Life, Against Apion*. London: Heinemann, 1926.

Secondary Literature

Aldrich, S., and C. Eccleston. 2000. "Making Sense of Everyday Pain." *Social Science & Medicine* 50:1631–41.

Alekseenko, E. A. 1984. "Some General and Specific Features in the Shamanism of the Peoples of Siberia." In *Shamanism in Eurasia*, edited by M. Hoppál, 85–96. Göttingen: Herodot.

Alexander, Desmond. 1986. "The Old Testament View of Life after Death." *Themelios* 11.2:41–46.

Allison, Dale C. 1993. "What Was the Star That Guided the Magi?" *Bible Review* 9.6:20–24, 63.

———. 1998. *Jesus of Nazareth: Millenarian Prophet*. Minneapolis: Fortress.

Almog, Oz. 1998. "The Problem of Social Type: A Review." *Electronic Journal of Sociology* 3.4:1–20.

American Psychiatric Association DSM-IV. 1994. *Diagnostic and Statistical Manual of Mental Disorders*. 4th ed. Washington, DC: American Psychiatric Association.

Ankersmit, F. R. 1989. "Historiography and Postmodernism." *H&T* 28:137–53.

Arnal, William. 1997. "Major Episodes in the Biography of Jesus: An Assessment of the Historicity of the Narrative Tradition." *Toronto Journal of Theology* 13:201–26.

Ashton, John. 2000. *The Religion of Paul the Apostle*. New Haven: Yale University Press.

Atkinson, Jane M. 1987. "The Effectiveness of Shamans in an Indonesian Ritual." *AmAnth* 89:342–55.

———. 1992. "Shamanisms Today." *ARA* 21:307–30.

Aune, David E. 1980. "Magic in Early Christianity." In *ANRW* II.23.2:1507–57.

———. 1994. "Human Nature and Ethics in Hellenistic Philosophical Traditions and Paul: Some Issues and Problems." In *Paul in His Hellenistic Context*, edited by T. Engberg-Pedersen, 291–312. Edinburgh: T. & T. Clark.

Austin, James H. 1998. *Zen and the Brain: Towards an Understanding of Meditation and Consciousness*. Cambridge: MIT Press.

Avalos, Hector. 1995. *Illness and Health Care in the Ancient Near East: The Role of the Temple in Greece, Mesopotamia, and Israel*. Harvard Semitic Monographs 53. Atlanta: Scholars.

———. 1999. *Health Care and the Rise of Christianity*. Peabody: Hendrickson, 1999.

Bailey, Kenneth E. 1991. "Informal Controlled Oral Tradition and the Synoptic Gospels." *Asia Journal of Theology* 5:34–54.

———. 1995. "Middle Eastern Oral Tradition and the Synoptic Gospels." *Expository Times* 106:363–67.

Baird, William. 1985. "Visions, Revelations, and Ministry: Reflections on 2 Cor 12:1–5 and Gal 1: 11–17." *JBL* 104:651–62.

Balla, Peter. 2001. "What Did Jesus Think About His Approaching Death?" In *Jesus, Mark and Q: The Teaching of Jesus and Its Earliest Records*, edited by M. Labahn and A. Schmidt, 239–58. JSNTSup 214. Sheffield: Sheffield Academic.

Balzer, Marjorie. 1991. "Doctors or Deceivers? The Siberian Khanty Shaman and Soviet Medicine." In *The Anthropology of Medicine: From Culture to Method*, edited by L. Romanucci-Ross, D. E. Moerman, and L. R. Tancredi, 56–80. 2nd ed. New York: Bergin & Garvey.

Bar-Ilan, Meir. 1992. "Illiteracy in the Land of Israel in the First Centuries C.E." In *Essays in the Social Scientific Study of Judaism and Jewish Society*, Vol. 2, edited by S. Fishbane, S. Schoenfeld, and A. Goldschläger, 46–61. Hoboken: Ktav.

Barraclough, Geoffrey. 1978. *Main Trends in History*. New York: Holmes & Meier.

Bauckham, Richard. 2006. *Jesus and the Eyewitnesses: The Gospels as Eyewitness Testimony*. Grand Rapids: Eerdmans.

Berger, Peter L., and Thomas Luckmann. 1966. *The Social Construction of Reality: A Treatise in the Sociology of Knowledge*. Harmondsworth: Penguin.

Bernstein, Richard J. 1983. *Beyond Objectivism and Relativism: Science, Hermeneutics, and Praxis*. Oxford: Blackwell.

———. 1991. *The New Constellation: The Ethical-Political Horizons of Modernity/Postmodernity*. Cambridge: MIT Press.

Blackburn, Barry L. 1994. "The Miracles of Jesus." In *Studying the Historical Jesus: Evaluations of the State of Current Research*, edited by Bruce Chilton and Craig A. Evans, 353–94. NTTS 19. Leiden: Brill.

Bloch-Smith, Elizabeth. 1992. "The Cult of the Dead in Judah: Interpreting the Material Remains." *JBL* 111:213–24.

Bloomquist, L. Gregory. 1997. "The Rhetoric of the Historical Jesus." In *Whose Historical Jesus?*, edited by William E. Arnal and Michel Desjardins, 98–117. SCJ 7. Waterloo, ON: Wilfred Laurier University Press.

Bogin, Barry. 1991. "The Evolution of Human Nutrition." In *The Anthropology of Medicine: From Culture to Method*, edited by L. Romanucci-Ross, D. E. Moerman, and L. R. Tancredi, 158–95. 2nd ed. New York: Bergin & Garvey.

Bonanno, G . A. 1990. "Remembering and Psychotherapy." *Psychotherapy* 27.2:175–86.

Borg, Marcus J. 1986. "A Temperate Case for a Non-Eschatological Jesus." *Forum* 2.3:81–102.

———. 1987. *Jesus a New Vision: Spirit, Culture, and the Life of Discipleship*. San Francisco: Harper & Row.

———. 1994a. "Jesus and Eschatology: Current Reflections." In *Jesus in Contemporary Scholarship*, 69–96. Valley Forge: Trinity.

———. 1994b. *Meeting Jesus Again for the First Time: The Historical Jesus and the Heart of Contemporary Faith*. San Francisco: HarperSanFrancisco.

———. 1994c. "Root Images and the Way we See: The Primordial Traditional and Biblical Tradition." In *Jesus in Contemporary Scholarship*, 127–39. Valley Forge: Trinity.

———. 1995. "The Historian, the Christian, and Jesus." *ThTo* 52:6–16.

———. 1999. "Seeing Jesus: Sources, Lenses, and Method." In *The Meaning of Jesus: Two Visions*, by Marcus J. Borg and N .T. Wright, 3–14. San Francisco: HarperSanFrancisco.

Boring, M. Eugene. 1983. "Christian Prophecy and the Sayings of Jesus: The State of the Question." *NTS* 29:104–12.

Botha, Pieter J. J. 1992. "Greco-Roman Literacy as Setting for New Testament Writings." *Neot* 26:195–215.

———. 1993. "The Social Dynamics of the Early Transmission of the Jesus Tradition." *Neot* 27:205–31.

———. 1994. Review of *The Social World of Luke-Acts: Models for Interpretation*, edited by Jerome H. Neyrey. *Neot* 28:251–55.

———. 1998a. "Die Menigte Rondom Jesus." *Skrif en Kerk* 19.1:11–28.

———. 1998b. "Rethinking the Oral-Written Divide in Gospel Criticism: The Jesus Traditions in the Light of Gossip Research." *Voices: A Journal for Oral Studies* 1:28–58.

———. 2000. "Submission and Violence: Exploring Gender Relations in the First-Century World." *Neot* 34:1–38.

Bourguignon, Erika. 1968. "World Distribution and Patterns of Possession States." In *Trance and Possession States*, edited by Raymond Prince, 3–34. Montreal: Burke Memorial Society.

———. 1972. "Trance Dance." In *The Highest State of Consciousness*, edited by J. White, 331–43. New York: Anchor.

———. 1979. *Psychological Anthropology: An Introduction to Human Nature and Cultural Differences*. New York: Holt, Rinehart and Winston.

Boyer, L. Bryce. 1969. "Shamans: To Set the Record Straight." *AmAnth* 71:307–9.

Brody, H. 1988. "The Symbolic Power of the Modern Personal Physician: The Placebo Response under Challenge." *The Journal of Drug Issues* 18.2:149–61.

Brown, John Pairman. 1981. "The Mediterranean Seer and Shamanism." *Zeitschrift für die alttestamentliche Wissenschaft* 93:374–400.

Brown, Peter. 1988. *The Body and Society: Men, Women and Sexual Renunciation in Early Christianity*. London: Faber and Faber.

Brown, P. J., and M. C. Inhorn. 1990. "Disease, Ecology, and Human Behavior." In *Medical Anthropology: Contemporary Theory and Method*, edited by T. M. Johnson and C. F. Sargent, 187–214. New York: Praeger.

Brown, Raymond E. 1973. *The Virginal Conception and Bodily Resurrection of Jesus*. New York: Paulist.

———. 1977. *The Birth of the Messiah: A Commentary on the Infancy Narratives in Matthew and Luke*. Garden City, NY: Doubleday.

———. 1994. *The Death of the Messiah: A Commentary on the Passion Narratives in the Four Gospels*. New York: Doubleday.

Brown, S. Kent. 1992. "Soul, Preexistence Of." In *ABD* 6:161.

Brown, Walter A. 1998. "The Placebo Effect." *Scientific American* (January 1998) 68–73.

Brown, Warren S. 1998. "Cognitive Contributions to Soul." In *Whatever Happened to the Soul? Scientific and Theological Portraits of Human Nature*, edited by Warren S. Brown, Nancey Murphy, and H. Newton Malony, 99–125. Minneapolis: Fortress.

Bryson, Bill. 2003. *A Short History of Nearly Everything*. New York: Doubleday.

Bultmann, Rudolf. 1980. *Theologie des Neuen Testaments*. 8., durchgesehene, um Vorwort und Nachträge wesentlich erweiterte Auflage. Edited by Otto Merk. Uni-Taschenbücher 630. Tübingen: Mohr/Siebeck.

Burke, Peter. 1987. *The Historical Anthropology of Early Modern Italy: Essays on Perception and Communication*. Cambridge: Cambridge University Press.

———. 1990. "Historians, Anthropologists, and Symbols." In *Culture Through Time: Anthropological Approaches*, edited by E. Ohnuki-Tierney, 268–83. Stanford: Stanford University Press.

———. 1991. "Overture: The New History, Its Past and Its Future." In *New Perspectives on Historical Writing*, 1–23. Cambridge: Polity.

———. 1992. *History and Social Theory*. Cambridge: Polity.

Burkert, Walter. 1962. "*Goēs*: Zum Griechischen 'Schamanismus.'" *Rheinisches Museum* 105:36–55.

Bystrina, Ivan. 1991. "Das Erbe des Shamanismus im alten Palästina." In *Hungrige Geister, Rastlose Seelen: Texte zur Schamanismus-Forschung*, edited by M. Kuper, 181–213. Hamburg: Reimer.

Cannon, Walter B. 1942. "'Voodoo' Death." *AmAnth* 44.2:169–81.

Capra, Fritjof. 1982. *The Turning Point: Science, Society, and the Rising Culture*. New York: Simon and Schuster.

———. 2002. *The Hidden Connections: Integrating the Biological, Cognitive and Social Dimensions of Life into a Science of Sustainability*. New York: Doubleday.

Caragounis, Chrys C. 1992. "Kingdom of God/Kingdom of Heaven." In *Dictionary of Jesus and the Gospels*, edited by Joel B. Green and Scot McKnight, 417–30. Downers Grove: InterVarsity.

Carney, T. F. 1975. *The Shape of the Past: Models and Antiquity*. Lawrence, KS: Coronado.

Carr, Edward Hallett. 1961. *What is History?* Middlesex: Penguin.

Carroll, Noël. 1998. "Interpretation, History, and Narrative." In *History and Theory: Contemporary Readings*, edited by Brian Fay, Philip Pomper, and Richard T. Vann, 34–56. Malden, MA: Blackwell.

Charlesworth, James H., editor. 1983. *The Old Testament Pseudepigrapha*. Vol. 1: *Apocalyptic Literature and Testaments*. Garden City, NY: Doubleday.

———, editor. 1985. *The Old Testament Pseudepigrapha*. Vol. 2: *Expansions of the 'Old Testament' and Legends, Wisdom and Philosophical Literature, Prayers, Psalms and Odes, Fragments of Lost Judeo-Hellenistic Works*. Garden City, NY: Doubleday.

Cheetham, R. W. S., and J. A. Griffiths. 1982. "Sickness and Medicine: An African Paradigm." *SAMJ* 62:954–56.

Cheetham, R. W. S., and A. Rzadkowolski. 1980. "Crosscultural Psychiatry and the Concept of Mental Illness." *SAMJ* 58:320–25.

Chilton, Bruce. 1999. "Assessing Progress in the Third Quest." In *Authenticating the Words of Jesus*, edited by B. Chilton and C. A. Evans, 15–25. NTTS 28/1. Leiden: Brill.

———, and Craig A. Evans, editors. 1994. *Studying the Historical Jesus: Evaluations of the State of Current Research*. NTTS 19. Leiden: Brill.

Clow, A. 2001. "Behavioural Conditioning of the Immune System." In *Understanding the Placebo Effect in Complementary Medicine: Theory, Practice and Research*, edited by David Peters, 51–66. New York Churchill Livingstone.

Cohn, Bernard S. 1980. "History and Anthropology: The State of Play." *CSSH* 22:198–221.

———. 1982. "Anthropology and History in the 1980s: Toward a Rapprochement." In *The New History: Studies in Interdisciplinary History*, edited by T. K. Rabb and R. I. Rotberg, 227–52. Princeton: Princeton University Press.

Collingwood, R. G. 1946. *The Idea of History*. Oxford: Oxford University Press.

Collins, John J. 1983. "Apocalyptic Eschatology as the Transcendence of Death." In *Visionaries and Their Apocalypses*, edited by Paul D. Hanson, 61–84. Issues in Religion and Theology. Philadelphia: Fortress.

———. 1997. *Seers, Sibyls and Sages in Hellenistic-Roman Judaism*. JSJSup 54. Leiden: Brill.

———. 2000. "Eschatologies of Late Antiquity." In *Dictionary of New Testament Background*, edited by C. A. Evans and S. E. Porter, 330–37. Downers Grove, IL: Intervarsity, 2000.

Comaroff, John, and Jean Comaroff. 1992. *Ethnography and the Historical Imagination*. Studies in Ethnographic Imagination. Boulder, CO: Westview.

Cornelius, Izak. 1994. "The Visual Representation of the World in the Ancient Near East and the Hebrew Bible." *Journal of Northwest Semitic Languages* 20:193–218.

Cotter, Wendy. 1998. *Miracles in Greco-Roman Antiquity: A Sourcebook*. London: Routledge, 1998.

Cousins, Norman. 1989. *Head First: The Biology of Hope*. New York: Dutton.

Craffert, Pieter F. 1995. "Is the Emic-Etic Distinction a Useful Tool for Cross-Cultural Interpretation of the New Testament?" *R&T* 2:14–37.

———. 1996. "On New Testament Interpretation and Ethnocentrism." In *Ethnicity and the Bible*, edited by Mark G. Brett, 449–68. BibIntSer 19. Leiden: Brill.

———. 1999a. "Jesus and the Shamanic Complex: First Steps in Utilising a Social Type Model." *Neot* 33:321–42.

———. 1999b. *Meeting the Living among the Dead: Perspectives on Burials, Tombs and the Afterlife*. Pretoria: Biblia.

———. 2001a. "An Exercise in the Critical Use of Models: The 'Goodness of Fit' of Wilson's Sect Model." In *Social Scientific Models for Interpreting the Bible: Essays by the Context Group in Honour of Bruce J. Malina*, edited by John J. Pilch, 21–46. BibIntSer 53. Leiden: Brill.

———. 2001b. "Jesus Van Nasaret as Historiese Figuur: Die Rol Van Wêreldbeelde en Interpretasiestyle." *Fragmente* 7:101–15.

———. 2002. "Religious Experience and/as (Alternate) States of Consciousness from a Biopsychosocial Perpsective." In *Brain, Mind and Soul: Unifying the Human Self*, edited by C. W. du Toit, 53–97. Pretoria: Unisa.

———. 2005a. "How Historiography Creates (Some)Body: Jesus, the Son of David: Royal Stock or Social Construct?" *Scrip* 90:608–20.

———. 2005b. "What on Earth (or in Heaven) is a Resurrected Body? The Outline of a Historical-Anthropological Answer." In *One Text, a Thousand Methods: Essays in Memory of Sjef van Tilborg,* edited by P. Chatelion Coumet and U. Berges, 227–52. BibIntSer 71. Leiden: Brill.

———, and Pieter J. J. Botha. 2005. "Why Jesus Could Walk on the Sea but He Could not Read and Write: Reflections on Historicity and Interpretation in Historical Jesus Research." *Neot* 39:5–35.

Craig, William Lane. 1995. "Did Jesus Rise from the Dead?" In *Jesus Under Fire,* edited by M. J. Wilkins and J. P. Moreland, 141–76. Grand Rapids: Zondervan.

Crossan, John Dominic. 1991a. *The Historical Jesus: The Life of a Mediterranean Jewish Peasant.* San Francisco: HarperSanFrancisco.

———. 1991b. "The Life of a Mediterranean Jewish Peasant." *The Christian Century* (December, 18–25):1194–200.

———. 1994a. "The Historical Jesus in Earliest Christianity." In *Jesus and Faith: A Conversation on the Work of John Dominic Crossan,* edited by J. Carlson and R. A. Ludwig, 1–21. New York: Orbis, 1994.

———. 1994b. *Jesus: A Revolutionary Biography.* San Francisco: HarperSanFrancisco.

———. 1997. "What Victory? What God? A Review Debate with N.T. Wright on *Jesus and the Victory of God.*" *SJT* 50:345–58.

———. 1998. *The Birth of Christianity: Discovering What Happened in the Years Immediately after the Execution of Jesus.* San Francisco: HarperSanFrancisco.

———. 1999. "Historical Jesus as Risen Lord." In *The Jesus Controversy: Perspectives in Conflict.* John Dominic Crossan, Luke Timothy Johnson, and Werner H. Kelber, 1–47. Harrisburg, PA: Trinity, 1999.

———. 2003a. "Methodology, Healing, Story, and Ideology: Response to the Articles by Pieter Craffert and Johan Strijdom." *R&T* 10:296–307.

———. 2003b. "Virgin Mother or Bastard Child?" *HTS* 59:663–91.

———. 2006. "Bodily-Resurrection Faith." In *The Resurrection of Jesus: John Dominic Crossan and N. T. Wright in Dialogue,* edited by R. B. Stewart, 171–86. Minneapolis: Fortress.

———, and Jonathan L. Reed. 2001. *Excavating Jesus: Beneath the Stones, Behind the Texts.* San Francisco: HarperSanFrancisco.

Csordas, T. J., and A. Kleinman. 1990. "The Therapeutic Process." In *Medical Anthropology: Contemporary Theory and Method,* edited by T. M. Johnson and C. F. Sargent, 11–25. New York: Praeger.

Cullmann, Oscar. 1991. "Infancy Gospels." In *New Testament Apocrypha.* Vol. 1: *Gospels and Related Writings,* edited by Wilhelm Schneemelcher, 414–69. Rev. ed. Translated by R. McL. Wilson. Louisville: Westminster John Knox.

Cupitt, Don. 1995. *The Last Philosophy.* London: SCM.

d'Aquili, Eugene G., and C. Laughlin. 1975. "The Biopsychologial Determinants of Religious Ritual Behavior." *Zygon* 10:32–58.

d'Aquili, Eugene G., and Andrew B. Newberg. 1993. "Liminality, Trance, and Unitary States in Ritual and Meditation." *Studia Liturgica* 23:2–34.

Davies, Philip R. 1977. "Hasidim in the Maccabean Period." *JJS* 28:127–40.

———. 1997. "Qumran and the Quest for the Historical Judaism." In *The Scrolls and the Scriptures: Qumran Fifty Years After,* edited by S. E. Porter and C. A. Evans, 24–42. JSJSup 26. Sheffield: Sheffield Academic.

Davies, Stevan L. 1995. *Jesus the Healer: Possession, Trance, and the Origins of Christianity.* New York: Continuum.

Davila, James R. 2001. *Descenders to the Chariot: The People Behind the Hekhalot Literature.* JSJSup 70. Leiden: Brill.

Davis, Natalie Zemon. 1982. "Anthropology and History in the 1980s: The Possibilities of the Past." In *The New History: Studies in Interdisciplinary History,* edited by T. K. Rabb and R. I. Rotberg, 267–75. Princeton: Princeton University Press.

Davis, Stephen T. 1997. "'Seeing' the Risen Jesus." In *The Resurrection: An Interdisciplinary Symposium on the Resurrection of Jesus,* edited by Stephen T. Davis, Daniel Kendall, and Gerald O'Collins, 126–47. Oxford: Oxford University Press.

———, Daniel Kendall, and Gerald O'Collins, editors. *The Resurrection: An Interdisciplinary Symposium on the Resurrection of Jesus.* Oxford: Oxford University Press.

De Craen, A. J. M., A. J. E. M. Lampe-Schoenmaekers, and J. Kleijnen. 2001. "Non-Specific Factors in Randomized Clinical Trials: Some Methodological Considerations." In *Understanding the Placebo Effect in Complementary Medicine: Theory, Practice and Research,* edited by David Peters, 179–87. New York: Churchill Livingstone.

Degenaar, J. J. 1979. "Some Philosophical Considerations on Pain." *Pain* 7:281–304.

Deist, F. E. 1987. "Genesis 1:1–2:4a: World Picture and World View." *Scrip* 2:1–17.

Delaney, Carol. 1986. "The Meaning of Paternity and the Virgin Birth Debate." *Man* 21:494–513.

Denton, Donald L., Jr. 2004. *Historiography and Hermeneutics in Jesus Studies: An Examination of the Work of John Dominic Crossan and Ben F. Meyer.* JSNTSup 262. London: T. & T. Clark.

Derrett, J. D. M. 1995. "The Evil Eye in the New Testament." In *Modelling Early Christianity: Social-Scientific Studies of the New Testament in Its Context,* edited by Philip F. Esler, 65–72. London: Routledge.

Dixon, R. B. 2004. "Some Aspects of the American Shaman." In *Shamanism: Critical Concepts in Sociology.* 3 vols. Edited by Andrei A. Znamenski, 2:3–14. London: Routledge.

Dodds, E. R. 1951. *The Greeks and the Irrational.* Berkeley: University of California Press.

———. 1971. "Supernormal Phenomena in Classical Antiquity." *Proceedings of the Society for Psychical Research* 55.202:189–237.

Dow, James. 1986. "Universal Aspects of Symbolic Healing: A Theoretical Synthesis." *AmAnth* 88:56–69.

Downing, F. Gerald. 1987. "The Social Contexts of Jesus the Teacher: Construction or Reconstruction." *NTS* 33:439–51.

Du Toit, David S. 2001. "Redefining Jesus: Current Trends in Jesus Research." In *Jesus, Mark and Q: The Teaching of Jesus and Its Earliest Records*, edited by Michael Labahn and Andreas Schmidt, 82–124. JSNTSup 214. Sheffield: Sheffield Academic.

———. 2002. "Der Unähnliche Jesus: Eine kritische Evaluierung der Entstehung des Differenzkriteriums und seiner geschichts- und erkenntnistheoretiechen Voraussetzungen." In *Der Historische Jesus: Tendenzen und Perspektiven der Gegenwärtigen Forschung*, edited by Jens Schröter and Ralph Brucker, 89–129. BZNW 114. Berlin: de Gruyter.

Dubos, R. 1977. "Determinants of Health and Disease." In *Culture, Disease, and Healing: Studies in Medical Anthropology*, edited by David Landy, 31–41. New York: Macmillan.

Duling, Dennis C. 1992. "Kingdom of God, Kingdom of Heaven." In *ABD* 4:49–69.

Dunn, James D. G. 1975. *Jesus and the Spirit: A Study of the Religious and Charismatic Experience of Jesus and the First Christians as Reflected in the New Testament.* London: SCM.

———. 1999. "Can the Third Quest Hope to Succeed?" In *Authenticating the Activities of Jesus.* Bruce Chilton and Craig A. Evans, 31–48. NTTS 28/2. Leiden: Brill.

———. 2002. "'All That Glisters is not Gold': In Quest of the Right Key to Unlock the Way to the Historical Jesus." In *Der Historische Jesus: Tendenzen und Perspektiven der Gegenwärtigen Forschung*, edited by Jens Schröter and Ralph Brucker, 131–61. BZNW 114. Berlin: de Gruyter.

———. 2003a. "Altering the Default Setting: Re-Envisaging the Early Transmission of the Jesus Tradition." *NTS* 49:139–75.

———. 2003b. *Jesus Remembered.* Christianity in the Making 1. Grand Rapids: Eerdmans.

Edwards, S. D., R. W. S. Cheetham, E. Majozi, and A. J. Lasich. 1982. "Zulu Culture-Bound Psychiatric Syndromes." *South African Journal of Hospital Medicine* 8:82–87.

Ehrman, Bart D. 2005. *Misquoting Jesus: The Story Behind Who Changed the Bible and Why.* New York: HarperSanFrancisco.

Eilberg-Schwartz, Howard. 1990. *The Savage in Judaism: An Anthropology of Israelite Religion and Ancient Judaism.* Bloomington: Indiana University Press.

Eisenberg, Leon. 1977. "Disease and Illness: Distinctions Between Professional and Popular Ideas of Sickness." *Culture, Medicine and Psychiatry* 1:9–23.

Eliade, Mircea. 1961. "Recent Works on Shamanism: A Review Article." *History of Religion* 1:152–86.

———. 1964. *Shamanism: Archaic Techniques of Ecstasy.* Princeton: Princeton University Press.

———. "Shamanism." 1987. In *ER* 13:201–8.

Elliott, John H. 1988. "The Fear of the Lear: The Evil Eye from the Bible to Li'l Abner." *Forum* 4.4:42–71.

———. 1993. *What Is Social-Scientific Criticism?* GBS. Minneapolis: Fortress.

Ellis, E. Earle. 1999. *The Making of the New Testament Documents.* BibIntSer 39. Leiden: Brill.

Engel, George L. 1977. "The Need for a New Medical Model: A Challenge for Biomedicine." *Science* 196.4286:129–36.

———. 1997. "From Biomedical to Biopsychosocial: Being Scientific in the Human Domain." *Psychosomatics* 38:521–28.

Ernst, Edzard. 2001. "Towards a Scientific Understanding of Placebo Effects." In *Understanding the Placebo Effect in Complementary Medicine: Theory, Practice and Research*, edited by David Peters, 17–29. New York: Churchill Livingstone.

Esler, Philip F., editor. 1995. *Modelling Early Christianity: Social-Scientific Studies of the New Testament in Its Context*. London: Routledge.

Evans, Richard J. 2002. "From Historicism to Postmodernism: Historiography in the Twentieth Century." *H&T* 41:79–87.

Fabrega, Horacio Jr. 1971. "The Study of Medical Problems in Preliterate Settings." *Yale Journal of Biology and Medicine* 43:385–407.

———. 1982. "Culture and Psychiatric Illness: Biomedical and Ethnomedical Aspects." In *Cultural Conceptions of Mental Health and Therapy*, edited by Anthony J. Marcella and Geoffrey M. White, 39–68. Dordrecht: Reidel.

Fay, Brian. 1998. "The Linguistic Turn and Beyond in Contemporary Theory of History." In *History and Theory: Contemporary Readings*, edited by Brian Fay, Philip Pomper, and Richard T. Vann, 1–12. Malden, MA: Blackwell.

Fenwick, Peter. 2001. "Psychoneuroimmunology: The Mind-Brain Connection." In *Understanding the Placebo Effect in Complementary Medicine: Theory, Practice and Research*, edited by David Peters, 215–26. New York: Churchill Livingstone.

Fish, Stanley. 1990. "Rhetoric." In *Critical Terms for Literary Study*, edited by Frank Lentricchia and Thomas McLaughlin, 203–222. Chicago: University of Chicago Press.

Flusser, David. 1957. "Healing through the Laying-on of Hands in a Dead Sea Scroll." *Israel Exploration Journal* 7:107–8.

Fowl, Stephen. 1990. "Reconstructing and Deconstructing the Quest of the Historical Jesus." *SJT* 42:319–33.

Fredriksen, Paula. 1995. "What You See Is What You Get: Context and Content in Current Research on the Historical Jesus." *ThTo* 52:75–97.

Freyne, Sean. 1997. "Galilean Questions to Crossan's Mediterranean Jesus." In *Whose Historical Jesus?*, edited by William E. Arnal and Michel Desjardins, 63–91. SCJ 7. Waterloo, ON: Wilfred Laurier University Press.

Friedman, M. 1990. "Psychoneuroimmunology." *SA Family Practice* 11:350–54.

Friedman, Richard Elliott, and Shawna Dolansky Overton. 2000. "Death and Afterlife: The Biblical Silence." In *Judaism in Late Antiquity, Part 4: Death, Life-After-Death, Resurrection and the World-to-Come in the Judaisms of Antiquity*, edited by A. J. Avery-Peck and Jacob Neusner, 35–59. Leiden: Brill.

Funk, Robert W. 1996. *Honest to Jesus: Jesus for a New Millennium*. San Francisco: HarperSanFrancisco.

———, Roy W. Hoover, and The Jesus Seminar. 1993. *The Five Gospels: The Search for the Authentic Words of Jesus*. New York: Macmillan.

————, and The Jesus Seminar. 1998. *The Acts of Jesus: The Search for the Authentic Deeds of Jesus*. San Francisco: HarperSanFrancisco.

Furst, Peter T. 1972. "Introduction." In *Flesh of the Gods: The Ritual Use of Hallucinogens*, edited by Peter T. Furst, vii–xvi. New York: Praeger.

García Martínez, Florentino. 1994. *The Dead Sea Scrolls Translated: The Qumran Texts in English*. Leiden: Brill. 2nd ed. 1996.

Geertz, Clifford. 1973. "Thick Description: Toward an Interpretive Theory of Culture." In *The Interpretation of Cultures: Selected Essays*, 3–30. New York: Basic Books.

Gilberg, R. 1984. "How to Recognise a Shaman Among Other Religious Specialists." In *Shamanism in Eurasia*, edited by Mihály Hoppál, 21–27. Forum 5. Göttingen: Herodot.

Gill, Sam D. 1986. "Shamanism, North American." In *ER* 13:216–19.

Goldammer, Kurt. 1972. "Elemente des Shamanismus im Alten Testament." *Ex Orbe Religiorum* 22.2:266–85.

Good, Byron J. 1994. *Medicine, Rationality, and Experience: An Anthropological Perspective*. Cambridge: Cambridge University Press.

————, and Mary-Jo DelVecchio Good. 1981. "The Meaning of Symptoms: A Cultural Hermeneutic Model for Clinical Practice." In *The Relevance of Social Science for Medicine*, edited by Leon Eisenberg and Arthur Kleinman, 165–96. Culture, Illness, and Healing 1. Dordrecht: Reidel.

————, and Mary-Jo DelVecchio Good. 1982. "Toward a Meaning-Centered Analysis of Popular Illenss Categories: 'Fright Illness' and 'Heart Distress' in Iran." In *Cultural Conceptions of Mental Health and Therapy*, edited by Anthony J. Marcella and Geoffrey M. White, 141–66. Culture, Illness, and Healing 4. Dordrecht: Reidel.

Goodman, Felicitas D. 1987. "Visions." In *ER* 15:282–88.

Goulder, M. D. 1991. "The Visionaries of Laodicea." *JSNT* 43:15–39.

Grabbe, Lester L. 1995. *Priests, Prophets, Diviners, Sages: A Socio-Historical Study of Religious Specialists in Ancient Israel*. Valley Forge, PA: Trinity.

————. 2000. *Judaic Religion in the Second Temple Period: Belief and Practice from the Exile to Yavneh*. London: Routledge.

Gray, Rebecca. 1993. *Prophetic Figures in Late Second Temple Jewish Palestine: The Evidence from Josephus*. Oxford: Oxford University Press.

Green, Joel B. 1998. "'Bodies—That is, Human Lives': A Re-Examination of Human Nature in the Bible." In *Whatever Happened to the Soul? Scientific and Theological Portraits of Human Nature*, edited by Warren S. Brown, Nancey Murphy, and H. Newton Malony, 149–73. Minneapolis: Fortress.

Grim, John A. 1983. *The Shaman: Patterns of Siberian and Ojibway Healing*. Civilizations of the American Indian Series 165. Norman: University of Oklahoma Press.

Groth-Marnet, G., and R. Summers. 1998. "Altered Beliefs, Attitudes and Behaviors Following Near-Death Experiences." *Journal of Humanistic Psychology* 38.3:110–25.

Gruenwald, Ithamar. 1980. *Apocalyptic and Merkavah Mysticism*. AGAJU 14. Leiden: Brill.

Gumede, M. V. 1989. "Healers Modern and Traditional." In *Afro-Christian Religion and Healing in Southern Africa*, edited by G. C. Oosthuizen et al., 319–28. Lewiston, NY: Mellen.

Habermas, Gary R. 1995. "Did Jesus Perform Miracles?" In *Jesus Under Fire*, edited by Michael J. Wilkins and J. P. Moreland, 117–40. Grand Rapids: Zondervan.

Hachlili, Rachel. 1977. "The Zodiac in Ancient Jewish Art: Representation and Significance." *Bulletin of the American Schools of Oriental Research* 288:61–71.

Hadot, Pierre. 2001. "Shamanism and Greek Philosophy." In *The Concept of Shamanism: Uses and Abuses*, edited by Henri-Paul Francfort and Roberte N. Hamayon, 389–401. Bibliotheca Shamanistica 10. Busapest: Akadémiai Kiadó.

Hahn, Robert A. 1984. "Rethinking 'Illness' and 'Disease'." *Contributions to Asian Studies* 18:1–23.

Hamayon, Roberte N. 1993. "Are 'Trance,' 'Ecstasy' and Similar Concepts Appropriate in the Study of Shamanism?" *Shaman* 1.2:3–25.

Hanson, John S. 1980. "Dreams and Visions in the Graeco-Roman World and Early Christianity." In *ANRW* II.23.2:1395–427.

Harner, M. 1988. "What Is a Shaman?" In *Shaman's Path: Healing, Personal Growth, and Empowerment*, edited by Gary Doore, 7–15. Boston: Shambhala.

Harris, Sam. 2004. *The End of Faith: Religion, Terror, and the Future of Reason*. New York: Norton.

Haskell, Thomas. 1998. "Objectivity Is not Neutrality: Rhetoric Versus Practice in Peter Novick's *That Noble Dream*." In *History and Theory: Contemporary Readings*, edited by Brian Fay, Philip Pomper, and Richard T. Vann, 299–319. Malden, MA: Blackwell.

Hayman, Paul. 1991. "Monotheism: A Misused Word in Jewish Studies?" *JJS* 42:1–15.

Helman, Cecil G. 2001. "Placebos and Nocebos: The Cultural Construction of Belief." In *Understanding the Placebo Effect in Complementary Medicine: Theory, Practice and Research*, edited by David Peters, 3–16. New York: Churchill Livingstone.

———. 2004. *Suburban Shaman: A Journey Through Medicine*. Cape Town: Double Storey.

Heron, John. 2001. "The Placebo Effect and a Participatory World View." In *Understanding the Placebo Effect in Complementary Medicine: Theory, Practice and Research*, edited by David Peters, 189–212. New York: Churchill Livingstone.

Herzog, William R. II. 2005. *Prophet and Teacher: An Introduction to the Historical Jesus*. Louisville: Westminster John Knox.

Hesse, M. 1990. "Beyond Relativism in the Natural and Social Sciences." In *Knowledge and Method in the Human Sciences*, edited by J. Mouton and D. Joubert, 13–25. Pretoria: Human Sciences Research Council.

Hock, Ronald F. 1995. *The Infancy Gospels of James and Thomas*. Santa Rosa, CA: Polebridge.

Holmberg, Bengt. 2004. "Questions of Method in James Dunn's *Jesus Remembered*." *JSNT* 26:445–57.

Horsley, Richard A. 1996. *Archaeology, History, and Society in Galilee: The Social Context of Jesus and the Rabbis*. Valley Forge, PA: Trinity.

———. 2003. *Jesus and Empire: The Kingdom of God and the New World Disorder*. Minneapolis: Fortress.

———. 1983. "Moses' Throne Vision in Ezekiel the Dramatist." *JJS* 34:21–29.

———. 1994. "Sarah's Seminal Emission." In *Hellenism-Judaism-Christianity: Essays on Their Interaction*, 203–23. Kampen: Kok Pharos.

Horton, R. 1967. "African Traditional Thought and Western Science (Part I)." *Africa* 37:50–71.

Hughes, C. C. 1985. "Culture-Bound or Construct-Bound? The Syndromes and DSM-III." In *The Culture-Bound Syndromes: Folk Illnesses of Psychiatric and Anthropological Interest*, edited by R. C. Simons and C. C. Hughes, 3–24. Dordrecht: Reidel.

Hulse, E. V. 1975. "The Nature of Biblical 'Leprosy' and the Use of Alternative Medical Terms in Modern Translations of the Bible." *Palestine Exploration Quarterly* 107:87–105.

Hultkrantz, Åke. 1967. "Spirit Lodge, a North American Shamanistic Séance." In *Studies in Shamanism*, edited by C-M. Edsman, 32–68. Stockholm: Almqvist & Wiksell.

———. 1973. "A Definition of Shamanism." *Temenos* 9:25–37.

———. 1984. "Shamanism and Soul Ideology." In *Shamanism in Eurasia*, edited by M. Hoppál, 28–36. Göttingen: Herodot.

———. 1985. "Comments." *CurrAnth* 26:453.

———. 1988. "Shamanism: A Religious Phenomenon?" In *Shaman's Path: Healing, Personal Growth, and Empowerment*, edited by G. Doore, 33–41. Boston: Shambhala.

———. 2004. "Ecological and Phenomenological Aspects of Shamanism." In *Shamanism: Critical Concepts in Sociology*, edited by A. A. Znamenski, 3:146–71. London: RoutledgeCurzon.

Hurtado, Larry W. 1997. "A Taxonomy of Recent Historical-Jesus Work." In *Whose Historical Jesus?*, edited by William E. Arnal and Michel Desjardins, 272–95. SCJ 7. Waterloo, ON: Wilfred Laurier University Press.

Huxley, Aldous. 1972. "Visionary Experiences." in *The Highest State of Consciousness*, edited by J. White, 34–57. Garden City, NY: Anchor.

Iggers, G. G. 1997. *Historiography in the Twentieth Century: From Scientific Objectivity to the Postmodern Challenge*. Hanover: Wesleyan University Press.

Iggers, G. G., and K. Von Moltke. 1973a. "Introduction." In *The Theory and Practice of History: Leopold von Ranke*, edited by G. G. Iggers and K. Von Moltke, xv–lxxi. New York: Bobbs-Merrill.

———. 1973b. "Preface." In *The Theory and Practice of History: Leopold Von Ranke*, edited by G. G. Iggers and K. Von Moltke, xi–xiv. New York: Bobbs-Merrill.

James, William. 1902. *The Varieties of Religious Experience*. New York: Modern Library.

Jeremias, Joachim. 1958. *Heiligengräber in Jesu Umwelt: Eine Untersuchung Zur Volksreligion der Zeit Jesu*. Göttingen: Vandenhoeck & Ruprecht.

————. 1971. *New Testament Theology.* Translated by John Bowden. London: SCM, 1971.

Johnson, A. G. 1994. "Surgery as a Placebo." *Lancet* 344.8930:1140–42.

Johnson, Luke Timothy. 1996. *The Real Jesus: The Misguided Quest for the Historical Jesus and the Truth of the Traditional Gospels.* San Francisco: HarperSanFrancisco.

Jones, R. L. 1976. "Limbu Spirit Possession and Shamanism." In *Spirit Possession in the Nepal Himalayas,* edited by J. T. Hitchcock and R. L. Jones, 29–55. Warminster: Aris and Phillips.

Kalweit, H. 1992. *Shamans, Healers, and Medicine Men.* Boston: Shambhala.

Kapelrud, A. S. 1967. "Shamanistic Features in the Old Testament." In *Studies in Shamanism,* edited by C-M. Edsman, 90–96. Stockholm: Almqvist & Wiksell.

Kasser, Rudolphe, Marvin Meyer, and Gregor Wurst. *The Gospel of Judas: From Codex Tchacos.* Washington, DC: National Geographic, 2006.

Kee, Howard Clark. 1992. "Medicine and Healing." In *ABD* 4:659–64.

Keel, Othmar, and Christoph Uehlinger. 1998. *Gods, Goddesses, and Images of God in Ancient Israel.* Minneapolis: Fortress.

Kehoe, A. B. 2000. *Shamans and Religion: An Anthropological Exploration in Critical Thinking.* Prospect Heights, IL: Waveland.

Kelber, W. H. 1987. "The Authority of the Word in St. John's Gospel: Charismatic Speech, Narrative Text, Logocentric Metaphysics." *Oral Tradition* 2:108–31.

————. 1994. "Jesus and Tradition: Words in Time, Words in Space." *Semeia* 65:139–67.

Kiefer, C. W. 1985. "Comments." *CurrAnth* 26:454.

King, Karen L. 1987. "Kingdom in the Gospel of Thomas." *Forum* 3.1:48–97.

Kingsley, P. 1994. "Greeks, Shamans and Magi." *Studia Iranica* 23:187–98.

————. 1995. *Ancient Philosophy, Mystery, and Magic: Empedocles and Pythagorean Tradition.* Oxford: Clarendon.

Kleinman, A. 1986. "Concepts and a Model for the Comparison of Medical Systems as Cultural Systems." In *Concepts of Health, Illness and Disease: A Comparative Perspective,* edited by C. Currer and M. Stacey, 29–47. New York: Berg.

————, and L. H. Sung. 1979. "Why Do Indigenous Practitioners Successfully Heal?" *Social Science and Medicine* 130:7–26.

————, P. E. Brodwin, B. J. Good, and M-J. DelVecchio Good. 1992. "Pain as Human Experience: An Introduction." In *Pain as Human Experience: An Anthropological Perspective,* edited by M-J. DelVecchio Good et al., 1–28. Berkeley: University of California Press.

————, L. Eisenberg, and B. Good. 1978. "Culture, Illness, and Care: Clinical Lessons from Anthropologic and Cross-Cultural Research." *Annals of Internal Medicine* 88:251–58.

————, H. A. Guess, and J. S. Wilentz. 1990. "An Overview." In *The Science of the Placebo: Towards and Interdisciplinary Research Agenda,* edited by H. A. Guess, 1–32. BMJ.

Koester, Helmut. 1990. *Ancient Christian Gospels: Their History and Development*. Philadelphia: Trinity.

Koriat, A., M. Goldsmith, and A. Pansky. 2000. "Towards a Psychology of Memory Accuracy." *Annual Review of Psychology* 51:481–537.

Kriel, J. R. 1997. "Transforming Medicine's Clinical Method: A Critical Assessment of the Influence of the Natural Science World-View on Medicine." *Scrip* 61:179–92.

———. 2000. *Matter, Mind, and Medicine: Transforming the Clinical Method*. Amsterdam: Ropodi.

———. 2002. "And the Flesh Became Mind: Evolution, Complexity and the Unification of Animal Consciousness." In *Brain, Mind and Soul: Unifying the Human Self*, edited by C. W. du Toit,135–78. Pretoria: Unisa.

Krippner, S. 1972. "Altered States of Consciousness." In *The Highest State of Consciousness*, edited by J. White, 1–5. New York: Anchor.

———. 1985. "Comments." *CurrAnth* 26:453–54.

———. 1988. "Shamans: The First Healers." In *Shaman's Path: Healing, Personal Growth, and Empowerment*, edited by G. Doore, 101–14. Boston: Shambhala.

Krüger, J. S. 1995. *Along Edges: Religion in South Africa: Bushman, Christian, Buddhist*. Pretoria: Unisa.

Kuemmerlin-McLean, J. K. 1992. "Magic: Old Testament." In *ABD* 4:468–71.

Kümmel, Werner Georg. 1975. *Introduction to the New Testament*. Rev. ed. Translated by Howard Clark Kee. Nashville: Abingdon.

Lambek, M. 1989. "From Disease to Discourse: Remarks on the Conceptualization of Trance and Spirit Possession." In *Altered States of Consciousness and Mental Health: A Cross-Cultural Perspective*, edited by C. A. Ward, 36–61. London: Sage.

Lang, Bernhard. 2002. *The Hebrew God: Portrait of an Ancient Deity*. New Haven: Yale University Press.

Laughlin, C. D. 1997. "The Cycle of Meaning: Some Methodological Implications of Biogenetic Structural Theory." In *Anthropology of Religion: A Handbook*, edited by S. D. Glazier, 471–88. Westport, CT: Greenwood.

Laughlin, C. D., J. McManus, and E. G. d'Aquili. 1990. *Brain, Symbol & Experience: Towards a Neurophenomenology of Human Consciousness*. Boston: New Science Library.

Lee, M.-K. 1999. "A Man of High Degree: An Exploration of Jesus as Shaman in the Synoptic Gospels." D.Phil. dissertation, University of Sheffield.

Lenski, Gerhard, and Jean Lenski. 1987. *Human Societies: An Introduction to Macrosociology*. 5th ed. New York: McGraw-Hill.

Lesses, R. M. 1998. *Ritual Practices to Gain Power: Angels, Incantations, and Revelation in Early Jewish Mysticism*. Harrisburg, PA: Trinity.

Lewis, I. M. 1984. "What Is a Shaman?" In *Shamanism in Eurasia*, edited by M. Hoppál, 3–12. Göttingen: Herodot.

———. 1986. *Religion in Context: Cults and Charisma*. Cambridge: Cambridge University Press.

————. 1989. *Ecstatic Religion: A Study of Shamanism and Spirit Possession.* London: Routledge.

Lewis-Williams, J. D. 1995. "Seeing and Construing: The Making and 'Meaning' of a Southern African Rock Art Motif." *Cambridge Archaeological Journal* 5:3–32.

Lightstone, J. N. 1984. *The Commerce of the Sacred: Mediation of the Divine Among Jews in the Graeco-Roman Diaspora.* Chico, CA: Scholars.

Lock, M., and N. Scheper-Hughes. 1990. "A Critical-Interpretive Approach in Medical Anthropology: Rituals and Routines of Discipline and Dissent." In *Medical Anthropology: Contemporary Theory and Method,* edited by T. M. Johnson and C. F. Sargent, 47–72. New York: Praeger.

Loeb, E. M. 1929. "Shaman and Seer." *AmAnthr* 31:60–84.

Lorenz, C. 1998a. "Can Histories be True? Narrativism, Positivism, and the 'Metaphorical Turn'." *H&T* 37:309–29.

————. 1998b. "Historical Knowledge and Historical Reality: A Plea for 'Internal Realism.'" In *History and Theory: Contemporary Readings,* edited by edited by Brian Fay, Philip Pomper, and Richard T. Vann, 342–76. Malden, MA: Blackwell.

Lüdemann, Gerd. 1995. *What Really Happened to Jesus: A Historical Approach to the Resurrection.* Translated by John Bowden. London: SCM.

Ludwig, A. M. 1968. "Altered States of Consciousness." In *Trance and Possession States,* edited by Raymond Prince, 69–95. Montreal: Burke Memorial Society.

MacIntyre, A. 1971. "The Idea of a Social Science." In *Against the Self-Images of the Age: Essays on Ideology and Philosophy,* 211–29. London: Duckworth.

Mack, Burton L. 1993. *The Lost Gospel: The Book of Q and Christian Origins.* San Francisco: Harper.

Malina, Bruce J. 1991. "Interpretation: Reading, Abduction, Metaphor." In *The Bible and the Politics of Exegesis: Essays in Honor of Norman K Gottwald on His Sixty-Fifth Birthday,* edited by David Jobling et al., 253–66, 355–58. Cleveland: Pilgrim.

————. 1995. *On the Genre and Message of Revelation: Star Visions and Sky Journeys.* Peabody: Hendrickson.

————. 1997. "Jesus as Astral Prophet." *BTB* 27:83–98.

————. 1999. "Assessing the Historicity of Jesus' Walking on the Sea: Insights from Cross-Cultural Social Psychology." In *Authenticating the Activities of Jesus,* Bruce Chilton and Craig A. Evans, 351–71. NTTS 28/2. Leiden: Brill.

————. 2001a. *The New Testament World: Insights from Cultural Anthropology.* 3rd ed. Louisville: Westminster John Knox.

————. 2001b. *The Social Gospel of Jesus: The Kingdom of God in Mediterranean Perspective.* Minneapolis: Fortress.

————. 2002a. "Exegetical Eschatology, the Peasant Present and the Final Discourse Genre: The Case of Mark 13." *BTB* 32:49–59.

————. 2002b. "Social-Scientific Methods in Historical Jesus Research." In *The Social Setting of Jesus and the Gospels,* edited by Wolfgang Stegemann, Bruce J. Malina, and Gerd Theissen, 3–26. Minneapolis: Fortress.

————, and Jerome H. Neyrey. 1988. *Calling Jesus Names: The Social Value of Labels in Matthew*. Sonoma: Polebridge.

————, and Jerome H. Neyrey. 1996. *Portraits of Paul: An Archaeology of Ancient Personality*. Louisville: Westminster John Knox.

————, and Richard L. Rohrbaugh. 1992. *Social Science Commentary on the Synoptic Gospels*. Minneapolis: Fortress.

————, and Richard L. Rohrbaugh. 1998. *Social-Science Commentary on the Gospel of John*. Minneapolis: Fortress.

Marsh, C. 1997. "Quests of the Historical Jesus in New Historicist Perspective." *Biblical Interpretation* 5:403–37.

————. 1998. "Theological History: N.T. Wright's *Jesus and the Victory of God*." *JSNT* 69:77–94.

Martin, Dale B. 1995. *The Corinthian Body*. New Haven: Yale University Press.

Martin, L. H. 2004. "History, Historiography, and Christian Origins: The Jerusalem Community." In *Redescribing Christian Origins*, edited by Rod Cameron and Merrill P. Miller, 263–273. Atlanta: Society of Biblical Literature.

Mason, Steve. 1995. "Method in the Study of Early Judaism: A Dialogue with Lester Grabbe." *Journal of the American Oriental Society* 115:463–72.

McCloskey, M., C. G. Wible, and N. J. Cohen. 1994. "Is There a Special Flashbulb-Memory Mechanism?" In *Experimenting with the Mind: Readings in Cognitive Psychology*, edited by L. K. Komatsu, 474–91. Pacific Grove: Brooks/Cole.

McCullagh, C. B. 2004. "What Do Historians Argue About?" *H&T* 43:18–38.

Medick, H. 1987. "'Missionaries in the Row Boat'? Ethnological Ways of Knowing as a Challenge to Social History." *CSSH* 29:76–98.

Meeks, Wayne A. 1972. "The Man from Heaven in Johannine Sectarianism." *JBL* 91:44–72.

Meier, John P. 1991. *A Marginal Jew: Rethinking the Historical Jesus*. Vol. 1: *The Roots of the Problem and the Person*. New York: Doubleday.

————. 1994. *A Marginal Jew: Rethinking the Historical Jesus*, Vol. 2: *Mentor, Message, and Miracles*. New York: Doubleday.

————. 1999. "The Present State of the 'Third Quest' for the Historical Jesus: Loss and Gain." *Biblica* 80:459–87.

Metzger, Bruce M. 1971. *A Textual Commentary on the Greek New Testament*. London: United Bible Societies.

Michaelsen, P. 1989. "Ecstasy and Possession in Ancient Israel: A Review of Some Recent Contributions." *Scandinavian Journal of the Old Testament* 2:28–54.

Milgrom, Jacob. 1989. "Rationale for Cultic Law: The Case of Impurity." *Semeia* 45:103–9.

Miller, Robert J., editor. 1992 *The Complete Gospels: Annotated Scholars Version*: Revised and Expanded Edition. San Francisco: HarperSanFrancisco.

————. 1999. *The Jesus Seminar and Its Critics*. Santa Rosa, CA: Polebridge.

————. 2003. *Born Divine: The Births of Jesus and Other Sons of God*. Santa Rosa, CA: Polebridge.

Moerman, D. E. 1991. "Physiology and Symbols: The Anthropological Implications of the Placebo Effect." In *The Anthropology of Medicine: From Culture to Method*, 2nd ed., edited by L. Romanucci-Ross, D. E. Moerman, and L. R. Tancredi, 129–43. New York: Bergin & Garvey.

———. 2002. *Meaning, Medicine and the 'Placebo Effect.'* Cambridge: Cambridge University Press.

———. 2005. "Explanatory Mechanisms for Placebo Effects: Cultural Influences and the Meaning Response." In *The Science of the Placebo: Towards and Interdisciplinary Research Agenda*, edited by Harry A. Guess, 77–107. London: BMJ.

Monberg, T. 1975. "Fathers Were not Genitors." *Man* 10:34–40.

Morray-Jones, C. R. A. 1992. "Transformational Mysticism in the Apocalyptic-Merkabah Tradition." *JJS* 43:1–31.

———. 1993. "Paradise Revisited (2 Cor 12:1–12) The Jewish Mystical Background of Paul's Apostolate. Part 2: Paul's Heavenly Ascent and Its Significance." *HTR* 86:265–92.

Moxnes, Halvor. 1988. *The Economy of the Kingdom: Social Conflict and Economic Relations in Luke's Gospel*. Reprinted, Eugene, OR: Wipf & Stock, 2004.

———. 2000. "Placing Jesus of Nazareth: Towards a Theory of Place in the Study of the Historical Jesus." In *Text and Artifact in the Religions of Mediterranean Antiquity: Essays in Honour of Peter Richardson*, edited by Stephen G. Wilson and M. Desjardins, 158–75. Waterloo, ON: Wilfred Laurier University Press.

———. 2001. "The Construction of Galilee as a Place for the Historical Jesus—Part I." *BTB* 31:26–37.

———. 2003. *Putting Jesus in His Place: A Radical Vision of Household and Kingdom*. Louisville: Westminster John Knox.

Mutwa, V. C. 1996. *Song of the Stars: The Lore of a Zulu Shaman*. Barrytown, NY: Station Hill Openings.

Neufeld, Dietmar. 1996 "Eating, Ecstasy, and Exorcism (Mark 3:21)." *BTB* 26:152–62.

Neusner, Jacob. 1994. "Who Needs 'The Historical Jesus'? An Essay-Review." *Bulletin for Biblical Research* 4:113–26.

Newberg, A., Eugene d'Aquili, and V. Rause. 2001. *Why God Won't Go Away: Brain Science and the Biology of Belief*. New York: Ballantine.

Neyrey, Jerome H. 1988. "Bewitched in Galatia: Paul and Cultural Anthropology." *CBQ* 50:72–100. Reprinted in *Paul, In Other Words: A Cultural Reading of His Letters*, 181–206. Louisville: Westminster John Knox, 1990.

———, editor. 1991. *The Social World of Luke-Acts: Models for Interpretation*. Peabody, MA: Hendrickson.

Nickelsburg, George W. E. 1992a. "Resurrection: Early Judaism and Christianity." In *ABD* 5:684–91.

———. 1992b. "Son of Man." In *ABD* 6:137–50.

Niditch, Susan. 1980. "The Visionary." In *Ideal Figures in Ancient Judaism: Profiles and Paradigms*, edited by John J. Collins and George W. E. Nickelsburg, 153–79. Chico, CA: Scholars, 1980.

Niehr, Herbert. 1995. "The Rise of YHWH in Judahite and Israelite Religion: Methodological and Religio-Historical Aspects." In *The Triumph of Elohim: From Yahwisms to Judaisms*, edited by Diana V. Edelman, 45–72. Kampen: Pharos.

Nipperdey, T. 1978. "Can History be Objective?" *Historia* 23:2–14.

Noll, R. 1985. "Mental Imagery Cultivation as a Cultural Phenomenon: The Role of Visions in Shamanism." *CurrAnth* 26:443–51, 457–61.

Nordland, O. 1967. "Shamanism as an Experiencing of 'the Unreal.'" In *Studies in Shamanism*, edited by C-M. Edsman, 166–85. Stockholm: Almqvist & Wiksell.

Obeng, E. A. 1992. "The Significance of the Miracles of Resuscitation and Its Implication for the Church in Africa." *Bible Bhashyam* 18:83–95.

O'Collins, Gerald. 1978. *What Are They Saying about the Resurrection?* New York: Paulist.

Ogilvie, R. M. 1969. *The Romans and Their Gods: In the Age of Augustus*. London: Chatto & Windus.

Öhler, M. 2001. "Jesus as Prophet: Remarks on Terminology." In *Jesus, Mark and Q: The Teaching of Jesus and Its Earliest Records*, edited by M. Labahn and A. Schmidt, 125–42. JSNTSup 214. Sheffield: Sheffield Academic.

Overholt, Thomas W. 1985. *Prophecy in Cross-Cultural Perspective: A Sourcebook for Biblical Researchers*. Atlanta: Scholars.

Peacock, J. L. 1986. *The Anthropological Lens: Harsh Light, Soft Focus*. Cambridge: Cambridge University Press.

Peacocke, Arthur. 2000. "DNA of Our DNA." In *The Birth of Jesus: Biblical and Theological Reflections*, edited by George J. Brooke, 59–67. Edinburgh: T. & T. Clark.

Pentikäinen, J. 1984. "The Sámi Shaman—Mediator Between Man and Universe." In *Shamanism in Eurasia*, edited by M. Hoppál, 125–49. Göttingen: Herodot.

Perrin, Norman. 1976. *Jesus and the Language of the Kingdom: Symbol and Metaphor in New Testament Interpretation*. London: SCM.

Peters, L. G., and D. Price-Williams. 1980. "Towards and Experiential Analysis of Shamanism." *American Ethnologist* 7:397–418.

Peters, T. 2006. "The Future of the Resurrection." In *The Resurrection of Jesus: John Dominic Crossan and N. T. Wright in Dialogue*, edited by R. B. Stewart, 149–69. Minneapolis: Fortress.

Pfifferling, J-H. 1981. "A Cultural Prescription for Medicocentrism." In *The Relevance of Social Science for Medicine*, edited by L. Eisenberg and A. Kleinman, 197–222. Dordrecht: Reidel.

Pilch, John J. 1981. "Biblical Leprosy and Body Symbolism." *BTB* 11:108–13.

———. 1988. "Understanding Biblical Healing: Selecting the Appropriate Model." *BTB* 18:60–66.

———. 1995. "The Transfiguration of Jesus: An Experience of Alternate Reality." In *Modelling Early Christianity: Social-Scientific Studies of the New Testament in Its Context*, edited by Philip F. Esler, 47–64. London: Routledge.

———. 1996. "Altered States of Consciousness: A 'Kitbashed' Model." *BTB* 26:133–38.

————. 1998. "Appearances of the Risen Jesus in Cultural Context: Experiences of Alternate Reality." *BTB* 28:52–60.

————. 2000. *Healing in the New Testament: Insights From Medical and Mediterranean Anthropology.* Minneapolis: Fortress.

————, editor. 2001. *Social Scientific Models for Interpreting the Bible: Essays by the Context Group in Honor of Bruce J. Malina,* edited by John J. Pilch, 21–46. BibIntSer 53. Leiden: Brill.

————. 2002a. "The Nose and Altered States of Consciousness: Tascodrugites and Ezekiel." *HTS* 58:708–20.

————. 2002b. "Paul's Ecstatic Trance Experience Near Damascus in Acts of the Apostles." *HTS* 58:690–707.

————. 2002. "Altered States of Consciousness in the Synoptics." In *The Social Setting of Jesus and the Gospels,* edited by Wolfgang Stegemann, Bruce J. Malina, and Gerd Theissen, 103–15. Minneapolis: Fortress.

————. 2004. *Visions and Healing in the Acts of the Apostles: How the Early Believers Experienced God.* Collegeville: Liturgical.

Piper, A. 1994. "Multiple Personality Disorder." *British Journal of Psychiatry* 164:600–612.

Popper, Karl. 1970. "Normal Science and Its Dangers." In *Criticism and the Growth of Knowledge: Proceedings of the International Colloquium in the Philosophy of Science,* edited by I. Lakatos and A. Musgrave, 51–58. Cambridge: Cambridge University Press.

Prince, Raymond. 1982a. "The Endorphins: A Review for Psychological Anthropologists." *Ethos* 10:303–16.

————. 1982b. "Shaman and Endorphins." *Ethos* 10:409–23.

Rahmani, L. Y. 1982. "Ancient Jerusalem's Funerary Customs and Tombs: Part 4." *BA* 45:109–19.

Reinhard, J. 1976. "Shamanism and Spirit Possession: The Definition Problem." In *Spirit Possession in the Nepal Himalayas,* edited by J. T. Hitchcock and R. L. Jones, 12–20. Warminster: Aris and Phillips.

Remus, Harold. 1997. *Jesus as Healer.* Understanding Jesus Today. Cambridge: Cambridge University Press.

Rhodes, L. A. 1990. "Studying Biomedicine as a Cultural System." In *Medical Anthropology: Contemporary Theory and Method,* edited by T. M. Johnson and C. F. Sargent, 159–65. New York: Praeger.

Riches, D. 1994. "Shamanism: The Key to Religion." *Man* 29:381–405.

Ridley, M. 1999. *Genome: The Autobiography of a Species in 23 Chapters.* London: Fourth Estate.

Riley, Gregory J. 1995. *Resurrection Reconsidered: Thomas and John in Controversy.* Minneapolis: Fortress.

————1997. *One Jesus, Many Christs: How Jesus Inspired not One True Christianity, but Many.* Reprinted, Minneapolis: Fortress, 2000.

Ripinsky-Naxon, M. 1993. *The Nature of Shamanism: Substance and Function of a Religious Metaphor*. Albany: State University of New York Press.

Robinson, J. A. T. 1976. *Redating the New Testament*. London: SCM.

Robinson, James M. 2001. "The Critical Edition of Q and the Study of Jesus." In *The Sayings Source Q and the Historical Jesus*, edited by A. Lindemann, 27–52. Bibliotheca Ephemeridum Theologicarum Lovaniensium 158. Leuven: Peeters.

Rochberg-Halton, F. 1992. "Astrology in the Ancient Near East." In *ABD* 1:504–7.

Rohrbaugh, Richard L. 1978. *The Biblical Interpreter: An Agrarian Bible in an Industrial Age*. Philadelphia: Fortress.

———. 1995. "Legitimating Sonship? Test of Honour: A Social-Scientific Study of Luke 4:1–30." In *Modelling Early Christianity: Social-Scientific Studies of the New Testament in Its Context*, edited by Philip F. Esler, 183–97. London: Routledge. Reprinted as "Luke's Jesus: Honor Claimed, Honor Tested." In *The New Testament in Cross-Cultural Perspective*, 31–44. Matrix. Eugene, OR: Cascade, 2007.

———. 2001. "Gossip in the New Testament." In *Social Scientific Models for Interpreting the Bible: Essays by the Context Group in Honour of Bruce J. Malina*, edited by J. J. Pilch, 239–59. BibIntSer 53. Leiden: Brill. Reprinted as "Gossip in the New Testament." In *The New Testament in Cross-Cultural Perspective*, 125–46. Matrix. Eugene, OR: Cascade, 2007.

———. 2002. "Ethnocentrism and Historical Questions About Jesus." In *The Social Setting of Jesus and the Gospels*, edited by Wolfgang Stegemann, Bruce J. Malina, and Gerd Theissen, 27–43. Minneapolis: Fortress. Reprinted as "What Did Jesus Know about Himself and When Did He Know It?" In *The New Testament in Cross-Cultural Perspective*, 61–76. Matrix. Eugene, OR: Cascade, 2007.

———. 2007. *The New Testament in Cross-Cultural Perspective*. Matrix. Eugene, OR: Cascade.

Rosemont, H. Jr. 1988. "Against Relativism." In *Interpreting Across Boundaries: New Essays in Comparative Philosophy*, edited by G. J. Larson and E. Deutsch, 36–70. Princeton: Princeton University Press.

Rousseau, John J., and Rami Arav. 1995. *Jesus and His World: An Archaeological and Cultural Dictionary*. Minneapolis: Fortress.

Roussin, L. A. 1997. "The Zodiac in Synagogue Decoration." In *Archaeology and the Galilee: Texts and Contexts in the Graeco-Roman and Byzantine Periods*, edited by D. R. Edwards and C. T. McCollough, 83–96. Atlanta: Scholars.

Rowland, Christopher. 1982. *The Open Heaven: A Study of Apocalyptic in Judaism and Early Christianity*. London: SPCK.

Russel, D. S. 1964. *The Method and Message of Jewish Apocalyptic*. London: SCM.

Rüsen, J. 1994. *Studies in Metahistory*. Pretoria: Human Science Research Council, 1993.

Safrai, S. 1994. "Jesus and the Hasidim." *Jerusalem Perspective* 42, 43, 44:3–22.

Salman, D. H. 1968. "Concluding Remarks." In *Trance and Possession States*, edited by Raymond Prince, 197–200. Montreal: Burke Memorial Society.

Sanders, E. P. 1985. *Jesus and Judaism*. London: SCM.

————. 1992. *Judaism: Practices and Belief 63 BCE—66 CE*. Minneapolis: Fortress.

————. 1993. *The Historical Figure of Jesus*. London: Penguin.

Schinkel, A. 2004. "History and Historiography in Process." *H&T* 43:39–56.

Schneemelcher, Wilhelm, and R. McL. Wilson, editors. 1991. *New Testament Apocrypha.* Vol. 1: *Gospels and Related Writings.* Rev. ed. Louisville: Westminster John Knox.

Schoffeleers, M. 1994. "Christ in African Folk Theology: The *Nganga* Paradigm." In *Religion in Africa: Experience and Expression,* edited by T. D. Blakely, W. E. A. Van Beek, and D. L. Thomson, 73–88. London: Currey.

Schröter, Jens. 1996. "The Historical Jesus and the Sayings Tradition: Comments on Current Research." *Neot* 30:151–68.

————. 2001. "Die Frage Nach dem Historischen Jesus und der Charakter Historischer Erkenntnis." In *The Sayings Source Q and the Historical Jesus,* edited by A. Lindemann, 207–54. Leuven: Peeters.

————. 2002. "Von der Historizität der Evangelien: Ein Beitrag zur Gegenwärtigen Diskussion um den Historischen Jesus." In *Der Historische Jesus: Tendenzen und Perspektiven der Gegenwärtigen Forschung,* edited by Jens Schröter and Ralph Brucker, 163–212. BZNW 114. Berlin: de Gruyter.

Schüssler Fiorenza, Elisabeth. 1997. "Jesus and the Politics of Interpretation." *HTR* 90:343–58.

Scott, Bernard Brandon. 1994. "From Reimarus to Crossan: Stages in a Quest." *Currents in Research: Biblical Studies* 2:253–80.

Searle, J. R. 1995. *The Construction of Social Reality*. London: Penguin.

Segal, Alan F. 1980. "Heavenly Ascent in Hellenistic Judaism, Early Christianity and Their Environment." In *ANRW* II.23.2:1333–94.

————. 1992. "Some Observations About Mysticism and the Spread of Notions of Life after Death in Hebrew Thought." In *SBL 1996 Seminar Papers,* edited by E. H. Lovering, 385–99. Atlanta: Scholars.

————. 2004. *Life after Death: A History of the Afterlife in the Religions of the West*. New York: Doubleday.

————. 2006. "The Resurrection: Faith or History?" In *The Resurrection of Jesus: John Dominic Crossan and N. T. Wright in Dialogue,* edited by Robert B. Stewart, 121–38. Minneapolis: Fortress.

Sellew, Philip. 1992. "Aphorisms of Jesus in Mark: A Stratigraphic Analysis." *Forum* 8.1–2:141–60.

Siiger, Halfdan. 1967. "Shamanistic Ecstasy and Supernatural Beings: A Study Based on Field-Work Among the Kalash Kafirs of Chitral." In *Studies in Shamanism,* edited by C.-M. Edsman, 69–81. Stockholm: Almqvist & Wiksell.

Siikala, A.-L. 1987. "Siberian and Inner Asian Shamanism." In *ER* 13:208–215.

Skinner, Q. 1985. "Introduction: The Return of Grand Theory." In *The Return of Grand Theory in the Human Sciences,* 3–20. Cambridge: Cambridge University Press.

Smith, Huston. 1976. *Forgotten Truth: The Primordial Tradition*. New York: Harper & Row.

Smith, Jonathan Z. 1982. "In Comparison a Magic Dwells." In *Imagining Religion: From Babylon to Jonestown*, 19–35. Chicago: University of Chicago Press.

———. 1990. *Drudgery Divine: On the Comparison of Early Christianities and the Religions of Late Antiquity.* Chicago: University of Chicago Press.

Smith, Mark S. 1990. *The Early History of God: Yahweh and the Other Deities in Ancient Israel.* San Francisco: Harper & Row.

Smith, Morton. 1978. *Jesus the Magician.* San Francisco: Harper & Row.

———. 1980. "The Origin and History of the Transfiguration Story." *Union Seminary Quarterly Review* 36:39–44.

———.1981. "Ascent to the Heavens and the Beginning of Christianity." *Eranos Jahrbuch* 50:403–29.

———. 1982. "Helios in Palestine." *Eretz Israel* 16:199–214.

———. 1984. "Transformation by Burial (1 Cor. 15:35–49; Rom 6:3–5 and 8:9–11)." *Eranos Jahrbuch* 52:87–112.

Solomon, G. F. 1979. "Comments." *Cultural Anthropology* 20:74.

Spiro, M. E. 1968. "Virgin Birth, Parthenogenesis and Physiological Paternity: An Essay in Cultural Interpretation." *Man* 3:242–61.

Spurrett, D. 2002. "The Human Self as a Coalition of Distributed Agencies." In *Brain, Mind and Soul: Unifying the Human Self*, edited by C. W. du Toit, 191–223. Pretoria: Unisa.

Stanford, M. 1986. *The Nature of Historical Knowledge.* Oxford: Blackwell.

Stegemann, Wolfgang, Bruce J. Malina, and Gerd Theissen, editors. 2001. *The Social Setting of Jesus and the Gospels.* Minneapolis: Fortress.

Stenschke, C. 2002. "Der Stern von Bethlehem: Ein Kritishes Gespräch mit Konradin Ferrari D'Occhieppo." *R&T* 9:309–26.

Stevens, Maryanne. 1990. "Paternity and Maternity in the Mediterranean: Foundations for Patriarchy." *BTB* 20:47–53.

Strauss, D. F. 1999. "History and Myth." In *The Historical Jesus Quest: A Foundational Anthology*, edited by G. W. Dawes, 87–111. Leiden: Deo.

Sussman, M. 1992. "Sickness and Disease." In *ABD* 6:6–15.

Swinburne, R. 1997. "Evidence for the Resurrection." In *The Resurrection: An Interdisciplinary Symposium on the Resurrection of Jesus*, edited by S. T. Davis, D. Kendall, and G. O'Collins, 191–211. Oxford: Oxford University Press.

Talbert, Charles H. 1975. "The Concept of Immortals in Mediterranean Antiquity." *JBL* 94:419–36.

Tart, C. T. 1980. "A Systems Approach to Altered States of Consciousness." In *The Psychobiology of Consciousness*, edited by J. M. Davidson and R. J. Davidson, 243–69. New York: Plenum.

Taves, Ann. 1999. *Fits, Trances, & Visions: Experiencing Religion and Explaining Experience from Wesley to James.* Princeton: Princeton University Press.

Taylor, C. 1985. "Understanding and Ethnocentricity." In *Philosophy and the Human Sciences: Philosophical Papers 2*, 116–33. Cambridge: Cambridge University Press.

————. 1991. "The Dialogical Self." In *The Interpretive Turn: Philosophy, Science, Culture*, edited by J. F. Bohman, D. R. Hiley, and R. Shusterman, 304–14. Ithaca, NY: Cornell University Press.

Taylor, R. P. 1985. *The Death and Resurrection Show: From Shaman to Superstar*. London: Anthony Blond.

Telford, W. R. 1994. "Major Trends and Interpretive Issues in the Study of Jesus." In *Studying the Historical Jesus: Evaluations of the State of Current Research*, edited by Bruce Chilton and Craig A. Evans, 33–74. NTTS 19. Leiden: Brill.

Theissen, Gerd. 1992. *Lokalkolorit und Zeitgeschichte in den Evangelien: Ein Beitrag zur Geschichte der synoptischen Tradition*. 2nd ed. Göttingen: Vandenhoeck & Ruprecht.

————. 1996. "Historical Scepticism and the Criteria of Jesus Research." *SJT* 49:147–76.

————. 1999. "Jesus—Prophet einer Millenaristischen Bewegung? Sozialgeschichtliche Überlegung zu einer sozialanthropologischen Deutung der Jesusbewegung." *Evangelishe Theologie* 59:402–15.

————, and Annette Merz. 1997. *Der Historische Jesus: Ein Lehrbuch*. Göttingen: Vandenhoeck & Ruprecht.

————, and Annette Merz. 1998. *The Historical Jesus: A Comprehensive Guide*. Minneapolis: Fortress.

————, and D. Winter. 1997. *Die Kriterienfrage in der Jesusforschung: Vom Differenzkriterium zum Plausibilitätskriterium*. Göttingen: Vandenhoeck & Ruprecht.

Thompson, M. P. 1993. "Reception Theory and the Interpretation of Historical Meaning." *H&T* 32:248–72.

Thorpe, S. A. 1993. *Shamans, Medicine Men and Traditional Healers: A Comparative Study of Shamanism in Siberia Asia, Southern Africa and North America*. Pretoria: Unisa.

Toews, J. E. 1987. "Intellectual History After the Linguistic Turn: The Autonomy of Meaning and the Irreducibility of Experience." *American Historical Review* 92:879–907.

Tonkin, E. 1990. "History and the Myth of Realism." In *The Myths We Live By*, edited by R. Samuel and P. Thompson, 25–35. London: Routledge.

Toorn, Karel van der. 1996. *Family Religion in Babylonia, Syria and Israel: Continuity and Change in the Forms of Religious Life*. Leiden: Brill.

Tosh, John. 1984. *The Pursuit of History: Aims, Methods and New Directions in the Study of Modern History*. London: Longman.

Townsend, J. B. 1997. "Shamanism." In *Anthropology of Religion: A Handbook*, edited by S. D. Glazier, 429–69. Westport, CT: Greenwood.

Tuckett, C. M. 2002. "Q and the Historical Jesus." In *Der Historische Jesus: Tendenzen und Perspektiven der Gegenwärtigen Forschung*, edited by Jens Schröter and Ralph Brucker, 213–41. BZNW 114. Berlin: de Gruyter.

Twelftree, G. H. 1993. *Jesus the Exorcist: A Contribution to the Study of the Historical Jesus*. Peabody: Hendrickson.

Unnik, W. C. van. 1973. "Once More St Luke's Prologue." *Neot* 7:7–26.

Van Aarde, Andries G. 2001. *Fatherless in Galilee: Jesus as Child of God.* Harrisburg, PA: Trinity.

Van Blerkom, L. M. 1991. "Zoonoses and the Origins of Old and New World Viral Diseases." In *The Anthropology of Medicine: From Culture to Method,* edited by L. Romanucci-Ross, D. E. Moerman, and L. R. Tancredi, 196–218. 2nd ed. New York: Bergin & Garvey.

Van der Horst, P. W. 1976/77. "Peter's Shadow: The Religio-Historical Background of Acts v.15." *NTS* 23:204–12.

Van der Walde, P. H. 1968. "Trance States and Ego Psychology." In *Trance and Possession States,* edited by Raymond Prince, 57–68. Montreal: Burke Memorial Society.

Van Lommel, P., R. Van Wees, V. Meyers, and I. Elfferich. 2001. "Near-Death Experience in Survivors of Cardiac Arrest: A Prospective Study in the Netherlands." *Lancet* 358:2039–45.

van Tilborg, Sjef, and Patrick Chatelion Counet. 2000. *Jesus' Appearances and Disappearances in Luke 24.* BibIntSer 45. Leiden: Brill.

VanderKam, James C. 1994. *The Dead Sea Scrolls Today.* Grand Rapids: Eerdmans.

Vermes, Geza. 1973. *Jesus the Jew: A Historian's Reading of the Gospels.* London: SCM.

———. 1993. *The Religion of Jesus the Jew.* Minneapolis: Fortress.

———. 2000. *The Changing Faces of Jesus.* London: Penguin.

Vitebsky, P. 1995. *The Shaman.* Boston: Baird.

Voigt, V. 1984. "Shaman—Person or Word?" In *Shamanism in Eurasia,* edited by M. Hoppál, 13–20. Göttingen: Herodot.

Von Ranke, L. 1973. "Preface to the First Edition of Histories of the Latin and Germanic Nations." In *The Theory and Practice of History.* Indianapolis: Bobbs-Merrill.

Vorster, J. N. 2000. "(E)mpersonating the Bodies of Early Christianity." *Neot* 34:103–24.

———. 2002. "Bodily Parts Vying for Power: Hierarchies and Bodies in Early Christianity." *Scrip* 80:287–306.

———. 2002. *Wat Sê die Bybel Regtig Oor . . . Seks?* Pretoria: C B Powell Bybelsentrum.

Wallace, A. F. C. 1972. "Mental Illness, Biology and Culture." In *Psychological Anthropology,* edited by F. L. K. Hsu, 363–402. Cambridge, MA: Schenkman.

Walsh, R. 1989a. "The Shamanic Journey: Experiences, Origins, and Analogues." *ReVision* 12.1:25–32.

———. 1989b. "Shamanism and Early Human Technology: The Technology of Transcendence." *ReVision* 12.1:34–40.

———. 1989c. "What is a Shaman? Definition, Origin and Distribution." *Journal of Transpersonal Psychology* 21:1–11.

———. 1990. "Shamanic Cosmology: A Psychological Examination of the Shaman's Worldview." *ReVision* 13.2:86–100.

———. 1993. "Phenomenological Mapping and Comparisons of Shamanic, Buddhist, Yogic, and Schizophrenic Experiences." *Journal of the American Academy of Religion* 56:739–69.

Walters, R. G. 1980. "Signs of the Times: Clifford Geertz and Historians." *Social Research* 47:537–56.

Ward, C. A. 1989. "Possession and Exorcism: Psychopathology and Psychotherapy in a Magico-Religious Context." In *Altered States of Consciousness and Mental Health: A Cross-Cultural Perspective*, edited by C. A. Ward, 125–44. London: Sage.

Watkins, J. G, and H. H. Watkins. 1986. "Hypnosis, Multiple Personality, and Ego States as Altered States of Consciousness." In *Handbook of States of Consciousness*, edited by B. B. Wolman and M. Ullman, 133–58. New York: Van Nostrand Reinhold.

Webb, R. L. 1994. "John the Baptist and His Relationship to Jesus." In *Studying the Historical Jesus: Evaluations of the State of Current Research*, edited by Bruce Chilton and Craig A. Evans, 179–229. NTTS 19. Leiden: Brill.

Wedenoja, W. 1990. "Ritual Trance and Catharsis: A Psychobiological and Evolutionary Perspective." In *Personality and the Cultural Construction of Society: Papers in Honor of Melford E. Spiro*, edited by D. K. Jordan and M. J. Swartz, 275–307. Tuscaloosa: University of Alabama Press.

Weiner, H., and I. F. Fawzy. 1989. "An Integrative Model of Health, Disease, and Illness." In *Psychosomatic Medicine: Theory, Physiology, and Practice, Vol I*, edited by S. Cheren, 9–44. Madison: International Universities Press.

Wessels, W. H. 1985. "Understanding Culture-Specific Syndromes in South Africa: The Western Dilemma." *Modern Medicine of South Africa* 9:51–63.

———. 1989. "Healing Practices in the African Independent Churches." In *Afro-Christian Religion and Healing in Southern Africa*, edited by G. C. Oosthuizen, S. D. Edwards, W. H. Wessels, and I. Hexham, 91–108. Lewiston, NY: Mellen.

White, G. M., and A. J. Marsella. 1982. "Introduction: Cultural Conceptions in Mental Health Research and Practice." In *Cultural Conceptions of Mental Health and Therapy*, edited by A. J. Marcella and G. M. White, 1–38. Dordrecht: Reidel.

Winkelman, M. J. 1990. "Shamans and Other 'Magico-Religious' Healers: A Cross-Cultural Study of Their Origins, Nature, and Social Transformations." *Ethos* 18:308–52.

———. 1992. *Shamans, Priests and Witches: A Cross-Cultural Study of Magico-Religious Practitioners.* Tucson: Arizona State University.

———. 1997. "Altered States of Consciousness and Religious Behavior." In *Anthropology of Religion: A Handbook*, edited by S. D. Glazier, 393–428. Westport: Greenwood.

Winthrop, R. H. 1991a. "Animism." In *Dictionary of Concepts in Cultural Anthropology*, 10–12. New York: Greenwood.

———. 1991b. "Shamanism." In *Dictionary of Concepts in Cultural Anthropology*, 255–57. New York: Greenwood.

Withers, R. 2001. "Psychoanalysis, Complementary Medicine and the Placebo." In *Understanding the Placebo Effect in Complementary Medicine: Theory, Practice and Research*, edited by D. Peters, 111–29. New York: Churchill Livingstone.

Wong, G. 2003. *Penicillin, the Wonder Drug.* Http://www.botany.hawaii.edu/faculty/wong/BOT135/Lect21b.htm.

Worsley, P. 1982. "Non-Western Medical Systems." *ARA* 11:315–48.

Wright, M. R. 1995. *Cosmology in Antiquity.* London: Routledge.

Wright, N. T. 1992a. *The New Testament and the People of God.* Minneapolis: Fortress.

———. 1992b. "Quest for the Historical Jesus." In *ABD* 3:796–802.

———. 1996. *Jesus and the Victory of God.* Minneapolis: Fortress.

———. 1999a. "Born of a Virgin?" In *The Meaning of Jesus: Two Visions*, edited by Marcus J. Borg and N. T. Wright, 171–8. San Francisco: HarperSanFrancisco.

———. 1999b. "Knowing Jesus: Faith and History." In *The Meaning of Jesus: Two Visions*, by M. J. Borg and N. T. Wright, 15–27. San Francisco: HarperSanFrancisco.

———. 1999c. "The Transforming Reality of the Bodily Resurrection." In *The Meaning of Jesus: Two Visions*, by M. J. Borg and N. T. Wright, 111–27. San Francisco: HarperSanFrancisco.

———, and John Dominic Crossan. 2006. "The Resurrection: Historical Event or Theological Explanation? A Dialogue." In *The Resurrection of Jesus: John Dominic Crossan and N. T. Wright in Dialogue*, edited by R. B. Stewart, 16–47. Minneapolis: Fortress.

Wright, S. G, and J. Sayre-Adams. 2001. "Healing and Therapeutic Touch: Is It All in the Mind?" In *Understanding the Placebo Effect in Complementary Medicine: Theory, Practice and Research*, edited by D. Peters, 165–75. New York: Churchill Livingstone.

Wulff, D. M. 1997. *Psychology of Religion: Classic and Contemporary.* New York: Wiley.

Young, A. 1982. "The Anthropologies of Illness and Sickness." *ARA* 11:257–85.

Zevit, Ziony. 2001. *The Religions of Ancient Israel: A Synthesis of Parallactic Approaches.* London: Continuum.

Zias, J. 1991. "Death and Disease in Ancient Israel." *BA* 54:147–59.

Zinberg, N. E. 1977. "The Study of Consciousness States: Problems and Progress." In *Alternate States of Consciousness*, edited by N. E. Zinberg, 1–36. New York: Free Press.